53

Y

?7

Alison Holst

The Ultimate
RECIPE COLLECTION

In loving memory of my mother and father,
Margaret and Henry Payne,
who loved me steadfastly,
were always there to support me,
and who taught me from the beginning
that there were no things in life more important than food and family!

First published in 2000 in UK by New Holland Publishers (UK) Ltd
Auckland • Sydney • London • Cape Town

218 Lake Road, Northcote, Auckland, New Zealand
14 Aquatic Drive, Frenchs Forest, NSW 2086, Australia
24 Nutford Place, London W1H 6DQ, United Kingdom
80 McKenzie Street, Cape Town 8001, South Africa

ISBN: 1 85974 742 6

Cover design: Glyn Bridgewater
Cover photograph: John Pettitt
Managing editor: Renée Lang
Design: Barbara Nielsen, Stylus
Project co-ordinator: Amy Palmer
Editor: Susan Brierley

Photographic Credits

INL (Sal Criscillo): 4–5, 20, 23, 40, 44, 50, 53, 55, 59, 60, 65, 69, 75, 78, 79, 83, 84, 87, 88, 93,
94, 95, 100, 102, 107, 108, 111, 114, 116, 121, 124, 133, 137, 140, 143, 144, 149, 151, 152,
173, 185, 190, 193, 198, 204, 210, 213, 214, 217, 218, 220, 221, 223, 226, 228, 235, 240, 242,
245, 246, 252, 254, 256, 258, 270, 271, 272, 275, 276, 279, 282, 285, 286, 288, 292, 293, 300,
303, 307, 308, 310, 314, 318, 322, 328, 332, 337, 339, 340; **Hyndman Publishing** (Lindsay Keats):
1, 3, 24, 31, 43, 47, 51, 56, 66, 72, 105, 113, 130, 134, 139, 154, 155, 156, 159, 171, 181, 189,
224, 232, 250, 251, 260, 261, 265, 266, 267, 269, 277, 280, 291, 294, 296, 298, 334; **Hodder
Moa Beckett Publishers Ltd** (Sal Criscillo): 70; **Watties** (Sal Criscillo): 38, 164, 167, 209;
Hyndman Publishing (Sal Criscillo): 304, 313; **Natural Gas** (Sal Criscillo): 76, 90, 110, 201;
Food Media (Sal Criscillo): 63, 97, 118, 123, 126, 163, 174, 194, 202, 233, 302, 317, 325, 326

Colour reproduction by Colourscan (Singapore)
Printed by Tien Wah Press (Pte) Ltd

The recipes in this book have been carefully tested by the author. The publisher and the author
have made every effort to ensure that the instructions are accurate and safe, but cannot accept
liability for any resulting injury or loss or damage to property whether direct or consequential.
Because ovens and microwave ovens vary so much, you should take the cooking times
suggested in recipes as guides only. The first time you make a recipe, check it at intervals to
make sure it is not cooking faster, or more slowly than expected.
Always follow the detailed instructions given by manufacturers of your appliances and
equipment, rather than the more general instructions given in these recipes.

Page 1: East-West Beef Salad with Coriander Dressing (p. 162)
Page 3: Lamb Rack with Fruited Couscous (p. 105)
Pages 4–5: Dee's Ultimate Cheesecake (p. 221)

Alison Holst

The Ultimate
RECIPE COLLECTION

NEW
HOLLAND

INTRODUCTION

This book, my eightieth, is unlike any of my others. It is a very personal collection of the recipes I like best, and which I have used most over the past 50 years! I hope that, in time, my children and grandchildren will hunt through it for their personal favourites too, and smile as particular recipes remind them of the many happy times we have had together – in my kitchen, around various dining tables, in the garden, at a picnic or camp site – enjoying the food as well as the company of friends and extended family.

I have always found food and cooking to be wonderfully interesting work and an absorbing hobby, exciting to explore in my own kitchen, and very satisfying to share with others. The recipes in this book record many of my personal kitchen experiences. These started when, as a teenager, I helped my mother during the week, and made sweets on wet Sunday afternoons. I moved on to the challenge of cooking on a tight budget when I became an impecunious student, then to experimenting with more sophisticated cooking as an enthusiastic young graduate. I think I learned as much as I taught when I began to teach 'Foods' to university students by day, and groups of keen homemakers at evening classes! As my own situation changed, I became interested in the cooking problems and pleasures of young parents and home gardeners. A leap into the media world of television and radio cooking programmes, newspaper and magazine articles, and live cooking shows in front of hundreds of people broadened my communication skills! Travel and day-to-day living in other countries introduced me to exciting new ideas, yet more careful budgeting, and good friends from different backgrounds. Returning home again, I juggled the demands of fast-growing children and a busy husband with the writing of new books about innovative labour-saving kitchen machines, and extensive travel to promote New Zealand's high quality primary products.

I hope that you will enjoy the wide range of recipes in this book – from old favourites, new ideas, short cuts, vegetarian food and inexpensive family standbys, to spectacular special-occasion treats.

From the large number of options presented here, I hope you will select and cook, with great success, those of my recipes which suit your own style of living, and your present interests. Enjoy 'talking food' with your friends and workmates, and encourage your children to learn to cook. Tell them that it is not only fun and creative, but if they cook for themselves and later, their families, they will have more to spend on other things, and have more control over their lives, knowing exactly what they are eating!

I would like to thank the many people who have shared their good ideas and recipes with me, and the much smaller group who have worked with me and provided efficient backup over the years. I hope I have helped the people who have bought, and cook from, more than three million copies of my books. And, most importantly, I thank my husband, sisters, children and grandchildren for their enduring love, thoughtfulness, friendship and support.

Contents

GLOSSARY

baking bran – wheat bran

baking paper – non-stick baking paper

baking soda – bicarbonate of soda

baking tin – baking pan

baking tray – baking sheet

Basmati rice – aromatic long-grain rice

bench – kitchen worktop or counter

biscuit – cookie

blender – liquidiser

bouillon cubes – stock cubes

bottling – canning

bread flour – strong flour, bakers' flour, high-grade flour

broad beans – fava beans

canola oil – rapeseed oil

chickpeas – garbanzo beans

chilli powder – ground dried chillies with no added flavourings

cling wrap – microwave-safe transparent film

crayfish – rock lobster (salt water)

cream – light whipping cream

crème fraîche – rich, cultured sour cream

custard powder – replace with cornflour (cornstarch)

eggbeater – egg whisk

eggplant – aubergine

essence – extract

evaporated milk – unsweetened condensed milk

feijoa – subtropical fruit, substitute apples in pies

frypan – frying pan, pan

golden syrup, treacle – molasses

green prawns – raw prawns

green/red pepper – green/red bell pepper/capsicum

grill – broil

haricot beans – navy beans

hogget – mature lamb

icing sugar – confectioner's sugar

icing – frosting

instant coffee – instant coffee powder

instant stock – concentrated powdered stock, replace with stock cubes

jam setting mix – powdered pectin

Kikkoman soy sauce – Japanese light soy sauce

Kremelta – copha, solid coconut oil

kumara – orange-fleshed sweet potato

mandarins – satsumas or clementines

minced beef – ground beef

oreganum – oregano

oysters – shucked or shelled oysters

paper towel – kitchen paper

paua – abalone

pipi – bivalve mollusc, replace with cockles

pot – saucepan

reduced cream – 20% milk fat, sterilised and canned

rice bubbles – rice crispies

rolled oats – oatmeal

savoury tomatoes – diced tomatoes

schnitzel – very thinly sliced meat (from a variety of animals)

scones – American biscuits

self-raising flour, 1 cup = 1 cup plain flour + 2 tsp baking powder

sieve (verb) – strain

sieve (noun) – strainer

silver beet – Swiss chard, spinach beet

smoked cod's roe – tarama

snow pea – mange tout

soft butter – softened butter

spirits – whisky, gin, brandy, rum

spring onion – scallion

sultanas – seedless raisins

swede – rutabaga

tangelo – cross between tangerine and grapefruit

tasty cheese – sharp cheese

teatowel – dish towel

Teflon liner or sheet – use non-stick baking paper

telegraph cucumbers – long, tender-skinned cucumber

tomato paste – tomato concentrate

tomato purée (22–24% tomato solids) – tomato sauce

tomato sauce (10–12% tomato solids) – tomato ketchup

top milk – single cream

Trim milk – low-fat milk

Trim pork – New Fashioned Pork in Australia, Pork in the United Kingdom

tuatua – oval bivalve mullusc, replace with cockles

vanilla – vanilla extract

Vegemite or Marmite – yeast extract

wholemeal flour – whole wheat or graham flour

yeast, surebake or muripan – replace with two thirds as much easy blend yeast or active dried yeast

zucchini – courgette

SYMBOLS **M** can be prepared in a microwave **V** suitable for vegetarians

OTHER IMPORTANT INFORMATION

Soup Mixes
Soup mixes used in some recipes in this book make 3–4 servings of soup. The packets tend to weigh around 30 g (1 oz).

Cultured Dairy Products
A 250 g (8 oz) carton of cottage cheese, cream cheese and sour cream is equivalent to 1 cup.

Coconut Cream
The coconut cream used in these recipes is unsweetened and available canned or in tetrapaks. Replace with liquid made by soaking desiccated coconut in boiling water or dissolve a cake of compressed creamed coconut in warm water.

Meat Cuts
If you are not familiar with a meat cut in this book, talk to your butcher about it.

Can Sizes
You may find that you cannot buy cans of the exact size specified in this book. Do not worry if the cans are a little larger or smaller than those specified. Small variations are unlikely to make a difference to your recipe.

Food Processors
A food processor with a large mixing bowl and a strong motor was used for testing and preparing the recipes in this book. Some food processors would not cope with such large amounts. Follow the instructions given by the maker of your food processor.

The following measures and equivalents have been used in this book:

1 tsp . . . .5 ml

1 Tbsp . . .3 tsp . . . . . .15 ml

4 Tbsp . . .1/4 cup . . . .60 ml

8 Tbsp . . .1/2 cup . . .125 ml

16 Tbsp . .1 cup . . . .250 ml

Graduated sets of standard metric measuring cups and spoons have been used throughout this book unless otherwise stated.

Always use level measures – rounded or heaped measures will upset the balance of ingredients.

When measuring flour, stir it in its original container, using a fork, then spoon it lightly into the measure. Level it off without shaking or banging, since this packs down the flour and means that too much is used. Individual 1/4 and 1/2 cup measures make measuring small amounts quicker.

Small amounts of ingredients have been measured by spoons. Larger quantities have been given in cups or in metric and imperial weights.

Weights have been rounded off to convenient amounts and are approximate only.

Conversions through the book may not always appear to be consistent, since recipes were considered individually when conversions were made.

Abbreviations Used

cm . . . . .centimetre
C . . . . .Celsius
F . . . . .Fahrenheit
ml . . . . .millilitre
g . . . . .gram
kg . . . . .kilogram
oz . . . . .ounce
fl oz . . . . . . .fluid ounce
lb . . . . .pound
in . . . . .inch
tsp . . . . . . .teaspoon
Tbsp . . . . . . .tablespoon

Oven Temperatures and Approximate Equivalents

Celsius	Fahrenheit	Gas
100°C	225°F	1/4
125°C	250°F	1/2
150°C	300°F	2
160°C	325°F	3
170°C	325°F	3
180°C	350°F	4
190°C	375°F	5
200°C	400°F	6
210°C	425°F	7
220°C	425°F	7
230°C	450°F	8
250°C	500°F	9

Always bring the oven to the required temperature before putting in the food which is to be cooked, unless otherwise specified.

Most of the oven-based recipes in this book were cooked in an oven with a fan. The fan circulates heat so that no parts of the oven are much hotter or colder than other parts.

If you use an oven which does not have a fan, you may find that you need to allow a slightly longer cooking time, or slightly higher temperature. A fan oven set to 180°C (350°F) is equivalent to a setting of about 190°C (375°F) in an oven without a fan. Individual ovens vary, however.

To help you judge when food is cooked, other indications of readiness have been given, wherever possible, as well as an indication of the probable time required.

When baking, always position the oven rack so the top of the food being cooked is just above the middle of the oven, unless other instructions are given in the recipe.

MICROWAVE COOKING

Microwave cooking times vary, and cannot be given precisely. Microwave instructions have been given for a 730 Watt microwave oven with a turntable.

High (Full power) 100% power, about 730 Watts
Medium High 70% power, about 510 Watts
Medium 50% power, about 360 Watts
Defrost 30% power, about 220 Watts

Check the power levels and percentages on your own microwave oven, and alter cooking times accordingly, if your oven is different.

The first time you microwave a new recipe, always watch it carefully during the second half of its cooking time, in case it is cooking more quickly. As soon as you can smell the food, you know that it is nearly cooked.

If the instructions given by the microwave oven manufacturer are not the same as those given here, always follow those for your particular oven, rather than these general instructions.

Standing Time

Microwaved food continues to cook after it is taken out of a microwave oven, e.g. a potato keeps baking for 1–2 minutes longer.

If you wait until food looks and feels completely cooked before you take it from the oven, it may overcook on standing.

ONE CUP EQUIVALENTS

In the following list where ingredients are described as chopped, grated, mashed, etc, this should be done before they are measured in a 250 ml (8 fl oz) cup. All measures are approximate.

1 cup	grams	ounces
allbran	100	3 1/2
slivered almonds	112	4
chopped dried apricots	150	5
asparagus pieces (cooked)	115	4
mashed banana	250	8
barley	200	6 1/2
beans, black-eyed	180	6
beans, cooked red kidney	175	6
chopped green beans	115	4
beans, haricot	200	6 1/2
beans, red kidney	180	6
beans, soya	170	6
biscuit crumbs	100	3 1/2
bran, baking (wheat bran)	45	1 1/2
bran, oat	120	4
breadcrumbs, dry	130	4
breadcrumbs, fresh	150	5
bulgar	165	5 1/2
butter	225	7

	grams	ounces
chopped cabbage	115	4
grated carrot	170	6
cashew nuts	120	4
cauliflower pieces	115	4
sliced celery	125	4
grated cheese	100	3 1/2
chickpeas	200	6 1/2
chocolate pieces	160	5 1/2
cocoa	125	4
coconut	100	3 1/2
cornflour	100	3 1/2
cornmeal, coarse yellow	170	6
cottage cheese	250	8
cream cheese	250	8
croutons	50	2
diced cucumber	120	4
currants	135	4 1/2
diced eggplant	100	3 1/2
flour, pea	140	5
flour, self-raising	125	4
flour, soya	90	3
flour, white	125	4
flour, wholemeal	140	5
chopped herbs	25	1
kibbled wheat	160	5 1/2
kibbled rye	160	5 1/2
lentils, brown	190	6 1/2
lentils, split red	190	6 1/2
macaroni	110	4
chopped marrow	100	3 1/2
mixed fruit	140	5
moong dahl	185	6
chopped mushrooms	85	3
oats, whole grain	90	3
diced onion	140	5
grated Parmesan cheese	125	4
pasta, dry large	60	2
pasta, dry small	130	4
frozen peas	110	4
peanuts	140	5
crushed pineapple	250	8
pine nuts	140	5
mashed potato	250	8
pumpkin purée	250	8
chopped rhubarb	150	5
rice, brown (cooked)	190	6 1/2
rice, brown (raw)	195	6 1/2
rice, short-grain (cooked)	150	5
rice, short-grain (raw)	185	6
rolled oats	90	3
sesame seeds	120	4
cooked spinach	200	6 1/2
split peas, green	200	6 1/2
split peas, yellow	200	6 1/2
frozen strawberries	150	5
sugar	220	7
sugar, brown (packed into measure)	200	6 1/2
sugar, castor	210	7
sugar, icing	110	4
sultanas	160	5 1/2
sunflower seeds	135	4 1/2
chopped tomato	175	6
frozen mixed vegetables	150	5
whole walnuts	75	3 1/2
chopped walnuts	100	3 1/2
wheatgerm	75	2 1/2
grated zucchini	150	5
sliced zucchini	110	4

Breakfasts and Brunches

Breakfast should get every day off to a good start! Workday breakfasts should be quick and simple, tempting and nutritious, to set children up for a happy and successful time at school and help adults cope with whatever the day has in store. Weekend breakfasts and brunches can be fun, creative and varied, anticipated with pleasure and sometimes shared with friends. The next few pages are full of good ideas to lure the sleepiest of cooks into the kitchen!

MUESLI

Banish breakfast boredom by trying different mueslis.

Nature's Best Muesli

This muesli appeals to people who want uncooked, unsweetened grains in their breakfast mixtures. When I make this for my own use, I bake the first five ingredients until the oats lose their raw flavour, then add the fruit.

For 5¹/₂ cups:
2 cups wholesome rolled oats
1 cup coconut threads
¹/₂ cup pumpkin kernels
¹/₂ cup sunflower seeds
¹/₂ cup raw Redskin peanuts
¹/₂ cup sultanas
¹/₂ cup chopped dried apricots

Measure all the ingredients into a large bowl or plastic bag and mix well. Store in an airtight container.

Variation: Bake the first five ingredients at 150°C (300°F) for 15–20 minutes or, for crispness without sweetness, mix them with a little olive or canola oil before baking.

Swiss Muesli

This nutritious mixture makes an excellent complete meal, at any time of the day.

For 2 small or 1 large serving:
2–3 Tbsp finely chopped almonds (skin on)
2–3 Tbsp chopped sultanas
¹/₄ cup rolled oats, fine or regular
¹/₂ cup low-fat fruit-flavoured yoghurt
¹/₂ apple

Mix the chopped almonds and sultanas together, stir in the rolled oats and yoghurt. Quarter and core the apple, leaving the skin on. Grate it coarsely or chop it finely. Stir it into the mixture.

Refrigerate for up to 24 hours. Eat as is, or with sliced strawberries or grapes.

Clockwise from left: Malted Swiss Muesli, Light Muesli, Swiss Muesli, Nature's Best Muesli

Light Muesli

This light-coloured mixture of precooked cereals, seeds and fruit often appeals to children. It keeps well in an airtight jar.

For 6 cups:
1 cup puffed wheat
1 cup puffed corn
1 cup Allbran
1 cup cornflakes
1 cup coconut threads
1 cup pumpkin kernels
¹/₂ cup chopped papaya chunks
¹/₂ cup sliced dried apple

Mix all the ingredients together until evenly combined. Store in an airtight container at room temperature. Serve topped with milk or yoghurt and slices of fresh fruit.

Note: Check the crispness of cereals. If necessary, mix the first six ingredients in a large roasting pan and heat at 125°C (250°F) for about 10 minutes, before adding everything else.

Malted Swiss Muesli

You won't believe how good this is until you try it! The malted milk gives it special character.

For 2 servings:
1 large apple
about ¹/₄ cup (60 ml/2 fl oz) orange juice
¹/₂–³/₄ cup rolled oats
¹/₄ cup coconut threads (optional)
1–4 Tbsp lightly toasted almonds
¹/₄ cup malted milk powder

Place the unpeeled, roughly sliced apple in a food processor, add the orange juice and process in short bursts until the apple is chopped. Add the remaining ingredients and process again briefly. Add a little extra juice if you like. Pile into bowls and serve immediately with fruit-flavoured yoghurt or milk, and with other fresh fruit if you wish.

Variation: Alter the proportions to suit your taste.

Mix-in-the-Pan Muesli

This was the first cooked muesli I 'invented'. My family ate it in large quantities for years!

For 8 cups:
4 cups rolled oats
2 cups wheatgerm
1 cup coconut or wheat bran
1 cup brown sugar
1 tsp salt
1 tsp cinnamon
1 tsp mixed spice
¹/₄ cup (60 ml/2 fl oz) canola oil
¹/₂ cup (125 ml/4 fl oz) milk

Turn the oven to 180°C (350°F). Measure all the dry ingredients into a large roasting pan and mix together with your hands. Drizzle the oil and milk over the dry ingredients, then mix thoroughly with your hands until the mixture is evenly dampened. Break up large lumps which go hard when baked.

Bake for 15 minutes, stir well, bake for another 10 minutes, then stir again. Bake 10 minutes longer, remove from the oven, stir once more and leave to cool. When quite cold, store in airtight containers. Serve with fruit, yoghurt, etc. for breakfast or dessert.

Scrunch

This dehydrated mixture makes a great breakfast or snack for hungry trampers.

3 cups wholegrain oats
2 Tbsp honey
2 Tbsp lemon juice
2–3 grated apples
2 Tbsp oil
1¹/₂–2 cups apricot yoghurt
2 Tbsp toasted sesame seeds

Mix together all the ingredients except the sesame seeds, in the order given. Spread onto solid dehydrator trays and sprinkle with sesame seeds. Dehydrate for about 20 hours or until firm enough to break in pieces when cold. Store in airtight plastic bags.

Crisp and Crunchy Muesli   M

This light muesli, enriched with nutrient-rich wheatgerm and seeds, is a favourite with children.

For 4–6 cups (8–12 servings):
1/4 cup honey
1 Tbsp canola oil
2 cups rice bubbles
2 cups malted wheatflakes
2 cups cornflakes
3/4 cup wheatgerm
3/4 cup pumpkin kernels and/or sunflower seeds
1/4 cup coconut threads
about 1/2 cup chopped dried fruit

Warm the honey and oil together in a small container until it is hot enough to pour easily. Mix remaining ingredients except dried fruit in a large roasting pan or large (27 cm/11 in) flat-bottomed microwave dish. Drizzle the syrup over the cereals, stirring until all the wheatgerm is sticking to the cereals. Spread the coated cereal evenly so it is about 1 cm (3/8 in) deep.

Microwave on High (100%) power for 5–6 minutes, or bake at 150°C (300°F) for 10–12 minutes, stirring occasionally and watching that the mixture does not burn. The muesli is cooked when a teaspoonful spread on a cold surface is crisp when cold.

Stir in finely chopped dried fruit – try apples, apricots, peaches, pears, pineapple or papaya. When cold, store in airtight containers.

Everyday Muesli

Dress up this basic muesli with fruit and nuts if you like.

For 4 cups (16 servings):
1/4 cup water
3 Tbsp white or brown sugar
1 Tbsp golden syrup
1/2 tsp salt
1/4 cup (60 ml/2 fl oz) oil
4 cups large rolled or wholegrain oats
1/4–1/2 cup wheatgerm (optional)
dried fruit and nuts (optional)

Turn the oven to 180°C (350°F). Measure the first 5 ingredients into a large pot and heat until blended. Take off the heat and stir in the oats and wheatgerm. Spread in an oiled roasting pan and bake for about 20 minutes or until evenly browned, stirring every few minutes. Add (chopped) dried fruit and nuts if you like. Cool, then store in an airtight container.

Frypan Muesli

You can cook this muesli all at once in a large electric frypan, or in two batches in a smaller pan on the stove.

For 3–4 cups (about 12 servings):
2 heaped household Tbsp honey
1/4 cup (60 ml/2 fl oz) soy or canola oil
1 cup wholegrain oats or rolled oats
1 cup oatbran
1 cup wheatgerm
1/2 cup coconut (optional)
1/2 tsp salt
1/4 cup chopped nuts
1/4 cup sesame seeds
dried fruit (optional)

Melt the honey, stir in the oil, and mix with all the remaining ingredients except the dried fruit. Stir over moderate heat for 5–10 minutes, until the mixture turns golden. Allow to cool, add dried fruit if desired, then store in airtight jars.

Munchy Muesli   M

This muesli contains many healthful 'goodies' and tastes great!

For 8 cups (32 servings):
4 cups wholegrain oats
1/2 cup wheatgerm
1/2 cup oatbran or fibre-rich bran
1/2 cup fine or medium coconut threads
1/2 cup pumpkin kernels
1/2 cup sunflower seeds
1/2 cup sliced almonds
1/2 cup honey
1/4 cup sugar
1/2 tsp salt
2 Tbsp water
1/4 cup (60 ml/2 fl oz) canola or other oil
1 cup chopped dried fruit

Turn the oven to 150°C (300°F). Mix the first 7 ingredients in a large bowl. Heat together the honey, sugar, salt, water and oil in a pot or microwave dish, stirring until the sugar has dissolved. Pour the hot liquid over the dry mixture and stir in.

Spread in two large, shallow baking pans and bake for 20 minutes, or until lightly browned. Stir if the edges darken.

OR spread half the mixture on a microwave turntable, leaving the centre uncovered. Microwave, uncovered, on High (100%) power for 4–6 minutes or until lightly browned, checking after about 3 minutes to make sure it is browning evenly. Add dried fruit, cool and store in an airtight container.

PLATES OF PORRIDGE

The microwave oven has revolutionised porridge making, as porridge lovers realise they can mix and cook porridge in the bowl from which they eat it, without messy pots!

Traditional Porridge

Porridge is nutritious, easy and the cheapest breakfast cereal you can prepare. Add wheatgerm for a super-nutritious breakfast that will set you up for the day, especially in cold weather.

For 4 servings:
1 cup rolled oats
1/4 cup wheatgerm
1/4 tsp salt
about 3 cups (750 ml/24 fl oz) water

Measure everything into a medium-sized pot. Bring to the boil, stirring most of the time, then allow the porridge to simmer gently for 2–5 minutes. (Frequent stirring while simmering gives a smoother texture.) Serve with milk, brown or white sugar or golden syrup.

Variations: Alter proportions of water and rolled oats for thinner and thicker porridge.

Use wholegrain oats for a rougher textured porridge.

Add a mixture of flaked and kibbled grains to the rolled oats.

Serve with fresh or dried fruit, Cinnamon or Sesame Sugar (p. 11).

Microwave Porridge   M

When cooking your porridge in the microwave, it's easiest to make it in individual bowls. Use a deep bowl rather than a wide, shallow one, so that the porridge won't bubble over the sides.

For 1 serving:
4 Tbsp rolled oats
pinch of salt
8 Tbsp hot water

Put the dry ingredients in your bowl and add the hot water. Cook on Medium (50%) power for 1–1 1/2 minutes, stir, then cook until the porridge in the middle of the bowl looks cooked (1/2–2 minutes, depending on the temperature of the water).

Variations: Add wheatgerm or other ingredients to suit your taste.

Apple Cinnamon Porridge

Dried apple and cinnamon make porridge really interesting.

For 1 large or 2 small servings:
1/2 cup rolled oats
1 1/2 cups (375 ml/12 fl oz) water
1–2 Tbsp chopped dried apple
pinch of salt
1 tsp Cinnamon Sugar (p. 11)

Combine the rolled oats, water, apple and salt in a pot. Bring to the boil, stirring frequently, then simmer for 5 minutes. Remove from the heat and stir in the Cinnamon Sugar. Serve with extra Cinnamon Sugar and fresh or evaporated milk.

Millet Porridge

Finely ground millet makes smooth, creamy porridge which some people love, but others find rather strange! I think millet is underrated; it flourishes in arid areas, can be eaten by some people with allergies to other grains, and has more iron than most other cereals.

For 2 servings:
½ cup finely ground millet
1 cup (250 ml/8 fl oz) cold water
½ cup (125 ml/4 fl oz) milk or water
4 tsp brown sugar
4 tsp butter or oil (optional)
pinch of salt

Mix the millet with the cold water and bring to the boil, stirring all the time. When thick, add the milk or water and bring back to the boil. Remove from the heat and stir in the sugar, butter or oil and salt. Top with Sesame or Cinnamon Sugar (below) if you like, and serve with milk, yoghurt or cream, or fresh or stewed fruit.

Brown Rice Porridge

Brown rice, cooked until very soft, makes porridge with a lovely nutty flavour. Bake the rice when you have the oven on for something else, then reheat it as required.

For 4 servings:
1 cup brown rice
¾ tsp salt
4 cups (1 litre/32 fl oz) hot water
Cinnamon Sugar (below)

Cook the rice in the salted water for about 1½ hours in a covered casserole in a moderate oven (or 20 minutes in a pressure cooker), until well cooked and slightly mushy. Refrigerate until needed. (It will absorb extra water during this time.) When needed, stir in about 2 tsp Cinnamon Sugar per serving and reheat in a microwave or pot. Serve topped with fresh fruit, more Cinnamon Sugar or Sesame Sugar (below), milk or a little cream.

Mixed-Grain Porridge M

Keep a selection of kibbled and flaked grains handy so you can make different mixed-grain porridges easily. Add wheatgerm as an inexpensive nutrient booster, and high-fibre bran as you think you need it!

For 1 large or 2 medium servings:
2 Tbsp wholegrain oats
1 Tbsp kibbled wheat or kibbled rye
1–2 Tbsp wheatgerm
1–3 Tbsp wheat bran
about 1 cup (250 ml/8 fl oz) hot water
pinch of salt

Combine the cereals in a microwave jug or a deep bowl. Add the hot water and the salt, and stir to mix. Microwave for 1 minute on High (100%) power. Stir then

Top to bottom: Millet Porridge, Apple Cinnamon Porridge, Brown Rice Porridge, Cinnamon Sugar, Mixed-Grain Porridge with Sesame Sugar

cook for 4–6 minutes on Medium (50%) power, until the grains are tender. Add more hot water if it looks dry. Stir the porridge briefly for a grainy texture, and often if you like it smooth. Serve with Sesame or Cinnamon Sugar (below) and milk, plain or fruity yoghurt, or a little cream.

Variation: Add chopped dried apricots, sultanas or nuts at any time during cooking.

Cinnamon Sugar

¼ cup brown sugar
¼ cup white sugar
1 Tbsp cinnamon

Shake ingredients together and store in an airtight jar.

Sesame Sugar

2 Tbsp toasted sesame seeds
2 Tbsp brown sugar
2 Tbsp white sugar
pinch of salt

Grind the sesame seeds with a pestle and mortar or in a coffee grinder. Mix with the brown and white sugar, add the salt and grind together briefly.

Store this in an airtight jar in a cool place.

Note: Always toast sesame seeds as soon as you buy them, by heating them until they are a light golden brown in a dry frypan, under a grill, or in a moderate oven.

WONDERFUL WAFFLES

Waffles can be made ahead of time and frozen. They can then be taken out at any time and heated in the toaster for a quick, no-fuss breakfast treat.

Note: If you don't have a waffle iron, try these waffle recipes cooked as pancakes.

Banana Waffles

Mash the banana well or the waffles will brown unevenly, although this does not really matter.

For 6–8 servings:
50 g (2 oz) butter, melted
¼ cup sugar
2 eggs
1 ripe banana, mashed
½ tsp salt
1 cup (250 ml/8 fl oz) milk
1 cup self-raising flour

Add the sugar and eggs to the melted butter and beat lightly with a fork. Stir in the mashed banana, salt and milk, then fold in the flour, mixing just enough to combine the ingredients.

Heat a waffle iron according to the manufacturer's instructions. Spray with non-stick spray. Pour the batter into the prepared iron, close the lid and cook for about 5 minutes, until evenly cooked and golden brown. Serve warm or hot with mixed fresh or canned fruit and a dusting of icing sugar, or with maple or golden syrup and a dollop of flavoured yoghurt or sour cream.

Crisp Coconut Waffles

These waffles, cooked slowly, are crisp, like an icecream cone. Be prepared, they stick easily!

For 1 large waffle:
1 cup (250 ml/8 fl oz) coconut cream
½ cup self-raising flour
2 Tbsp sugar

Mix all the ingredients together until just combined. The mixture should be cream consistency – thin with about 1 Tbsp of water if it is too thick. Heat a waffle iron according to the manufacturer's instructions, spray with non-stick spray, and pour the mixture in until it covers the waffle pattern; close the lid. Cook slowly, for longer than other waffles, until golden brown. If you open the iron too soon, the waffle may split. Cut it into portions while it is hot and flexible. These crunchy waffles are delicious served with fresh fruit, and sprinkled with toasted coconut.

Top to bottom: Banana Waffles, Crisp Coconut Waffles, Almondy Waffles, Oaty Waffles

Almondy Waffles

I like the crunchy nuts in these. Serve them with something sweet to bring out their full flavour.

For about 4 waffles:
1 cup self-raising flour
¼ tsp salt
¼ cup sugar
¾ cup chopped toasted almonds
2 eggs, separated
1¼ cups (310 ml/10 fl oz) milk
¼ tsp almond essence
50 g (2 oz) butter, melted

Measure the flour, salt, sugar and chopped almonds into a large bowl and toss together with a fork. Beat the egg yolks, milk and essence together in a separate bowl. Pour the egg mixture and the melted butter into the dry ingredients and fold together. Beat the egg whites until stiff then fold them into the batter.

Heat a waffle iron according to the manufacturer's instructions, spray with non-stick spray, and pour the batter into the centre of the prepared iron, filling it until the waffle pattern is just covered. Close the iron and cook quite slowly for about 5 minutes, until golden brown. These are delicious served with fresh berries or sliced banana, and maple syrup.

Oaty Waffles

Rolled oats are a good addition to waffles.

For 6–8 servings:
¾ cup rolled oats
1 cup (250 ml/8 fl oz) milk
2 eggs
½ tsp salt
¼ cup sugar
½ cup plain flour
2 tsp baking powder
25–50 g (1–2 oz) butter, melted

Pour the milk over the rolled oats. Add the rest of the ingredients and mix briefly with a fork, stirring just enough to combine the ingredients. Cook as for Almondy Waffles above. These waffles are good with grilled bacon or sausages, canned peaches and maple or other syrup.

PANCAKES PLEASE

Ever-popular pancakes get the weekend off to a great start!

Cottage Cheese Pancakes

These soft-textured, nutritious little pancakes are good finger food for small children.

For 10–12 small pancakes:
2 Tbsp plain flour
2 eggs

2 tsp sugar
1 Tbsp wheatgerm
2 tsp oil
½ cup cottage cheese

Combine all the ingredients in the order given, using a food processor or egg beater, until they are just mixed but still lumpy. Cook on a preheated griddle or non-stick frypan spread with more oil or butter than normal. Pour about 2 Tbsp of batter into the pan and cook until bubbles break on the surface. Turn the pancakes carefully and cook the other side until golden brown. Serve while hot, topped with sliced raw fruit or spoonfuls of thick apple or apricot purée. These pancakes are very tender and are nice rolled up and eaten in the fingers.

Blueberry Buttermilk Pancakes

These pancakes are soft and tender, with blueberries dotted through them. They are best eaten just after they are cooked.

For 3–4 servings:
¾ cup plain flour
2 Tbsp sugar
½ tsp salt
½ tsp baking soda
1 egg
1 cup (250 ml/8 fl oz) buttermilk
50 g (2 oz) butter, melted
1 cup frozen or fresh blueberries

Fork the first 4 ingredients together in a large bowl, mixing thoroughly. In another container, beat the egg, buttermilk and melted butter together. Fold the mixtures together without overmixing.

Heat a heavy griddle or frypan and brush with a little butter on a paper towel. The pan is hot enough when a drop of water breaks into several smaller balls which dance around the pan. Form pancakes then drop a few berries on top of each. Turn carefully when the first side is cooked. Serve stacked, with syrup.

Fruity Pancakes

Add an apple or two, or some leftover canned or stewed fruit to these pancakes. Topped with syrup, they go down a treat!

For 4 servings:
1 cup rolled oats
¼ cup wheatgerm
¾ cup (185 ml/6 fl oz) milk
2 eggs
1–2 apples, grated, or ½ cup well-drained cooked fruit, chopped
2–3 Tbsp brown sugar
½ tsp salt
50 g (2 oz) butter, melted
½ cup plain flour
2 tsp baking powder

Measure the first 4 ingredients into a large bowl and mix with a fork to combine. Add grated apple or chopped cooked fruit, sugar and salt, and mix again. Add the melted butter. Measure the flour and baking powder into a sieve and shake into the mixture. Stir to combine. Do not beat until smooth. Cook as for Blueberry Buttermilk Pancakes.

Giant Baked Pancake

If you don't want to cook pancakes in a frypan, what about trying a baked one. This spectacular pancake makes a good weekend brunch. Be warned, it will disappear fast!

For 2 large or 4 small servings:
2 eggs
2 Tbsp sugar
½ cup (125 ml/4 fl oz) milk
½ cup plain flour
50 g (2 oz) butter
lemon juice and sugar, to taste

Turn the oven to 230°C (450°F).

Beat the first 4 ingredients together until smooth. Put the butter in a sponge-roll tin or roasting pan of about the same size, and heat it in the oven until the butter is melted and bubbly but not brown. Watch it carefully! Pour the batter into the pan and bake for 15 minutes, or until the pancake has set and has puffed up in some places. Don't leave it to bake until crisp. Remove from the oven, sprinkle with lemon juice and sugar, and cook for 5 minutes longer. Cut in pieces (with kitchen scissors) and serve immediately.

Orange French Toast

When stale bread is dipped in an orange-flavoured egg mixture, then cooked gently until it has puffed up and is golden brown, it turns into something wonderful.

For 4 servings:
2 eggs
½ cup (125 ml/4 fl oz) milk
2 Tbsp orange juice
1 tsp grated orange rind
2 Tbsp sugar
1 tsp vanilla
pinch of salt
8 slices french bread, cut diagonally,
  1 cm (½ in) thick

Place all the ingredients except the bread in a bowl, and whisk until well mixed. Place the bread in a large, shallow dish and cover with the egg mixture. Leave for 20–30 minutes, turning occasionally.

Heat a little butter in a large frypan. Add the soaked bread and cook over a low heat for 5–10 minutes each side, turning when golden brown. Serve immediately, topped with berries, a dusting of icing sugar and a trickle of maple syrup, or serve with jam or jelly.

BREAKFAST IN A GLASS

A 'meal in a glass' is comforting, soothing and filling – often the perfect solution if you are tired, out of sorts, or passing through the kitchen 'on the run', and find it an effort even to think about chewing solid food.

The following drinks taste best when they are drunk as soon as they are made. After trying these, concoct your own mixtures.

Golden Whirl

Puréed apricots are satin-smooth, and make good drinks.

For 2 large drinks:
1 can (400 g/14 oz) apricot halves
about 1 cup (250 ml/8 fl oz) plain or
* flavoured yoghurt*
2–3 rounded tsp honey
orange juice
fresh mint and grated orange rind, to
* garnish*

Put the apricots, yoghurt and honey into a blender or food processor. Blend until smooth and creamy, dilute with orange juice to the desired thickness, and serve garnished with fresh mint and grated orange rind.

Orange Julia

I concocted this years ago in an effort to recreate an American drink I loved. I have long since forgotten the original, but I always have takers for this!

For 1 large or 2 smaller drinks:
4 ice cubes
1 cup (250 ml/8 fl oz) orange juice
1/2 cup skim milk powder
1 Tbsp vanilla instant pudding (optional)
1/2 tsp vanilla essence

Drop the ice cubes into the rotating blades of a food processor. (The loud noise will only last a few seconds.) Before the chopped ice melts, add the orange juice, skim milk powder, instant pudding (if you want a thick mixture) and vanilla essence. Process until really frothy. Sweeten to taste with honey or sugar if necessary.

Strawberry Dream Cream

This 'slush' depends on the strawberries being frozen rock hard!

For 1–2 drinks:
1 cup frozen strawberries
1/4 cup icing sugar
1/2 cup (125 ml/4 fl oz) chilled yoghurt

Cut the frozen strawberries into 1 cm (1/2 in) cubes, then chop them to dust in the food processor (expect an initial loud noise). Add the icing sugar, process until mixed, then add the yoghurt, stopping when the mixture is smooth and semi-liquid. Quickly spoon into glass(es) and consume promptly.

Sal's Special

A friend makes this for breakfast every morning, and swears that it cures all ills!

For 1–2 drinks:
2–3 Tbsp Milo
1 heaped tsp honey
1/4 cup (60 ml/2 fl oz) yoghurt
1 small banana, mashed
1 egg
2 cups (500 ml/16 fl oz) cold milk
1 scoop icecream (optional)

Mix the Milo, honey, yoghurt, mashed banana and raw egg in a blender or food processor until smooth. Add the milk, and in hot weather a generous scoop of icecream, and process until mixed.

> Raw eggs aren't good for young babies, but unless your doctor has said otherwise, they won't hurt an older child. Do not give raw egg to children under two.

Malted Banana Float

Malted milk adds body, richness and flavour to this mixture.

For 2 drinks:
2–3 Tbsp malted milk powder
1 mashed banana
2 scoops vanilla icecream (plus extra for
* topping)*
2 cups (500 ml/16 fl oz) very cold milk

Mix all the ingredients together vigorously in a specially designed shaker, or whiz in a food processor or blender until smooth. Pour into glasses and top with extra scoops of icecream.

Orange and Banana Cream

The perfect start to a summer day!

For 1 drink:
1 mashed banana
1 egg
1/2 cup (125 ml/4 fl oz) orange juice
about 1/2 cup vanilla icecream

Blend all the ingredients in a food processor or blender until smooth.

Tofu Temptation

The tangy flavour of dried apricots gives new life to tofu. The best dried apricots to use are the large, bright orange ones from Central Otago, which purée beautifully. The small Turkish dried apricots won't purée.

For 1 drink:
1/2 cup New Zealand dried apricots
1/2 cup (125 ml/4 fl oz) orange juice
100 g (31/2 oz) soft tofu
milk, soy milk or orange juice, to taste

Soak the dried apricots in hot water until soft (or chop then boil them until soft if you are short of time). Purée the softened apricots in a food processor or blender, adding 1/2 cup orange juice to thin the mixture. Drop in the tofu and continue processing until smooth and creamy. Thin down to the thickness you like with milk, soy milk or more orange juice. Taste and sweeten if necessary.

Variation: Replace the dried apricots with 1/2–1 cup of drained canned apricot pieces or halves.

Prunaroonie

This has a dark colour, but a good flavour.

For 4 drinks:
1 cup soaked or stewed prunes
1–1½ cups (250–375 ml/8–12 fl oz)
  orange juice
½–1 cup (125–250 ml/4–8 fl oz) yoghurt

Combine the prunes and orange juice in a food processor. Mix until smooth, then add the yoghurt slowly, tasting at intervals. Stop when the flavour and texture suit you.

Orange Milk Shake

This 'instant' breakfast is fat-free, quick, and a good start to a hot day for those who feel they can't face a solid breakfast.

For 1 serving:
½ cup (125 ml/4 fl oz) chilled orange juice
2–4 Tbsp non-fat dried milk powder
1–2 ice-blocks (optional)

Shake all the ingredients together in a screw-topped jar, or process in a food processor, and drink immediately. Alter the amount of milk powder to suit your taste.

Raspberry Smoothie

Pink and popular!

For 1 large drink:
½ cup frozen raspberries
about ½ cup (125 ml/4 fl oz) berry-
  flavoured yoghurt
1 scoop icecream

Chop the frozen raspberries finely in a food processor then add the yoghurt and icecream. Purée until smooth, stir in sugar or honey to taste and serve immediately.

Tofu Shake

Here's a nutritious meal in a glass that is almost as quick to make as it is to drink!

For 2 medium shakes:
about 125 g (4½ oz) tofu
1 banana
2 Tbsp brown sugar
1 cup (250 ml/8 fl oz) orange juice or milk
½ tsp vanilla essence

Put the tofu and pieces of banana in a blender or food processor and process until well mixed. Add the sugar, orange juice or milk, and vanilla. Process again until the mixture is smooth and creamy. Pour into two glasses, and serve with thick straws and/or long-handled spoons.

Kiwi Smoothie

Try this for an interesting, different, and creamy drink.

About 4 servings:
2 tsp grated fresh root ginger
¼ cup sugar
½ cup (125 ml/4 fl oz) water
1 soft, ripe kiwifruit
½ cup coconut cream
1 cup (250 ml/8 fl oz) apple juice

Mix the ginger, sugar and water together in a cup and microwave on High (100%) power for 2–3 minutes or until boiling briskly. Remove the skin and core from the kiwifruit and chop roughly. Blend the kiwifruit, hot ginger syrup, coconut cream and apple juice in a food processor until smooth. Sieve to remove the seeds. Serve over ice.

Variation: Add ½–1 ripe banana.

Banana Egg Nog

When my children were toddlers I found banana egg nogs a wonderful standby. They are easy to swallow, and never seem as substantial as the separate ingredients.

For 1 serving:
1 ripe banana
¾–1 cup (185–250 ml/6–8 fl oz) cold milk
1 egg
grated nutmeg or vanilla essence to taste

For best results drop all ingredients into a blender and run it until the banana has disintegrated completely. If you don't have a blender, choose a soft, ripe banana, and mash it with a fork in a bowl. Add the milk, egg and flavouring and beat with a rotary beater until smooth. Serve with a straw.

Variation: Add a dash of orange juice, some maple syrup, or a scoop of icecream.

Banana Smoothie

Froth Top milk makes amazingly thick smoothies so get some if you possibly can!

For 3–4 large smoothies:
1 small banana
½ cup (125 ml/4 fl oz) orange juice
½ cup (125 ml/4 fl oz) fat-free milk
about 1 tsp maple syrup or sugar
¼ tsp vanilla essence (optional)

Mash the banana with a fork and put it in a food processor. Add the orange juice and process until smooth. Pour in the cold milk and keep processing until very thick. Add maple syrup or sugar to taste, and vanilla if you like. Pour into glasses and serve with thick straws and teaspoons.

Golden Morning

Extra good on a lazy summer morning when you can sit in the sun to drink it!

For 2 servings:
1 tsp honey
1 egg
¾ cup (185 ml/6 fl oz) cold milk
¼–½ cup (60–125 ml/2–4 fl oz) orange
  juice
½ tsp vanilla essence

Put the honey in a bowl just big enough to hold the egg beater. Warm the bowl if the honey needs softening. Add the egg and beat until very thick, then add the milk, orange juice and vanilla. Beat just enough to mix everything. Pour into two glasses containing ice cubes, and sprinkle some nutmeg on top if you like.

Variation: Add ¼ cup dried milk powder when you add the milk.

From left to right: Golden Whirl, Orange Julia, Strawberry Dream Cream, Sal's Special, Orange and Banana Cream, Tofu Temptation, Malted Banana Float, Raspberry Smoothie, Prunaroonie

BREAKFAST EGGS

A fresh egg, simply cooked, can get any weekend off to a good start! Don't just stick with one egg recipe – try some of our family favourites!

Boiled Eggs

Pierce or tap the rounded end of an egg with a metal skewer or large needle to prevent the shell breaking when you put it in the hot water. Lower the egg carefully into enough gently boiling water to cover it. With the water simmering, cook the egg for 5–7 minutes, depending on the size of the egg, its initial temperature, and the softness of yolk you like.

Serve straight away so the egg does not harden on standing. If you don't have an egg cup, run cold water briefly over the shell, shell the egg immediately, and quarter it or chop it onto lightly buttered toast.

Hard-boiled eggs: Prepare as above but cook for about 10 minutes.

Poached Eggs

A good poached egg should be oval, with the yolk almost surrounded with white. Break a fresh egg into a saucer – if the white is compact and lying close to the yolk, without spreading, the egg will poach well.

Bring to the boil enough water to cover the eggs. Add ½ tsp salt and 1 Tbsp cider or white wine vinegar (to help the whites set quickly), then slip the eggs into the simmering water.

Simmer for about 5 minutes, until the white and yolk are set as you like them. Lift out carefully. (A potato masher lifts a poached egg from a small pot efficiently.)

Serve straight away, on hot, lightly buttered toast, plain or with a spoonful of salsa or sauce. If you don't want to serve the eggs immediately, slip them into cold water. You can reheat them later, without hardening the yolks, by standing them in very hot water for 2–3 minutes.

Cupped Eggs

When an egg in a ramekin or little bowl is cooked in a covered pan, you can make sure it cooks exactly to the stage you want. Eat it straight from the bowl to minimise dishwashing.

Top to bottom: Watercress Scrambled Eggs with Salmon, Avocado Baked Eggs, Herby Cheese Baked Eggs, Puffy Omelet, French Omelet with Mushroom and Sour Cream Filling

Stand a small bowl, cup or ramekin in about 1 cm (1/2 in) of water in a pot with a lid. Put 1/4–1/2 tsp butter in the ramekin, put the lid on the pot and bring the water to the boil, warming the container and melting the butter. Break in an egg, replace the lid and simmer until the egg is set as desired, 6–8 minutes depending on the size and coldness of the egg. Place the ramekin on a plate with fingers of hot buttered toast and serve immediately.

Variations: Add chopped tomato, ham, avocado, etc. to the butter.

Top the cooked egg with your favourite sauce.

'Comfort' Eggs

For an easy, comforting meal for a toddler, cook a cupped egg, cube a slice of buttered bread, stir it through the just-cooked egg, and serve warm, with a teaspoon.

Eggs Benedict

This rich recipe suits a very special occasion!

For 4 servings:
4 poached eggs
Hollandaise Sauce (p. 345)
2 English muffins
bacon or ham to taste

Prepare the poached eggs, cooking them ahead, as above, if you like. Make the Hollandaise Sauce. Split and toast the muffins, and grill enough bacon or ham to cover each muffin generously.

To serve, top each toasted muffin with cooked bacon, a hot poached egg and a spoonful of sauce. Serve immediately.

Herby Cheese Baked Eggs

Flavour a baked egg with herb-flavoured cream cheese.

For 1 serving:
1–2 tsp cream cheese
2 tsp chopped fresh herbs
1 egg
1 tsp fresh or sour cream

Rub a small ramekin with butter. Place the cream cheese and herbs in the bottom of the ramekin, mix briefly, then break the egg on top. Spoon the fresh or sour cream over the yolk, and bake as above. Garnish with paprika and fresh herbs and serve immediately.

Basic Microwave Scramble   M

The easiest and most reliable way to microwave an egg!

Break an egg into a small bowl or cup. Add 2 Tbsp milk and beat with a fork

until blended. Add seasoning and/or chopped parsley or chives if you like, then microwave on High (100%) power for 30–40 seconds. Gently stir the cooked egg into the centre, then cook for about 30 seconds longer, until the volume suddenly increases. Stir gently, then leave to stand for about a minute to finish cooking. If not firm enough, cook in 10-second bursts until it is!

Two eggs plus 1/4 cup (60 ml/2 fl oz) milk cook in 2–3 minutes.

Four eggs plus 1/2 cup (125 ml/4 fl oz) milk cook in about 4 minutes.

Avocado Baked Eggs

A good way to cook eggs for a group of people. Prepare these ahead and bake them when required.

For 1 serving:
1 small tomato, seeds removed, chopped
* or sliced*
1/4 avocado, sliced
2 small or 1 large egg
1 tsp fresh or sour cream

Rub a small ramekin with butter. Place the tomato and avocado in the bottom and break the eggs on top. Spoon the fresh or sour cream over the yolk. Put aside until required.

To bake, heat the oven to 200°C (400°F). Stand the ramekin in a baking pan containing about 2 cm (3/4 in) of hot water. Bake for 10–12 minutes, or until the egg is set as you like it. Serve immediately, garnished with fresh herbs, with warm toast alongside.

Watercress Scrambled Eggs with Salmon

These scrambled eggs are really special.

For 2 servings:
2 tsp butter
2 large eggs
1/4 cup sour cream
1/4 cup watercress leaves, chopped
* (or 2 tsp chopped chives)*
about 1/4 cup chopped smoked salmon
* pieces*

Melt the butter in a small frypan. Lightly beat the eggs and sour cream together and pour into the pan. Stir in most of the chopped watercress. Cook over moderate heat, pushing and lifting the mixture from the bottom of the pan with a fish slice as it sets. Do not stir the eggs at any stage. When the eggs are nearly set on top sprinkle in the salmon. Gently lift the eggs onto freshly prepared toast, an English muffin or bagel, just before the top of the mixture is completely set; the mixture will finish cooking off the heat. Garnish with the remaining watercress.

French Omelet with Mushroom and Sour Cream Filling

A french omelet takes only a few seconds to mix and cook. Omelet fillings take a little longer and are optional but nice.

For 1 serving:

Filling
1/2 cup sliced button mushrooms
water
1 tsp chopped parsley
1–2 tsp sour cream

Omelet
2 eggs
2 Tbsp water, milk or cream
pinch of salt
2 tsp butter

Cook the sliced mushrooms in a little water in a small pan until wilted. Stir in the parsley and sour cream and cook over low heat while making the omelet. Add water if the mixture looks dry, then raise the heat until nearly all the liquid evaporates.

To make the omelet, beat the eggs, water (or milk or cream), and salt together with a fork until the egg whites and yolks are just combined. Heat the butter in a 20 cm (8 in) omelet pan until straw-coloured, then tip in the egg. Stir the mixture for the first 5 seconds only. Tilt the pan and lift the edges as they set, so that the uncooked mixture runs underneath. When the surface is still moist but will no longer run, place the hot mushroom mixture on one half of the omelet. Fold the uncovered side over and slide onto a plate (or fold up the unfilled omelet and serve the mushroom mixture on top). Serve immediately.

Puffy Omelet

It is not hard to produce a good puffy omelet, but it takes a bit longer to make than a french omelet.

For 1 serving:
1 egg
pinch of salt
1 Tbsp water
1 tsp butter

Separate the egg into two small bowls. Beat the white until foamy, add the salt then beat until it forms a peak with a turned-over tip when you lift up the beater. Beat the egg yolk and water until very thick.

Heat a small frypan, and fold the egg yolk into the white until well blended. Swirl the butter round the hot pan, tip in the omelet mixture, and cook over low heat until the omelet is almost completely set and is golden brown on the bottom. Place under a hot grill to dry the top if you like. Fold the omelet in half and serve immediately.

Apple Fritters

Wonderfully popular with all age groups!

For 4 servings:

1 egg
3/4 cup (185 ml/6 fl oz) milk
1 cup self-raising flour
1–2 apples

Beat the egg and milk together with a fork. Add the flour and mix until smooth.

Using an apple corer, remove the core from the peeled or unpeeled apples, then slice them into rings about 7 mm (3/8 in) thick. Pat them dry then dip into the batter. Fry in hot oil about 5 mm (1/4 in) deep until the batter is golden brown on both sides and the apple is just tender-crisp, not so soft that the slices are falling apart. Serve sprinkled with Cinnamon Sugar (p. 11) with bacon or sausages, and maple syrup if you like.

Banana Fritters

Although you can dip whole bananas, halved bananas, or sliced bananas in batter before frying them, I think you get the best results using beaten egg and fine, dry breadcrumbs.

Beat an egg with a fork and prepare a shallow dish of dry breadcrumbs for dipping. Cut banana into diagonal slices, dip into the beaten egg, then the breadcrumbs. Fry in hot oil, 5 mm (1/4 in) deep, until the breadcrumbs are golden brown and crisp. Serve as soon as possible, with crisp grilled bacon.

Hint: If you deepfry in a wok, you use less oil than you do in a flat-bottomed pan. The sides of the wok catch spatters, too.

Summer Frittata

This frittata makes a good summer brunch.

For 3–4 people:

1/2 large red onion, sliced 5 mm (1/4 in)
   thick
1 Tbsp olive oil
3 roast peppers (see p. 346)
3 eggs
1/4 tsp salt
about 1 tsp chopped fresh herbs
about 1 Tbsp Parmesan cheese (optional)

Cook the onion in the oil in a covered, medium-sized pan, until tender but not browned. Add the sliced roasted peppers and heat through. Beat the eggs with the salt, herbs and Parmesan cheese, then pour the egg mixture over the vegetables in the pan. Jiggle the pan to distribute the egg mixture, and cook over moderate heat, lifting the sides regularly to let uncooked mixture run underneath, until it is all set. Dry the top of the frittata under the grill if necessary. Serve hot, warm, or at room temperature.

HEARTY BREAKFASTS

Few of us need large breakfasts regularly but we can usually justify traditional breakfast treats occasionally!

Mixed Grill

A good mixed grill is made up of small amounts of different foods cooked together under a grill. Aim for quality rather than quantity, include several vegetables, and make sure chops are small and lean.

Try to work out which foods take longest to cook, and partly cook them before adding the others. Alternatively, transfer the cooked food to warmed plates as soon it is ready.

Start grilling uncooked sausages first. Do not separate link sausages before cooking, since they keep their shape best cooked this way, and may be easily cut apart later. When half-cooked, add halved trimmed lambs' kidneys, bacon, and small, well-trimmed lamb cutlets. (Add halved or whole precooked sausages at this time too.) When these are partly cooked add halved tomatoes and mushrooms (preferably the large open-cupped variety). Brush mushrooms lightly with bacon fat or oil, or put a small knob of butter in each. Watch carefully, brushing anything that looks dry with a little oil, turning food when necessary and transferring cooked foods to serving plates, one at a time.

Bacon, Kidneys and Tomatoes

An occasional treat for kidney lovers!

Allow one lambs' kidney per serving. Cut in half lengthways, remove the white parts from the middle, and arrange on a grill tray, or thread several halves lengthways on skewers, so the kidneys stay flat during cooking. Grill each side until nicely browned, and until the juices run clear when the kidneys are pierced deeply. When the kidneys are partly cooked, place the bacon under the grill. Add firm, halved tomatoes a few minutes before the kidneys and bacon are ready. If anything is cooked before the others, remove it from the grill tray and keep warm.

Black Pudding, Tomatoes and Fried Egg

You will sometimes find horseshoe-shaped black puddings in the 'deli' section of super-markets or at specialist butchers' shops.

Heat just enough oil in a frypan to prevent sticking. Add halved tomatoes, cut side down, then break in the eggs. Add about 1 tsp water per egg, and cover the pan. Cook over moderate heat until the yolks are filmed over, then remove the lid and transfer the cooked eggs and tomatoes to plates in a warm oven. Add to the pan 1 cm (1/2 in) thick, diagonally cut slices of black pudding from which the skin has been removed. Sauté in a film of butter or oil for about a minute a side, until each side is dark and slightly crusted. Arrange slices on plates with the eggs and tomatoes and serve immediately.

Breakfast Potato Cakes

These potato cakes don't need to be made to an exact formula.

about 1 cup cooked mashed potato
about 1/2 cup self-raising flour
1/2 tsp of any flavoured salt
1 chopped spring onion
milk to mix

Just before cooking the cakes, mix together the mashed potato, flour and seasonings, adding enough milk to form a firm dough. Form into a cylinder on a floured board, then cut into 6–8 slices, and flour each slice. Cook in a frypan with a little very hot oil until golden brown on both sides. Good with grilled bacon, tomatoes and mushrooms.

Breakfast Kidneys   M

This recipe is unbelievably quick and easy, as well as being very rich in iron.

For 2–3 servings:

4 lambs' kidneys
2 rashers bacon
50 g (2 oz) button mushrooms
2 tsp dark soy sauce
2 tsp cornflour
2 Tbsp water or sherry

Halve, trim and slice the kidneys thinly. Place in a small microwave dish with the chopped, derinded bacon, thickly sliced mushrooms, and remaining ingredients. Stir to mix.

Cover and microwave for 5–6 minutes on High (100%) power, until the sauce has thickened and the kidneys are firm. Serve on toast, sprinkled with finely chopped fresh herbs.

Bacon, Eggs and Tomatoes

Good timing is the secret of this.

Rub the bottom of a large frypan with a film of oil. Cook bacon rashers over moderate heat from cold, then push them aside or put on plates in a warm oven. Put halved tomatoes, cut side down, in any remaining pan drippings. Break eggs into the pan, add 1–2 tsp water and cover. Cook the eggs until the yolks film over and the whites set. Turn the tomatoes while the eggs cook. Arrange the eggs and tomatoes on plates with the bacon, and serve immediately.

Lambs' Liver with Bacon

Lambs' liver (or fry) is wonderful value for money, iron-rich, and moist and delicious as long as it is not overcooked.

Cut lambs' liver into 5 mm (¼ in) slices. Trim away and discard any pieces that are not smooth and fine-textured. Allow about 50 g (2 oz) per serving. Rinse in cold water then pat dry with paper towels.

Arrange rashers of bacon and halved tomatoes under a grill. When both are cooked arrange them on heated plates in a warm oven.

Save the bacon drippings and heat them with a little oil, so the bottom of a large, non-stick frypan is barely covered. Turn the dry lambs' liver in flour seasoned with a little salt and pepper, and place in the pan. Cook over high heat, turning several times, until no pink beads appear on the top, and no pink juices run when the liver is pierced. The cooking time is short, 1–2 minutes. (Overcooked liver is dry and grainy, while well-cooked liver is tender and moist.) Serve straight away.

Hash Browns

These are best made with potatoes which have been barely cooked the day before.

Coarsely grate (using the largest holes on the grater) the required amount of potato. Heat a little butter to straw colour in a non-stick frypan. Turn the potato into the pan, and pat it down lightly to form a cake. Brown, uncovered, over moderate heat, and slide out of the pan onto a plate when the first side has a crisp brown crust. Flip back into the pan, uncooked side down. Slip a little extra butter down the side of the pan and cook, uncovered, until a crust forms on this side. Serve hot, cut into wedges, with bacon, an egg and/or tomatoes.

See also

Creamy Tomato Toast Topping, p. 34

Curried Corn on Toast, p. 34

Grilled Tomatoes on Toast, p. 34

Mushrooms on Toast, p. 34

Bagels, p. 36

Pan-Cooked Bacon, p. 99

Microwaved Bacon, p. 99

Microwaved Savoury Kidneys, p. 117

Special Spanish Omelet, p. 192

Birds' Nest Potatoes, p. 194

Make a Muffin, pp. 262–271

V9 Juice, p. 320

Top to bottom: Black Pudding, Tomatoes and Fried Egg; Mixed Grill; Summer Frittata; Bacon, Kidneys and Tomatoes

Starters and Snacks

It is a pity to serve 'a little something' only before 'special occasion' meals. There are many simple mixtures, dips in particular, that you can offer to children before a meal, to assuage hunger pangs and to make sure they eat plenty of vegetables. Crisp, raw vegetable sticks often disappear like magic when served in front of a television set, and dunked into a favourite dip. They seem much more acceptable to many children than the same vegetable cooked and presented on a dinner plate! In the following pages, I hope you find plenty of ideas for simple starters, as well as interesting nibbles to serve to your friends.

Alison's Dukkah   V

My dukkah is a highly flavoured mixture of seeds, nuts and spices. I serve it in shallow bowls with pieces of good, crusty bread that are dipped in olive oil then in dukkah.

Try dukkah sprinkled on an oiled chicken before roasting, and on cooked, oiled vegetables such as green beans.

For about 2 cups:
1/2 cup sesame seeds
1/2 cup sunflower seeds
1/2 cup pumpkin kernels
1 cup blanched almonds
1/4 cup cumin seeds
1/4 cup coriander seeds
1 1/2 tsp rock salt
1 Tbsp ground paprika
1 1/2 tsp ground turmeric

Heat the oven to 180°C (350°F). Put the seeds and almonds in to roast, in separate foil dishes, in the order given. I find the first few take longer than those listed last. Watch carefully, checking them at least every 5 minutes, and take out each container when the seeds have darkened a little and have an appetising aroma. Most will take about 10 minutes, but sesame and sunflower seeds take longer.

Leave to cool, then grind with the salt, paprika and turmeric in one or two batches in a food processor, using the pulse button, or grind in a mortar and pestle. The mixture should have some texture – it should not be ground to an oily powder.

Store in airtight containers in a cool place, away from bright light. It will gradually lose its flavour during long storage, but is still good after a couple of months.

Lentil Dahl

Lentil Dahl   V

This is the tastiest dahl I have ever made.

For about 2 cups:
1 cup red lentils
2 1/2 cups (600 ml/20 fl oz) water
1 large onion, chopped
2 cloves garlic, chopped
1 tsp each turmeric, ground coriander, ground cumin, grated fresh ginger
1 or 2 small dried chillies, crushed
1 Tbsp oil
1–2 tsp Spice Mix (see below)
1 tsp each salt and sugar
2 Tbsp lemon juice
1 Tbsp butter (optional)

Wash and drain the lentils, then simmer them in a covered pot with the next 8 ingredients for 20–30 minutes, until thick and mushy.

While this cooks, heat the oil in a small frypan, add the Spice Mix and cook until the spices brown lightly and smell aromatic. Remove from the heat and add the salt, sugar and lemon juice.

When the lentils are almost cooked, stir in the spice mixture. Adjust seasonings to taste, adding a tablespoon of butter if you like. The dahl will thicken on cooling and standing. Serve it warm or cold as a dip or as a filling in flatbread rollups. Refrigerate in a covered container for up to 4 days.

Spice Mix

Mix equal volumes of black mustard seeds, cumin seeds, fennel seeds and fenugreek (from a store stocking Indian ingredients). Store in an airtight jar.

Flatbread Rollups

Spread dahl on naan or mountain bread. Add grated carrot, lettuce leaves, sliced celery (and grated cheese if you like). Roll up tightly, wrap in cling film until needed, then cut into short lengths with a really sharp knife. Best eaten within 30 minutes of making.

Good Old Onion Dip   V

(Photo p. 26)

Dips like this have been around for a long time, but are still quick, easy and popular.

For about a cup:
1 packet (about 30 g/1 oz) onion soup mix
1 carton (250 g/8 oz) sour cream

Stir the soup mix and sour cream together with a fork until no lumps of powder remain. Leave to stand for at least half an hour, until the pieces of onion soften.

Use straight away or cover and refrigerate for up to 2 days, thinning with milk or yoghurt if it thickens too much. Serve with vegetable dippers (see below).

Variations: Replace half the sour cream with plain, unsweetened yoghurt. Stir one or more of the following into the dip: chopped chives, spring onions, parsley or other fresh herbs, curry powder or paste, pesto, finely chopped walnuts, chopped roasted peanuts, chutney or tabasco sauce.

Vegetable Dippers   V

Serve a colourful selection of crisp, cold vegetable pieces, slices or sticks, e.g. carrots, celery, red and green peppers, cauliflower, young green beans, radishes, button mushrooms, daikon, young turnips, tender asparagus heads and snow peas.

To keep vegetables crisp, wash them, cut up as desired and rinse with cold water, leaving a little remaining, then refrigerate in sealed plastic bags until required.

Pesto Dips   V

For extra-easy pesto dips, simply stir 2–3 Tbsp of your favourite pesto through 1 cup of sour cream, cream cheese or plain unsweetened yoghurt. Thin with milk if required and adjust seasonings to taste.

Serve with raw vegetables, potato wedges, corn chips, crostini (p. 27), melba toast (p. 344), crisp-baked pita bread wedges or baked, grilled or fried tortilla wedges.

Easy Guacamole V

A dollop of this guacamole will improve almost any snack. Use a ripe avocado – its flesh will 'give' slightly when it is ready to use.

For about 1 cup:
1 ripe avocado
2–3 Tbsp Easy Tomato Salsa (p. 346)
  or 2 Tbsp lemon juice
1 finely chopped spring onion
1/4 tsp salt
tabasco sauce
chopped fresh coriander (optional)

Cut around the centre of the avocado lengthways, then gently twist the two halves apart. Chop a sharp knife into the stone and twist it to remove the stone.

Spoon the flesh into a bowl, scraping out the greenest flesh close to the shell. Mash with a fork, and add the salsa and other ingredients in quantities to suit your taste.

Use immediately or cover with cling film touching the surface and leave for no longer than an hour. Use as a dip for corn chips, a topping for Mexican foods, crackers, crostini (p. 27), and in any other ways you like.

Green Pea Guacamole V

Frozen peas make this surprisingly good, brilliant green, nearly instant dip.

For about 2 cups:
1/4 cup roughly chopped fresh coriander
1 Tbsp chopped pickled jalapeno peppers
1 Tbsp liquid from jar of jalapeno peppers
1/2 tsp ground cumin
1 tsp herb, onion or garlic salt
2 spring onions, roughly chopped
1 Tbsp lime or lemon juice
400–500 g (about 1 lb) frozen peas (baby
  peas if possible)
about 3 Tbsp olive oil

Put the first 7 ingredients in a food processor. Use fresh lime or lemon juice, or the (unsweetened) lime juice in plastic bottles.

Partly thaw the peas and get rid of any ice by putting them in a sieve (in several batches) and running hot water over them. Process the nearly thawed (uncooked) peas with the other ingredients until evenly chopped and fairly smooth, adding the oil while processing. Taste and add more flavourings if you want a more highly seasoned dip.

Use immediately as a dip for corn chips, potato chips, wedges or toasted pita bread, or spread on crostini (p. 27), crisp crackers, etc., and eat straight away. Refrigerate leftovers in a covered container for up to 24 hours.

Dreamy Bean Dip V

Olive oil is necessary to give this light-coloured dip a good flavour. It makes an ideal summer lunch or dinner starter.

For 2 cups:
1 cup haricot beans or chickpeas
4 cups (1 litre/32 fl oz) boiling water
seasonings
1 tsp each salt and sugar
1 large onion, chopped
2 cloves garlic, chopped
1/2 tsp ground cumin
1/4 cup (60 ml/2 fl oz) olive oil
1/2 cup chopped fresh herbs (parsley,
  oreganum, thyme, etc.)
juice of 1 lemon

Pour the boiling water over the dried beans or chickpeas and leave to soak for at least 8 hours. Drain, cover with fresh water and add seasonings such as several garlic cloves, a sprig of celery and parsley, etc., if available. Cook for 45–75 minutes, until the beans are soft and mealy, or for 10–15 minutes on high pressure in a pressure cooker. Add the salt and sugar to the cooked beans and leave to cool in their cooking liquid.

Gently cook the onion, garlic and cumin in the olive oil in a covered pot or pan for 5–10 minutes, until tender but not browned.

Mexican Cheese and Tomato Dip V

Keep the ingredients for this easy, delicious hot dip on hand so you can make it at short notice. Served with plenty of corn chips it is always popular!

For 4–8 servings:
1 medium onion, chopped
1 green pepper, chopped
1 Tbsp oil
1 Tbsp chopped jalapeno peppers
1 can (425 g/15 oz) Mexican tomatoes
1 Tbsp plain flour
2 cups grated tasty cheese
1/4–1/2 cup low-fat sour cream
fresh coriander or spring onions to garnish

Cook the onion and green pepper in the oil, without browning, for 2–3 minutes.

Add the jalapeno peppers (available in a jar from supermarkets) and tomatoes, and bring to the boil.

Toss the flour through the cheese, then stir into the hot tomato mixture until melted and smooth.

Serve hot in a shallow dipping bowl, topped with sour cream and garnished with chopped coriander or finely chopped spring onions. Surround with corn chips.

Variations: Replace Mexican tomatoes with whole tomatoes and add cumin and oreganum to taste. Drain the beans,

reserving the cooking liquid, and purée with the onion mixture, herbs and lemon juice, adding enough cooking liquid to make a mixture of dip consistency. Taste and add salt as needed. Refrigerate for up to 3 days.

Serve with corn chips and vegetable dippers (p. 21).

Zesty Red Bean Dip V

I like to take a can of red beans from my store cupboard and make this lively dip in just a few minutes. Its flavour depends on the seasonings used, so add more or less to suit your taste.

For 1 3/4 cups:
1 large clove garlic
1/4 red onion or 2 spring onions
1/4 cup roughly chopped parsley
2 Tbsp roughly chopped fresh coriander
1 tsp ground cumin
2 tsp pickled jalapeno peppers
2 tsp lime (or lemon) juice
1 Tbsp tomato paste
2 Tbsp olive oil (optional)
1 can (400 g/14 oz) kidney beans, drained
bean liquid, to thin mixture

Roughly chop the garlic and red onion, or cut the spring onion into 2 cm (3/4 in) lengths. Put into a food processor with the parsley, coriander, cumin, jalapeno slices and lime or lemon juice. Chop finely, then clean the sides of the processor and add the tomato paste and olive oil and process again briefly.

Drain the bean liquid into a suitable container, then add the beans to the processor and process until mixed but not completely smooth. Add enough bean liquid to thin the dip to the consistency you like, then taste to see if it needs more seasoning. You may need none – it depends on the seasoning of the beans and the peppers. If it is bland, add a little salt and more lime or lemon juice, or more tomato paste. If it is too zesty, add enough sour cream to 'soften' the flavours.

Refrigerate and use within 3 days. Serve with corn chips, vegetable dippers (p. 21) or toasted wedges of flour tortillas.

Liptauer Cheese V

My version of this tasty Austrian spread is wonderful on crackers, melba toast (p. 344), crostini (p. 27), or flat slices of raw vegetables.

For about 1 1/2 cups:
1 cup cottage cheese
100 g (3 1/2 oz) butter, softened
1 tsp paprika
1 tsp ground caraway seeds
2 tsp chopped capers
1–2 tsp chopped anchovies
1 tsp mixed mustard
2 Tbsp chopped chives

Beat all the ingredients together until light, well mixed and creamy, using a food processor or a bowl and a wooden spoon. Refrigerate in a covered container until required. It tastes best when eaten within 24 hours, but can be kept for up to a month.

Note: Grind the caraway seeds with a pestle and mortar (or hammer) just before using them.

Creamy Vegetable Dip   V

A creamy dip flavoured with dill leaves is wonderful with crisp vegetable dippers (p. 21). It is worth hunting for dried dill leaves since their flavour is intense – much stronger than fresh dill leaves.

For 1 cup:
½ cup (125 ml/4 fl oz) unsweetened plain yoghurt
½ cup sour cream
1 Tbsp finely chopped parsley or spring onion
1 tsp dried dill leaves
½–1 tsp plain or seasoned salt

Stir the first 4 ingredients together and leave to stand for half an hour or longer, then add plain or seasoned salt to taste, remembering that the dip will be diluted by the vegetables dipped in it.

Surround the dip with carrot sticks, celery sticks, cauliflorets, slices of turnip or swede, radishes, cucumber sticks and green pepper strips. To ensure all the vegetables are really cold and crisp when served, put them in plastic bags with a little water, shake to coat, then refrigerate until required.

Layered Festive Dip   V

This spectacular layered dip can be prepared up to 24 hours before a party, without the avocado discolouring.

For 6 servings:
2 cloves garlic, finely chopped
¼ tsp chilli powder
1 tsp each ground cumin and oreganum
¼ tsp salt
1 Tbsp oil
1 can (440 g/15 oz) baked beans
2 Tbsp tomato paste
1 or 2 avocados
3–4 Tbsp lemon juice
½–1 cup low-fat sour cream
hot chilli sauce to taste
fresh coriander, black olives, spring onions and hot chilli sauce to garnish

Cook the garlic and seasonings in oil for about a minute. Add the baked beans and tomato paste, mashing well as the mixture heats through. Remove from the heat and leave to cool, then spread evenly in one or more straight-sided glass dishes.

Mash the avocado and lemon juice and spread evenly over the bean mixture.

Season the sour cream with chilli sauce, then spread over the avocado. Cover and refrigerate until required.

Just before serving, decorate with chopped coriander, sliced pitted black olives and/or spring onions and a dribble of hot chilli sauce. Serve with corn chips or crostini (p. 27), scooping deep to get several layers.

Variation: Stir 1 cup grated cheese into the hot bean mixture.

Sesame Eggplant Dip   V

This dip (or relish) has an amazing flavour even though its appearance is rather drab. It is well worth trying, and is addictive!

For about 1½ cups:
300 g (10½ oz) eggplant
1 tsp grated fresh ginger
1 large clove garlic, finely chopped
2 spring onions, finely chopped
1 Tbsp finely chopped fresh coriander
1 Tbsp light soy sauce
1 Tbsp wine vinegar
½ jalapeno pepper, finely chopped
1½ tsp sesame oil
1 Tbsp olive or other oil (optional)
1–2 tsp toasted sesame seeds

Cut unpeeled eggplant into small cubes and, as they are prepared, drop them into a small amount of boiling water in a covered pot. Stir after each addition. When tender, after 5–10 minutes, drain off any remaining water.

While the eggplant cooks, mix together all the remaining ingredients except the toasted sesame seeds. Add to the warm, drained eggplant, tossing thoroughly to mix. (If you prefer smaller pieces, chop in a food processor.)

Refrigerate in a covered container for up to 4 days. Serve piled in a bowl, topped with the toasted sesame seeds and extra chopped coriander. Dip corn chips, crostini (p. 27) or melba toast (p. 344).

Sesame Eggplant Dip

Herbed Chicken Liver Pâté

Herbed Chicken Liver Pâté

This easily prepared, smooth and creamy pâté is the best I have ever made.

For about 2 cups:

100 g (3½ oz) butter
1½ tsp minced or very finely chopped garlic
350–400 g (12–14 oz) chicken livers
2 fresh or dried bayleaves, if available
2–4 Tbsp finely chopped fresh herbs, e.g. thyme and oreganum
2 Tbsp chopped fresh parsley
2 Tbsp Thai sweet chilli sauce
¼ cup (60 ml/2 fl oz) cream
2–4 Tbsp brandy or sherry (or a mixture)
freshly ground pepper
½ tsp salt

Melt the butter over moderate heat in a fairly large, non-stick frypan. Stir in the garlic then add the chicken livers, straight from their pack. (Use a little more or less as desired.)

Add the bayleaves, fresh herbs and chilli sauce and cook over moderate heat until the livers are cooked right through, about 5 minutes. As they cook, chop them into small pieces (in the pan) with kitchen scissors. When the cut surfaces show no pink, they are ready.

Add the cream, bring the mixture back to the boil, then add the sherry and/or brandy and simmer for a minute longer. Turn off the heat, add the pepper and salt.

Remove the bayleaves then purée the hot mixture in a food processor. Sieve the mixture, a third at a time, to remove any fibrous pieces. (Bang the sieve above the bowl for easiest sieving.) Pour into suitable containers, cover and chill until firm. Refrigerate for up to a week or freeze for up to 2 months.

Note: Freezing alters the flavours of the herbs; if freezing the pâté for long, omit the herbs for a mild flavour.

Pretend Pâté   V

This vegetarian pâté seems 'meaty', and is always popular. If you are serving it for a large party give it a vegetarian label, since it is unlikely to be recognised as such!

For about 1½ cups:

¼ cup (60 ml/2 fl oz) olive oil
2 cloves garlic, chopped
1 large onion, chopped
¼ cup celery, chopped
1 cup chopped walnuts
pinch of chilli powder
¼ tsp dried thyme
4 hard-boiled eggs
½ tsp salt
freshly ground black pepper

Heat the oil in a small frypan, add the garlic, onion and celery, and cook over moderate heat until the vegetables are lightly browned. Add the chopped walnuts and continue to cook until they

brown slightly. Stir in the chilli powder and thyme, remove from the heat, then transfer the mixture to a food processor fitted with a metal chopping blade. Process briefly then add the roughly chopped eggs, salt and pepper and process until the mixture is fairly smooth – whatever you consider to be pâté texture. Taste and adjust seasonings as desired.

Serve at room temperature or chilled, with melba toast (p. 344), crackers and/or vegetable dippers (p. 21).

Baked Bread Savouries   V

It is easy to forget how good some simple foods are. Bread, baked until crisp, can be turned into many different sorts of savouries, all of which are good. Here are some of the variations I make. Bake them all at 150°C (300°F) for 15–30 minutes, until the bread has dried out, or put them in an oven that is cooling down after being used for something else.

Store your baked bread savouries in airtight containers. They are nicest eaten soon after they are made, but should all keep quite well for several days.

•Make melba toast to serve with pâté and dips by baking sandwich-sliced bread in whole slices, halves or triangles. For a chunkier dipper use toast-sliced bread in fingers or triangles.

- Place slices of bread on an oven tray, spray lightly with oil, then sprinkle lightly with one or more flavoured salts (e.g. celery, garlic, herb-flavoured) before baking.
- Cut thin diagonal slices from bread rolls. Season if desired, then sprinkle lightly with grated tasty cheese and bake. (Place slices close together on the baking tray, then grate cheese over the whole tray, separating the slices after cooking.)
- Mix together 100 g (4 oz) cheese, 50 g (2 oz) softened butter, 1 tsp garlic or onion salt, 1 tsp celery salt and 1 tsp paprika or curry powder in a food processor bowl; process with the metal blade until smooth. Alternatively, grate the cheese and mix the ingredients well using a wooden spoon. This amount of filling will coat 12 large sandwich-slices of bread. Cut each slice into 4 or 5 fingers after spreading. For straight fingers remove crusts from the long sides of the fingers. Bake as above.

Note: If bread savouries get soft, you can always crisp them up again in a warm oven.

Flatbread Crisps V

The growing number of flatbreads on the market, including pita breads, various tortillas, Indian naan and mountain bread, make interesting and varied snacks.

When fresh and soft these flatbreads can easily be rolled up or folded around fillings, but if they stand around too long they tend to crack when folded or rolled, especially when cold.

When fresh, or after a few days in the refrigerator, they may be left flat, cut into smaller pieces and baked, grilled or heated in a frypan until crisp. They then make great dippers.

Thin flour tortillas make excellent crisps, cut into squares, rectangles or wedge shapes, or sometimes heated in large rounds, then broken into small pieces for dipping. Brush or spray both surfaces lightly but evenly with a little olive or canola oil. Heat in a heavy, dry, preheated frypan, about 3–4 minutes per side, until there are darker flecks on each side (they will become crisper as they cool on a rack),

OR heat for about the same time under a grill until golden brown, turning after 2 minutes,

OR heat on an oven tray at 180°C (350°F) for about the same time, until evenly golden brown, without turning.

Cool on a rack.

Note: The time taken to crisp flatbreads varies with their thickness and freshness. Thin or stale breads will take a shorter time.

Thicker flatbread crisps are best grilled or baked. Grill under lower heat, or further from the heat than thinner breads; their cooking time will also be longer.

Poppadoms V

Since uncooked poppadoms may be kept in a cupboard for months, then cooked very quickly and easily, they make useful dippers. Microwave on High (100%) power, on a folded paper towel, until puffed over the whole surface. You will smell them just before they are ready. Stop cooking them if you see them turning brown.

Large poppadoms take 40–70 seconds each. Cook one at a time and break them into pieces before dipping.

Very small poppadoms (the size of a 50-cent coin) take about 30 seconds for 8–10, arranged in a circle on a paper towel.

Note: For extra crispness, spray poppadoms lightly with canola oil before heating them.

Cheese and Onion Crisps V

These crisps taste best if left for a few hours (or overnight) before being eaten.

1 packet (30 g/1 oz) onion soup mix
¼ cup (60 ml/2 fl oz) milk
100 g (3½ oz) cold butter
1 cup plain flour
1 cup grated cheese

Turn the oven to 180°C (350°F). Mix the soup and milk together and leave to stand for 15 minutes.

Meantime in another bowl, or a food processor, cut or rub the cold butter into the flour until it looks like rolled oats. Mix in the cheese and the onion soup mixture. Add a little extra flour or milk if necessary to make a firm dough. Roll out on a floured board and cut into squares, fingers or interesting shapes. Push any scraps together and roll out again.

Bake on an ungreased oven tray for 10–15 minutes, until lightly browned. Cool on a wire rack, then put in an airtight tin.

Zingy Cheese Straws V

Cheese straws are always popular! This mixture is fairly highly seasoned, so the cheese flavour is intensified. Leave out any seasonings you don't have, but this combination is good!

The cheese doesn't have to be in prime condition. This is the perfect way to use up bits and pieces which have dried up somewhere at the back of your refrigerator!

2 cups plain flour
1 tsp celery salt
1 tsp garlic or onion salt
1 tsp paprika
1 tsp curry powder
1 tsp dry mustard
125 g (4½ oz) cold butter
1–2 cups grated tasty cheese
about ½ cup (125 ml/4 fl oz) cold water

Turn the oven to 220°C (425°F). Sift together the flour, salts, paprika, curry powder and mustard. (Replace the seasoned salts with half the quantity of plain salt if desired.) Cut the cold butter into the seasoned flour or rub it in with your fingers until the mixture resembles coarse breadcrumbs.

Toss the grated cheese into this mixture until the cheese is well coated with flour.

Gradually add a tablespoon of cold water to the dry ingredients, tossing with a fork or processing briefly. Repeat with more water, adding just enough to make the dough stick together to form a ball when pressed with the fingertips. The amount of water will vary with the type of flour – the quantity suggested is a guide only. (Take care not to overmix in a food processor.) Place the ball of dough in the refrigerator for 5 minutes then roll out thinly, using just enough extra flour to stop it sticking to the board and rolling pin.

Cut the dough into strips (or other dipping shapes), place on an ungreased oven tray, and bake until golden. Watch them carefully after they have baked for 5 minutes, because they change colour quickly.

Remove from the oven tray as soon as they are taken from the oven, cool on a rack, then store in airtight jars.

Mountains of Mousetraps V

Mousetraps are so popular it is worth making them in bulk every so often! Long, slow cooking is needed if cheese-topped bread savouries are to remain crisp during long storage.

1 medium-sliced loaf
300–500 g (10 oz–1 lb) grated tasty cheese

Turn the oven to 150°C (300°F), or 130°C (250°F) if fan-baking. Lay the slices of bread close together on oven trays that have been lightly sprayed with non-stick spray, olive or canola oil. Sprinkle with cheese.

Bake for 30 minutes, then turn the oven a little higher if they are very light in colour, and bake for about 30 minutes longer until completely dry and crisp. If you are cooking several trays at once, change the tray positions every 10 minutes.

Cool on a rack and store in airtight plastic bags or jars as soon as they are cold. They will keep for 1–2 weeks.

Savoury Crackers　　V

Try to leave these little biscuits for an hour or two after they are baked – they taste best if you can wait!

Cut them into long thin sticks, into stars, circles or any other shape you like. They make excellent dippers but are good plain, too.

1 cup plain flour
2 tsp baking powder
1 tsp salt
1 tsp paprika
1/4 cup sesame seeds
25 g (1 oz) cold butter
1/2–1 cup grated tasty cheese
about 1/4 cup (60 ml/2 fl oz) cold water

Turn the oven to 200°C (400°F). Measure the flour, baking powder, salt and paprika into a sieve and shake into a large bowl.

Brown the sesame seeds lightly over moderate heat in a dry frypan, then tip them into the bowl.

Rub the butter into the flour mixture until it looks like rolled oats. Stir in the grated cheese, then add the water a few drops at a time while stirring with a fork. Stop adding water when the mixture is wet enough to stick together in a ball.

Roll out very thinly on a floured board, adding extra flour if necessary so the dough doesn't stick. Cut into whatever shapes you like.

Bake until the edges brown, watching after 5 minutes – very thin, small biscuits cook very quickly; big, thick ones take longer.

Cheesy Pastry　　V

This cheese pastry may be used for dippers, cheese straws or crackers. Children often like to help to cut the pastry into small fancy shapes.

1 cup plain flour
1 tsp baking powder
75 g (2½ oz) cold butter
½ cup cottage cheese
2 Tbsp grated Parmesan cheese
¼ cup grated tasty cheese
1–2 Tbsp cold water

Turn the oven to 200°C (400°F). Put all the ingredients except the water into a bowl or food processor. Rub in or process until the butter and cheeses are well mixed through the flour.

Gradually add enough water to dampen the dough while stirring or processing in bursts, using the pulse button.

Roll out very thinly. Cut into shapes with small pastry cutters, or into long, thin strips. Place carefully on an oven tray covered with a non-stick liner and bake for 5–10 minutes, or until lightly browned. Watch carefully, since they brown very quickly.

When cold, store in an airtight container.

Stuffed Eggs　　V

These disappear fast whenever I make them. I serve them for lunch with salady things, or with other snacks before a vegetable main course for evening entertaining.

To stop eggshells from splitting as you boil the eggs, tap a tiny hole in the rounded end with a metal skewer or any sharp metal tool. Cover the eggs with water and simmer for about 12 minutes, then stand them in cold water until cool enough to handle, tap gently all over to crack the shells evenly, then peel off the shells.

Halve lengthways and gently lift out the yolks. Mash these with a fork, adding ½ tsp butter per egg, and enough milk to soften them to a smooth, spoonable consistency. Add a few capers, chopped herbs or olives if you like, season carefully, then spoon the filling back into the whites.

Anchovy Stuffed Eggs

8 hard-boiled eggs
2 anchovy fillets, drained
25 g (1 oz) butter, at room temperature
2 tsp chopped chives or spring onion
1 Tbsp milk

Mix the egg yolks with the drained anchovy fillets, butter, chives or spring onion and milk in a food processor bowl. Process until smooth, adding more milk if necessary, then spoon into the egg whites.

Quick Tapenade　　V

This mixture has a very strong, concentrated flavour. Its colour varies with the darkness of the olives used.

For about 1 cup:
1 cup sliced black olives
2–4 cloves garlic, peeled
2 or 3 anchovy fillets (omit for a
　vegetarian version)
1 Tbsp capers
1 Tbsp caper liquid
1 Tbsp lemon or lime juice
2–3 Tbsp olive oil

Finely chop (but do not purée) all the ingredients except the olive oil, using a food processor.

Add 2 Tbsp of oil to the mixture and spoon into a jar. Pour the remaining oil over the top, and close with an airtight screw-on top.

Use as a spread on melba toast (p. 344), etc. or stir into unsweetened, plain yoghurt, sour cream or mayonnaise, in proportions to suit your taste, to make dips and milder-flavoured spreads. (Unflavoured yoghurt and tapenade produce a dip with the strongest tapenade flavour.) Store in the refrigerator for up to a month.

Variation: Add 2–3 Tbsp chopped sun-dried tomatoes.

Good Old Onion Dip (p. 21),
Stuffed Eggs

Potted Cheese V

Small quantities of this strongly flavoured cheese mixture team well with pears, nuts, grapes, apples, crackers and celery.

Matured cheddars 'pot' well. So do milder cheddars when mixed with blue cheese, although they have a greenish-grey colour.

50 g (2 oz) blue and/or matured cheddar cheese
25 g (1 oz) unsalted butter, at room temperature
pepper, mace or nutmeg
1–3 Tbsp sherry, brandy or port

Mash, grate or process the cheese with the butter. Add a little pepper, mace or nutmeg, then add whatever liquid you want to use, about a teaspoon at a time, until you have a soft, spreading texture.

Store in the refrigerator for up to a week, and serve in small, covered pots. Spread on crackers, or slices of apples, pears, etc.

Marinated Mushrooms V

Many people find marinated mushrooms quite irresistible! Drain them, spear with cocktail sticks, and place on a plate with other finger food.

about 300 g (10 oz) small, tightly closed button mushrooms
¼ cup (60 ml/2 fl oz) wine vinegar
1 tsp balsamic vinegar (optional)
1 tsp (1–2 cloves) minced garlic
1 tsp oreganum
½ tsp salt
1 tsp sugar
1 Tbsp tomato paste
½ cup (125 ml/4 fl oz) olive oil

Brush the mushrooms clean if necessary, and trim the stems level with the caps. Halve large mushrooms if desired.

Measure the remaining ingredients into a small pot and bring to the boil, stirring to mix. Add the mushrooms, and stir until they soften and are covered with the hot liquid. (At first there will not seem to be enough liquid, but liquid comes from the mushrooms as they cook.) Simmer for about 3 minutes, then transfer to a jar, making sure the liquid covers the mushrooms. Cover and leave to cool.

Serve warm or at room temperature within 3 days, refrigerating meantime.

Notes: Olive oil turns cloudy when refrigerated, but will clear again when warmed a little.

Mushrooms reduce down considerably when cooked; what starts out as a large quantity will end up a lot smaller.

Sliced, marinated mushrooms make great toppings for pizzas. For very easy individual pizzas, halve hamburger buns or use small round pita breads. Spread with sun-dried

Crostini, Marinated Mushrooms

tomato pesto or tomato paste, then add a selection (2 or 3 is usually enough!) of your favourite toppings, including marinated mushrooms, and sprinkle generously with grated cheese. Bake at 200°C (400°F) or grill until the cheese bubbles and browns, then serve immediately.

Crostini V

You can make these popular dippers or savoury bases before you need them and store them in an airtight container.

1 loaf french bread
flavourings (e.g. Parmesan cheese, pesto, tapenade, mixed mustard, ground cumin, tabasco sauce)
¼ cup (60 ml/2 fl oz) olive oil

Turn the oven to 150°C (300°F). Slice the bread diagonally into 1 cm (½ in) slices. Mix the flavourings of your choice with the olive oil in a shallow bowl and brush or spread evenly over the sliced bread, on one or both sides.

Arrange on a baking tray that has been lightly sprayed or covered with a non-stick or Teflon liner and bake for 5–10 minutes, until golden brown and crisp. When cold, store in airtight containers for up to a week.

Variation: Use slices of any other interestingly shaped or flavoured breads. This is a good way to use up the ends of loaves which are a little stale.

Sinfully Rich Potato Wedges V

These rich but absolutely delicious potatoes should be served as an occasional treat. They are coated with a heavily herbed and spiced mixture and baked until crisp.

For 3–4 servings:
4 large potatoes (1 kg/2 lb)
25 g (1 oz) butter
¼ tsp salt
3 Tbsp olive oil
2 tsp finely chopped garlic
2 tsp ground cumin
1 tsp oreganum
¼–½ tsp chilli powder

Microwave or boil the scrubbed potatoes until barely tender. Cool if you have time, then cut each potato lengthways into 8 wedges.

Melt the butter in a large roasting pan, add the remaining ingredients and mix well.

Turn the potato wedges in the roasting pan, mixing them gently but thoroughly with your hands until they are well coated. Spread in a single layer then bake at 180°C (350°F) for 1–1½ hours, until crisp, turning once. Drain well and serve hot or warm with your favourite tomato-based salsa.

Twice-Baked Potato Skins

Twice-Baked Potato Skins   V

Loved for their crispness, twice-baked potato skins are made from potatoes which have previously been baked whole.

If baking only a few potatoes, microwave them on High (100%) power, allowing about 10–12 minutes for 500 g (1 lb), or 20 minutes for 1 kg (2 lb). Bake larger numbers of potatoes in the oven at 200°C (400°F) for 45–60 minutes.

In either case, potatoes are cooked when they 'give' slightly when squeezed (use a cloth to avoid burns).

Quarter medium-sized potatoes lengthways. Cut bigger potatoes lengthways into sixths. Scoop or cut out the flesh, leaving 5–8 mm (¼ in) of potato on the skins. (Use the flesh in other recipes.)

Brush the skins with olive or other oil, then season with salt and pepper or your favourite seasoning mix. (Prepare ahead to this stage if you like.)

Heat the oven to 230°C (450°F) and bake in one layer in a shallow roasting pan or metal baking pan for 15–20 minutes, or until crisp with golden-brown edges. If

desired sprinkle with a little grated cheese, chopped olives, etc. before lifting off the baking pan.

Serve hot or warm with your favourite dip, sweet chilli sauce, sour cream (plain or flavoured with chopped herbs or pesto), etc.

Jacket Wedges   V

These easy, tasty and filling snacks seem to be popular with all age groups. Ring the changes by adding different spices to flavour them, then serve them with bought or homemade dips – the sky's the limit!

For 3–4 servings:
4 large potatoes (about 1 kg/2 lb)
3 Tbsp olive oil
1 Tbsp Kikkoman soy sauce
1 tsp minced garlic (1–2 cloves)
1 tsp ground cumin
1 Tbsp grated Parmesan cheese
1 Tbsp plain flour

Turn the oven to 200–220°C (400–425°F). Scrub but do not peel the potatoes. Cut them into halves, quarters, then eighths lengthways. Put the prepared wedges into a bowl of cold water and leave to stand

while you mix all the other ingredients together in another bowl.

Drain the potatoes and pat them completely dry between several layers of paper towels. Drop the dried potatoes into the seasoning mixture then, using your fingers, gently turn them until they are thoroughly coated.

Lie the wedges in one layer on baking paper in a large, shallow roasting dish or other baking pan, or in a baking pan with a good non-stick finish, drizzled with a little oil.

Bake for 35–40 minutes, or until tender and golden brown, turning after 20 minutes.

If you like, sprinkle with a little salt, seasoned salt, and/or grated cheddar cheese before lifting them off the baking pan. (I have found that wedges salted before cooking are less crisp.)

Serve straight away, with dips such as guacamole (p. 22), salsa (p. 346), satay sauce (p. 346) or sour cream.

Variation: Add different herbs and spices to suit your taste.

Filo Pastry Savouries   V

Filo pastry gives a feeling of lightness and crunchiness to savouries. This traditional filling of spinach and feta cheese is hard to beat, but you can use creamed corn instead of spinach if you prefer.

Filling
½ cup well-squeezed cooked spinach
½ cup crumbled feta cheese
1 egg
¼ cup toasted pinenuts (optional)

Turn the oven to 180°C (350°F). Chop the drained spinach finely and mix it with the cheese, egg and nuts, using a fork to combine them.

To make small triangular savouries, sandwich 2 sheets of filo pastry together with a small amount of melted butter. Cut the double sheet into 6 strips, each about 6–7 cm (2½–3 in) wide. Put a teaspoonful of filling on the end of one strip, about a centimetre from one edge and the bottom. Fold the corner with the filling over, so the bottom edge is against the side, and the filling is enclosed. Keep folding the pastry over and over until the filling is enclosed by all the pastry in the strip. Fold any ends under, or cut them off. Brush the top surface with melted butter, and place on a lightly buttered oven tray or a sponge-roll pan.

Make as many triangles as you want, then bake them, uncovered, for 10–20 minutes, or until the pastry is crisp and golden brown. Serve immediately, or reheat when required.

Crispy Pork Wontons

These little wontons are always popular and are not difficult to make, once you locate the wonton skins. Look for them in stores which stock Asian supplies if they are not in the freezer at your supermarket.

40–50 wonton skins
400 g (14 oz) pork mince
1 Tbsp sherry or lemon juice
2 Tbsp soy sauce
1 Tbsp cornflour
1 tsp sesame oil
2–3 spring onions
canola or other oil
dipping sauce

Thaw the wonton skins if necessary, keeping them wrapped.

Put the minced pork in a bowl and mix in the next 4 ingredients with a fork. Chop the spring onions into thin slices, add them to the mixture, and mix well. Divide this filling into 4 parts, then each part into 10 small blobs.

Heat 1 cm (1/2 in) of oil in a small pot or heat the oven to 225°C (425°F). Taking 4 wonton skins at a time, put one blob of filling in the middle of each. Dampen one side with a little water, then fold the edge over, pressing the sides together. Leave flat for easier frying, or fold over, dampening parts which touch. Lower carefully into the hot oil, and adjust the heat so the wontons brown in 1 minute, OR brush both sides with oil and bake on baking paper for 10 minutes.

Drain cooked wontons on paper towels, and eat hot with a chilli or sweet-sour sauce for dipping.

Shaping Wontons

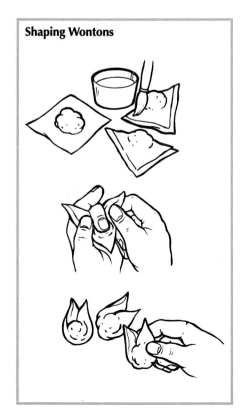

Parmesan Meatballs

These are always popular, and may be made ahead and reheated in a microwave oven or frypan.

For about 40 small meatballs:
1 toast-slice bread
350–400 g (12–14 oz) lean beef mince
1/4 cup grated Parmesan cheese
1/4 cup chopped parsley
1/2 tsp freshly grated nutmeg
salt and pepper to taste
1 large egg
olive or other oil for cooking

Break up the slice of bread and process until crumbed in a food processor. Add the remaining ingredients and process only until combined. If you do not have a food processor, leave the bread to stand in a bowl with the egg, then mash it with a fork before mixing it with the remaining ingredients.

With wet hands, shape the mixture into balls the size of small walnuts. Heat enough oil to cover the bottom of a medium-sized frypan. Cook the meatballs in batches over medium heat, jiggling the pan to turn them, until they are golden brown and cooked in the centre; about 5 minutes.

Serve warm, on toothpicks, with a tomato or chilli dipping sauce.

Crispy Popcorn   V

You can make about 6 cups of lovely, crisp popcorn from 1/4 cup of popping corn in a few minutes, so it pays to keep a jar of popping corn on hand. Plain popcorn is easiest and fastest to make (and is best for you), but you can season and lightly butter popcorn too.

Put 1/4 cup of popping corn and 1 Tbsp of oil in a large pot. Cover, preferably with a glass lid, and heat, tossing the corn every 30 seconds or so. After a few minutes the corn should start popping. Turn the heat to low, and do not lift the lid as very hot corn can pop right out of the pan into someone's eye! Shake the pot occasionally so that the unpopped corn falls to the bottom.

After you have heard no popping for 2 minutes, open the pot, keeping small faces well out of the range of the popping corn. Serve the popcorn just as it is, straight away.

Curried Popcorn   V

Pour about 1 Tbsp of melted butter over the popped corn in the pot. Toss to mix then sprinkle with a mixture of 1/2 tsp seasoned salt, 1/2 tsp curry powder and 1 tsp icing sugar which has been well stirred together. Eat within an hour of making.

Firedust Popcorn   V

Pour half a Tbsp each of melted butter and hot oil over the hot popcorn. Using a small sieve, sprinkle over a previously stirred together mixture of 1 tsp icing sugar, 1/2 tsp five-spice powder, 1/2 tsp salt and 1/8–1/4 tsp cayenne pepper.

Variation: Stir any of the flavoured popcorns through good quality roast mixed nuts for interesting party pass-arounds.

Spiced Almonds   V

Almonds are delicious when given a spicy, sweet coating.

1 cup almonds
2 tsp lightly beaten egg white
1/4 cup castor sugar
1 tsp cinnamon
1 tsp mixed spice
1/4 tsp ground cloves
pinch of salt

Turn the oven to 125°C (250° F). Put the (dry) nuts into a large bowl. Add the egg white, which has been beaten very lightly with a fork. Using your fingers, coat the nuts with the egg. Leave to stand for 4–5 minutes, until the nuts soak up some of the egg and have a 'tacky' surface.

Meanwhile mix the castor sugar with the remaining ingredients. Put half this mixture in with the nuts, shake to coat lightly, then arrange the nuts in one layer on a Teflon liner or baking paper on an oven tray. Shake or finely sieve more coating mixture over the nuts (do not turn the nuts over).

Bake, without fan if possible, for 15 minutes. When cool transfer to airtight jars, plastic or cellophane bags.

Devilled Almonds   V

The combination of flavours in this coating is unusual and very tasty.

1 cup almonds
1 tsp olive or other oil
1 tsp light soy sauce
1 tsp tabasco sauce
1/2 tsp each garlic and celery salt
1/2 tsp curry powder
1/2 tsp five-spice powder (optional)
pinch of cayenne pepper (optional)

Turn the oven to 125°C (250°F). Toss the almonds, oil, soy and tabasco sauces together in a large bowl. Leave to stand for 5 minutes.

Mix the remaining flavourings together, adding the cayenne if you want extra 'heat'. Sprinkle this mixture over the nuts, tossing to coat evenly.

Spread on a Teflon liner or baking paper on an oven tray, and bake for 15 minutes. When cool pack in screw-topped jars or in plastic or cellophane bags.

Stuffed Grape Leaves V

Although dolmades, or stuffed grape leaves, may seem exotic, they are easy and inexpensive to make if you or your friends have the right things growing in your garden.

For 36 dolmades:
about 40 young grape leaves
1 onion, finely chopped
1/2 cup (125 ml/4 fl oz) olive oil
1/2 cup uncooked rice
1/2 cup dried currants
1/4–1/2 cup pinenuts
1/4 cup (60 ml/2 fl oz) lemon juice
1–2 Tbsp chopped fresh mint
1–2 Tbsp chopped fresh parsley
1–2 Tbsp chopped fresh dill leaves
1 tsp salt
1 cup (250 ml/8 fl oz) water

Turn the oven to 150°C (300°F). Put young, light green grape leaves into a pot of boiling water, and hold them under the surface until they will fold easily without breaking. Cool in cold water.

Cook the onion gently in half the olive oil for 2–3 minutes. Add the rice, currants and pinenuts, stir for a minute longer, then remove from the heat and add half the lemon juice, 2 or more of the herbs, and the salt.

With the shiny side of the leaves down, put a teaspoon of rice mixture in the centre of each leaf. Fold the stem ends then the sides of the leaf over the filling, and roll up loosely into cylinders.

Arrange stuffed leaves side by side, joins down, in one layer in a baking dish. Drizzle with the remaining oil and lemon juice then pour the water round them. Cover with flat grape leaves then with a lid or foil. Bake for 1–1 1/2 hours, or until the rice is cooked and the stuffed leaves are tender. Drain, cover with cling film and leave to cool. Refrigerate up to 4 days, and serve at room temperature.

Marguerite's Salmon Roll

This recipe came to me with the enthusiastic recommendation of a friend.

1 can (about 200 g/7 oz) salmon
1 carton (250 g/9 oz) firm cream cheese
1 packet (30 g/1 oz) onion soup mix
1 Tbsp lemon juice
1/2 cup finely chopped toasted almonds or
 1/4 cup finely chopped spring onions
2 Tbsp capers, chopped
parsley, nuts or sesame seeds for coating

Drain the liquid from the salmon, reserving it.

Beat the cream cheese until creamy in a food processor or a large bowl. Add the drained salmon, soup mix and lemon juice, and combine. Do not mix until everything is uniformly pulverised since it is good to have some variety in texture.

Toast the almonds under a grill until light brown, then chop finely; or chop spring onions or chives finely. Stir into the salmon mixture with the capers, and 1 or 2 tsp of the caper liquid.

Taste the mixture. If it is not particularly salty, thin it down to a creamier consistency with some of the salmon liquid. If it is salty, add a little sherry or table wine to thin it. If it is too salty, add soft white breadcrumbs and milk until you get the right balance.

Refrigerate for 30 minutes. In this time, the soup mix will firm up the mixture, and you will find it easier to work with.

Roll it into one or two cylinders 3–4 cm (about 1 1/2 in) in diameter. Coat with finely chopped toasted or plain nuts, finely chopped parsley, or lightly toasted sesame seeds. Cover lightly and refrigerate until required.

Serve with melba toast (p. 344) or crackers, and crisp vegetable slices.

Alternatively, stand for at least 24 hours, then cut into slices about 7 mm (1/4 in) thick. Arrange several of these on individual savoury or bread and butter plates, with melba toast and crisp, raw vegetables.

Smoked Salmon Pâté

Smoked salmon offcuts are considerably cheaper than perfect slices, but have the same delicious flavour. With small packets of offcuts in your freezer you can produce a luxury pâté in moments!

200 g (7 oz) fresh or frozen smoked
 salmon offcuts
100 g (3 1/2 oz) butter, at room temperature
2 Tbsp horseradish sauce or cream (p. 344)
2 Tbsp lemon juice
1 tsp tabasco sauce
2 spring onions, roughly chopped

Optional ingredients
2–3 tsp chopped fresh dill leaves
1/4 cup chopped telegraph cucumber (skin on)
2–3 tsp capers

Thaw the salmon if necessary. Chop it finely in a food processor, add the butter which should be softened but not melted, and process until light-coloured and creamy. Add the horseradish, lemon juice, tabasco and spring onions with one or more of the optional ingredients, and process enough to chop them without losing all their texture. Refrigerate in a covered container until required.

Serve chilled, while the mixture is just soft enough to spread, on crostini (p. 27), melba toast (p. 344), crackers or slices of french bread. Garnish with a small piece of lemon, dill or cucumber.

Sushi

Interesting, tasty, attractive, and low-fat as well – what more could you ask!

For 24–30 pieces of sushi:
1 cup medium-grain rice
2 cups (500 ml/16 fl oz) boiling water
2 Tbsp sherry

Stuffed Grape Leaves

2 Tbsp water
1 Tbsp wine or rice vinegar
1 Tbsp sugar
1 tsp salt
¹/₂ avocado
cold-smoked salmon
cucumber
pickled (pink) ginger (optional)
3 sheets yaki nori (grilled seaweed sheets)
wasabi paste (green horseradish paste)
Kikkoman soy sauce

Dipping Sauce
2 Tbsp water
1 Tbsp wine vinegar
1 tsp sugar
¹/₂ tsp salt

Pour the boiling water over the rice then cover and microwave on 50% power for 15 minutes. Mix the sherry, second measure of water, vinegar, sugar and salt together and stir through the almost-cooked rice. Heat on High (100%) power for 1 minute, then leave to stand for 10 minutes. At this stage the grains should be completely tender, quite sticky, and have a good flavour.

Make the dipping sauce by mixing together the water, vinegar, sugar and salt. Cut the avocado, smoked salmon, cucumber and ginger into long thin strips, and turn them in the dipping sauce.

Place a sheet of nori on a bamboo sushi mat or a sheet of cling film. Working with dampened fingers, spread a third of the rice in an even layer on the nori. Work with one of the longer edges nearest you, and leave a 2–3 cm (1 in) strip on the other side uncovered with rice.

Spread a little wasabi paste on the rice on the nearest edge, then lay lines of pickled ginger, avocado, cucumber and smoked salmon on or close to it. Using the cling film or bamboo mat to help you, roll up the sushi firmly, starting at the edge closest to you.

Dampen the uncovered nori with a little water or dipping sauce before rolling it up. Repeat with the remaining rice, nori, etc.

Using a sharp, serrated knife, cut each roll of sushi into 8–10 slices. Serve within a few hours, with a dipping sauce made by mixing wasabi and soy sauce.

Smoked Roe Savouries

Smoked roe has a distinctive flavour and texture, and is ready to serve as a gourmet snack after minimal preparation.

Roes vary in size and texture. Small, firm, thin roes may be sliced crossways into oval slices. Larger roes may be scooped or spooned out of their containing skin, or may be pressed through a coarse sieve to produce an attractive, light-textured product.

Sushi

Sliced, sieved or mashed roe may be spooned or scooped on to crackers or melba toast within an hour of serving, garnished with a few capers, a parsley sprig or sliced green or black olives, but I think its flavour and texture is best when it is served mounded on hot buttered wholegrain toast.

To serve with drinks, quarter small slices of warm toast, pile on the prepared roe, add a little lemon juice and pepper and a tiny parsley garnish.

Lunches and Light Meals

During school holidays and at weekends, many family cooks feel that one meal is no sooner cleared away than another one is called for! Look through this section for practical ideas which are a little different, and often easy enough for children to prepare for the rest of the family. You will find more ideas in other parts of the book too, so don't forget to check out the suggestions on page 43.

Crêpes V

Crêpes are thin, delicate, tender pancakes, made in a small frypan. They make wonderful wrappers for a variety of mixtures.

Don't be discouraged if the first crêpes you make are not perfect. You will soon find you can turn out a pile of crêpes remarkably quickly and easily. As long as you don't let them dry out, they may be made ahead and refrigerated or frozen until required.

Batter
For 12–20 small crêpes, each about 15 cm (6 in) in diameter:
2 eggs
3/4 cup (185 ml/6 fl oz) milk
1/2 cup plain flour
1/2 tsp salt

Combine the ingredients in the order given, in a blender or food processor. If mixing in a bowl, add the eggs then the milk to the dry ingredients, and beat until smooth.

Heat a small, smooth, well-sprayed or buttered frypan, and pour in a measured quantity (e.g. 2 Tbsp) of the batter. Immediately tilt the pan so the batter covers the bottom in a thin film. If it does not spread thinly, add more milk to the mixture before making the next crêpe. Don't worry if they are not perfect circles.

When the batter no longer looks wet in the centre, ease the edges of the crêpe from the pan. Lift and turn carefully. Dry the second side, without necessarily browning it. Remove from the pan, stacking the crêpes until required. Put them on a plate in a plastic bag to prevent them drying out.

Note: If freezing or refrigerating crêpes, place pieces of plastic between them.

Savoury Apple Filling V
Sauté sliced onions in butter until tender, then add sliced apple and brown lightly.

Crêpes with Savoury Apple Filling

Add a little white wine and chopped sage if available. Cook until tender. Taste and season. Spread on cooked crêpes. Fold or roll the filled crêpes, sprinkle with Parmesan cheese if desired and reheat if necessary. Serve with maple syrup.

Bacon and Mushroom Filling
For 4 servings:
2 Tbsp butter or oil
2–3 rashers bacon, chopped finely
2 large onions, sliced
2–3 cups mushrooms, sliced

Prepare and cook the crêpe batter as for Savoury Apple Crêpes.

Heat the butter or oil in a large frypan, add the bacon and vegetables and cook over a low heat, stirring frequently, for about 5 minutes, until the onions are quite tender but only lightly browned.

Divide the filling between the cooked crêpes, folding or rolling them up, as above.

Spinach and Cheese Crêpes V

This is another dish that can be prepared ahead and baked when required. For really successful spinach crêpes, you need to thicken the spinach and season it carefully.

For 4–6 servings:
1 recipe crêpe batter
1–2 cups cooked, drained, squeezed and chopped spinach
3 Tbsp butter
3 Tbsp plain flour
1/2 tsp salt
1 tsp grated nutmeg
11/2 cups (375 ml/12 fl oz) milk
11/2 cups grated cheese
sprinkling of paprika or Parmesan cheese

Prepare and cook crêpes as for Savoury Apple Crêpes, using a small frypan.

Prepare the spinach.

To make the sauce, melt the butter, add the flour, salt and nutmeg. Add the milk half a cup at a time, boiling and stirring

between additions. After the last boiling, add the grated cheese.

Mix a third of the cheese sauce with the spinach. Spread this mixture over the crêpes and roll up. Place the filled crêpes in a well-sprayed oven pan. Pour over the remaining sauce (thinned a little if necessary), and sprinkle with paprika or Parmesan cheese.

Cook immediately, or refrigerate until required. Bake at 200°C (400°F) for 20 minutes, or until bubbly. Brown the surface under the grill before serving.

Kumara and Corn Cakes V

A great way to serve vegetables for a weekend lunch.

For 4 servings:
500 g (1 lb 2 oz) kumara (sweet potatoes)
1 Tbsp oil
1 onion, roughly chopped
2 cloves garlic, chopped
1 cup cooked corn (fresh, frozen or canned)
1–2 tsp ground cumin
about 1/2 tsp salt
2–3 Tbsp chopped fresh coriander
1 large or 2 small eggs
3 Tbsp self-raising flour

Peel the kumara and cut it roughly into 2 cm (3/4 in) slices.

Heat the oil in a large pot and cook the onion and garlic until soft. Add the sliced kumara and as little water as you need to stop it burning while it cooks. Cover and cook over moderate heat until the kumara is just tender when pierced with a sharp knife. Drain, then finely chop the cooked vegetables in the pot with a sharp knife.

Add the drained corn and remaining ingredients and stir with a fork to mix.

Using a dessertspoon, form the mixture into about 12 patties, then transfer half of these to a large, hot frypan containing a film of oil. Cook uncovered for about 5 minutes, until nicely browned, then turn and cook the other side for a similar time. Repeat with the remaining cakes.

Creamy Tomato Toast Topping   V

A little cream cooked down to a glaze makes tomatoes very special. Make it without a guilty conscience, as long as you don't butter the toast on which you serve it.

For 2 servings:
½ tsp butter
3–4 large tomatoes, cut into quarters
pinch each of sugar, salt and pepper
2 Tbsp water
1 Tbsp cream
chopped fresh herbs

Heat the butter in a medium-sized frypan. Place the quartered tomatoes cut-side down in the pan and sprinkle with sugar, salt and pepper. Cook for about 1 minute then turn the tomatoes and add the water. Turn the heat to high and bring to the boil.

Add the cream and fresh herbs then boil briskly until the mixture thickens, turning the tomatoes regularly. If it is not thick by the time the tomatoes are cooked, put them on the toast and continue to boil the sauce.

Serve on unbuttered toast with extra liquid spooned over the top, and fresh herbs to garnish.

Holiday Hash

This makes a good, easy holiday meal.

For 4 servings:
800 g (1¾ lb) cooked potatoes (4 fairly large potatoes)
1–2 cups finely cubed cooked meat or luncheon sausage
¼ cup chopped gherkins or other pickle or relish
4 spring onions, chopped
¼ cup chopped parsley (optional)
1 egg (optional)
1–2 tsp oil

Mash the cooked potatoes with a fork. Mix them with the chopped meat, gherkins, white and green parts of the spring onions, and parsley. Add an egg if the mixture does not hold together well.

If you use meat that has not been salted, add a sprinkling of celery or garlic salt for extra flavour.

Heat a 20–23 cm (8–9 in) non-stick frypan. Add the oil, swirl round to coat the bottom and sides of the pan, then add the potato mixture, levelling the top. Cover the pan for more even heating.

Cook over slow to moderate heat until the hash forms a golden brown crust; about 10 minutes. Carefully run a knife around it so it does not stick, then slip it onto a plate so the uncooked side is still up. Invert it into the pan again, with a little extra oil, and cook the second side. Cut into quarters and serve with tomatoes, salad and tomato sauce or other relish.

Mushrooms on Toast   V

If you can, use two different types of mushrooms in this classic dish.

For 1 serving:
about 100 g (4 oz) mushrooms
½ tsp butter
about 1 tsp cream or sour cream
about ¼ tsp mixed mustard
fresh herbs (optional)

Clean and trim the mushrooms. Keep some whole and slice others.

Heat the butter in a frypan and add the mushrooms. Brown for 1–2 minutes, ignoring the fact that they seem dry, then add enough water to make steam. Cover the pan tightly and cook on high until the mushrooms have wilted, softened, and produced their own juice.

Stir in the cream or sour cream and the mustard, add a little more water to mix, and stir in some fresh herbs for extra flavour if desired. Cook uncovered until the liquid has almost disappeared, then turn the mushrooms to glaze them. Serve on unbuttered toast, garnished with herbs, alone or with bacon.

Curried Corn on Toast   V

Open a can of corn for a tasty, high-fibre lunch.

For 2–4 servings:
1 can (440 g/15 oz) whole kernel corn
2 tsp butter
½ tsp curry powder
2 tsp plain flour
pinch of salt
1–2 tsp Parmesan cheese (optional)
chopped fresh herbs (optional)

Drain the corn, reserving the liquid. Melt the butter in a hot frypan, add the curry powder and flour, and cook, stirring all the time, for about 20 seconds. Stir in the reserved corn liquid and bring to the boil.

Cook briskly until the sauce reduces and thickens (you should have about half a cup of sauce). Add the drained corn and the salt, and cook until the corn is heated through. Stir in the Parmesan cheese and/or chopped herbs if you like. Serve at once on unbuttered, wholemeal toast.

Grilled Tomatoes on Toast   V

Oval Italian tomatoes are excellent for grilling; they are redder, with a stronger, fuller flavour and less juice than most round, ordinary tomatoes.

Cut thick slices of large, ripe tomatoes, place them on a grill tray or sponge-roll tin and brush lightly with oil. Sprinkle with a little salt, pepper and sugar. Cook under the grill, without turning, until the tops of the tomatoes bubble.

If you like, grill a slice of bacon per serving alongside the tomatoes, and toast bread, halved rolls or English muffins at the same time. Pile the tomatoes onto the unbuttered toast, spoon over any cooking liquids, and sprinkle with parsley.

Pears and Cheese on Toast   V

Arrange several slices of unpeeled, ripe pear on hot toast. Cover with thin slices of gruyère or other cheese and grill until the cheese melts. Serve straight away.

Ring the changes by varying the cheese used. Melted plain or blue brie on the pear makes a real breakfast treat, or try elsberg for a lovely nutty flavour. Raclette is another good melting cheese with a lovely aroma and plenty of flavour.

Cheese and Corn Savouries   V

1 cup creamed corn
2 eggs
2 spring onions, chopped
2 cups grated cheese

Mix the corn, eggs and spring onions together with a fork. Stir over low heat until the mixture thickens, then stir in the cheese.

Spoon onto crispbreads, toast or toasted bread cases (as for Potato and Tuna Savouries, but bake the unfilled cases until lightly browned and crisp.)

Potato and Tuna Savouries

These savouries make great snacks at any time of the day!

For 24:
6 slices fresh, sandwich-sliced bread
softened butter
1 cup mashed potato
1 small can (about 100 g/4 oz) tuna, any flavour
1 egg
2 spring onions, chopped
1 Tbsp chopped parsley
salt and pepper to taste

Turn the oven to 180–190°C (350–375°F).

Butter the bread evenly, remove the crusts, and press butter-side down into muffin pans. Combine the remaining ingredients with a fork, seasoning as necessary, and pile into the uncooked bread cases. Bake for 20–30 minutes, or until the cases and filling are golden brown. Serve hot, garnished with parsley.

Note: These savouries are very hot inside. Watch that you do not burn your mouth!

From top to bottom: Pears and Cheese on Toast, Mushrooms on Toast, Grilled Tomatoes on Toast, Curried Corn on Toast, Creamy Tomato Toast Topping

Filled Croissants

Hot croissants are deliciously flaky and buttery, but they disintegrate easily – if you are going to fill them it is safer to split croissants before you heat them. Use a sharp, serrated knife when you cut them.

A few fillings may be added before heating, but most of the following are best added after the croissants are heated. Heat croissants at 100°C (225°F) for about 15 minutes, depending on their size; check the centres are hot before serving. Do not heat filled or unfilled croissants in a microwave.

Pastrami Croissant: Fill a split, heated croissant with several thin slices of pastrami. Add lettuce, watercress and dill pickles to taste. Serve immediately.

Creamy Pesto and Sun-Dried Tomato Croissant: Before or after heating, spread with cream cheese, a thin layer of pesto and sun-dried tomatoes.

Pepper and Pesto Croissant: Spread a warmed croissant with pesto. Fill generously with pepper slices (red, green, yellow and orange) and sliced black olives. Garnish with fresh basil. (Roast pepper slices are best – see p. 346.)

Ham and Cheese Croissant: Stuff a split croissant with thick slices of ham and cheese (I use gruyère). Heat through as above, then garnish with watercress or dill pickles.

Salami and Witloof Croissant: Fill heated croissant with salami, fresh witloof leaves and mayonnaise.

Crunchy Apple and Celery Croissant: Chop equal amounts of unpeeled apple and celery into small cubes. Add chopped walnuts and mix with mayonnaise. Spoon into heated croissants and garnish.

Salmon and Avocado Croissant: Fill heated croissant with smoked salmon and thick slices of avocado. Garnish will dill leaves or dill flowers.

Smoked Chicken and Asparagus Croissant: Fill heated croissant with thick slices of smoked chicken and cooked asparagus tips.

Creamy Mushroom Croissant: Fry 1 rasher of chopped bacon in 1 tsp oil, add 100 g (4 oz) chopped mushrooms and cook over fairly high heat until mushrooms have wilted. Stir in 1–2 tsp mixed mustard and 1/4 cup sour cream, and cook over high heat until the sauce reduces and thickens. Spoon hot mixture into 3 or 4 preheated croissants.

Bagels

Bagels are doughnut-shaped breads that are boiled before baking and have a glazed surface and a deliciously chewy,

dense texture. Warm fresh bagels in the oven, or split and toast bagels which are not perfectly fresh. (Microwaving is not recommended.)

Lox and Bagels: This is a traditional bagel topping. Spread halved, very fresh or toasted bagel with cream cheese, and top with thin slices of cold-smoked salmon. Use enough to give flavour. Depending on your taste, garnish with thinly sliced red onion, a little tomato, fresh dill or coarsely ground black pepper. Add a squeeze of lemon juice.

Bacon Bagel: Top a warm or toasted halved bagel with warm, crisp, grilled bacon. Eat as is or top with slices of creamy avocado or garden-fresh tomato. Cream cheese under the bacon tastes very good.

Strawberry Cream Bagels: To celebrate summer, spread half an oven-fresh bagel with a layer of cream cheese. Top with whole, halved or thick slices of strawberries. (If strawberries are not available, try other fruit such as oranges, pears, apples or apricots.)

Creamy Date and Nut Bagels: Mix half a cup of quark or cream cheese with 1 tsp finely grated orange rind and enough yoghurt to make a creamy mixture. Stir in about a quarter of a cup each of chopped dates, dried apricots and chopped walnuts. Add about 2 Tbsp finely chopped preserved ginger. Refrigerate for up to a week. Spread on toasted bagels.

SANDWICHES FOR LUNCH

Homemade sandwiches make good, inexpensive lunches to take to school, work, picnics, or to eat at home.

The amounts needed vary with age, activities and appetite. As a guide, allow 4 slices of bread (making 4 sandwiches per person) per day. School children may prefer to eat one sandwich mid-morning, two at lunchtime, and one after school.

The texture of sandwich fillings is important. They must spread easily, they should hold together well, and they must not seem dry when they are eaten.

Sometimes you can mix the spread and filling ingredients together, which can speed up sandwich making. Unlikely mixtures often taste good!

Fillings made up of 2 or 3 different foods seem more satisfying and interesting than those made with only one.

Use the fillings in '2-slice' sandwiches, filled rolls or stuffed pita breads, in rolled flatbreads, or in rolled crustless slices of bread.

Alternative Sandwich Spreads

As a change from butter or margarine, try the following occasionally:

- Low-fat cream cheese
- Low-fat cream cheese mixed with horseradish
- Cottage cheese, plain or flavoured. (Cottage cheese can also form the main part of a filling, used in larger amounts.)
- Cheese spreads
- Peanut or other nut butters
- Well-seasoned bean spreads
- Hummus
- Well-seasoned tofu mixtures
- Mayonnaise, plain or flavoured (use sparingly)
- Meat or liver pâté (use sparingly), fish pâté and spreads
- Unsweetened yoghurt, after straining through a lined sieve to thicken it
- Mustard spreads
- Marmite, etc.

Fillings to Use Sparingly, with Salad Vegetables

- Thinly sliced luncheon sausage, cold meat or poultry
- Chopped hard-boiled egg mixtures
- Thinly sliced sausage and salami
- Crumbled cooked bacon
- Grated cheese or soft, sliced cheeses
- Fresh herbs

Fillings for Generous Use

- Lettuce and other leafy salad greens
- Finely shredded cabbage
- Grated carrot
- Thinly sliced celery
- Beetroot
- Cucumber
- Radishes
- Tomatoes
- Thinly sliced cauliflower
- Asparagus
- Sweetcorn, plain or creamed
- Chopped peanuts or other nuts
- Dried fruit, chopped or minced, with fruit juice to moisten
- Dates or date spread
- Beansprouts and alfalfa
- Cracked wheat salads
- Green and red peppers
- Raw or marinated mushrooms
- Potato salads
- Bean salads
- Avocado slices (coated with lemon juice)

Filling Mixtures to Use Alone or with Salad Greens

- Cream cheese or cottage cheese, chopped gherkin and beansprouts, with a little chilli sauce or chutney
- Cooked (dried) beans mashed with chopped celery, spring onion, chilli sauce and mayonnaise
- Peanut butter, mashed baked beans and cooked bacon

Filled Croissants

- Grated cheese, chopped celery or spring onion and mayonnaise
- Crunchy peanut butter, toasted chopped sunflower seeds, finely chopped sultanas, with a little honey
- Grated cheese with cottage cheese and chopped celery
- Baked beans mashed with grated cheese
- Dates, heated with orange juice to soften them, cooked and mixed with chopped nuts, or peanut butter and/or cottage or cream cheese
- Chopped or minced cooked meat mixed with pickles or tomato sauce, with shredded cabbage or lettuce
- Tuna mashed with mayonnaise, with chopped cucumber or celery and lettuce
- Sweetcorn with relish, cream cheese and lettuce
- Peanut butter with grated carrot
- Cream cheese, chopped nuts and/or chopped sultanas
- Cheese and marmite
- Cheese spread with tomato and sprouts
- Peanut butter (or other nut butters) and tahini in equal quantities, mixed with honey, tofu or chopped sunflower seeds
- Coleslaw, raisins and cheese
- Peanut butter, cheese and sprouts
- Tomato and cottage cheese
- Egg filling and tomato with sprouts

Egg Sandwich Filling   V

This filling makes sandwiches that taste just the way egg sandwiches should!

4 hard-boiled eggs
2 Tbsp milk
1 Tbsp butter, at room temperature
1/4 cup finely chopped chives, spring onions or parsley
1/4–1/2 tsp salt
pepper to taste

Peel the eggs and put them into a food processor with the milk, butter and herbs; process until smooth, adding salt and pepper to taste. Or you can mash the eggs with a fork then mix well with the remaining ingredients, adding salt and pepper to taste. Cover and refrigerate for 3–4 days.

Note: It is not necessary to butter the bread when using this filling.

Open Sandwiches

One of the most useful, quick snacks you can make is an open sandwich. Start with a bread base, remembering that you have many choices as far as texture, colour and flavour go. Try some of the following:

- Heavy-textured wholegrain bread
- Lighter, softer-crumbed brown bread
- Fruit bread
- Interesting white bread
- English muffins
- Crumpets
- Pita or pocket bread
- Halved hamburger buns
- Long (hot dog) rolls, halved
- Lengths of french bread, halved
- Crispbread
- All of the above, toasted

Here are some open sandwiches that are worth trying.

- Thickly sliced ripe, red tomato on hot toasted rye or mixed grain bread spread with butter, cottage cheese or quark. Top with freshly ground black pepper, basil leaves or alfalfa sprouts.
- Sliced tomato on a split length of french bread, topped with sliced mozzarella or gouda, browned under a grill, or heated in a microwave until the cheese melts. Add lettuce or watercress if you like.
- Sliced avocado on fresh french bread, with plenty of black pepper or several shakes of not-so-hot chilli sauce. Sprinkle with alfalfa sprouts if available.
- Mashed avocado on hot toast or a toasted English muffin.
- Drained, canned beans mixed with pickle, chopped hard-boiled egg, and chilli mayonnaise, on a fresh crusty roll.
- Canned beans, drained and chopped, mixed with chopped spring onion and sprinkled with Mexican seasoning or cumin. Top with a slice of cheese and a few thin slices of red pepper, and heat under the grill until the cheese melts.
- Fresh, crunchy peanut butter (or a mixture of tahini and peanut butter) and honey on crispbread.
- Peanut butter sprinkled with toasted sunflower seeds, on fruit bread, topped with sliced banana, drizzled with honey or a sprinkling of light brown sugar and a little cinnamon, then grilled.
- Hot refried beans on toast, topped with grated cheese, shredded lettuce, and a slice of tomato.
- Hot refried beans, sliced avocado and a little sour cream, sprinkled with hot pepper sauce, on a flour tortilla.

Toasted Rollups

Microwaved Hot Meat Sandwiches   M

A delicious way to use up leftover cold meat or poultry.

For 1 serving:
1 crusty bread roll
mayonnaise or butter
1–2 slices roast or corned beef, chicken
  or other cold meat
gravy (optional)
1 Tbsp mild mixed mustard
1 Tbsp relish or tomato sauce

Split the bread roll not quite all the way through and spread the cut surface with mayonnaise or butter. Slice, chop or fold the meat, adding a little leftover gravy if desired. Place the meat in the roll. Add mustard and relish, tomato sauce, etc. Fold a paper towel around the roll and heat in the microwave on High (100%) power for 30 seconds, or until the meat is hot and the roll warm.

Note: If the meat is dry, spread it with relish before placing in roll.

Toasted Rollups   V

These are economical and very popular with children.

fresh sandwich bread
melted butter
grated cheese
canned creamed corn
canned spaghetti

Turn the oven to 200°C (400°F). Cut crusts from bread and lightly brush the edges and one side with melted butter. Spread the other side with corn, sprinkle with grated cheese then lay canned spaghetti across diagonally. Garnish with strips of red pepper if desired, then fold the two opposite corners over the spaghetti and secure with toothpicks. Bake for about 10 minutes or until golden brown and crisp.

Pineapple Toasties   V

Toasted cheese and pineapple is a great combination!

4 slices toast
1 cup grated cheese
¼ cup crushed pineapple, drained

Preheat the grill. Make the toast.

Mix the cheese and pineapple together with a fork and spread on the toast, right to the edges. Grill until bubbly, then cut in half or in fingers. Eat while hot.

Barbecue Buns   V

Cook these inside, in the oven, if the weather is cold outside.

25 g (1 oz) soft butter
2 cups grated tasty cheese
3 Tbsp tomato sauce or relish
1 Tbsp onion juice

Put the butter, grated cheese and tomato sauce in a mixing bowl. Cut an onion in half crosswise, without skinning it. Scrape the cut surface with a teaspoon to get onion juice, or grate the onion on the cheese grater. Mix everything together thoroughly with a wooden spoon.

Cut bread rolls in half and spread thickly with this mixture.

Wrap each roll in foil and heat over the barbecue or in a hot oven for 5–10 minutes. Undo the aluminium foil and eat while hot.

OR cut french bread nearly through into slices, spread the mixture between the slices, wrap in foil, and heat the same way.

OR spread the mixture on toasted bread or rolls and heat under the grill until bubbly.

Put the rest of the spread in a covered dish in the refrigerator until required.

Mediterranean Toasties

Good for lunch or a late-night snack.

For 1 serving:
1 red onion, sliced
2 tsp oil
1/4 tsp paprika
1 crusty bread roll, halved
4–6 slices cheese
4–6 flat anchovies
2–3 green or black olives, sliced
fresh basil or parsley, chopped

Put the onion in a bowl and mix through the oil and paprika. Cover and microwave on High (100%) power for 1 1/2 minutes.

Brush the cut surface of the roll with a little of the oil mixture. Place the roll on a paper towel and arrange the cheese, anchovies, onion and sliced olives on the cut surface. Brush with the remaining oil. Microwave for 30 seconds to 1 minute, until the cheese melts and the bread is warm.

Toasted Cheese Sandwiches   V

A toasted sandwich is so much more exciting than a plain sandwich made with stale bread. It is good on any cold day, by itself or served with soup.

Butter 2 slices of bread evenly (but not thickly).

Spread the unbuttered side of 1 slice with about 1/4 cup grated cheese or with thin slices of cheese.

Spread the unbuttered side of the other piece with your favourite chutney, relish, mustard or tomato sauce, add creamed corn, thinly sliced ham, or leave it plain.

Put the slices together, buttered sides out, and place on a warmed or cold frypan.

Heat the uncovered pan over moderate heat until the bread is golden brown, then carefully turn the sandwich and cook the second side to the same stage. By this time the cheese in the middle should have melted. Cut the hot toasted sandwiches in halves, triangles or fingers, and eat while warm.

Variation: Try serving toasted sandwiches American-style. Pile 2 or 3 fairly large sandwiches on lettuce leaves. Skewer small, colourful savoury foods (such as a wedge of tomato and an olive) and impale the sandwiches. Serve carrot, celery or cucumber sticks alongside.

Spaghetti Savouries

Make these savouries in whatever size suits you, depending on what bread and baking tins you have.

For 4 servings:
sliced bread
butter

2 eggs
1–2 cups grated cheese
2–3 rashers rindless bacon, chopped
1 small onion, chopped
1 tomato, chopped

Use 12 medium-sized slices of bread. Butter the bread, cut off the crusts and press the slices, buttered side down, into 12 muffin pans.

OR use 6 large slices of sandwich-bread. Butter the bread, cut off the crusts and cut each slice into 4 square quarters. Press the slices, buttered side down, into 24 small patty tins.

OR use 4 large slices of bread. Butter the bread, cut off the crusts and press each slice, buttered side down, into 4 individual pie tins.

Heat the oven to 220°C (425°F). Break the eggs into a mixing bowl. Add the cheese, bacon, onion and tomato, and mix together with a fork. Divide the filling between the bread cases. Bake for about 10 minutes, until the bottoms of the bread cases are golden brown. Eat while hot.

Crunchy Cheese and Corn Rolls   V

This mixture makes a lot of spread. Use it to turn nearly a loaf of sandwich bread into rolls, then freeze them until you want to cook them. Serve with soup, or raw fruit or vegetables, to make a complete meal.

3 cups grated cheese or 350 g (12 oz)
  cheese broken into small chunks
1 can (310 g/11 oz) creamed corn
1 cup unsweetened condensed
  (evaporated) milk
1 packet (30 g/1 oz) onion soup mix
fresh loaf of thinly sliced sandwich bread
softened butter

Stir grated cheese together with the other filling ingredients, or put small chunks of cheese in a food processor with the other ingredients and process until it is finely chopped.

Cut the crusts off the bread and spread one side of each piece with softened butter. (For easy rolling, work on a metal oven tray laid over a sink of hot water.) Place the buttered side down and spread over the cheese mixture, making sure you reach the edges. Roll up, then place the shaped rolls close together in rows in a plastic bag. This keeps them rolled. They can be refrigerated or frozen like this. A brief warming, in a microwave oven or by putting the bag under a hot tap, ensures the rolls separate without breaking.

Heat the oven to 220°C (425°F). Place the rolls, edges down, on a sponge-roll tray, about 1 cm (1/2 in) apart. Bake for about 15 minutes, until lightly browned, turning once, or brown under a grill, at least 10 cm (4 in) from the heat. Frozen rolls will

take a little longer, but may be thawed in a microwave oven on Defrost (30% power). Unused mixture will thicken on standing and may be used in sandwiches, on crackers, to stuff celery stalks, etc.

Puffy Cheese Rolls   V

This glamorised version of toasted cheese sandwiches makes a quick and tasty lunch dish.

For 6 servings:
6 bread rolls
250 g (9 oz) cheese, grated
1/2 tsp salt
1/2 tsp Worcestershire sauce (optional)
1/2 tsp baking powder
2 eggs, separated
about 2 Tbsp milk

Split the rolls. Arrange cut-side down on the griller rack and toast both sides until golden brown.

Prepare the filling by combining the cheese, seasonings, baking powder and egg yolks in a medium-sized bowl. Mix with a fork, adding enough milk to get the consistency of creamed butter. Beat the egg whites to a stiff foam, then add to the cheese mixture and combine thoroughly.

Spread the filling nearly to the edges of the rolls and grill about 10 cm (4 in) from the heat until puffy and golden brown. Serve immediately.

Toasted Cheese Savouries

These savouries go well with soup in cold weather, and are easy enough for children to make for themselves.

For 4 servings:
4 slices bread
1 egg
1 1/2–2 cups grated cheese
shake pepper

Optional Ingredients
1 rasher bacon, cooked and chopped
several slices salami or other luncheon
  sausage
1–2 Tbsp chopped gherkins
1–2 Tbsp chopped pickled onions
1–2 Tbsp chopped tomatoes

Toast the bread lightly in a toaster, or on one side only under a grill. While it is toasting, break the egg into a medium-sized bowl and beat it with a fork, just enough to combine the yolk and white. Add the cheese, seasoning and any of the optional ingredients.

Spread the mixture on the toast (or the untoasted side of the grilled toast), making sure it goes right to the edges. Place it under a grill (about 7–8 cm/3 in away from the heat) and grill it for 3–5 minutes or until the cheese turns golden brown.

Cut into fingers while hot, and serve promptly, alone or with soup.

Crispy Coin Purse Eggs

Crispy Coin Purse Eggs V

In San Francisco I learned that there are more ways to fry an egg than 'easy over' and 'sunny side up'! These eggs are purse-shaped, with a soft 'gold coin' inside, and a crisp brown coating, well worth a little practice to perfect.

For 1 serving:
2 tsp canola or olive oil
1 large, fresh egg
pepper and salt or spicy salt (see Note)
about a cup of hot cooked rice
sweet chilli sauce (or oyster sauce)
spring onion curls or chopped spring
  onions

Preheat a wok or a small rounded frypan over a fairly high heat. Add the oil, and tilt the wok or pan to coat a saucer-sized area. Break the egg into a small bowl or saucer, and when the oil is almost smoking hot, carefully slide the egg into the wok. Take care, because the egg and hot oil splutter and sizzle. Sprinkle the egg with a little pepper and salt, or with spicy salt, as it cooks.

When the bottom and edges of the egg white are browned and crusty, slide a spatula under half the egg and flip it over to make a half-moon shape. Gently press the edges together until the two sides set and hold the egg in a purse shape.

Lower the heat and cook for 10–20 seconds longer, until the white round the

yolk has just set, the yolk is still runny, and the outside surfaces are crisp and brown.

Place a cupful of hot rice on a plate and top with the hot egg. Drizzle with sweet chilli sauce or oyster sauce, and garnish with spring onion curls or chopped spring onions.

Notes: To make spicy salt, heat 2 Tbsp Szechwan peppercorns on foil under a grill until they smoke slightly. Using a coffee grinder or a mortar and pestle, grind them with 2 Tbsp salt and 1 tsp black peppercorns. Store in an airtight jar.

To make spring onion curls, shred spring onions lengthways. Soak the pieces in iced water until they curl.

Convent Eggs V

This simple recipe is 'comfort food' to me, since it was one of the recipes my mother cooked regularly on Sunday nights.

For 4 servings:
2 large onions, sliced
2 Tbsp butter
1 Tbsp oil
1/4 cup plain flour
2 cups (500 ml/16 fl oz) milk
2 Tbsp Parmesan cheese
salt and pepper
4–6 hard-boiled eggs

Cook the onions gently in the butter and oil

in a covered pot until they are tender but not brown (5–10 minutes). Add the flour, stir well, then add the milk in 3 portions, stirring well and bringing to the boil after each addition.

Add the cheese, taste, and season with pepper and salt if necessary. Slice the eggs into the sauce, thinning it with a little extra milk if it is very thick. Serve on toast, pasta or rice, sprinkled with a little parsley and paprika.

Baked Cheese Fondue V

A baked fondue is like a soufflé, but has more body because of the added breadcrumbs. It is not difficult to make but, like a soufflé, it should not be kept waiting after it is cooked.

For 4 servings:
1 cup (250 ml/8 fl oz) milk
1 cup soft breadcrumbs
1 Tbsp butter, melted
1 cup grated cheddar cheese
3 large eggs
1/2 tsp salt
shake of pepper

Turn the oven to 180°C (350°F). Scald the milk in a medium-sized pot. Remove from the heat and add the breadcrumbs (made by crumbling stale bread), butter and cheese.

Separate the eggs and beat the whites and salt until they form peaks which turn over when the beater is lifted.

Beat the yolks and pepper until thick. Mix the yolks with the ingredients in the pot, and fold in the whites carefully but thoroughly.

Pour the mixture into a large, ungreased oven dish. Stand in a pan of hot water and bake for 30–45 minutes, until the centre is firm when pressed, or a knife inserted in the middle comes out clean.

Variations: Pour the mixture over chopped cooked ham, asparagus, corn, broccoli, etc. in the baking dish. Add chopped herbs to the egg mixture if desired.

Cheese and Broccoli Soufflé V

Practise making soufflés until you find them trouble-free. Make this one in a regular baking dish if you don't care about a traditional soufflé shape.

For 4–5 servings:
250 g (9 oz) prepared broccoli (see below)
3 Tbsp butter
1/2 tsp salt
1/2 tsp celery salt
1/2 tsp Dijon mustard
1/4 cup plain flour

1¹/₂ cups (375 ml/12 fl oz) milk
1¹/₂ cups grated tasty cheese
3 large eggs, separated

Preheat the oven to 190°C (375°F). Prepare the broccoli, peeling the stems and cutting them into short lengths; cook, drain and cool it.

Melt the butter, add the salts and mustard, then the flour. Stir over low heat until the flour bubbles. Add the milk, half a cup at a time, bringing it to the boil and stirring well after each addition. Add the grated cheese, remove from the heat and stir until smooth.

Separate the eggs, putting the whites in a medium-sized bowl and stirring each egg yolk into the sauce. Add the drained, chopped broccoli to the sauce.

Beat the egg whites until the peaks turn over at the tips when the beater is removed; fold into the sauce. Butter the bottom only of a 6-cup soufflé dish (or shallower baking dish) and pour in the sauce.

Run a knife through the mixture in a circle 2 cm (³/₄ in) in from the edge of the dish.

Bake for 40–45 minutes, or until a knife inserted in the centre comes out clean. Serve immediately, with a salad if desired.

Variation: Replace the broccoli with cooked, well-drained, chopped spinach, asparagus, fennel, etc.

Asparagus Squares　　V

Grated zucchini provides the bulk, and canned asparagus the flavour!

For 8 servings:
1 can (340 g/12 oz) asparagus
2 cups grated zucchini
1 large red onion
4 large eggs
1¹/₂ cups grated tasty cheese
salt and pepper to taste
1 cup self-raising flour
¹/₄ cup (60 ml/2 fl oz) liquid from
* asparagus*
salt and pepper to taste

Turn the oven to 200°C (400°F). Drain the asparagus (reserving ¹/₄ cup of the liquid) and chop it.

Grate the zucchini and the red onion into a large bowl, add the eggs, cheese and seasonings, and mix together thoroughly. Stir in the flour, chopped asparagus and reserved liquid, and mix to combine. Pour the mixture into a shallow, lined or buttered 20 cm (8 in) square baking dish.

Bake for 30 minutes, or until the top is evenly browned and firm to touch. Stand for 5 minutes before cutting into serving-sized pieces. Serve in smaller pieces as finger food if preferred. Reheat if desired.

Easy Vegetable Square　　V

Make this useful recipe with canned or leftover cooked vegetables, or 'purpose cooked' vegetables. The pesto and Parmesan cheese ensure a good, interesting flavour. Serve for lunch or dinner.

For 6 smaller or 4 large servings:
2–3 cups cooked, drained vegetables*
4 large eggs
³/₄ cup low-fat or regular sour cream
6 Tbsp Parmesan cheese
3 Tbsp basil pesto
3 Tbsp couscous or dry breadcrumbs
2 tomatoes (optional)
about ¹/₂ cup grated cheddar cheese

* Suitable vegetables include asparagus, cabbage, cauliflower, young green beans, broccoli, whole kernel corn, kumara, squeezed spinach, well-drained silverbeet, young carrots, pumpkin, new potatoes, peas, frozen mixed vegetables, zucchini and mushrooms. (Tomatoes and eggplant are too wet to use.)

Turn the oven to 180°C (350°F).

Cook raw vegetables until just tender, or use cooked leftovers or canned vegetables. Cut the cooked vegetables into 1 cm (¹/₂ in) cubes.

Put the eggs, sour cream, Parmesan cheese and pesto in a bowl. Stir with a fork or whisk until well mixed.

Lightly butter or spray with non-stick spray a baking pan about 20 cm (8 in) square. Sprinkle the base with couscous or breadcrumbs, so any liquid that comes from the vegetables during baking will be soaked up. (Use couscous if you have it; it works well and makes the base firmer.)

Sprinkle the well-drained vegetables evenly over the base of the pan, then pour over the egg mixture. Jiggle the pan so the liquid surrounds the vegetables. Cover the surface with slices of tomato then sprinkle with grated cheese. Bake (on fan bake if possible) for 30 minutes, or until the top is golden brown and nicely risen, the sides are golden brown, and the centre feels firm. Leave for a few minutes before cutting into serving-sized pieces.

Easy Vegetable Square

Quesadillas   V

I keep flour tortillas in the freezer so I can make these crisp savouries at short notice. With crusted brown cheesy toppings flecked with colourful tomato and avocado they are irresistible – like a pizza with a very thin, crisp base.

Lie flour tortillas on a grill pan or oven tray. Brush the edges lightly with olive oil. Cover with grated cheese. Chop several of the following into pea-sized pieces: red onions, olives, tomatoes, red or green peppers, brown flat mushrooms, avocado. Sprinkle these on evenly, and if you like add spoonfuls of Spicy Mexican Filling (see below) or any canned Mexican bean mixture. Add more cheese on top.

Grill 5–8 cm (2–3 in) from the heat or bake at 180°C (350°F) for 5–8 minutes, until the cheese melts and browns slightly and the edges of the tortilla are brown and crisp.

Quesadilla 'Sandwiches'   V

To make these crisp, thin, cheese-filled tortilla sandwiches, lightly oil a fairly large flour tortilla. With the oiled side down, put grated cheese (and extra flavourings as in quesadillas if you like) on one half.

Fold the unfilled half over the 'topped' part, then pan-cook in a preheated frypan, pressing the top down as the tortilla softens, and turning to cook the other side when the bottom has browned lightly. Alternatively, grill (turning once) or bake at 180°C for 5–8 minutes, or until lightly browned and crisp.

Cut into smaller wedges soon after cooking, and eat while still fairly crisp. Eat just as they are, or use as dippers, especially for guacamole (p. 22) and salsa.

Variations: Depending on the size of the tortillas and the size of your frypan, sandwich together two small tortillas, or use one tortilla folded in half (as above). If your pan is small and your tortillas large, cook half a tortilla at a time, folding it so you finish with a quarter shaped Quesadilla Sandwich.

Tacos and Tostadas

Taco shells are corn tortillas that are folded over into a U shape and fried or baked until crisp. A tostada is simply a tortilla (usually corn), cooked in the same way but left flat. Instead of being filled, like tacos, tostadas simply have the same 'fillings' piled on top.

Fillings/Toppings
Spicy Mexican Filling (see below)
grated cheddar cheese
very finely shredded lettuce
finely grated carrot
guacamole (p. 22)
sour cream
chilli sauce

Fry corn tortillas flat (for tostadas) or folded (for tacos), or buy them already prepared.

Give everyone their own shells and paper plates and have them help themselves from bowls of fillings.

Start with the warm Spicy Mexican Filling then add cheese, then lettuce, etc., finishing with guacamole, sour cream and chilli sauce.

Be warned, there is no easy and/or neat way to eat tacos and tostadas. Use your fingers and accept a little mess as part of the fun!

Burritos

A burrito is the Mexican equivalent of a filled roll – a soft flour tortilla wrapped around selected fillings. It is eaten informally (as a hamburger is).

Soft flour tortillas vary quite widely in size from fairly small (about 20 cm/8 in across) to quite large (about 40 cm/16 in across) and can be bought packaged in several different ways. Some imported varieties come in vacuum packs (sold separately, or as part of 'dinner kits') which have long shelf-lives, and now locally made products are appearing (at a considerably lower price). These have a shorter shelf-life and are often found in or near the bread departments of supermarkets.

Fillings for burritos are exactly the same as for tacos and tostadas; however, if you are filling extra-large tortillas, you may want some rice for added bulk.

To fill a burrito, lay the tortilla on a flat surface. Arrange the fillings in a line that runs down the centre, leaving the bottom 2 cm (3/4 in) clear. Don't be too generous with the fillings or your burrito will be difficult to roll and almost impossible to eat!

When you have finished adding fillings, fold the bottom (the unfilled bit) up over the filling, then fold one edge in, followed by the other (a bit like making a tall, skinny envelope). These can be assembled on a large paper plate at the table or on a board in the kitchen.

Wrapping this whole construction in a paper napkin, paper towel or even foil will make it easier to eat with your fingers, or it can be tackled on a plate with a knife and fork.

Nachos

Nachos are deservedly popular and are sure to be received with great enthusiasm by all age groups! In their simplest form they are just corn chips with melted cheese over them, but by adding Spicy Mexican Filling and other optional extras you can turn them in a substantial meal.

Optional Extras
Spicy Mexican Filling (see below)
sliced mushrooms
chopped olives
diced tomatoes
diced peppers (or chillies)
sliced avocado/guacamole (p. 22)
sour cream
chilli sauce or salsa
chopped fresh coriander
chopped spring onions

Place a pile of the heated (quite thick) Spicy Mexican Filling in the centre of a flat plate and pile corn chips around it. Sprinkle the corn chips with grated cheese and grill (or microwave) until the cheese has melted. Top the Mexican Filling with a dollop of sour cream and/or guacamole. Arrange any of the other optional additions around the plate and serve immediately.

For one large platter, pile corn chips and cheese on an oven tray and grill or bake it until the cheese melts. Heap onto a large tray with a bowl of heated Spicy Mexican Filling, and serve with smaller bowls (or a platter) of other optional ingredients.

Spicy Mexican Filling

This spicy mince and bean mixture is great for delicious nachos, tacos, tostadas, burritos and other Mexican treats.

For 2–4 servings:
1 Tbsp oil
1 large red onion, chopped
2 cloves garlic, chopped
250 g (9 oz) minced beef
1 red or green pepper, diced
1/2–1 tsp chilli powder
2 tsp ground cumin
1 tsp oreganum
1 tsp salt
1 tsp sugar
1 can (about 440 g/15 oz) kidney beans
2 Tbsp tomato paste
about 1/2 cup (125 ml/4 fl oz) water

Heat the oil in a large pot, add the onion, garlic and mince and cook over fairly high heat until browned. Add the diced pepper to the pot with the spices and cook for a further 2 minutes.

Reduce the heat, add the remaining ingredients, including the liquid from the can of beans, and simmer for about 15–20 minutes. Stir occasionally to prevent sticking, and add extra water if necessary.

Sesame Beef Wraps

Use flour tortillas to make these 'wraps'.

For 2–3 servings:

*about 250 g (9 oz) rump or sirloin steak,
  cut 2 cm (¾ in) thick
2 tsp olive oil
1 tsp Kikkoman soy sauce
1 clove garlic, crushed
1 tsp sesame oil
wheat tortillas
chopped tomato
shredded lettuce
diced cucumber
Tahini (or other) Dressing*

Trim any visible fat from the steak and snip
the edges. Put the steak and the next
4 ingredients in a plastic bag, squeeze out
the air, and marinate for at least 30 minutes.

Remove the steak from the marinade and
cook in a very hot frypan for 1–2 minutes
per side, to the stage you like. Leave the
steak to cool for about 5 minutes, then
cut it diagonally into slices.

Lie several slices of warm steak on warmed
tortillas. Add the prepared salad vegetables,
drizzle with dressing, roll up, wrap in paper
serviettes and eat in your fingers.

Tahini Dressing

*2 Tbsp tahini
2 Tbsp lemon juice
¼ tsp salt
½ tsp sugar
few drops sesame oil (optional)
2–4 Tbsp cold water*

Combine the first 5 ingredients in a bowl
and mix until smooth, adding water until
the dressing is the consistency of thin
cream. Taste and adjust the seasonings.

Quesadilla 'Sandwiches' and Burritos

Satisfying Soups

It is hard to think of anything more warming and comforting on a cold day than a steaming bowl of homemade soup. No longer regarded merely as meal starters, soups have moved up the ranks and are often enjoyed as the main part of lunch or evening meals. Many of the following soups contain a large proportion of vegetables, in a form that many picky eaters consider acceptable, so they are particularly useful if you are looking for ways to include more vegetables in your family meals.

Mariners' Mussel Soup

Mussels are nutritious, full of flavour, tender and succulent. Try this easy recipe to impress your guests!

Buy cultivated mussels the day you are going to cook and eat them. Select mussels that are closed or close when tapped, and avoid any with cracked or broken shells.

For 4 servings:
1.5 kg (3 lb 5 oz/about 24 fairly large) cultivated mussels
2 large onions
1 Tbsp olive or other oil
1 tsp finely chopped garlic
pinch of saffron (optional)
1/2 cup (125 ml/4 fl oz) white wine
1 can (425 g/15 oz) savoury tomatoes
chopped parsley or coriander

Scrub the live mussels, pulling out the beards and discarding any that do not close when tapped.

Chop the onions finely. Heat the oil in a large pan with a lid, and cook the onions and garlic until transparent, but not browned. Add the saffron (if available), wine and tomatoes.

Bring to the boil, add half the mussels, cover and simmer until the shells open about 1 cm (1/2 in). Watch carefully, turning the mussels so they heat evenly, and lifting each mussel out with tongs as soon as it is ready. Arrange the opened mussels in individual bowls, and keep them warm while you cook the remaining mussels.

The tomato mixture will be diluted by liquid from the mussels, which adds extra flavour. Boil the broth briskly for about 2 minutes, then spoon it evenly over the mussels in the bowls. Sprinkle with chopped parsley or coriander, and serve with chunks of crusty bread.

Hint: For maximum flavour and colour from the saffron threads, grind them in a pestle and mortar before adding them to the onion mixture.

Cream of Mussel Soup

Cream of Mussel Soup

Serve this creamy gourmet soup with pride! It has a lovely flavour, quite similar to that of oyster soup, but is cheap enough to serve often.

For 4 servings:
500–600 g (1 lb 2 oz–1 lb 5 oz) cultivated mussels
1–2 cloves garlic
25 g (1 oz) butter
3 Tbsp plain flour
1/2 tsp freshly grated nutmeg
milk to make the mussel stock up to 3 cups (750 ml/24 fl oz)
salt and pepper

Check the mussels, discarding any that are cracked or do not shut immediately if tapped. Cook by steaming in about 1/4 cup of water in a covered pan until they open. Remove the first to open with tongs, then cover the pan again and steam the remainder. (Overcooked mussels shrink and toughen.) Strain the liquid from the pan, and make it up to 3 cups with milk.

In a clean pot, cook the finely chopped garlic in butter until straw-coloured. Stir in the flour and nutmeg and cook until bubbling, then add half the milk-and-stock mixture. Stir constantly over medium heat until the sauce thickens and boils, then add the rest of the liquid and bring back to the boil, stirring often. Simmer gently for 2–3 minutes, then remove from the heat.

Shell the mussels and chop them in a food processor, blender or mouli until puréed, adding some of the sauce from the pot to thin the purée. Sieve this mixture into the sauce, discarding the mussel solids after pressing them firmly. Mix well and season to taste. Cool, then refrigerate if not serving immediately.

Just before serving, gently reheat without boiling in a pot or microwave bowl. (The flavour is best after the soup has stood for a few hours.) For special occasions, swirl a spoonful of softly whipped cream into each bowl. Top with sprigs of dill if available, and serve with tiny croûtons (p. 344), crackers or toast.

Oyster Chowder

Only recently have I produced an oyster chowder which really delights me.

For 4 main-course servings:
4 rashers bacon
2 Tbsp butter
2 large onions, chopped in 1 cm (1/2 inch) cubes
2 large cloves garlic, finely chopped
1 large potato, chopped in 1 cm (1/2 inch) cubes
1 cup (250 ml/8 fl oz) liquid (see below)
1 tsp green herb stock powder or 1/2 tsp salt
2 dozen oysters
2 cups (500 ml/16 fl oz) milk
2 Tbsp cornflour
black pepper or hot pepper sauce
fresh herbs (parsley, chives, dill, etc.)

Cut the rind off the bacon. Put the rind in a large frypan or pot over low heat. Chop the bacon into neat 5 mm (1/4 in) pieces and add to the pan; cook until lightly browned. Add the butter, onion and garlic to the lightly browned bacon and cook for 5 minutes without browning while you prepare the potatoes.

Put the oysters in a sieve, draining their liquid into a bowl. Rinse the oysters with water, collecting it in the bowl too. Make up to 1 cup with water or white wine. Add the potatoes to the pan, stir for 30 seconds, then add the liquid and stock powder or salt. Cover and simmer for 10 minutes or until the potatoes are tender. Discard the bacon rinds.

Add the oysters and milk to the pan, then add the cornflour mixed to a paste with more milk. Bring to the boil, stirring constantly, then remove from the heat. The oysters will toughen and shrink if over-cooked. Add finely chopped herbs to taste.

Adjust the seasonings. Reheat it briefly and serve in large, deep bowls, with crusty bread, crackers or toast. Never leave the chowder simmering.

Note: If they are available, use 'cut' oysters (damaged as they are opened) for this soup.

Seafood Chowder

This chowder (or chunky soup) is quickly made from ingredients from your store cupboard, and embellished with fresh seafood if available. Even without these additions, however, the flavour is excellent, especially if the soup is allowed to stand for a few hours to enable the flavours to blend.

For 2 servings:
2 medium onions
2 stalks celery
1 carrot
25 g (1 oz) butter
2 medium potatoes
1 cup (250 ml/8 fl oz) water
1 tsp each herb and chicken stock powder
   or 1 tsp salt
1 can (125–200 g/4–8 oz) shrimps or
   salmon
2 cups (500 ml/16 fl oz) milk
6–12 raw oysters (optional)
6–12 steamed mussels (optional)
about 2 Tbsp cornflour
chopped parsley

Chop the onions and celery coarsely and slice the carrot thinly. Cook gently in butter for 5 minutes. Scrub the potatoes and cut them into small cubes. Add the water, stock powders or salt and the potatoes to the pan. Cover and simmer gently for 10–15 minutes, until the vegetables are tender.

Add the shrimps or salmon and any liquid from the can, the milk, whole or halved oysters, and mussels cut into chunks. Bring back to the boil, then thicken with the cornflour mixed to a paste with cold milk. Remove from the heat and serve sprinkled with chopped parsley.

Creamy Fish Chowder

This main-meal chowder is well worth the several steps involved, and is a great way to serve inexpensive whole fish, or better still, a fish which you have caught, but do not want to fillet.

For 4–6 servings:
1 large onion
2 stalks celery
1–2 carrots
3 Tbsp butter
1 cup (250 ml/8 fl oz) water
2 tsp chicken or green herb stock powder
   or 1 tsp salt
about ½ cup whole kernel corn
about ½ cup frozen peas
about 600 g (1 lb 5 oz) whole fish
½ cup (125 ml/4 fl oz) white wine or
   water
3 Tbsp plain flour
1–2 cups (250–500 ml/8–16 fl oz) milk

Chop and slice the onion, celery and carrots and cook gently in 1 Tbsp butter in a large, covered pot for 3–4 minutes, without browning.

Add the water and stock powder or salt and cook until the vegetables are tender, then add the corn and peas and cook a little longer.

In a large, covered pot or pan, cook the whole or halved fish in the water or wine until it flakes, then strain the liquid through a sieve into the vegetables. Flake the fish, discarding the skin and bones, and add the flaked fish to the pot with the vegetables.

Clean the pan in which the fish was cooked then melt the remaining butter in it, and stir in the flour, heating until it bubbles. Add 1 cup of milk and bring to the boil, stirring constantly.

Add all the liquid from the fish and vegetables and cook until the sauce is smooth and boiling, stirring all the time. Add extra milk or water if it is too thick. Simmer for about 5 minutes then gently stir in the fish and vegetables and check the seasoning.

Reheat carefully when ready to serve. Garnish with fresh herbs and serve with garlic bread (p. 344).

Note: The fish should be gutted, but need not have its skin or scales removed before cooking.

Chunky Vegetable Chowder V

Vegetable chowder makes a substantial meal. By adding canned and frozen vegetables to fresh vegetables you get a good mixture of flavours, textures and colours in a short time.

For 4–6 servings:
1 medium carrot
1 medium onion
1 leek and/or celery stalk
1 potato
1 cup (250 ml/8 fl oz) water
1–2 tsp stock powder, any flavour
50 g (2 oz) butter
3 Tbsp plain flour
½ cup (125 ml/4 fl oz) milk
1 can (440 g/15 oz) creamed corn
1–2 cups frozen peas

Cut all the raw vegetables into small chunks. Cook in the water until tender, then add stock powder.

In another pot melt the butter, stir in the flour and cook briefly. Add the milk, and stir constantly until the sauce boils.

Stir the sauce into the cooked vegetables, add the corn and peas, and bring the mixture back to the boil. Simmer gently for 2–3 minutes. Serve with bread rolls or Toasted Cheese Sandwiches (p. 39).

Variation: Add pieces of leftover cooked chicken to the mixture just before serving.

Green Pea and Potato Chowder

This bright green, rich, creamy soup is easily and quickly made from everyday ingredients!

For 4 servings:
1 large onion
2 cloves garlic
1 rasher bacon
1 Tbsp butter
2 medium potatoes
2 cups (500 ml/16 fl oz) water
1½ tsp chicken or vegetable stock powder
1 tsp sugar
3–4 sprigs mint
1 cup frozen peas
about ½ cup (125 ml/4 fl oz) cream

Chop the onion, garlic and bacon and cook gently in the butter in a medium to large pot without allowing anything to brown.

Scrub and cube the potatoes. Add to the onion, cover and cook gently for 5 minutes, stirring occasionally.

Add the water, stock powder, sugar and mint. Cover and simmer until the potatoes are tender, 5–10 minutes. Add the peas and cook for 5 minutes longer.

Reserve ½ cup of the cooked vegetables for garnish if you like, then purée the soup in a blender or food processor, adding up to ½ cup cream to get the flavour, colour and richness you want. Reheat if necessary, without boiling, adding the reserved vegetables for garnish.

Creamy Green Pea Soup V

With peas from the freezer and a carton of cream cheese, you can make a bright green, tasty, substantial and filling soup.

For 3–4 large servings:
1 tsp (1–2 cloves) minced garlic
1 Tbsp olive oil or butter
4 cups free-flow frozen peas
1 cup (250 ml/8 fl oz) water
1 tsp herb-flavoured salt or stock powder
1 carton (250 g/8 oz) cream cheese
   (low-fat or regular)
1–2 cups (250–500 ml/8–16 fl oz) milk
seasonings to taste

Heat the garlic in oil or butter until bubbling but not brown, add the frozen peas and water, cover and cook for 4–5 minutes, until the peas are tender but still bright green.

Purée in a food processor with the salt or stock powder, and previously stirred cream cheese. Thin with milk to the consistency you like.

Adjust seasonings, adding salt, pepper and tabasco to taste. If you like, sieve part or all of the soup to make it smoother.

Refrigerate for up to 2 days, thinning with water or milk as necessary.

Top each serving with spoonfuls of sour cream and basil pesto (p. 346), or with tiny croûtons (p. 344), sour cream and tomato salsa. Serve with warmed, crusty, crunchy bread.

Variation: If you have them, cook several chopped lettuce leaves and/or spring onions, and a dozen or so fresh mint leaves with the peas.

'Dinner For One' Soup M

This soup for one is a real treat! It has a wonderful flavour, is a complete, low-fat meal, and is well-balanced nutritionally.

For 1 large (main) serving:
1 cup cooked brown or white rice,
* or 50 g (2 oz) uncooked instant noodles*
75 g (2½ oz) boneless, skinless salmon or
* other fish, or cooked chicken*
1 large or 2 small spring onions
4–6 button mushrooms
¼–½ ripe avocado (optional)
1½ cups (375 ml/12 fl oz) chicken stock,
* or 1 cup (250 ml/8 fl oz) canned*
* chicken consommé with ½ cup*
* (125 ml/4 fl oz) water*
½ tsp grated fresh root ginger (optional)
1 tsp Kikkoman soy sauce
1 tsp sesame oil
1 tsp Thai sweet chilli sauce (optional)
2 Tbsp chopped fresh coriander, basil,
* parsley or other herbs*
salt and pepper to taste

If you are using instant noodles pre-cook them by pouring over 2 cups (500 ml/ 16 fl oz) of boiling water, leaving them to stand for 2 minutes, then draining them. Cut the raw salmon or other fish into 1 cm (½ in) cubes, or cut the cooked chicken into chunky but manageable pieces. Slice the spring onions diagonally, about 5 mm (¼ in) thick. Cut the mushrooms and avocado into pieces about the same size as the fish.

Put all the ingredients except the salt and pepper in a large, fairly deep, microwave-safe soup bowl, or in a medium-sized pot.

Microwave for about 5 minutes, until the soup is very hot but has not boiled. The fish will cook in this time. OR bring all the ingredients in the pot to the boil and simmer gently for 5 minutes. Season and serve immediately.

Notes: Freeze 1-cup lots of cooked brown rice so you always have it on hand.

Canned consommé makes excellent soup.

Sour, Sweet and Hot Soup V

This Asian soup is easy to make despite its long list of flavourings. Soured with lemon juice, sweetened with a little sugar, and heated with chilli, it is deliciously different. It is well worth making with good stock.

'Dinner for One' Soup

For a vegetarian option use homemade vegetable stock and add strips or cubes of firm tofu with the suggested vegetables.

For 4–6 servings:
6 cups (1.5 litres/48 fl oz) chicken stock
1 lemon or lime
2 Tbsp fish sauce
2 Tbsp sugar
2 Tbsp very finely sliced lemon grass*
1 tsp finely chopped garlic*
2 tsp minced or grated fresh ginger*
2 tsp ground coriander
½ tsp minced chilli*
salt and pepper to taste
500 g (1 lb 2 oz) chicken breast, fish
* fillets or prawns (optional)*
8–10 button mushrooms (optional)
1 carrot (optional)
2 small zucchini (optional)
4 spring onions
2–3 Tbsp chopped fresh coriander

* Use fresh or from jars.

Measure the stock into a large pot. Cut the lemon or lime into quarters and add these to the stock with the next 7 ingredients. Bring to the boil, turn the heat down and simmer gently for 15 minutes.

Remove the lime or lemon quarters, squeezing the remaining juice into the soup. Taste carefully, adding salt and pepper if necessary.

The soup tastes good like this, without any more solids, but the optional ingredients add extra flavour and substance. Slice the boneless, skinless chicken or fish and the mushrooms thinly, and cut the carrot and zucchini into long, thin matchsticks. Stir whatever you are using into the soup, bring it back to the boil and simmer until the additions are cooked.

Just before serving, stir in the finely chopped spring onions and coriander.

Oriental Coconut Soup   V

Eastern soups are excitingly different! This one takes only 20 minutes from start to finish. Choose a chicken, fish or vegetarian option.

For 2 large main or 4 starter servings:
1 can (400 ml/14 oz) coconut cream
2 cups (500 ml/16 fl oz) chicken, fish or vegetable stock, or 2 tsp stock powder in 2 cups water
1 cup (250 ml/8 fl oz) water
1 tsp minced or grated fresh ginger
2 Tbsp fish sauce or Kikkoman soya sauce
2–3 tsp curry powder or Thai curry paste
finely grated rind and juice of 1 lime
1/2 tsp minced chilli or 1 small fresh chilli, finely chopped
1 Tbsp very finely sliced lemon grass
125–150 g (4½–5 oz) egg noodles*
4 tsp sesame oil
200 g (7 oz) chicken breast, fish fillets, tofu or prawns
6 button mushrooms, thinly sliced
1 cup bean sprouts (optional)

* Use yellowy, fresh egg noodles from Asian food stores or instant dried noodles (without flavour sachets).

Measure the first 8 ingredients (including minced chilli) into a medium-sized pot. Add the lemon grass. (If using fresh lemon grass, grate or finely chop the base of the stem only.) Stir to mix, bring to the boil, then simmer gently for 20 minutes.

Cook dried noodles according to the packet instructions, or cook fresh noodles briefly in salted, boiling water. Drain and stir in 2 tsp of the sesame oil. Toss to mix and put aside.

Finely slice the chicken, fish or tofu. Mix these or the prawns with the remaining sesame oil and put aside.

Just before serving, add the mushrooms, bean sprouts, noodles, chicken, fish, tofu or prawns to the hot stock, bring it back to the boil and simmer for a few minutes, until the additions are cooked.

If you like, serve one or more of these prepared ingredients as accompaniments: spring onions, chopped fresh coriander, Vietnamese mint, hard-boiled eggs, roasted peanuts or lime wedges.

'Dieter's Delight' Soup

This delicious, low-calorie, highly flavoured soup is a real boon for dieters. Despite the long ingredient list it takes less than half an hour to make.

For 12 cups, 6–8 large servings:
1–2 large onions
2 tsp olive or other oil
1 tsp oreganum
2 tsp ground cumin
1/4 tsp thyme
2 tsp finely chopped garlic*

1 tsp minced or grated fresh ginger*
1–1½ tsp Thai green curry paste
4–6 large stalks celery
1–2 green or red peppers (optional)
500 g (1 lb 2 oz) cabbage
6 cups (1.5 litres/48 fl oz) hot water plus 1 cup (250 ml/8 fl oz) cold water
1 packet Cream of Chicken soup
1 Tbsp cornflour
2 cans (400 g/14 oz each) Italian or Mexican-style tomatoes
2–3 Tbsp tomato paste
chopped fresh herbs
1 Tbsp pesto (optional)
salt, pepper and sugar to taste

* Ready-prepared chopped or puréed garlic and ginger in jars gives this soup a better flavour than the fresh product.

Chop the onion and cook it in the oil in a large pot, over moderate heat, for 5 minutes. Stir in the next 6 seasonings, and cook with the onion while you chop, then add as each is prepared, the celery, peppers and cabbage. (Chop the cabbage into small chunks.) Add the hot water, bring to the boil and simmer for 5 minutes.

Mix the powdered soup, cornflour and cold water to a smooth paste, then stir into the boiling vegetable mixture. When the soup thickens, add the tomatoes, tomato paste, herbs and pesto. Bring to the boil then remove from the heat. Add salt, pepper and sugar until the soup has a really good flavour.

When cool, refrigerate for up to a week, or freeze. Heat only enough for each meal.

Gazpacho   V

Is gazpacho a cold soup full of salad, a salad in a soupy sort of dressing or a cross between a salad and a soup? Anyway, it's a great start to a summer meal or barbecue!

For 6 servings:
3 slices wholemeal or white bread
1 kg (2 lb 3 oz) ripe, red tomatoes
5–6 cm (2–2½ in) length of telegraph cucumber
3 Tbsp wine vinegar
2–3 Tbsp olive oil
1–2 cloves garlic
1 tsp sugar
2 tsp salt
1 Tbsp tomato paste
about 1 cup (250 ml/8 fl oz) water
fresh basil or coriander

Soak the bread in cold water, squeeze it to extract most of the moisture, then mash it with a fork until broken up.

Peel the tomatoes by standing them in boiling water for a minute, then in cold water. Halve them, then shake out and discard the seeds and surrounding watery liquid before chopping them finely.

Grate the peeled cucumber and mix with

the tomatoes. Add the bread, vinegar and olive oil. Mash or purée the garlic with the sugar and salt and mix in. Stir in the tomato paste. Add the water if the mixture looks and tastes too concentrated, otherwise leave it out.

Add a few chopped basil or coriander leaves, adjust the seasonings (tomato mixtures often need extra sugar) and chill for at least an hour.

Prepare small dishes of each of the following, allowing at least a spoonful of each for every diner: chopped red, yellow and green peppers, cubed cucumber, chopped red onions, small croûtons (p. 344), diced avocado, pesto (p. 346), chopped basil or coriander.

Serve the chilled gazpacho in bowls which contain one or two ice cubes, and pass around the bowls of accompaniments.

> For best colour and flavour, instead of refrigerating tomatoes, keep them in a basket at room temperature on your benchtop so they can ripen fully.

Artichoke Soup   V

The tubers of Jerusalem artichokes look like knobbly potatoes, have a definite, mild but interesting flavour, and make wonderful soup.

For 4 servings:
500–600 g (1–1¼ lb) Jerusalem artichokes
1 Tbsp butter
2 cloves garlic
1½ cups (375 ml/12 fl oz) chicken or vegetable stock
1 tsp sugar
1/2 tsp salt
1–1½ cups (250–375 ml/8–12 fl oz) milk
about 1/4 cup (60 ml/2 fl oz) cream

Scrub the unpeeled artichokes, then slice them 1 cm (1/2 in) thick.

Melt the butter in a medium-sized pot, add the finely chopped garlic and cook gently for about a minute, without browning. Add the sliced artichokes, stock, sugar and salt.

Cover and simmer for 10 minutes, or until the artichokes are tender.

Lift the pieces of artichoke from the pot with a slotted spoon and purée in a food processor, blender or mouli, gradually adding the cooking liquid after the vegetables are puréed. Add 1 cup of milk to the purée, process again, then pour through a sieve to remove any pieces of skin.

Stir in the cream, then add milk until the soup is the consistency you like.

Reheat just before serving, adjusting the seasonings to bring out the full artichoke flavour. Garnish with whipped or plain cream and some finely chopped parsley or chives.

Note: If the greyish colour of this soup bothers you, cook a little spinach or pumpkin with the artichokes.

Warning: Jerusalem artichokes upset some people's stomachs, causing wind! Do not give guests large servings of soup without telling them what they are eating!

Roasted Corn Soup   V

Roasting corn intensifies its fresh flavour. I associate this with late summer, and the pleasures of wayside stalls!

For 4 servings:
4 large corn cobs
25 g (1 oz) butter
4 cloves garlic
1 red pepper (optional)
1 large potato
4 cups (1 litre/32 fl oz) chicken or
* vegetable stock*
1/4 cup (60 ml/2 fl oz) cream (optional)
seasonings

Turn the oven to 220°C (425°F). Pull back the husks from the corn cobs and remove the silk. Melt the butter and brush it over the kernels, then pull the husks back to cover the cobs again. Place the corn cobs in one layer in a roasting pan, with the whole, unpeeled garlic cloves and the halved red pepper. Bake for 20 minutes.

While the corn roasts, peel and roughly chop the potato and cook it in the chicken stock in a large pot, until tender. Using a slotted spoon, lift out the cooked potato and put in a food processor, blender or mouli.

Pull the husks off the roasted corn cobs. With a sharp, serrated knife, cut the kernels off the cobs, then scrape the remaining corn flesh from the cobs using a dessertspoon held bowl down.

Purée the kernels and flesh from 3 cobs with the potato, add the pulp squeezed from the garlic cloves, then return the mixture to the pot with the chicken stock.

Finely dice the red pepper, discarding the stem and seeds. Add to the soup with the corn cut from the last cob, and the cream, and bring to the boil. Adjust the seasonings to taste, adding a little salt, sugar, tabasco sauce and freshly ground black pepper if necessary.

Reheat just before serving. Top individual servings with finely chopped parsley or coriander.

Variations: Add a little chipotle powder, paste or sauce to the potatoes if you have it and like the idea of its subtle, smoky flavour in your soup.

Barbecue the corn, garlic (on a skewer) and red pepper.

Chunky Corn Chowder   V

Add a large can of creamed corn to a few basic vegetables for a substantial and interesting soup in a short time.

For 4–5 large servings:
2 large onions
1 cup finely chopped celery (optional)
2 Tbsp butter or olive oil
2 medium potatoes
1 1/2 cups (375 ml/12 fl oz) chicken or
* vegetable stock, or 1 1/2 tsp stock powder*
* in 1 1/2 cups water*
1 can (410 g/14 oz) creamed corn
1/2 cup (125 ml/4 fl oz) water
1 cup (250 ml/8 fl oz) milk
1/2 cup (125 ml/4 fl oz) sour cream,
* cream, cream cheese or evaporated milk*
1 Tbsp basil pesto (optional, p. 346)
1/2 tsp or more salt
pepper and tabasco sauce to taste

Chop the onions and celery into 5 mm (1/4 in) cubes. Cook in a medium-sized pot in the butter or oil, without browning, while you prepare the potatoes.

Scrub the potatoes, cut them into 5 mm (1/4 in) cubes, and add to the onions. Add the stock, cover and simmer over moderate heat for 4–5 minutes, until the potato is tender.

Add the creamed corn, rinse out the can with the water and add it, the milk, and the sour cream, cream, cream cheese or evaporated (unsweetened condensed) milk. Stir or whisk everything together. Bring to the boil, simmer for about a minute, then remove from the heat and stir in the pesto. Season to taste with the salt, pepper and tabasco.

Reheat briefly when required, adding chopped parsley, fresh herbs or thinly sliced spring onion leaves if available. Serve with buttered toast or warmed crusty rolls.

Variations: For extra flavour and colour chop half a red or orange pepper finely, and add to the butter or oil before the potatoes. A few green beans or some broccoli, chopped finely and added at the same stage, are also good.

Chunky Corn Chowder

Dot's Mysterious Beer Soup

Dot's Mysterious Beer Soup

Whenever I serve this soup I am asked what is in it. My friends and family find the combination of carrots, cream cheese and lager delicious – but cannot identify the individual flavours.

For 6 servings:
2 large onions
2 large carrots
25 g (1 oz) butter
¼ cup plain flour
2 cups (250 ml/8 fl oz) chicken or vegetable stock
1 carton (250 g/8 oz) cream cheese
about 2 cups (500 ml/16 fl oz) lager
chopped parsley

Finely chop or grate the onions and carrots. Melt the butter in a large pot, add the onion, and cook over low heat until very lightly browned and quite soft. Add the carrots, cover and cook for 5–10 minutes longer, until the carrot is soft.

Stir in the flour, cook another minute, then add the stock. Stir over gentle heat until the soup boils and thickens.

Remove from the heat and allow to cool slightly, then purée in a food processor or blender, in several batches if necessary. Pour back into the pot.

Put the cream cheese and lager in the (unwashed) food processor or blender and blend until smooth. Add to the vegetable purée in the pot, stirring to combine. Reheat before serving.

Serve topped with finely chopped parsley or coriander and cheesy pastry croûtons or plain croûtons (p. 344).

Spinach Soup V

This soup has a wonderful bright green colour. A little cream 'softens' its flavour and makes it popular with many people who do not enjoy plain spinach.

For 4 large servings:
1 Tbsp butter
1 large onion, finely chopped
½ tsp freshly grated nutmeg
2 large potatoes
3 cups (750 ml/24 fl oz) chicken or vegetable stock, or 3 tsp stock powder in 3 cups water
250 g (9 oz) spinach
½ cup (125 ml/4 fl oz) cream
½ cup (125 ml/4 fl oz) milk
salt and pepper

Melt the butter in a fairly large pot and add the onion. Add nutmeg if available, then cover and cook gently for 5–10 minutes without browning.

Scrub the potatoes and cut them into 1 cm (½ in) cubes. Add to the pot with the stock, cover and simmer for about 15 minutes, until the potatoes are tender. Add the well-washed, roughly chopped spinach and simmer 3–4 minutes longer, until tender but still bright green.

Purée everything in a food processor, blender or mouli, in several batches if necessary, then pour back into the pot. Whisk in the cream and milk, adding more milk if you want it thinner. Season if necessary, adding extra salt, freshly ground pepper and nutmeg.

Reheat briefly just before serving. Serve plain, with a swirl of plain or lightly whipped cream, or with croûtons (p. 344) or melba toast (p. 344).

Brown Mushroom Soup V

This soup is wonderful made with large, freshly picked mushrooms or with the large, flat brown-gilled mushrooms from your supermarket.

For 6 servings:
3 Tbsp butter
2 medium onions, finely chopped
2 cloves garlic, finely chopped
4–6 large (150 g/5 oz) flat, brown mushrooms, finely chopped
¼ tsp thyme
3 Tbsp plain flour
2 cups (500 ml/16 fl oz) chicken stock or 2 tsp stock powder in 2 cups water
½ tsp salt
pepper to taste
1 Tbsp sherry (optional)
1 Tbsp wine vinegar
2 cups (500 ml/16 fl oz) milk

Melt the butter in a large pot, add the onion and cook over medium heat for about 5 minutes, until evenly browned. Add the garlic, cook 1–2 minutes longer, then add the mushrooms and thyme. Cook for 5 minutes, stirring frequently.

Stir in the flour and cook until lightly browned, then add the stock, salt, pepper, sherry and vinegar. Stir well to mix, and bring to the boil. Simmer for 5–10 minutes. Add the milk, heat until almost boiling, then serve.

Leek and Potato Soup V

This is a good, filling winter soup, using vegetables that are in season. This version may not be traditional, but it is quick to make and tastes very good.

For 4–6 servings:
50 g (2 oz) butter
1 clove garlic, crushed
3 medium leeks, sliced thinly
2–3 medium potatoes (300–450 g/10 oz–1 lb)
4 cups (1 litre/32 fl oz) water
3 tsp chicken or vegetable stock powder
1 tsp sugar
¼–½ cup (60–125 ml/2–4 fl oz) cream
salt and pepper to taste

Melt the butter in a large pot. Gently cook the garlic and leeks for about 10 minutes, without letting them brown. (Use all the white and light green inner leek leaves, but none of the dark green parts.) Peel the potatoes, slice them thinly and add to the leeks with the water, stock powder and sugar, and simmer for about 10 minutes until the vegetables are just tender. (Overcooking spoils the colour and flavour.)

Blend or process the mixture or, for a chunky soup, mash with a potato masher. Add cream, according to your taste and conscience! Taste and adjust the seasonings carefully.

Serve immediately or reheat. For a special occasion add a spoonful of whipped cream to each bowl. Sprinkle with chopped chives or paprika.

Quick Tomato Soup   V

If you have found the perfect ready-made tomato soup at a reasonable price, you won't need this recipe. If you haven't, try this 7-minute version, which I think is well worth the little effort involved!

For 4 large servings:
1 Tbsp olive or other oil
1 tsp (2 cloves) minced garlic
1 tsp ground cumin or curry powder
2 Tbsp plain flour
1 can (425 g/15 oz) tomato purée made up
  to 4 cups (1 litre/32 fl oz) with hot water
grated rind of 1/2 lemon (optional)
1 1/2 tsp sugar
1 carton (250 g/8 oz) sour cream
salt and tabasco sauce to taste
1–2 Tbsp basil pesto

Heat the oil in a medium-sized pot. Add the garlic, cumin or curry powder and flour, and stir until bubbling. Stir in about a cup of the purée mixture then bring to the boil, stirring all the time. Add the remaining purée mixture with the grated lemon rind and sugar, and bring to the boil.

Whisk or beat the sour cream in with a fork, remove from the heat and season to taste. Add some basil pesto (p. 346) if you want a stronger herb flavour.

Just before serving, reheat without boiling. Serve with buttered toast, toasted cheese sandwiches (p. 39), warmed bread rolls or sliced french bread.

Variations: Top each serving with a little plain, unsweetened yoghurt and a sprinkling of fresh herbs or thinly sliced spring onions.

Kumara, Pumpkin and Peanut Soup   V

This combination makes a popular and interesting soup with a complex flavour. Made with vegetable stock, it is good for a vegetarian main course.

For 4–6 servings:
1 large onion
1 tsp finely chopped garlic
2 Tbsp butter or oil
1/2 tsp curry powder
1/2 tsp freshly ground coriander seed
1/8–1/2 tsp chilli powder or minced chilli
1 fairly large kumara (about 250 g/9 oz)
250 g (9 oz) pumpkin
4 cups (1 litre/32 fl oz) chicken or
  vegetable stock, or 2 tsp stock powder in
  4 cups water
1/2 tsp salt
2 Tbsp peanut butter

Cook the chopped onion and garlic over low heat in butter or oil, in a medium-sized pot, until the onion is transparent. Add the curry powder, coriander and chilli powder (as much as you like for hotness) and stir over moderate heat for about a minute.

Peel the kumara and pumpkin and chop the flesh into 1 cm (1/2 in) cubes. (Do not use more kumara or the soup will be too sweet.) Add the vegetables to the pot with the stock, bring to the boil and simmer for about 15 minutes or until the vegetables are tender. Add the salt then peanut butter. (Too much overpowers the vegetables.)

Purée in a food processor, blender or mouli (or use a potato masher). Adjust the seasonings and reheat. Serve topped with a swirl of yoghurt or coconut cream, or with a few finely chopped roasted peanuts.

Thai Pumpkin Soup   V

Its colour, interesting flavour and 'velvet smooth' texture make this a wonderful soup to serve to guests.

For about 8 large servings:
2 medium onions
2 Tbsp olive oil
2 tsp Thai green curry paste
4 cups (1 litre/32 fl oz) chicken or
  vegetable stock or 4 tsp stock powder in
  4 cups water
2 medium carrots
1 kg (2 lb 3 oz) peeled and seeded
  pumpkin
2 medium kumara
1 can (400 ml/13 fl oz) coconut cream
1 Tbsp fish sauce or Kikkoman soy sauce
fresh coriander

Chop the onions finely and cook in the oil in a large pot until transparent but not browned. Add the curry paste and cook for 2–3 minutes longer, stirring often, then add the stock.

Slice the carrots thinly (5 mm/1/4 in thick) and add to the pot so they start cooking while you cut the pumpkin and kumara into 1 cm (1/2 in) cubes, then add them too. Cover and cook for 10–12 minutes, or until the vegetables are tender. (For best flavour and colour, do not cook longer than necessary.)

Blend or process in batches, then pour through a sieve into a clean pot. Add the coconut cream and fish or soy sauce, and bring back to the boil. Adjust seasonings.

Serve immediately or reheat when required, garnishing each serving with a sprig of fresh coriander, or with finely chopped coriander.

Thai Pumpkin Soup

Chilled Summer Vegetable Soup   V

Make the smooth soup base ahead but add the fresh green vegetables at the very last minute.

For 4 servings:
2 fairly large potatoes
2 cups (500 ml/16 fl oz) milk
1 clove garlic, finely chopped
1/4 tsp salt
1/2 cup cream cheese
1/4 cup (60 ml/2 fl oz) dry white wine
1/4 cup (60 ml/2 fl oz) cream
1/4 cup chopped watercress
1/4 cup shredded lettuce
1/4 cup finely chopped spinach leaves
  (optional)
1/4 cup coarsely grated telegraph
  cucumber
2 spring onions, finely chopped
1/4–1/2 cup chopped bean or snow pea
  sprouts

Peel and cube the potatoes and cook them gently in the milk, with the garlic and salt, until tender.

Measure the cream cheese, wine and cream into a food processor, add the hot, cooked potatoes and process until smooth. Add the cooking liquid, and pour the mixture through a sieve to remove any lumps. Refrigerate until well chilled.

Just before serving, add the finely chopped green vegetables to the chilled soup. They should be as crisp as possible when they are chopped and added to the soup. If you can, wash, trim and discard the stalks from the watercress and spinach straight after you make the soup base. Remove the excess water by shaking the vegetables in a tea towel or rolling them up in a paper towel, then chill them. Shred then chop everything except the cucumber very finely, using a sharp knife. Taste, adjust seasonings and serve.

Fresh Tomato Soup   M V

I microwave this easy soup in the bowl into which I pick the tomatoes. Its success is partly due to a secret ingredient – bread!

For 4–6 servings:
1–1.5 kg (2–3 lb) ripe, red tomatoes
1 slice bread, broken up
1 tsp salt
1 Tbsp sugar
1/2 tsp basil
1/2 tsp oreganum
1–2 cloves garlic, chopped
1 onion, chopped
parsley, bayleaf, thyme (optional)
about 2 tsp wine vinegar

Put the tomatoes in a large microwave casserole, halving large ones. Add the bread. Sprinkle with the salt, sugar, basil and oreganum, replacing the dried herbs with fresh ones if you have them.

Add the chopped garlic and onion, and small quantities of the other herbs if you like.

Cover and cook until tender and mushy. Cook on High (100%) power for about 10 minutes, then lower the power to 50% if you think the mixture may boil over, and cook for 10 minutes longer. If there is no danger of overflow, leave on High power.

Break up the mixture with a potato masher, leave it to stand for about 5 minutes, then shake and press it through a coarse sieve. Add 1 tsp vinegar and taste, adding more if necessary. Cover and chill in the refrigerator. Adjust seasonings if necessary.

If serving as a cold soup, pour into individual bowls just before serving. Pass round bowls of crisp croûtons (p. 344), diced celery, diced peppers, cubed tomato, cubed avocado, chopped cucumbers, etc.

If serving hot, stir in parsley or chives if desired, or as much cream, crème fraîche or sour cream as you like.

Swede and Bacon Soup   V

Swedes give a surprising, unrecognisable flavour to this soup, which is equally good as a dinner party starter or a family weekend lunch.

For 4 large servings:
2–3 rashers bacon
1 Tbsp olive oil or butter
1 onion
2 cloves garlic
1/2 carrot
1/2 celery stalk
400 g (14 oz) swede
2 cups (500 ml/16 fl oz) chicken or
  vegetable stock
1 tsp sugar
freshly ground black pepper
1/4 tsp freshly grated nutmeg (optional)
2 Tbsp cream cheese (optional)
25 g (1 oz) butter
2 Tbsp plain flour
1 1/2 cups (375 ml/12 fl oz) milk
1/2–1 tsp salt
1/4–1/2 cup (60–125 ml/2–4 fl oz) cream
  (optional)

Chop the bacon finely, discarding the rind, then cook in a large pot with the oil or butter. Chop the onion, garlic, carrot and celery, and stir into the bacon. Cover and cook over a low heat for 5–10 minutes, without browning.

While the vegetables 'sweat', peel the swede and cut it into cubes no bigger than 1 cm (1/2 in). Add to the pot with the stock, sugar, pepper and nutmeg. Simmer for 5–10 minutes, just until the swede is tender. Do not overcook.

Transfer the vegetables with a little of the liquid to a food processor or blender, add the optional cream cheese, then purée until smooth. Save the rest of the liquid.

In another pot, melt the second measure of butter, add the flour, cook for 30 seconds, then add half the milk and bring to the boil, stirring all the time. When thick and smooth, add the rest of the milk and the vegetable cooking liquid and stir until boiling again. Add the swede purée and season carefully to taste. Add cream to the thickened soup until it is the required richness.

Serve garnished with croûtons (p. 344), chopped parsley or spring onions, or a spoonful of whipped cream and a sprinkling of paprika.

Variation: If you are using the extra cream, you can leave out the white sauce. This makes less soup, however.

Red Lentil, Carrot and Kumara Soup   V

Red lentils cook fast, without soaking, so you can make this tasty and substantial soup in about half an hour.

For 4 large servings:
1 large onion
2 Tbsp olive oil or butter
1 tsp (1–2 cloves) minced garlic
1/4–1/2 tsp minced red chilli
2 tsp ground cumin
1 tsp turmeric (optional)
4 cups (1 litre/32 fl oz) vegetable stock or
  4 tsp stock powder in 4 cups water
3/4–1 cup red lentils
2 medium carrots
2 stalks celery
1 large kumara
1/4–1/2 cup (60–125 ml/2–4 fl oz) cream
  (optional)
salt and freshly ground black pepper
basil pesto

Chop the onion in 1 cm (1/2 in) chunks and cook in the oil or butter for 5 minutes, without browning. During this time, stir in the next 4 ingredients; the spices should smell fragrant, but should not burn.

Add the stock and lentils (more makes a thicker soup), and simmer, stirring now and then, while you cut the carrots and celery into 5 mm (1/4 in) slices, and the thinly peeled kumara into 1 cm (1/2 in) cubes. Add the vegetables to the pot and cook gently, with the lid tilted, for 15–20 minutes, until everything is tender.

Leave the soup chunky or purée all or part of it, as you like. Thin with extra stock, water or milk if it is very thick. Add cream or sour cream if you like. Taste and season last of all. To serve, top with spoonfuls of basil (or other) pesto (p. 346).

Variations: A few minutes before serving, stir small cubes of tofu into the soup; sprinkle Parmesan cheese on individual servings; replace the kumara with potatoes.

Lentil Soup with Coriander V

This soup is one of my all-time favourites! Serve it with bowls of colourful and tasty extras.

For 8–10 servings:
1½ cups brown or green lentils
10 cups (2.5 litres/80 fl oz) water
2 bayleaves (optional)
2 small dried chillies
2 large onions
3–4 stalks celery
1 green pepper
½ cup (125 ml/4 fl oz) olive or other oil
4 cloves garlic
1 tsp oreganum
1 tsp ground cumin
2 Tbsp chopped fresh coriander
3 Tbsp wine vinegar (red for preference)
about 1 tsp salt
black pepper

Simmer the lentils, water, bayleaves and chillies in a large pot for 45–60 minutes, or until the lentils are very soft. (Lentils which have been pre-soaked for 8 hours or longer will be tender in 20 minutes.)

Meanwhile, chop the onions, celery and pepper into small pieces about the size of the lentils. Heat the oil in a large frypan, cook the vegetables without browning for about 10 minutes, then leave to stand.

While these mixtures are cooking, chop the garlic and add half to the pot with the lentils, and half to the mixture in the pan. Add half the oreganum and cumin to each container.

When the lentils are soft add the mixture from the frypan, bring to the boil and simmer 15 minutes longer. Remove from the heat, take out the bayleaves and chillies, add the chopped coriander and the vinegar, then add salt and freshly ground black pepper to taste. Serve immediately or reheat when needed.

If you like, serve topped with croûtons (p. 344), pesto (p. 346), grated Parmesan cheese or sour cream.

Pork and Bean Soup

A few times each year, I make a large pot of this wonderful pale, creamy soup.

For about 10 servings:
2½ cups haricot beans
10 cups (2.5 litres/80 fl oz) water
1 bacon hock
2 cloves garlic, chopped
2 onions, sliced
2 stalks celery, sliced (optional)
seasonings

Put the beans into the soup pot, picking out any discoloured ones. Either pour cold water over them and leave them to stand overnight, or pour over boiling water and leave them to stand for an hour.

Mediterranean Bean Soup

Add the bacon hock and vegetables, cover and simmer for about 2 hours, until the meat and beans are very tender. (If the meat becomes tender before the beans, lift it out; if the beans become tender before the meat, you can finish cooking it in another pot with some of the liquid if you like.) Lift the hock from the liquid, remove the skin, and chop the meat into cubes. Purée the vegetables and cooking liquid, then add the meat. Season very carefully to bring out the flavour.

Serve in large bowls, topped with a knob of butter and a sprinkling of chopped parsley, or a spiral of cream and a sprinkling of paprika, chives or parsley.

Mediterranean Bean Soup V

To most of us, 'Mediterranean' means a blazing sun in a clear blue sky and sparkling blue sea. This soup, however, is eaten in the cold Mediterranean winter.

For 8 servings:
1½ cups haricot or baby lima beans
10 cups (2.5 litres/80 fl oz) water
2–3 cloves garlic
2–3 bayleaves
2 large onions
2 carrots
2–3 stalks celery
1 can (400 g/14 oz) whole tomatoes in juice
1½ tsp salt
¼ cup (60 ml/2 fl oz) olive oil
pepper
3–4 Tbsp freshly chopped parsley

Soak the dried beans in the water overnight. Pour off and measure the soaking water and replace with the same volume of fresh water.

Add the chopped garlic and the bayleaves and simmer for about half an hour. Chop the onions, carrots and celery, add to the pot and simmer for 30 minutes longer, until the beans are very soft. (For a thicker soup, purée all or half the solids.) Add the tomatoes and juice, salt, olive oil, plenty of pepper, and the chopped parsley.

For the best flavour, leave to stand for a few hours then adjust the seasonings, adding about a tsp of brown sugar if needed. Remove the bayleaves and serve with crusty, solid bread.

Variations: For a half-hour soup, pressure cook the beans, water, garlic and bayleaves for 20 minutes, add the vegetables and pressure cook for 5 minutes.

Granny's Chicken Soup

Old fowls make wonderful soup! Hunt them down if you are a serious soup-maker! You will find these 'retired layers' at some supermarkets and butchers' shops, at Asian food suppliers and egg farms.

For 6–8 servings:
*1 roasting fowl or roasting hen
   (about 1.5 kg/3 lb)
8 cups (2 litres/64 fl oz) water
1–2 tsp finely chopped garlic
1 tsp grated or minced fresh ginger
2 Tbsp soy sauce
2 Tbsp sherry (optional)
1 onion
1 carrot
1 stalk celery
1/2 cup macaroni
1 Tbsp rolled oats
1 small potato
chopped parsley and/or other fresh herbs
salt and pepper*

Place the bird (and its giblets) in a large pot, add the next 4 ingredients and the optional sherry. Cover, bring to the boil, then simmer for about 4 hours. Prepare the onion, carrot and celery, adding the tops, bottoms and any peelings at this stage. The vegetables themselves are chopped finely and added later.

Lift the bird from the pot and when cool enough separate the flesh from the skin and bones, using your fingers. Put the bones and trimmings back in the liquid to cook for 30–60 minutes longer.

Strain off the liquid, discard the debris, and skim off the fat which rises to the top.

Bring the cleared stock back to the boil, add the finely chopped onion, carrot and celery, bring back to the boil again and add the macaroni and rolled oats. Simmer for 20–30 minutes, or until the macaroni and vegetables are tender. Grate the unpeeled potato and add to the soup with the chopped herbs; season carefully to taste. The potato will thicken the soup, and must not be added before the other vegetables are cooked.

Add some (or all) of the cold chopped chicken if you like, and warm through. Refrigerate or freeze leftovers.

Quick Beef and Vegetable Chowder

Yes, it really is possible to make a wonderfully warming, nutritious and filling chowder (a cross between a soup and a stew) in less than half an hour! Serve it plain for an easy meal, or turn it into something really special by adding exciting toppings!

For 4 large servings (8 cups):
*1 large onion
1 Tbsp oil*
*500 g (1 lb 2 oz) lean minced beef
1 clove garlic
1 medium carrot
2 stalks celery
1/2 red or yellow pepper (optional)
1 can (about 400 g/14 oz) whole
   tomatoes in juice
2 cups (500 ml/16 fl oz) chicken stock
   plus 2 cups water, or 4 cups (1 litre/32 fl
   oz) water plus 2 tsp stock powder
2 bayleaves (optional)
1/2 tsp oreganum
1 tsp each salt and sugar
1/2 cup orzo (rice-shaped pasta) or other
   small pasta
2 Tbsp tomato paste
about 1/4 cup chopped parsley or other
   fresh herbs*

Chop the onion finely. Heat the oil in a large pot, cook the onion for 1–2 minutes until lightly browned, then add the mince. Cook over fairly high heat until no longer pink, adding the other vegetables as you prepare them. Chop them very finely by hand or in a food processor, or grate the carrot.

Stir in the tomatoes and juice, the stock and water, bayleaves and remaining seasonings. Bring to the boil, then add the pasta. Bring back to the boil, then reduce the heat and simmer covered for 15 minutes, or until the pasta is tender.

Remove and discard the bayleaves, then stir in the tomato paste and fresh herbs.

Taste and add extra salt, pepper, a little sugar and a little lemon juice if it seems bland.

Serve in large bowls, accompanied by good crusty bread, bread rolls or toast.

If the chowder is the main part of the meal serve a selection of toppings, which should be added in generous spoonfuls to individual servings; e.g. unsweetened yoghurt or sour cream (or a mixture of the two), chopped fresh coriander or more parsley, chopped raw tomato or a simple tomato salsa, chopped avocado in lemon juice, tiny croûtons (p. 344) or crackers, basil or other pesto (p. 346), Parmesan cheese, hot sauce or chilli sauce.

Pea Soup with Bacon

This is a meal in itself, especially if topped with a few slices of sizzling sausage.

For 8–10 servings:
*250–500 g (8 oz–1 lb) bacon pieces
2 large onions
2–3 stalks celery
2 medium carrots
1 tsp finely chopped garlic
8–10 cups (2–2.5 litres/64–80 fl oz) water
3/4 cup split yellow peas
1/2 cup red lentils
3 Tbsp butter*
*1/4 cup plain flour
milk, water or stock to thin
salt and pepper*

Chop the bacon finely, discarding the rind. Brown, adding a little oil if necessary, in the pot in which the soup is to be cooked. Add the coarsely chopped vegetables and the garlic and cook for 2–3 minutes, then add the water, peas and lentils. Cover, leaving the lid ajar, and cook gently for about 2 hours (or 30 minutes in a pressure cooker), until the peas are tender. (Use the smaller amount of water if the soup is pressure cooked.) Purée in batches in a food processor, blender or mouli.

Rinse out the pan and melt the butter in it. Add the flour, cook briefly, then add a cup of the puréed mixture. Bring to the boil, stirring constantly, then add another cup of the mixture and bring back to the boil. Add the remaining purée, bring to the boil again, and simmer for 5 minutes.

The resulting soup is very thick. I store it in jars in the refrigerator or in cartons in the freezer, and thin it as I use it with milk, water or stock. (The amount of these depends on the thickness you want.) Taste the soup critically after thinning it and adjust the seasonings.

Serve very hot, garnished with slices of cooked sausage browned in a little oil in a frypan, with crumbled, cooked bacon, or croûtons (p. 344).

Barley Broth

This is the soup of my childhood, remembered very fondly!

For 12 or more servings:
*1 large bag soup bones (about 2 kg/4 1/2 lb)
water to cover
3 large onions
3 stalks celery
3 large carrots
3 large cloves garlic
1 tsp black peppercorns
1 cup barley
3–4 cups finely chopped vegetables
chopped fresh herbs (optional)
salt and pepper to taste
1 cup chopped parsley*

Place the bones in a very large pot and cover with water. (For a browner soup, first grill or roast the bones in a large roasting dish in a very hot oven, until the edges and rough bits turn dark brown and char.)

Add to the pot the unpeeled onions, roughly chopped celery, scrubbed carrots, garlic and peppercorns.

Place the barley in a large sieve and lower it into the pot so it is immersed in the stock. (This allows you to lift it out before you strain the stock.) Cover and simmer very slowly for 4–5 hours.

Remove the pot from the heat, then take out and put aside the sieve of barley. Strain the stock, discard the bones and vegetables, and put the stock back in the pot. Skim the fat from the top.

Tip the barley into the stock, add a mixture of chopped vegetables and herbs, and simmer for about 30 minutes, until the vegetables are tender. Add salt and pepper to taste during the last 15 minutes. You will probably need several teaspoons of salt.

Serve topped with finely chopped parsley, with crusty bread. Refrigerate or freeze any soup not used immediately.

Minestrone   V

This popular, colourful soup is made from stock with added tomatoes, and filled with vegetables, beans and pasta. For speed, start with precooked (canned) beans, using whatever you think will look and taste best, and frozen or instant stock.

For 6 servings:
1 large onion
1 carrot
1 stalk celery
2 Tbsp olive or other oil
1/2 tsp finely chopped garlic
4 cups (1 litre/32 fl oz) chicken, beef or vegetable stock (see Note)
1 can (400 g/14 oz) tomatoes in juice
1/4 cup macaroni
1 cup chopped zucchini
1 cup chopped green beans
1 cup chopped cabbage
1 can kidney or other beans (any size)
sugar, pepper and salt to taste
freshly chopped herbs
Parmesan cheese

Chop the onion, carrot and celery into small cubes and cook in the oil in a large pot for about 15 minutes, until the onion is tender and the vegetables lightly browned. Stir in the garlic and cook a few seconds longer.

Add the stock and the tomatoes, squashing them to break them up if necessary. Bring to the boil, add the macaroni and cook for a few minutes while you prepare the green vegetables. Add these, simmer a few minutes longer, then add the canned beans.

Cook gently for a few minutes then taste and adjust the seasonings, adding a little sugar to intensify the tomato flavour. Add any finely chopped herbs you like.

Serve immediately or reheat, topping individual servings with grated Parmesan cheese.

Note: Use homemade stock (p. 343), bought stock, or 4 tsp stock powder in 4 cups (1 litre/32 fl oz) of water.

Shank Soup

Shank Soup

This old-fashioned soup is packed full of cereals, pulses and vegetables, and is very substantial. A large, two-cup serving with a crusty bread roll makes a complete warming meal on a winter's evening.

For 5–6 servings:
2–3 lamb or hogget shanks
1 large onion
2–3 large cloves garlic
2 carrots
12 cups (3 litres/96 fl oz) water
1/2 cup each barley, 'soup mix' and split peas or brown lentils
1 tsp each celery seed, oreganum and ground cumin
1/2 tsp thyme
1/8 tsp chilli powder
freshly ground black pepper
11/2 tsp salt
3 cups chopped vegetables
1/2 cup chopped parsley

Brown the shanks in a large pot, turning several times, while you chop the onion and garlic finely. Add the onion and garlic with a tsp of butter or oil, if no fat has come from the meat.

Cut the carrots into 1 cm (1/2 in) cubes and add to the browned shanks. Next add the water and everything else except the last 3 ingredients. Cover, leaving the lid ajar so the soup will not boil over, then simmer for 11/2 hours if you are in a hurry, or 2 hours for maximum flavour.

Lift the shanks from the soup. Add the salt to the soup, and a good selection of chopped raw vegetables, such as potato, kumara, pumpkin, cauliflower, cabbage.

While these cook, cut the shank meat into chunky pieces. Return these to the soup. Discard the bones and any trimmings. When the vegetables are tender check the level of the liquid, adding a few more cups of water if necessary. Simmer for a little longer, then adjust the seasonings carefully, add the parsley and serve. Refrigerate or freeze any leftovers.

Note: The soup thickens on standing, and may need thinning with extra water before later use.

Fabulous Fish

We may live in a country surrounded by sea, but until recently many of us tended to follow the example of our parents and grandparents, who considered the meat we produce so efficiently to be much more important than fish. Ideas change, however, and we now realise that we should be enjoying at least two fish meals a week, to take advantage of all the nutritional benefits fish offers. Experiment with some of the many varieties available, cooking them in some of the following ways.

Marinated Grilled Fish

Turn plain fish into a special occasion dish which will cook in 5 minutes!

For 2 servings:
2 pieces boneless, skinless fish such as
salmon or snapper, about 15 mm (¾ in)
thick, each weighing 150–200 g (5–7 oz)

Marinade
½ tsp ground cumin
¼ tsp oreganum
¼ tsp chilli powder
½ tsp salt
1 Tbsp Dijon mustard
2 Tbsp lime or lemon juice
1 Tbsp chopped fresh coriander
1 clove garlic, finely chopped
2 tsp olive or other oil

If you prefer to avoid last-minute work, prepare the marinade the night before.

Combine all the marinade ingredients, in the order given, in an unpunctured plastic bag big enough to hold the fish. Squeeze the bag to mix. Place the fish in the bag and massage it so the marinade coats all surfaces, and leave to stand for 10–20 minutes.

Heat a solid grill tray about 10 cm (4 in) from the heat. Meanwhile take a doubled piece of foil, fold over the edges and coat the surface with butter or oil. Take the fish from the marinade and place it on the foil. Spread any remaining marinade over the fish.

About 6 minutes before you plan to eat, slip the fish, on the foil, onto the heated grill tray. Cook close to the heat until the fish flakes or has changed colour in the centre, usually after 5 minutes. The mixture on the outside of the fish is unlikely to change colour very much. Do not turn the fish, since the underside should be cooked by this time.

Serve with new potatoes and asparagus or salad vegetables.

Marinated Grilled Fish

Basic Pan-Fried Fish Fillets

When you have plenty of top-quality, well-flavoured fish (such as fine-textured flatfish fillets or tarakihi), the simplest cooking method is the best!

For 1 serving:
about 150 g (5 oz) fish fillets
milk (optional)
about ¼ cup plain flour
about ½ tsp salt
2–3 tsp olive oil
2–3 tsp butter

Trim away any ragged edges of fish. Pat fish dry if necessary, and cut in smaller pieces if too large to turn over easily. When ready to cook, dip fish in a shallow dish of milk then turn it in a mixture of flour and salt.

Preheat a frypan, preferably non-stick, over moderate heat. Swirl a little olive oil over the base of the pan, add butter and tilt the pan as it melts. As soon as it bubbles, but before it darkens, add the fish. Immediately jiggle the pan to prevent the fish sticking.

Cook thin fillets over high heat, and thicker pieces over moderate heat, turning them once. When the fish is ready it should be lightly browned and the flesh milky rather than translucent in the thickest part. Thin fillets may take just 45 seconds a side, while thicker fillets, slices or cutlets may take 2–3 minutes per side.

Serve immediately with wedges of lemon or lime, fresh crusty bread and a salad, or in a warm, split, buttered bun.

Rosy Fish Fillets

Easy enough to prepare after work, tasty enough to serve to someone special, and less than 5 minutes' cooking time!

For 2 servings:
250 g (9 oz) boneless, skinless fish fillets
2 Tbsp plain flour
1 tsp ground cumin
1 tsp oreganum
½ tsp garlic salt
½ tsp paprika

about 1 Tbsp oil
½ cup (125 ml/4 fl oz) white wine
1 Tbsp tomato paste
2 Tbsp cream

Cut the fillets diagonally into 4–6 even-sized pieces. Mix the next 5 ingredients together and coat the fish with this mixture. Preheat a little oil in a frypan and fry the fish until it is barely cooked. Remove from the pan, pour off any extra oil, then add the wine and tomato paste and boil down to half the original volume. Stir in the cream, return the fish to the pan, and turn it to coat with sauce.

Serve straight away, with fresh asparagus and new potatoes, or with bread rolls or garlic bread (p. 344) and a green salad.

'Instant' Herbed Fish

This recipe is as delicious as it is quick. You don't need to buy expensive fish, as long as the fillets are fresh. Insist that your family be ready and waiting before you start cooking! The total cooking time should be less than 2 minutes.

For 4 servings:
500–600 g (1 lb 2 oz–1 lb 5 oz) fish fillets
50 g (2 oz) butter
2–3 cloves garlic, finely sliced
¼–½ cup chopped parsley (and other
fresh herbs, if available)
½ tsp salt
pepper

Cut the fish into thin (5 mm/¼ in) strips across the fillets. Prepare the garlic and herbs before starting to cook.

Warm a large frypan, add the butter and garlic, and heat until the butter is bubbling but not brown. Add the slivers of fish and the herbs, and turn the mixture with a fish slice until the fish is milky white and the flakes start to break. Do not overcook. The fish should cook for 20–30 seconds.

Remove from the heat, stir in salt and pepper, then taste and add extra salt if necessary. Serve immediately on rice or piled into warm bread rolls.

Herbed Fish Fillets

The first time I tasted this I thought it was the best fish I had ever eaten! It is very quick to prepare, easy and 'unmessy'. The total cooking time is 3–4 minutes.

Alter the herb quantities if you like, but don't reduce them too much, or leave out the parsley, sage and garlic.

For 4 servings:
500–600 g (1 lb 2 oz–1 lb 5 oz) fish fillets
25–50 g (1–2 oz) butter
2 Tbsp chopped parsley
4 fresh sage leaves
sprig each marjoram and thyme
1–2 cloves garlic
1/2 tsp salt
pepper
1/2 cup (125 ml/4 fl oz) white wine
1 tsp plain flour

Cut each fillet in two, removing the strip of bones near the midline. If the fillets are large, cut the smaller part in two pieces and the larger in three. Cut at an angle, with the knife blade slanted rather than upright, so each piece tapers like a smaller fillet. Trim sole fillets and cut each one into several smaller 'fillets' if desired.

Put about a teaspoonful of the butter aside. Chop the herbs very finely. Crush the garlic with the salt, then melt most of the butter in a large frypan with the herbs and garlic. Do not let the butter brown at any stage during the cooking. Lay the pieces of fish in the pan, turning them after about a minute. Add pepper to taste and pour in the wine (replace it with 2 Tbsp lemon juice in water if you prefer).

Cover and cook for 1–2 minutes, until the fish is milky white, then lift it onto warmed plates or a serving dish. Mix the reserved butter with the flour and add to the sauce. Stir until smooth, then spoon the sauce over the fish. Serve immediately, with hot, crusty bread rolls and a tomato side salad or with creamy mashed potatoes and green beans.

Fish Fillets with Curry Cream Glaze

Although this mixture seems rich and creamy, it actually contains little fat.

For 2 servings:
1 clove garlic
1 tsp butter
1/2 tsp curry powder
1/2 cup (125 ml/4 fl oz) white wine
2 boneless, skinless fish fillets
2 Tbsp lite sour cream
1 tsp chopped fresh dill or 1/2 tsp dried dill leaf
1 tsp cornflour

Chop the garlic very finely and cook it gently in the butter, in a pan big enough to hold the fish in one layer, for about a minute. Stir in the curry powder, then the wine, and bring to the boil. Cut the fish into pieces, and add with the sour cream and the dill.

Turn the fish to coat it with cooking liquid, cover the pan and simmer gently for about 5 minutes, or until the thickest part of the fish is opaque. Turn after about 2 minutes.

Mix the cornflour with a little more wine, and pour about half of it into the fish, shaking the pan gently. Add the rest if necessary. The sauce should coat the fish. Taste the sauce, and adjust seasonings.

Serve with rice, green beans, and a salad.

Spicy Cajun Fish

A Cajun-style coating gives grilled fish an interesting colour and flavour.

For 4 servings:
1 Tbsp paprika
1/4 tsp chilli powder
2 tsp ground cumin
1 tsp garlic salt
1 tsp oreganum
1 tsp thyme
1/2 tsp turmeric
1 Tbsp plain flour
600 g (1 lb 5 oz) boneless, skinless fish fillets
olive or other oil

Measure all the seasonings and the flour into a dry jar with an airtight top. Shake well to mix. Cut each fillet lengthways into strips about 5 cm (2 in) wide, then cut each of these pieces diagonally into pieces 10–12 cm (4–5 in) long.

Preheat the grill and grill tray. Brush the fish lightly with oil, then coat evenly with the seasoning mixture. Use most of the seasoning mix to coat this amount of fish. Place the fish pieces close together on a piece of lightly oiled foil, twist up the corners, transfer to the preheated grill tray, and cook close to the grill until the thickest flesh is milky when tested with a fork, probably 3–5 minutes. It should not be necessary to turn the fillets if they are put on a hot grill tray.

Serve with wedges of fresh lime or lemon, hot vegetables or salad and garlic bread (p. 344).

Creamy Paprika Fish

This recipe has been one of my favourites for more than twenty years.

For 4 servings:
2 medium onions, finely chopped
25 g (1 oz) butter
2 tsp paprika
2 Tbsp plain flour
1/2 tsp salt
1/2 cup (125 ml/4 fl oz) milk
1/2 cup (125 ml/4 fl oz) cream, sour cream or evaporated milk
750 g (1 lb 10 oz) firm-fleshed, boneless, skinless fish fillets
2 Tbsp chopped parsley

Cook the onion gently in the butter in a covered pan until tender.

Stir in the paprika, cook for 30 seconds longer then add the flour and salt. Add the milk and bring to the boil, stirring constantly, then add the cream, sour cream or evaporated milk and bring to the boil again, still stirring.

Cut the fish into 2 cm (3/4 in) squares about 1 cm (1/2 in) thick. Gently stir the fish and parsley into the sauce, cover again, and cook very gently for 3–5 minutes, until the fish is cooked. Taste and adjust seasonings if necessary.

Serve spooned over pasta, or pile on toasted, buttered split rolls and accompany with a salad.

Coconut Fish Curry

Coconut cream gives a wonderful richness to fish curries. For preference make this recipe using fish with a medium to firm texture so the pieces do not fall apart.

Do not use fish with a particularly delicate flavour since it will be overwhelmed by the sauce.

For 4 servings:
2 onions, chopped
2 cloves garlic, chopped
25 g (1 oz) butter
2 tsp curry powder
1 can (about 420 g/15 oz) coconut cream
600–700 g (1 lb 5 oz–1 lb 9 oz) fish fillets
1/4–1/2 tsp salt

Melt the butter in a large frypan and cook the onion and garlic over low heat, covered, until tender but not browned. Stir in the curry powder, cook 1 minute longer over moderate heat, then add the coconut cream, using 1–2 cups depending on the can size. Cook uncovered for 5–10 minutes, until the sauce thickens.

Cut the fish into pieces about 10 cm (4 in) long and up to 4 cm (2 in) wide. Turn the pieces in the sauce and pack into the pan, preferably in one layer. Cover and simmer until the centre of the fish is opaque and it will flake fairly easily, 5–10 minutes. Add salt to taste.

Serve the curried fish on rice or noodles, with a crisp salad alongside.

Note: If your curry sauce is not thick enough, lift out the cooked fish and boil the sauce vigorously until it thickens, then return the fish to it, or thicken it with cornflour paste. Don't keep boiling the fish in the sauce, since this will just overcook the fish and produce more liquid to thin the sauce further.

Oven-Baked Fish and Chips

If you don't like deep-frying fish and chips, try 'oven frying' both the fish and the chips.

For 4 servings:

4 large potatoes
2–3 Tbsp oil
4 boneless, skinless fish fillets (150 g/5 oz each)
½ cup self-raising flour
½ tsp salt
½ tsp sugar
½ tsp ground cumin (optional)
½ tsp oreganum (optional)
½ tsp paprika (optional)
2–3 Tbsp oil
1 or 2 eggs, beaten

Turn the oven to 230°C (450°F) and position two shelves, one a little below the middle, the other above the first.

Scrub the potatoes and cut them lengthways into eighths. Put the pieces in a bowl of cold water. When ready to cook, drain the potatoes and dry them with paper towels. Dry the bowl and put in the first measure of oil. Using your fingers, turn the potato pieces to coat with oil.

Bake the potatoes in a large, shallow metal baking dish for about 30 minutes, turning once or twice.

While the chips cook, for spicy fish, combine the flour and seasonings in a shallow bowl. For less flavoured fish, use only the flour, salt and sugar. Rub the surface of another shallow metal dish which will hold the fish in one layer, with a quarter of the second measure of oil.

When the chips are nearly cooked (about 12 minutes before you want to eat), heat the oiled baking dish in the oven for about 1 minute. While it heats, pat the fillets dry and coat them first with the seasoned flour, then the beaten egg, then again with the flour. Working fast, put the fillets in the preheated, oiled dish and drizzle the remaining oil over them. Cook on the shelf above the chips for about 8 minutes altogether, turning after 5 minutes.

Serve with lemon wedges and a salad.

Fried Battered Fish Fingers

If you cut boneless fillets into fingers, the fish will go further, there is plenty of crisp coating and the pieces cook quickly. Everybody should be happy!

For 4 servings:

600 g (1 lb 5 oz) fish fillets
1 egg
½ cup (125 ml/4 fl oz) beer or lager
1 Tbsp oil
¼ tsp salt
½ tsp curry powder (optional)
½ cup plain flour
oil for frying

Fried Battered Fish Fingers with Chips (p. 195)

Remove skin and bones from the fillets if necessary, and cut them lengthways into strips 2 cm (1 in) wide. Cut the strips into shorter lengths, each about 5 cm (2 in), cutting diagonally rather than straight across so that each little fish finger tapers at the ends and looks rather like a small fish. Pat dry on a paper towel.

To make the batter, put the egg, beer, oil, salt and curry powder, if used, into a fairly large, shallow bowl, and mix with a fork. Sprinkle the flour over, then stir again with the fork until there are no dry lumps of flour.

If you are cooking chips, don't start to cook the fish until the chips are ready. Heat clean oil at least 5 mm (¼ in) deep, preferably a little deeper. When it is hot, but not hot enough to smoke, toss the pieces of fish that are to be cooked together in flour, shake off the excess, then dip each in the batter. The batter should coat the fish thinly. If the coating of batter is too thick, thin the batter with a little more beer. If it is thinner than you like, stir in a little more flour.

Drop each batter-coated piece of fish into the hot oil, taking care that no water drops in, and making sure nothing splashes. Cook for 1–2 minutes, until the batter is evenly golden brown. Put the cooked fish on paper towels in a warm place until all the pieces are cooked. Serve as quickly as possible.

Serve with whatever your family considers essential, e.g. tomato sauce, lemon wedges, vinegar and pepper. Do not use more salt than necessary.

Poached Salmon with Zucchini Ribbons

When poaching fish:

- always choose very fresh fish
- choose a well-flavoured variety
- poach chunks rather than thin fillets
- always cook gently
- never overcook
- serve with small amounts of concentrated sauce
- add colour with fresh herbs, etc.

Poached salmon is a favourite of mine, because I love its texture, flavour, and its pretty colour. It is also fast, easy and deliciously light and fresh.

For 4 servings:
1/4 cup (60 ml/2 fl oz) lemon juice
1/4 cup (60 ml/2 fl oz) white wine
1/4 cup (60 ml/2 fl oz) water or fish stock
1 bayleaf
6 green peppercorns
2 shallots or 1 clove garlic, chopped
1 large sprig fresh dill
500–600 g (1 lb 2 oz–1 lb 5 oz) fresh salmon fillet

Put the first 7 ingredients in a medium-sized frypan and boil until the liquid has reduced by half. Strain.

Cut the boneless salmon fillet diagonally or crosswise into 4 slices, place in the pan, cover, and cook gently in the reduced liquid for 2–3 minutes, turning once, until the fish feels firm rather than raw; when a sharp, pointed knife is pushed into the thickest part you should not see the darker colour of uncooked flesh. If the pan does not have a lid, cover it with 2 layers of aluminium foil, pressed down close to the fish.

Lift the cooked fish carefully onto a serving plate and keep it warm. Boil the liquid in which the fish was cooked down to 1/4 cup if necessary, then taste and season. This liquid may be spooned over the salmon as is, or you can add finely chopped fresh herbs such as dill; swirl it round in the pan with 1–2 tsp butter, or stir about 1–2 Tbsp of cream into it and boil down to 1/4 cup again.

Spoon the sauce over the salmon and serve with Zucchini Ribbons (p. 202) and baby new potatoes or warmed bread rolls.

Fish Fillets in Lemon and Caper Sauce

When fish fillets are turned in a caper sauce thickened with mustard, they have a lovely, tangy flavour. Use a medium-textured fish.

For 2 servings:
300–350 g (10–12 oz) boneless, skinless fish fillets
1/4 cup plain flour
1 Tbsp butter
1 Tbsp olive or other oil

Poached Salmon with Zucchini Ribbons (p. 202)

2 cloves garlic, chopped
¼ cup (60 ml/2 fl oz) white wine
1 Tbsp lemon juice
1 Tbsp each capers and caper liquid
pinch of salt
freshly ground black pepper
2 tsp Dijon mustard
1 Tbsp finely chopped parsley

If necessary cut large fillets diagonally into even pieces, so you end up with 2–3 pieces of almost equal size from each fillet. Lightly coat with flour, patting it onto the surface so the fish is evenly covered.

Melt the butter and oil in a large frypan and cook the garlic for about a minute. Remove the garlic and put half the fish pieces into the hot, garlicky oil. Cook the fish until lightly browned, about 1 minute each side. Lift out and keep warm. Repeat with the remaining fish, then make the sauce.

To the drippings in the pan add the wine, lemon juice, capers and liquid, salt, pepper and mustard, and boil until reduced slightly. Return the cooked fish to the pan, turn in the sauce, and sprinkle with parsley.

Nice served with sautéed potatoes, green beans and tomatoes.

Smoked Fish in White Sauce

This simple mixture is often very popular with children, especially if it is served with pasta.

For 3–4 servings:
25 g (1 oz) butter
3 Tbsp plain flour
1 can (300–400 g/10–14 oz) smoked fish fillets
about 1½ cups (375 ml/12 fl oz) milk
¼–½ cup chopped parsley

Melt the butter in a medium-sized pot and stir in the flour. Strain the canned fish and make the liquid up to 2 cups with the milk. Add ½ cup of this liquid to the flour and butter, bring to the boil, and stir until smooth. Add the remaining liquid in 2 separate additions, stirring and bringing the sauce to the boil each time.

Break up the fish with a fork and stir it into the sauce. Heat without boiling. Just before serving add the chopped parsley. Serve on rice, pasta or toast.

Reddened Fish Fingers

This is a good way to cook soft-textured fish which might otherwise break up when fried.

For 4 servings:
600 g (1 lb 5 oz) boneless, skinless fish fillets
1 egg
2 tsp paprika
2 tsp oreganum

1 tsp salt
½ tsp sugar
¼–½ tsp chilli powder
3 Tbsp plain flour
about ¼ cup (60 ml/2 fl oz) oil

Cut the fish fillets lengthways into long, thin pieces. With the knife at a 45° angle to the board, cut each strip diagonally into diamond-shaped pieces. Aim to finish up with about 24 pieces.

Beat the egg with a fork to combine the white and yolk, then coat the fish in it evenly. Mix the seasonings and flour together. (Adjust the amount of chilli powder to suit – the larger amount will be too hot for most children.)

Heat the oil in a frypan until it is hot but not smoking, then, working quickly, lift the fish from the egg, a piece at a time, turn it in the seasoning and place it in the pan. About half the fish will fill the pan. The first piece of fish should be ready to turn soon after the last piece is put in. As soon as the fish is cooked, remove it from the pan, drain on kitchen paper, and keep warm while you cook the remaining fish. Serve immediately, sprinkled with lemon juice.

Soy-Seared Salmon

In spring, I often cook and serve freshly grown and harvested foods plainly with no sauces, so that the food flavours 'shine'.

For 4 servings:
4 slices fresh salmon (150 g/5 oz each)
1 Tbsp light soy sauce
1 Tbsp lemon juice
½ tsp turmeric
2 tsp olive oil

If possible, buy salmon slices that have been cut crosswise from a large fillet. The skin may be left on. If the slices weigh less than specified, cook them for a shorter time. Mix the other ingredients in a dish just large enough to hold the fish, then place the fish in the mixture for about 10 minutes, turning it several times.

Heat a large, non-stick frypan until very hot. Film the surface with a little oil, then add the salmon pieces, skin-side down, without crowding them. Keeping the heat high, cook the salmon for 4–6 minutes in total, depending on its thickness; turn the fish when each surface is browned. Add the remaining marinade to the pan in the last minute. (When cooked, the centre of each piece of fish should still be the original pink colour, and the fish should not break.)

Orange Fish Steaks

These steaks are popular with everyone who eats them! For a stronger orange flavour add more orange rind, or for a milder one, less.

For 1 serving:
1 small or ½ a large fish steak (about 200 g/7 oz)
plain flour for coating
2 tsp oil
2 Tbsp orange juice
1 tsp light soy sauce
½ tsp finely grated orange rind
1 spring onion, chopped

Lightly coat the steak with flour. Heat the oil and brown the steak on each side in the hot pan. Add the remaining ingredients, turn the steaks in the liquid as it thickens, then cover the pan and cook very gently until the steak is cooked in the centre. Pour the remaining glaze over the steak when serving.

Grilled Salmon Steaks with Hollandaise Sauce

Grilled salmon steaks are a good choice for a special dinner.

For 4 servings:
4 salmon steaks or fillets (100–150g/ 3½–5 oz each)
about 25 g (1 oz) butter
2 tsp Kikkoman soy sauce
2 tsp lemon or lime juice
about ¼ tsp tabasco sauce
Hollandaise Sauce (p. 345)

Place the steaks or fillets in one layer on a piece of unpunctured foil which has had its edges folded over, turned up and twisted at the corners.

Melt the butter and stir in the soy sauce, lemon or lime juice and tabasco. Brush the fish with this, covering all surfaces. Cover and refrigerate the fish if you are not going to cook it straight away, then bring it to room temperature before you cook it. Brush with remaining marinade if desired. Don't start cooking the fish until everything else is ready.

Make the Hollandaise Sauce and leave it to stand in a bowl of warm (not hot) water while you cook the fish.

Preheat the grill and a solid grill tray. (If your grill has racks only, heat the removable base of a cake tin or something similar.) Slide the foil container holding the fish onto the preheated surface. Unless the fish is very thick, this should ensure the bottom part of the fish cooks and you will not need to turn it over.

Grill until the salmon loses its translucency, feels firm rather than spongy when you press it, and the flesh flakes when a small fork or sharp knife is twisted in the thickest part. This may happen in about a minute with a fairly thin steak or fillet under a really hot grill.

Carefully lift the cooked fish onto warmed plates. Add any remaining cooking juices to the Hollandaise Sauce and spoon it over the salmon.

Baked Whole Fish

This is an easy and delicious way to cook salt- or freshwater fish. Try whole sea fish such as kahawai, snapper, tarakihi, gurnard, etc. Gut the fish but scale it only if you want to eat the skin, since you can easily lift off the skin and scales after the fish is cooked.

You will need to alter cooking times to suit the size of your fish. The important thing about cooking fish is not to overcook it.

For 4–6 servings:

1 cleaned fish, skin on, bone in (1 kg/
  2 lb 3 oz after cleaning)
1 tsp celery salt
1 tsp garlic salt
1 tsp onion salt
1 tsp hickory smoke salt
1 tsp lemon pepper
1 tsp ground cumin
1 tsp oreganum
2 lemons
sprigs of parsley and dill, if available
about 1 Tbsp butter

Turn the oven to 180°C (350°F). For even cooking, cut several slashes down to the bone on each side of the fish where the flesh is thickest. Sprinkle the dry seasonings, one after the other, both inside the cavity and over the skin. Squeeze one of the lemons and pour the juice over the inside and outside of the fish. Slice the other lemon and place slices evenly along the cavity of the fish, then fill the cavity with sprigs of parsley and dill, if you have them. Dot the butter around, some inside and some outside the fish.

Wrap carefully in 2 layers of foil, sealing the edges carefully so you can turn the parcel over halfway through cooking. Place in a large, shallow baking dish, just in case any of the juices leak during cooking.

Bake for 20–40 minutes for a fish weighing 1–2 kg (2 lb 3 oz–4 lb 7 oz) after cleaning, and 5 cm (2 in) thick from side to side. The exact time will vary with the size and shape of the fish. At intervals, test the thickest flesh to see if it has turned milky and will flake. Only a little liquid should form around the fish if it is cooked for the right period of time.

Once cooked, allow the fish to cool for about 10–15 minutes to make handling easier. Pour off, strain and save any juice from around the fish. Lift away the head, tail and the large and small fins, peel away the skin, then lift the flesh from the bones in chunks. Put the flesh onto clean foil or in an oven bag and pour over any juice, after squeezing the lemon slices. Taste critically. If you feel it is bland, sprinkle the flesh with a little more of any or all of the seasonings used in the cooking. Turn the pieces, without breaking them up further.

Serve the fish at room temperature with Kiwifruit Salsa (p. 346), either served alongside or tossed through the pieces of fish, OR serve with mayonnaise flavoured with chives, parsley and fresh dill and thinned with small amounts of leftover cooking liquid.

Soused Trout

Sousing is an excellent method of cooking fish which is to be eaten cold. As well as giving extra flavour and interest to fish with a very mild or rather nondescript flavour of its own, it tends to soften small bones, particularly if strong vinegar is used and if the fish is left to stand in it.

Trout, salmon, herring, mackerel and eel are suitable for sousing.

2 trout
1–2 onions, sliced
1/2 bayleaf
2 cloves
6 peppercorns
1 tsp salt
about 1 cup (250 ml/8 fl oz) wine vinegar
about 1 cup (250 ml/8 fl oz) water

Turn the oven to 150°C (300°F). Place the cleaned fish in a casserole dish. They can be left whole or cut into pieces, but should be arranged so that they almost fill the dish. Add the onion, herbs, spices and seasonings, and cover the fish with vinegar and water, using more or less than the 2 cups as necessary.

Cover and bake for 1 hour, then allow the fish to cool in the cooking liquid.

Serve whole fish on a flat plate garnished with cucumber slices, or flake it and serve in a salad, e.g. coat flaked soused trout and diced cucumber with mayonnaise and serve in lettuce cups.

Variations: Replace the bayleaf and cloves with several sprigs of dill or other fresh herbs. Use less vinegar if preferred.

Microwaved Herbed Fish   M

The microwave oven has made life easier for cooks with a fishing enthusiast in the family.

It is easy to cook a small fish, exactly as it came from the water an hour or so earlier, then to lift off and discard the skin and scales, and remove the flesh carefully, leaving the skeleton and gut intact. The cooked fish may be seasoned and eaten as is, or stirred into batter and fried.

Larger whole fish also microwave well. Gut the fish, scaling it only if you want to eat the skin. Make several slashes down to the bone on each side, where the flesh is thickest, for more even cooking. Fill the central body cavity with fresh herbs, slices of lemon, chopped onion or shallot and crushed garlic.

Turn the fish in plain or garlic-flavoured melted butter, then wrap in greaseproof paper or parchment, or cover both the fish and plate with cling film. Vent this in several places, and microwave on High (100%) power, allowing 45–50 seconds per 100 g (3½ oz) fish.

If the whole fish is too big to fit in the microwave, remove its head and tail before weighing and preparing it. (You can always cook these briefly, then arrange them at each end of the cooked fish before serving, with large parsley garnishes to mask your surgery!)

The time given here is a guide only. Before the estimated time has been reached, test the thickest flesh to see if it has turned milky, and will flake.

Skin and fillet the cooked fish before serving it with its buttery cooking juices.

Sautéed Whitebait

A treat for anyone lucky enough to have at least half a cup of whitebait per person.

For 1 serving:
1 Tbsp butter
1–2 cloves garlic, chopped
1/2 cup whitebait
plain flour
2–3 Tbsp chopped parsley
freshly ground black pepper
lemon juice

Heat a fairly heavy frypan, and cook the butter and garlic over low heat for 3–4 minutes. Spread the whitebait on a clean, dry teatowel. Sprinkle the dry whitebait with flour, lifting the sides of the teatowel to coat the fish evenly. Raise the heat of the garlic butter and add the whitebait (but no loose flour) when the butter turns straw-coloured. Toss with a fish slice until the fish turns milky white – this takes just a few seconds.

Sprinkle with the parsley, pepper and lemon juice. Eat immediately.

Whitebait Omelet for One

This recipe makes a small amount of whitebait go further.

Proceed as for Sautéed Whitebait, using a small frypan and allowing at least 1/4 cup of whitebait. Beat an egg with a pinch of salt and a tablespoon of water, and pour this over the whitebait as soon as they turn milky. Shake the pan to spread both the whitebait and the egg, and lift the edges to let uncooked egg run underneath. As soon as the egg will no longer run when the pan is tilted, fold the omelet in half and serve immediately.

Sautéed Whitebait

Fish and Macaroni Casserole

It is not necessary to select skinless, boneless fillets, as the skin and bones can easily be removed after cooking.

For 6 servings:
500 g (1 lb 2 oz) fish fillets
1½ cups (375 ml/12 fl oz) liquid (see below)
2–3 hard-boiled eggs
½ cup raw macaroni
1 Tbsp chopped spring onion
3 Tbsp butter
3 Tbsp plain flour
¼ cup finely grated cheese
½ tsp salt
parsley
paprika

Turn the oven to 180°C (350°F). Wrap the fish in buttered foil and place it in a frypan with enough water to stop it burning. Cover the pan and simmer for 3–8 minutes, or until the fish is milky white all through and will flake readily. Drain and save the liquid, making it up to 1½ cups with milk. Lift off and discard any skin, then flake the fish with 2 forks, removing any bones. Keep the pieces chunky.

Halve the hard-boiled eggs and separate the whites from the yolks. Cook the macaroni and mix it with the fish and the chopped egg whites. Add the chopped spring onion.

To make the sauce, melt the butter, add the flour and stir in the mixture of milk and fish liquor; add half a cup of liquid at a time, stirring well and boiling after each addition. Add the cheese and salt, stir well, and remove from the heat immediately.

Place half the fish, egg and macaroni mixture in a casserole dish and cover with half the sauce, then repeat with the rest of the ingredients. Cover and heat through in the oven for 20–30 minutes. Sprinkle with paprika and parsley before serving.

Salmon, Egg and Celery Savoury

This recipe is one of the most useful I have. I make it time and time again. Serve the mixture on rice or pasta.

For 4 servings:
3 Tbsp butter
¼ cup chopped onion
1 cup sliced celery
2 Tbsp plain flour
1 cup (250 ml/8 fl oz) salmon juice and milk
3–4 hard-boiled eggs
1 can (100 g/3½ oz) salmon
1 Tbsp chopped parsley

Melt the butter in a pot with a well-fitting lid and add the onion and celery. Cover and cook over medium heat for 5–10 minutes, until the vegetables are tender.

Cook for a few minutes longer without the lid, then stir in the flour. Gradually add the liquid (the juice from the salmon made up to 1 cup with milk), stirring the sauce and bringing it to the boil after each addition.

A few minutes before serving add the hard-boiled eggs and salmon, broken into medium-sized pieces. Add the chopped parsley, adjust the seasonings and reheat. Serve immediately on rice or spaghetti, or fold into shell-shaped pasta.

Old-Fashioned Fish Pie

As this fish pie contains potatoes and leeks, you need serve nothing else with it to have a satisfying, well-balanced main course.

For 4 servings:
2 leeks (about 600 g/1 lb 5 oz)
2 tsp butter
¼ cup (60 ml/2 fl oz) water
*1 can (310 g/11 oz) smoked fish fillets**
2 hard-boiled eggs
milk
2 Tbsp butter
½ tsp curry powder
2 Tbsp plain flour
750 g (1 lb 10 oz) potatoes, cooked and mashed
2 Tbsp grated Parmesan cheese

* Use 2 cans if you prefer more fish.

Turn the oven to about 175°C (325°F). Wash the leeks and cut them into 1 cm (½ in) slices. Cook with the butter and water, covered, for about 5 minutes, then drain, reserving the liquid.

Drain the fish, reserving the liquid, break it into chunks and place in a lightly buttered casserole dish, about 18 x 23 cm (7 x 9 in). Spread the leeks over the fish, and add the chopped hard-boiled eggs.

Put the reserved fish and leek liquids into a measuring cup and make up to 1½ cups (375 ml/12 fl oz) with milk. Melt the second measure of butter with the curry powder, add the flour and heat until it bubbles. Stir the liquid in gradually, bringing it to the boil between each addition, and simmer for 5 minutes. Pour over the fish, leeks and eggs.

Mash the potato, beat it with a little butter and milk and season carefully. Spoon it over the fish and sauce mixture, and sprinkle the top with the Parmesan cheese. Bake uncovered until the potato topping is lightly browned and crisp and the bottom is bubbling; about 20 minutes. Serve alone or with a salad.

Variation: Use canned salmon in place of smoked fish.

Stewart Island Seafood Pie

Although not strictly a fish pie, this is a delicious mixture, well worth making occasionally.

For 4–5 servings:
500 g (1 lb 2 oz) boned, skinned, blue cod fillets
12 oysters
1½ cups fresh breadcrumbs
grated nutmeg (optional)
3–4 Tbsp butter
4 Tbsp plain flour
1 cup (250 ml/8 fl oz) milk
½ cup oyster liquor (125 ml/4 fl oz) and dry sherry
pepper, salt and seasoned salt
1 Tbsp butter
½ cup grated cheese
paprika

Turn the oven to 190°C (375°F). Cut the fish into 5 cm (2 in) cubes. Drain the oysters, reserving the liquor. Sprinkle half a cup of the breadcrumbs in a buttered, shallow casserole, and arrange the raw fish and oysters on top. Sprinkle over a small amount of grated nutmeg if desired.

Melt the first measure of butter, add the flour, then half the milk. Bring to the boil, stirring constantly, then add the remaining milk. After the sauce has boiled again add the oyster liquor made up to half a cup with dry sherry, or a mixture of sherry and milk. Boil again, then adjust the seasonings, adding pepper, salt or seasoned salt to taste. Pour the sauce evenly over the fish. Rinse the pot and melt the second measure of butter. Toss the remaining cup of breadcrumbs in the melted butter, then add the grated cheese. Sprinkle this over the sauce, and sprinkle with paprika if desired.

Bake, uncovered, for 20–30 minutes, until the top is golden brown and the sauce bubbly.

Variation: Replace the cod and oysters with other fish, chopped mussels, prawns, etc.

Curried Fish Pie

This is a good family meal which may be made ahead and reheated when required. You can use salt- or freshwater fish.

For 4–6 servings:
50 g (2 oz) butter
1–2 tsp curry powder
1 tsp salt (if using fresh fish)
¼ cup plain flour
2 cups (500 ml/16 fl oz) milk and fish cooking liquid
2 cups cooked rice or macaroni
2 cups cooked (fresh or canned), flaked fish
2 Tbsp chopped parsley or chives
2 hard-boiled eggs, sliced
2–4 sliced tomatoes

Turn the oven to 180°C (350°F). To make the sauce, melt the butter, add the curry powder, salt if you are using fresh fish, mix well, then stir in the flour. Add the liquid in thirds, stirring well and bringing to the boil between each addition.

Mix together the rice or macaroni, fish and herbs, and place half this mixture in a greased casserole dish. Cover with 1 cup of the curry sauce, and spread the sliced egg over this. Add the remaining rice mixture, then the rest of the curry sauce.

Cover and heat through in the oven for 20–30 minutes. Arrange the tomato slices around the edge of the dish (or on top) and cook uncovered until they heat through.

Kedgeree

Kedgeree is a tasty mixture of smoked fish, curry and rice. For maximum flavour, eat it soon after the fish is mixed with the rice.

For 4–5 servings:
1 Tbsp butter
1 large clove garlic, sliced
1/4 cup (60 ml/2 fl oz) white wine
freshly ground black pepper
600–700 g (1 lb 5 oz–1 lb 9 oz) smoked fish fillets
3 hard-boiled eggs
2 Tbsp butter
2 onions, finely chopped
1 tsp curry powder
1/2 tsp turmeric
1 cup basmati rice
2 1/4 cups (560 ml/18 fl oz) liquid (reserved fish stock made up to this quantity with water)
1/2 tsp salt
freshly ground black pepper
1 Tbsp lemon juice
fresh dill and parsley, chopped
3 spring onions, chopped

Heat the first measure of butter in a frypan big enough to hold the fish. Add the sliced garlic and cook gently for a few minutes, then add the wine, pepper and fish fillets. Cover the pan and poach the fillets gently for 5–7 minutes, or until the fish will flake easily. Turn the fish once, after 4–5 minutes.

Drain off the liquid, sieve it to remove any bits and pieces, and put it aside. Flake the fish, removing and discarding the skin and bones. Put the flaked fish aside.

Hard-boil the eggs while the fish cooks.

Cook the chopped onions in a pot with the second measure of butter, until soft but not browned. Stir in the curry powder and turmeric. Add the uncooked rice, the reserved fish stock made up to 2 1/4 cups with water and, unless the fish stock is very salty, the salt and pepper.

Cover and cook gently over low heat for 10–15 minutes, until the rice is tender and the liquid absorbed. Remove from the heat.

Just before serving, fold into the hot rice the warm flaked fish, chopped hard-boiled eggs, pepper, lemon juice and herbs. Reheat in a microwave or over very low heat if necessary. Sprinkle with the chopped spring onions and garnish with wedges of lemon.

Note: The seasoning is very important in a recipe like this. Unless you use enough salt, the mixture will taste bland and uninteresting. Since the smoked fish is sometimes quite salty, however, you have to watch and taste as you go along.

Variation: Replace the smoked fish with canned smoked fillets. Use the liquid from the can to replace the fish cooking liquid when cooking the rice.

Tuna and Tomato Casserole

Keep a few cans of fish in your store cupboard to make filling, relatively inexpensive family meals.

For 3–4 servings:
100 g (3–4 oz) uncooked pasta (about 1 cup of small shells)
2 cups (500 ml/16 fl oz) water
1/2 tsp salt
1 medium onion, chopped
2 stalks celery or 1 red/green pepper, chopped
1 can (425 g/15 oz) tomatoes
1 can (185 g/6 oz) tuna in water
1 Tbsp lemon juice
2 Tbsp chopped parsley
2–3 Tbsp cream cheese
freshly ground black pepper
about 1 cup grated tasty cheese
paprika

Cook the pasta in boiling, lightly salted water. While it cooks add the onion and celery or pepper, as each is prepared. Cook until the pasta is tender and most of the water absorbed. Drain if necessary, leaving about 1/4 cup of liquid in the pot. Chop the tomatoes and add them to the pasta with the liquid from the can, and the flaked tuna and its liquid. (If using tuna in oil, discard the oil.)

Stir the lemon juice, parsley and cream cheese together until smooth. Mix this and a generous amount of black pepper through the pasta mixture, then taste and adjust seasonings if necessary.

Transfer the mixture to a buttered or sprayed 20 cm (8 in) ovenware dish, sprinkle with grated cheese and add a little paprika for colour. Put aside until required, then bake, uncovered, at 170°C (325°F) for 20–30 minutes, or until the cheese is golden brown and the sauce heated through. Serve with a leafy green salad and crusty rolls.

Tuna and Tomato Casserole

Sesame Mussels

Sesame Mussels

A marinade based on Eastern ingredients gives mussels a very interesting flavour.

For 2 main courses or 4–6 starters:
12–18 fresh mussels
2 Tbsp fish sauce
1–2 Tbsp Thai hot chilli sauce
1 tsp sesame oil
2 Tbsp lemon or lime juice
1 Tbsp strained liquid from the mussels
2 cloves garlic, finely grated
2 tsp freshly grated fresh ginger
1–2 spring onions, very finely chopped
1–2 tsp finely chopped fresh coriander
¼ red pepper, raw or roasted, very thinly sliced

Cook the mussels about 6 at a time in a covered pan containing about a cup of water. Lift them out with tongs as soon as they open, and place them in a shallow bowl. Cook the remaining mussels in the same liquid.

Measure the remaining ingredients, except the red pepper, into a tough, unpunctured plastic bag with a zip-lock top, since the marinade surrounds the mussels better than it does in a bowl. Remove the mussels from their shells, discard the beards, etc., and put them into the marinade. Reserve shells for serving if you like.

Thinly slice some roasted red pepper if you have any, or slice raw pepper very thinly and simmer it for 1–2 minutes, until wilted. Add to the marinade.

Leave the mussels in the marinade for at least 30 minutes, or up to 24 hours, and serve them whole, or cut in 2 or 3 chunks if very large, in the reserved shells, or from a shallow serving dish.

Eat the mussels, with some of the liquid surrounding them, on crusty bread, such as ciabatta, or in a split bread roll.

Note: If you can buy small mussels, use about twice as many.

Mussels in Curried Tomato Sauce

This recipe is best made with small, fresh, green-lipped mussels, often sold live in larger supermarkets.

For 2–3 servings:
½ cup (125 ml/4 fl oz) dry white wine
½ cup (125 ml/4 fl oz) water
1 onion, finely chopped
2 cloves garlic, finely chopped
thyme, dill, fennel or parsley
12 mussels in the shell
1 Tbsp butter
½ tsp curry powder
1 Tbsp plain flour
½ cup (125 ml/4 fl oz) tomato juice
2 Tbsp cream
½ cup peeled, chopped tomato

Plain Marinated Mussels

Refrigerate freshly steamed, drained mussels in this simple marinade.

12–20 raw mussels in their shells
liquid from mussels made up to 1 cup (150 ml/8 fl oz) with water
1 tsp salt
1 tsp sugar
¼ cup (60 ml/2 fl oz) cider or wine vinegar

Heat the mussels in a lidded pan containing a very small amount of water. Lift them out as soon as they open, leaving all the liquid in the pan. Measure the mussel liquid and make up to 1 cup with water. Add the remaining ingredients, bring to the boil, then cool to room temperature.

Remove the cooked mussels from their shells and cover with the liquid. Refrigerate for up to 3 days.

Always cook bought mussels the day you buy them. Refrigerate them as soon as they are cooked and marinated.

Mustardy Pickled Mussels

Whether you pick them from the rocks on a clean beach or get them from the supermarket, mussels taste really good in this mixture. Eat them within a few days of pickling.

¼ cup sugar
1 Tbsp dry mustard powder
1 tsp salt
1 cup vinegar
cooked, shelled mussels

Stir the sugar, mustard powder and salt together in a pot, then add the vinegar. Bring to the boil, stirring all the time. The mustard will thicken the liquid slightly. Allow to cool.

Put well-drained, freshly cooked, shelled mussels in a jar, and pour over the cooled liquid. All the mussels must be covered by the pickling mixture. Make sure the liquid and mussels are well mixed by jiggling the jar gently. Cover and refrigerate. Leave for a few hours before eating, but do not keep longer than 3 days.

Combine the wine, water, onion and garlic in a large frypan. Simmer gently while chopping any or all of the fresh herbs mentioned. Put the mussels in the simmering liquid, cover, cook until the shells open wide, then remove. Take the mussels out of their shells, discarding beards, etc. Strain the cooking liquid into a bowl and discard the vegetables.

Melt the butter in the pan, add the curry powder and cook gently for about a minute, then stir in the flour, tomato juice and strained cooking liquid. Stir until smooth and thick, then add the cream. Bring back to the boil, add the cooked mussels and the chopped tomato and heat through. Do not leave the mixture simmering, or the mussels will shrink and toughen. Taste, adjust seasonings if necessary, and sprinkle with more of any of the fresh herbs used earlier.

Serve with bread rolls, on pasta or with rice, with a leafy green salad on the side.

Mariners' Mussels

Mussels make an interesting and inexpensive fish meal that is rich in iron!

For 4 servings:
2 large onions
2 cloves garlic
1 Tbsp oil
pinch of saffron (optional)
1/2 cup (125 ml/4 fl oz) white wine
1 can (425 g/15 oz) whole tomatoes
1.5 kg (3 lb 5 oz) fresh mussels (about 24)
1/4 cup chopped parsley

Chop the onions and garlic and cook in the oil in a large pan with a lid, until transparent. Add saffron if available, then add the wine and roughly chopped tomatoes and boil for 2 minutes.

Add half the mussels and simmer with the lid on until the shells open about 1 cm (1/2 in). Arrange the opened mussels in 2 individual serving bowls and keep them warm while you cook the remaining mussels the same way.

When cooked place the rest of the mussels in serving bowls, boil the broth briskly for about 2 minutes, then spoon evenly over the mussels. Sprinkle with chopped parsley.

Serve immediately with large amounts of french or garlic bread (p. 344) to dip in the broth.

Barbecued Garlic Mussels

Always popular with lovers of seafood, these make an inexpensive appetiser or meal.

For 4–6 servings:
24–36 fresh, uncooked mussels in the shell

50 g (2 oz) butter
3–4 cloves garlic, finely chopped
2 Tbsp lemon juice
4 drops hot pepper sauce
1/4 cup chopped parsley (or mixed fresh herbs)

Check that all the mussels you use are tightly closed. Scrub them, pulling away any hairy 'beards'.

Put the butter, garlic, lemon juice and hot pepper sauce in a small metal container and heat over the barbecue until the mixture bubbles.

Place the mussels on the rack of a barbecue, turning them every 30 seconds (so both sides heat) until the shells open. Lift one opened mussel at a time off the barbecue, using tongs. Pour off the liquid from the shell, remove and discard the upper part of the shell if desired, and spoon a little of the butter mixture around the partly cooked mussel. Replace on the barbecue to warm through. Watch carefully, removing the mussels from the rack before they shrink and toughen. Serve immediately with lemon wedges and buttered bread.

Oysters or Mussels with Mignonette Sauce

This simple sauce is delicious with cold cooked mussels or fresh Bluff oysters.

1/4 cup (60 ml/2 fl oz) white wine vinegar
1 Tbsp finely chopped spring onion
1/4 cup (60 ml/2 fl oz) white wine
freshly ground black pepper
salt to taste

Combine all the ingredients. Dip a mussel (or oyster) into the sauce and taste. Add salt if necessary.

When serving this sauce with oysters, make a small bowlful for every person and stand it on a larger plate containing oysters, a fork and brown bread. For mussels, make a larger quantity and marinate the mussels in half of it before serving. Put the remainder into small bowls for dipping. Drain the marinated mussels before serving.

Oyster Fritters

When you need to make oysters go further, try this recipe.

For 3–4 servings:
1 dozen oysters
2 eggs
1 cup plain flour
2 tsp baking powder
1 tsp salt
shake of pepper
1/2 tsp freshly grated nutmeg
oyster liquor to mix
lemon wedges

Drain the oysters, reserving the liquid. Slice the oysters and put them aside. Beat the eggs thoroughly in a medium-sized bowl, then fold in the sifted dry ingredients to make a batter of medium thickness. Add the oysters and fold into the batter. Thin with some of the reserved oyster liquor if it seems too thick.

Shallow-fry spoonfuls of batter in hot, clean oil; since the oysters only need heating through, the temperature can be fairly high. Turn the fritters, and cut through the centre of one with a vegetable knife to check whether the batter is cooked. If not, turn down the heat so they do not brown so quickly. Serve as quickly as possible, with lemon wedges.

Paua Steaks

Although paua shells are beautiful, the contents of the shells look almost inedible. Fresh pauas are, however, a delicacy when properly prepared and cooked.

Remove the fish from the shell by running a sharp, rather heavy knife around between the flesh and the shell. After you have removed the first paua from its shell, you will be able to see the area where the muscle was attached, and you will know exactly where to cut the rest. Discard all the softer parts of the fish that lie between the foot and the shell, and scrub the hard muscular foot with a stiff brush, removing grit, and some of the dark covering.

If you feel the oval foot carefully, you will probably feel one particularly hard 'beak' area. Cut this out with a v-shaped cut. If you cannot feel it, don't worry, because you will be able to find it more easily after the fish has been pounded, although after a lot of pounding it may be broken. Wrap the foot in a piece of clean sacking or other clean, heavy, rough material, place it on a flat rock, on concrete, or heavy board, and pound it with a mallet, a hammer, the back of a small axe, or a heavy piece of wood. About fifty bangs are necessary! It is important to bang hard enough to soften the muscle, but not so hard that the flesh disintegrates. After banging, the flesh will feel flexible, and will be bigger and flatter. Do not remove the dark green frilly edge, even though it feels so tough.

Coat each paua steak with flour seasoned with salt and pepper and fry over moderate heat in about a tablespoon of butter, allowing 30–60 seconds per side. Do not overcook. Miraculously, the frilly edge becomes tender during this short cooking, and you will probably find that you can cut the paua steak with the side of a fork, without using a knife at all.

Thai-Style Squid with Vegetables

This spicy, Thai-inspired dish is really very simple. The sauce is also delicious with chicken or even with vegetables alone.

For 2–3 servings:
2 squid tubes (about 180 g/6 oz)
1 Tbsp each sesame oil and light soy
*   sauce*
2 cloves garlic, finely chopped
1 cm (1/2 in) fresh ginger, grated
1 small onion
1 green pepper
2 cups broccoli florets
1 cup button mushrooms
1 Tbsp each Thai fish sauce, oyster sauce
*   and dark soy sauce*
1 tsp sugar
1–2 Tbsp chopped fresh coriander
2 Tbsp oil
1/2–1 tsp red curry paste (optional)
1 dried red chilli, sliced and deseeded
*   (optional)*
chopped coriander or spring onions to
*   garnish*

Halve the squid tubes lengthways, trim, and discard any remaining cartilage. Lay each half flat on a board with the inside facing upwards. With a sharp knife, score the surface into 1 cm (1/2 in) diamond shapes. Cut into rectangles about 2 x 4 cm (3/4 x 11/2 in). Place the scored squid in a bowl and toss with the sesame oil, light soy sauce, garlic and ginger. Set aside.

Halve and slice the onion and green pepper, cut the broccoli into bite-sized pieces and slice the mushrooms.

Measure the fish sauce, oyster and dark soy sauces, sugar and coriander into a small bowl. Heat the oil in a large wok or frypan. Add the onion, optional curry paste and chilli. Stir for about 1 minute, then add the broccoli, green pepper and mushrooms. Cook, stirring occasionally, until the broccoli is barely tender.

Add the squid and cook for 2–3 minutes, stirring frequently, then add the sauce mixture, toss and remove from the heat. It is important not to overcook the squid or it will become chewy and touch.

Serve immediately over fragrant Thai (jasmine) rice. Garnish with chopped coriander or spring onions.

Sweet Chilli Prawns

These prawns taste so good you won't mind the work involved in shelling them!

For 6 servings:
1.5 kg (3 lb 5 oz) green prawns
2 Tbsp honey
2 Tbsp Thai sweet chilli sauce
2 Tbsp lemon or lime juice
2 Tbsp oil
2 cloves garlic, finely chopped

Shell and devein the prawns, leaving the tails intact. Combine the remaining ingredients and put into a plastic bag with the prepared prawns. Refrigerate for at least 1 hour, but preferably longer.

Barbecue the prawns quickly, turning them at least once and brushing them with any leftover marinade while they cook. Serve immediately.

Skewered Satay Prawns

Take great care not to overcook these delicious morsels!

For 6 servings:
1.5 kg (3 lb 5 oz) green prawns
1–2 Tbsp lemon or lime juice
1 Tbsp light soy sauce
1–2 Tbsp sesame oil
1 tsp ground cumin
2 cloves garlic, finely chopped
2 Tbsp chopped fresh coriander

Soak 12 bamboo skewers in cold water. Shell and devein the prawns if necessary, leaving the tails intact.

Combine the remaining ingredients and marinate the prawns for at least 1 hour, but preferably longer. Thread the marinated prawns onto the skewers.

Barbecue quickly, close to the heat, until the prawns are cooked through. Brush with any leftover marinade during cooking. Serve immediately with bought or homemade satay sauce (p. 346).

Crab Patties

This recipe makes eight crab patties. As long as you are serving other food with them, such as salad and bread rolls, eight patties will serve four people. For three people, form the mixture into nine patties.

For 8–9 patties:
1 small pottle (250 g/8 oz) fresh or frozen
*   crabmeat*
2 eggs
2 tsp Worcestershire sauce
1/2 tsp salt
1/4 tsp hot pepper sauce
2 spring onions, finely chopped
2 Tbsp chopped parsley
about 1 cup soft breadcrumbs
1–2 Tbsp butter for frying

Thaw the crabmeat if necessary, check to make sure there are no pieces of shell in it, and put it aside. (For this recipe it does not matter if you have a little more or less than the amount specified. If you are measuring the volume, rather than weighing it, you need about a cup of fairly tightly packed flesh.)

Put the eggs, Worcestershire sauce, salt and hot sauce into a fairly large bowl. Beat with a fork until combined, then add the spring onion and the parsley. Stir in the crabmeat.

If possible use crumbs made from fairly stale white or light brown bread. Stir the crumbs into the mixture slowly and gently, until it is firm enough to drop from a spoon and keep its shape. Do not add more crumbs than you need.

Heat a large, heavy-bottomed frypan. Add the butter, let it melt then bubble, and drop in the crab patties before it browns. Adjust the heat so the first side browns in 2–3 minutes, then turn to brown the other side. Make sure the centres are firm before serving the patties, but do not overcook them. Serve as quickly as possible, with lemon wedges.

Variation: Vary the amounts of the seasonings to suit your taste.

Neptune's Patties

Mashed potatoes, well flavoured and mixed with a self-raising flour mixture, can be sautéed in a little butter or oil to make tasty, filling patties that everybody enjoys.

There is only one important thing to remember. After you mix the potatoes and flour you must cook the patties within ten minutes, since the mixture can soften and turn pasty if it stands too long before cooking.

For 4–6 servings:
1 kg (2 lb 3 oz) potatoes
1 tsp salt
1 Tbsp butter
1 can (310 g/11 oz) smoked fish fillets
3–4 spring onions
1/4 cup grated Parmesan cheese or 1 tsp
*   curry powder*
chilli sauce (optional)
11/2–2 cups self-raising flour
oil for frying

Peel the potatoes, cut into quarters and cook in a small amount of boiling, lightly salted water in a covered pot, until tender enough to mash. Take care not to overcook the potatoes, or to let them get soggy.

Mash the cooked, drained potatoes with the butter and 2 Tbsp of the liquid from the canned fish, using a potato masher first, then beating them with a fork to get them light and fluffy. (You should get about 4 cups of mashed potato.)

Discard the remaining liquid from the fish, flake the fish and mix it with the potato.

Add finely chopped spring onions, Parmesan cheese or curry powder, and a little chilli sauce if you like.

Add the flour just before you are ready to cook the patties, using as much as you need to make a mixture a little firmer than scone dough. Form the dough into a roll and cut into 8–12 slices, coating them with a little extra flour. Fry in a large, non-stick frypan, in 1–2 Tbsp of oil, until golden brown on both sides.

Serve soon after cooking, with sautéed mushrooms, grilled tomatoes, or tomato sauce or relish. Coleslaw is good with these patties, too.

Spicy Fish Cakes

These little fish patties are quickly mixed and cooked, and have a deliciously Oriental flavour.

For 4 main or 6 starter servings:
500 g (1 lb 2 oz) fresh fish fillets, skinned and boned
1 small onion, chopped
1 egg
2 tsp salt
1–2 tsp green curry paste
1 tsp sesame oil
2 Tbsp chopped fresh coriander
3 slices day-old bread
1 cup water
1 Tbsp lemon juice

Cut the fillets into 1–2 cm (1/2–3/4 in) cubes. Put into a food processor bowl and process with the onion, egg, salt, curry paste, sesame oil and coriander until finely minced. (Vary the amount of curry paste depending on the strength of flavour and hotness you prefer.)

Break the bread into small pieces, removing the crusts if you want a light-coloured mixture. Arrange evenly over the minced fish mixture.

Dribble three-quarters of the water and the lemon juice over the bread. Process until smooth, adding extra water if needed. Shape into 16 patties with wet hands.

Heat a non-stick pan with enough oil to cover the surface. When hot, add the patties and cook over high heat for 2–3 minutes per side, until lightly browned.

Serve hot or warm with lemon or lime wedges. Add rice and Oriental-style salads or vegetables for a more substantial meal.

Spicy Fish Cakes

Fishburgers

Fish Patty Burgers

A hot patty served in a hamburger bun is a convenient and easy meal, from the point of view of the cook as well as the recipient – who merely has to pick it up in his or her hands and eat it.

Fish makes wonderful patties, and these are especially good sandwiched between split buns which have been lightly toasted while the fish cooks. These burgers are made from raw fish.

For 6 burgers:
3 slices day-old bread
several sprigs parsley
1 small onion, chopped
500 g (1 lb 2 oz) boneless, skinless raw
  fish fillets
1 egg
1 tsp salt
pepper to taste
about 1 cup (250 ml/8 fl oz) milk
2 Tbsp canola or olive oil
6 hamburger buns or bread rolls

lettuce leaves
sliced tomato
sliced cucumber

Break each slice of bread into 4–6 pieces and chop in a food processor fitted with a metal chopping blade. Add the parsley, process until chopped then add the chopped onion and process again.

Remove any skin and bones from the fillets and cut them into about 2 cm (3/4 in) cubes. Add to the breadcrumbs in the processor with the egg and seasonings. Process in bursts, gradually adding three-quarters of the milk, until the fish is puréed and mixed evenly through the crumbs. (Do not process more than is necessary or the patties will be tough when cooked.) The mixture should be moist enough to hold together in patties when shaped with wet hands. Use more or less milk than specified to get them to this stage.

Heat the oil in a large frypan, add the patties and cook over moderate heat until lightly browned; turn and cook the other side (usually about 8–10 minutes altogether).

Toast 6 halved hamburger buns or bread rolls while the fish cooks, then place each patty on lettuce leaves on the warm bun. Top with some slices of tomato and cucumber, then with the rest of the toasted bun. Serve immediately.

Fishburgers

Canned or cooked fresh fish also make good burgers.

For 4 burgers:
1 cup cooked, flaked, drained fish
2 eggs
1 cup fresh breadcrumbs
2 spring onions
fresh parsley and dill (optional)
about 1/2 tsp salt (for fresh fish)

Drain all the liquid from the canned or cooked fish and flake it with 2 forks, making sure all the bones are removed from freshly cooked fish. Mix the fish with the unbeaten eggs in a medium-sized mixing bowl, using a fork.

Make the breadcrumbs using a food processor or by breaking up the bread and rubbing it between the palms of your hands. Chop the spring onions and herbs finely with a sharp knife, or by adding them to the crumbs in the processor. Tip the crumbs into the fish and egg mixture and add the salt if necessary. Mix well with a fork, leave to stand for 5 minutes, then add more crumbs if the mixture is too soft, or a little milk if it is too firm to form into 4 patties.

Cook the patties in a little oil in a large frypan, allowing about 5 minutes per side.

Toast 4 split hamburger buns or bread rolls while the fish cooks. Serve the patties in the toasted buns, with carrot and celery sticks alongside.

Barbecued Fish

It's hard to beat a meal of freshly caught fish, lightly cooked to perfection on the barbecue!

Because fish is delicate, it must be handled carefully for good results. Double-sided, hinged grilling baskets enable fish to be turned without breaking it, and make life easier for the barbecue cook.

Barbecued Fish Steaks

Fish steaks are best cooked in a hinged wire basket over a grill rack, or on a hot plate. Brush the surfaces with Lemon Butter Baste (p. 75) or Garlic Herb Butter (p. 344) before cooking. Steaks about 2 cm (3/4 in) thick may cook in 2 minutes per side in the hinged basket. If using a solid plate, preheat it before adding the steaks. Cook for about the same time that you would in a frypan on the stove.

Barbecued Fish Fillets

It is easier to barbecue fish steaks directly on a barbecue plate than it is to cook fish fillets, since the thinner edges of fillets may overcook before the thicker centres are cooked. Especially if the fish is a soft-fleshed variety, wrap fillets in foil, as in the following recipe.

Barbecued Foiled Fish Fillets

Fish barbecues well in foil parcels, without breaking up. In this recipe the fish is given a delicious Oriental flavour before it is enclosed in individual parcels.

For 4 servings:
750 g (1 lb 10 oz) boneless fish fillets, cut
  in pieces
3 Tbsp lemon juice
2 Tbsp light soy or fish sauce

1 tsp pepper sauce
1 Tbsp chopped fresh coriander or spring
  onion
1 Tbsp oil
2 tsp cornflour
1 tsp finely chopped garlic, optional

Combine the fish and all the other ingredients in an unpunctured plastic bag, and knead gently to mix. Refrigerate until required.

Make 4 squares of doubled foil, put a quarter of the fish on each, fold the foil over the fish and seal the edges, folding the foil over several times and excluding any air. The finished packages should be about 10 x 15 cm (4 x 6 in).

Cook over a grill rack for preference, or on a hot plate. In good conditions, the fish should cook in 2–3 minutes per side. Test one package if necessary; the flesh should be milky white, and the liquid slightly thickened.

Serve the packets on plates so diners can unfold or cut open their own portions. Accompany with lemon wedges, salad and heated bread rolls.

Barbecued Whole Round Fish

A curved, fish-shaped hinged basket is ideal for cradling your fish while it barbecues over the grill rack. The fresh fish should be gutted (from as small a slit as possible) and the body cavity cleaned and filled with herbs, lemon slices, crushed garlic, sliced onion, etc. for extra flavour. Wild fennel leaves, dill leaves, wild marjoram or wild mint from riverbanks add interesting flavours. (Use only herbs which you can identify.) These herbs are not to be eaten, but they delicately flavour the flesh.

It is not essential to scale the fish if you intend to peel back the skin before serving it. Some cooks like to make diagonal slashes in the thick flesh on each side of the fish, since this ensures more even cooking, while others prefer to serve the fish unmarked. Brush both sides of the fish with melted butter, or with Lemon Butter Baste (p. 75). A layer of grape leaves between the coated fish flesh and the grill basket produces more even cooking, and is worth trying if you barbecue fish often and have grape leaves available.

Cooking times vary enormously depending on the size and thickness of the fish, and the conditions. A thick fish will cook faster if a domed lid or foil tent is used to keep the top part warm while the bottom grills.

Spiced Barbecued Sole or Flounder

A fresh, small whole flatfish, quickly cooked on a barbecue, served with a warmed crusty bread roll and a cucumber and tomato salad, is hard to beat on a summer evening. Since a small fish cooks in 2–3 minutes, it is easy to cook one fish after another until everyone is served.

Mix together in a shaker:
1 tsp chilli powder
1 tsp paprika
1 tsp garlic powder
1 tsp ground cumin
1 tsp salt
1 tsp oreganum

For each fish to be cooked, warm together:
1 tsp butter
1 tsp light soy sauce
1 tsp lemon juice

Allow a 200–300 g (7–10 oz) scaled flatfish for each person. For more even cooking make 3 or 4 parallel diagonal cuts to the bone on each side of the fish. Brush each side with the butter mixture. Place 1 or 2 flatfish in a hinged flat grilling basket for easy turning, sprinkle each side with the seasoning mix, and barbecue over high heat until the thickest flesh will flake when tested with a fork. This may be as soon as 1 minute for a small fish. Turn and cook the second side. Serve immediately, with a squeeze of lemon or lime juice, and a little extra seasoning.

See also
Watercress Scrambled Eggs with Salmon, p. 17

Anchovy Stuffed Eggs, p. 26

Marguerite's Salmon Roll, p. 30

Smoked Salmon Pâté, p. 30

Smoked Roe Savouries, p. 31

Sushi, p. 31

Potato and Tuna Savouries, p. 34

Cream of Mussel Soup, p. 45

Mariners' Mussel Soup, p. 45

Oyster Chowder, p. 45

Creamy Fish Chowder, p. 46

Seafood Chowder, p. 46

Tuna and Tomato Casserole, p. 65

Paella, p. 80

Salmon Surprise Packages, p. 148

Salad Niçoise, p. 160

Salmon and Pasta Salad, p. 160

Fisherman's Salad with Kiwi Salsa, p. 161

Seared Scallop Salad, p. 161

Ten-Minute Salmon and Couscous Salad, p. 161

Salmon and Seashells, p. 180

Clam Sauce for Spaghetti, p. 183

Chicken and Other Poultry

Over the years, I have watched chicken become more and more popular. This has not surprised me, since it has so many advantages. Its flavour and texture are popular with all age groups, and it is sold in user-friendly cuts. Little judgement is needed when cooking chicken, apart from making sure that it is cooked right through – that is, its juices must run clear, not pink, when it is pierced to the bone, or to the centre of the thickest part – and keen cooks can enjoy using chicken as the base for a wide variety of recipes.

TIPS FOR GRILLED AND BARBECUED CHICKEN

Suitable Cuts to Use

Tenders/tenderloins: Small, very lean; cook quickly, close to the heat. Use marinade; glaze when nearly cooked. Take care not to overcook.

Boneless, skinless breast: Very lean – use marinade to keep moist. Cook further from the heat as the centre is thick. Cooks more quickly and evenly if beaten out first. Glaze at end of cooking time.

Boneless, skinless thighs: Juicy and moist. Snip the underside to prevent curling during cooking. Marinate. Cook quickly, close to the heat.

Whole legs, thighs, drumsticks – skin-on, bone-in: These are thick. Use lower heat or cook further from the heat. Slash to the bone for more even cooking. When barbecued, large pieces of skin-on chicken cooked from raw may cause 'flare-ups' – pre-cook to prevent this. (See 'Shortcut' Barbecued Chicken Legs, p. 74.) When grilled, fat from the skin usually drips away without problems.

Whole chickens: These are hard to cook evenly in a short time. Cut down the centre back and open flat; slash thick parts. They are likely to drip fat if barbecued. May be grilled if cooked some distance from the heat for a long time.

Barbecued and grilled chicken is delicious, but not always trouble-free. To avoid problems:

- Precook larger pieces of skin-on chicken before you grill or barbecue them.
- Choose smaller skinless, boneless cuts which cook quickly and evenly.
- Skin (then marinate) larger cuts which are to be barbecued, to prevent flare-ups.

'Shortcut' Barbecued Chicken Legs (p. 74)

Cooking Times

These vary with the heat, and how far the chicken is from it. For small boneless pieces, use higher heat and place close to the heat source. For larger pieces, lower the heat or move the chicken further from it.

> Chicken is cooked when the juices run clear, not pink, when the thickest part is pierced.

Marinades

These add flavour to chicken before cooking, and can be brushed on during cooking to add more. Marinades often contain oil to prevent the surface drying out and burning.

To make the best use of a small amount of marinade, put the marinade ingredients and the chicken in an unpunctured plastic bag before cooking, squeeze out the air and leave it to stand. It will add definite flavour to small pieces in as little as 5 minutes. Large pieces are best marinated for at least 30 minutes; marinate in the refrigerator for longer than 30 minutes. Brush on extra marinade during cooking if desired.

Do not use leftover marinade as a sauce over cooked chicken unless it has been brought to the boil and simmered for several minutes after the chicken has been removed.

Use the following marinades with 500 g (1 lb 2 oz) of the chicken of your choice – flattened breasts; boneless, skinless thighs; tenders/tenderloins, or drumsticks. Put the marinade ingredients and the chicken in a plastic bag, as above, then barbecue or grill it.

Satay Marinade

1–2 Tbsp lemon or lime juice
1 Tbsp each soy sauce and fish sauce
1–2 tsp sesame oil
1 tsp ground cumin
2 cloves garlic, finely chopped
1 tsp grated fresh ginger
1 Tbsp chopped fresh coriander (optional)

Sweet Chilli Marinade

2 Tbsp oil
2 Tbsp light soy sauce
2 Tbsp Thai sweet chilli sauce

Green Marinade

1/4 cup (60 ml/2 fl oz) olive oil
1 tsp minced garlic
1 tsp oreganum
2 Tbsp lemon juice

Thai Marinade

2 Tbsp oil
1 tsp finely chopped garlic
2 spring onions, chopped
1 Tbsp fish sauce
2 Tbsp rice or wine vinegar
1/4 tsp chilli powder or 1/2 tsp minced chilli
2 tsp sugar

Sesame Marinade

1 Tbsp sherry
2 tsp sesame oil
2 tsp brown sugar
1 clove garlic, finely chopped
1/2 tsp grated root ginger

Glazes

These are brushed onto nearly cooked meat. They usually contain sugar (juice, jam, sauce, etc.) which causes the surface to brown attractively. Glazes will cause chicken to burn if brushed on too soon.

Apricot Glaze

2 Tbsp apricot jam
2 tsp Dijon mustard
1 Tbsp each orange juice, olive or other oil, and light soy sauce
1/2 tsp minced garlic

Stir together, warming if necessary to mix thoroughly.

Traditional BBQ Glaze

2 Tbsp each tomato sauce and oil
1 Tbsp lemon juice
1 Tbsp Worcestershire sauce
1 tsp each paprika and garlic salt

Stir together until well blended.

'Shortcut' Barbecued Chicken Legs

Pre-cook chicken legs before you take them outside to barbecue, offer a choice of glazes, and serve the tasty, sizzling chicken only 10 minutes later.

chicken legs (about 350 g/12 oz each)
soy sauce

Mustardy Citrus Glaze

1 Tbsp grainy mustard
2 Tbsp lemon or lime juice
1 tsp grated lemon or lime rind
1 Tbsp olive or other oil
1 large clove garlic, finely grated

Hot Sesame Glaze

2 Tbsp light soy sauce
2 Tbsp lemon juice
1 tsp brown sugar
2 tsp sesame oil
1 small fresh chilli, finely sliced, or 1 Tbsp
  Thai hot chilli sauce

Sun-Dried Tomato Glaze

1 Tbsp sun-dried tomato pesto
1 large clove garlic, finely grated
1 Tbsp balsamic or wine vinegar
½ tsp oreganum
1 Tbsp olive oil

In advance, microwave the chicken legs two at a time. Brush the legs with enough soy sauce to coat them, then wrap in greaseproof or baking paper, or oven bags. Microwave each pair of legs at 70% power for 7 minutes, turning once during cooking.

Combine the glaze ingredients in screw-topped jars, shake well and refrigerate until needed. They will keep, refrigerated, for a week. Brush each chicken leg with one of the glazes and barbecue (or grill) for 8–10 minutes, turning to brown both sides. Brush with more glaze at intervals if desired.

Sesame Chicken M

Small bone-in chicken pieces cook in a short time in this sauce, whether microwaved, baked, grilled or barbecued.

For 2 servings:

about 300 g (10 oz) chicken wings or
  drumsticks
2 Tbsp each soy sauce and sherry
1 Tbsp each sugar and sesame oil
1 clove garlic, finely chopped
½ tsp cornflour (if microwaving)
2 Tbsp toasted sesame seeds

To microwave:

Put the chicken pieces in an oven bag, then add all the other ingredients except the sesame seeds. (Use dark soy sauce for a browner glaze.) Leave for 5 minutes to 24 hours before cooking.

Place the bag flat in the microwave, with the chicken pieces in one layer, leaving a finger-sized opening for steam to escape.

Microwave on High (100%) power for about 6 minutes. Flip the bag over, stand for about 2 minutes, then pierce the thickest piece. If the juice runs pink, cook for longer, in 1-minute bursts, until it is clear. Remove from the bag and sprinkle with toasted sesame seeds before the glaze sets.

To cook conventionally:

Bag the chicken and marinade ingredients, using dark or light soy sauce, but omit the cornflour. Marinate as above. Fasten the bag with a twist tie, leaving a finger-sized hole. Lie the bag flat and bake at 180°C (350°F) for 20–30 minutes, then test and coat with sesame seeds as above.

To barbecue or grill:

Marinate the chicken as above but without adding cornflour or sugar. Cook close to the heat for about 20 minutes, turning and brushing with marinade during cooking. Test as above.

Serve with a salad of your choice.

Sesame Soy-Glazed Chicken Thighs

This favourite family barbecue recipe requires next to no preparation, is amazingly quick to cook, and tastes delicious. Gone are the days of charred skin and underdone inside flesh.

For 4 servings:

6–8 skinless, boneless chicken thighs
3 Tbsp light soy sauce
2 Tbsp sesame oil
1 tsp finely chopped garlic
fresh parsley or coriander and lemon
  wedges to garnish

Put the chicken in a bowl with the other ingredients. Leave to stand for at least 5 minutes, ideally about half an hour.

Preheat the barbecue or grill and cook the chicken on a rack for about 3 minutes a side. When the thickest part of the meat is pierced and no pink liquid emerges, the chicken is cooked.

Stand the chicken in a warm place for 5 minutes, then place it on a board and cut each thigh into about 5 diagonal slices. Arrange these on a serving plate, garnish with parsley or coriander, and lemon wedges if desired, and serve hot or warm.

This chicken is good dropped into pockets of pita bread, or served on rice or noodles with a spoonful of chicken juice on top.

Grilled Lemon Chicken

This recipe is always popular. Make it with chicken pieces or with drumsticks, thighs, etc.

For 4 servings:

2–4 Tbsp butter
2 Tbsp lemon juice
½ tsp paprika
about 8 chicken pieces, bone-in

Melt the butter over low heat, add the lemon juice and paprika. Heat gently. Line a sponge-roll tin with foil and place the chicken on it, skin-side down. Brush with the butter mixture. Cook 15 cm (6 in) from the grill, turning after about 15 minutes, and brushing with the remaining butter mixture. If the pieces brown too quickly, move them slightly further from the heat. Cook for about 30 minutes altogether, or until the juice from a pierced drumstick is clear rather than pink. Serve hot or cold.

Variation: Barbecue on a rack, brushing at intervals with the butter mixture.

Grilled Chicken Breasts

These chicken breasts are good served alone, with apricot sauce or with a little sun-dried tomato paste spread over them or on the fresh crusty bread served with them.

For 4 servings:

2 boneless, skinless chicken breasts
1 Tbsp olive oil
1 Tbsp light soy sauce
1 Tbsp Thai sweet chilli sauce

Put 1 chicken breast between 2 sheets of plastic. Using a rolling pin, bang gently until the breast is of even thickness and double its original length and width. Repeat with the second breast.

Combine the oil, soy and chilli sauce and brush over the chicken. Grill or barbecue for about 5 minutes each side, or until cooked through. (Take care not to overcook.)

Serve sliced, with bread rolls, Tomato Salsa (p. 346) or Sun-Dried Tomato Paste (p. 346).

Barbecued Chicken Kebabs

If you find it difficult to judge when a whole chicken breast is cooked, make kebabs instead. You can make good kebabs by threading cubes of skinless chicken breast, or boneless, skinless thigh meat, onto soaked bamboo skewers. If you have time, marinate them (see p. 73), then barbecue them for a short time. Brush kebabs with olive oil or melted butter; with a mixture of 1 Tbsp each of honey, lemon juice and oil, warmed together, or with Lemon Butter Baste (see opposite). Oil the grill rack or spray it with non-stick spray. Place the kebabs fairly close together on the hottest part of the grill rack, cook for 2 minutes, then turn and cook 2 minutes longer. The kebabs are cooked as soon as they feel fairly firm when pressed, and when a cube of chicken, cut in half, has no translucent, uncooked part in the middle.

Red-Cooked Chicken

They should be lightly browned, and marked with dark lines from the hot rack if the barbecue was hot enough to start with. Cook for a little longer if necessary, but take care not to overcook, since the lean breast meat, which is very tender and moist if cooked to the right stage, dries out quickly if overcooked. Kebabs with the honey glaze will be darker brown than those brushed with butter or oil.

Variation: Chicken kebabs cook well and very quickly on a double-sided contact grill.

Lemon Butter Baste

1 large clove garlic
1 Tbsp butter
2 tsp light soy sauce or fish sauce
1 Tbsp lemon juice

Finely chop or crush the garlic, and heat with the butter until it bubbles. Stir in the soy or fish sauce and the lemon juice. Brush on chicken (or fish) before and during cooking.

Variations: Try the various glazes on p. 73 when barbecuing kebabs.

Red-Cooked Chicken   M

Barbecued chicken with a difference! Here the chicken is pre-cooked in a strongly flavoured sauce, before it is barbecued or grilled.

For 4 servings:

4 chicken legs
1 cup (250 ml/8 fl oz) cold water
½ cup (125 ml/4 fl oz) dark soy sauce
½ cup (125 ml/4 fl oz) light soy sauce
2 Tbsp sherry
1 walnut-sized piece fresh ginger, peeled and sliced
1 clove garlic, peeled
1 star anise 'flower'
1½ Tbsp sugar

To microwave:

Combine all the ingredients except the chicken in an unpunctured oven bag. Add the chicken legs and microwave on High (100%) power for 12–14 minutes, or until the juices run clear when the thighs are pierced deeply. Turn the legs 2 or 3 times during cooking.

To cook conventionally:

Simmer the chicken legs in the marinade in a covered pan for 15–30 minutes, turning once or twice. Test as above.

Pour off the cooking liquid, strain and refrigerate for re-use within a week, or freeze for later use. Barbecue or grill the chicken soon after cooking, or refrigerate until required. The chicken can now be cooked quite close to the heat, as it only needs reheating. Serve hot with barbecued fresh vegetables, warmed bread rolls and a leafy green salad.

Peanutty Chicken Kebabs

400–500 g (about 1 lb) boneless chicken thighs, cubed
½ cup peanut butter
2 Tbsp Kikkoman soy sauce
4 Tbsp sherry
1 clove garlic, very finely chopped
2 Tbsp toasted sesame seeds

Soak bamboo skewers then thread on the cubes of chicken. Combine the peanut butter, soy sauce, sherry and garlic, and brush this paste onto the meat. Sprinkle with toasted sesame seeds. Grill, turning several times, until cooked.

Apricot-Glazed Chicken Breasts

Apricot-Glazed Chicken Breasts

This is one of my standbys when I want a quick and easy recipe for dinner guests.

Even when the weather is less than perfect, I barbecue the chicken and bring it inside to serve at the table.

For 4 servings:
4 skinless, boneless chicken breasts
1 large clove garlic, crushed
4 tsp light soy sauce
1 Tbsp olive or other oil
2 Tbsp apricot jam
2 tsp Dijon mustard
1 Tbsp orange juice

Put the chicken breasts in a heavy, unpunctured plastic bag with the garlic, half the soy sauce and the oil. Turn to coat all sides with marinade and leave for at least 10 minutes, preferably longer.

Barbecue on a rack over moderate heat, turning after 4 minutes. When the second side has cooked for 4 minutes, pierce the deepest part of the flesh with a sharp knife. If it is cooked, no pink liquid will appear. Keep cooking until this stage is reached.

Meanwhile make a glaze by heating together the remaining soy sauce, the apricot jam, mustard and orange juice until bubbling (either in a small metal container on the barbecue or in the kitchen). Brush both sides of the chicken breasts with the glaze, and serve as soon as it has browned attractively on both sides.

Note: If you find it hard to tell when the chicken breast is cooked, cut it in half lengthwise, with a very sharp knife, parallel to the board and if necessary barbecue, cut sides down, until both surfaces are cooked.

Orange Chicken with Cashews

This tasty 'east-west' recipe is ideal when you are late home from work and want to make something that is quick and delicious.

For 2 servings:
250 g (9 oz) chicken breast meat, thinly
*   sliced*
1 tsp grated root ginger
1 tsp chopped garlic
1 spring onion, finely chopped
grated rind of 1/4–1/2 tangelo or orange
1 Tbsp sherry
1 Tbsp light soy sauce
1 tsp brown sugar
1/2 tsp salt
2 medium/large zucchini
1 stalk celery

1/4 cup (60 ml/2 fl oz) chicken stock
2 Tbsp tangelo or orange juice
2 tsp cornflour
2 Tbsp oil
1/4 cup roasted cashews

Put the sliced chicken into an unpunctured plastic bag or a bowl with the next 8 ingredients. Leave for at least 5 minutes (or up to 24 hours) before cooking.

Cut the zucchini and the celery diagonally into 5 mm (1/4 in) slices and cook in 2–3 Tbsp of boiling water in a covered pan until barely tender; drain.

Mix the chicken stock, juice and cornflour in a small bowl and put aside.

Heat the oil in a large frypan or wok and add the cashews. Add the chicken and cook, stirring all the time until it is milky white. Add the cooked, drained vegetables and the stock, juice and cornflour mixture and bring to the boil. Serve immediately over noodles or cooked rice.

Two-Minute Chicken Breasts

This is a wonderfully quick recipe when you don't have the energy to make anything elaborate or time-consuming.

For 2 servings:
3 chicken breasts
1 Tbsp sherry
2 tsp sesame oil
2 tsp brown sugar
1 clove garlic, finely chopped
1/2 tsp grated root ginger
1–2 Tbsp oil
1 tsp cornflour
1 Tbsp sherry
1 Tbsp water
chives, spring onions or fresh coriander

Cut each chicken breast crosswise into 6 or 9 pieces.

Mix together the first measure of sherry, the sesame oil, brown sugar, garlic and root ginger. Marinate the chicken pieces in this mixture for at least 5 minutes, preferably longer. (If you like to work ahead, and want an instant meal without any last-minute chopping or grating, refrigerate the chicken in its marinade in a plastic bag.)

Heat the oil in a heavy, non-stick frypan, add the chicken and the liquid around it, and stir-fry for about 2 minutes, or until the chicken is opaque right through.

Mix together the cornflour, extra sherry and water, pour over the chicken and toss to coat. Sprinkle with chopped chives, spring onion or fresh coriander and serve immediately. Serve with bread rolls and a salad, or on rice or noodles.

Stuffed Chicken Breasts

When making stuffing, consider the colour as well as the flavour of the mixture.

If you want a meal that looks impressive, slice these cooked breasts before you serve them. This is only possible if you have a knife sharp enough to slice the meat easily. I use a smallish serrated knife.

For 4 servings:
4 boneless, skinless chicken breasts

Stuffing
1 Tbsp butter
1 small onion, chopped
1–2 rashers bacon, finely chopped
½ cup finely chopped mushrooms (optional)
2 Tbsp soft breadcrumbs
12–20 sweet pickled walnuts (optional)

Coating
plain flour
1 egg, lightly beaten
fine dry breadcrumbs

Melt the butter and cook the onion until tender. Add the bacon and mushrooms, and cook until the bacon is done. Stir in the crumbs.

Prepare the coating ingredients and find strong toothpicks or string.

Prepare the breasts the same day you plan to eat them. Place them between 2 layers of plastic and bang them with a rolling pin to flatten them. Spread the filling over the inner surface of each breast, work out the easiest way to roll them, and arrange the walnuts.

Roll up, trying to keep the chicken in one piece. Skewer or tie in position. Coat with flour, then lightly beaten egg, then crumbs.

Refrigerate until required, then sauté for about 5 minutes in a frypan with a little butter or oil, turning often. Leave to stand for 1–2 minutes then remove fastenings and slice.

'Two for One' Chicken Breasts

When you are cooking for a small number of people, you can use techniques that are not always practical for larger numbers.

For 2 meals for 2 people:
4 boneless, skinless chicken breasts

Stock
¼ cup (60 ml/2 fl oz) water
¼ cup (60 ml/2 fl oz) white wine
1 clove garlic, crushed
1 spring onion, chopped

2–3 thin slices root ginger
2 tsp light soy sauce
¼ tsp sesame oil
3–4 drops hot pepper sauce

Put stock ingredients in a medium-sized pot and bring to the boil. Add the chicken breasts, cover, and simmer very gently for 5 minutes after the liquid bubbles. Turn off the heat and leave to stand for 20 minutes.

Lift out the chicken and put it in a plastic bag if not using immediately, to prevent it drying out.

For chicken salad: slice the room-temperature chicken into diagonal slices 5 mm (¼ in) thick. Dip each slice in good homemade herbed mayonnaise then arrange overlapping slices on plates containing prepared salad vegetables.

For sauce-glazed chicken slices: boil the cooking liquid briskly until it has reduced to about ¼ cup. Strain, discarding the vegetables. Add 2 Tbsp cream to the stock, boil until it is thick and syrupy. Stir in very finely chopped fresh herbs if desired. Slice 2 chicken breasts, turn them in the sauce, and serve straight away if possible. If not, arrange them in a dish in which they may be reheated when required. Cover and refrigerate.

The ingredients used in this stock are not usually associated with either mayonnaise or cream, but both combinations work well.

Note: Chicken breasts are very tender and cook very quickly. If they are cooked at too high a temperature or for too long, they will be dry and tough. Treat them carefully.

Lime Chicken with Mango Salsa

Although limes cost more than lemons, one small lime gives more zip and zing to a recipe like this than a lemon twice its weight.

For 4 servings:
4 chicken breasts (125 g/4 oz each)
¼ cup self-raising flour
2 Tbsp butter
1 Tbsp very finely chopped shallots
juice and grated rind of 1 lime (or lemon)
¼ cup (60 ml/2 fl oz) white wine
salt and freshly ground black pepper
1 lime, thinly sliced, to garnish

Remove the skin, and bone the chicken breasts if necessary. Place them between 2 plastic bags and pound with a rolling pin until they are of even thickness and almost twice their original size. Take care not to pulverise the meat, which is very tender.

Sprinkle the breasts with a light coating of flour and pat it to coat evenly.

Heat the butter in a large frypan. Stir in the shallots, cook about 30 seconds, then add the chicken and cook over medium heat for about 2 minutes per side, or until the chicken is firm and light golden-brown. It is cooked as soon as the thickest flesh springs back and the centre has lost its translucent appearance.

Sprinkle the lime juice over the chicken, turn so both sides have a hint of lime flavour, then remove it from the pan. Let the shallots brown if necessary, then add the wine and finely grated rind and cook until the liquid reduces and forms a slightly thickened, light brown sauce. Season to taste with salt and pepper.

To serve, pour the sauce over the chicken and garnish with lime slices. (For a stronger lime flavour, use both limes in the sauce and garnish with something else!) Serve with Mango Salsa (p. 346) and vegetables of your choice.

Stir-Fried Chicken

When tender chicken breast is cut into thin strips it cooks very quickly. Teamed with tender-crisp, colourful vegetables, it tastes as good as it looks.

For 2 servings:
about 200 g (7 oz) chicken breast meat
1 tsp grated root ginger
1 clove garlic, sliced
1 Tbsp light soy sauce
1 Tbsp sherry
1 tsp brown sugar
1 tsp chicken stock powder
1 tsp cornflour
2 Tbsp oil
2–3 cups prepared vegetables*
1–2 Tbsp water

* Choose a selection of quick-cooking vegetables, e.g. spinach, mushrooms, celery, spring onions, green and red peppers. Slice them into pieces about the same size as the chicken.

Cut the chicken breast across the grain into 5 mm (¼ in) thick slices. Put in a plastic bag with the next 7 ingredients. Knead lightly to combine, and allow to stand for at least 15 minutes.

Heat the oil in a large frypan over a very high heat. Add the prepared vegetables and toss until coated with oil and heated through. Add the water, cover and cook until the vegetables are barely tender, then remove from pan. Add a little extra oil if necessary, then stir in the chicken. Stir over a very high heat until the meat turns white, then return the vegetables to the pan. Toss gently to mix.

Serve immediately on noodles or rice.

Curried Chicken with Kumara

Curried Chicken with Kumara

This flavourful chicken curry can be cooked on the stovetop as described, or baked in the oven at 180°C (350°F) for about 1½ hours in a roasting pan covered with foil.

For 4–8 servings:
1–2 kg (2 lb 3 oz–4 lb 7 oz) chicken
* pieces or drumsticks*
2–3 Tbsp oil
2–3 large onions, sliced
2–3 large cloves garlic, chopped
1 tsp salt
2 tsp sugar
2 Tbsp curry powder
12 star anis petals (optional)
1 cinnamon stick (optional)
10 cardamom pods (optional)
3–4 cups (750 ml–1 litre/24–32 fl oz)
* water*
2–3 large kumara

Pat the chicken dry if necessary. Heat the oil in a large pot or frypan, add the onions and garlic and cook over a moderate heat until the onion is evenly browned. Add the salt, sugar, curry powder and optional spices and heat for a minute longer, stirring constantly. Add the chicken pieces and water, using less water for a smaller quantity of chicken. Cover and simmer for 20–30 minutes for skinless, boneless chicken, or about 1 hour for chicken pieces with bone; turn occasionally.

Peel the kumara and cut into 2 cm (3/4 in) cubes; add to the chicken 15 minutes before it is cooked (or, if baking, 30 minutes before).

Serve on a generous pile of rice, spooning on the sauce so it flavours the rice as well. Serve with curry accompaniments if you like.

Note: The optional ingredients give this curry a very special character. Use them if you can.

Thai Green Chicken Curry

Thai cooking does require some special ingredients, but most keep well and once you have them they can be used to produce a variety of quick and delicious meals.

For 3–4 servings:
3 or 4 kaffir lime leaves
2 Tbsp oil
1–2 Tbsp Thai green curry paste
1 cup (250 ml/8 fl oz) coconut cream
300–400 g (10–14 oz) boneless, skinless
* chicken thighs or breasts*
1 medium onion, sliced
2 Tbsp fish sauce
1 tsp sugar
2 or 3 zucchini, sliced
½ cup peas or green beans, fresh or
* frozen*
1 can (150–200 g/5–7 oz) bamboo shoots,
* drained (optional)*

Cover the lime leaves with a little boiling water, soak for a few minutes, then cut into 1 cm (½ in) slices. Cut the chicken into 2 cm (3/4 in) cubes.

Heat the oil in a frypan or wok, stir in the curry paste and cook for 1–2 minutes, then add the lime leaves. Pour in the coconut cream, then add the chicken. Add the onion, fish sauce and sugar and simmer for 5 minutes, stirring occasionally.

Add the vegetables and bamboo shoots, and ¼–½ cup water to thin the sauce if necessary. Simmer until the chicken is cooked through and the vegetables are just tender.

Serve over fragrant Thai (jasmine) rice, garnished with chopped basil or spring onion and curry accompaniments of your choice.

Variation: For a vegetarian alternative, omit the chicken and add 1–2 cups assorted vegetables (cubed potato, eggplant, cauliflower, broccoli, etc.) and replace the fish sauce with light soy sauce.

Tandoori Chicken

This popular Indian dish is best prepared ahead and left in its marinade overnight (or at least for 1–2 hours). It cooks with little last-minute fuss.

For 4 servings:
3 or 4 cloves garlic
1–2 cm (½–3/4 in) root ginger
½ tsp chilli powder
1 tsp each ground cumin, coriander,
* paprika, turmeric, garam masala and*
* mint*
1 tsp salt
1 cup unsweetened yoghurt
8 small or 4 large chicken pieces (skin
* removed if you like)*

Crush and chop the garlic and grate the ginger. Combine with the spices, mint and salt in a shallow container large enough to hold the chicken pieces in a single layer, or in an unpunctured plastic bag.

Stir in the yoghurt to make a paste. Add the chicken pieces, turning to make sure they are well coated. Cover and leave to stand for 1–2 hours, or refrigerate overnight if possible.

Arrange the chicken on a rack. Grill 12–15 cm (5–6 in) away from the grill or barbecue for 10–20 minutes per side, depending on the thickness.

Serve with plain rice or Spicy Rice Pilaf (p. 172), a salad and your favourite Indian breads.

Thai-Style Chicken

This recipe has a mild and very interesting flavour, but is not a curry.

For 3–4 servings:
4 chicken breasts (300–400 g/10–14 oz)
2 Tbsp oil
1 tsp finely chopped garlic
2 spring onions, chopped
1 Tbsp fish or light soy sauce
2 Tbsp rice or wine vinegar
1/4 tsp chilli powder
2 tsp sugar
1/4 cup (60 ml/2 fl oz) water
1/2 tsp chicken stock powder
1 tsp cornflour
1–2 Tbsp Thai chilli sauce (optional)
2–3 Tbsp chopped fresh coriander or basil
  (optional)

Slice each chicken breast crosswise, with your knife at an angle to the board, into about 8 slices. Mix with the oil, garlic, spring onion, fish or soy sauce, vinegar, chilli powder and sugar.

Heat a wok or large frypan and cook over high heat, stirring all the time, for about 2 minutes, until the chicken is milky white and has lost its translucency.

Mix together the water, stock powder and cornflour. Remove the cooked chicken from the pan and keep it hot. Add the cornflour mixture to the pan and stir until the sauce thickens and has boiled down to about half its volume. Return the chicken to the pan and toss to coat in the sauce.

Serve like this, or add Thai chilli sauce and stir to coat. Toss with the chopped herbs and serve immediately, on rice or noodles, with a salad.

Balti Chicken Curry

This curry cooks very quickly in a heavy frypan or wok, using tender chicken cuts that need very little cooking.

For 2 servings:
300 g (10 1/2 oz) boneless, skinless chicken
  breasts or thighs
1–2 Tbsp oil
2 cloves garlic, finely chopped
1 large onion, finely chopped
1–2 Tbsp curry paste*
1/2 cup (125 ml/4 fl oz) chicken stock or
  water
1–2 tsp garam masala
1 Tbsp chopped fresh coriander
salt to taste

* Use bought Indian curry paste or make your own (see below).

Cut the chicken into long strips about 1 cm (1/2 in) thick. In a wok or large frypan, heat the oil over medium heat and cook the garlic very briefly (about 30 seconds). Add the onion and cook until lightly and evenly browned,

4–5 minutes. Stir in the curry paste, add the chicken, then raise the heat and stir-fry until the chicken loses its raw look, 3–5 minutes.

Add the stock or water and simmer, stirring, on a lower heat for 5 minutes. Test a piece of chicken to check that it is cooked right through. If not, cook for a few minutes longer. Add the garam masala and coriander, mix well, and add salt to taste. Serve immediately with rice, poppadoms and other curry accompaniments.

Curry Powder and Paste

This curry mixture is interesting and mildly hot. For a more fiery mixture, double the amount of chilli powder. Roasting the whole seeds before you grind them gives a really aromatic mixture which will make tasty curries for six months or so.

To make about 100 g (3 oz):
2 Tbsp coriander seeds
1 1/2 Tbsp cumin seeds
5 cm (2 in) piece cassia or cinnamon bark
1 tsp fennel seeds
1 tsp black mustard seeds
1 tsp cardamom seeds
1/2 tsp celery seeds
1/4 tsp wild onion seeds (if available)
3–4 whole cloves
2–3 bayleaves

Balti Chicken Curry

Ground Spices
2 tsp turmeric
2 tsp garlic powder
1 tsp powdered ginger
1/4–1/2 tsp chilli powder

Heat the whole spices in a dry frypan or under a preheated grill, stirring them at intervals until they smell aromatic and you see them lightly smoking. Then grind them finely, mix them with the ground spices and store them in an airtight container in a cool place away from the light, or make curry paste as follows:

Put the curry powder in a bowl, mix in 1/2 cup mild vinegar, and leave to stand for at least 10 minutes.

Heat 1/2 cup oil in a frypan or wok and add the paste (it will splatter, so take care). Heat, stirring all the time to prevent the paste sticking, until the water has boiled away (about 5 minutes). At this stage the paste will make a regular bubbling noise when you don't stir it. Take off the heat and leave to stand for 3–4 minutes. If the oil floats to the top, the spices are cooked. If not, add a little more oil and carry on cooking and stirring.

Bottle in sterilised jars and top with a little more heated oil. Cover tightly and refrigerate up to 6 months.

Mexican Chicken

This tasty and popular chicken is very easy to make using a homemade seasoning mix.

For 6 servings:

6–8 skinless, boneless chicken thighs or
  4 chicken breasts
1 tsp butter, melted
1 tsp oil
about 2 Tbsp Mexican Coating Mixture

Make sure all skin and bone is removed from the chicken, place it between 2 pieces of plastic or cling film, and beat with a rolling pin until it is 1 cm (1/2 in) thick. Make sure thighs will lie flat, snipping the meat if necessary. Brush with, or turn in, a mixture of melted butter and oil.

Five to 10 minutes before cooking, sprinkle the chicken on both sides with the Mexican Coating Mixture, adjusting the quantity to taste (about 1 tsp per side for each piece gives a good flavour).

Barbecue on a rack close to the heat until the juices no longer run pink when the thickest part is pierced. Slice thighs diagonally before serving, if you like.

Mexican Coating Mixture

If you like the flavour of the herbs and spices used in Mexican cooking, keep this mixture on hand to flavour chicken for a quickly prepared meal.

1 Tbsp paprika
1 Tbsp oreganum
1 Tbsp ground cumin
1 Tbsp onion or garlic salt
1 Tbsp plain flour
2 tsp castor sugar
about 1 tsp chilli powder

Mix all the ingredients together, crumbling leaves of oreganum if you like, and store in an airtight container. Use less chilli powder for less hotness. Makes about 1/3 cup.

Cuban Chicken

Interesting marinades from other parts of the world make lean, skinned, boned chicken breasts really exciting. Lime juice and fresh coriander make this chicken unforgettable!

For 4 servings:

4 skinless, boneless chicken breasts
3 cloves garlic, finely chopped
1/2 tsp ground cumin
1/4 tsp oreganum
1/4 tsp thyme
1 Tbsp finely chopped fresh coriander
3 Tbsp lime juice
3 Tbsp olive oil
1 tsp sugar
1/2 tsp salt

Pat the chicken breasts dry with absorbent paper and trim if necessary. Place each breast between plastic and bang gently with a rolling pin until it is one and a half times its original size. Place the chicken in a sponge-roll tin big enough to hold it all in one layer.

Mix the remaining ingredients together in a screw-top jar, or combine them in a food processor. Brush this mixture over both sides of the chicken, and leave to marinate for at least 15 minutes, or up to 24 hours in the refrigerator, covered with cling film.

Preheat a heavy pan or barbecue plate, brush or rub it with a film of oil, and cook the chicken until brown on both sides and just cooked in the middle. This should only take 2 minutes per side if you have beaten the chicken out thinly. Serve with a spicy bean or rice salad.

Paella

Paella is a mixture which originates in Spain. Made of meat, fish and rice, it is a very practical dish combining small quantities of local, inexpensive fresh foods. The ingredients vary according to what is on hand.

It is important to cook the rice mixture just before it is to be eaten – paella made ahead and reheated loses a lot of its 'oomph'. Brown the meat earlier if you like, but don't do the main part of the cooking ahead of time.

The paella is served without other vegetables, so the quantities given are generous. Each plate should be piled high.

For 4 servings:

8 small or 4 large chicken pieces
3–4 Tbsp oil
2 chorizos or other spicy sausages
1–2 rashers bacon, chopped
2 onions, chopped
2 cloves garlic, chopped
1 green pepper, chopped (optional)
1 red pepper, chopped (optional)
2–3 tomatoes, chopped, or 1 Tbsp tomato
  paste
3/4 cup long- or medium-grain rice
2 1/2 cups (600 ml/20 fl oz) salted chicken
  stock, or 1 Tbsp chicken stock powder in
  2 1/2 cups hot water
turmeric (or saffron)
1 cup frozen peas
8 fresh mussels
shrimps, etc. if available

Brown the chicken evenly in the oil in a large (electric if you have it) frypan. This will take 10–15 minutes. Remove when well browned.

Chop the sausages and bacon and brown in the same pan. Put aside with the chicken. Brown the chopped onion and garlic, without burning, add the peppers and tomato, and cook until hot but not browned.

Add the rice to this mixture, and cook until it turns milky white. Add the stock and enough turmeric to make the liquid bright yellow.

Return the chicken, sausage and bacon to the pan, cover and cook for about 15 minutes, until the rice and chicken are cooked. Add the frozen peas and mussels and cook 2–3 minutes longer, then add any cooked shrimps or other seafood and allow to heat through. Serve as soon as these are hot.

Herbed Roasted Chicken Legs

There are times when you want to 'dress up' chicken for a special meal. One of the nicest ways of doing this is to make a creamy stuffing, spread it between the skin and the flesh of the chicken, then roast (or bake).

For 4 servings:

4 whole chicken legs (drumsticks and
  thighs joined)

Stuffing

2 spring onions, chopped
1 tsp finely chopped fresh thyme
2 cloves garlic, finely chopped
1/2 cup cream cheese
1 tsp tomato paste

Choose chicken legs (sometimes called Chicken Marylands) with unbroken skin.

Turn the oven to 180°C (350°F). Starting at the end where the leg was cut away from the body, separate the skin from the flesh, without breaking the skin or damaging the flesh (using the handle of a spoon helps). Work down to the lower (drumstick) part of the leg, separating some, if not all, of the skin. Leave the skin around the 'ankle' attached.

Prepare the stuffing by mixing together all the ingredients, preferably in a food processor (or chop the spring onions, thyme and garlic very finely and mix them with the cream cheese and tomato paste). Divide the stuffing in four and carefully spread it in the pocket of each leg, so it is above the flesh and below the skin. At the top of the leg, secure the skin to the flesh with small toothpicks. Gently knead the legs to spread the stuffing evenly.

Bake, uncovered, in a shallow baking pan (lined with baking paper if you have it), for 30–45 minutes, or until cooked. Remove the toothpicks before serving and spoon the juices over and around the chicken.

Tangy Chicken

I like to keep a couple of packets of chicken drumsticks in the freezer. These thaw quickly in the microwave or a bowl of warm water, and are delicious when cooked using the following recipe.

For 4–6 servings:
8–12 chicken drumsticks
1/2 cup apricot jam
2 Tbsp Dijon mustard
2 Tbsp dark soy sauce
1 tsp Worcestershire sauce
1/2 tsp hot pepper sauce
1 clove garlic, chopped
1 tsp freshly grated root ginger

Turn the oven to 190°C (375°F). Place the chicken pieces in a non-stick or foil-lined roasting pan.

Combine the remaining ingredients in a small pot and stir over the heat until the mixture boils. Brush this glaze over the chicken and bake uncovered for 20–30 minutes, turning occasionally and glazing with the remaining sauce. Check the chicken is cooked by piercing with a skewer; the juices should run clear.

Oven-Fried Chicken

The coating on this chicken is very similar to that on conventionally fried chicken, but this is much easier to cook.

For 4–6 servings:
8–12 chicken pieces
1 Tbsp butter
1 Tbsp oil
1/2 cup plain flour
1 tsp salt
freshly ground black pepper

Select large chicken pieces or joint a chicken so that each piece is the right size for one serving.

Measure the butter and oil into a shallow non-stick baking or roasting pan, or one lined with baking paper, and heat in the oven until the butter melts. Dry the joints thoroughly with paper towels, then turn in the butter mixture.

Heat the oven to 200°C (400°F). Toss the remaining ingredients together in a large plastic bag, then turn the chicken pieces in this mixture. Arrange, skin-side down, in the baking pan and bake uncovered for 20 minutes. Turn and bake for another 20 minutes, basting once. Test by piercing the thickest part – if the juices have any hint of pinkness, cook a little longer.

Baked Chicken and Rice

This easy recipe makes one of my favourite chicken dinners. It looks after itself as it cooks, tastes wonderful and the ingredients can be varied.

Baked Chicken and Rice

For 4 generous servings:
8 large chicken drumsticks
1 Tbsp olive or canola oil
1–2 onions
2 carrots
1 1/2 cups long-grain rice
1–2 tsp chopped garlic
1/2–1 tsp minced chilli (from a jar)
1–2 tsp ground cumin
1 tsp oreganum
3 1/2 cups (875 ml/28 fl oz) boiling water
2 tsp salt
1–2 cups chopped green beans, zucchini, broccoli or other green vegetables
paprika and extra cumin

Turn the oven to 210°C (425°F), or 200°C (400°F) for fan-bake, and select a baking or roasting pan just big enough to hold the chicken in one layer. Pat the drumsticks dry, and brown them evenly in the oil in a large, preheated frypan. Meanwhile quarter the carrots lengthways and chop them, and chop the onions.

Put the chicken aside and put the onions, carrots and rice in the pan. Cook over moderate heat until the rice is milky white. Stir in the garlic, chilli, cumin and oreganum, then cook 1 minute longer. Add the boiling water and salt, then pour the mixture into the baking or roasting pan. Stir the green vegetables into the rice, then arrange the chicken pieces on top, best side up.

Sprinkle the chicken with a little extra cumin and paprika. Bake uncovered for 50–60 minutes, until the rice is tender (with all the liquid absorbed) and the chicken juices run clear when it is pierced to the bone. Serve immediately.

Variations: Replace chicken drumsticks with a smallish chicken, quartered.

Replace the vegetables with celery, pumpkin, mushrooms, cauliflower, etc. Add long-cooking vegetables with the rice, and quicker-cooking vegetables later. Change the amounts and varieties of spices and herbs to taste.

Note: If the chicken does not cover all the rice in the baking pan, place foil over the uncovered rice (but not the chicken).

Country Captain Chicken

Country Captain Chicken

This is a traditional American recipe that is good when you have friends coming for a meal.

For 6 servings:
12 bone-in chicken pieces
1/2 cup plain flour
3–4 Tbsp oil
1 large onion, sliced
1 clove garlic, sliced
1 green pepper, sliced
1 Tbsp brown sugar
2 tsp curry powder
1 tsp salt
1/2 tsp thyme
1 can (425 g/15 oz) whole tomatoes
1/4 cup currants

Coat the chicken evenly with flour, then heat the oil in a frypan and brown over high heat, turning when necessary. Remove from the pan.

Lower the heat and add the onion, garlic and green pepper. Cook for 2–3 minutes without browning, then replace the chicken pieces in the pan, skin-side down. Add the sugar, curry powder, salt, thyme and roughly chopped tomatoes and juice. Cover and cook over a low heat for 15 minutes. Turn the chicken, add the currants, and cook for a further 10–15 minutes, or until the juices run clear.

Serve with bread rolls and a green salad.

Variation: For larger numbers, arrange browned chicken pieces best-side down in a roasting dish. Prepare the remaining ingredients in the pan then pour over the chicken. Cover with foil, bake at 180°C (350°F) for 30 minutes, then uncover, turn and cook 15 minutes longer. (If the mixture is refrigerated before baking, allow 15 minutes longer.)

Creamy Chicken and Mushroom Casserole

For 3–4 servings:
6–8 chicken pieces
1/4 cup plain flour
2–3 tsp butter or oil
1 clove garlic, sliced
about 12 button mushrooms
1 cup (250 ml/8 fl oz) white wine or water
1/2 tsp salt
1/4 tsp thyme
1/4 cup (60 ml/2 fl oz) cream
1 Tbsp finely chopped parsley

Turn the oven to 180°C (350°F). Pat the chicken pieces dry and toss in the flour in a plastic bag. Brown the floured chicken evenly in butter or oil in a hot frypan, then transfer to a casserole. Pour most of the remaining fat from the pan, then lightly brown the garlic and halved mushrooms. Add the wine or water and salt, scrape the pan to remove any drippings, and pour over the chicken pieces.

Sprinkle with thyme, cover tightly and bake for 1 hour. Test to see if the chicken is cooked through, and if necessary cook a little longer.

Just before serving add the cream, mix into the liquid, season carefully and spoon the sauce over the chicken. Sprinkle with parsley and serve immediately.

Spring Chicken and Vegetable Casserole

This tasty family dinner may be prepared ahead and left to turn itself on in an automatic oven, or assembled just before baking.

For 4 servings:
8 bone-in chicken pieces or 1 jointed chicken
1 Tbsp oil
4 small new potatoes
8–12 small carrots
12–20 button mushrooms
2 tsp chopped fresh tarragon or 1/2 tsp dried tarragon (or thyme)
1 cup (250 ml/8 fl oz) dry white wine
1 cup (250 ml/8 fl oz) chicken stock or 2 tsp chicken stock powder in 1 cup water
cornflour to thicken
1/2 cup finely chopped parsley

Turn the oven to 180°C (350°F). Heat the oil in a frypan and brown the chicken evenly on all sides. Transfer to a large casserole and arrange the unpeeled potatoes and whole carrots around it. Sauté the mushrooms lightly and add to the casserole.

Sprinkle with tarragon, add the wine and stock, and cover tightly. Bake until the potatoes and chicken are cooked (about 1 1/2 hours). Thicken the juices lightly with a paste made of cornflour and water.

Just before serving, stir chopped parsley through the liquid. Serve with green beans.

Easy Oriental Simmered Chicken

Here is a very popular and unusual recipe, originally from an American friend with Korean parents.

For 4–6 servings:
8–12 bone-in chicken pieces
1/2 cup (125 ml/4 fl oz) light soy sauce
1 Tbsp honey
1/4 cup sugar
1 cup (250 ml/8 fl oz) water
2 Tbsp grated root ginger
2–3 cloves garlic, crushed
4–8 star anise petals
2 Tbsp sherry
4 spring onions, chopped
cornflour to thicken

Put the chicken in a pot (preferably a stovetop-to-table variety) with all the ingredients except the spring onion and cornflour.

Bring to the boil then simmer on a very low heat for about an hour, or until the chicken is very tender. Add the spring onions and thicken the liquid as desired with cornflour mixed to a paste with cold water. Serve over rice with a green salad.

30-Minute Chicken Dinner

This recipe is good when you have limited energy and want a meal on the table within 30–40 minutes. I make it for two or three people in a large frypan on the cooktop, or for more people in a larger electric frypan.

For 2–3 servings:

4–6 boneless, skinless chicken thighs
plain flour to coat
2–3 tsp olive oil or butter
2 large cloves garlic, finely chopped
1 tsp ground cumin
2 tsp oreganum
1/2 tsp thyme
3/4–1 tsp salt
1/8–1/4 tsp chilli powder
1/2 cup (125 ml/4 fl oz) orange or other
 juice, or white wine
1/2 cup (125 ml/4 fl oz) water
6–9 small potatoes
8 small or 2 large carrots
1 stalk celery, sliced (optional)
1 cup chopped green beans (optional)
1/4 cup finely chopped parsley

Dry the chicken thighs with paper towels, then turn them in flour and pat it in well. Heat the oil or butter in a large frypan and brown the chicken pieces on both sides over fairly high heat. Reduce the heat, add the garlic, dried herbs and salt. Add chilli powder to suit your taste – the smaller amount gives a slight bite, the larger amount a definite hotness that is likely to be too much for young children. Add the juice and water, turn the chicken so all sides are seasoned, cover and leave to simmer while you prepare the vegetables.

Scrub the potatoes, leaving them whole if small, halving or quartering larger ones. Scrub the carrots and cut larger ones into pieces that will cook in the same time as the potatoes. Add to the chicken as soon as you have prepared them, cover again and cook for about 15 minutes. During this time, chop the celery and prepare the beans (or broccoli or zucchini). Add these to the pan and turn the chicken, potatoes and carrots at the same time. Add more water if the sauce has boiled down and thickened too much. Cook about 10 minutes longer, until all the vegetables are tender, and the chicken has cooked for about half an hour altogether. Thin or thicken the sauce again if necessary.

Sprinkle generously with chopped parsley and serve in shallow bowls, with warmed bread rolls alongside.

Herbed Chicken Casserole

This easy family-style casserole cooks without attention in the oven. Fresh herbs add colour and flavour to the sauce.

For 4 servings:

4 large or 8 small jointed chicken pieces
4 potatoes
4 small onions
4 carrots
2 cups chopped celery (optional)
2 tsp chicken stock powder or 1 tsp salt
1 1/2 cups (375 ml/12 fl oz) warm water
2–4 Tbsp chopped fresh herbs
cornflour to thicken
chopped parsley or other fresh herbs

Turn the oven to 180°C (350°F). Peel the potatoes, halving large ones and leaving small ones whole. Peel and quarter the onions; peel and halve the carrots lengthways. Place the vegetables in a large casserole.

Dissolve the stock powder or salt in the water and pour over the vegetables. Add chopped celery if desired. Arrange the chicken pieces, skin-side up, over the vegetables. Sprinkle with the fresh herbs and cover with foil or a tightly fitting lid.

Bake for 1 1/2 hours or until the chicken is cooked.

Drain the juices from the chicken and vegetables into a pot and thicken with a little cornflour mixed to a paste with cold water. Heat until the liquid thickens to gravy consistency. Serve in bowls, garnished with more chopped fresh herbs.

Variation: Replace 1 cup of water with white wine.

Bacon-Wrapped Chicken with Mushrooms

Mushrooms, bacon and chicken are a delicious combination!

For 2 servings:

4 boneless, skinless chicken thighs
4 rashers side bacon
1 clove garlic, finely chopped
about 10 mushroom cups, chopped
fresh herbs (thyme, basil, tarragon)
4 slices soft, white-crusted cheese
 (e.g. brie, camembert)
1/4–1/2 (60–125 ml/2–4 fl oz) cup red wine
pepper

Place each chicken thigh between 2 pieces of plastic and beat gently with a rolling pin until it is one and a half times as big as it was. Lie the flattened chicken skin-side down, fold a thigh in half, and see what length of bacon is needed to wrap around it and be secured with toothpicks. Cut the extra length from the 4 bacon slices, chop finely, and put in a pan big enough to hold the rolls of chicken. Add the garlic, half the mushrooms, and a little water if the mixture looks dry. Cook until the bacon is cooked and the mushroom soft.

Divide this mixture between the 4 chicken pieces, add fresh herbs, then top the stuffing with a slice of cheese. Fold the chicken over the stuffing, wrap the bacon round, and fasten with toothpicks. Brown in the pan used before. Add the rest of the mushrooms, the wine (or some lemon juice and water) and a grinding of pepper.

Cover and simmer for about 20 minutes, turning occasionally, until the chicken is cooked. Adjust the seasonings, and thicken very lightly with a little cornflour or boil down until it thickens slightly.

Remove the toothpicks and serve immediately, whole or sliced.

Variation: For a stronger mushroom flavour, replace mushroom cups with about half the number of brown flats.

If you keep a packet of dried porcini mushrooms in your freezer, bring out and soak a few, adding the soaking liquid and chopped rehydrated mushrooms to the fresh mushrooms.

Bacon-Wrapped Chicken with Mushrooms

Granny's Roasting Fowl Stew

Granny's Roasting Fowl Stew

Roasting fowls are 'retired layers' which are available in some large supermarkets, butchers' shops and Asian food stores. This stew has a very good chicken flavour, although the flesh is not as tender as that of young chicken.

For 4–5 servings:

1 small roasting fowl
2 cups (500 ml/16 fl oz) water
2–3 cloves garlic, chopped
2 onions
2 carrots
2 stalks celery
1 tsp salt
2 Tbsp cornflour
chopped parsley or other herbs

Remove the giblets, etc. from the chicken, then place it in a pot with the water and

garlic. Cover tightly, bring to the boil and simmer gently for 2–3 hours, adding the tops, bottoms and any peelings from the vegetables as they are prepared.

Slice the vegetables into small chunks and cook until barely tender in a small amount of water in another pot. Leave to cool.

Remove the bird from the pot, strain the cooking liquid and leave it for the fat to rise to the top. Cool the bird until it can be handled easily. Remove and discard the skin, then take the flesh from the bones, cutting it into even pieces.

Put the chicken and drained vegetables in a pot with enough of the cooled, skimmed cooking liquid to cover everything. Bring to the boil, add enough salt to bring out the flavour, then thicken with the cornflour mixed to a paste with water. Season carefully, add the parsley and serve with mashed potatoes, rice or pasta.

Nana's Chicken Casserole

The best container for this type of casserole is an oval one made of heavy metal which can be put directly on the burner to brown the bird, then put in the oven. If you do not have a heavy metal casserole, brown the chicken in a frypan then transfer it to an ovenproof casserole. It may take a little longer to cook in this, so adjust the cooking times accordingly.

For 4–6 servings:

1.5 kg (3 lb 5 oz) chicken
2 Tbsp oil
2 cloves garlic, sliced (optional)
½ cup (125 ml/4 fl oz) white wine or stock
½ cup (125 ml/4 fl oz) water or stock
pepper and paprika
2–3 rashers bacon
1 bunch fresh herbs*
6–8 small potatoes
6–8 small carrots

2 stalks celery, chopped
6–8 whole small onions
about 6 small wedges pumpkin
cornflour
chopped parsley

* If you have fresh herbs, tie together a selection with a string long enough to remove easily before the chicken is served; if not, use dried herbs.

Turn the oven to about 180°C (350°F). Pat the chicken dry, then place it breast up and push down firmly so the breast is flattened and will brown more evenly. Heat the oil in a large, heavy, metal casserole with a lid, then brown the breast side of the chicken. Turn and brown the back, adding the garlic just before the chicken is ready. Turn off the heat and add the liquids. Sprinkle with pepper and paprika, and put the bacon (whole or cut into short lengths) around the chicken. Add the herbs.

Cover the casserole, and bake in the oven for 30 minutes. Cut the vegetables into even sizes so they will cook evenly, and add at this point. Cover and cook for another 30–45 minutes, until the chicken is well cooked and the vegetables just cooked.

Skim any visible fat from the liquid around the chicken, and thicken the remaining liquid with cornflour paste, taking care not to break up the vegetables. Stir in a generous amount of parsley, and serve from the casserole.

Fast Orange Chicken   M

Mix and cook this in an oven bag for a no mess, no wash-up main course.

For 4 servings:
4 chicken legs
1 Tbsp brown sugar
1 Tbsp cornflour
1 Tbsp tomato ketchup
1–2 cloves garlic, sliced
1 tsp dark soy sauce
1/4 tsp grated nutmeg
1/2 cup (125 ml/4 fl oz) orange juice

Halve the chicken legs for easier mixing and serving. Put them in an oven bag with the brown sugar and cornflour, and shake to coat. Add the remaining ingredients in the order given, kneading the bag gently to mix. Secure the bag with a rubber band, leaving a finger-sized opening, and lay it flat on a dinner plate so the chicken is in one layer. Microwave on High (100%) power for 15 minutes, turning the bag over after 8 minutes. Leave to stand for 5 minutes, check the chicken is cooked, knead the bag again to mix, then serve.

Note: Although dark soy sauce gives a better colour, you can use light soy sauce.

Spiced Chicken and Tomatoes

Ring the changes with this easy but tasty chicken and tomato mixture. Serve it as it is, on rice or add pasta or beans. Whichever you choose, you will finish up with a trouble-free dinner for two.

For 2 servings:
about 500 g (1 lb 2 oz) bone-in chicken
 pieces (nibbles, drumsticks or thighs)
2 tsp oil
1 large onion, chopped
1 tsp minced garlic
1/2 tsp minced chilli or chilli powder
1–2 tsp ground cumin
1/2 tsp oreganum
1 can (425 g/15 oz) tomatoes in juice
1 cup (250 ml/8 fl oz) water
1/2–1 tsp salt
2 tsp brown or white sugar
1–2 cups sliced zucchini, green beans or
 broccoli
1 cup frozen or fresh corn kernels (optional)

Brown the chicken evenly in the oil in a non-stick pot or frypan. Add the onion and cook until lightly browned, then stir in the garlic, chilli, cumin and oreganum. Cook about 30 seconds longer.

Add the tomatoes, water, 1/2 tsp salt, and sugar. Cover and simmer for about 20 minutes, or until the chicken is almost cooked. Add vegetables of your choice and cook 10 minutes longer. If using fresh corn, remove the husks and silk, then cut the kernels off the cob. As the 'rafts' of kernels cook, they separate.

Use this basic recipe in one of the following three ways.

Spiced Chicken on Rice

Thicken the sauce slightly with a little cornflour mixed with water. Serve straight away or reheat when required. Spoon the mixture over plain rice in bowls, top with chopped spring onions or fresh coriander.

Spiced Chicken and Pasta

Add 2 extra cups water and the larger amount of salt to the recipe above. When the chicken and tomato mixture has simmered for 10 minutes, add 150 g large macaroni or other pasta. Stir at intervals so the pasta cooks evenly, and add vegetables 10 minutes after the pasta. Taste and adjust seasonings if necessary; add a little extra boiling water if the mixture seems dry. For the best flavour, serve soon after cooking, topped generously with chopped parsley.

Spiced Chicken with Beans

Add the tomatoes, etc. as above, using the smaller amount of salt. Simmer for 15 minutes, then add a can of kidney beans (and liquid) or a can of chilli beans. Add the green vegetables and/or corn only if desired. Simmer for 15 minutes longer. Check everything is cooked and adjust seasoning. Serve immediately or reheated, in bowls, alone or on rice. Top with sour cream and grated cheese if desired.

Microwaved Herbed Chicken   M

A whole chicken can be microwaved successfully in less than 30 minutes. It is best cooked in an oven bag, as it cooks more evenly and faster than if uncovered.

For 4 servings:
1 whole chicken, about 1 kg (2 lb 3 oz)
rind from 1/2 lemon
2 tsp butter
2 tsp Dijon mustard
2 tsp Worcestershire sauce
2 tsp dark soy sauce
2 tsp finely chopped fresh thyme or 1/2 tsp
 dried thyme
2 tsp lemon juice
1–2 tsp finely chopped fresh tarragon or
 1/2 tsp dried tarragon
2 Tbsp finely chopped parsley

Remove the giblets from the chicken, tuck the wing tips behind the neck, and wipe dry with a paper towel. Remove the rind from the lemon using a potato peeler.

Put the remaining ingredients in an unperforated oven bag and microwave on High (100%) power for about 1 minute, or until the butter has melted. Put the chicken in the bag, turning to coat all surfaces. Add the lemon rind, then close the bag with a rubber band, leaving a finger-sized hole so steam can escape. Estimate the cooking time, allowing 10 minutes per 500 g (1 lb).

Put the bagged chicken, breast-side down, in a dish with low sides and cook for 10 minutes on High (100%) power. Turn the chicken over and cook for the rest of the estimated time, then leave it to stand for at least 10 minutes, or up to 20 minutes, turning it at intervals. Test at the end of this time, piercing a thigh to check that the liquids run clear. If not, cook for 5 minutes longer.

Serve with the skimmed cooking liquids or thicken with 1 tsp cornflour mixed with 2 Tbsp water or white wine.

Chicken microwaves very successfully. Tough oven bags make excellent containers for whole birds or pieces, eliminating messy cleanups, allowing easy viewing during cooking. Because they enclose only a small amount of surrounding air, they ensure faster cooking and a more even heat spread. For best appearance, add some colourful ingredients to disguise the lack of natural browning in cooking.

ROASTING CHICKEN

Roasting Times for Chicken

- Read the instructions on the wrapper of the fresh or frozen bird carefully.
- Chicken cooks more quickly in a fan-bake oven than an oven without a fan.
- A bagged bird roasts more quickly than an uncovered bird.
- An unstuffed bird roasts more quickly than a stuffed bird.

Because ovens vary, allow a little longer than the estimated time. You can always put the chicken aside, covered with foil and a clean teatowel, if it cooks more quickly than you expect. If you have no instructions to go by, use the following times as a guide:

At 180–200°C (350–400°F):

Weight	Stuffed	Unstuffed
about 1 kg (2 lb 3 oz)	1¼–1½ hrs	1–1¼ hrs
about 1.5 kg (3 lb 5 oz)	1½–1¾ hrs	1¼–1½ hrs
about 2 kg (4 lb 7 oz)	2–2¼ hours	1½–2 hrs
about 2.5 kg (5 lb 8 oz)	2¼–2½ hrs	2–2¼ hrs

These times are for uncovered birds in a shallow pan, without an oven fan. The chicken is cooked when the juice from the thickest part of the drumstick runs clear, rather than pink, when it is pierced deeply with a sharp knife.

Roast Stuffed Chicken with Gravy

A stuffed roast chicken is often the centrepiece of a special-occasion family meal.

For 6 servings:
1 chicken (about 1.5 kg/3 lb 5 oz)
stuffing (see below)
1 Tbsp light soy sauce
1 Tbsp lemon juice
3 Tbsp plain flour
2 cups (500 ml/16 fl oz) chicken stock
2 Tbsp sherry (optional)

Thaw the chicken slowly if necessary, take off the wrapping, remove the giblets, neck, etc., and pat dry inside and out. (To make stock for the gravy, simmer the giblets and any trimmings in 3 cups (750 ml/24 fl oz) water with vegetable trimmings.) Pull away and discard any fat from around the large cavity.

Turn the oven to 180–200°C (350–400°F).

Just before cooking, pack the prepared stuffing into the main cavity of the bird. If there is some left over, pack it into the front cavity and/or wrap it in buttered foil to

bake beside the chicken for 30 minutes. Secure openings with toothpicks or sew with a heavy needle and thread. Place the bird breast-side up on baking paper or a non-stick liner.

Mix the soy sauce and lemon juice together and rub over all the outer surfaces. Bake the chicken for about 1½ hours, surrounded by roast vegetables if you like. (See notes above – a stuffed bird takes longer to cook than an unstuffed one.) Baste the chicken with the remaining soy and lemon while it cooks.

Transfer the bird (and roast vegetables) to a serving plate. Drain off most of the fat, leaving the pan drippings and about a tablespoon of fat. Stir the flour into this and heat until it bubbles and browns. Add about 2 cups of strained stock and/or vegetable cooking liquid, with a dash of sherry. Simmer for at least 5 minutes, then season and strain into a serving jug.

Traditional Herbed Stuffing

1 onion, finely chopped
1 stalk celery, very finely chopped
1–2 Tbsp butter
1 tsp grated orange or lemon rind (optional)
¼ cup chopped parsley
1 tsp chopped fresh thyme or ½ tsp dried thyme or other herbs
1 yolk, white, or whole egg
salt and pepper (optional)
4 slices stale bread, crumbled

Cook the onion and celery in a covered pan for 3–5 minutes without browning. Remove from the heat, add the remaining ingredients and mix well.

Variations: Replace the breadcrumbs with 1½ cups cooked brown or white rice, cooked orzo (rice-shaped pasta), or cooked couscous.

Cook ½–1 chopped apple with the onion and celery.

Replace half the breadcrumbs with chopped cooked mushrooms.

Add chopped ham, cooked bacon, etc.

Use minced chicken stuffing (see Easy Carve Christmas Chicken, p. 88).

Dried Apricot and Pinenut Stuffing

1 onion, finely chopped
1 Tbsp butter or oil
¼ cup currants
¼ cup pinenuts
3 thick slices bread, crumbled
¼–½ cup dried apricots, chopped and soaked
1 yolk, white or whole egg (optional)

Cook the onion in butter or oil until transparent, add the currants and pinenuts and cook until plumped and lightly

browned. Stir in crumbled bread and apricots. For a firmer stuffing, stir in a lightly beaten egg.

Roast Stuffed Chicken Legs

Make a small amount of stuffing. Separate the skin from the flesh on the outer side of a leg, pack the stuffing in between the flesh and skin, and secure with a toothpick.

Roast stuffing-side up, at 180°C (350°F), for 45 minutes or until the juices run clear when the chicken is pierced deeply.

Baked Foil-Wrapped Stuffing

Roast chickens cook more quickly and evenly when unstuffed. Prepare the stuffing and wrap it in buttered foil, forming a cylinder. Fold the edges over to seal. Bake for 45 minutes in the oven with the chicken, then slice and serve with it.

Stuffing Balls

These are always popular and make a roast, unstuffed chicken go further.

For 20–30 balls:
1 large onion, finely chopped
1 egg
about 500 g (1 lb 2 oz) sausage meat
1 tsp oreganum
1 tsp garlic salt
1 tsp celery salt
1 cup dry breadcrumbs
1 can (440 g/15 oz) creamed corn
¼ cup (60 ml/2 fl oz) tomato paste
1 cup (250 ml/8 fl oz) water

Turn the oven to 170°C (325°F). Thoroughly mix together all the ingredients except the tomato paste and water.

Mix the tomato paste and water in a shallow baking dish that will hold 20–30 little meat balls in one layer. Form the meat mixture into small balls and place them in the liquid in the dish. Bake, uncovered, for about 40 minutes, turning halfway through if you like. Serve with roast chicken.

30-Minute Roasted Chicken Legs with Summer Vegetables

A great recipe for those who love a roast chicken dinner but don't have the time to roast a whole bird with chunky vegetables.

For 2 servings:
fresh rosemary sprigs
2 chicken legs
2 peppers (red, green or yellow)
1 large red onion
2 small eggplants
2 Tbsp orange juice
2 Tbsp light soy sauce
2 Tbsp olive oil

Festive Chicken in Pastry

Turn the oven to 220°C (425°F). Spread the sprigs of rosemary over the bottom of a roasting dish lined with baking paper or a non-stick liner. Place the chicken on top, and put in the oven to start cooking while you prepare the vegetables.

Quarter the peppers and remove the seeds. Peel and quarter the onion, leaving the root end intact. Quarter the eggplants lengthways. Put the vegetables around the chicken.

Mix together the orange juice, soy sauce and oil. Brush the chicken and vegetables with this mixture once or twice as they cook.

Bake for 25–30 minutes, then test the chicken by piercing the thickest part with a skewer. It is cooked when the juices run clear, not pink.

Serve hot or at room temperature, with warmed bread rolls.

Variation: Add spices or other flavourings to the mixture brushed over the chicken, e.g. 1 tsp ground cumin plus 1 tsp finely chopped garlic.

Festive Chicken in Pastry

Prepare this recipe for a festive dinner for a small group. It looks special, but is not too complicated or time-consuming.

For 3–5 servings:
4 boneless, skinless chicken breasts
2 Tbsp olive oil
1 large onion
1 cup parsley sprigs
1 tsp chopped fresh sage
¼ cup pinenuts
6 spinach leaves
12–15 pieces semi-dried tomatoes or a jar of sliced red peppers, drained
400 g (14 oz) puff pastry
1 egg, beaten

Turn the oven to 220°C (425°F). Place each chicken breast between 2 sheets of plastic and beat gently with a rolling pin until it is twice its original width and length.

To make a green stuffing layer, chop the onion, parsley and sage finely and cook in the heated oil until the onion is soft and transparent. Add the pinenuts and brown very lightly. Wash and chop the spinach, cook briefly until wilted, then drain and stir into the onion mixture.

To make a red layer, use semi-dried tomatoes or sliced red peppers, soaking the chopped tomatoes in a little boiling water for 15 minutes.

Roll the pastry out until it is 45 cm (20 in) square. Place 2 of the flattened chicken breasts side by side in the centre, patting them into an oval shape. Spread the spinach mixture evenly on top, leaving the edges clear, then arrange the tomatoes or peppers on this. Place the remaining chicken on top. Pat into a neat shape.

Cut 4 diagonal lines from the corners of the pastry to the chicken. Fold the pastry over the chicken, trim away the excess, but leave enough to fold under the ends. Try to finish up with an oval package. Brush with beaten egg and bake for 45–60 minutes, until golden brown. Cover loosely if the top browns too quickly.

Allow to stand for 10 minutes before serving with seasonal vegetables.

Easy-Carve Christmas Chicken with Ham and Mushroom Stuffing

Easy-Carve Christmas Chicken

Although it takes just 15 minutes, a little patience and a sharp knife to bone a chicken, the resulting bird is very easy to carve and is a great talking point. If you don't feel that you can do it yourself, order one from your butcher or supermarket.

For 6–8 servings:
1 chicken, about 1.8 kg (4 lb)
400 g (14 oz) minced chicken or breast meat
1 egg
¼ cup (60 ml/2 fl oz) cream
2 Tbsp dry sherry
1 tsp salt
½ cup finely chopped fresh herbs
1 onion
2 tsp butter
2 Tbsp tomato paste

Turn the oven to 180°C (350°F). To bone the chicken, start by cutting from neck to tail down the centre back, cut around the rib cage, then remove all the bones except the leg and wing bones. Lie the chicken flat, skin-side down. (Boil the bones and scraps to make stock for gravy.)

In a food processor, purée together the minced chicken or chopped breast, the egg, cream, sherry and salt. Remove half the purée, add the herbs to the processor and mix thoroughly. Put the herb mixture in spoonfuls on the boned chicken.

Chop the onion, cook until tender in the butter, then add with the tomato paste to the remaining puréed chicken. Put this in spoonfuls between the herbed mixture. Bring the edges of the skin to the centre and sew or skewer together, closing all openings.

Roast the chicken breast-side up, in a roasting dish lined with baking paper or a non-stick liner, for 1½ hours, basting occasionally with oil, melted butter or pan juices.

To carve, cut off the legs and wings, then carve into 1 cm (½ in) slices, starting from the front of the bird. Serve hot with seasonal vegetables or cold with a salad.

Variations: Replace the tomato paste with 1 cup finely chopped, cooked mushrooms, or make double the quantity of herb stuffing.

Ham and Mushroom Stuffing

Here is another stuffing for a boned chicken. The different layers are clearly visible when the chicken is carved.

250 g (9 oz) chicken breast meat (2 large breasts) or minced chicken
1 egg, lightly beaten
¼ cup (60 ml/2 fl oz) cream
1 tsp salt
¼ cup chopped fresh herbs, e.g. parsley, thyme, dill, basil
1 or 2 slices ham
1 Tbsp olive or other oil
1 clove garlic, chopped
3–4 large mushrooms, chopped
½ cup cooked rice or 1 cup fresh breadcrumbs

Chop the chicken breasts into smaller pieces and put them or the minced chicken in the food processor with two-thirds of the beaten egg, the cream, salt and coarsely chopped herbs. Process until the ingredients are puréed. Spread the herbed chicken mixture evenly over the fleshy chicken meat. On top of this put the sliced ham, with the rind removed.

Sauté the garlic and mushrooms in the oil until almost cooked, then remove from the heat and stir in the rice or breadcrumbs and the remaining egg. Spread this mixture over the ham.

Roast Glazed Duckling

Domestic ducklings, bred for meat, are consistently tender at all times of the year.

Ducks have solid, heavy frames, and should not be compared with chickens in terms of servings per bird. A 2 kg (4 lb 7 oz) duckling yields 3–4 servings.

Thaw duckling completely and pat dry, inside and out. Cut off the wings at the 'elbow' joint, and while the duckling roasts simmer these with the neck (from the body cavity) in a covered pot with 4 cups (1 litre/32 fl oz) of water, vegetable trimmings and seasonings, to make stock for gravy.

Prick the duckling all over so oil from the skin will escape during cooking. Rub the skin with lemon juice. If desired, place a sliced lemon or orange, 2–3 sliced garlic cloves and fresh herbs in the body cavity. Place the duckling breast-side up, uncovered, on a rack over a roasting pan containing 2 cups (500 ml/16 fl oz) of water. Roast near the bottom of the oven at 180°C (350°F) for 1¾–2 hours. Lower the heat if the skin browns too much.

Twenty minutes before the end of the cooking time, tilt the duckling, pour the juices from the body cavity into the pan, and return the duckling to the oven in another baking dish. Pour away and discard nearly all the oil from the pan, leaving the drippings. To make gravy, brown 2–3 Tbsp flour in the drippings, add the strained duck stock and simmer for about 15 minutes, adjusting seasonings and thinning with wine if desired.

To glaze the duckling, brush it several times during the last 20 minutes of cooking with one of the glazes below. Just before serving, add leftover glaze and drippings to gravy.

To serve roast duckling, divide it into 4 more or less equal portions. Cut down the central breastbone and lift the breast meat, with the remaining wing bone attached, away from the bone. Bend the leg down and out and lift or cut it away from the carcass. Serve portions like this, with gravy, or carve into slices.

Oriental Glaze

Combine ¼ cup sherry, 2 Tbsp light soy sauce and ½ tsp five-spice powder. Two minutes before the end of cooking, brush with 1 Tbsp warmed honey.

Gingered Orange Glaze

Combine ¼ cup orange juice, 2 Tbsp light soy sauce, 1 tsp each grated root ginger and orange rind. Two minutes before the end of cooking, brush with 1 Tbsp warmed honey.

Chilli Marmalade Glaze

Heat 2 Tbsp each marmalade and sweet Thai chilli sauce with 1 tsp light soy sauce until blended.

Apricot Glaze

Mix 2 Tbsp apricot jam with 1 tsp each orange juice, rind and light soy sauce.

Bagged Roast Duckling

Thaw, dry and prick the duckling skin as in the previous recipe. Turn the oven to 180°C (350°F).

Rub the duckling all over with lemon juice or a mixture of 1 Tbsp each lemon juice and light soy sauce and 1 tsp powdered ginger. Place in a roasting bag and close with a twist tie, leaving a finger-sized hole for the steam to escape.

Stand the bag in a roasting pan so the duckling is breast-side up, and roast for 1¾ hours. Carefully lift the bag from the pan, snip a corner and pour off all the liquid. Discard the oil and save the juices. Cut the bag away from the duckling.

To make gravy, brown 2–3 Tbsp flour in the drippings, add duck stock, wine and a little soy sauce to darken it if necessary.

Stuffing for Ducklings

Although it is not traditional to stuff ducklings, you may like to serve a fruity stuffing with your roast or bagged duckling. Stuff the body cavity, or bake the stuffing separately.

½ cup finely chopped dried apricots
¼ cup (60 ml/2 fl oz) orange juice
1 onion, finely chopped
1 Tbsp butter
¼ cup currants (optional)
2 cups crumbled stale bread
¼ cup finely chopped fresh herbs
1 egg, beaten

Cook the dried apricots in the orange juice until the juice is absorbed. Cook the onion in the butter until transparent. Add currants if you like, and heat through. Combine the apricot and onion mixtures with the breadcrumbs, herbs and beaten egg.

Place in a loaf tin that has been buttered or lined with baking paper. Cover loosely and bake beside the duck for 30–45 minutes. Cut in slices or spoon out and serve with the duckling.

Wild Duck

I like wild duck braised at a low heat until it is tender, then reheated. This recipe is delicious served with braised red cabbage, mushrooms and mashed potatoes.

For 4 servings:
2 wild ducks
plain flour for coating
2 Tbsp oil
2 cloves garlic, chopped
1–2 onions, sliced
2 cups (500 ml/16 fl oz) apple and orange juice
1 tsp fresh or ½ tsp dried thyme (or other herbs)
1 tsp salt
1 Tbsp redcurrant jelly or jam
sherry or port
extra stock or water
pepper
1–2 tsp cornflour
1–2 tsp grated orange rind (optional)

Turn the oven to 180°C (350°F). Coat the ducks with flour and brown on each side in oil. Add the garlic and onions and cook until lightly browned. Pour off the surplus fat, and add apple and orange juice, herbs according to taste, and salt. Cover and cook in the oven, basting occasionally, until the ducks are tender. Place on a clean dish to cool.

Add the redcurrant or other red jelly to the remaining liquid and stir in the sherry or port. Bring to the boil then press through a sieve, adding extra water or stock if there is less than 1½ cups. Taste and season carefully, adding extra salt, pepper or jelly if necessary. Thicken slightly with cornflour paste if desired.

Cut the cooled ducks down the middle, then lift away all the bones except the main leg and wing. Lay the halved ducks, cut-side down, in a shallow dish and pour over the sauce. When required (up to 2 days later), cover and place in the oven just long enough for the meat to heat through.

Pork, Ham and Bacon

There is something really special about pork, especially now that so many lean cuts are available. Some of my favourite cuts, like pickled pork, require long, slow cooking, but others, like schnitzels, take only minutes to cook, and seem just as popular. I regard ham as a treat and a convenience food 'par excellence', and I would hate to live without bacon! I hope that you will try, and enjoy, many of my pork recipes.

Barbecued Pork Ribs

It's no use planning a slow-cooking pork rib recipe for a barbecue, because people who are addicted to them just can't wait that long! Although this recipe calls for preliminary work in the kitchen, it is worth it.

For 4 servings:
1–1.5 kg (2 lb 3 oz–3 lb 5 oz) meaty pork ribs
1 cup (250 ml/8 fl oz) water
sprinkling of ground cumin

Sauce
1 onion
2 cloves garlic
1 Tbsp oil
1 tsp ground cumin
1/2 tsp ground coriander seed
1/2 cup (125 ml/4 fl oz) tomato sauce
2 Tbsp Worcestershire sauce
2 Tbsp soft brown sugar
1 Tbsp wine or cider vinegar
1 Tbsp tomato concentrate
1/2 tsp cornflour
1/2 cup (125 ml/4 fl oz) water
about 1/4 tsp chilli powder

Cut the ribs into sections of 3–4 bones each, and place in a large pot with the water and cumin. Cover tightly and simmer for 1 1/2 hours, or until the meat is very tender.

OR Put ribs, cumin and water in a roasting pan, cover tightly with foil, then bake at 150°C (300°F) for 2–3 hours or until tender.

While the pork cooks, make the sauce. Put the first 5 ingredients into a food processor, chop very finely, transfer to a pan and cook over moderate heat for about 5 minutes. Add the remaining ingredients to the pan and simmer for about 15 minutes.

When required, place the rib sections on the barbecue, heat on each side until they sizzle, then brush with the warm sauce and heat again on both sides.

Serve with crusty bread, warmed on the barbecue, or with corn cobs. Coleslaw is also good.

Barbecued Pork Ribs

Pineapple Pork Ribs

This is a recipe I learnt in Chinatown, San Francisco. It fast became a family favourite.

For 4 servings:
1.5 kg (3 lb 5 oz) meaty pork ribs
2 cups (500 ml/16 fl oz) water
1 can (350–450 g/12 oz–1 lb) pineapple pieces in syrup
3 Tbsp vinegar
3 Tbsp brown sugar
1/4 tsp salt
2 onions, chopped
1 green pepper, chopped
1–2 Tbsp cornflour

If possible, have your butcher chop the ribs into 5 cm (2 in) lengths. Cut them into sections of 3–4 bones, brown as evenly as possible over moderate heat in a heavy frypan, then add the water. Cover tightly and simmer over low heat until the meat lifts off the bones easily, 1–2 hours. When the meat is tender add the pineapple syrup, vinegar, sugar and salt. (Cover and leave at this stage if desired.) Reheat, adding the onion, pepper and pineapple pieces. Boil the syrup down so it is concentrated, then season to taste. Thicken with a little cornflour if necessary, and serve on rice.

Herbed Pork Chops

I have tried a lot of pork chop recipes, but I keep returning to my favourite, which is so simple it is scarcely a recipe.

Snip the edges of pork chops so they will not curl up during cooking. Brown both sides of the chops at a high temperature in an electric frypan or any large pan. Add about 1/4 cup (60 ml/2 fl oz) water for each chop, sprinkle with a little dried or chopped fresh thyme, lower the heat, cover the pan tightly and simmer gently for 45 minutes. Add extra water occasionally if it evaporates during cooking.

After 40 minutes check that there is about 2 Tbsp stock to each chop. Add a little extra water, or raise the heat to concentrate the cooking liquid, if necessary. Season with freshly ground black pepper, chopped parsley (and other fresh herbs), and sprinkle with a little seasoned salt. Turn the chops so both sides are seasoned, leave them to stand in the pan for 2–3 minutes, then serve with mashed potatoes and fresh asparagus or broccoli.

Pork Chops with Corn Topping

This recipe provides a change from the usual methods of cooking pork chops. I find it good because it needs no last-minute attention, and is useful when friends come to dinner.

I like to use shoulder or wide rib chops, since the meat in these stays moister during cooking.

For 4 servings:
4 pork rib or shoulder chops, about 1 cm (1/2 in) thick
1/2 cup (125 ml/4 fl oz) boiling water
1 cup soft breadcrumbs
3/4 cup creamed corn
1–2 Tbsp onion pulp or juice
1 Tbsp finely chopped celery or green pepper
1/2 tsp salt
1/2 tsp dry mustard
1/4 tsp pepper

Turn the oven to 180°C (350°F). Brown the chops in a dry frypan for 5–10 minutes, until golden brown on both sides. Place them in an ovenware dish (preferably just big enough to hold the chops in one layer).

Pour any fat from the frypan, pour the boiling water into the hot pan, and pour this liquid around the chops, adding more if necessary to nearly cover the chops.

Make the breadcrumbs from stale bread, and combine with the remaining ingredients. (Scrape the cut surface of a halved onion to get onion juice or pulp.) Spread this mixture over the chops so that all the lean portion is covered but the fatty edge is uncovered. Bake uncovered for 1 1/4–1 1/2 hours (1–1 1/4 hours if the chops are thinner).

Serve with baked or mashed potatoes, carrots or pumpkin, and brussels sprouts, broccoli, pan-cooked cabbage or peas.

Pork and Apple Casserole

It is not always necessary to brown stews and casseroles in added butter or oil if the liquid in which the meat simmers is well-flavoured. Fruit and vegetables that simmer with the meat make servings look larger, as well as adding to the favour.

For 4–6 servings:
500 g (1 lb 2 oz) cubed pork
1 large apple, cubed
1 large onion, chopped
2 celery stalks, sliced
2 Tbsp Worcestershire sauce
3 Tbsp tomato sauce
1 Tbsp brown sugar
3/4 tsp salt
1/2 tsp thyme
1 tsp sage
1 1/2 cups (375 ml/12 fl oz) water
cornflour to thicken
chopped parsley

Turn the oven to 150°C (300°F). Put all the ingredients except the cornflour and parsley in a casserole dish with a well-fitting lid. Place in the oven, below the middle, and cook for 1 1/2 hours, stirring once. When the meat is tender, thicken with cornflour paste and sprinkle with chopped parsley. Serve on pasta or with mashed potatoes, with pan-cooked cabbage and carrots.

Peter's Pork Cassoulet

This recipe is a speciality of my husband's. To my delight, he makes it several times each winter, refrigerating or freezing part of it, or inviting friends to share it with us.

A warming, delicious and satisfying cold-weather meal, it simmers in the oven, virtually untended, filling the house with wonderful aromas! It does, however, require some thought and organisation to get it to this stage, but I think you will agree the end result justifies this!

For 6–8 servings:
2 cups dried haricot beans
2–3 rashers bacon, chopped
2–3 large onions, sliced
1–2 tsp finely chopped garlic
olive oil if required
about 800 g (1 lb 12 oz) pork slices or
*   fingers*
2 cups (500 ml/16 fl oz) chicken stock
2 Tbsp tomato paste
2 cans (each 400 g/14 oz) tomatoes in
*   juice*
2–3 carrots
1 tsp each thyme and sage
3–4 bayleaves
3–4 sprigs rosemary, about 10 cm (4 in)
*   long, if available*

Haricot beans are small white beans – the same type as used in canned baked beans. Pick them over, removing and discarding any discoloured beans. Pour 8 cups (2 litres/64 fl oz) boiling water onto the beans in a large pot, and leave them to stand in a warm place for 2 hours or longer. Drain off and discard the soaking water, add 4 cups (1 litre/32 fl oz) fresh hot water (but don't add any salt) and simmer until tender, about an hour. (If you have a pressure cooker, cook the unsoaked beans in 8 cups water for 40 minutes.)

Meanwhile, turn the oven to 150°C (300°F). Brown the bacon, onions and garlic over moderate heat, adding a little olive oil if the mixture is dry. Put this mixture aside.

Brown the pork in the same way, then cut in short lengths and put in a large casserole with the onion and bacon mixture, drained beans, stock, tomato paste, tomatoes and juice, and the carrots cut in 2–3 cm (about 1 in) slices. Add the bayleaves and rosemary.

Cover and bake for 3 hours, stirring occasionally, until the pork and carrots are tender and the liquid has thickened slightly. (It usually looks very runny until the last 15 minutes of cooking, when it seems to thicken up quickly.)

Season to taste and serve in bowls or on dinner plates, alone, with bread and a side salad, or with mashed potato and broccoli or brussels sprouts.

Refrigerate up to 4 or 5 days, or freeze leftovers in meal-sized amounts for up to 2 months.

Spicy Pork on Noodles

Ready in just half an hour, this recipe is always popular.

For 4 servings:
2 onions, chopped
2 cloves garlic, chopped (optional)
1–2 tsp oil
500 g (1 lb 2 oz) minced pork
1 can (425 g/15 oz) Italian seasoned
*   tomatoes*
1/2 cup (125 ml/4 fl oz) water, white wine
*   or stock*
pinch of cayenne or chilli powder
2–3 Tbsp sour cream
1–2 tsp cornflour
300 g (10 oz) zucchini

Brown the onion and garlic in as little oil as necessary, add the minced pork and stir over high heat, then stir in the tomatoes, liquid and cayenne or chilli powder. Cover and simmer for about 20 minutes, then add the sour cream, bring to the boil, and thicken with a little cornflour mixed to a thin paste with cold water.

Serve on fettuccine, spaghetti or other noodles. Cut the zucchini into matchsticks and cook with the pasta during its last few minutes of cooking, or add sliced zucchini to the mince mixture 5 minutes before adding the sour cream.

Simmered Pork with Apricots

This mixture has a lovely flavour and texture and needs no browning.

For 4 servings:
500–600 g (1 lb 2 oz–1 lb 5oz) cubed pork
2 onions, chopped
2 cloves garlic, chopped (optional)
1 stalk celery or 1 green pepper, chopped
1 cup (250 ml/8 fl oz) water
1 Tbsp soy sauce
1 Tbsp Worcestershire sauce
1/4 cup chopped dried apricots
1 Tbsp brown sugar
about 1 Tbsp cornflour

Put the first 7 ingredients in a medium-sized pot, cover and simmer for 30 minutes. Add the dried apricots and simmer for about 15 minutes longer, or until the pork is tender. Do not overcook.

Stir in the sugar and thicken with cornflour mixed to a thin paste with water. Serve with rice, noodles or mashed potatoes, beans or broccoli, and carrots.

Porky Parcels

This minced pork recipe, served in lettuce leaf packages, makes a great summer outdoors meal. If lettuce packages are not for you, put the mixture on little pancakes, baked potato halves, split toasted buns, pita breads or burritos.

For 4 servings:
500 g (1 lb 2 oz) minced pork
1 large onion, finely chopped
2 cloves garlic, finely chopped
2 Tbsp tomato sauce
1 Tbsp dark soy sauce
1 Tbsp wine or cider vinegar
1/2–1 tsp five-spice powder
about 1 tsp hot pepper sauce
1/2 cup (125 ml/4 fl oz) water
2 tsp cornflour
1 tsp chicken stock powder
1/2 cup (125 ml/4 fl oz) water
salt
3 or 4 spring onions, chopped
chopped fresh coriander (optional)

Heat a large, non-stick frypan, and add the pork and onion. Stir over high heat, breaking the meat into small pieces and browning the onion in the pork fat. Add the garlic and stir for about a minute before adding the next 5 ingredients.

Add the first measure of water, cover, and simmer for 5–10 minutes to cook the meat and onion. Mix the cornflour and stock powder into the second measure of water and stir into the mixture. Cook a few minutes longer then taste and add salt and more of any of the flavourings as necessary. Heat, uncovered, until the mixture is dry enough to spoon into a lettuce leaf without dripping.

Serve immediately, or reheat when required. Just before serving, stir in the chopped spring onion and coriander, or serve these separately in small bowls.

To serve lettuce packages:
Wash and remove the leaves from any loose-leafed lettuce. Serve the lettuce leaves on a large, flat plate or shallow bowl, beside the hot meat.

Each diner should take a lettuce leaf, put a dessertspoon of pork in the centre of it, fold the stem end over the meat, the sides over this, then roll up the rest of the leaf. Hold the roll firmly while eating it, with a plate or paper serviette underneath, to catch dribbles!

Kirsten's Spiced Pork

This recipe is one my daughter makes regularly for her family. It is interestingly spiced but contains no 'hot' ingredients. You can add chilli for hotness, but I like it just the way it is.

For 4–6 servings:
2 Tbsp oil
2 tsp mustard seeds
2 large onions, coarsely chopped
2 cloves garlic, chopped
1 Tbsp grated fresh root ginger
2 tsp ground coriander seed
2 tsp ground cumin
2 tsp ground turmeric
1 tsp cinnamon
1 tsp ground cardamom
½ tsp ground cloves
about 750 g (1 lb 10 oz) cubed pork
1 cup (250 ml/8 fl oz) chicken stock
500–600 g (about 1¼ lb) potatoes or kumara
about 2 tsp cornflour
1 Tbsp coconut cream powder or 2–4 Tbsp coconut cream
1 Tbsp lemon juice

Heat the oil and mustard seeds in a large pot, then add the onion, garlic and ginger.

Add the rest of the spices, keeping the heat high so the spices and onion brown slightly. Add the pork and stir over high heat until it loses its raw appearance. Add the stock, and simmer for 45 minutes.

Scrub the potatoes or peel the kumara, cut in cubes about the same size as the meat, and add to the pot. Simmer gently for 45 minutes longer, until the pork and vegetables are tender. Add the cornflour mixed to a paste with the coconut cream powder and a little cold water, or with coconut cream. Add the lemon juice and season with pepper, salt and a little sugar if necessary.

Serve with rice, poppadoms and several vegetable side dishes.

Pork Stir-Fry Salad

This mixture is a cross between a stir-fry and a salad. It contains an interesting mixture of flavours and textures, and cooks very quickly in a large pan or wok. It is an excellent meal for a warm summer's evening.

For 4 servings:
2 Tbsp olive or canola oil
1–2 Tbsp chopped lemon grass stem (see below)
1 tsp finely chopped garlic
1 red onion, finely sliced
500 g (1 lb 2 oz) minced pork
2 tsp freshly ground coriander seed
½ cup chopped roasted peanuts
2 Tbsp lime or lemon juice
1 Tbsp fish sauce
2 tsp sesame oil
¼ cup (60 ml/2 fl oz) Thai sweet chilli sauce
1 Tbsp cornflour
1 Tbsp water
about 100 g (3–4 oz) bean sprouts
1–2 Tbsp chopped fresh coriander
Chinese or chicken noodles
cabbage (optional)

Assemble all the ingredients before you start cooking. Use bottled lemon grass, garlic, lime juice and coriander leaves if these are not available fresh.

Before you start to cook the pork, cook enough thin Chinese noodles for 4 servings (these are like 2-minute noodles, without the seasonings), or cook 2 packets of 2-minute chicken noodles, adding generous amounts of finely shredded cabbage after 1 minute, and adding seasoning as usual. Keep the noodles and cabbage warm while the pork mixture cooks.

Heat the oil in a wok or large frypan, add the lemon grass, garlic and onion, and stir-fry for about 30 seconds. Add room-temperature minced pork and the ground coriander, and stir-fry for 3–4 minutes over very high heat until the pork is cooked. Add the chopped nuts, juice, fish sauce, and sesame oil.

Mix the chilli sauce and cornflour with the water and stir through the pork mixture. Heat until the liquid thickens. Just before serving, stir the bean sprouts and fresh coriander through the mixture.

Serve over or stir through the cooked noodles, or the noodle cabbage mixture, and serve immediately.

Variations: Add diagonally sliced snow peas or young beans, strips of spring onion, or julienne strips of celery after thickening the pork.

Kirsten's Spiced Pork

East-West Pork and Vegetables

For 4–5 servings:
2 onions, finely chopped
2 cloves garlic, finely chopped
2–3 tsp oil
600 g (1 lb 5 oz) lean minced pork
3 Tbsp light soy sauce
3 Tbsp sherry
1 Tbsp brown sugar
2 Tbsp sweet chilli sauce or a few drops
  of hot pepper sauce
1 cup (250 ml/8 fl oz) water
2 stalks celery
4 carrots
1 red pepper
1 green pepper
200 g (7 oz) green beans or 1 can
  (425 g/15 oz) baby corn, drained
about 200 g (7 oz) cauliflower
about 200 g (7 oz) cabbage
1 Tbsp cornflour
1/4 cup (60 ml/2 fl oz) water

Lightly brown the onions and garlic in the oil, then raise the heat and add the mince. Stir, without breaking up the lumps of meat too much, until the meat has lost its raw look, then add the next 5 ingredients.

Cover the pan, chop the celery and carrots diagonally, stir them into the meat mixture and cover the pan again. While these cook over fairly high heat, slice the peppers and beans (or drain the corn). Toss them through the mixture, cover and cook over fairly high heat.

Break the cauliflower into florets and chop the cabbage coarsely. By this time, all the vegetables in the pan should be half cooked. Stir the cauliflower and cabbage into the mixture, cover, and cook

about 5 minutes longer, until the cabbage is tender but still bright green.

Mix the cornflour with the water and stir in about half of it. Add more if necessary, but just enough to glaze the vegetables. Serve with noodles, or on brown or white rice.

Variations: Replace the pork with lean minced beef.

Vary the vegetables, adding them at appropriate times so they are all tender-crisp when the dish is served.

Sweet and Sour Meatballs

This is an interesting pork meal, colourful as well as tasty, which can be put together quickly after work.

For 2 servings:
1 slice toast-thickness bread
1 large onion
1 Tbsp oil
3 pineapple rings
1/2 tsp oreganum
1 tsp chicken stock powder
1 tsp dark soy sauce
250 g (9 oz) minced pork
1/2 red pepper
1/2 green pepper
1/4 cup (60 ml/2 fl oz) pineapple juice
3 Tbsp tomato sauce
2 tsp cornflour

Crumb the bread in a food processor, add about a third of the onion, and chop the rest into 1 cm (1/2 in) pieces and cook gently in the oil in a non-stick frypan.

Chop the pineapple into pieces about the size of the onion in the pan. Put the equivalent of half a ring in the food processor with the bread and onion, and chop finely. Add the oreganum, half the

stock powder, the soy sauce and pork, and process just enough to mix evenly.

Form into 16 small balls and arrange in a ring around the edge of a flat plate. Microwave, uncovered, on High (100%) power for 4–5 minutes, or until evenly firm. Alternatively, cook the meatballs in a little extra oil in a large frypan for about 10 minutes.

Cut the red and green peppers into chunks and add to the partly cooked onion in the pan. Add the remaining pineapple and stir over moderate heat. Add the juice, remaining stock powder and tomato sauce. Taste and add more of anything you think necessary. Mix the cornflour to a paste with a little water, and stir enough into the sauce to thicken it slightly.

Tip the cooked meatballs and any liquid into the sauce. Stir to coat. To serve, spoon the mixture over noodles.

Note: If you do not have a food processor, run the bread under the tap, squeeze out all the liquid, and break it into little bits. Chop everything else as finely as you can.

Variation: Try the same recipe with minced beef.

Microwaved Pork and Pineapple   M

This is another flavoursome, colourful combination quickly prepared and cooked.

For 4 servings:
500 g (1 lb 2 oz) pork schnitzel
2 cloves garlic, chopped
2 tsp grated root ginger
2 Tbsp oil
2 onions, sliced
2 stalks celery, sliced
1–2 peppers, sliced (optional)
1 can (225 g/8 oz) pineapple pieces
2 Tbsp cornflour
1 Tbsp brown sugar
2 Tbsp light soy sauce
1 tsp beef stock powder or 1/2 tsp salt

Trim the schnitzel of any fat and gristle, and cut into slices. Combine the pork, garlic, ginger and half the oil in a small bowl and put aside.

Combine the remaining oil, the onion, celery and peppers in a casserole dish, cover and microwave on High (100%) power for 5 minutes. Stir in the meat mixture and the drained pineapple (reserve the juice). Cover and cook for 4 minutes, or until the pork is no longer pink.

Mix together the cornflour, sugar, sauce, stock or salt and the juice from the pineapple made up to 1 cup with water or white wine. Heat until the sauce thickens and boils, stirring after 1 minute. Stir into the casserole dish and heat until the sauce bubbles, taking care not to overcook. Serve on rice or noodles.

East-West Pork and Vegetables

Pork Medallions, Peanutty and Plain

These are delicious if not overcooked.

For 4 servings:
4 pork medallions (about 500 g/1 lb)
2 tsp Kikkoman soy sauce
1 tsp sesame oil
about 1/4 tsp hot pepper sauce
1 clove garlic, crushed
1 egg yolk or 1/2 egg (optional)
about 1/4 cup roasted peanuts, finely chopped (optional)
2 tsp olive oil
1 tsp sesame oil

Place the pork medallions between 2 plastic bags and bang with a rolling pin to flatten to half their original thickness. Place them in a plastic bag with the next 4 ingredients, turn to mix, and leave to stand for at least 5 minutes.

Peanutty Pork Medallions

Just before cooking add an egg yolk (or half a lightly beaten egg) to the pork in the marinade. Turn to coat evenly. Coat with the peanuts, and cook in the mixture of olive and sesame oils for about 2 minutes per side over moderate-high heat. Take care not to overcook.

Plain Pork Medallions

Cook as above without the coating of egg and nuts. Serve immediately with new potatoes and fresh asparagus.

Peachy Pork Schnitzels

Pork schnitzels are very tender and moist, as long as you don't overcook them.

For 2 servings:
2 Tbsp sherry
2 tsp dark soy sauce
1 clove garlic, crushed
a grating of fresh nutmeg
200 g (7 oz) pork schnitzels
about 1/4 cup canned peach segments
2 tsp butter

Mix the sherry, soy sauce, garlic and nutmeg together in a large, shallow dish.

Trim any small pieces of connecting tissue and fat from the pork and flatten the schnitzels evenly with a meat hammer. Turn in the sherry mixture and leave to stand for at least 5 minutes, while you slice the peach segments into thinner pieces.

Heat a frypan until very hot, add the butter then, before it burns, add the schnitzels. Cook for 15–20 seconds per side, until lightly browned, then remove from the pan and add the peaches and any remaining marinade to the pan drippings. Return the schnitzels to the pan and turn to coat with the peach mixture. Heat through and serve.

Beans or broccoli and kumara or pumpkin go well with this.

Pork Stir-Fry

Oriental Pork Schnitzels

These delicious marinated schnitzels must be cooked quickly on a very hot, heavy frypan or griddle, otherwise they overcook and toughen. Serve them with rice and vegetables, slice them and pile them in a split bun or pita bread, or toss them with salad vegetables.

For 4 servings:
500 g (1 lb 2 oz) pork schnitzel
2 Tbsp dark soy sauce
1 Tbsp honey
1 Tbsp sesame oil
1 Tbsp lemon juice
2–3 cloves garlic, crushed

Cut the schnitzels into pieces about 4 x 10 cm (1 3/4 x 4 in). Mix the remaining ingredients together in an unpunctured plastic bag, warming it to dissolve the honey if necessary. Add the schnitzels, mix gently, squeeze out the air and fasten the bag. Leave to stand for at least 10 minutes, then cook the drained schnitzels for a few seconds on each side in a VERY hot frypan. The pork should just have lost its pinkness, but must not dry out.

Serve as suggested above. To serve with salad vegetables, slice the warm schnitzels onto vegetables, then toss with a little lemon juice and sesame oil.

Pork Stir-Fry

You don't need to have special equipment for stir-frying. You can do almost as good a job with a large frypan as with a wok.

For 2–3 servings:
250 g (9 oz) pork schnitzels
2 tsp raw or brown sugar
1 tsp cornflour
1 Tbsp dark soy sauce

1 Tbsp sherry
1 Tbsp oil
1–2 cloves garlic
2 slices fresh ginger, cut in slivers
2 Tbsp oil
1 large onion, sliced
4 cups prepared vegetables*
1/4–1/2 cup (60–125 ml/2–4 fl oz) water
1 tsp chicken stock powder
1 tsp sugar
1 tsp cornflour

* Choose fast-cooking vegetables, e.g. red and green peppers, broccoli or spinach, celery, mushrooms, cauliflower, snow peas, bean or snowpea sprouts and green and yellow zucchini. Slice thinly.

Cut the schnitzel thinly across the grain and put in a bowl with the next 7 ingredients. Leave to stand as long as possible, but at least 5 minutes.

Heat 1 Tbsp of the second measure of oil in a wok or large frypan, add the onion and prepared vegetables and cook over high heat until tender but crisp, stirring continuously. Alternatively, cook the vegetables with the oil in a covered microwave dish on High (100%) power for 3–4 minutes, while cooking the meat in the wok, as below.

When the vegetables are tender-crisp remove them from the wok and cover while cooking the meat. Add the other Tbsp of oil to the wok and stir-fry the meat and the marinade until the meat has browned slightly and lost its pinkness, taking care not to overcook it. Mix together the water, stock, sugar and cornflour and add to the meat with the cooked vegetables. Heat just until the meat and vegetables are coated and the sauce has thickened. Serve on rice or noodles.

Barbecued Pork Kebabs

Use lean cubed pork for these kebabs, or choose foreloin or medallion pork steaks, and cut into cubes.

For 4–6 servings:

Kebabs
750 g (1 lb 10 oz) lean pork
3–4 pineapple rings (optional)
1 red pepper (optional)
1 green pepper (optional)

Marinade
1 Tbsp dark soy sauce
1 rounded Tbsp honey
1 Tbsp sherry
1 Tbsp sesame oil
1 tsp grated fresh ginger
1 tsp hot pepper sauce
2 cloves garlic, crushed

Cut the pork into 2 cm (3/4 in) cubes and place in an unpunctured plastic bag. Add the marinade ingredients, knead gently to mix, squeeze out all the air, fasten with a rubber band and leave to stand at room temperature for at least an hour, or in the refrigerator overnight.

Divide the cubes into 12 even groups and thread on 12 soaked bamboo skewers, alone or with cubes of pineapple and squares of blanched red and green pepper between them. Barbecue over a high heat, turning after 2 minutes, brushing with marinade before and after turning.

The kebabs are cooked as soon as the pork feels firm, and is no longer pink in the centre. Test after 4 minutes.

Peanutty Pork Kebabs

For 4 servings:
1/2 cup peanut butter
2 Tbsp light soy sauce
4 Tbsp sherry
1 Tbsp brown sugar
1 clove garlic, finely chopped
about 500 g (1 lb) pork (any tender cut)
2 Tbsp toasted sesame seeds (optional)

Combine the peanut butter, soy sauce, sherry, sugar and garlic, mixing until smooth. Refrigerate in a covered container until required, keeping any leftover mixture for up to a week. Thin with a little more sherry or water just before use.

Cut the pork into 2 cm (3/4 in) cubes and thread onto soaked bamboo skewers. Brush the peanut butter mixture over evenly, and sprinkle all over with toasted sesame seeds if you like.

Grill or barbecue 6–8 cm from the heat, turning several times, for 5–6 minutes altogether, or until the thickest part of the meat is no longer pink. Test by cutting a cube in half if you are not sure.

Serve immediately – the kebabs will be tough if they overcook or are reheated.

Barbecued Pork Fillet Dinner

Pork fillets cook in about 15 minutes on a preheated, oiled barbecue plate. Accompany with corn cobs cooked in their husks on the barbecue rack, bread rolls warmed on the rack for a few minutes, and a green salad.

For 2–3 servings:
2 cloves garlic
2 tsp olive oil
2 tsp balsamic vinegar
1 pork fillet (about 400 g/14 oz)

Crush the garlic and mix it with the oil and vinegar. Rub over all surfaces of the pork fillet.

Barbecue for 10 minutes on a lightly oiled, preheated, heavy barbecue plate, turning frequently. When the outside is evenly browned, slice the fillet lengthways, cutting about three-quarters of the way through. Press the opened surface onto the hot plate and cook for about a minute longer to ensure the centre is cooked. Remove the fillet from the heat and leave to stand for 5 minutes before slicing diagonally.

Stuffed Pork Fillet

Stuffed pork fillet makes a good special occasion dinner for two.

For 2 servings:
250 g (9 oz) pork fillet
mixed mustard
light soy sauce
oil
2–4 prunes
2–4 dried apricots
1/4 cup (60 ml/2 fl oz) orange juice
grated rind of 1/2 orange (optional)
1 Tbsp brandy (optional)
2 Tbsp pinenuts or chopped blanched almonds
fresh rosemary and/or sage (optional)
pepper
butter

Turn the oven to 180°C (350°F). Cut the fillet open lengthways, leaving a hinge. Brush both sides with a mixture of mustard, light soy sauce and oil. Leave to stand for about 15 minutes.

Open the prunes flat and quarter the dried apricots. Add to the orange juice and rind and microwave or simmer until the fruit is soft. Add the brandy, cool the fruit, then place down the centre of one side of the fillet. Top with nuts, add a little finely chopped rosemary and/or sage if you like, then cover with the remaining meat.

Skewer the fillet together with a few toothpicks then tie more firmly with string, looping it like blanket stitch. Coat with coarsely ground black pepper and/or lemon pepper.

Stand the pork in a roasting pan on sprigs of rosemary and sage, if available. Top with several knobs of butter and roast uncovered for 25–30 minutes. Leave to stand for 5 minutes then remove the string or skewers and slice with a sharp knife. Serve with pan drippings and/or a light, fruity chutney.

Japanese Pork Fillet

Don't be put off by the large amount of sesame oil in this delicious recipe. The flavour of the pork is wonderful when the exact amounts given in the recipe are used.

For 3–4 servings:
400–500 g (about 1 lb) pork fillet
1 Tbsp grated fresh ginger
1 large clove garlic, finely chopped
2 Tbsp light soy sauce
pinch of cayenne
1/4 cup (60 ml/2 fl oz) sesame oil
3 Tbsp wine vinegar
1 tsp cornflour
2 Tbsp water

Trim the pork of any fat and untidy ends if necessary. Put the whole fillet in an unpunctured plastic bag with the next 6 ingredients. Turn the bag to mix well and coat the pork with the marinade. Marinate for at least 30 minutes, or up to 24 hours (refrigerate if marinating for the longer time).

Preheat a barbecue or grill to a high heat. Remove the pork from the bag, and reserve the marinade. Cook for 4 minutes each side, then leave to stand for about 10 minutes before carving into 1 cm (1/2 in) slices. The outside of the meat should be lightly browned, and the inside light beige, with only a slight rosy glow in the centre. If you are not sure, cut the fillet in two, crosswise, at the end of the cooking time – if there is any bright pink flesh, cook a little longer.

Mix the cornflour and water together, add the reserved marinade and heat until the mixture boils and thickens.

Serve the sliced pork with rice or bread rolls and a salad, drizzling a little of the sauce over the meat.

Pickled Pork

If you don't see pickled pork on display, ask for it. It may be called pickled pork, cured pork, or salted pork. It is salted by soaking in brine, but is not smoked like a ham.

If you want fairly lean meat, buy pork from the shoulder rather than the belly.

For 4–6 servings:
a piece of pickled shoulder pork
  (1–1.5 kg/2 lb 3 oz–3 lb 5 oz)
1 onion, roughly chopped
1–2 cloves garlic
1 carrot, roughly chopped

Pickled Pork, Parsley Sauce (p. 345)

1 stalk celery, chopped
about 10 peppercorns
about 6 juniper berries
about 6 allspice seeds
1 bayleaf
1 sprig thyme
1 sprig parsley
1–2 small chillies

Place the pork in a large container, cover with cold water, and leave to stand for 1–3 hours, changing the water after 30 minutes.

Place in a large pan or cast-iron casserole, preferably one in which it fits snugly, and cover with fresh water. Add any of the flavourings listed, or use others that you like. Do not add salt. Spices may be crushed if you like more flavour.

Bring to the boil and simmer very gently with the lid on, turning the meat occasionally. The meat is cooked when a skewer goes through it easily. This may be as soon as an hour for young shoulder meat, or up to 2 hours.

Lift the cooked pork out of the casserole or pan and put it in a roasting bag with a few spoonfuls of liquid to stop it drying out. (If not eating immediately, reheat in the bag in a microwave or conventional oven.)

Put aside some of the cooking liquid to make a parsley sauce (p. 345) and throw out the rest. Serve with new or mashed potatoes, small whole carrots, and cabbage or leeks.

Brawn from a Salted Pig's Head

This bargain-priced brawn may be served as a cold meat, and makes an excellent sandwich filling.

half a salted pig's head
5 cups (1.25 litres/40 fl oz) water
2–3 onions, coarsely chopped
1 Tbsp chicken stock powder or 1½ tsp salt
¼ tsp dried sage or 1 sprig fresh sage,
  finely chopped
pepper

Boil the head in the unsalted water for about 3 hours in a large, covered pot, or bake with the water in a covered roasting pan at 150°C (300°F) for 3 hours, or until very tender. Leave until cool enough to handle. Pour the stock into a bowl, and remove all fat from the surface.

With the skin-side down, lift all the bones from the meat, making sure all pieces of meat are removed from the bone. Discard any dark or discoloured meat, the skin and the eye.

Mince the meat with the onions and place in a pot with the stock powder or salt, sage, pepper and 3 cups (750 ml/ 24 fl oz) of stock from the first boiling. Bring the mixture to the boil, simmer for 1–2 minutes, then pour into bowls or loaf tins and leave to set.

Pig's Trotters

Some people love trotters, while others run a mile if invited to eat them! If you are partial to them, watch or ask for them at your butcher or supermarket. They are often very cheap at a time when hams are being prepared – a fraction of the price of cooked trotters in a deli. Enjoy them skin and all!

Brine

4 cups (1 litre/32 fl oz) water
2 Tbsp salt
2 Tbsp brown sugar
3–4 cloves garlic, squashed
1 bayleaf
6 peppercorns
6 allspice berries (optional)
6 juniper berries (optional)
6 cloves (optional)

To cook unsalted trotters, make up a well-flavoured brine using the ingredients above. Cook in the brine in a large pot.

If the trotters are salted, boil them in unsalted water, with or without flavourings.

Cook the trotters for 2–3 hours, until they are so tender they look as if they are starting to fall apart, and you can lift the meat from the bones. Cool in the cooking mixture, then refrigerate the cooked trotters in separate plastic bags, ready to eat. Enjoy them as a lunchtime snack, or as desired.

Pennywise Roast Pork

You can sometimes buy half a fresh pig's head for next to nothing! If you are prepared to work on it, you will get a delicious meal for 2 people very cheaply.

Buy an uncured (fresh) half pig's head with the cheek intact. Lay it on a board, cut-side down. To make crackling, cut parallel lines 5 mm (¼ in) deep and 5 mm (¼ in) apart over the cheek area. Rub 1 Tbsp salt over the cut area, and brush ¼ cup (60 ml/2 fl oz) oil over the scored skin.

Turn the grill to high, and grill the cheek 10–12 cm (4–5 in) away from it. It will take 10–20 minutes for the crackling to bubble and brown, and you'll have to move the head and prop it up with metal spoons or measuring cups for even browning. In a gas oven you cannot do this, but you can get the same effect by turning the oven heat to high for the first 20–30 minutes of cooking.

Turn the oven to 150°C (300°F), and roast the half head skin-side up, uncovered, for 2½–3 hours, roasting vegetables around it if you like.

Lift the head from the roasting pan and allow it to cool until you can handle it. Place it skin-side down on a wooden board. It should be so well cooked that you can lift the bones away from the meat quite easily. To do this, bend it lengthways so the skin of the lower jaw is folded against the skin of the upper jaw, then lift away and discard the upper part of the skull. Make sure the muscle that runs from the lower jaw to under and behind the eye is not discarded with the skull, as it is excellent meat. With the skin-side down, find the lower jawbone and pull it out. Turn the boned cheek over so the crackling is uppermost. Cut away and discard the front end of the lower jaw. Trim away any nasty bits and tuck pieces of detached meat underneath. Discard the debris then forget about the operation you have performed! The remaining roast meat is worth your work!

Roast Pork with Crackling

One of favourite special-occasion meals is a boned loin of pork, rolled, stuffed and roasted, served with crunchy crackling.

Prunes, bacon and marmalade give the stuffing plenty of flavour, and spinach is added for extra colour.

A few days before you want to cook this roast, ask your butcher to prepare a 2 kg (4 lb 7 oz) piece lean pork loin. Ask to have the skin removed, and closely scored for crackling. Ask for some of the flap to be left attached to the loin, so it can be rolled around the eye of meat and the stuffing.

Be clear about details when you are planning a special, festive meal and want everything to be just right.

For 8–12 servings:
12 prunes
2 Tbsp whisky or orange juice
6 water chestnuts (optional)
4 rashers bacon
about 6 spinach leaves
2 kg (4 lb 7 oz) loin of pork
2 tsp finely grated orange rind
1 Tbsp marmalade
2 tsp dark soy sauce
1 tsp Dijon mustard
2 Tbsp oil
1 tsp salt
2–3 Tbsp plain flour

Turn the oven to 180°C (350°F). Cut the prunes open and check no stones remain. Pour the whisky or orange juice over the prunes, turn them in it, and leave to stand for at least 30 minutes.

Slice the water chestnuts. Fry or grill the bacon, remove the rind, and chop. Remove the stalks from the spinach and blanch the leaves in boiling water for about 30 seconds, then drain and refresh with cold water.

Place the meat on a board and unroll the flap. Cover the meaty surface of the flap with the blanched spinach, leaving the edge farthest from the main muscle of the meat clear. Sprinkle over the bacon and water chestnuts. Lay the prunes along the flap, right beside the muscle.

Stir the orange rind into the marmalade, and spread over the prunes. Roll up the loin so that the flap surrounds the eye and secure firmly with string and skewers. Mix the soy sauce and mustard to a smooth paste and brush over the surface of the meat in a large roasting pan. Bake, uncovered, for about 1½ hours.

Crackling

To make the crackling, rub the surface of the skin lightly with the oil, then rub in the salt. Put this in a sponge-roll tin soon after the meat has been put in to cook. Check regularly – the crackling is ready when the surface has blistered and it is crisp and golden. Take it out, drain on paper towels, and break or cut into pieces with kitchen scissors.

Gravy

Pour any fat from the roasting pan, keeping the juices and brownings from the meat. Add the flour to the pan and heat, stirring constantly, until it just starts to bubble, then add about 3 cups (750 ml/24 fl oz) of liquid. Use a mixture of vegetable cooking liquid, water and a little wine or orange juice. Bring to the boil, then leave to cook very gently for 10 minutes.

Pan-Cooked Bacon

It's surprising what a little bit of bacon can do to brighten up a slice of toast, piece of bread or a crusty roll! Bacon can be put with all sorts of foods to make satisfying texture and flavour combinations.

Cut the rind off bacon with kitchen scissors if desired. Lay the bacon in a cold, preferably non-stick, frypan, then heat the pan. Have the heat hot enough to keep the bacon 'frizzling', but not so hot that you scorch parts of it before others are cooked. Turn over occasionally. Save leftover bacon fat to add bacon flavour to other foods.

Note: Some bacon is 'wet' and makes liquid in the pan as it is cooked. Avoid types or brands that do this, if you can.

Bacon Mushroom Burgers

Cook bacon in a frypan until crisp, then remove it and add mushrooms to the pan. Add a squeeze of lemon juice and a dash of water and cover the pan, since the mushrooms wilt more quickly in a steamy atmosphere. Once they have wilted remove the lid and raise the heat, turning the mushrooms occasionally so they absorb pan liquids.

Split a wholemeal or plain roll, or a length of french bread, and heat briefly. Arrange the mushrooms on the bacon in the (unbuttered) bread and sprinkle with chopped parsley or chives.

Microwaved Bacon

You can microwave bacon on the plate from which you will eat it. This is a real bonus for the person who does the washing up! Sit a paper towel loosely over the bacon on the plate to avoid spattering.

American recipes often call for bacon to be cooked between paper towels. Because our bacon is so much leaner, if you do this the meaty part of the bacon can stick to the paper towel.

Cooking times vary with the size and thickness of the bacon. Start with 1 minute per slice (or rasher) on High (100%) power and cook a little longer if necessary.

M

Roast Pork with Crackling, Banded New Potatoes (p. 195), baby beets and sugarsnap peas

Bacon, Potato and Bean Savoury; Cornmeal Muffins (p. 271)

Bacon, Potato and Bean Savoury

This simple but delicious summer dinner dish is especially good made with home-grown vegetables. Multiple the quantities to suit the people being fed.

For 1 serving:

3 rashers bacon
1 small onion, chopped
1–2 tsp butter or oil
2–3 small–medium new potatoes, scrubbed
about 2 Tbsp water
¼ tsp salt
oreganum or ground cumin to taste
100–150 g (3–5 oz) green beans, cut into 5 cm (2 in) lengths
about 1 tsp cornflour

Chop the bacon, removing the rind, and cook in a frypan until crisp, adding a little oil or butter if it seems dry. Remove most of the bacon and reserve it for garnishing. Add the onion and butter or oil to the pan, and cook until the onion is transparent and lightly browned.

Add the potatoes (whole, halved or quartered depending on size), water, salt and herbs. Cover and simmer until the potatoes are tender, about 20 minutes. Add the beans 10 minutes after the potatoes, and if necessary add a little extra water during cooking. Aim to finish up with about 2 Tbsp of liquid. Thicken the juices with just enough cornflour paste to coat and glaze the vegetables. Adjust seasonings.

Serve in a large, shallow bowl, sprinkled with the reserved bacon, as a complete main course, with a tomato salad alongside if you choose.

Hawaiian Ham Steaks

Ham steaks make a good, easy dinner when time is short. Since they are already cooked, they only need heating through.

For 4 servings:

4 ham steaks (about 5 mm/¼ in thick)
2 tsp butter or oil
onion juice or pulp
1 Tbsp brown sugar
½ cup (125 ml/4 fl oz) pineapple juice
1 tsp soy sauce
4 large or 8 small pineapple rings

Heat a large, heavy-bottomed frypan. Snip the edges of the steaks with a sharp knife or kitchen scissors so they will not curl up as they cook. Oil or butter the surface of the pan and cook the steaks over high heat for 1–2 minutes a side, until they are heated through but not brown.

Lift them from the pan and keep warm. Cut an unpeeled onion in half crosswise and scrape the cut surface with a teaspoon straight into the hot pan. The resulting onion pulp and juice will brown in the remaining film of fat. For a stronger onion flavour, cut off another slice and scrape again. Add the sugar, juice and soy sauce to the pan and cook over medium heat until the liquid has reduced by half and is thick and syrupy. Turn the steaks quickly in this glaze then turn the pineapple rings in it, adding a little extra pineapple juice and soy sauce if necessary.

Serve immediately, with the pineapple rings on top of the steaks.

Barbecued Glazed Ham Steaks

This glaze adds a little sweetness to ham steaks. You can use pre-cut ham steaks, or cut thick slices from a boneless, pressed ham and cook them the same way.

For 4 servings:

4 ham steaks
pineapple rings (optional)

Glaze

¼ cup (60 ml/2 fl oz) pineapple juice
1 Tbsp tomato or barbecue sauce
1 tsp smooth mixed mustard
1 tsp cornflour
1 tsp light soy sauce
1 Tbsp maple syrup or brown sugar

Mix the glaze ingredients together and heat until boiling, stirring until the mixture is thick and clear. Snip the edges of each steak in 4 to 6 places so they will not curl up as they cook. Pour the glaze over the steaks in an unpunctured plastic bag or a shallow dish. Make sure all the ham surfaces are coated. Leave for at least 15 minutes.

Remove the steaks from the bag and barbecue over high heat on a hot plate or oiled grilling rack until they are hot and lightly browned on both sides, 3–5 minutes per side. Do not overcook.

If you like, barbecue canned pineapple rings to serve with the steak. Place them on an oiled, heated plate, or in a hinged wire basket, since they break easily when turned. If you are barbecuing fresh pineapple, sprinkle slices or cubes lightly with sugar first.

Glazing and Decorating Small Rolled Hams

As the festive season approaches, give some thought to the type of ham that suits your family best. Some of the smaller hams and ham products may suit you better than a large, bone-in, whole ham. If you are not feeding large numbers, consider buying one or more small rolls of ham, such as a 2 kg (4 lb 7 oz) roll of shoulder ham.

It is difficult to give an exact number of servings from any piece of meat – this depends on the ages and appetites of the diners, the skills of the carver and the sharpness of the knife, and the amounts of other foods served alongside.

From a 2 kg (4 lb 7 oz) boneless ham you will get nearly thirty 70 g (2 oz) servings, or twenty 100 g (3 1/2 oz) servings. If you are an inexperienced carver, cut and weigh one portion ahead, then use it as a guide for the size of the following portions.

Keep your ham in its original wrapping in the refrigerator until the day you intend to glaze and decorate it. Do this three hours before the ham is to be served, so you eat it at room temperature. The meat is then softer and juicier than if it is served straight from the refrigerator.

To glaze a small 'ham', mix in a small pot: 1/2 cup brown sugar, 1/4 cup (60 ml/2 fl oz) orange juice, 1/4 tsp ground cloves and 1/2 tsp mixed spice. Bring to the boil and simmer for 5 minutes until thick and syrupy.

Preheat the grill of an electric stove and adjust the rack so the upper surface of the ham is 7–8 cm (about 3 in) from the hot elements.

Score the whole of the ham diagonally, forming diamonds with 2 cm (3/4 in) sides, and making cuts about 5 mm (1/4 in) deep. Although it is hard to see where you have cut before the meat is heated, the surface shrinks as it browns, emphasising the diamond shapes.

Part of a small ham roll may be coated with skin; if so, position the skin so it is uppermost for glazing, etc. Put the scored meat in a shallow pan, prop it in place with a few toothpicks, and brush it with the hot syrup. Watch it carefully as it cooks under the grill since you want it to brown evenly and quickly on the outside without overheating inside. Brush more glaze over the meat after 5 minutes and turn it a quarter turn every 8 minutes.

In half an hour the ham should be nicely brown and smell delicious. Remove it from the oven and position it best-side up. Skewer cherry pieces and small pineapple wedges on half toothpicks, and use these to decorate any accessible diamonds. Brush the decorated ham with glaze and heat it again briefly, then arrange it on a platter for serving and slicing.

Alternatively, if you are serving glazed ham to fewer people over a longer period, stud each diamond with a clove before glazing it. Serve with pickled pineapple as a relish, rather than decorating the surface with pineapple and cherries.

Don't cut the ham too thinly or you won't enjoy its texture fully. Don't cut even rings of ham – they look unnatural. Cut tapering slices and turn the roll between slices, removing the decorations first, if necessary.

If you can't fit the glazed ham under the grill to brown it, put it in a hot oven – about 220°C (425°F) – instead. Don't overcook it though, or the meat may dry out.

If you have a microwave, make sure you enjoy some of your ham hot – put slices in split rolls with mustard and relish, wrap in a paper towel or serviette and microwave briefly. A slice of brie or camembert is a good addition. The filling heats before the bread, and the result is delicious.

And last but not least, don't leave your ham buying until the last days before Christmas, or you will have a poor selection!

Ham Fried Rice

Fried rice with added ham is a popular, quick and economical summer meal.

For 3–4 servings:
1/2–1 cup diced ham
1/2–1 cup diced raw summer vegetables (young carrots, beans, zucchini, mushrooms, etc.)
3–4 spring onions, sliced
1–2 cloves garlic, very finely chopped
2 Tbsp oil
2–3 cups cooked rice, preferably basmati
1 Tbsp light soy sauce
1 Tbsp sherry
1/2 tsp sugar
1–2 eggs
sesame oil (optional)
oyster sauce (optional)

Cut up the ham and the vegetables, and assemble all the ingredients before you start cooking. (The rice is best if cooked several hours, or longer, ahead.) Use vegetables which cook quickly, and cut them in very small pieces.

Cook the vegetables with the white parts of the spring onions, and the garlic, in half the oil, in a large, covered, non-stick frypan. Cook on a fairly low heat, until barely tender. Add a tablespoon of water to make steam during cooking if necessary. Remove from the pan.

Fry the ham in the remaining film of oil, over higher heat, until just starting to brown, then remove, and add the rest of the oil. When it is very hot add the rice,

and cook over high heat until hot right through, turning frequently.

Clear a space in the middle of the rice, and break in the egg(s). Stir until half set, then stir through the rice. Stir in the spring onion greens, then shake in sesame oil and oyster sauce if you like.

For best flavour, cover and leave to stand for 5–10 minutes before serving.

Ham Encores

Ham is one of the best meats for 'easy reheating', so you should never be short of ideas for serving the ham that remains after the first few meals of 'plain ham' over the holiday period.

Ham sandwiches, spread with mild mustard, with added cucumber pickles, can be made very quickly if you work with frozen slices of bread. Wrap the sandwiches in a damp teatowel, then a plastic bag, if you need them later.

If you haven't tried french bread split and filled with ham, chutney, and a few salad vegetables, then wrapped tightly in a paper towel or serviette and microwaved until the bread is warm, and the ham hot, you don't know what you are missing.

To make a small amount of ham go further, add small cubes to the nearly cooked vegetables in a frittata.

Lean and Lovely Lamb

It's easy to take lamb for granted, and forget that in many parts of the world a grilled lamb chop or tender roast is expensive and exotic. I hope my lamb recipes will encourage you to experiment with a variety of lamb cuts, to try something a little different, and to make the most of this tender and tasty meat. Tucked in amongst my favourite lamb recipes are some delicious 'variety' meat recipes, and a few good value-for-money mutton recipes too. I hope you won't pass them by!

Roast Lamb and Kiwi Sauce

It is nice to be able to serve overseas guests a dish that contains several special New Zealand foods.

Well-trimmed lamb is good served pink. Even if you think you like it well cooked, I hope you will try lean lamb served pink at least once!

For 4–6 servings:
1 leg of lamb
1/2 cup (125 ml/4 fl oz) dry white wine
2 Tbsp butter
2 cloves garlic, crushed
stock or more wine

Turn the oven to 165°C (325°F). Trim most visible fat from the surface of the lamb, and stand it in a roasting pan just large enough to hold it. Heat the wine, butter and garlic until the butter melts. Pour over the lamb.

Roast uncovered, allowing 25–35 minutes per 500 g (1 lb), basting every 30 minutes with the wine mixture. If necessary add more liquid (vegetable or meat stock or wine) during cooking so there is always some liquid around the lamb.

Remove the cooked leg to the carving dish. Skim the pan juices and thicken slightly with cornflour, or make Kiwi Sauce.

Kiwi Sauce
2 kiwifruit, chopped or sliced
1 Tbsp butter
1/4 tsp cinnamon
1/2 tsp ground ginger
1 Tbsp orange juice
1 tsp tomato paste

Sauté the kiwifruit in the butter and spices. Add the pan juices from the meat, the orange juice and tomato paste. Stir to combine. Adjust the seasonings, and serve very hot with lamb.

Roast Leg of Lamb

The traditional roast leg of lamb is popular and delicious, and quite at home in the most untraditional situations.

1 leg of lamb
1 Tbsp olive or other oil
2 Tbsp Worcestershire sauce
juice of 1 lemon
2 cloves garlic, crushed
1 tsp finely chopped rosemary

Trim the leg of nearly all visible fat. Put the leg with the other ingredients in an unpunctured plastic bag and marinate for at least an hour, overnight if possible.

Turn the oven to 160–180°C (325–350°F). Remove the leg from the marinade, lie it on sprigs of rosemary if available, and roast uncovered for 11/2–2 hours (longer if you like it well done), basting occasionally with marinade. Leave to stand in a warm place for 15 minutes before carving.

Roast Stuffed Lamb Forequarter

For about 4 servings:
1 boned lamb forequarter
2–3 cloves garlic, slivered
1 onion, finely chopped
1 Tbsp butter
2 cups fresh breadcrumbs
1–4 Tbsp chopped fresh herbs
2 tsp dry mustard
2 Tbsp soy sauce

Turn oven to 160–170°C (325°F). Trim any extra fat off the meat if necessary, make small cuts over the surface, and insert the garlic slivers (or chop it and cook with the onion). Cook the onion in the butter until tender. Stir in the breadcrumbs and herbs. Season lightly.

Pack the stuffing lightly into the cavity left by the blade bone. Secure the meat with skewers and string. Make a paste with the mustard and soy sauce and brush over the lamb for extra flavour (and an appetising smell as the meat cooks). Score the surface lightly if you like.

Roast uncovered, preferably on a rack, for about 2 hours. Do not add extra fat. Roast vegetables under or around the roast during the last 1–11/2 hours. Strain the pan drippings to make gravy.

Robyn's Lavender Lamb

This lamb is baked in a nest of fragrant hay and lavender. If the idea of cooked grass worries you, just think of it as a herb. It is well and truly sterilised during the cooking, and its flavour is almost as special as that of the lavender.

When buying meat for this recipe, ask your butcher to tunnel-bone a chump-on leg of lamb.

Important: Use only English lavender.

For 4–6 servings:
1 long (full) leg of lamb, tunnel-boned
freshly cut hay, washed (if available)
about 10 stems of English lavender
2 large cloves garlic
2 Tbsp melted butter or olive oil

Turn the oven to 200°C (400°F). Make a nest of the hay and about 6 stems of lavender in a large roasting pan. Dampen the hay with half a cup (125 ml/4 fl oz) of hot water, so there is some steam around the lamb as it cooks.

Trim all visible surface fat from the lamb. Put the remaining lavender stems and 1 garlic clove in the cavity. Cut the remaining garlic clove into slivers and push these into small cuts on the surface of the lamb. Place the lamb, best side up, in the 'nest' of hay. Drizzle the butter or olive oil over the meat. Cover tightly, with a piece of foil under the lid if necessary.

Bake for 30 minutes, then reduce the temperature to 150°C (300°F) and cook a further 11/2–2 hours, until very tender. Remove from the roasting dish and carve. Pour off, skim and strain the pan juices, and pour over the carved lamb. Serve with whole new potatoes and a green salad.

Robyn's Lavender Lamb

Heavenly Roast

This is one of my favourite lamb roasts.

For 4–6 servings:
1 lamb or hogget forequarter, boned
2 Tbsp plain flour
2 Tbsp sugar
2 tsp dry mustard
3 Tbsp wine vinegar
¼ cup fresh mint leaves
1 cup (250 ml/8 fl oz) stock or water
Angostura bitters
cornflour

Turn the oven to 170°C (325°F). Trim most of the visible fat from the lamb. Make a paste with the flour, sugar, mustard and enough vinegar to make it spreadable, and brush about half over the meaty inner surface of the lamb. Sprinkle with whole young mint leaves and roll up. Secure with string and/or skewers. Spread remaining paste over the outside.

Roast uncovered on a rack for 2–2½ hours, depending on size. If you like, put vegetables to roast under the rack after an hour, adding oil if necessary.

When cooked, transfer to a serving dish and pour the fat from the pan drippings. Add the rest of the vinegar, the stock or water and a few drops of bitters. Bring to the boil, thicken if desired with a little cornflour paste, and adjust seasonings. Remove string/skewers before carving into fairly thick slices. Do not serve mint sauce with this lamb or you will lose the more subtle flavours.

> Hogget is meat from one- or two-year-old sheep.

Soy-Glazed Bagged Lamb

The meat from the forequarter is sweet, tender and juicy. A boned forequarter may be used in many ways – this is one of my favourites, and one of the easiest.

For 3–4 servings:
1 lamb or hogget forequarter, boned
¼ cup (60 ml/2 fl oz) dark soy sauce
2 cloves garlic, flattened

Trim as much visible fat as possible from the meat, and place it in an unpunctured oven bag. Pour the soy sauce around the meat, add the garlic, squeeze out all the air and leave to marinate for at least half an hour, or up to 36 hours. The meat can thaw in this marinade.

Turn the oven to 150°C (300°F). Close the bag with a twist tie, leaving a finger-sized hole so steam can escape. Place the bagged meat in a roasting pan and cook for about 3 hours for lamb, and 3½–4 hours for hogget, until the meat is VERY tender, and glazed a rich brown.

Remove from the oven, loosen the tie, and

pour all the liquid into a bowl. Skim the fat from this liquid, dilute it with water or unsalted vegetable cooking liquid, and thicken as desired with cornflour.

Leave the meat in the bag for a few minutes to firm up, then carve it in thick slices with a sharp knife. (It has a tendency to break up easily unless a good sharp knife is used.) Spoon a little sauce over each serving.

Barbecued 'Butterflied' Leg of Lamb

You cannot always walk into a supermarket and buy a boned rolled leg, as you can a boned rolled forequarter. You can, however, ask any butcher to 'butterfly' a leg (or the shank end of a leg) of lamb or hogget for you. If you explain that you want to barbecue it in one flattish piece, you may be able to get the outer fatty side trimmed too. Use Tex-Mex or Mediterranean Marinade and leave the boned leg to marinate for 24–48 hours before barbecuing. The cooking time should be about 30–40 minutes (under good conditions), since the meat is thicker. The meat should feel springy, not spongy, when cooked. If in doubt, cut a thick part with a sharp knife and see if the centre is done to the stage you like it. Leave to stand, covered, for 10–15 minutes, then carve in slices across the grain of the meat.

Tex-Mex Marinade
1 Tbsp ground cumin
2 tsp oreganum
½–1 tsp chilli powder
juice of 2 or 3 lemons
2 Tbsp Worcestershire sauce
2 Tbsp oil
2–3 cloves garlic, crushed

Mediterranean Marinade
Leave out the chilli and replace the cumin with at least 2 Tbsp chopped fresh rosemary or thyme.

Orange-Glazed Lamb Leg

A golden glazed leg of lamb or hogget is a good choice for a special dinner.

For 6–8 servings:
1 boned leg of lamb or hogget

Marinade
½ cup (125 ml/4 fl oz) dry white wine
¼ cup (60 ml/2 fl oz) orange juice
grated rind of 1 orange
1 Tbsp Worcestershire sauce
2 cloves garlic, crushed

Stuffing
1 onion, chopped
¼ cup chopped almonds
2 Tbsp butter
¼ cup currants
¼ cup chopped mint

grated rind of 1 orange
2 cups soft breadcrumbs
salt and pepper
1 egg, beaten

Glaze
¼ cup (60 ml/2 fl oz) orange juice
¼ cup (60 ml/2 fl oz) white wine
¼ cup apricot jam
2 tsp soy sauce

Trim the boned leg of any excess fat and place it in a strong, unpunctured plastic bag with the marinade ingredients. Squeeze all the air from the bag, secure with a rubber band, and refrigerate for 1–3 days. When ready to cook, remove from the refrigerator and put the marinade in a roasting pan. Turn the oven to 170°C (325°F).

To make the stuffing, heat the onion and almonds in the butter until the almonds start to turn light brown. Remove from the heat and add the currants, mint, orange rind and breadcrumbs. Season with salt and pepper then add enough egg to mix to a moist but not sticky consistency. Stuff and reshape the leg, securing it with cocktail sticks and heavy thread.

Roast uncovered for 2–3 hours, basting occasionally with the marinade, and adding a little extra wine if the liquid evaporates. If the leg browns too quickly, cover it lightly with a foil hood.

Make the glaze while the lamb cooks. Simmer all the ingredients in a small pan until thick, syrupy and golden brown. Darken slightly with gravy browning if it is not brown enough.

Remove the lamb to a serving platter 15 minutes before serving. Remove the cocktail picks and string, and brush on the hot glaze with a pastry brush. Make gravy from the pan juices after removing fat.

Apricot-Stuffed Lamb Loin

Serve this delicious lamb dish to anyone who is not convinced that lamb is a gourmet food.

For 4 servings:
2 boneless lamb or hogget short loins
½ cup dried apricots, chopped
½ cup (125 ml/4 fl oz) white wine
½ cup finely chopped onion
1 Tbsp butter
½ cup soft breadcrumbs
¼ tsp chopped fresh thyme
¼ cup toasted pinenuts or chopped almonds (optional)
freshly ground black pepper
¼ cup (60 ml/2 fl oz) white wine

Sauce
2 Tbsp each apricot jam, sherry and water

Ask the butcher to bone out the loin, or do it yourself. Remove the large muscle from the loin, keeping it in one piece, and pull it free of surrounding fat. (Trim off the fillet from the other side of the bone, and use it later for stir-frying, etc.)

If it has not already been removed, carefully trim away the silvery coating on one side of each boneless loin, since it shrinks a lot during cooking. Cut a pocket down the centre of each loin, using a long-bladed, sharp knife.

To make the stuffing, soak the chopped apricots in the 1/2 cup wine while cooking the onion in the butter for 3 minutes without browning. Add the apricots and wine to the onion and simmer until all the liquid has evaporated. Stir in the breadcrumbs, thyme and nuts. Pack the stuffing into the pockets in the meat. Secure the ends with toothpicks or with a needle and thread, if desired. Refrigerate until required.

Before cooking, season the lamb with freshly ground black pepper. Cook in a lightly oiled frypan for 10 minutes altogether, turning frequently. Add 1/4 cup wine to the pan in the last 2 minutes of cooking, boil down, and turn the meat in the small amount of liquid to glaze it. Leave the lamb to stand for 5 minutes before carving diagonally into thin slices and serving on a pool of sauce.

To make the sauce, add the apricot jam, sherry and water to the pan drippings. Boil until thick and syrupy.

Lamb Rack with Fruited Couscous

Cook this for a special occasion dinner for two.

For 2 servings:
1 chined, trimmed rack of lamb or
* 6–8 small chined lamb cutlets*
1 Tbsp orange or lemon juice
1 tsp olive oil
1/2 tsp ground cumin
1/2 tsp crushed coriander seeds (optional)
pinch of chilli powder

Check the lamb has been well trimmed (fat and bones other than rib bones removed). If using cutlets, put them between plastic and flatten by banging with a rolling pin. Combine the remaining ingredients and brush over the lamb. Leave to stand for at least 10 minutes, longer if possible.

Cook rack before the couscous, and cutlets after. For rack, heat the oven to 220°C (425°F), put the meat on a rack above a roasting pan, and bake for 20–25 minutes, depending on size and how you like it. Remove from the oven, cover with foil and leave to stand in a warm place for 10 minutes before slicing into cutlets.

To cook cutlets, heat a heavy pan until very hot. Brush with a little oil, then cook the cutlets, in 2 batches if necessary, until browned on both sides, probably 1–2 minutes per side. Serve immediately.

Fruited Couscous

For 2–4 servings:
1 cup quick-cooking couscous
6 dried apricots, finely chopped
2 cups (500 ml/16 fl oz) boiling chicken stock
1 Tbsp olive oil
1/4 cup (dried) currants
1/4 cup pinenuts or chopped almonds
1/2 tsp ground cumin
about 1/4 cup chopped fresh coriander or mint

Put the couscous in a bowl and add the apricots. Pour in the boiling stock and leave to stand in a warm place for 6–10 minutes.

Meanwhile, heat the currants and nuts in the oil in a medium-sized frypan, until the currants have puffed up and the nuts have browned lightly. Add the cumin, toss over heat for a few seconds, then stir the mixture through the couscous. Adjust seasonings. Add herbs just before serving.

A loin of lamb is often cut into two pieces: the front, rib end is called a 'rack', and the back end is called the 'short loin'. When a rack is 'chined', the backbone is removed in one piece. When it is 'frenched', the thin strip of meat between the rib bones is cut away.

Lamb Rack with Fruited Couscous

Crusty Lamb Rack M

This rack has a well-flavoured coating. It cooks very quickly in either a conventional or a microwave oven.

For 2 servings:
1 rack of lamb, frenched and chined
2 tsp dry mustard
1¹/₂ tsp dark soy sauce
1 clove garlic, crushed
1 Tbsp dry breadcrumbs
¹/₂ tsp paprika
¹/₄ tsp curry powder
about 1 tsp finely chopped thyme (or other herb)

If necessary trim away the outer coating of fat from the rack. Make a paste with the mustard, soy sauce and garlic, and brush over the exposed meaty surface of the lamb.

Combine the crumbs, paprika, curry powder and thyme. Sprinkle evenly over the meat.

Stand the lamb, bone-side down, in a shallow pan, and bake uncovered at 200°C (400°F) for 20–25 minutes.

To microwave, stand the lamb on a ridged dish or inverted plate. Microwave on High (100%) power for 4¹/₂–5 minutes, depending on the size of the rack. (A rack taken straight from the refrigerator may need 1 minute longer.)

Leave the baked or microwaved rack for 5–10 minutes before cutting into chops.

Note: For a hogget rack at room temperature, increase the cooking time to 5¹/₂ minutes, and give it 30 seconds longer if the meat in the centre seems undercooked. Roast a hogget rack conventionally for 25 minutes.

'Mini' Leg Cuts of Lamb

When a leg of lamb or hogget is 'seam-boned' you get four neat, compact cuts from each leg. These have no fatty outer layer, and are wonderful for small families.

The cuts are lamb rump or chump, lamb topside, lamb silverside and lamb thick flank. All can be barbecued very successfully. For faster, even cooking, the chunky, thick flank and topside may be cut open and laid flat.

Marinate the meat for at least 15 minutes, using Tex-Mex or Mediterranean Marinade (p. 104) or the following marinade.

Sesame Marinade
¹/₄ cup (60 ml/2 fl oz) Kikkoman soy sauce
¹/₄ cup (60 ml/2 fl oz) lemon juice
2 Tbsp sesame oil
1–2 tsp tabasco sauce
2 cloves garlic, crushed

Barbecue the marinated meat over high heat on the grilling rack, preferably covered with a domed lid or foil tent, for 8–12 minutes per side, depending on the conditions and how you like the meat cooked. Leave to stand for 10 minutes before slicing diagonally into thick slices.

Lamb Kebabs with Ginger-Soy Marinade

Kebabs are a marvellous stand-by to have in the freezer. Lean lamb kebabs can be cooked with or without marinades, but a marinade like this brings out the flavour of the meat and tenderises it. Kebabs may be threaded and frozen before or after marinating.

Meat from a lamb shoulder makes excellent kebabs. It is worth learning how to bone a shoulder yourself if you want to produce good, economical lamb meals.

For 4 servings:
500–600 g (1 lb 2 oz–1 lb 5 oz) lean lamb
2 Tbsp soy sauce
1 Tbsp oil
1–2 tsp lemon juice or vinegar
1 tsp sugar
1 clove garlic, crushed or thinly sliced
1 tsp grated fresh root ginger

Cut the lamb into 2–3 cm (about 1 in) cubes, and thread onto bamboo or metal skewers. Mix the remaining ingredients in a shallow dish. Turn the skewered meat in the liquid or brush the liquid over the meat with a pastry brush. Cover and leave to stand for several minutes – or several hours if you have time.

Grill or barbecue the kebabs close to the heat source, turning once. Depending on the fierceness of the heat, they should cook in 4–10 minutes.

Variation: Thread pieces of bacon, kidney, liver or cooked sausage between the cubes of lamb.

Glazed Lamb Riblets

This recipe is the result of my experiments to make a lamb equivalent of pork spare ribs!

For 4 servings:
2 hogget flaps
grated rind and juice of 2 oranges
2 Tbsp Kikkoman soy sauce
1 Tbsp Worcestershire sauce
2 cloves garlic, crushed
¹/₄ cup (60 ml/2 fl oz) wine or water
1 tsp sesame oil

Turn the oven to 160°C (325°F). Lay the flaps bone-side up. Using a sharp knife, cut either side of the rib bones and remove them in a sheet, then trim away any large areas of fat. Score the upper and lower surfaces of the meat to form 1 cm (¹/₂ in) diamonds, cutting about 5 mm (¹/₄ in) deep.

Put the remaining ingredients in an unpunctured oven bag and add the lamb so it lies flat. Turn the bag so that all surfaces are coated with the liquid. Fasten a twist tie around the opening, leaving a finger-sized hole, lay it flat on a sponge-roll tin and bake for about 1¹/₂ hours, or until the meat is very tender, flipping the bag over several times. Check there is always some liquid in the bag (as well as the fat which will be poured off later); if necessary, add extra water.

When the meat is cooked, drain off all liquid, skim off and discard the fat, and keep the small amount of concentrated glaze. Cut the lamb into fingers, drizzle with the glaze, and serve hot.

Variation: Add smoke-flavoured salt or liquid to the cooking liquid for a barbecued flavour.

Mediterranean Lamb Kebabs

Whether you cook them outdoors on a barbecue, or indoors under a grill, kebabs are perfect for relaxed summer entertaining. Prepare them the night before or in the morning, when it's cool, refrigerate them, then cook them in a few minutes. Mediterranean Lamb Kebabs are always popular.

For 4 servings:
600–700 g (1 lb 5oz–1 lb 9 oz) lamb cubes, cut from shoulder chops or a boned shoulder
1 large onion, chopped
2 Tbsp salad or corn oil
2 Tbsp Worcestershire sauce
¹/₂ tsp salt
1 tsp basil
1 tsp oreganum

Cut the lamb into 2 cm (³/₄ in) cubes and thread onto 8 bamboo or metal skewers. Leave a little space between them so they cook evenly.

Put the remaining ingredients in a blender or food processor and process until smooth. Pour over the lamb, cover and refrigerate, turning the meat occasionally.

Barbecue or grill close to the heat for 5–10 minutes, until the outside is crusty and brown. Do not overcook.

Variation: For more colourful kebabs, skewer 1 cm (¹/₂ in) slices of young zucchini, button mushrooms, small or quartered tomatoes, or pieces of red or green pepper between the pieces of meat. Double the amount of oil in the marinade if you are going to coat vegetables as well as meat.

> Bamboo skewers should be soaked for 5–10 minutes before being threaded for grilling or barbecuing.

Honey-Glazed Skewered Lamb Fillets

Although lamb fillets cost more than other lamb cuts, they are very lean and tender, and may be cut in pieces and threaded on kebabs or skewers with very little time and effort.

For 2 servings:

250–300 g (9–11 oz) lamb fillets
2 Tbsp lemon juice
1 Tbsp honey
1 Tbsp oil
1 clove garlic, finely chopped

Cut the meat into 2 cm (3/4 in) slices, trimming off any fat. Put the cubes in an unpunctured plastic bag.

Heat the remaining ingredients in a microwave on High (100%) power for 20 seconds, or in a small pot until the honey has melted. Stir well and cool to room temperature, then pour over the bagged meat and leave to stand while you prepare accompaniments.

Thread the marinated lamb onto 4 soaked bamboo skewers. Cook on a barbecue rack, or under a preheated grill close to high heat, for a short time. The kebabs are ready when the outside is brown and the inside pink but not red – they cook quickly and dry out easily if overcooked.

Lamb Satay

Cook this lamb dish on the barbecue or under the grill.

For 4 servings:

500 g (1 lb 2 oz) lamb shoulder meat
2 Tbsp soy sauce
2 Tbsp lemon juice
1 Tbsp grated root ginger
1 Tbsp brown sugar
1 Tbsp oil
1/4 tsp salt
1/2 tsp turmeric
1 onion, grated
2 cloves garlic, crushed
1/4 cup crunchy peanut butter
1/2 cup (125 ml/4 fl oz) coconut milk
tabasco sauce

Cut the meat from shoulder chops (or forequarter) into 2 cm (3/4 in) cubes. Thread on bamboo or metal skewers and arrange in a shallow dish. Combine the remaining ingredients, except the peanut butter, coconut milk and tabasco, and pour over the meat. Stand for at least 30 minutes, preferably overnight in the refrigerator.

Grill or barbecue close to the heat. The outside should brown quickly, while the meat near the skewers remains pink.

Add the peanut butter, coconut milk and tabasco to the remaining marinade and simmer until it has a sauce consistency. Add more coconut milk or water if

Honey-Glazed Skewered Lamb Fillets, Salsa (p. 346)

necessary. Extra salt, sugar and tabasco sauce may be needed to balance the flavours. Stir pan drippings into the sauce.

Place the skewered meat on a bed of rice. Pour over sauce and serve with salads of your choice.

Minted Lamb or Hogget Kebabs

In late summer and autumn it is nice to thread cubes of hogget on skewers with cubes of eggplant. Both benefit from a marinade based on yoghurt, flavoured with mint and garlic.

For 4 servings:

half a boned forequarter of large lamb or hogget
1 eggplant
1/2 cup plain (sweetened or unsweetened) yoghurt
1/4 cup mint leaves, chopped
2 garlic cloves, chopped
juice of 1/2 lemon

Cut the meat and the eggplant into 2 cm (3/4 in) cubes, removing excess fat from the meat. Do not peel the eggplant.

Combine the remaining ingredients, preferably in a food processor. Pour the mixture over the meat and eggplant and mix well to coat all surfaces. Leave to stand for at least 30 minutes, or up to several hours, then thread meat and eggplant alternately onto 8–12 bamboo skewers. Grill or barbecue close to the heat for 3–4 minutes per side, turning once. The eggplant should have a golden brown crust and the meat should be nicely browned on the outside, and pink in the middle. Serve immediately.

Lamb Kebabs with Orange Rosemary Sauce

Lamb kebabs skewered with vegetables and dried apricots, and flavoured with rosemary, have a delicious Middle Eastern accent. The combination is a welcome change at barbecues and at dinner parties in not-so-warm weather.

For 4 servings:

500 g (1 lb 2 oz) lean, boneless shoulder lamb
1/2 cup (125 ml/4 fl oz) Orange Rosemary Sauce
1 onion
1 red pepper
18–24 dried apricots

Cut the trimmed lamb into 3 cm (1 1/4 in) cubes and marinate in Orange Rosemary Sauce for 30 minutes.

Cut the onion and pepper into 3 cm (1 1/4 in) squares. Put the apricots in a bowl and pour boiling water over them to plump them. Drain well.

Decide how many kebabs you want and divide the lamb, onion, pepper and apricots into this number of piles. Thread them alternately onto bamboo skewers or onto lengths of rosemary stems stripped of their leaves, apart from a few at the end. Grill or barbecue, turning frequently, brushing with marinade at intervals, until the lamb is cooked to your liking. Do not overcook.

Serve with Pilaf (p. 344) and a salad of sliced oranges and small lettuce leaves tossed in a little vinaigrette.

Orange Rosemary Sauce

1 tsp grated orange rind
1/2 cup (125 ml/4 fl oz) orange juice
1/4 cup (60 ml/2 fl oz) olive oil
2 Tbsp white wine vinegar
1 Tbsp light soy sauce
2 Tbsp grated raw onion or onion juice
1 clove garlic, finely chopped
2–3 tsp very finely chopped fresh rosemary

Combine ingredients in a screw-top jar. Shake well.

Barbecued Lamb Chop Know How

In Mediterranean countries the delicious smell of pieces of lamb cooking over open fires has wafted through the countryside for thousands of years.

On a barbecue you can quickly and easily cook lamb chops cut from the shoulder, ribs, or middle loin. Like all meat that is to be barbecued, the chops should be trimmed of as much visible fat as possible. Well-trimmed meat cooks much faster than meat surrounded by thick layers of fat, and does not drip fat and cause flare-ups.

Rib and middle loin chops are more tender than shoulder chops and may be cooked without marinating, although a marinade will add flavour. Shoulder chops and cubes of shoulder meat will be more tender if marinated at room temperature for at least an hour.

Rib Chops and Cutlets

Cut away nearly all outer fat. Cut off knobbly bone with pruners or cutting pliers if you like. (This bone will probably already be removed from cutlets.)

Middle Loin Chops

Trim off as much fat as possible, without detaching the tail of the chop. So the tail meat does not overcook, roll it up towards the small eye of very tender meat and secure it with a toothpick.

Noisettes

Trim fat from middle loin chops as above, then cut around the T-shaped bone and remove it. Wind the tail around both eyes of meat, and push a bamboo skewer through the rolled chop, from one side to the other. Cut off the skewer, and push the remaining half through at right angles to the first. The crossed skewers will keep the roll of lamb flat and in place as it cooks.

Shoulder Chops

Cut off all outer fat and any bones that are near the edge of the chop. Snip the edges

Lamb Kebabs with Orange Rosemary Sauce, Pilaf (p. 344)

to prevent curling during cooking. Bang a few times on both sides with a meat hammer to tenderise if desired. Turn in the marinade of your choice and leave to stand at room temperature for an hour, or up to 24 hours in the refrigerator.

East-West Marinade

This marinade is good for all chops and cubes of lamb.

1 Tbsp light soy sauce
1 Tbsp lemon juice
1 tsp honey
1–2 cloves garlic, crushed and chopped finely
1 tsp sesame oil or ¹/₄ tsp crumbled dried thyme

Combine all ingredients in an airtight jar and shake. Brush over lamb, following the general directions above.

Note: If sesame oil is added the marinade has a definite Eastern accent. If thyme is used, it has a Western flavour.

Lemon-Honey Lamb Cutlets

Cutlets are well-trimmed rib chops from which the upper (angled) bone has been removed.

For 2 servings:
6 lamb cutlets
about 2 tsp soy sauce
¹/₄ cup (60 ml/2 fl oz) lemon juice
¹/₂ tsp tarragon or ¹/₄ tsp dried mint
1 Tbsp honey
¹/₄ tsp black pepper
1 tsp mustard
1 tsp butter

Trim all fat from the cutlets, brush with soy sauce and leave to stand for 5 minutes.

Cook in a non-stick frypan for 3–4 minutes, depending on their thickness. Remove the cutlets from the pan, add the lemon juice and tarragon (or mint) and bring to the boil, stirring the sediment off the bottom of the pan. Add the honey, pepper and mustard and mix thoroughly. Swirl in the butter.

Return the chops to the pan and turn to coat with the sauce.

Easy Grilled Lamb

This is a very easy, and very good, lamb recipe. Combine the seasoning ingredients ahead and put the mixture in an empty spice jar with a shaker top. Label it 'Lamb Seasoning', and keep it within easy reach on your spice shelves.

lamb chops, or cubed lamb on skewers
lemon juice
1 Tbsp curry powder
1 Tbsp garlic salt
1 Tbsp ground ginger

Place well-trimmed chops or kebabs in a shallow dish. Sprinkle or lightly brush with lemon juice, then shake the seasoning mixture lightly over all surfaces.

Grill or barbecue close to the heat so the meat is nicely browned on the outside and pink in the middle. Serve immediately.

Variation: Sprinkle the seasoning mix over lamb roasts just before cooking.

Minted Mustardy Chops

These chops have a delicious mild minty flavour. The mustard in the marinade gives them a slight crustiness.

For 4 servings:
8 lamb loin chops
juice of 1 lemon
1 Tbsp oil
¹/₄ cup mint leaves, finely chopped
2–3 tsp mixed mustard

Trim the fat from the chops. Combine the remaining ingredients, preferably in a food processor. Turn the chops in this mixture, cover and leave to stand for at least 15 minutes, preferably an hour.

Grill the chops in a shallow grill pan, brushing on marinade during cooking if desired. More mustard will give the chops a crustier surface.

Hawaiian Lamb Chops

These chops can be grilled or pan-grilled. Make the sauce in another pan while they cook, and combine the two when serving.

I like to serve them with plain rice and a green, leafy side salad. Other vegetables are unnecessary because of the onions, peppers and pineapple in the sauce.

If you are making these for a special dinner, consider boning the chops and curling the tails around the eyes to make noisettes. If you like, wrap them in bacon before skewering them.

For 4 servings:
8 middle loin lamb chops
2 Tbsp dark soy sauce
1 Tbsp oil
2 Tbsp lemon juice
1 Tbsp brown sugar
1 tsp grated root ginger
1–2 cloves garlic, crushed
1–2 onions, sliced
1 cup cubed pineapple
1 red pepper, sliced (optional)
1–2 green peppers, sliced
¹/₂–1 (125–250 ml/4–8 fl oz) cup pineapple juice
cornflour to thicken

Trim skin and any excess fat from the chops. Put them in a shallow dish or plastic bag with the next 6 ingredients

and leave to stand for at least 30 minutes, or up to 24 hours.

Sauté the onion, pineapple and peppers in a little extra oil until the onion is transparent, about 5 minutes. Keep the heat moderate so the vegetables do not brown. Lift the chops from the marinade and grill or pan-grill. Add the remaining marinade and the pineapple juice to the vegetable mixture and simmer for 3–5 minutes. Use the larger quantity of juice if cooking in a large pan, or if you want plenty of sauce. Thicken with a little cornflour paste.

Serve as soon as the chops are cooked, spooning the vegetables and sauce over the meat.

Moroccan Cutlets

Lamb cutlets marinated in these interesting spices are tender, delicious and very quickly cooked.

For 4 servings:
8 frenched lamb cutlets, well trimmed
2 Tbsp lemon juice
1 Tbsp olive oil
¹/₂ tsp ground cumin
¹/₂ tsp paprika
1 clove garlic, crushed

Flatten the cutlets by pounding them between 2 sheets of plastic with a meat hammer or rolling pin.

Put the remaining ingredients in a plastic bag, add the cutlets, squeeze out the air, and leave to stand for 10–20 minutes.

Cook in a hot, non-stick pan for about 2 minutes each side then serve with Fruity Couscous (p. 105).

Greek Marinated Lamb Chops or Noisettes

For 4 servings:
8–12 middle loin lamb chops
juice of 1 lemon
2 cloves garlic, finely chopped
1 tsp oreganum
1–2 Tbsp olive oil

Trim any outer fat from the chops without detaching the tail of the chop. If you want noisettes, trim off the fat, then cut round the T-shaped bone and remove it. Wind the tail around the outside of the tender 'eyes', and push 2 bamboo skewers through the rolled chops, from one side to the other, at right angles.

Place the prepared lamb in a shallow dish in one layer. Combine the remaining ingredients, pour over the lamb, and leave to stand, turning once or twice, for at least 30 minutes.

Grill or barbecue close to the heat, turning once or twice, until brown on the outside but still pink in the middle. Brush with extra marinade during cooking.

Glazed Bacon-Wrapped Noisettes

Glazed Bacon-Wrapped Noisettes

When the weather warms up and it's time to get out the barbecue, what better way to celebrate than with glazed noisettes made from succulent young lamb chops.

For 4 servings:
8 middle loin lamb chops
8 thin rashers side bacon
juice of 2 lemons
1/4 cup redcurrant or cranberry jelly
2 tsp Dijon mustard

Cut the T-bones from the chops and trim away any fat if necessary. Cut the bacon rashers so they are as wide as the chops are thick.

Roll the tails of the chops around the 'eyes' of muscle, then wrap the bacon strips around the noisettes, securing them and keeping the chops flat by pushing 2 bamboo skewers or half-skewers through the meat at right angles. Sprinkle with a little of the lemon juice and refrigerate until required.

Barbecue or grill the chops for about 5 minutes each side, 8–10 cm (3–4 in) from the heat, so the outside browns nicely, without overcooking the eye of the noisette. Heat the remaining lemon juice with the jelly and mustard and brush over the noisettes in the last 2–3 minutes of cooking.

Variation: Add a filling when rolling up the noisettes. Use one or more interesting, colourful ingredients, e.g. pieces of cooked peach, strips of red pepper, wedges of kiwifruit, sautéed mushrooms, water chestnuts.

Noisettes with Lemon-Sesame Sauce

Noisettes can be left plain or wrapped in a strip of bacon before skewering, as above, and they can also be coated with seasoned egg and breadcrumbs. Without the crumb coating they can be barbecued, grilled, pan-grilled or baked. After coating, noisettes are usually fried in a small amount of hot oil, or baked.

With or without coatings, grilled, fried or baked, noisettes are delicious with this lemony sauce – the same type of sauce that is sometimes served with chicken in Asian recipes.

Lemon-Sesame Sauce
For 8 chops:
1/4 cup sugar
2 Tbsp cornflour
grated rind and juice of 1 lemon
1 Tbsp corn or soy oil
2 Tbsp mild vinegar
1/2 tsp sesame oil
1 cup (250 ml/8 fl oz) water

Mix the sugar and cornflour together in a small pot. Add the remaining ingredients and bring to the boil, stirring constantly. Thin with extra water if necessary. Pour over cooked noisettes from which the skewers or toothpicks have been removed.

Sautéed Lamb with Chilli

This recipe calls for cubes of well-trimmed lamb shoulder meat, or the striploins or fillets from mutton, hogget or lamb, cut in cubes or slices. (Mutton striploins are sometimes called mutton backs.) The mutton in particular should be marinated before cooking for maximum tenderness and flavour.

The meat should be cooked briefly in a preheated, lightly oiled frypan (or a pan with a non-stick finish) in small quantities. Meat for more than three servings should be cooked in several batches.

For 3 servings:
400–500 g (about 1 lb) lean lamb, hogget or mutton, cubed
1 Tbsp dark soy sauce
1 tsp brown sugar
1/2 tsp sesame oil or 1 tsp corn oil
2 onions, sliced
2 cloves garlic, chopped
2 Tbsp corn oil
pinch cayenne, chilli powder or tabasco sauce, or finely chopped fresh chilli to taste
2 Tbsp water
juice of 1 lemon

Mix cubed meat with the soy sauce, brown sugar and oil. Cover and leave at room temperature for up to 4 or 5 hours, or in the refrigerator for 6 to 24 hours.

Lightly brown the onion and garlic in the corn oil in a fairly large frypan over a moderate heat, then add the cayenne or chilli to the onion as it cooks.

Remove the onion mixture from the pan and raise the heat until the pan is very hot. Add the meat a few pieces at a time, shaking or stirring the pan to prevent sticking. Keep the heat high. Turn all pieces so they brown evenly. When well coloured on all sides, add the water and lemon juice, and the cooked onion mixture. The meat should be evenly coated in a glaze which forms as the liquid evaporates. The meat should cook in 4–5 minutes.

Serve immediately on rice, with a salad, lightly cooked beans or stir-fried broccoli.

Chinese Lamb and Vegetables

For 3–4 servings:
about 300 g (10–11 oz) lean, tender lamb
2 cloves garlic, chopped
4 slices root ginger, finely chopped
2 Tbsp water
1 Tbsp cornflour
2 Tbsp oil
¼–½ cup toasted cashew nuts

Vegetables
300 g (10–11 oz) of a mixture of the
  following:
green and red pepper
spring onions
cabbage or spinach
cauliflower
celery
mushrooms

Marinade
1 Tbsp soy sauce
1 Tbsp sherry
1 tsp beef stock powder
1 tsp brown sugar

Combine the marinade ingredients. Slice the lamb thinly across the grain. Mix with half the garlic and ginger, and the marinade ingredients. Leave to stand for at least 15 minutes.

Mix the water and cornflour in a small bowl and put aside. Slice all the vegetables so they are suitable for stir-frying.

Heat 1 Tbsp oil in a large frypan, add the remaining garlic and ginger, then the vegetables, adding the slower-cooking ones first. Stir-fry until tender-crisp, then remove from the pan.

Reheat the pan again with the remaining oil, add the lamb and stir-fry over high heat until the meat changes colour. Add the cashew nuts, cooked vegetables, and enough of the cornflour paste to glaze both the meat and vegetables. Serve immediately, on rice or pasta.

Mexican Lamb

This recipe comes from 'sheep country' in Central Mexico. I like to make it with large, boned lamb forequarters, but a shoulder or leg of hogget or lamb works equally well.

Cooking meat slowly in a covered container is easy and troublefree, as long as you look at it occasionally to make sure the liquid around it has not evaporated. Some fat usually comes out of the meat as it cooks and this is poured away before the meat is shredded and served.

Meat cooked in an oven bag loses little liquid, and it is easy to see the different layers of liquid and fat through the clear bag. When the meat is ready, both fat and liquid may be poured into a container and the fat removed and discarded. For these reasons I usually cook this recipe in an oven bag rather than a casserole dish.

For 6–8 servings:
4 large onions, thinly sliced
2–3 Tbsp oil
1 boned shoulder of lamb (about 1.3 kg/
  2 lb 14 oz)
4 cloves garlic, sliced
1 cup (250 ml/8 fl oz) dry white or red
  wine
¼ cup (60 ml/2 fl oz) white or red wine
  vinegar
2 tsp ground cumin
2 tsp oreganum
½ tsp ground cinnamon
½ tsp chilli powder

Turn the oven to 180°C (350°F). Heat the oil in a large frypan and cook the onion over moderate heat until evenly browned.

Meanwhile, put the meat in an unpunctured oven bag or a casserole. Add the garlic, then the remaining ingredients. Add the browned onions. Close the bag, leaving a finger-sized hole, and place it in a roasting pan, or cover the casserole first with a sheet of foil then with a lid. Bake for 3 hours, or until the meat is so tender that it falls apart easily. Check there is always some liquid in the bag or casserole, adding a little water if necessary. (Do not mistake melted fat for liquid.)

Lift out the meat and shred it with 2 forks, discarding any fatty pieces. Place the shredded meat in a serving bowl.

Strain the liquid to remove the onion, then skim off all the fat. Arrange the onion over the meat, spoon over the skimmed juices, and cover until needed.

Serve the meat fairly hot, reheating it if necessary. Serve it on rice or piled into flour tortillas, topped with fresh coriander, lime juice and a little sour cream if desired. Accompany with Mexican Salad (p. 176) or with tossed salad.

Grilled Lamb Leg Steaks

This is the sort of meal I dream about in cold weather. It is especially good for an easy barbecue, or one away from home. Marinate the chops before you leave, and take pita bread to warm on the barbecue alongside the lamb.

For 4 servings:
4 lamb leg steaks
1 Tbsp olive oil
2 Tbsp light soy sauce
3 Tbsp lemon juice
2 cloves garlic, crushed

Trim any visible fat from around the lamb and snip the edges. Put the meat between 2 layers of plastic and bang with a rolling pin or meat hammer until it is about half its original thickness.

Mix the remaining ingredients and brush over both sides of the lamb, or turn the lamb in the mixture in a shallow container. Leave to stand at least 5 minutes, but preferably for several hours, in the refrigerator or a cool place.

Grill or barbecue close to the heat, remembering that lean, trimmed, beaten-out meat is likely to cook in only a few minutes. Grill red onion rings alongside if you like. Serve with Tabbouleh (p. 170) and lightly toasted pita bread.

Grilled Lamb Leg Steaks and Tabbouleh (p. 170)

Lamb Shoulder Pot Roast

This pot roast is one I cooked regularly when my children were of school age.

For 4–6 servings:

1 boned forequarter or shoulder of lamb
or hogget
1 Tbsp dry mustard
2 cloves garlic, finely chopped
2 Tbsp dark soy sauce
2 Tbsp lemon juice
1 Tbsp finely chopped fresh rosemary plus
extra sprigs

Turn the oven to 170°C (325°F). Trim all visible fat from the meaty side of the lamb, and cut away as much fat and outer membrane from the skin-side as possible. It is worth taking 15–20 minutes to do this thoroughly.

Mix together the next 5 ingredients, spread half over the inner surfaces of the meat and roll up evenly. Tie securely into an even roll, using heavy thread or string. Rub or brush the remaining mixture over the surface of the meat. Wrap it in foil with the extra sprigs of rosemary, or place it in an oven bag or a cast-iron casserole dish with a tightly fitting lid.

Bake for 2–2½ hours, depending on the size and age of the lamb or hogget, until it is very tender. Pour off the cooking liquid and strain it, skimming off and discarding the fat. Thicken the juices with a little cornflour paste. Cut the roll of meat into thick slices and serve with a little of the sauce.

Boiled Leg of Mutton

An old-fashioned English favourite, this recipe is excellent as long as you allow plenty of cooking time to ensure the meat is tender.

For 6 servings:

1 boned leg of mutton
2 onions
2 cloves garlic
2 carrots
6 cloves
6 peppercorns
sprig each thyme and parsley
50 g (2 oz) butter
¼ cup plain flour
2 tsp Dijon mustard
1 Tbsp vinegar (any variety)
2 Tbsp milk or cream
salt and pepper
2–3 tsp capers or chopped parsley (optional)

Trim the surface fat from the mutton and if you like tie it into a compact shape. Place it in a large pot, outer side up. Cover with water and add the onions, garlic, carrots, spices and herbs. Cover and simmer gently for 3–4 hours, until the meat is tender.

When the meat is ready, melt the butter in another pot. Add the flour and mustard,

gradually add 2 cups of stock strained from the meat, and stir until the sauce boils. Add the vinegar and milk, then season to taste, remembering that no salt has been added. Add the capers or chopped parsley if desired.

Slice the cooked meat quite thickly across the grain and pour over the sauce.

Note: Use the remaining stock for soup, sauces or as liquid for other stews or casseroles.

Seam-Boned Mutton

The following recipes are made from a leg of mutton that has been 'seam-boned' into four cuts: the thick flank, topside, silverside and rump or chump. You will need the cooperation of a helpful butcher for this. You may consider buying a side of mutton, asking for the leg to be 'seamed out', the loin muscle to be boned out in one piece, and the rest of the side to be boned, trimmed then minced. This produces well-flavoured meat that is excellent value for money, as long as it is cooked carefully.

Stir-Fried Mutton

If you slice the long, thin muscles from a boned loin of mutton very thinly, you can marinate the meat, then stir-fry it as you would tender cuts of lamb and beef. Take care not to overcook it or it will be tough.

For 2 servings:

about 200 g (7 oz) mutton
1 Tbsp dark soy sauce
1 Tbsp oil
1 tsp brown sugar
1 clove garlic, chopped
¼ tsp salt
1 onion
2 stalks celery
about 100 g (4 oz) cabbage
other vegetables (optional)
2 Tbsp oil
water
1 Tbsp cornflour

Slice the mutton into very thin slices across the grain of the muscle. Put it in an unpunctured plastic bag with the next 5 ingredients, and knead the bag gently to mix. Fasten the bag and refrigerate for 24–48 hours. (It becomes more tender as it stands.)

Cut the onion, celery and cabbage into even strips suitable for stir-frying, adding any other quick-cooking vegetables (e.g. red pepper, cauliflower and mushrooms) if you have them. Heat the second measure of oil in a large, heavy frypan, add the vegetables, and toss to coat with the oil. Add about 1 Tbsp water and cover the pan so the vegetables wilt and soften in the resulting steam. As soon as they are tender-crisp, remove them from the pan.

Heat the frypan again, tip in the marinated meat, adding a little more oil if it sticks, and stir-fry until it loses its red colour. Working fast, put the vegetables back in the pan and mix. Add the cornflour, mixed to a thin paste with water, to coat and glaze both the meat and the vegetables.

Serve immediately, on rice.

Mutton Schnitzels

Mutton schnitzels, coated and cooked the following way, are delicious. The compact and chunky thick flank and topside can be cut across the muscle in very thin slices, then banged even thinner with a rolling pin or meat hammer.

Each muscle, served as schnitzel, makes about 4 servings.

mutton schnitzels
1 Tbsp cider or wine vinegar
1 Tbsp soy sauce
plain flour
seasoned, beaten egg
breadcrumbs
oil

Place the meat in a plastic bag with the vinegar and soy sauce, leave to marinate for 24 hours, then coat and cook as schnitzels.

For a thick coating, dip each slice first in flour, then in seasoned, beaten egg, then in fine, dry breadcrumbs or crumbs made from stale bread. Cook in a few tablespoons of very hot oil until lightly browned on both sides.

Variation: Cook lamb, beef or pork schnitzels in the same way.

Mutton Steaks

The topside and thick flank muscles from a leg of mutton can easily be cut with a sharp knife into neat, meaty steaks, ideally about 1 cm (½ in) thick.

For 2 servings:

250 g (9 oz) mutton steaks
2 tsp soy sauce
2 tsp cider or wine vinegar
1 tsp sugar
1 tsp sesame or other cooking oil

Bang the steaks with a meat hammer or rolling pin. Combine the remaining ingredients and marinate the steak for several hours (or overnight). Cook it briefly in a lightly oiled frypan over high heat for 1–2 minutes each side. Take care not to overcook or the steaks will toughen.

Note: The larger of the two muscles from the loin may be treated the same way. Because it is quite a thin muscle, cut the steaks diagonally rather than crosswise, so they look bigger. Slices from the rump may cooked the same way.

Hot and Spicy Lamb Shanks

Hot and Spicy Lamb Shanks

These shanks simmer gently, untended, to make a memorable meal.

For 4–6 servings:
4–6 lamb shanks
1 tsp Szechwan peppercorns
1 Tbsp sesame oil
1 medium onion, chopped
3 cloves garlic, chopped
1 walnut-size piece fresh ginger, thinly sliced
1 cinnamon stick
1 whole star anise
2 whole cloves
2 small dried chillies
peel of ½ an orange and ½ a lemon
3 cups (750 ml/24 fl oz) water
3 Tbsp light soy sauce
2 Tbsp sherry
1 Tbsp brown sugar

For the best appearance and easy serving, ask your butcher to cut the lamb shanks in half crosswise.

Crush the peppercorns with a rolling pin or mortar and pestle, then heat in a large dry pot until aromatic. Add the sesame oil, onion, garlic and ginger, and cook over moderate heat for 3–4 minutes, until the onion is golden brown. Add the meat

and the remaining ingredients in the order given. Bring to the boil, reduce the heat and simmer gently for about 2 hours, or until the meat is very tender and falling from the bones.

Remove from the heat, lift out the shanks and strain the liquid through a sieve. Leave liquid to stand for a few minutes before skimming the fat from the surface. Boil the liquid down to a smaller amount if desired, or thicken it lightly with a little cornflour mixed to a paste in cold water. Put the shanks back in the pot, pour over the sauce and reheat before serving. Serve on rice with stir-fried vegetables.

Lamb Shanks with Macaroni

This is a great cold-weather family dinner! In the hour before dinner, the house is filled with delicious savoury aromas.

For 4 large or 8 smaller servings:
8 lamb or hogget shanks
3 medium onions, quartered
4 cloves garlic, chopped
1 jar (190 g/7 oz) tomato paste (nearly 1 cup)
4 cups (1 litre/32 fl oz) boiling water
1–2 tsp oreganum
1 Tbsp Worcestershire sauce (optional)
1 Tbsp sugar
1½ tsp salt
3–4 sprigs rosemary (optional)
1 cup small macaroni shapes
chopped parsley

Turn the oven to 170°C (325°F). Put the whole or halved shanks in a large roasting pan with the onion and garlic. Mix together the tomato paste, boiling water, oreganum, Worcestershire sauce, sugar and salt, and pour over the meat. Lay the rosemary sprigs over the meat, then cover the pan tightly, using a lid or 2 strips of foil folded together where they join.

Bake until the meat is tender (1¾–2 hours), then remove and discard the rosemary and sprinkle the macaroni evenly around the meat, making sure it is all under the surface of the liquid. Cover the pan again loosely, and cook for 30 minutes longer, until the macaroni is tender.

Lift the shanks out of the pan and gently stir the macaroni evenly through the thickened sauce. Thin a little with vegetable cooking liquid or water if necessary.

If possible, serve the shanks, macaroni and sauce in bowls rather than on flat plates, sprinkled with parsley.

Fruited Lamb Casserole

Fruited Lamb Casserole

This lamb stew has a Middle Eastern flavour, with almonds for added texture, dried apricots for tartness, and small amounts of spices which add interest without overpowering other flavours.

For 4 servings:
600–700 g (1 lb 5 oz–1 lb 9 oz) lean lamb
about 2 Tbsp plain flour
2 Tbsp olive or other oil
1–2 onions, sliced
1/2 tsp ground coriander
1/2 tsp ground cumin
1/2 tsp ground cinnamon
1/4 tsp ground allspice
about 1/4 cup blanched almonds
1/2 cup dried apricots, quartered
1/2 cup (125 ml/4 fl oz) water
1/2 cup (125 ml/4 fl oz) white wine
salt and pepper if necessary
about 1 Tbsp chopped fresh coriander
about 1 Tbsp chopped mint

Cut lamb from the shoulder or leg into 15 mm (1/2 in) cubes, removing fat, etc. Pat the meat dry if necessary, then sprinkle with the flour, tossing to coat and patting the flour into the meat. Discard excess flour.

Heat the oil in a heavy pot or frypan, then brown the onion evenly, adding the spices as the onion cooks. Remove this mixture from the pan, raise the heat and brown the meat on all sides, in several batches if necessary. Add the browned onions to the meat mixture.

Add the almonds, apricots, water and wine, cover and simmer gently for 30–45 minutes, or until the lamb is tender. Add extra water if the meat looks dry at any time.

Taste the lamb, adjust seasonings and thickness if necessary, then stir in the fresh herbs. Serve with couscous (p. 170).

Orange Lamb Casserole M

This microwaved lamb and vegetable casserole has a good colour and an interesting flavour.

For 4–5 servings:
1 kumara (about 250 g/9 oz)
25 g (1 oz) butter
1 green pepper
600 g (1 lb 5 oz) lean lamb
grated rind and juice of 1 orange
1 Tbsp cornflour
2 tsp chicken stock powder
1 Tbsp soy sauce
2 tsp grated root ginger
1 cup (250 ml/8 fl oz) hot water

Peel the kumara and cut it into 2 cm (3/4 in) cubes. Place it in a lidded microwave dish with the melted butter, cover and cook on High (100%) power for 5 minutes, stirring after 2 minutes. Dice the pepper, cut the lamb into cubes, and add to the cooked kumara.

In a jug mix the orange rind and juice, cornflour, stock powder, soy sauce, ginger and hot water to a smooth paste. Stir into the meat mixture.

Cover and cook on High (100%) power for 3 minutes, stir well, then cook on Medium (50%) power for 20 minutes, or until the meat is tender.

Leave to stand for 15 minutes before adjusting the seasonings. Serve on rice.

Lots-of-Lamb Casserole

This easy casserole has a very good flavour and colour, and is put together with the minimum of effort. If you like to cook ahead, make it the day before you want it. Leftovers may be refrigerated for up to a week and reheated easily in an oven or microwave.

If you don't have time to cut up and trim the meat yourself, ask your butcher to do this for you. (Many butchers charge very little for such work, as long as you buy a reasonable amount of meat.)

For 10 servings:
1 large hogget forequarter, boned
2 rashers bacon
2 Tbsp plain flour
1 jar (400–600 g/14 oz–1 lb 5 oz) any tomato-based pasta sauce
1/2 cup (125 ml/4 fl oz) white wine or stock
1/2 cup dried currants

Turn the oven to 180°C (350°F). Trim the fat from the meat and cut it into 15 mm (1/2 in) cubes.

Chop the bacon finely and put it with the lamb in a large casserole dish. If you do not have a large enough casserole, use a roasting pan and cover it with foil, folding 2 pieces together if necessary. Sprinkle the flour over the meat and toss with your fingers to coat fairly evenly.

Mix in the remaining ingredients, cover, and cook for about 2 hours, stirring every half hour if the casserole dish is deep. (Try a piece of meat after 1 1/2 hours. If you are using a wide, shallow dish, the meat may be cooked in this time.) If the meat has been carefully trimmed, no fat should rise to the top. If the trimming has not been particularly thorough, spoon off any fat that has risen to the top before you stir the mixture.

Variation: For extra colour, stir in several lightly cooked red peppers and zucchini just before serving.

Cranberry Lamb Casserole

This American recipe was sent to me by a woman living in Maine, who had seen me promoting lamb in Honolulu.

For 6–8 servings:

1 kg (2 lb 3 oz) lamb, cut from the
  shoulder
2 large onions, sliced
2 cloves garlic, chopped
1 tsp salt
pepper
½ cup (125 ml/4 fl oz) dry red wine
1 cup (250 ml/8 fl oz) water
2 Tbsp tomato paste or concentrate
1 Tbsp wine vinegar
½–1 cup (125–250 ml/4–8 fl oz) whole
  cranberry sauce
¼ tsp ground ginger
¼ tsp oreganum

Cube the lamb, removing most visible fat. Brown the meat in 2 batches over a high heat in a heavy-bottomed pot. Lightly brown the onion and garlic in the remaining fat, return the browned meat to the pan and add the salt, pepper, wine, water and tomato concentrate. Simmer for 45 minutes, with the lid of the pot ajar to allow some evaporation of the liquid. Add the remaining ingredients, cover tightly and simmer very gently for 30 minutes more. The liquid should be the right consistency at the end of the cooking time, but thin or thicken it if it is not.

Serve on rice, with green peas or beans and a crisp side salad if desired.

Lamb and Tomato Casserole

Neck chops are often great value for money, but need to be well cooked, so the meat falls off the bone.

For 4 servings:

1 kg (2 lb 3 oz) lamb or hogget neck
  chops
2 onions, sliced
2 cloves garlic, sliced
2–3 tsp oil
½ tsp sage, thyme or dill
1 cup (250 ml/8 fl oz) tomato purée
1 cup (250 ml/8 fl oz) water
salt, pepper and brown sugar to taste
2 Tbsp cornflour
2 Tbsp chopped parsley

Turn the oven to 160°C (325°F). Trim as much fat as possible from the chops. Brown them well, turning frequently, then transfer to a casserole dish. Cook the onion and garlic in a little oil until the onion is transparent and straw-coloured. Add to the meat with the herbs. Add the tomato purée and water, cover tightly and cook in the oven until the meat is tender enough to fall from the bones (2–3 hours). Leave to cool, then remove the fat and bones.

Reheat the meat and sauce, seasoning very carefully with salt, pepper and sugar. Thicken with cornflour paste as necessary. Sprinkle with parsley and serve on rice, or with mashed or baked potatoes.

Variation: Replace the chops with 600 g (1 lb 5 oz) cubed lean lamb and cook for 45–60 minutes, or until tender.

Spiced Lamb and Lentils

This economical mixture is particularly good made with small pieces of lamb cut from shoulder chops or from part of a shoulder or forequarter. Trim off most but not all of the fat, since the lentils absorb lamb fat as well as the lamb flavour. If you like, you can use more lamb and fewer lentils, leaving the other ingredients unchanged.

Garam masala is a type of mixed spice – whole coriander, cloves, cumin, cardamom, cinnamon, nutmeg and pepper, toasted or roasted, then ground. If you don't have garam masala, try adding some of its ingredients.

For 8–10 servings:

500–600 g (1 lb 2 oz–1 lb 5 oz) lamb
2–3 Tbsp oil
2 onions, chopped
2–3 cloves garlic, chopped
1 tsp garam masala
1 tsp turmeric
1 tsp ground cumin
1 tsp ground coriander seed
1 tsp ground ginger
1½ cups lentils
2 cups (500 ml/16 fl oz) water
2 tsp salt
1 cup (250 ml/8 fl oz) plain yoghurt

Cut the meat into very small cubes. Heat the oil in a large pot, then add the onion, garlic and spices. Stir over moderate heat for about 5 minutes, then add the meat. Stir over slightly higher heat for 5 minutes, browning but not burning anything, then add the lentils and water. Cover and simmer until the lentils are tender and the water absorbed.

Add the salt and yoghurt (or some extra water), cover again and simmer for about an hour, until the lamb is tender. Serve on rice, with salad vegetables.

LAMB VARIETY MEATS

Liver and kidneys are excellent value for money and are very nutritious, but we often ignore them, perhaps because they do not look or feel like other raw meat. They cost so little that it is well worth a try! Sometimes lambs' liver (lambs' fry) is sold by the kilogram or pound but when it is plentiful it is often sold (more cheaply) by the whole liver. Lambs' liver is at its best, moist and tender, when very lightly cooked. If overcooked, it is dry, tough and

chewy. The total cooking time of thinly sliced liver is about 2 minutes.

Pan-Fried Lambs' Liver

It is not essential to marinate liver, but it gives a good flavour and colour. Because liver cooks so fast, you should have the rest of your meal ready to serve before you start to cook it. Choose popular vegetables if your family or friends are not sure whether they like lambs' liver.

For 4 servings:

400 g (14 oz) lambs' liver, thinly sliced
oil
plain flour for coating
juice of ½ lemon or orange
chopped fresh herbs

Marinade
2 tsp soy sauce
2 tsp brown sugar
½ tsp garlic salt or ¼ tsp salt

Combine the marinade ingredients and add to thin slices of liver in an unpunctured plastic bag. Leave to stand for at least 5 minutes, or up to 24 hours.

Heat a large frypan with a thin film of oil. Lift 1 slice of liver at a time from the marinade, dip it in flour to coat both sides lightly, then place in the pan. Repeat with 4 or 5 pieces, working quickly. Cook for about 1 minute per side, until browned on the outside and pink in the middle. Take care not to overcook. Keep the cooked liver warm while you cook the rest in the same way.

Serve as is or put all the cooked liver back in the pan, squeeze over the juice, add whatever fresh herbs you like, and turn the slices until the liquid disappears.

Crumbed Lambs' Liver

For 4 servings:

400 g (14 oz) lambs' liver, thinly sliced
marinade (see above)
lightly beaten egg
2 Tbsp water
1 tsp curry powder
plain flour
fine dry breadcrumbs
oil

Marinate the liver as above. Mix the lightly beaten egg with the water and curry powder. Dip the drained slices of liver first in flour, next in the egg mixture, then in the breadcrumbs. If possible leave the crumbed slices to stand on a rack for about 5 minutes.

Heat about ¼ cup of oil in a large frypan. When it is very hot, but not smoking, add the crumbed liver. Cook for 1–2 minutes per side, until the crumbs are evenly golden. (Cut one piece in half to check the liver is cooked.) Serve as soon as possible with a selection of vegetables.

Patricia's Terrine

This tasty terrine makes a good summer first course, and an excellent topping for crusty bread with cucumber pickles, pickled walnuts, little radishes and spring onions.

For 4–6 servings:

about 400 g (14 oz) lambs' liver
2 small onions
3 cloves garlic
300 g (10½ oz) ham, cubed
1 cup (250 ml/8 fl oz) cream
1 egg, lightly beaten
freshly ground black pepper
1 tsp salt
½ tsp ground allspice
1 Tbsp fresh thyme, chopped

Trim the liver, discarding any tough bits and skin. Slice into about 2 cm (¾ in) strips. Soak for about 30 minutes in cold water.

Turn the oven to 150°C (300°F). Finely chop the quartered onions and garlic in the food processor, then put aside in a large mixing bowl.

Drain the water from the liver, place the liver in the unwashed food processor and, using the pulse button, purée until smooth. Add the ham and process again briefly. Add to the chopped onion. Add the cream, lightly beaten egg and seasonings, and stir lightly until well combined.

Line a terrine or loaf pan about 7-cup (1.75 litres/56 fl oz) capacity with baking paper or spray lightly with non-stick spray. Pour in the liver mixture, smooth the surface and cover with a lid or foil. Place in a roasting pan. Add water to the pan until it is at least halfway up the sides of the terrine. Check frequently during cooking, adding more water if necessary.

Cook for 1–1½ hours, or until the mixture feels firm when you press it in the middle. Remove from the oven, lift out of the water bath and weigh down with a suitable weight, e.g. a piece of wood or polystyrene, wrapped in cling film, then weighed down with several cans of food, or a loaf pan of similar size filled with water or stones.

Leave until cold, then refrigerate. Use within 3 or 4 days. The colour of your terrine may not be too exciting, but the flavour is wonderful!

Variation: Line the bottom of the terrine or loaf tin with several rashers of bacon before pouring in the liver mixture.

Lambs' Liver in Sour Cream

Liver with onions, paprika and sour cream just has to taste good!

For 4 servings:

400 g (14 oz) lambs' liver
1 large onion
2 Tbsp butter
2 tsp paprika
½ tsp salt
pepper to taste
½ cup sour cream

Cut the liver into 5 mm (¼ in) slices. Soak for 15 minutes in cold water, drain and pat dry. Cut the slices into strips about the thickness of a pencil. Halve then slice the onion thinly.

Melt 1 Tbsp of the butter in a medium-sized frypan and cook the onion until tender and golden, covering the pan loosely. Remove the cooked onion from the pan.

Heat the remaining butter in the same pan, add the strips of liver and cook on high heat for 3 to 4 minutes, stirring constantly, until evenly browned on all sides. Return the onion to the pan, add the paprika, salt, pepper and sour cream. Turn so the sauce coats the onion and liver, and heat through (but do not boil) before serving.

Serve on wide green ribbon pasta that has been tossed with a little butter or oil and finely chopped fresh herbs or parsley. Serve a green, leafy salad on a side dish.

Patricia's Terrine

Herbed Lambs' Liver

Sage and liver is an excellent combination.

For 4 servings:
400–500 g (about 1 lb) lambs' liver
2 tsp soy sauce
1 clove garlic, very finely chopped
1–2 onions, thinly sliced
1 Tbsp butter
1 rasher bacon, very finely chopped
about 4 fresh sage leaves, finely chopped,
* or ¼ tsp dried sage*
1 Tbsp lemon juice
½ cup (125 ml/4 fl oz) water
freshly ground black pepper
hot pepper sauce
about ¼ cup plain flour
a little oil or clarified butter

Cut the liver into 5 mm (¼ in) slices, trimming off and discarding any pieces that are not smooth and fine-textured. Cut large pieces into smaller, leaf-shaped pieces if you think they look nicer. Pat dry between paper towels, then put in a shallow dish with the soy sauce and garlic while you make the sauce.

Cook the onion in the butter in a medium-sized pan, until evenly browned. Add the bacon and cook for 2–3 minutes longer, then add the sage, lemon juice and water and simmer for 2–3 minutes. During this time, add pepper and a dash of hot pepper sauce. Put the sauce aside while you cook the liver.

Put the flour in another shallow container, heat a thin film of oil or clarified butter in a large, preferably non-stick frypan, and when very hot, dip each piece of liver lightly in the flour and put it in the pan. Cook for about 1 minute per side, or until no pink juice comes to the surface when it is pierced. (Turn the pieces at least twice). Remove each piece of liver as soon as it is cooked. As soon as all the liver is cooked, put the sauce in the pan, bring it to the boil, then replace the liver and turn to glaze it.

Note: Always flour slices of liver just before putting them in the pan.

Microwaved Savoury Kidneys   M

This recipe is unbelievably quick and easy, as well as being rich in iron. It is the perfect recipe for a small household.

For 2–3 servings:
4 lambs' kidneys
2 rashers bacon
50 g (2 oz) button mushrooms
2 tsp dark soy sauce
2 tsp cornflour
2 Tbsp water or sherry

Halve, trim and slice the kidneys thinly. Chop the bacon, discarding the rind, and slice the mushrooms thickly. Place the kidneys in a small microwave dish with the bacon, mushrooms, soy sauce, cornflour and water or sherry. Stir gently but thoroughly to mix.

Cover and microwave for 5–6 minutes on High (100%) power, until the sauce has thickened and the kidneys are firm. Serve on toast, sprinkled with finely chopped fresh herbs.

East-West Lambs' Kidneys

Although this recipe contains an odd combination of ingredients, they all mix well together!

For 2 servings:
4 lambs' kidneys
1 Tbsp sherry
1 Tbsp dark soy sauce
1 clove garlic, crushed
½ tsp grated root ginger (optional)
1 rasher bacon
2 tsp tomato paste
1 Tbsp mixed mustard
1 Tbsp cream
1 tsp oil

Slice the kidneys lengthways, remove and discard the cores, then slice thinly crosswise. Put them in a small container with the sherry, soy sauce, garlic and ginger. Leave to stand at room temperature for at least 10 minutes or refrigerate for up to 24 hours.

Chop the bacon into small pieces, discarding the rind. Stir the tomato paste, mustard and cream together in a small glass until completely mixed.

Heat a wok or heavy, non-stick frypan on high heat, add the oil, and coat the cooking surface with it. Add the drained kidneys (reserving the marinade) and the bacon. Stir-fry for about 2 minutes, until the kidneys and bacon are firm and the pieces separate. Add the remaining marinade and keep cooking until most of it has disappeared. Taste a kidney to see if it is cooked, then stir the tomato mixture and add to the pan. Continue to cook until the sauce thickens and coats the kidneys.

Serve on or with triangles of toast, or piled on halved baked potatoes.

Spicy Lambs' Kidneys

I regard kidneys as a treat but my family doesn't share my views, so I decided to add ingredients which would modify the kidney flavour without adding much to the cost. My experiment seemed to succeed, as this dish has proved very popular. I suggest serving the kidneys on plain rice, or a rice risotto mixture, with beans and carrots, or with coleslaw.

For 4 servings:
500–600 g (1 lb 2 oz–1 lb 5oz) lambs'
* kidneys*
1 Tbsp butter or oil
1 large onion, sliced
1 or 2 cloves garlic, sliced
1 tsp curry powder
½ tsp ground ginger
4 cloves
2–3 cm (1 in) cinnamon stick or ¼ tsp
* ground cinnamon*
1 Tbsp Worcestershire or soy sauce
1 cup (250 ml/8 fl oz) water
cornflour for thickening
salt to taste

Slice the kidneys lengthways, remove and discard the cores, then slice thinly crosswise.

Melt the butter or oil in a medium-sized pot. Add the onion, garlic, curry powder, ginger, cloves and cinnamon, and cook for 5 minutes over moderate heat, stirring frequently. Add the sliced kidneys, stir well to coat, then add the Worcestershire or soy sauce and water. Cover and simmer for 1–1½ hours, until the kidneys are tender.

Remove the cloves and cinnamon stick, thicken with a paste made from cornflour and cold water, then taste critically and add as much salt as you need to bring out the flavour. Serve immediately, or refrigerate until required, then reheat, stirring frequently.

Bravo for Beef

Next time you want beef for dinner, cast your eyes over the varied selection of recipes in this chapter. Whether you want a quick steak, stir-fry or schnitzel, a simmered stew or an impressive roast, I hope you will find something to whet your appetite. At the end there are a couple of tasty venison recipes as well, included here because there aren't enough to put in a separate section, and because they may also be made with beef.

Barbecuing Steak

Steaks that have been cut 1–2 cm (1/2–3/4 in) thick are best cooked on a preheated thick metal plate rather than on a grill rack, since it is hard to get the heat on a rack high enough to brown the outside of a thinnish steak without overcooking the centre.

A steak that is 3–5 cm (1¼–2 in) thick can be cooked on a grill rack or solid plate, and should be carved diagonally into thin slices after it is cooked.

All steaks will be more tender if they are marinated before they are cooked. The longer they stand in the marinade, the more tender they will be. In other words, the tougher the steak cut, the longer it should be marinated.

Marinades tenderise fastest at room temperature, so this is best if you have only a few hours in which to marinate the steak. You can leave steak in a marinade in the refrigerator for several days if you like. Trim the steak of nearly all visible fat, put it in an unpunctured plastic bag with the marinade, squeeze out all the air, and secure the bag with a rubber band.

- Fillet steak is the most tender.
- Rib eye and sirloin steaks are not quite as tender as fillet, but have more flavour.
- Rump steaks and cross-cut blade steaks have excellent flavour but are tougher, and require marinating and brief cooking for best results. A thick piece of marinated rump is excellent carved after cooking.
- Thin flank or flank skirt steak may be marinated and cooked fairly rare, in one piece, on a hot plate, then thinly sliced across the grain.

Barbecued Beef Fillet

For this special-occasion barbecued beef, see the recipe on p. 125.

Barbecued Rump Steak

Wine Marinade

¼ cup (60 ml/2 fl oz) red or white wine
1 Tbsp wine vinegar
1–2 cloves garlic, crushed
1 tsp dried oreganum
1–2 Tbsp corn or olive oil

If you are using a cut of steak that is not so tender, and have little marinating time, tenderise it with a meat hammer. Mix all the marinade ingredients together, and marinate the steak as above.

When ready to cook, preheat a thick metal plate or a heavy pan on the barbecue. Pat the steak dry, oil its surface lightly, then brown it on both sides on the thoroughly preheated plate. If necessary lower the heat until the centre is cooked to your liking. It may take as little as 3 minutes under good conditions. Brush with a glaze at the end of the cooking time if you like.

Note: Soy-based marinades are also good for beef.

Barbecued Rump Steak

Although rump steak is not as tender as steaks from the loin, its flavour is excellent. Treat the steak very carefully so you can enjoy its flavour without toughening it.

A thick slice of rump, marinated, barbecued, then sliced thinly, is delicious!

For 2 servings:
1 rump steak, 4 cm (1¾ in) thick
2 Tbsp dark soy sauce
strip of lemon or lime rind
2 Tbsp lemon or lime juice
1 Tbsp oil
2 cloves garlic, crushed
1 tsp honey or brown sugar
hot pepper sauce
1–2 tsp grated fresh root ginger (optional)

Trim the thick steak, removing all outer fat. Snip any membrane, since it shrinks faster than the meat, causing it to curl during cooking. Put the meat between 2 pieces of cling film or plastic, and bang it evenly from one side to the other with a rolling pin, then turn it at right angles and bang it again in the same way.

Measure all the remaining ingredients into a heavy, unpunctured plastic bag. Add the steak, squeeze out the air, fasten the bag with a rubber band, and refrigerate, preferably for 1–2 days, but for at least half an hour, turning it occasionally. An hour before cooking, bring to room temperature. Lift the steak from the marinade and drain off the liquid.

Put the steak in a grilling basket and position it so that the surface of the meat is about 8 cm (3¼ in) from the heat. Alternatively, cook the steak on a preheated, solid plate lightly brushed with oil. Cook for about 6 minutes then turn and cooking another 4–6 minutes. Press the centre of the meat at intervals. At first it will be spongy, then it will become springier as it cooks. If you are not sure if it is cooked, cut a small slit and check the colour.

Leave to stand for at least 6 minutes then, using a very sharp knife, cut in thin diagonal slices, across the grain of the meat. Serve hot or at room temperature, with mustard or horseradish sauce, and your favourite vegetables or salads.

You don't have to travel far from home to find meat cuts with unfamiliar names. If in doubt, ask a butcher's advice. Butchers know a great deal about meat and are often happy to help a prospective customer.

When my daughter moved to another town and started buying and cooking food for flatmates, I suggested that she arrange with a nearby butcher to watch him disjoint a carcass, learn the names he gave to different meat cuts, listen to his cooking suggestions, and find what he felt was best value for her (limited) budget. She did as I suggested, learned a lot, and benefited from the butcher's interest in her future purchases.

London Broil

A beef skirt flank steak is leaf-shaped, about 30 cm (12 in) long and 20 cm (8 in) wide. You can see the muscle fibres running down its length. After it is scored and marinated for 24 hours, it may be pan-grilled very successfully, but it must be slightly undercooked – it will be tough if well done.

Skirt flank comes from the belly area of the beef carcass. There are two pieces on each carcass. Do not buy thick flank for this recipe.

For 3–4 servings:
1 whole beef skirt flank steak
2 Tbsp oil
2 Tbsp lemon juice
2 Tbsp soy sauce
2 tsp sugar
½ tsp salt
2 cloves garlic, crushed

Score the surface of the steak on both sides in 2 cm (³/4 in) diamonds, making cuts not more than 5 mm (¹/4 in) deep.

Mix the remaining ingredients in an unpunctured plastic bag. Add the steak and press so that all the air is removed. Tie the bag tightly and refrigerate for 24 hours.

Grill or barbecue the meat on a solid plate, allowing 5–6 minutes per side. It should be browned outside, but pink in the middle. Leave it to stand for 5 minutes after cooking, then slice diagonally across the grain.

Quick Beef Satay

Make these kebabs with a tender cut of steak.

For 4 servings:
750 g (1 lb 10 oz) sirloin or rump steak

Marinade
1 tsp ground cumin
1 tsp ground coriander
2 Tbsp soy sauce
2 Tbsp lemon juice
2 Tbsp oil
2 cloves garlic, crushed
about ¹/4 tsp chilli powder

Peanut Sauce
¹/4 cup peanut butter
½ cup (125 ml/4 fl oz) water
2 Tbsp soft brown sugar
1 Tbsp lemon juice
1 Tbsp dark soy sauce

Cut the steak into 2 cm (³/4 in) cubes and mix with the marinade ingredients in a plastic bag. Refrigerate for 12–24 hours.

Thread the steak onto 12 bamboo skewers, then barbecue on an oiled grill rack over high heat for about 4 minutes per side. Stir the remaining marinade into the peanut sauce ingredients and bring to boil, thinning with more water if necessary. Brush the kebabs with peanut sauce during the second half of cooking. Serve extra sauce with the skewered beef.

> Soak bamboo skewers in water for 5–10 minutes before using for kebabs.

Pan-Grilled Steak

Learn how to perfect this way of cooking steak – it is a very useful skill. Select steaks for pan-grilling as you would steaks for barbecuing (see Barbecuing Steak, p. 119).

For 4 servings:
4 steaks, cut 2 cm (³/4 in) thick

Marinade
1 Tbsp lemon juice
1–2 Tbsp soy sauce
1–2 cloves garlic, crushed
1 tsp brown sugar
1–2 tsp oil

If the steaks are not the most tender cut, pound them with a meat hammer before marinating. Mix the marinade ingredients together and turn the steaks in this. Put them in plastic bags or cover them closely if they are to be left to stand for long.

Marinate fillet steak for a few minutes (for flavour).

Marinate rib and sirloin steaks for 30 minutes or longer.

Marinate rump steak (or heart) for at least 3–4 hours.

Marinate cross-cut blade in the refrigerator for 24 hours.

Bring the steak to room temperature before cooking it. Heat a heavy pan, add just enough oil to form a thin film on the pan, then add the steaks. Brown one side, turn and brown the other side, then lower the heat and cook to the degree you like. If in doubt cut through the thickest part of the steak and check its colour. Remove the cooked steaks to serving plate.

Add the remaining marinade to the pan with a little water, wine or stock and seasoning. Stir until the bottom of the pan is clean and 3 or 4 Tbsp of liquid remain. Remove from the heat, add some freshly chopped herbs if you like, then add 1–2 tsp of butter. Turn the pan until the butter dissolves and the mixture looks syrupy, then pour it over the steaks.

Notes: Marinades may be added to frozen steaks, so they thaw and marinate at the same time.

Steaks such as cross-cut blade, for barbecues, may be pounded, marinated, then frozen, so they can be cooked as soon as they have thawed.

Sesame Steaks

I cook these on the barbecue, or pan-grill them on the stove. See Barbecuing Steak, p. 119, for selecting steaks.

For 4 servings:
4 steaks
¹/4 cup (60 ml/2 fl oz) soy sauce
2 Tbsp sugar
2 tsp sesame oil
1 onion, grated
2 cloves garlic, crushed
few drops tabasco sauce

Snip the edges of the steaks to prevent them curling, and put them in an unpunctured plastic bag. Put the remaining ingredients in a blender or food processor, process until evenly mixed, then pour over the steaks. OR measure the soy sauce, sugar and oil into the bag with the steaks, add the finely chopped or grated onion and garlic, and the tabasco.

Move the meat around so it is all coated with marinade, squeeze out the air, seal the bag and refrigerate until required. Lift the steaks from the marinade and bring to room temperature before cooking. Reserve the marinade.

Heat a heavy frypan until very hot, oil the surface, then add the steaks and cook 2–4 minutes each side, turning once. Remove to a serving dish.

Add the remaining marinade to the pan, bring to the boil, evaporate it until it is thick and syrupy, and spoon a small amount over each steak.

OR barbecue the steaks, brushing them with extra marinade as they cook.

Slice the steak and serve it with rice or hot bread rolls, tomatoes and cucumber, or a green salad.

Mexican Beef with Peppers

Mexican seasonings are interesting, but not necessarily hot. Alter the hotness to suit yourself in this recipe, varying the amount of chilli powder you use, and the make, type and quantity of chilli sauce.

For 4 servings:
500 g (1 lb 2 oz) rump steak (in one piece)
3 peppers, preferably 1 green, 1 red and 1 yellow
1 red onion
about 2 Tbsp sweet chilli sauce

Seasoning
1 Tbsp paprika
2 tsp oreganum
½ tsp rosemary
1 Tbsp ground cumin
½–1 tsp chilli powder
2 tsp garlic powder
1 tsp brown sugar
1 tsp salt

Trim all visible fat from the meat and cut it across the grain into 5 mm (1/4 in) slices. Halve the peppers lengthways, then cut crosswise into slices about 1 cm (1/2 in) thick. Chop the onion finely.

Combine all the seasoning ingredients, mixing thoroughly in a food processor, blender or small grinder, or simply shaking everything together. Mix most of the seasoning with the sliced meat, coating it as evenly as possible.

Preheat a heavy frypan or wok with a little oil and stir-fry the vegetables over high heat for 2–4 minutes, or until barely tender, then add the coated meat, with a little more oil if necessary. Toss the mixture so the meat loses it pinkness and is lightly browned all over. Add the chilli sauce, toss to coat, and serve immediately with a salad of sliced tomatoes, avocado and spring onions, and with corn chips, rice or bread rolls.

Variations: For a less highly seasoned mixture use half the seasoning. Keep the rest in an airtight jar.

Tip the stir-fried vegetables out of the pan before cooking the meat, and combine the meat, vegetables and chilli sauce later.

Note: When the full quantity of chilli powder is used, this dish is too hot for many people. With half the seasoning it is too hot for most children. Use chilli with care!

Beef Schnitzels

A meal of schnitzels is generally cheaper than a steak meal as a little thinly sliced beef goes a long way if you beat it even thinner, then coat it with a substantial crust. Beef schnitzels are cut from thick flank or topside. Because these aren't particularly tender cuts, you must be careful not to overcook and toughen them. To ensure tenderness, serve them as soon as the coating is cooked.

For 4 servings:
350–400 g (12–14 oz) beef schnitzels
1 tsp garlic salt or 1/2 tsp salt
1/2 tsp curry powder (optional)
1 Tbsp water
1 egg
plain flour (optional)
1 cup fine dry breadcrumbs

Cut the schnitzels into manageable pieces and trim, cutting any connective tissue at the edge to prevent the meat curling during cooking. To make the schnitzels thinner, place them between sheets of plastic or cling film and bang with a meat hammer or rolling pin.

In a shallow bowl, mix the salt and curry powder with the water, then add the egg. Stir with a fork until the egg white and

Mexican Beef with Peppers

yolk are mixed, but not overbeaten (overbeaten egg will not stick to the meat so well). Dip the schnitzels into the egg mixture, then into the crumbs. For a thicker coating, first dip the meat in flour, then egg, then crumbs. Stand the schnitzels on a rack for about 5 minutes to set the coating.

Heat a frypan until very hot, with enough oil to cover its bottom, and cook the schnitzels briefly until golden brown on both sides. Take care not to overcook. By the time the coating is golden brown, the meat will be cooked.

Veal Schnitzels

White veal is the meat from young calves. It is light in colour, lean, with a delicate flavour, and should not be overcooked or served with foods that are very strongly flavoured.

For 2 servings:
2 or 4 white veal schnitzels
plain flour for coating
1 Tbsp oil
1 Tbsp butter
1/4 cup sliced mushrooms
2 tsp plain flour
1/4 cup (60 ml/2 fl oz) white wine
1/4 cup (60 ml/2 fl oz) chicken stock
1 Tbsp capers (optional)
2 Tbsp cream

Lightly flour the schnitzels. Cook them in the oil and butter in a pan over moderate heat until very lightly browned on both sides. Remove the meat from the pan and keep it warm.

Add the mushrooms and 2 tsp flour to the drippings in the pan, and cook until straw-coloured. Stir in the wine, chicken stock, capers and cream and stir until smooth, diluting with extra wine or water if desired. Pour over the veal and serve.

Curried Stir-Fried Beef

This rather unusual recipe calls for stir-frying thinly sliced beef, then stirring it into a hot curry mixture. Keep the heat very high when you make a mixture like this.

For 2 servings:
250 g (9 oz) rump or skirt steak
2 tsp cornflour
1 Tbsp dark soy sauce
1/2–1 tsp sesame oil
1/4–1/2 tsp tabasco sauce
2 Tbsp oil
1 large clove garlic, sliced
2–3 tsp curry powder
1 tsp sugar
1 Tbsp sherry

Slice the meat across the grain, no more than 5 mm (1/4 in) thick. Mix with the next 4 ingredients, leave to stand for at least 15 minutes, then stir-fry in the oil over very high heat in a large frypan or wok. Cook the meat in 2 lots if the pan is not very big. Remove from the pan as soon as it has lost its pinkness.

Add a little more oil to the pan if necessary, so you have 1 Tbsp left. Add the sliced garlic then the curry powder and the sugar. Add the sherry. If necessary add about a tablespoon of water if there isn't enough liquid to dissolve the curry mixture.

Add the meat, toss for no more than 1 minute, then serve on rice.

Steak Teriyaki

For 2 servings:
250 g (9 oz) beef schnitzels
1–2 cloves garlic, crushed
1/2 tsp beef stock powder
2 Tbsp hot water
2 Tbsp sugar
2 Tbsp sherry
2 Tbsp Kikkoman soy sauce
about 1/2 tsp cornflour

Trim the schnitzels, cutting them into smaller pieces if desired. Combine all the other ingredients except the cornflour in the order given, in a shallow dish. Turn the steak in the marinade, and leave for about 30 minutes.

Barbecue or grill the steak close to the heat, or brown on both sides in a non-stick frypan. Add the cornflour to the remaining marinade and bring to the boil to thicken. Spoon a little sauce over the cooked steaks.

Extra-Quick Beef Stroganoff

Beef stroganoff is a very rich, quickly cooked mixture, made with tender steak which is sliced thinly, browned quickly, and served in a sauce containing mushrooms, tomato paste (or concentrate) and sour cream. Any of the suggested cuts make good stroganoff, but fillet is the most tender.

To prepare this in a very short time, cook the onions and mushrooms ahead.

For 4 servings:
4 Tbsp butter
2 large onions, halved and sliced
250–500 g (9 oz–1 lb 2 oz) button mushrooms, sliced
3/4 tsp salt
2 tsp cornflour
2 Tbsp tomato paste
1/2 cup (125 ml/4 fl oz) water
500–600 g (1 lb 2 oz–1 lb 5 oz) fillet, porterhouse or scotch fillet
1/2–1 cup sour cream

Heat 1 Tbsp of the butter in a heavy frypan, add the onion and cook over moderate heat until tender and browned at the edges. Add the mushrooms and cook over fairly high heat until they are hot, stirring occasionally. Add the salt, cornflour, tomato paste and water, stir until the mixture boils and thickens, then remove from the pan and refrigerate until required.

Cut the steak into strips of pencil thickness and matchstick length and put aside.

Ten minutes before you want to serve, heat a heavy frypan until very hot. Drop 1 Tbsp of the butter into the pan, and add a third of the steak. Stir over high heat until the steak loses its red colour – do not overcook. Put aside in a bowl. Cook the next third in another Tbsp of butter, repeat with the remaining meat, and again empty the pan.

Put the sauce back in the pan to heat. When it is close to boiling, stir in the beef and the sour cream. Warm through thoroughly but do not boil or leave to simmer. Serve as soon as possible, on cooked noodles that have been drained, buttered and mixed with chopped parsley, and with green beans.

Stir-Fried Steak and Mushrooms

Stir-fried meat dishes like this one cook in a few minutes.

For 4 servings:
400–500 g (about 1 lb) skirt steak
2 cloves garlic, finely chopped
2 slices fresh ginger
2 Tbsp dark soy sauce
2 Tbsp sherry
100 g (4 oz) button mushrooms
6 spring onions
2 Tbsp oil

Slice the steak very thinly with a very sharp knife. Place in a plastic bag with the garlic, ginger, soy sauce and sherry. Squeeze air from the bag and leave to marinate for a few minutes, or for up to 24 hours.

When ready to cook, wash and drain the mushrooms and gently push them down the feed tube of a food processor, slicing

them with the slicing disk. Cut the spring onions with a knife into diagonal pieces 3–4 cm (1 1/2 in) long.

Heat the oil in a large frypan or wok. When the oil starts to smoke, add the steak and stir it with a fish slice until it has all changed colour. Keeping the heat, add the mushrooms and spring onions. Keep stirring the mixture gently, lifting and turning it with the fish slice.

Serve as soon as the mushrooms and onions have heated through, with rice or noodles and one or two vegetables.

Stir-Fried Beef and Vegetables   M

When you are really in a hurry, a stir-fried meal is one of the quickest and most practical meals you can cook.

For 4 servings:
400–500 g (about 1 lb) beef schnitzel
2 cloves garlic
2 Tbsp corn or soy oil
1 Tbsp sherry
1 Tbsp dark soy sauce
2 tsp cornflour
1 tsp beef stock powder
500 g (about 1 lb) mixed vegetables
2 Tbsp oil

Slice the schnitzels into strips 1 cm (1/2 in) wide, removing any fat and fibrous tissue. Mix with next 6 ingredients, cover and leave to stand at least 5 minutes.

Select quick-cooking, colourful vegetables, and slice them into strips. Heat 2 Tbsp of oil in a large frypan or wok, add the vegetables, and toss to coat with oil. Cover and cook at high heat for 2–4 minutes, until crunchy tender. (Add 1–2 Tbsp of water to make steam if necessary.) Remove the vegetables from the pan.

Add the marinated meat to the pan and stir over high heat until it loses its pinkness. Add the vegetables, stir to mix, and serve immediately on rice.

For a microwaved 'stir-fry', marinate the meat in an oven bag. Toss the vegetables in 1–2 Tbsp of oil in a covered microwave dish, and microwave on High (100%) power for 3–4 minutes, until crunchy tender.

Secure the mouth of the oven bag with a rubber band, leaving a finger-sized hole. Microwave for 3–4 minutes, until the meat is no longer pink. Combine the meat and vegetables, and serve immediately.

Beef Port Casserole

This full-flavoured casserole requires little attention as it cooks.

For 4 servings:
4 cross-cut blade steaks
2 medium onions

2 Tbsp oil
2 Tbsp plain flour
1 Tbsp honey
½ cup (125 ml/4 fl oz) water
½ cup (125 ml/4 fl oz) port
2 tsp beef stock powder or 1 tsp salt
2 tamarillos, peeled and sliced (optional)

Turn the oven to 150°C (300°F). Lay the steaks in one layer in a casserole dish. Slice the onions into rings and brown in a frypan in the oil. Add the flour to the onions, stir until evenly brown, then add the honey and let it turn golden brown as well. Remove from the heat, add the water, port and stock powder, and pour over the meat. Cover tightly and bake for 1 hour.

Add the tamarillos and cook 30 minutes longer. Serve with baked potatoes and brussels sprouts or beans.

Variations: Replace port with sherry.

Replace tamarillos with pineapple rings or other fruit, and add 1 Tbsp tomato paste.

One-Step Beef Casserole

I'm sure everyone must have days when they want to get the easiest dinner possible on to cook so they can get on with more pressing things. This is a casserole that you can throw together and put in the oven as you rush out the door. It's good to arrive home and smell the casserole, ready to eat!

For 4 servings:
600 g (1 lb 5 oz) blade steak, cubed
1 packet (about 30 g/1 oz) tomato soup
  mix
1 Tbsp wine vinegar
2 tsp mixed mustard
2 tsp dark soy sauce
1 tsp marjoram or oreganum
½ tsp thyme
2 cloves garlic, chopped
1½ cups (375 ml/12 fl oz) water

Toss the meat in the soup mix then put in a casserole with all the other ingredients, in the order listed. Stir well.

Cover the casserole, putting a piece of foil under the lid, and put in a cold or preheated oven. Cook at 150°C (300°F) for 2 hours, stirring once during this time if possible. Leave to stand for 10 minutes before serving if time allows.

Although you may find they overcook a bit, you can put large chunks of potatoes and carrots in with the casserole as well. Sprinkle them generously with chopped parsley before serving.

Drip Stew

A 'drip stew' needs no attention as it cooks. The resulting mixture has a flavour which is intensely beefy, and like all stews, it tastes even better when reheated.

For 4 servings:
600 g (1 lb 5 oz) chuck steak
1 onion
1 Tbsp Worcestershire sauce
bunch of herbs (optional)
freshly ground black pepper
¼ tsp salt
2 tsp cornflour
2 Tbsp sherry or water

Select a bowl made of heat-resistant glass or stainless steel, or a small casserole dish that you can sit on a plate inside a large covered pot. During the cooking the bowl or casserole should be covered by a plate, an inverted lid, or a piece of foil that is depressed in the middle. The idea is that the steam will condense on the cover and drip back down onto the meat from its lowest point, the centre.

Slice the steak into thin strips, discarding fat and thick pieces of gristle. (Small pieces will disappear during cooking.) Slice the onion thinly. Put the meat, onion and Worcestershire sauce in the container and mix together.

Make a herb bundle by tying together any fresh herbs you like, e.g. thyme, oreganum, lovage, a bayleaf and parsley, or add a pinch of dried herbs. Bury the bundle of herbs in the meat. Add the pepper, cover, and pour warm water around the bowl so that it comes halfway up the side. Simmer for 1½ hours, until the meat is tender, but look at the meat after an hour, stirring it and removing the bundle of herbs.

When the meat is tender, add salt to taste, and stir in the cornflour mixed with the sherry or water. Cook a little longer until the stew has thickened, then serve with a selection of vegetables. Try spooning the meat and gravy over noodles, too.

Drip Stew

Swiss Steak

This is a beef casserole that I have made regularly for 30 years. I like the fact that I can prepare it when it suits me, leave it to cook while I am busy with other things, then refrigerate the leftovers to serve later in the week.

For 4 servings:

¼ cup plain flour
600 g (1 lb 5 oz) cross-cut blade steak,
  1 cm (½ in) thick
2–3 Tbsp oil
2 medium onions
½–1 tsp salt
2 tsp sugar
1 cup (250 ml/8 fl oz) tomato purée
½ cup (125 ml/4 fl oz) water

Turn the oven to 180°C (350°F). Sprinkle the flour on a large board and turn the steaks in it. Pound the floured meat on both sides with a kitchen mallet, using extra flour as the initial amount is absorbed, until the meat is half its original thickness. Discard any remaining flour.

Brown the steaks evenly in oil, using as little as necessary, then place them in a casserole.

Slice the onions into rings and lightly brown them in a little more oil. Layer the onions and meat in the casserole, sprinkle with salt and sugar, pour on the tomato purée and water and cover tightly, putting a sheet of foil under the lid if it is not tight-fitting.

Bake for about 1 hour, or until the meat is tender, turning once. Add a little water if it thickens too much.

Variation: Use chuck steak instead of cross-cut blade, but don't use topside steak as it produces a rather dry result.

Big Beef Casserole

Cooking for larger numbers than usual can pose problems for inexperienced cooks. Although the quantities given in many recipes can be doubled, this is not always successful, and few hostesses want to run risks when they are entertaining. What's more, it is often hard to find larger recipes for family-style cooking. This casserole is just mixed, marinated (if you have time) and cooked slowly. It needs no attention as it cooks.

For 10–12 servings:

2 kg (4 lb 7 oz) stewing beef
2 packets (each about 25 g/1 oz) brown
  onion sauce mix
1 packet (30 g/1 oz) mushroom soup mix
1 Tbsp dry mustard
1 Tbsp soy sauce
1 Tbsp Worcestershire sauce
2 cups (500 ml/16 fl oz) water
1 cup (250 ml/8 fl oz) dry red or white
  wine (or extra water)
½ tsp dried thyme (or fresh), other herbs
  to taste
cornflour paste

Trim any fat from the meat, cut it into bite-sized pieces and place it in a large, deep casserole. Sprinkle with the dry mixes and mustard, and stir to coat evenly. Add the sauces, water and wine, then add thyme and small quantities of other herbs if you like.

Cover tightly. Leave to stand for several hours at room temperature if possible, especially if wine has been added, as this will make the meat more tender.

Cook at 150°C (300°F) for 2–3 hours, depending on the cut of meat used, until tender.

If the casserole is to be cooled then reheated, remember that the meat will cook more while cooling. Reheat for about 45 minutes at 130°C (250°F). If desired, thicken with cornflour paste 5 minutes before serving.

Swiss Steak

Curry for Crowds

This easy casserole is useful if you are entertaining a number of guests. It is spiced with curry and a mixture of other flavourings, and can be made and refrigerated one or two days before it is needed. It will improve on standing.

This is not an authentic Indian or Asian curry, but a curry-flavoured mixture which always seems popular.

For 15–20 servings:
2–3 kg (4 lb 7 oz–6 lb 10 oz) lean chuck
  or blade steak
¼ cup curry powder
¼ cup plain flour
4 onions
2 large cloves garlic
oil
1 packet (30 g/1 oz) mushroom soup mix
1 packet (30 g/1 oz) leek and potato soup
  mix
1 Tbsp soy sauce
¼ cup marmalade
1 cup fruit chutney
juice of 1 lemon
4–5 cups (1–1.25 litres/32–40 fl oz) water

Turn the oven to 150°C (300°F). Trim the meat carefully, removing fat, and cut it into small, even cubes. Shake in a large plastic bag with the curry powder and flour. Cut the onions into chunks the same size as the meat, and cut the garlic into thin slices. Heat a little oil in a very hot frypan and brown the meat in 4 batches, each with some of the onion and garlic. Do not hurry this step.

Tip the meat and onion into a large, heavy casserole dish, preferably one you can use for cooking, storing and serving. If the coating sticks to the pan, add some of the water, scrape the bottom clean with a fish slice, then add this to the meat. When all the meat and onion has been browned, sprinkle the soup mixes over the meat and stir to coat evenly.

In the same frypan, simmer the soy sauce, marmalade, chutney and lemon juice with half the remaining water. When evenly mixed, pour over the meat. Add enough water so that the liquid almost covers the meat. Cover and cook for 2–3 hours, stirring after 30 minutes, until the meat is tender. Serve on rice with assorted side dishes and salads.

Steak and Kidney Pudding

When nights are long and days cold, really warming meals are called for. Steak and kidney pudding may take quite a long time to cook, but it doesn't take long to make. All you need is 20 minutes in the kitchen, four or five hours before you want to eat your winter dinner! As long as the pot doesn't boil dry, you won't have to do anything to your main dish before you serve it.

Crust
1½ cups self-raising flour
1 Tbsp chopped fresh herbs, or 1 tsp dried
  thyme
½ tsp salt
50 g (2 oz) butter
about ¾ cup (185 ml/6 fl oz) milk or
  water

Filling
600 g (1 lb 5 oz) blade steak
100 g (4 oz) ox or lambs' kidney
100 g (4 oz) mushrooms (optional)
1 large onion
2 Tbsp plain flour
1 tsp beef stock powder
1 tsp chopped fresh thyme or ½ tsp dried
  thyme
2 tsp Worcestershire sauce
¼ cup (60 ml/2 fl oz) water

Select a bowl or other container in which to cook the pudding, and a pot large enough to hold it. Any metal bowl will do, or a deep pyrex or similar casserole dish. It should hold at least 8 cups (2 litres/64 fl oz).

Spray or butter the container well. Put enough water in the pot to come halfway up the sides of the bowl when it is standing on a stand, saucer, or piece of crumpled foil which will keep it off the bottom of the pot.

Mix together the flour, herbs and salt for the crust. Cut or rub in the butter, then add enough milk or water to make a fairly stiff dough. Roll out three-quarters of the dough and line the bowl. It should come to the rim. Roll out the rest to cover the bowl later.

Cut the steak, kidney, mushrooms and onion into 1 cm (½ in) cubes. Sprinkle over the flour, stock and thyme, then toss to coat thoroughly. Pack into the lined bowl, pour over the Worcestershire sauce and water, then fold the edges in over the filling. Dampen the dough which will cover the pudding, and press it firmly into place.

Cover the pudding with foil, smoothing it firmly round the top rim and down the sides of the bowl. Place carefully on the stand in the water in the pot, cover the pot tightly, and boil gently for 3½–5 hours. Serve in wedges from the bowl, or unmould onto a large plate before cutting.

Variation: Replace the beef with lean shoulder lamb or hogget. Allow 3 hours for lamb, 4 hours for hogget.

Barbecued Beef Fillet

A small fillet of beef, or part of a large one, carefully cooked whole on a well-regulated barbecue, makes a wonderful festive meal in summer. Allow 150–200 g (5–7 oz) per person. Leftovers make excellent cold meat.

Marinade
2 Tbsp wine vinegar or ¼ cup (60 ml/
  2 fl oz) red or white wine
2 Tbsp lemon or orange juice
2 cloves garlic, squashed
1 Tbsp light soy sauce
2 Tbsp olive or other oil
fresh herbs, bruised, or crumbled dried
  herbs, e.g. fresh citrus-flavoured thyme
  and crushed tarragon

Trim the meat, carefully cutting away the silvery membrane that appears on one side. This takes a little time but it is worth it, since if it is left on it shrinks as it cooks, and twists the meat into a curved shape. Tie the trimmed fillet into a compact shape, folding the narrow end back on itself, tying it in place with firm string or thread. Place the meat in the marinade, transfer it to an unpunctured plastic bag and refrigerate for 1–2 days, or for at least an hour.

Take the meat from the refrigerator 1 hour before you want to cook it, and put it on a preheated barbecue rack about 15–18 cm (6–7 in) from the heat. Cover the meat as it cooks with a domed barbecue lid or a tent of doubled foil (this speeds up cooking). Have the heat high until the meat has browned on all sides. If you like, throw a few sprigs of the herb used to flavour the marinade on the barbecue bricks during cooking – this gives a smoky, herby flavour.

Do not turn the meat too soon – wait for about 7–8 minutes for a small fillet or 12 minutes for a large, thick piece, so that it has heated through. The total cooking time for a fillet weighing about 1 kg (2 lb) is likely to be about 20 minutes, but part of a large fillet will probably take 30 minutes or longer since it is much thicker. Once the meat is evenly browned turn down the heat until it has cooked to the stage you like it. With experience, you can judge when the meat is cooked by pressing it – it should start to feel springy instead of spongy. Alternatively, make a cut in the thickest part and check the colour, or pierce it and check the colour of the juices. They should be pink but not bloody.

Leave the meat to stand for 5–10 minutes before carving it into diagonal slices. If you like, serve it with Fresh Plum Sauce.

Fresh Plum Sauce
3–6 fresh plums, sliced
1 Tbsp smooth mixed mustard
vegetable cooking liquid or wine to thin
salt and pepper
sugar to taste

Simmer the sliced plums in the remaining beef marinade, add the mixed mustard, and thin with vegetable liquid or wine. Strain through a sieve and season to taste carefully, adding a little sugar to bring out the flavours.

Corned Beef

A traditional corned beef dinner is popular with many people. Try this recipe when you see a nice piece of corned beef on special.

For 6–8 servings:

1½–2 kg (3 lb 5 oz–4 lb 7 oz) corned
 silverside
1 onion, stuck with cloves
2 cloves garlic
1 or 2 bayleaves
1 sprig parsley
1 stalk celery
1 sprig thyme
1 sprig dill or ½ tsp dried dill
6 peppercorns

Put the meat in a deep pot. Cover with cold water. Add all the seasonings, bring to the boil, cover, and simmer gently, so that the surface of the water barely moves, for about 2½ hours.

Select the vegetables you want to serve with the corned beef, e.g. carrots, cabbage, brussels sprouts, white turnips, potatoes and onions, and cook them separately, using some of the corned beef cooking liquid instead of lightly salted water. Drain the vegetables and butter them very lightly.

If desired, serve Parsley Sauce (p. 345) or Mustard Sauce (p. 345) with the corned beef, using some of the cooking stock, or simply serve the meat with mild mustard or horseradish cream.

Loin Beef Roasts

My first choices for easy, reliable and popular beef roasts for four to ten people are rib-eye (sometimes called Scotch fillet or cube roll) and strip-loin (sometimes called boneless loin). They are not quite as tender as roasted fillet of beef, but they

have even better flavour, and are good roasts for special occasions.

A rib-eye roast does not have a fatty layer on the outside. When it is carved, there is a thin streak of fat curving across each slice. The strip-loin roast has an outer fat cover on one side, and the carved slices are evenly lean. The slices from both these roasts tend to be oval. For best results buy a rib eye or sirloin roast which does not have a thin strip of streaky, not-so-tender meat wrapped around it.

Tie a 1½–3 kg (3 lb 5 oz–6 lb 10 oz) roast at intervals to keep it compactly round. Brush the surface with 1 Tbsp mustard mixed to a paste with 2–3 tsp dark soy sauce, then place the meat in an uncovered roasting pan (with no extra fat, water, sugar or flour) and cook in a preheated oven at 160–170°C (325°F) for 1½ hours. Lift the meat from the roasting

Corned Beef

pan, leave it to stand in a warm place for 15 minutes before carving, and make gravy from the nicely browned pan drippings.

Mustard Gravy

A small amount of dark, thin, well-flavoured gravy is delectable with rare roast beef.

pan drippings
1 Tbsp Dijon mustard
¼–½ cup (60–125 ml/2–4 fl oz) red wine
½–¾ cup (125–185 ml/4–6 fl oz) vegetable cooking liquid or stock

Lean beef roasts should produce very little fat. Drain off any fat, leaving pan drippings only, add the mustard to the pan, then stir in the wine and vegetable liquid or stock. Stir over moderate heat until reduced to ½–¾ (125–185 ml/4–6 fl oz) cup. Serve with thinly sliced beef.

Beef Mini Rump Roast

The whole rump is a huge cut of meat, and roasts and steaks cut from it tend to be unwieldy. Because of this, some butchers divide the large rump into individual muscle cuts:

• eye of rump (which weighs about 800 g/1 lb 12 oz and looks rather like a piece of fillet);
• centre-cut rump (a lean, egg-shaped roast weighing 1–1.4 kg/2 lb 3 oz–3 lb);
• rump cap (a flattish piece weighing about 800 g/1 lb 12 oz).

These all make good roasts, or they can be cut into neat slices for steaks, with the grain running the way you want it. They have a lot of flavour, but are not as tender as the loin cuts, so they should not be overcooked.

To cook, brush the room-temperature roast with a little oil. Brown it on all sides in a hot pan, which should take 5–10 minutes. Roast in an uncovered pan, without water or added oil or fat, at 160–170°C (325°F).

A centre-cut rump takes 45 minutes to cook, and the other two smaller rump roasts take about 30 minutes. To test whether a roast is cooked, feel it – an undercooked roast feels spongy rather than springy. When you pierce it, the juice should be pinkish red, but not bloody.

Leave the roast in a warm place for about 10 minutes before carving. Serve with Mustard Gravy if desired.

Rare Roast Topside/Silverside

Traditional roasts of beef are not cheap. Silverside and topside are tougher cuts than normal roasts, but produce good results when cooked this way – as long as the meat is cooked to the rare or slightly underdone stage. (If cooked until well done, the roast will be tough and dry.)

For 6–8 servings:
1 piece silverside or topside (about 2 kg/4 lb 7 oz)
1–2 cloves garlic (optional)
1 Tbsp dry mustard
1 Tbsp soy sauce
1 Tbsp oil

Turn the oven to 160°C (325°F). If you like a slight garlic flavour to your meat, cut small slits over the surface and insert slivers of garlic into them. Mix the dry mustard, soy sauce and oil to a thick paste and brush evenly over the meat. Place it, fat side up, in a roasting pan.

Roast uncovered for 1½ hours. If you have a meat thermometer, put it in the meat before you start cooking it. It is not necessary to add any extra fat or baste the roast as it cooks. Remove the roast from the oven when the thermometer registers rare or medium-rare beef, and leave it to stand for 10–15 minutes before slicing thinly. Use the pan drippings to make a thin, brown gravy.

A meat thermometer is a good investment if you are fussy about your roast meat. It will read 50°C (125°F) for rare, to 60°C (140°F) for medium. These thermometers are often calibrated in Fahrenheit.

Push the thermometer into the thickest part of the raw meat, taking care that it does not touch bone, and place the meat in the oven so the dial can be read easily. The meat is cooked when the thermometer reaches the temperature indicated on the scale for the kind of meat you are cooking.

BEEF VARIETY MEATS

If you enjoy beef heart, tongue, sweetbreads and tripe, use the following recipes to make some tasty, nutritious and value-for-money treats.

'Hearty' Steaks

When you slice the meaty part of an ox heart diagonally or crosswise into 1 cm (½ in) thick steaks, bang them briefly with a meat hammer, then marinate them and pan-cook them, you finish up with tender, interesting meat.

Slice the heart then trim it well, removing outer membrane, fat, and any uneven or stringy pieces. Cut the resulting pieces into steak-like shapes, bang briefly with a meat hammer, and marinate for at least 5 minutes, or up to 2 days, ensuring all surfaces come in contact with the marinade.

Marinade
1 Tbsp soy sauce
1 tsp oil
1 tsp lemon juice
1 clove garlic, finely chopped

Pan-grill the meat in an unoiled, very hot frypan, pressing the surface of the meat against the pan so that it browns evenly. Take care not to overcook.

Note: Save all trimmings, mince in a food processor or chop very finely, cover with water and simmer to make a rich meat broth for a toddler or to use in gravy, sauce or stock.

Spiced Jellied Ox Tongue

For me, this recipe is a summer treat. I prefer it to any other cured meat.

1 pickled ox tongue
water
1 tsp black peppercorns
1 tsp allspice berries
1 clove garlic
6 juniper berries
2 tsp gelatine
1 Tbsp cold water
½ cup finely chopped fresh herbs

If you are not sure about the saltiness of the tongue, rinse it, cover it with cold water and leave to stand for about an hour, then drain.

Put the tongue in a pressure cooker with 2 cups of water and the seasonings, and cook at the highest pressure for 45 minutes. OR put it in a pot, cover with water, add the seasonings, and cook for about 3 hours, until the meat feels really tender when pierced, and the skin peels off easily. When the tongue is cooked, run it under the cold tap and remove the skin.

Measure out half a cup of stock, tasting it first. If it is very salty, dilute it with water. You want a well-flavoured, but not salty liquid. Soften the gelatine in the cold water, then add the stock. Heat on the stovetop or on High (100%) power in the microwave until the liquid boils. Stir in the fresh herbs. Add salt to taste, if necessary.

Cut the skinned and trimmed tongue into large cubes or slices. Place them in a loaf tin 5- to 6-cup (1.25–1.5 litre/40–48 fl oz) capacity, pour the liquid over and mix gently. Top with an inverted lid or a board a little bigger than the loaf tin, and weigh this down with a few cans until the liquid covers the highest pieces of tongue. Refrigerate for at least 6 hours before unmoulding, slicing, and serving with salads, etc.

Variation: Replace ox tongue with 12 pickled lambs' tongues.

Note: Cooking times, yield, and tin sizes are given as a guide only. These vary with the age and size of the tongue.

Sweetbreads in White Wine Sauce

Sweetbreads are not always displayed in supermarkets or butchers' shops, so it pays to ask for them if you cannot see them. This is a classic and delicious way to cook sweetbreads.

For 2–3 servings:
250 g (9 oz) sweetbreads
1 cup (250 ml/8 fl oz) white wine
1 bayleaf
1 clove garlic
1/2 tsp salt
2 Tbsp butter
2 Tbsp plain flour
2 Tbsp cream
1/4 cup chopped parsley

Soak the sweetbreads for 30 minutes in cold water with a little salt and vinegar. Drain and put in a small pot with the wine, bayleaf, garlic and salt. Cover and simmer for 5–10 minutes, until just firm.

Drain the sweetbreads into a sieve, reserving the stock and discarding the bayleaf and garlic clove. Leave the sweetbreads to cool.

Melt the butter in a pot, add the flour, and cook till the flour bubbles. Add the reserved stock and cook over moderate heat, stirring constantly, till the sauce boils and thickens.

Remove the membranes from the cooled sweetbreads and cut them into bite-sized pieces. Add the cream and parsley to the sauce, and stir in the sweetbreads. Reheat to serve, but do not boil.

Serve on noodles, rice or in baked potato halves, or spoon into hollowed-out, halved bread rolls which have been brushed with butter and baked until crisp, or use the mixture as a filling for crêpes.

Note: To make sweetbreads go further, add sautéed button mushrooms not long before serving.

Tripe Greek-Style

Although I had never really liked tripe, when I came across a Greek recipe I decided I should experiment with it as it sounded interesting, and tripe is cheap, low in fat, and fairly high in protein.

When my butcher commented that tripe was good for delicate stomachs I thought that the smell of it cooking would make my stomach feel somewhat delicate, but I found to my surprise that this recipe didn't have the characteristic tripe smell. My herbed tripe turned out to be quite delicious, so if you like tripe, have a delicate stomach, like Greek food, or are poor but adventurous, try herbed tripe!

For 3–4 servings:
2 Tbsp olive or other oil
2–3 large onions, sliced
2–3 large cloves garlic, crushed and chopped
about 600 g (1 lb 5 oz) tripe
2 cups (500 ml/16 fl oz) water
1 1/2 tsp salt
2 tsp sugar
1 tsp thyme
1 can (400 g/14 oz) tomatoes in juice
fresh herbs (e.g. parsley, basil and/or marjoram)

Heat the oil in a large, heavy-bottomed pot or frypan, and brown the onions and garlic over moderate heat, stirring them frequently until they are evenly coloured. Cut the tripe into strips 1 x 4 cm (1/2 x 1 3/4 in), add to the browned vegetables and stir over fairly high heat for 3–4 minutes. Stir in all the remaining ingredients except the fresh herbs, cover and simmer very gently for 1 1/2 hours, stirring occasionally. Add extra water, white wine or chicken stock during cooking if the mixture looks dry.

When the tripe is as tender as you like it, remove the lid and raise the heat so the sauce evaporates and thickens. Stir in the freshly chopped herbs if you have them.

Serve in shallow bowls, on rice or noodles, or with crusty bread rolls, with or without a green salad.

Variation: Do not let the sauce evaporate and thicken, and serve the soupy tripe mixture in soup bowls, sprinkled with herbs.

VENISON

Naturally lean, with a distinctive (but not strong) flavour, farmed venison is juicy and tender as long as you take care not to overcook it.

Stir-Fried Venison

Any cut of farmed venison can be thinly sliced across the grain, marinated and stir-fried.

For 2 servings:
about 300 g (10 oz) venison
2 Tbsp dark soy sauce
2 Tbsp oil
2 Tbsp sherry
2 tsp brown sugar
2 cloves garlic, crushed
300 g (10 oz) vegetables
2 tsp cornflour

Slice the venison across the grain into very thin strips. (The meat slices most easily if partly frozen.) Put it in a plastic bag with the next 5 ingredients. Knead gently to mix, squeeze out the air, and leave to marinate for at least 24 hours.

Select vegetables that cook quickly. Slice them thinly, stir-fry in a large frypan or wok using 2 Tbsp extra oil, add 2 Tbsp water, cover and steam until they are tender-crisp.

Remove from the pan.

Stir-fry the venison until it loses its raw appearance. Add the cooked vegetables, toss, and thicken with a little cornflour mixed to a paste with cold water. Serve with rice.

Pan-Grilled Venison Steaks

Venison leg can be 'seam boned' the same way as legs of lamb and beef. The individual muscles are removed from the leg and trimmed of fat, then the tough silvery membranes that surround the muscles are cut away. This leaves absolutely lean meat, which is aged and often vacuum packed. After all this treatment the meat is not cheap, but there is no waste and the minimum of cooking is needed.

The flavour of farmed venison is just a little stronger than that of beef. All the cuts from a seam-boned 'Denver leg' are tender enough to be sautéed, pan-grilled or roasted, as long as they are not overcooked.

I like serving venison with blueberry sauce, and I freeze blueberries each year so that I can serve the sauce with venison or beef steaks, and occasionally with wild duck.

Start with a piece of venison from a Denver leg. If necessary have it cut smaller so that you have a piece of meat no thicker than 3–4 cm (1–1 1/2 in). Make sure the sauce, and the rest of the meal, is ready before you start cooking the venison, since it should not be kept standing after it is cooked.

Brush both sides of the venison with oil. Heat a film of oil in a large, heavy frypan until it starts to smoke, then add the meat. Brown it evenly, then turn and brown the other side. Reduce the heat to moderate and cook the meat until it is rare or medium. Judge this by pressing the meat, which becomes firmer and springier as it cooks, or make a cut near the middle and check the colour. Total cooking time should be 6–8 minutes.

During the last few minutes, dribble a little lemon juice or fruit-flavoured or balsamic vinegar over the meat, then turn it, so most of the liquid evaporates. With your knife at an angle to the board, slice the cooked steak into pieces the thickness of steak (thinner if you prefer). If you find the meat is too rare for your taste, very briefly brown the cut surfaces in the hot pan.

Venison Schnitzels

For deliciously tender, tasty venison, cook marinated schnitzels briefly in a very hot pan.

Stir-Fried Venison with plain white rice

For 4 servings:
8–12 venison schnitzels
2 cloves garlic, crushed
¼ cup (60ml/2 fl oz) white wine
2 Tbsp Worcestershire sauce
¼ cup redcurrant or cranberry jelly
¼ cup (60 ml/2 fl oz) orange juice

Cut thin slices of venison from topside or thick flank. (The meat is easier to slice if partly frozen.) Lay the schnitzels in a shallow dish containing the next 3 ingredients. Cover closely with cling film and leave to marinate for at least 12 hours in the refrigerator.

Drain the marinade from the venison and boil rapidly until it has reduced to about a tablespoon. Remove the garlic. Melt the jelly over high heat, add the orange juice and reduced marinade and boil for 2–3 minutes.

Cook the schnitzels two at a time in a very hot pan with ½ tsp butter per schnitzel (about 30 seconds per side). Add about a teaspoon of the prepared glaze for each schnitzel, swirling the pan so the meat browns lightly on both sides. You may need to rinse the pan briefly with hot water before cooking more schnitzels.

Serve immediately with a garnish of redcurrants, cranberries or sliced orange.

See also

Parmesan Meatballs, p. 29

Spicy Mexican Filling, p. 42

Sesame Beef Wraps, p. 43

Quick Beef and Vegetable Chowder, p. 54

Mince Magic, pp. 130–139

Simply Sausages, pp. 140–145

Cheesy Pieburgers, p. 154

Little Meat Pies, p. 155

East-West Beef Salad with Coriander Dressing, p. 162

Mediterranean Meat Salad, p. 162

Oriental Steak Salad, p. 162

Thai Beef Salad, p. 162

Economical Lasagne, p. 184

Quick Bolognese Sauce, p. 184

Mince Magic

Most of us include a package of minced meat in our weekly shopping. Mince is versatile and good value for money, and even fussy children usually give it the thumbs up. Many of the recipes in this section are favourites with my family, and were made by my children when they first went flatting and wanted easy meals that could be stretched when friends dropped in. I hope that many of these recipes will prove firm favourites in your household, and that you will encourage your family to learn to make them for themselves.

Macaroni Mix-Up

This tasty one-pan dinner is easy enough for a 'learner cook' to make, and ideal for anyone who hates lots of dirty dishes after they cook!

For 4–5 servings:
1 Tbsp oil
500 g (1 lb 2 oz) minced beef
1 tsp oreganum
1½ tsp salt
2 tsp sugar
2 cups uncooked macaroni
4 cups (1 litre/32 fl oz) boiling water
½ cup tomato paste
3 cups frozen peas or mixed vegetables

Heat the oil in a large, non-stick frypan and cook the mince over high heat until it has lost its pinkness, stirring it all the time and breaking up any lumps. Add the oreganum, salt and sugar, then the uncooked macaroni, and the boiling water. Stir to mix.

Cook with the lid on for 10 minutes, stirring once or twice and making sure the mixture is bubbling gently all the time but is not sticking to the bottom. Stir in the tomato paste and the frozen vegetables, turn up the heat until the mixture starts to boil again, then lower it, replace the lid, and cook gently for 10 minutes longer, adding more water if it looks dry before the macaroni and vegetables are tender.

Serve in bowls, sprinkled with grated cheese or chopped parsley if you like.

Variation: Use fresh rather than frozen vegetables. Before you start cooking anything, cut carrots and celery into 5 mm (¼ in) cubes until you have 3 cups altogether, and add them to the mince with the macaroni. If you have some broccoli, cut the stems and the tops into little pieces and add them with the tomato paste.

'Buttons and Bows' Frypan Dinner

'Buttons and Bows' Frypan Dinner

After a long and tiring day, a well-balanced family dinner that can be cooked in half an hour in one pan seems a great idea!

For 4–5 servings:
2 tsp oil
1 large onion, chopped
1 tsp chopped garlic
500 g (1 lb 2 oz) minced beef or lamb
3 medium carrots
3 cups (750 ml/24 fl oz) water
150 g (5 oz) bow-shaped pasta
½ tsp salt
4 medium zucchini
1 can (about 430 g/15 oz) concentrated chicken soup*
2–3 Tbsp chopped parsley and/or other fresh herbs

* Or any concentrated creamy soup, e.g. tomato, pumpkin or mushroom.

Heat the oil in a large frypan. Add the onion, garlic and mince and brown, stirring to break up the mince.

Cut the carrots into 5 mm (¼ in) slices (the red buttons), add to the pan with the water and bring to the boil. Add the pasta and salt, cover, and simmer for 15 minutes.

Slice the zucchini (green buttons) a little thicker than the carrots, and stir into the mixture. Cover and cook for 3–5 minutes longer, until the pasta and zucchini are just tender.

Add the soup (stir it first if solidified), then add the herbs and bring to the boil. Turn off and leave to stand for 5 minutes.

Serve in bowls, sprinkled with chopped parsley or a little grated cheese if you like.

Variations: For a richer, creamy sauce, add ¼ cup cream with the soup.

Replace zucchini with green beans or broccoli.

Anne's Stroganoff

This is a great recipe to make ahead and serve when entertaining a family with children.

For 8 servings:
250 g (9 oz) small lasagne noodles or other pasta shapes
50 g (2 oz) butter
2 large onions, chopped
2 cloves garlic, chopped
about 300 g (10 oz) button mushrooms, quartered
1 kg (2 lb 3 oz) minced beef or lamb
1 packet (30 g/1 oz) mushroom soup mix
2 cups (500 ml/16 fl oz) water, or ½ cup (125 ml/4 fl oz) white wine and 1½ cups (375 ml/12 fl oz) water
2 Tbsp tomato paste
1 carton (250 g/9 oz) sour cream
about 1 tsp salt
about ¼ cup Parmesan cheese

Cook the pasta in plenty of boiling, salted water until barely tender. Drain, rinse with cold water (to stop it cooking) and spread in a large, shallow, lightly sprayed ovenware dish.

While the pasta cooks, melt the butter in a large frypan and cook the onions, garlic and mushrooms until the onions are transparent. Remove from the pan then brown the mince until it has lost all its pinkness. Stir in the soup mix, then add the water (or white wine and water) and stir until the mixture boils. Simmer for 5 minutes, then mix in the onion mixture, tomato paste and sour cream. Taste and add salt as needed to bring out the flavour.

Spoon the mixture over the pasta (it will soak up some of the sauce later). Sprinkle with Parmesan cheese, cover and refrigerate until required.

To reheat, cover and bake at 180°C (350°F) for 20 minutes, then bake uncovered for another 20 minutes, or until the mixture has heated right through and is bubbling around the edges. Serve with a crisp, green salad.

Dinner for One, Please James M

This easy meal can be mixed, microwaved, and served in the same dish in a matter of minutes. Freeze 100 g (3½ oz) packets of mince so you can remove one, thaw it in the microwave, make your additions, then serve it for anyone who wants a quick meal at a time when no-one else is eating.

For 1 serving:
100 g (3½ oz) mince
1 or 2 cloves garlic or ¼ onion, chopped
¾ cup mixed vegetables
1 Tbsp tomato soup mix (about ¼ packet)
¼ tsp dark soy sauce
paprika, oreganum, marjoram or thyme
  (optional)
¼ cup small pasta, e.g. small shells,
  macaroni or orzo
1 cup (250 ml/8 fl oz) boiling water

In a shallow 15–20 cm (6–8 in) microwave dish mix together everything except the pasta and water. Add the pasta, then the boiling water, and mix again.

Cover and microwave on High (100%) power for 10 minutes, then leave for 3–4 minutes before serving.

Variations: For 4 servings, multiply the quantities by 4, and microwave in a covered casserole on High (100%) power for 30 minutes. For a stronger tomato flavour, add 2 tsp tomato paste.

Hamburgers

These hamburgers are big and juicy, and don't take long to make.

For 6 hamburgers:
6 burger buns
butter

Patties
1 thick or 2 thin slices bread
¼ cup (60 ml/2 fl oz) milk
2 spring onions, chopped finely, or
  ½ onion, grated
2 Tbsp tomato sauce
2 tsp soy sauce
500 g (1 lb 2 oz) minced beef

Extra Fillings
tomato or barbecue sauce
prepared mustard
shredded lettuce
sliced cheese
sliced tomatoes

If you have a food processor, mix all the pattie ingredients in it until blended. If not, break the bread into small pieces and stir with the milk in a large bowl, using a fork. Mix the spring onion or grated onion and the sauces through the soft bread. Add the meat, broken into 10–12 blobs, and stir until everything is well mixed. With wet hands, make 6 equal patties, shaping them so they are as wide as the buns.

Prepare the extra fillings to go in the buns. Split and butter the buns. Brown the cut sides in a hot pan or under the grill.

Heat a large oiled frypan, and add 2 or 3 patties. Cook on high heat until brown on both sides, turning after 2 minutes.

Put the patties in the warm buns with your favourite toppings. Enjoy!

Bonza Budget Burgers

This recipe makes 8 generous burgers which are good served in hamburger buns with plenty of lettuce, relish, etc. If you prefer, serve your burgers with mashed potatoes and cooked vegetables.

For 8 large burgers:
1 egg
1 Tbsp Worcestershire sauce
1 tsp curry powder
1 onion
1 apple
1 medium potato
300 g (10½ oz) sausage meat
300 g (10½ oz) beef mince
oil for cooking

Assemble all the ingredients before you start mixing, since the apple and potato may brown if left to stand too long before mixing and cooking.

Break an egg into a bowl, add the Worcestershire sauce and curry powder. Grate in the onion, unpeeled apple and scrubbed potato (skin and all). Stir well.

Mix in the sausage meat and mince. Divide into 8–10 patties with wet hands. The patties will be soft but will firm up when cooked.

Pan-cook in a little oil over moderate heat, allowing at least 5 minutes per side. (These need much more cooking than other hamburgers.) Serve on toasted, halved hamburger buns with your favourite accompaniments, or top with sautéed pineapple rings and serve with mashed potatoes and other vegetables.

Variation: Use a food processor to chop the vegetables and apple, then add the meat, using the metal chopping blade.

> Burger Glazes: In the last couple of minutes of cooking, brush patties with tomato or barbecue sauce, or a mixture of apricot or plum jam and soy sauce. If the glaze is added too soon it may burn before the patties are cooked, so take care.

Basic Meatballs

These are good served with Devilled Meatball Sauce or Creamy Sauce for Meatballs.

For 4 servings:
1 large onion, chopped
sprig of parsley, chopped
½ tsp oreganum
1 egg
½ cup rolled oats
1 tsp garlic salt
500 g (1 lb 2 oz) minced beef or mutton
1 Tbsp soy or Worcestershire sauce

Mix everything until all the ingredients are combined. If the mixture looks dry, add a little milk. If it looks very wet, add more rolled oats.

With wet hands, shape into 36 small balls. Brown in a large heated and oiled frypan. Keep the heat high, shaking the pan regularly, until the balls have browned fairly evenly and cooked through, about 15–20 minutes. Serve with the sauce of your choice.

Devilled Meatball Sauce

2 Tbsp oil
1 onion
1 apple
¼ cup chutney
1½ cups (375 ml/12 fl oz) hot water
½ tsp salt
1 Tbsp brown sugar
1 Tbsp soy sauce
1–2 Tbsp cornflour

Heat the oil in a pot or in the pan used for the meatballs. Chop the onion finely and cook in the oil until tender and transparent. Add the grated apple, chutney and hot water. Bring to the boil, add the salt, sugar and soy sauce. Thicken with cornflour mixed to a paste with a little water. Taste and adjust seasonings if necessary. Pour over hot meatballs and serve on rice or pasta.

Creamy Sauce for Meatballs
For 4 servings:
75 g (2½ oz) butter
¼ cup plain flour
2 tsp beef or chicken stock powder
2 cups (500 ml/16 fl oz) boiling water
¼ cup light sour cream
1–2 Tbsp lemon juice (optional)

Melt the butter in a pot . Add the flour and stir it until it browns. Add the stock powder and 1 cup of boiling water, and stir until smooth and thick. Then stir in the remaining liquid, stirring until it thickens again. Just before serving, stir in the sour cream (and the lemon juice if you like a tangy sauce). Do not boil again. Pour over hot meatballs and serve on pasta or rice.

Japanese Meatballs

A Japanese friend showed me how to make these meatballs. Follow the instructions exactly, and I am sure you will enjoy them too.

For 3–4 servings:

500 g (1 lb 2 oz) minced beef or lamb
2 eggs
2 Tbsp cornflour
1–2 Tbsp cold water

Broth

2 cups (500 ml/16 fl oz) chicken stock
1 tsp sugar
3 Tbsp Kikkoman soy sauce
2 tsp oil
2–3 spring onions

Mix the mince and the unbeaten eggs in a medium-sized bowl. Mix the cornflour and cold water together and stir through the meat mixture. Leave to stand.

To make the broth, heat the first 4 ingredients in a (lidded) pot or pan large enough to hold the meatballs in one layer.

Divide the beef mixture into 12–16 balls, using 2 wet dessertspoons. If the mixture is too soft to work with, add up to 2 tsp extra cornflour, mixed with a very small amount of cold water.

Drop the soft meatballs carefully into the simmering broth. (It doesn't matter if they flatten slightly.) Cover and leave to simmer for 10 minutes.

While the meatballs cook, chop the spring onions (including the green leaves). Divide the cooked meatballs and broth between 3 or 4 bowls and sprinkle with the chopped onion.

Hedgehog Meatballs

Swedish Meatballs

These seem rich and luxurious but the sauce contains only a little cream.

For 4–5 servings:

3 slices stale rye (or other dark) bread
1 medium onion, roughly chopped
½ tsp ground allspice
½ tsp freshly grated nutmeg
1 tsp salt
freshly ground black pepper
1 large egg
400–500 g (about 1 lb) minced beef or lamb
¼ cup plain flour
about ¼ cup (60 ml/2 fl oz) water
250 g (9 oz) button mushrooms, quartered
1–2 Tbsp butter
¼ cup (60 ml/2 fl oz) water or stock
¼ cup (60 ml/2 fl oz) fresh or sour cream
2 Tbsp finely chopped parsley or fresh dill

Chop the bread to crumb consistency in a food processor. Add the onion, spices and seasonings and chop again.

Add the egg, and the mince in chunks. Process until evenly mixed, adding a little milk if the mixture is not moist enough to form into 20 smooth balls with wet hands.

Put the flour into a dry bowl. Drop balls, 4 or 5 at a time, in the bowl, rotating to coat them evenly. Repeat with the remaining balls.

Brown meatballs in a large, non-stick frypan in a little oil, jiggling the pan so they move around and brown evenly. Cook for about 10 minutes, adding about ¼ cup (60 ml/2 fl oz) of water and covering after about 6 minutes.

In another pan, over fairly high heat, brown the mushrooms in the butter, add the water or stock, cover and cook until the mushrooms are wilted and the water has disappeared. Tip the mushrooms into the meatball pan. Put aside at this stage if not serving immediately.

When required, heat the meatballs with a little extra water if necessary, then add the cream. Simmer for 5 minutes, season to taste, and add enough water or stock to make a creamy glaze. Sprinkle with finely chopped parsley or dill. Serve with mashed potatoes and broccoli.

Hedgehog Meatballs M

This popular recipe dates from my student days. It was especially useful when we had spent most of our food money, but wanted to have friends for dinner!

For 4 servings:

100 g (3½ oz) mushrooms, quartered
1 onion, chopped
1 green pepper, chopped (optional)
1 can (425 g/15 oz) chunky tomato soup
½ cup (125 ml/4 fl oz) water
500 g (1 lb 2 oz) minced beef or mutton
1 onion, very finely chopped
½ cup uncooked long-grain white rice
1 tsp chopped fresh thyme (optional)
1 tsp oreganum
1 tsp paprika
2 tsp dark soy sauce

To bake:
Turn the oven to 180°C (350°F). Put the mushrooms, onion, pepper, soup and water in a casserole dish. Mix the remaining ingredients and shape into 16 meatballs. Place in the dish with the sauce. Cover tightly and bake for 45 minutes.

To microwave:
Place all the sauce ingredients except the water in a large, shallow round or oval dish. Prepare the meatballs as above. Arrange them in one layer in the sauce. Cover with a lid or cling film. Cook on High (100%) power for 5 minutes, then on Medium-High (70%) power for 20 minutes. Leave for 5 minutes before serving.

To pressure cook:
Bring the sauce ingredients to the boil in the pressure cooker. Form the remaining ingredients into 8–10 larger meatballs. Place in the hot sauce and cook at high pressure for 10 minutes.

American Meat Loaf

Little Meatballs

This recipe makes a little meat go a long way, and still provides a high-protein meal. The meatballs can be served with or without the sauce.

For 4 servings:
1 onion, very finely chopped
about 400 g (14 oz) minced beef
1 egg
¼ cup (60 ml/2 fl oz) milk
¼ cup rolled oats
¼ cup wheatgerm
½ tsp salt
1 tsp basil
½–1 tsp oreganum
about 1 Tbsp oil
1 tsp dark soy sauce
¼ cup (60 ml/2 fl oz) hot water
fettuccine, spaghetti, etc.
a little butter or oil
chopped fresh herbs or Parmesan cheese
  (optional)

Sauce
2 tsp cornflour
chopped fresh parsley, spring onions and
  other herbs
1 can (400 g/14 oz) tomatoes

Combine the first 9 ingredients, down to the oreganum, in a large bowl or food processor and mix well, adding more rolled oats or wheatgerm if the mixture is too soft to handle, or a little extra milk if it is too dry.

Divide the mixture into about 40 little meatballs, working with wet hands to prevent them sticking.

Heat a large, preferably non-stick frypan, and add about a tablespoon of oil while you shake the pan backwards and forwards with one hand over fairly high heat. Drop the meatballs into the moving pan and cook until they are evenly browned and firm.

Mix the soy sauce and hot water together and add to the pan, still keeping it moving. This should dislodge any bits from the bottom of the pan, and glaze the meatballs nicely.

In a large pot, in a generous amount of boiling salted water, cook plenty of fettuccine, spaghetti, etc., then drain, rinse and toss it in a little butter or oil, adding fresh herbs or a little Parmesan cheese if you like.

For an easy sauce, put the cornflour, parsley, spring onions and other herbs, if you have them, in another pan. Add the tomatoes, breaking them up as they heat. Adjust the seasonings. Add the sauce to the meatballs and reheat them. Serve on the pasta.

American Meat Loaf

When living on a tight budget in North America, taught by my friends, I used to make this traditional 'comfort food' loaf instead of serving roasts.

For 4 servings:
¾ cup fine dry breadcrumbs
1 packet (30 g/1 oz) onion soup mix
¼ cup (60 ml/2 fl oz) hot water
¼ cup (60 ml/2 fl oz) tomato or barbecue
  sauce
1 egg
450–550 g (1 lb–1 lb 4 oz) minced beef
or lamb*

Optional Topping
1–2 rashers thinly sliced bacon
1 Tbsp tomato paste
2 Tbsp water

* Don't use extra-lean mince for this recipe.

Turn the oven to 180°C (350°F). Stir the crumbs and soup mix together in a medium to large bowl. Add the hot water and mix with a fork. Add the sauce and egg, mix again with the fork, then add the mince.

Line a sponge-roll or other shallow-sided baking tray with a piece of baking paper or a non-stick liner.

With a damp hand, mix the mince as evenly as possible through the other ingredients, then form the mixture into an oval shape about 20 cm (8 in) long and place it in the prepared baking tray.

To make the topping, cut any rind off the bacon and snip all around the edges. Lay the bacon over the roll, smoothing it down evenly. Mix the tomato paste with the water and brush or rub this over the bacon and exposed meat.

Bake uncovered for 1 hour if using fan-bake, or for 1¼ hours without a fan. (If you are not sure whether the loaf is cooked, bake for 10 minutes longer. When cut, there should be no pinkness in the centre.)

To serve, cut in 8 or 10 thick slices and serve with gravy (p. 345), mashed potatoes, a green vegetable and carrots.

Curried Meat Loaf   M

This prize-winning, economical meat loaf is as good microwaved as it is cooked conventionally. It can be served hot or cold, and travels well, so it is good for a picnic or a 'pot-luck' dinner.

For 4–6 servings:
1 onion
1 small carrot
1 tart apple (sturmer or granny smith)
2 cloves garlic (optional)
1 egg
½ cup (125 ml/4 fl oz) milk
1 Tbsp soy sauce
1–2 tsp curry powder
1 tsp sugar
½ tsp salt
2 sprigs parsley
500 g (1 lb 2 oz) minced beef or lamb
1 cup rolled oats
¼ cup sultanas

If baking conventionally, turn the oven to 190°C (375°F). Quarter the onion, carrot and apple and process with the garlic in a food processor, using the metal chopping blade, until finely and evenly chopped. Add the next 7 ingredients and process again until mixed.

Break the mince into golf-ball sized pieces and add to the food processor, then sprinkle with the rolled oats. Process in short bursts, just enough to blend, then stir in the sultanas.

To mix by hand, grate the onion, carrot and unpeeled apple into a large bowl. Add the finely chopped garlic, then the next 6 ingredients. Chop the parsley, and add with the minced beef, oats and sultanas. Mix together thoroughly with your hands.

Line a loaf tin with a strip of greaseproof paper, covering both the long sides and the bottom. Press the mixture into the tin.

Bake in the oven for 1 hour, or cover a microwaveable loaf pan with cling film and microwave on Medium-High (70%) power for 20 minutes, or until the loaf feels firm in the middle. Leave the baked or microwaved loaf to stand for 10 minutes before slicing.

Serve hot with vegetables and your favourite sauce, ketchup or chutney, or cold with salads or in sandwiches.

South Pacific Meat Loaf

Kumara and spices give this meat loaf an interesting flavour.

For 4 servings:
500 g (1 lb 2 oz) minced lamb or beef
1 egg
1 large onion
1 tsp ground coriander seed or ½ tsp curry powder
1½ tsp salt
500 g (1 lb 2 oz) kumara

Turn the oven to 180°C (350°F). Put the mince in a bowl with the egg. Grate the onion, or chop it finely in a food processor, then add to the meat with the seasonings (use coriander seed if you like a curry-orange flavour).

Scrub and grate the kumara without peeling them. Mix the grated flesh through the mince as soon as it is prepared, so it does not discolour on standing.

Line a loaf tin (about 23 x 10 cm / 9 x 4 in) with a sheet of baking paper so the paper goes across the long sides and the bottom, then oil the ends of the tin and press the loaf mixture evenly into it. Cover with foil and bake for 1 hour, then remove the foil and bake uncovered for 30 minutes. Cut into thick slices.

Stuffed Cabbage Leaves

Leaves make excellent, edible food wrappers. Cabbage leaves are particularly good because they are readily available all year round, are cheap, a good weight, come in a convenient size, and are not too fragile to work with.

For 4–5 servings:
8–12 cabbage leaves
350 g (12 oz) minced lamb or beef
1 egg
2 onions, finely chopped
½ cup long-grain rice
1½ tsp salt
4 Tbsp tomato paste or ½ cup tomato purée
2 Tbsp lemon juice
¼ cup currants
1 Tbsp butter
1½ cups (375 ml/12 fl oz) water

Cut the stem and core out of the cabbage using a small, sharp knife. (With the core removed, the outer leaves should lift away from the heart.) Put the cabbage (impaled on a carving fork) into a large bowl or bucket and cover it with boiling water. After about 30 seconds the outer leaves should be wilted and soft enough to lift away from the heart, one at a time, without splitting them. Trim the central ribs so the leaves are easier to wrap up later.

In a bowl, mix together the mince, egg, onion and rice, half the salt and tomato paste or purée, and all the lemon juice and currants, until well combined. Divide this mixture evenly between the cabbage leaves, then form each into a neat parcel, folding first the stem end, then the sides of each leaf over the filling. Roll each leaf up loosely. Place each package, smooth side up, in a large, buttered casserole dish or roasting pan, one layer deep. Dot with butter.

Combine the water, remaining tomato paste or purée and salt. Pour this around the parcels, then cover them with a few blanched leaves that have ripped or were not stuffed. (This prevents the tops of the rolls sticking to the lid or browning.) Cover tightly, with foil or a lid. (Refrigerate at this stage if desired.)

Bake at 180°C (350°F) for 1 hour. Remove from the oven and remove the lid and upper layer of leaves.

Place the cabbage rolls on a serving dish, then thicken the juice with cornflour paste and/or sour cream. Pour over the rolls and sprinkle with paprika. Serve alone or with mashed potatoes.

Mince Fried Rice

Make your own modifications to this useful rice dish. Just remember that if it is to be the main part of the meal, it must have enough additions and seasonings to give it a really good flavour. If possible, cook the rice ahead of time.

For 2–3 servings:
1 cup long-grain rice
2 cups (500 ml/16 fl oz) boiling water
¼ tsp salt
1 rasher bacon, chopped
2 onions, chopped
2 Tbsp oil
250 g (9 oz) minced beef or mutton
2 cups finely chopped vegetables*
½ tsp sesame oil
1–2 Tbsp soy sauce

* Use a mixture of quick-cooking vegetables, e.g. peppers, cabbage, mushrooms.

Put the rice, boiling water and salt in a heavy pot. Cover and cook gently until the rice is tender and the water absorbed.

In a large frypan or wok cook the bacon and onion in the oil until lightly browned. Add the mince. Stir over high heat until the meat is brown and in separate pieces. Add the vegetables. When the vegetables are barely cooked, add the rice, and stir over a high heat until the rice is hot. Sprinkle with the sesame oil and add soy sauce to taste.

Variation: Push the rice aside when hot and add 1 or 2 eggs to the pan. Scramble them through the rice as soon as they have set.

Cabbage-Topped Hot Pot

This is a good dinner for people who don't like washing pots!

For 4 servings:
1 Tbsp oil or butter
2 onions, chopped
400 g (14 oz) minced beef or mutton
1–2 tsp curry powder
¾ cup long-grain rice
1 Tbsp Worcestershire or soy sauce
3 cups (750 ml/24 fl oz) hot water
2 carrots, chopped
2 stalks celery, chopped
1 packet (30 g/1 oz) any creamy soup mix
about 300 g (10 oz) cabbage, finely shredded

Heat the oil or butter in a large pot. Add the onion, mince and curry powder and cook until browned. Add the next 5 ingredients, then cover and cook for 10 minutes, or until the rice is tender. Sprinkle the powdered soup over the mixture (or mix it with ½ cup water) and stir well. Put the finely shredded cabbage on top, cover and cook gently, without stirring, until the cabbage is bright green and tender.

Spicy Dark Chilli

This dish is perfect for a casual party meal. Use a good dark beer for maximum flavour!

For 4–6 servings (about 5½ cups):
1 large or 2 medium onions
2 large cloves garlic
1 Tbsp oil
1 large red, yellow or green pepper
2 tsp whole cumin seeds
500 g (1 lb 2 oz) minced beef or lamb
1 tsp oreganum
¼–¾ tsp chilli powder
1 can (about 400 g/14 oz) tomatoes in juice
¼ cup tomato paste
about 1½ cups (375 ml/12 fl oz) beer
salt and sugar to taste
2 medium carrots (optional)
2 stalks celery (optional)
2 bayleaves
2 Tbsp cornmeal (or flour)

Chop the onion and garlic finely and heat in the oil in a large pot while you chop the pepper finely.

Push the onion to the side, heat the cumin seeds until they brown a little and pop, then stir in the chopped pepper and the mince. Cook over high heat until the meat is no longer pink, adding the oreganum and chilli powder during this time.

Add the next 7 ingredients and simmer for 1 hour, stirring occasionally, then thicken with the cornmeal or flour mixed to a paste with a little water. Season to taste.

(I usually add 1 tsp salt and 2 tsp white or brown sugar.) Remove the bayleaves.

Serve immediately or reheat when required. Spoon over rice with toppings of sour cream (or sour cream mixed with plain yoghurt), chopped spring onions (with their green leaves), grated cheese and chopped canned jalapeno peppers. Serve corn chips alongside.

Variation: To make it go further, add 1–2 cans of baked beans or drained kidney beans.

Filo Lamb Samosas

Although samosas are traditionally made with a special crust, I usually wrap the spicy filling in parcels made of filo pastry and find them very popular. Serve them the same day they are made, as the pastry softens if it stands too long.

For 12 samosas:
250 g (9 oz) minced lamb
1 onion, finely chopped
1 tsp grated root ginger
½ tsp chilli powder
½ tsp turmeric
1 can (about 425 g/15 oz) Indian Tomatoes or whole tomatoes in juice
1 cup frozen peas
1 tsp garam masala
2 Tbsp chopped fresh coriander, if available
1 Tbsp cornflour
12 sheets filo pastry
melted butter or oil

Turn the oven to 200°C (400°F). Put the mince and onion into a preheated frypan and heat, stirring frequently, until the mince is no longer pink.

Stir in the ginger, chilli powder and turmeric as the meat cooks. Add the

---

Folding Filo Triangles

---

tomatoes and cook uncovered until almost dry, then stir in the peas, garam masala and coriander and cook 2 minutes longer. Thicken with cornflour mixed to a thin paste with water (to prevent the filo going soggy), then cool.

Layer 3 sheets of filo pastry with a little melted butter or oil. Cut crosswise into 4 strips. Put a twelfth of the filling mixture at the top of one strip, then fold the filo over it so the top touches the side, forming a triangle. Keep folding in triangles until the filling is completely enclosed by the pastry and you have folded up the whole strip.

Repeat with the remaining filo and filling, making 12 triangular parcels.

Bake in the oven for 8–10 minutes, until evenly browned. Serve warm or hot, reheating if necessary.

Tex-Mex Squares

These squares are interesting, different and tasty, and very popular with teenagers.

For 4–6 servings:

Topping
400–500 g (about 1 lb) minced beef or lamb
2 tsp ground cumin
1 tsp oreganum
1 tsp each onion and garlic salt
1 tsp sugar
½–1 tsp chilli powder
2 Tbsp tomato paste
1 can (440 g/15 oz) kidney beans
1½ cups grated tasty cheese

Crust
1½ cups self-raising flour
about ¾ cup (185 ml/6 fl oz) milk

Turn the oven to 200°C (400°F). Brown the mince in a large pot or frypan, adding the spices and seasonings, in the order listed, as it cooks. (Add ¾ tsp chilli powder the first time you make it.)

When browned, stir in the tomato paste, then the kidney beans. Stir over low heat until everything is mixed, then leave to simmer while you prepare the crust.

Measure the flour into a medium-sized bowl. Add most of the milk. Stir to make a dough about the consistency of cake batter, adding more milk if necessary. Spread thinly on a 20–23 cm (8–9 in) square baking pan which has a good non-stick finish. It should cover the whole surface but need not be evenly thick.

Spread the hot mince and beans over the uncooked flour mixture, cover lightly with a piece of baking paper and cook in the oven for 20–30 minutes, until the dough in the centre looks cooked when you push a knife into it.

Remove from the oven and immediately spread with the grated cheese, which should melt onto it.

Serve hot or warm, cut in 4–6 pieces. Top with a salad of shredded lettuce, tomato, spring onion and fresh coriander, with a spoonful of sour cream on the top.

Note: Although the mixture in the pot may seem very spicy, it is much milder when cooked and served.

Enchilada Casserole

This popular layered, one-dish dinner could be described as a Mexican lasagne.

For 4–6 servings:
1 large onion, chopped
1 large clove garlic, chopped
1 Tbsp oil
1 large red or green pepper (optional)
1 tsp ground cumin
½ tsp oreganum
¼–½ tsp chilli powder
*400–500 g (about 1 lb) minced beef or
  lamb*
1 Tbsp plain flour
1 can (about 400 g/14 oz) tomatoes in juice
1 can (440 g/15 oz) whole kernel corn
1–2 Tbsp tomato paste
2 tsp sugar
¾ tsp salt
100–150 g (4–5 oz) corn chips
2 cups grated tasty cheese

Turn the oven to 180°C (350°F). Cook the onion and garlic in the oil in a large pot over moderate heat for 3–4 minutes, until the onion browns lightly. Chop the pepper into small cubes and add to the onion.

Stir in the cumin, oreganum and chilli powder. Raise the heat, add the mince and cook, breaking the meat into small pieces as it browns.

Add the flour, then the next 5 ingredients, including all the liquid from the cans. Simmer for about 10 minutes.

Spray an ovenware dish that holds 8–10 cups with non-stick spray. Spread a third of the meat mixture over the bottom, cover with half the corn chips, then sprinkle over a third of the cheese. Cover with half the remaining meat, then with the rest of the corn chips. Top with the rest of the meat, then the remaining cheese.

Bake uncovered for 30 minutes, until heated through, then leave to stand for 5 minutes. Use a large spoon to serve from the dish.

Serve alone or with crusty bread and a green salad.

Note: This is a good way to use up broken corn chips!

Cornbread-Crusted Chilli

This recipe could be described as a southwestern or Tex-Mex version of shepherd's pie.

For about 6 servings:
2 Tbsp oil
2 onions, chopped
600 g (1 lb 5 oz) minced beef or lamb
½–1 tsp chilli powder
*1 tsp each oreganum, ground cumin and
  paprika*
1 can (400 g/14 oz) whole tomatoes in juice
1 can (440 g/15 oz) baked beans

Cornbread Topping
50 g (2 oz) butter, melted
1 onion, chopped
½ cup sour cream
¼ cup (60 ml/2 fl oz) milk or water
1 can (225 g/8 oz) creamed corn
1 egg
1 cup yellow cornmeal*
1 tsp each baking powder and salt
1 cup grated tasty cheese

* Use cornmeal that is the same coarseness as semolina.

Turn the oven to 180°C (350°F). Heat the oil in a large frypan and brown the onion. Add the mince and cook over high heat until it is no longer pink. Add the chilli powder (using the smaller amount for a mild chilli flavour), oreganum, cumin and paprika, and cook about a minute longer.

Stir in the tomatoes and baked beans, and simmer gently for about 10 minutes while you make the cornbread topping.

Melt the butter in a microwave dish or pot big enough to hold all the ingredients. Add the onion and cook until it is translucent but not browned. Remove from the heat and add the sour cream, milk or water, creamed corn and egg, and mix well with a fork. Stir in the cornmeal, baking powder, salt and grated cheese.

Spread the chilli in a large, shallow ovenware dish, and spread over the topping. Bake uncovered for about 30 minutes, until the topping is firm in the centre and browned on top.

Spoon onto individual plates and serve with a green salad or cooked green vegetable.

Cornbread-Crusted Chilli

Cottage Pie

All my family regard cottage pie as real 'comfort food'. It does involve a few steps, but it can be made ahead then refrigerated or frozen until needed, which is often useful. Nothing else is needed with it, because it has plenty of added vegetables.

For 4–5 servings:
750 g (1 lb 10 oz/4–6 medium) potatoes
2 cups (500 ml/16 fl oz) water
4 cups finely chopped fresh or frozen
 vegetables
1 large onion, chopped
about 500 g (1 lb 2 oz) minced lamb or
 beef
1/4 cup plain flour
1/2 tsp each paprika and oreganum
 (optional)
1 tsp salt
pepper to taste
1 Tbsp butter
1/4–1/2 (60–125 ml/2–4 fl oz) cup milk
about 1 cup grated tasty cheese

Turn the oven to 180°C (350°F). Peel and quarter the potatoes for the topping and cook in a little of boiling, salted water.

In another pot, heat the 2 cups of water. Finely chop about 4 cups of fresh vegetables such as carrots, celery, green beans, etc., or measure out the same amount of frozen vegetables. Add to the water to cook.

Brown the chopped onion and the mince lightly in a large, non-stick frypan over high heat, stir in the flour, paprika and oreganum and cook about a minute longer.

By this time the vegetables should be cooked. Drain all their cooking liquid into the meat and stir until the mixture thickens. Simmer for 2–3 minutes, then add the cooked vegetables, salt and pepper, and adjust seasonings to taste. Spread the mixture in a fairly large, sprayed or lightly buttered ovenproof dish.

Drain the cooked potatoes, discarding the cooking liquid. Mash, then, using a fork, beat in the butter, enough milk to make creamy mashed potatoes, and half the cheese. Spread evenly over the meat, then swirl or roughen the top attractively and sprinkle with the rest of the cheese.

Bake uncovered for 30 minutes, until the pie has heated through and has a crunchy, lightly browned crust.

Moussaka

Who can walk past a display of smooth, shiny, plump and purple aubergines! Many of the aubergines that I can't resist are turned into this Greek speciality. Moussaka reheats well, too, so don't hesitate to make more than you need.

For 4–6 servings:
2 aubergines (about 23 cm/9 in long)
olive oil
2 large onions
about 600 g (1 lb 5 oz) minced lamb or
 beef
2 Tbsp flour
2 cans (each 400 g/14 oz) whole
 tomatoes in juice
1/2 tsp salt
1 tsp sugar
1 tsp oreganum
about 1/4 cup grated Parmesan cheese

Cheese Sauce
3 Tbsp butter
3 Tbsp flour
1 tsp nutmeg
2 cups (500 ml/16 fl oz) milk
1 cup grated cheddar cheese
1 large or 2 small eggs

Cut the unpeeled aubergines into 1 cm (1/2 in) slices, brush lightly with olive oil and grill in batches until lightly browned on both sides.

Meantime, lightly brown the onions in 1 Tbsp olive oil, then add the minced meat and brown over a high heat. Stir in the flour, then add the tomatoes, salt, sugar and oreganum and simmer until the aubergines and cheese sauce are ready, and the meat sauce has thickened.

To make the cheese sauce melt the butter in a medium-sized pot, stir in the flour and nutmeg then half the milk. Bring to the boil, stirring constantly, then add the rest of the milk and heat again, still stirring, until smooth and thick. Take off the heat, stir in the cheese, then beat in the egg(s).

Spray or butter a rectangular ovenproof dish of 12-cup capacity. Overlap half the aubergine slices in it, sprinkle them with half the Parmesan, then spread half the meat sauce over them. Repeat these layers, then press the them down fairly firmly, removing any air spaces. Pour the cheese sauce over everything.

Refrigerate until later or bake straight away at 180°C (350°F) for 30–45 minutes or until the top is golden brown and the mixture is bubbling round the sides. Leave to stand for 10–15 minutes before cutting in rectangles and serving with a tossed salad and warm, crusty bread rolls.

Murphy's Moussaka

This potato-based moussaka always gets the thumbs up when made on a cold winter's night. Part of its appeal is the creamy, cheesy layer on top!

For 6 servings:
750 g (1 lb 10 oz) potatoes
500 g (1 lb 2 oz) minced beef or lamb
2 large onions, finely chopped
2 Tbsp oil
1/2 tsp salt
freshly ground black pepper
1 Tbsp plain flour
1 can (400 g/14 oz) Italian-style tomatoes
2 Tbsp tomato paste

Cheese Sauce
2 Tbsp each flour and butter
freshly ground black pepper
1/2 tsp freshly grated nutmeg
1 cup (250 ml/8 fl oz) milk
1 cup grated tasty cheese
1 egg, beaten

Turn the oven to 180°C (350°F). Scrub the unpeeled potatoes and cut them into 5 mm (1/4 in) slices. Cook in a microwave in a lidded dish with 1/4 cup of water, or in a covered pan with a little water.

Cook the mince with the onion in the oil in a large frypan until the meat is no longer pink. Stir in the seasonings and flour, cook briefly, then add the tomatoes and tomato paste. Heat until the mixture boils and thickens.

To make the sauce, melt the butter. Add flour and seasonings and cook briefly, stirring constantly. Add half the milk, return to the heat and stir continuously until the sauce thickens. Add the rest of the milk and stir and heat until the sauce boils and thickens again.

Stir in the grated cheese, removing the pan from the heat as soon as it melts. Beat in the egg with a fork.

Spray or butter a 10- to 12-cup capacity ovenproof dish and cover the base with a third of the sliced potatoes. Cover with half the mince, the next third of the potatoes, then the rest of the mince. Cover this with the rest of the sliced potatoes. Press down until fairly flat and compact.

Pour the cheese sauce over the top and bake for 30 minutes. (If using uncooked potatoes cook for 1 hour.) Cover with foil if the topping browns too quickly. Leave to stand for 5–10 minutes before serving.

Serve with a cooked green vegetable such as cabbage, broccoli or brussels sprouts or with a mixed green salad.

Mushroom Lasagne

This 'tomato-less' lasagne is a good recipe for young families, because of its mild flavour and soft texture. A boon for any busy mother at the end of a long day, it can be assembled in a short time, then popped into the oven to look after itself.

For 4–5 servings:
1 Tbsp oil
150 g (5 oz) mushrooms, chopped
350 g (12 oz) minced beef or lamb
1/2 tsp each oreganum and thyme
1 packet (30 g/1 oz) mushroom, onion or
 chicken soup mix
3/4 tsp salt
31/2 cups (875 ml/28 fl oz) water
2 Tbsp sherry (optional)
150 g (5 oz/3 cups) small lasagne shapes

Stuffed Peppers

Topping

1 Tbsp cornflour
1 cup (250ml/8 fl oz) milk
1 large egg
1 cup grated tasty cheese

Turn the oven to 180°C (350°F). Heat the oil in a non-stick pot or frypan. Add the mushrooms, then the mince and herbs, and stir over fairly high heat until the mince has broken up and is no longer pink. Sprinkle the soup mix over the meat, add the salt, water and sherry, and bring to the boil.

Spray a casserole or baking dish which will hold 8 cups, spread the uncooked lasagne evenly over it, then pour over the (sloppy) hot mince and mushroom mixture. Rearrange if the pasta is not evenly distributed through the dish. Cover with a lid or foil and bake for 35 minutes.

Mix the cornflour and milk until smooth, then beat in the egg. Pour over the nearly cooked lasagne mixture, sprinkle with cheese, then bake uncovered for 15 minutes, until the top is lightly browned.

Leave to stand for 5 minutes then serve with peas or broccoli, or with crusty bread rolls and a green salad.

Variations: Make without the topping. Cook for 45 minutes instead of 35 minutes, then sprinkle liberally with grated cheese, a little chopped parsley or spring onion and paprika for extra colour. Leave to stand for 5 minutes, then serve as above.

For a stronger flavour, add 1 tsp finely chopped garlic to the mince and about 1/4 tsp chilli powder to the herbs.

Stuffed Peppers

Middle Eastern flavourings give mince and rice lots of flavour. Prepare these ahead for a delicious, interesting, and inexpensive summer meal.

For 4 servings:
4 large or 8 small peppers of mixed colours
3 medium onions
2 cloves garlic
3 Tbsp oil
250 g (9 oz) minced lamb or beef
1 cup brown or white long-grain rice
1/2 cup pinenuts or chopped almonds
1/2 cup currants
1/4 cup each chopped mint and parsley
1/2 tsp each ground allspice, nutmeg and cinnamon
1 tsp salt
1 can (400 g/14 oz) tomatoes in juice
8 young grape leaves, if available

Halve large peppers lengthways. Remove and discard all seeds and pith.

Chop 2 of the onions and the garlic finely and cook in 1 Tbsp of the oil in a large frypan until the onions are transparent. Add the mince and the rice and cook for a minute or two longer. Add 2 cups (500 ml/16 fl oz) water, cover and simmer 30–45 minutes for brown rice, or about 15 minutes for white rice, adding extra water if the mixture looks dry before the rice is cooked.

While the rice cooks, stand the prepared peppers in boiling water for 5 minutes, then drain, discarding the water.

Brown the pinenuts or almonds lightly in the second Tbsp of oil in another pan. Add the currants and cook until they have plumped up.

Combine the nuts, currants, mint, parsley, allspice, nutmeg, cinnamon, salt, meat and cooked rice.

Lightly brown the last onion in the last Tbsp of oil, in the frypan or baking pan in which the peppers will cook. Add the tomatoes.

Pack the stuffing firmly into the peppers, so the tops are rounded and all or most of the filling is used. Arrange the peppers on the tomato in a frypan or baking pan, so that the stuffing is not in contact with the tomatoes. Cover each pepper with a small grape leaf, if available.

Cover the frypan and simmer very gently for 20–30 minutes, until the peppers are tender and the tomato mixture thickened, OR cover lightly with foil and bake at 180–200°C (350–400°F) for 30–45 minutes, adding extra liquid if the tomato dries out.

Serve hot, warm or at room temperature, alone or with salad and crusty bread.

See also

Crispy Pork Wontons, p. 29
Parmesan Meatballs, p. 29
Spicy Mexican Filling, p. 42
Cheesy Pieburgers, p. 154
Patricia's Pork Pie, p. 155
Easy Spaghetti'n'Meat Sauce, p. 183
Economical Lasagne, p. 184
Quick Bolognese Sauce, p. 184

Simply Sausages

Don't forget how popular sausages are! Enjoy them plainly cooked during the barbecue season, but try some of the recipes in this section too, especially when you want to make a small amount go further. There are many interesting sausages available nowadays, so it's worth looking around, sampling different ones until you find which you like best for different purposes.

Curried Sausage Pie

'Comfort food' with a capital C! Everybody seems to enjoy cheese-topped creamy potatoes over savoury sausages. I have found that visiting children and teenagers who show interest in little other food will eat this with gusto and return for seconds!

For 4–6 servings:
1 kg (2 lb 3 oz/6 medium) potatoes
2 medium onions
1 kg (2 lb 3 oz) sausage meat or skinned sausages
2 tsp curry powder
2 Tbsp brown sugar
1 can (400 g/14 oz) apple sauce
1 Tbsp butter
freshly ground black pepper
½ cup (125 ml/4 fl oz) milk
½–1 cup grated cheese

Turn the oven to 180°C (350°F). Peel the potatoes thinly, cut them into even pieces, and cook in a pot of lightly salted water.

Cut the onions in half from stem to root, then into wedges. Sprinkle about half of them into a roasting pan or a large, shallow baking dish. With wet hands, form the sausage meat into walnut-sized blobs. Arrange these in one layer over the onion wedges. Sprinkle over the remaining onion.

Mix the curry powder and brown sugar together and sprinkle evenly over the sausages and onions, then spread with the apple sauce.

Drain and mash the cooked potatoes with the butter, pepper and milk. Spread evenly over the sausages, swirl or roughen the top attractively, then sprinkle over the grated cheese.

Bake uncovered for 1 hour, then serve with cooked vegetables and/or salad.

Variation: Replace the apple sauce with any 400 g (14 oz) can of seasoned tomatoes.

Sausage and Kumara Dinner

This tasty mixture may be cooked in a casserole or on the stovetop. Once you have everything in the dish you can relax with your feet up or get on with something else until serving time.

For 4 generous servings:
800 g (1 lb 12 oz) kumara
450–500 g (about 1 lb) venison or other 'gourmet' sausages
1 large onion
2 stalks celery
1 large green-skinned apple
¾ cup (185 ml/6 fl oz) chicken stock or 1 tsp chicken stock powder and ¾ cup water
1 cup (250 ml/8 fl oz) orange juice
2 Tbsp brown sugar
½ tsp mixed spice
4 tsp cornflour
¼ cup (60 ml/2 fl oz) cold water

Cook the unpeeled kumara in a covered pot or microwave until just tender. Brown sausages evenly in a large pan then cut in thick diagonal slices.

Chop the onion, celery and unpeeled apple into 1 cm (½ in) cubes and place them on the bottom of the pan or in a large, fairly shallow, buttered casserole dish.

Skin the kumara, cut it into 1 cm (½ in) cubes and place over the raw vegetables. Place the sliced sausages on top.

Pour on the chicken stock and the orange juice. Mix the brown sugar and mixed spice and sprinkle over the kumara and sliced sausages.

Cover and simmer for 20 minutes, or bake at 180°C (350°F) for 1¼ hours, until the vegetables are tender. Turn carefully once or twice if you are nearby.

Mix the cornflour with the water and stir in enough to thicken the juices. Mix carefully and serve in shallow bowls, sprinkled with chopped parsley.

Apricot and Sausage Loaf

This flavourful loaf is baked in an oven bag, surrounded by an easy but interesting sauce which flavours and glazes it.

For 6–8 servings:

Sauce
1 Tbsp tomato sauce
1 Tbsp Thai sweet chilli sauce
1 Tbsp Worcestershire sauce

Loaf
8 dried apricots
½ cup (125 ml/4 fl oz) boiling water
4 thick slices stale bread
1 egg
¼ cup (60 ml/2 fl oz) orange juice
½ tsp grated orange rind (optional)
450–500 g (about 1 lb) sausage meat
1 packet (30 g/1 oz) cream of chicken soup mix
1 large onion, finely chopped

Turn the oven to 150°C (300°F). Chop the dried apricots into thin strips. Put them in a bowl, pour over the boiling water, and leave to stand.

Measure the sauce ingredients into an unpunctured oven bag, and stand the bag upright in a loaf tin or other suitable baking dish. Add the water drained off the apricots.

Add to the apricots in the bowl the crumbled bread (crusts and all), egg, orange juice and rind. Mash the bread with a fork to soften it. Add the sausage meat, soup mix and onion. Mix together thoroughly with your hand, then form the mixture into a big egg shape and put it in the bottom of the oven bag. Move it around so it is coated with the sauce, reshape if necessary, then stand the bag upright in the baking tin, with the top folded over loosely several times.

Bake for 45 minutes, then open the bag so that the top of the loaf will dry. Bake for 15 minutes longer. Leave to stand in the bag for 5–10 minutes before lifting it onto a board for slicing.

Serve hot or cold with rice or a rice salad, and broccoli or a green salad.

Curried Sausage Pie

Sultans' Sausages

These sausages are simmered in a well-spiced fruity sauce which turns them into something really special. You may like to use some of the gourmet sausages that are now readily available.

For 4 servings:

8 sausages (about 500 g/1 lb)
1 small onion, cut into wedges
1 tsp minced garlic
1 tsp grated root ginger
1 tsp grated orange rind
½ (125 ml/4 fl oz) cup orange juice
¼ tsp chilli powder (optional)
½ cup (125 ml/4 fl oz) white wine
1 cup (250 ml/8 fl oz) chicken stock or
  1 tsp chicken stock powder in 1 cup
  water
8 dried apple rings, halved
8 dried apricots, halved
8 prunes, halved
½ tsp each ground allspice and cinnamon
2 tsp brown sugar
1 Tbsp sour cream
salt and pepper to taste

Brown the sausages in a large, heavy pot, frypan or iron casserole, turning to colour evenly. Add the onion and garlic, with a dribble of oil if necessary, and cook until lightly browned, stirring occasionally.

Add all the remaining ingredients except the sour cream, salt and pepper. Cover and cook over a low heat for 20–30 minutes. Remove from the heat and stir in the sour cream. Season to taste.

This recipe may be made ahead and reheated. Serve with couscous cooked in chicken stock, rice, mashed or baked potatoes and a lettuce, tomato and cucumber salad.

Sausage-Meat Square

This square has quite a lot of fruit or vegetables baked with the sausage meat. It is a good way to hide vegetables from children who may leave salads packed in school lunches uneaten!

450–500 g (about 1 lb) sausage meat
1 large egg
1 tsp curry powder (optional)
2 Tbsp tomato (or plum) sauce
1 large onion
1 medium-large apple
1 medium-large potato
1 large carrot
grated cheese

Turn the oven to 180°C (350°F). Put the sausage meat in a bowl with the egg, curry powder and sauce, and stir to mix.

Grate the onion, unpeeled apple and the scrubbed, unpeeled potato and carrot by hand. Mix the vegetables and apple into the sausage meat until evenly combined. (You can use a food processor for this,

but because the shreds are bigger you will need to process the sausage meat and grated mixture together, in batches, so the vegetable pieces are chopped smaller.)

Press the mixture into a 23 cm (9 in) square baking pan lined with baking paper. Sprinkle lightly with grated cheese and bake for 30–45 minutes, or until the mixture feels firm in the centre. Leave to cool, then cut into 9–12 pieces.

OR bake the mixture in 12 medium-sized muffin pans. Because it tends to stick, the muffin pans should be well coated with non-stick spray or lined with cupcake liners. Top with a little grated cheese (too much makes the muffins stick badly) and bake at 170°C (325°F) for 35–40 minutes. Leave for 5–10 minutes before removing from the pans.

Serve warm or cold with chutney or sauce. Refrigerate for up to 3 days, or wrap individually and freeze for up to a month.

Kiwi Curried Sausages

These are the curried sausages most New Zealanders remember fondly from their childhood. By all means add extra ingredients such as coconut, chutney, etc. if this is what your mother did!

For 4 servings:

8 sausages (about 500 g/1 lb)
1 onion, chopped
1 apple, diced
2–3 tsp curry powder
1 cup sultanas
1 cup (250 ml/8 fl oz) water
1 tsp chicken stock powder
2 Tbsp apricot or plum jam
1 Tbsp wine vinegar
1 tsp cornflour

Brown the sausages gently in a large frypan or pot. Add the onion and cook until lightly browned. Add the apple and curry powder and cook for 3–4 minutes, stirring to coat the sausages, onions and apples.

Add all the remaining ingredients except the cornflour and stir well to combine. Cover and cook over a low heat for 20–30 minutes.

Mix the cornflour with a little water to make a thin paste. Stir into the sausage mixture and reheat, stirring until the mixture thickens slightly.

Serve with rice or mashed potatoes and a variety of fresh vegetables.

Variations: Add 1 Tbsp Worcestershire sauce.

If you have no jam handy, use 1 Tbsp brown sugar instead.

Creamy Curried Sausages

This 20-minute curry is mild enough for primary school children. The sliced sausages and vegetables simmer in a well-flavoured creamy sauce. Use bought, pre-cooked sausages or cook sausages gently in another pan while you make the sauce.

For 4–5 servings:

1 Tbsp butter
2–3 tsp mild curry powder
1 onion
1 carrot
2 stalks celery
1 cup (250 ml/8 fl oz) water
400–500 g (about 1 lb) pre-cooked
  sausages
1 cup frozen peas
2 Tbsp cornflour
1½ tsp chicken stock powder
½ tsp sugar
1 cup (250 ml/8 fl oz) milk

Melt the butter in a medium to large pot. Stir in the curry powder and cook gently, without browning, while you prepare the vegetables.

Cut the onion, carrot and celery into small (5 mm / ¼ in) cubes. As each is prepared, stir it into the curry and butter. (Make sure you have a least a cup of each prepared vegetable.) After the celery, add the water, cover and simmer for 5 minutes.

While the vegetables simmer, skin the pre-cooked sausages and slice them 5 mm (¼ in) thick. Add them with the frozen peas and cook 5 minutes longer. By this time, all the vegetables should be tender.

Using absolutely level measures, mix the cornflour, stock powder and sugar together, then add the milk and stir until smooth. Add to the curried vegetables and sausages and stir gently until the mixture thickens.

Serve in large bowls, on plain rice, spirals or other pasta. No other vegetables are necessary, although a crisp salad is nice.

Toad in the Hole

Properly made, this mixture consists of sausage patties (the toads!) partly buried in light, crisp and crunchy, well-risen Yorkshire Pudding batter. I have had trouble with Yorkshire Pudding batters in the past, but I have solved my problems with the following method. Follow it exactly!

For 4 servings:

1 large or 2 smaller eggs
1 cup (250 ml/8 fl oz) milk
1 cup plain flour less 2 Tbsp
¼ tsp salt
450–500 g (about 1 lb) sausage meat

Turn the oven to 190°C (375°F). Mix the egg(s) and (brimming) cup of milk together in a medium-sized bowl.

Vigorously beat the flour in its container, using a whisk or fork. Then, without shaking or packing it in any way, spoon it lightly into a cup of exactly the same size as the milk cup. Without shaking it, level off the top, then remove and discard 2 level measuring Tbsp of flour.

Tip the remaining flour into the egg and milk mixture and beat until smooth. Stir in the salt. Leave to stand.

Shape plain or seasoned sausage meat into 16 patties and place them in a high-sided 23 cm (9 in) square baking or cake pan coated with non-stick spray (or use 2 loaf tins).

Bake for 10 minutes (without using the fan) then stir the batter briefly and pour it into the hot tin(s) quickly. Bake at the same temperature for about 40 minutes, until the crust has risen (unevenly) around the 'toads' and is crisp, golden brown, and set.

Variation: Add 1 Tbsp grated Parmesan cheese to the batter.

Note: The batter is risen by steam, and does not contain baking powder, etc. It rises better in small, deep-sided tins.

Winter Sausages

Tamarillos make a sauce with character! When they are not available, use tomatoes instead.

For 4 servings:
8 sausages (about 700 g/1 lb 9 oz)
1 large onion, chopped
2–3 cloves garlic, chopped
4 tamarillos or large firm tomatoes
1 cup (250 ml/8 fl oz) liquid*
1/4 cup brown sugar
1/2 tsp salt
1 Tbsp tomato paste
1–2 tsp tabasco sauce

* Use a mixture of wine, tomato, orange or other fruit juice, and water. Or use 1 Tbsp wine vinegar or 2 Tbsp lemon juice made up to 1 cup with water.

Brown the sausages in a large, heavy frypan, turning to colour evenly. Add the onion and garlic, with a dribble of oil if necessary, and cook until lightly browned, stirring often.

Peel the tamarillos or tomatoes, chop them into chunky pieces and add, with the remaining ingredients, to the sausages. Cover and simmer for about 20 minutes, until the sauce is of gravy consistency, or thicken with a little cornflour paste. Adjust seasonings to taste.

Serve with pasta, rice or mashed potatoes, and a green vegetable.

Note: This recipe may be made ahead and reheated.

Winter Sausages

Devilled Sausages

This is one of my favourite sausage recipes! I have made it regularly over the years, with minor changes, and I am sure that my family would happily eat it, once or twice a month, for as many years as I like to cook it!

For 4–6 servings:
8–12 sausages (500–600 g/1 lb 2 oz–1 lb 5 oz)
4 Tbsp brown sugar
1 Tbsp cornflour
1 tsp ground cumin
1 tsp dry mustard
1 tsp celery salt
1/4 tsp salt
1 Tbsp soy sauce
1 Tbsp wine vinegar
2 Tbsp tomato paste
1 cup (250 ml/8 fl oz) water
1 large onion
1–2 green-skinned apples

Turn the oven to 180°C (350°F). Separate the sausages if necessary. In an ovenware dish or small roasting pan in which they will fit in one layer, mix the (level) spoons of sugar, cornflour, cumin, mustard, celery salt and salt. Add the liquids and stir until smooth.

Chop the onion and the unpeeled but cored apple(s) into 1 cm (1/2 in) cubes and stir into the mixture.

Place the sausages in one layer in the pan, cover tightly with a lid or foil, and bake at 180°C (350°F) for 1 hour or 170°C (325°F) for 1 1/2 hours, turning the sausages in the sauce once or twice. Stir in half a cup of extra liquid (water, beer or wine) before serving if the sauce is thicker than you like.

Serve on rice, with baked or mashed potatoes, and beans or broccoli.

Variations: Replace the tomato paste, vinegar and 1 Tbsp of the brown sugar with 1/4 cup tomato sauce.

Instead of baking, cook in a large, covered frypan for 20–30 minutes, after browning the sausages first.

Stretched Sausages

Stretched Sausages

Make this when you want to make a few sausages go a long way! It is also an inexpensive way to keep out winter chills.

For 3 servings:
3 fairly large onions
6 sausages
3 apples
2 Tbsp brown sugar
2 Tbsp wine vinegar
salt to taste
about 3 Tbsp Thai sweet chilli sauce
lots of chopped parsley

Cut the onions into wedges and cook in a large, non-stick frypan in the smallest amount of oil needed to stop them sticking. Do not hurry this step.

While the onion is cooking, cut the skin of each sausage, from end to end, and hold under a slow-running cold tap as you peel away the skin. With wet hands, break each skinned sausage into 3 or 4 even pieces, and roll each into a small ball. Cook in another frypan, turning to brown evenly. Pour off any fat.

Quarter and core the apples (peel them if you like). Cut each quarter into 3 or 4 wedges and add these to the pan with the

partly cooked onion. When the onion is evenly browned and the apple slightly browned, add the brown sugar and vinegar, then a little salt to taste. Stir the cooked sausage balls into the apple and onion mixture. If you like more sauce, add about 1/2 cup water, chicken stock or wine, thicken the mixture with a little cornflour paste, and adjust the seasonings again.

Leave the mixture in a serving dish in a low oven until ready to serve, or reheat in a large frypan when needed.

A few minutes before serving, stir in half the chilli sauce, then drizzle the rest over the top for extra colour. Sprinkle generously with chopped parsley just before serving.

'Home Alone' Special

Here is a recipe for any hungry person who wants an easy, filling, 15-minute meal to eat in front of the television set! It is equally useful to feed to a couple of kids before the babysitter arrives and you rush out the door!

For 1 large or 2 medium servings:
250 g (9 oz) sausage meat or 4 sausages
1 tsp minced garlic
1/2 tsp oreganum

1 can (400 g/14 oz) tomatoes
1 cup (250 ml/8 fl oz) water
1 1/2 cups (125 g/4 1/2 oz) pasta spirals
1/4 tsp salt
1/2 tsp sugar
1 cup frozen peas

Cut through sausage skins lengthways, hold under a cold tap and peel away the skins. Cut the sausage meat or sausages into about 12 chunks, then brown these in a medium-sized, non-stick frypan with the minced garlic (from a jar) and the oreganum.

Add half the tomatoes and their liquid, and all the water. Break up the tomatoes as the mixture comes to the boil, then stir in the uncooked pasta. Cover and cook for 10 minutes, turning with a fish slice or stirrer once or twice.

When the pasta is nearly cooked, add the salt, sugar and frozen peas. Mix to break up the peas, add a little extra water if the mixture looks dry, cover again and cook for 4 minutes. Pour the remaining tomatoes over the mixture, and leave for a few minutes until they warm through.

Serve in bowls with a crisp green salad on the side.

Note: If you keep a tube of sausage meat and peas in the freezer, a jar of minced garlic in the fridge, pasta and a can of savoury tomatoes in your cupboard, this meal may be made at any time. Teach everybody in your house how to make it!

Ferhoodled Sausage

'Ferhoodled' is a wonderful Pennsylvanian Dutch word meaning 'all mixed up'. In this recipe sausage patties are all mixed up with rice and vegetables in a one-pan dinner. You prepare the next ingredient while the previous one cooks – really easy!

For 4 servings:
250 g (9 oz) sausage meat
2 onions, finely chopped
1 green pepper
2 stalks celery
1 large carrot
1 cup long-grain rice
1 tsp each oreganum, thyme and ground cumin
3 cups (750 ml/24 fl oz) chicken stock or 2 tsp stock powder in 3 cups water
1 bayleaf (optional)

Shape the sausage meat into 12–16 small patties with wet hands, and brown in a large frypan (with a lid). Add the onions and cook until transparent and slightly browned.

Roughly chop and add, as each is prepared, the pepper, celery and carrot. Keep all the vegetable pieces about the same size.

Stir in the rice and herbs and cook until the rice looks translucent, then add the stock and bayleaf.

Cover and simmer for 15 minutes, or until the rice is cooked and the water absorbed. Check during cooking, adding extra water if the mixture looks dry before the rice is cooked.

Check seasonings, adding extra salt if necessary. Sprinkle generously with chopped parsley and serve immediately, alone or with a green salad or coleslaw.

Easy Sausage and Macaroni

This recipe requires few ingredients, little time and next to no energy! It is just the thing for an easy family dinner at the end of a busy day! What's more, it will probably be a hot favourite with your children.

For 4 servings:
450–500 g (about 1 lb) sausage meat
1 large onion
1 can (400 g/14 oz) whole tomatoes in juice
1 cup (250 ml/8 fl oz) water
1/2 tsp oreganum
1/2 tsp salt
1 tsp brown sugar
1 cup (100 g/4 oz) small macaroni

Form the sausage meat into 8 patties and brown on both sides in a large, non-stick frypan with a lid.

Chop the onion into pieces much the same size as the macaroni, add to the pan, cook for 1–2 minutes then add the tomatoes and juice, and the water. Stir in the oreganum, salt and sugar, and break up the tomatoes.

When the liquid boils, sprinkle in the macaroni, stir to mix well, cover tightly and leave to simmer very gently until the macaroni is tender and the liquid absorbed, about 15 minutes.

Turn the mixture carefully, sprinkle with chopped parsley or grated Parmesan cheese and serve immediately.

Spicy Sausages

If you keep a packet of pre-cooked sausages in the freezer, replacing it straight after use, you can put a meal on the table in just a few minutes.

For 4 servings:
about 500 g (1 lb) pre-cooked sausages
about 2 tsp oil
2 rashers bacon
1 medium onion
1/4 cup (60 ml/2 fl oz) tomato or barbecue sauce
2 tsp prepared mustard
about 1/4 cup (60 ml/2 fl oz) water
chopped parsley

If necessary, thaw the sausages on Defrost (30% power) in the microwave, in their packet or a plastic bag, until they are soft enough to slice. Peel off the skin and cut each into about 6 diagonal slices.

Meanwhile heat the oil in a large frypan. Cook the sausages over moderate heat, turning them at intervals so all the surfaces brown. Cut the rind from the bacon and chop the rashers into 1 cm (1/2 in) pieces. Chop the onion finely. Add the bacon and onion to the browned sausages and cook until the onions have browned slightly.

Stir in the sauce, mustard and water. Bring to the boil, turning the sausages until they are coated with glaze. Sprinkle generously with chopped parsley and serve.

South-of-the-Border Sausages

This spicy corn and sausage sauce is almost as good on rice as it is on pasta. If you are cooking for people who do not like hot food, just leave out the chilli powder. The other flavourings add flavour, not hotness!

For 4–6 servings:
500 g (1 lb 2 oz) pre-cooked sausages, sliced
1 tsp minced garlic
1 onion
1 green pepper
1 red pepper
1 tsp each oreganum and ground cumin
1/4–1/2 tsp chilli powder
1–2 tsp oil
1 cup (250 ml/8 fl oz) chicken stock or 1 cup water and 3/4 tsp chicken stock powder
2 Tbsp butter
2 Tbsp plain flour
1 cup (250 ml/8 fl oz) milk
1 can (310 g/11 oz) whole kernel corn
salt and sugar to taste
chopped parsley or fresh coriander

Slice the sausages diagonally and cook in a large, non-stick frypan over medium heat until lightly browned. As they brown, stir in the minced garlic, and the onion and pepper chopped into thumbnail-sized pieces.

Sprinkle the spices over the mixture as it cooks. Add the oil only if no fat comes out of the sausages. After 3–4 minutes add the chicken stock. Simmer for 3–4 minutes, until the vegetables are tender-crisp.

Melt the butter in a small pot or microwave dish, stir in the flour, then add the milk and heat, stirring often, until the sauce thickens.

Drain off and keep the liquid from the canned corn, then combine the corn, white sauce and sausage mixture. Thin with some of the corn liquid if it is too

thick, then taste, and if necessary add enough salt and sugar to bring out the flavours.

Serve over cooked rice or pasta, sprinkled with parsley or fresh coriander.

Sauces for Sausages

Interesting sauces make all the difference to plain barbecued or grilled sausages. Serve a selection, with different flavours and textures, so your friends have a choice.

Barbecue Bean Sauce
For about 12 servings:
2 medium onions, chopped
2 cloves garlic, finely chopped
1 Tbsp oil
1 can (440 g/15 oz) baked beans
1/4 cup tomato paste
1/4 cup brown sugar
2 Tbsp mixed mustard
1 Tbsp Worcestershire sauce
2 Tbsp cider vinegar
water or beer for thinning

Brown the onion and garlic evenly in oil in a large pan. Add the remaining ingredients and simmer for 10 minutes, stirring often. Thin with water or beer if desired. Spoon over burgers and barbecued sausages.

Refrigerate for up to 1 week.

Sage and Apple Sauce
For about 6 servings:
1 onion, chopped
2 Tbsp butter
2 large apples, peeled and sliced
1 Tbsp chopped fresh sage
2 Tbsp apple juice, white wine or water
2–3 tsp sugar
salt and pepper

Cook the onion in the butter over moderate heat until golden brown. Add the apple, sage, the liquid of your choice, and sugar. Cover and cook until the apples are tender. Mash or purée, then season with salt and pepper to taste.

Serve warm or hot with barbecued sausages, sausage loaf, etc. Refrigerate for up to 3 days.

See also:

Mixed Grill, p. 18

Paella, p. 80

Stuffing Balls, p. 86

Bonza Budget Burgers, p. 132

Minted Picnic Pie, p. 154

Sausage Braid, p. 154

Sausage and Potato Salad with Mustard Dressing, p. 163

Sizzled Sausage and Sage Muffins, p. 269

Savoury Pies

Never underestimate the power of the pie! When you make a pie, quiche, flan or filo package, you are using your cooking skills and imagination to turn basic ingredients into something that looks impressive and is sure to be popular! It is not difficult to make pastry for your pies, but if you don't want to do this you have a choice of filo pastry and a range of bought pastries. When you buy pastry compare the labels – some new commercially made pastries contain less fat than our old favourites. I use homemade short pastry regularly because it contains less fat than most other pastries. Filo is fun to work with and can be remarkably low in fat if you brush on oil with great restraint, but it is best eaten soon after it is cooked, and this may not always suit you.

Self-Crusting Zucchini Pie V

A popular way to serve yet more zucchini from your garden!

For 6–8 servings:
3 cups grated zucchini
1 onion, grated
4 large eggs
1½ cups grated cheddar cheese
½ tsp salt
¾ cup self-raising flour
pepper
herbs and tomato slices (optional)
grated cheddar or Parmesan cheese for top

Turn the oven to 200°C (400°F). Spray or butter a 23 x 25 cm (9 x 10 in) roasting pan, or two 23 cm (9 in) pie plates or flan tins.

Pat the grated zucchini and onion dry with a paper towel and place in a fairly large mixing bowl with the eggs, cheese and salt. Mix well with a fork.

Add the flour and as much pepper as you like, and chop in any fresh herbs.

Pour the mixture into the prepared pan(s). It will rise quite a lot as it cooks, so do not fill the pan more than two-thirds full; it does not matter if the pan is only filled to half its depth.

Top with sliced tomatoes if you wish, and sprinkle with grated cheddar or Parmesan cheese. Bake for 25–40 minutes, until the centre feels firm and the top has browned slightly. Leave to stand for at least 5 minutes before cutting into pieces.

Reheat leftovers in the microwave until warm, not hot.

Carol's Vegetable Strudel

Self-Crusting Corn Quiche V

For 4–5 servings:
1 can (450 g/16 oz) whole kernel corn, drained
¼–½ cup chopped spring onions
½–1 cup grated tasty cheese
½ cup self-raising flour
¾ cup (185 ml/6 fl oz) milk
2 large eggs
3 firm tomatoes, sliced (optional)

Turn the oven to 200°C (400°F). Spray a 20–23 cm (8–9 in) solid-bottomed flan tin or pie plate with non-stick spray. Arrange the corn, spring onions and cheese in the tin.

Using a fork or whisk combine the flour, milk and eggs, and pour over the corn mixture. Arrange slices of tomato on top if you like.

Bake for 25–30 minutes, or until the centre is set and the top golden brown.

Variations: Replace the corn with 1½ cups cooked zucchini, 2 cups sliced sautéed mushrooms, 2 cups chopped cooked broccoli or a drained can of asparagus.

Carol's Vegetable Strudel V

This is spectacular and really delicious, well worth making.

For 6 servings:
1 carrot, thinly sliced
125 g (4½ oz) green beans, sliced
150 g (5 oz) broccoli florets
1 small leek, finely sliced
1 small stick celery, sliced
4 medium-sized mushrooms, sliced
2 Tbsp canola oil
100 g (3½ oz) bean sprouts (optional)
9 sheets filo pastry
oil or melted butter for brushing

1 cup grated tasty cheese
2 slices toast bread, crumbled
½ tsp salt
2 Tbsp finely chopped fresh basil or
   1 Tbsp pesto

Turn the oven to 190°C (375°F). Cook the first 5 (prepared) vegetables in a little boiling salted water until barely tender, then drain.

In a small frypan cook the mushrooms for 2 minutes in the oil, then add the bean sprouts and vegetables. Toss well and cool.

Lie 3 sheets of filo pastry side by side, long sides together and slightly overlapping. Brush lightly with oil or butter. Cover with 3 more sheets, oil or butter them the same way, then top with the remaining 3 sheets. You will end up with a large rectangle, 3 layers thick.

Place the vegetable filling over the first third of the rectangle. Mix together the cheese, breadcrumbs, salt and basil or pesto and sprinkle over the vegetables. Roll up loosely, filling end first. Cover the ends of the roll with foil so no filling falls out during cooking.

Bake on an oiled oven tray for 30–35 minutes, until golden brown. Serve immediately, with a leafy green salad.

FILO PASTRY PIE CRUSTS

Filo pastry is fun to work with and eat. The pastries made from it are lighter and less fatty than similar products made from puff pastry, and what's more you know exactly what type of fat or oil is in the finished product because you've put it there yourself.

Filo pies are best eaten soon after they are made, although they may be reheated in an oven set to 150°C (300°F), usually for about 20 minutes.

Mediterranean Vegetable Pie V

This versatile pie is good made with roasted peppers, eggplant, red onion or zucchini, or a mixture of these.

For 5–6 servings:
2 large red, orange or yellow peppers, or vegetables mentioned above
2 Tbsp olive oil
1 tsp (1–2 cloves) minced garlic
2 Tbsp capers, chopped black olives, or vegetarian tapenade (optional)
1 cup cottage cheese
250 g (9 oz) feta cheese, crumbled
4 eggs, lightly beaten
1/2 tsp grated nutmeg
freshly ground black pepper to taste
8 sheets filo pastry
olive oil for brushing
2–3 Tbsp grated Parmesan cheese
sesame or poppy seeds (optional)

Cut the peppers lengthways into 4 large pieces; remove the pith and seeds. Mix the olive oil with the garlic, and turn the peppers in the mixture in a shallow roasting pan. Grill, or roast uncovered, at 200°C (400°F) for 20 minutes, until the skin darkens, or cook in a contact grill on high for 5–10 minutes. Cool and peel off the skin. (Roast other vegetables in slices, similarly.) Turn the oven to 190°C (375°F).

Combine the next 6 ingredients. (Do not add any salt.) Mix well, mashing with a fork. Do not mix in a food processor, as the mixture gets too runny.

Take 4 sheets of filo pastry, brush each with a little olive oil and sprinkle with grated Parmesan cheese. Stack the sheets and place in a roasting or baking pan big enough to hold the sheets with their edges turned up about 2 cm (3/4 in).

Pour in half the cheese mixture, add half the roasted vegetables, then repeat these layers.

Prepare the rest of the filo as before and use to cover the pie. Cut the filo top smaller or wrinkle it so it fits to the edge. Fold the edges of the filo from the bottom of the pie over the top. Brush lightly with oil and sprinkle with sesame or poppy seeds if you like.

Bake for 30–45 minutes. If the pastry browns too quickly cover it with foil for part of the baking time. Serve warm, with a leafy salad and crusty bread.

Curried Chicken Samosas

Deliciously spicy chicken wrapped in triangular filo parcels.

For 16 parcels, 8 servings:
12 sheets filo pastry
melted butter or oil

Filling
250 g (9 oz) minced chicken
1 onion, finely chopped
1 tsp grated fresh ginger
1/2 tsp chilli powder
1/2 tsp turmeric
1 can (425 g/15 oz) savoury tomatoes
1 cup frozen peas
1 tsp garam masala
2 Tbsp chopped fresh coriander
1 Tbsp cornflour

Turn the oven to 200°C (400°F). Put minced chicken and onion into a preheated frypan and brown well, adding the ginger, chilli powder and turmeric as the meat cooks. Add the tomatoes and cook uncovered until almost dry, then add next 3 ingredients and cook 2 minutes longer.

Mix the cornflour to a paste with a little cold water and stir into the chicken mixture to thicken it. Cool, then use as filling for 16 filo triangles.

To make the triangles, layer 3 sheets of filo pastry, brushing between each with butter or oil. Cut into 4 strips crosswise. Put a spoonful of filling at the top of 1 strip, then fold the filo over it so the top touches the edge, forming a triangle (see diagram). Keep folding in triangles to enclose the filling. Repeat with the remaining filo and filling, always using 3 sheets per 'sandwich'. Brush the tops lightly with a little more butter or oil.

Place triangles on a baking tray. Bake at 200°C (400°F) for 10 minutes then reduce the temperature to 180°C (350°F) and cook for 15–20 minutes longer, until evenly golden brown. Serve warm, as finger food.

Mushroom-Filled Filo Triangles

Savoury mushrooms wrapped in filo pastry can be served as a lunch dish or as a vegetable at a main meal.

For 4 servings:
12 sheets filo pastry
oil for brushing

Filling
about 1 Tbsp butter
2 cloves garlic, finely chopped
200 g (7 oz) mushrooms, quartered or chopped
2 slices ham, chopped
parsley, tarragon, thyme, etc.
2–3 spring onions, chopped
1 slice bread, crumbled
1–2 Tbsp sour cream
black pepper to taste

Turn the oven to 200°C (400°F). Make the filling. Heat the butter in a frypan. Cook the garlic and mushrooms in it for a few minutes. Raise the heat, add a few Tbsp water and cover the pan to wilt the mushrooms. Add the ham, herbs to taste, and spring onions. Cook until the onion

has heated through. Taste, season well, then add the bread (crumbled in a food processor) and the sour cream to bind the mixture, and black pepper to taste.

Prepare and fill filo triangles as for Curried Chicken Samosas, above.

Place, joins down, on an oven tray, brush lightly with more butter, then bake for 5–10 minutes, until golden brown.

Salmon Surprise Packages

These packages give a feeling of lightness to a special occasion meal. They also make a little smoked salmon go a long way.

For 4 servings:
60 g (2 oz) smoked salmon offcuts
4 medium-sized new potatoes, cooked
2 tsp horseradish sauce (optional)
2 Tbsp sour cream
1 Tbsp chopped spring onion
salt and pepper (optional)
4 slices soft mould-ripened cheese
8 sheets filo pastry
about 2 tsp soft butter
4 whole chives or other ties

Turn the oven to 190°C (375°F). Chop the salmon into small pieces, and the potato into pea-sized pieces. Mix with the horseradish sauce, sour cream and spring onion. Season lightly if you like. Keep the cheese separate.

Layer 2 sheets of filo pastry, brushing between the layers with butter, using about 1/2 tsp per sheet. Cut the sheets in half and place one half on top of the other, so there are 8 more-or-less equidistant corners. Put a quarter of the filling and 1 slice of cheese in the centre, then gather up the edges so the filling is surrounded. Tie a long chive or other tie around the pastry before baking. Repeat with remaining filo and filling.

Bake in lightly buttered or sprayed sponge-roll pans for about 10 minutes, or until lightly browned. Serve as a starter or lunch dish, with a salad.

Filo Nests V

Sometimes I shape filo to make nest-shaped savouries. These seem remarkably substantial, although each is made from only one tissue-paper-like sheet. You need nice, fresh filo to make these, since dried filo will crack and break when you roll it and gather it up. It is nice to flavour the cases as well as the filling by sprinkling finely grated Parmesan cheese onto the oiled layers.

For 12 nests:
12 sheets filo pastry
about ¼ cup (60 ml/2 fl oz) olive oil
* (1 tsp per sheet)*
about ¼ cup finely grated Parmesan
* cheese*
Herb Pâté (right)
wafer-thin slices of ham, smoked beef,
* pork, salmon or salami*

Turn the oven to 180°C (350°F). Take 1 sheet of filo pastry, and with the short end nearest you lightly brush one half with oil. Sprinkle with about 2 tsp Parmesan cheese and fold in half, so the short ends are together. (Keep the remaining sheets of filo covered, on a dry surface, so they don't dry out.)

Lay a dry, lightly floured wooden spoon handle along the folded edge of the filo. Roll the filo loosely around the handle, stopping when you have about 8 cm (3 in) of unrolled pastry left.

Gently push the filo along the handle until it's about three-quarters of its original length, gathering it up as you go. Slide the handle out of the gathered length then, leaving the filo roll flat on the work surface, gently turn the ends of the rolled part in to meet each other, forming a horse-shoe shape. The unrolled part should be lifted up in the air inside the horse-shoe.

The horse-shoe edge will form most of the outer rim of the 'nest'. Press the unrolled part down to make the centre of the nest, then fold the ends of the unfolded part over the gap between the ends of the horse-shoe and tuck them underneath. This should leave you with a raised edge round a flat centre.

Repeat with the remaining filo sheets, then place the shaped nests on a baking tray and coat them lightly with olive oil or canola oil spray.

Bake for 10–15 minutes or until crisp and golden, flecked with darker-coloured Parmesan cheese. Cool on a rack.

Just before they're required, warm the cooked nests then fill each one with about a tablespoon of Herb Pâté. Arrange thin slices of smoked meat or salmon, garnish with fresh herbs and serve.

Herb Pâté

100 g (3½ oz) butter, softened
2 large cloves garlic, crushed
⅛ tsp salt
¼ tsp sugar
freshly ground black pepper
¼ cup chopped chives
¼ cup chopped parsley
¼ cup chopped fresh basil or dill
250 g (9 oz) cream cheese
2 Tbsp lemon juice
2 Tbsp milk

Preferably using a food processor, otherwise a wooden spoon, cream the soft (but not melted) butter. Add the remaining ingredients one at a time in the order given, beating briefly each time and thoroughly after the last is added.

Refrigerate in a covered container until required, up to 3 or 4 days.

Filo Chicken Parcels

Filo parcels always look attractive. They may be prepared ahead and cooked when needed, or cooked straight away and reheated later.

For 2 servings:
2 small boneless, skinless chicken breasts,
* cooked and cut into 1 cm (½ in) cubes*
4–6 mushrooms, sliced
1 Tbsp olive oil
2 Tbsp white wine
1 Tbsp finely chopped parsley
2 tsp fresh thyme, finely chopped
4 sheets filo pastry
2 tsp butter, melted
slices brie or camembert cheese, cubed
oil for brushing

Brown the chicken lightly with the mushrooms in the oil for about 1 minute. Add the wine and herbs and cook 1 minute longer, until the liquid has evaporated. Leave to cool.

Brush 2 sheets of filo lightly with melted butter, cover with remaining filo. Place half the chicken mixture and half the cheese on each double sheet. Wrap up loosely as you would wrap a parcel. Place the parcels join-side down in a shallow oven tray and brush lightly with oil.

Bake at 180°C (350°F) for 12–15 minutes, until the filo is evenly golden brown. Serve immediately or reheat at the same temperature when required.

Filo Nests with Herb Pâté

PASTRY FOR PIES

Pies are always popular, but it is important to get the pastry crust right. Here are the pastry recipes I use for most pies I make.

(An easier and faster alternative to shaping traditional small pies is to make Pieburgers – see page 154.)

Short Pastry

- Short pastry makes good pie crusts (and Pieburgers) and is especially easy to make if you have a food processor.
- It is much cheaper than bought pastry, and can be made in less time than it takes to thaw frozen pastry.
- It makes a much better lower pie crust than flaky or puff pastries, which do not brown as well and do not have such good texture because they contain more fat.
- Short pastry also makes a good upper crust, especially if you brush it with egg before you bake it, although it is not as flaky as upper crusts made with flaky or puff pastry. (If you look carefully at a commercially made pie, you will notice that the bottom crust is often made with a different, shorter pastry than the top, which is flakier.)

For 1 large pie or 6 double-crust pies (each about 10 cm/4 in across):
2 cups plain flour
125–150 g (4½–5 oz) cold butter
¼–½ cup (60–125 ml/2–4 fl oz) cold water
2 tsp lemon juice (optional)

To make by hand:
Sift the flour into a bowl. Cut the butter into about 9 cubes and rub into the flour using either a pastry blender, 2 knives or your fingers, until the mixture looks like rolled oats. Add the lemon juice to ¼ cup cold water, and have another ¼ cup on hand.

Add the lemon-water to the flour in a thin stream while you toss the flour with a fork. Add just enough of the plain water to make a dough wet enough to stick together when you press it with your fingers.

To make in a food processor:
Measure the flour into the bowl fitted with the metal chopping blade. Add the cold butter, cut into about 9 cubes. Mix the lemon-water, as above, and begin to process as you start adding the lemon-water in a thin stream, then process in short bursts, using the pulse button. Overmixing makes pastry tough. Add some of the plain water in the same way, stopping and testing to see if the mixture, which will probably still look dry, is actually damp enough to hold together when you press it with your fingers.

Whichever way you have made the pastry, press it into a ball, then refrigerate it for at least 5 minutes before rolling out.

Cheese Pastry

This well-flavoured pastry has a more attractive colour and a better flavour than short pastry. It makes wonderful Pieburgers (p. 154) and pasties. Because it is a little richer than short pastry it is better used for pies which are baked on flat oven sheets rather than in pie dishes.

2 cups plain flour
125 g (4½ oz) very cold butter
1 cup grated tasty cheese
about ½ cup (125 ml/4 fl oz) cold water
2 tsp lemon juice

To make by hand:
Sift the flour into a large bowl. Cut or grate the cold butter into the flour until the mixture resembles rolled oats. Add the grated cheese and toss well to mix. Add the liquid as for handmade short pastry.

To make with a food processor:
Measure the flour into the bowl. Add the cubed cold butter and the grated cheese. Mix as for food-processor short pastry, stopping when the mixture holds together when pressed against the side of the bowl. Refrigerate for at least 5 minutes, or until ready to shape.

To make pieburgers:
See page 154.

Shaping Pasties

Use short pastry or cheese pastry. Cut saucer-sized circles, put cooked or uncooked filling in the centre (without using too much), dampen the edge with beaten egg and water, then fold over to make a half-circle shape. Press edges together, decorate if you like, brush with egg and cut one or more air holes in each. Bake at 200°C (400°F) for 20–30 minutes, until golden brown.

Margaret's Flaky Pastry

This easy pastry is richer than short pastry. Double the recipe when you are making a large double-crust pie.

For 200 g (7 oz) pastry:
¾ cup plain flour
¼ tsp baking powder
60 g (2 oz) cold butter
¼ cup (60 ml/2 fl oz) milk
½ tsp wine vinegar or 1 tsp lemon juice

Sift or toss the flour and baking powder together well. Cut the butter into cubes, using either a food processor or the coarsest blade on the grater. Do not chop too finely if using the processor.

Sour the milk with the vinegar or lemon juice. Add most of it to the flour and mix it in, using enough to make a dough that is a little moister than normal short pastry, but is firm enough to roll out. Roll out thinly, using just enough flour to prevent it sticking.

Leek Flan   V

This flan, freshly baked or reheated, is a popular main course for lunch or dinner.

For a 20–23 cm (8–9 in) quiche:
half recipe of Short Pastry (this page)
3 small leeks (about 500 g/1 lb)
1 clove garlic, diced
1 Tbsp butter
½ cup (125 ml/4 fl oz) water
3 eggs
1 cup grated emmentaler (or tasty) cheese
½ cup sour cream
½ cup (125 ml/4 fl oz) milk
¼ tsp salt

Turn oven to 220°C (425°F). Roll out the pastry thinly to line a 20–23 cm (8–9 in) flan tin or pie plate. Chill until required.

Wash the leeks carefully and slice 5 mm (¼ in) thick. Cook leeks and garlic in the butter for 2–3 minutes without browning, then add the water and cook until tender. Raise the heat and let the rest of the liquid evaporate.

Beat the eggs, grated cheese, sour cream, milk and salt together.

Remove the leeks from the heat and stir into the egg mixture. Pour the filling carefully into the prepared crust.

Bake for about 30 minutes, or until the filling has set in the centre. Sprinkle with chopped herbs and/or paprika before serving if desired.

Variation: Double the filling ingredients if using a 23 cm (9 in) flan tin with high sides and increase the cooking time until the filling sets.

Quiche Lorraine

This traditional quiche is good freshly cooked or reheated, cut in large slices or small pieces as finger food.

Crust
half recipe of Short Pastry (above)

Filling
2–3 rashers bacon
1 onion, thinly sliced
100 g (3½ oz) gruyère cheese
2 eggs
½ cup (125 ml/4 fl oz) milk
½ cup (125 ml/4 fl oz) cream

Make short pastry and chill until required. Turn oven to 220°C (425°F).

Fry or microwave the bacon until cooked, but not crisp. Remove from the pan and chop into pieces about 2 cm (¾ in) square. Cook the onion in the bacon fat until tender. Cut the cheese into slices about 5 mm (¼ in) thick.

Mix the eggs, milk and cream together in a small bowl, until just combined.

Tasty Tartlets

Roll the pastry out thinly to fit a 23 cm (9 in) pie or flan dish. Line the dish with pastry, taking care not to stretch it; neaten the edges. Place the cold bacon, onion and cheese on the uncooked crust and pour over the egg mixture. Bake at 220°C (425°F) for 10 minutes, then reduce heat to 180°C (350°F) and cook for a further 15–20 minutes, until firm in the centre.

Tasty Tartlets   V

These tartlets are ideal party food or for light meals. Try these fillings then invent your own, using the same pastry and savoury custard to surround them.

For 12 tartlets:
400 g Margaret's Flaky Pastry (opposite)

Broccoli and Brie Filling
*well-drained chopped cooked broccoli
small cubes of brie*

Smoked Salmon and Avocado Filling
*small cubes of avocado sprinkled with
  lemon juice
chopped smoked salmon
chopped dill leaves or spring onion*

Savoury Custard
*2 eggs
½ cup (125 ml/4 fl oz) milk
½ cup (125 ml/4 fl oz) cream
½ tsp salt*

Turn the oven to 200°C (400°F). Make the pastry. Refrigerate for 5 minutes, then roll out thinly and use to line about 12 small tartlet tins, or wide, shallow patty pans.

Place the chosen filling lightly into the uncooked pastry shells, leaving room for the savoury custard that will surround them.

Mix the savoury custard ingredients together until blended. Pour over the filling in the uncooked tartlets, using about 1½ Tbsp for each, or less if the shells are smaller.

Bake for about 10 minutes, until the pastry is golden brown and the filling set and puffed. Serve warm, reheating if necessary.

Country Onion Pie

crust. Top with asparagus spears (like spokes).

Bake at 220°C (425°F) for 15 minutes, then at 180°C (350°F) until the centre has set. Leave to stand for at least 15 minutes before cutting.

Country Onion Pie　　　V

When served with a salad this onion pie makes a satisfying meal. I like a crust flavoured with three different cheeses, but you can use a plain short pastry shell if you prefer.

Cheese Pastry Crust
½ cup plain flour
½ tsp baking powder
40 g (1½ oz) cold butter
¼ cup cottage cheese
1 Tbsp Parmesan cheese
2 Tbsp grated tasty cheddar cheese
1–2 Tbsp cold water

Filling
12–15 small (pickling) onions
¼ cup sour cream
1 egg
¼ cup (60 ml/2 fl oz) milk
¼ tsp salt
¼ tsp freshly grated nutmeg or ½ tsp caraway seeds
freshly ground pepper to taste

Preheat the oven to 200°C (400°F). First roast the onions. Cut off the root and stem ends, place the onions in a bowl or jug, pour over boiling water and leave for 1 minute. Pour off the water and peel off the skins. Halve the onions crosswise, and turn in a little oil in a roasting pan. Roast cut-side up for 20 minutes or until lightly browned, then leave to cool in the roasting pan.

To make the pastry, measure the first 3 ingredients into a bowl and cut, grate or rub the butter through the flour. Stir in the cheeses, then enough water to make a dough moist enough to press into a firm ball with your fingers. Refrigerate for 10 minutes, then roll out thinly on a floured board to form a 25 cm (10 in) circle. Trim, then ease into a well-sprayed 20 cm (8 in) pie plate. Turn under and decorate the edges.

Mix the remaining filling ingredients together in a food processor or bowl. (For a stronger caraway flavour, crush the caraway seeds first.) Arrange the cooked onions, cut-side up, on the unbaked pie shell. Pour the filling around the onions, until only their tops are visible. Sprinkle lightly with extra caraway seeds if you like.

Bake for 15–20 minutes, or until the pastry is evenly browned and the filling set. Turn down the heat if the crust browns before this time.

Serve warm, with a green salad.

Festive Quiche　　　V

Make this colourful quiche for an easy meal over the Christmas holidays.

For 6 servings:
200 g (7 oz) Margaret's Flaky Pastry (p. 150)
1 can (400 g/14 oz) whole tomatoes
3 cups broccoli florets
3 eggs
½ cup (125 ml/4 fl oz) cream
¼ cup (60 ml/2 fl oz) milk
¼ cup grated Parmesan cheese
½ tsp salt

Turn the oven to 220°C (425°F). Roll the pastry out thinly and line a 20 cm (8 in) flan tin with a removable base and 5 cm (2 in) sides. Run a rolling pin over the top to cut off the pastry edges.

Chop the tomatoes roughly and drain well. Cook the broccoli in a little water for about 2 minutes or until barely tender, then drain well.

Mix the eggs, cream, milk, Parmesan cheese and salt together with a fork until will combined.

Fill the uncooked pastry base with the cooled broccoli, pour over the egg mixture, and arrange the tomato pieces on top.

Bake at 220°C (425°F) for 15 minutes, until the pastry edge has browned, then lower the temperature to 175°C (350°F) and cook about 10 minutes longer, or until the mixture has set in the centre.

Remove the sides of the flan tin as soon as the quiche is taken out of the oven, so the pastry will remain crisp.

Serve warm or reheated with a salad and bread rolls.

Asparagus Quiche　　　V

Canned asparagus makes a quiche with a very good flavour.

For 4–6 servings:
½ recipe of Short Pastry (p. 150)
2 cloves garlic, sliced
1 Tbsp butter
1 large cooked potato, cut into small cubes
1 can (340 g/12 oz) asparagus spears
2 eggs
¼ cup (60 ml/2 fl oz) fresh or sour cream
½ cup grated cheese
¼ tsp salt

Turn the oven to 220°C (425°F). Make the pastry, chill for at least 5 minutes, then roll out to line a 20 cm (8 in) flan tin. Chill until required.

Sauté the garlic in the butter, add the potato, mix to blend the flavours, then cool. Drain the asparagus, adding ¼ cup of the liquid to the potato and discarding the rest. Cut 8 cm (3¼ in) from the head end of the asparagus spears and reserve for garnish. Chop the remainder and mix with the potato. Add the eggs, fresh or sour cream, cheese and salt. Mix well with a fork, then pour into the uncooked

152

Ham, Cheese and Asparagus Pie

This makes a good main dish to serve to friends on a warm day.

Serve it with a mushroom salad, a leafy tossed salad and bread rolls. The quiche may be made ahead and reheated.

For about 6 servings:
½ recipe of Short Pastry (p. 150)
100 g (3½ oz) ham pieces
4 spring onions
1 can (340 g/12 oz) asparagus spears
½ cup grated tasty cheese
5 eggs
1 cup (250 ml/8 fl oz) cream or evaporated milk
½ cup (125 ml/4 fl oz) asparagus liquid
freshly ground black pepper

Turn the oven to 220°C (425°F). Make the pastry, refrigerate it for at least 5 minutes, then roll it out thinly. Press into a 23 cm (9 in) flan or quiche pan.

Cut the ham into 5 mm (¼ in) pieces, chop the spring onions, and sprinkle over the pastry. Drain the asparagus well, reserving ½ cup of liquid. Arrange on top of the ham and onions in a spoke pattern, or chop into chunks for a more casual appearance. Cover with the grated cheese.

Lightly beat the eggs, cream and asparagus liquid with the pepper and carefully pour over the filling. Cook for 30 minutes, or until the centre is set and the quiche has browned.

Corn and Potato Pie   V

A good everyday family pie for a meatless meal!

For a 23 cm (9 in) pie:
400 g (14 oz) Margaret's Flaky Pastry (p. 150)
4 medium potatoes
1 large onion, sliced
25 g (1 oz) butter
1 can (440 g/15 oz) creamed corn
4 eggs
¾ tsp salt
¼ cup chopped parsley

Turn the oven to 220°C (425°F). Make the pastry. Roll two-thirds of it into a 35 cm (14 in) circle and line a buttered, round 23 cm (9 in) cake tin. Roll the remainder into a 25 cm (10 in) circle.

Scrub the potatoes and boil until tender. Cool and slice or cube. Cook the onion in the butter until transparent and barely tender, then remove from the heat. Add the corn, eggs (reserving a little to use for glaze), salt and parsley and stir with a fork until combined. Stir in the cold cooked potato.

Spoon the filling into the uncooked crust. Dampen the edges with a little water, and top with the smaller circle of pastry. Seal the edges, folding excess pastry down the sides of the tin. Glaze with the reserved egg, and cut a steam vent.

Bake at 220°C (425°F) for 30 minutes, or until brown, then at 180°C (350°F) for 30 minutes longer. Cool for 5 minutes before removing from the tin. Serve warm, with tomatoes, lettuce or coleslaw.

Cornish Pasties

Serve these popular pasties hot for dinner, warm as fingerfood for lunch, and cold in packed picnics.

For 6 pasties:
400 g (14 oz) Margaret's Flaky Pastry (p. 150)
400 g (14 oz) lean shoulder lamb, finely cubed or minced
¾ cup (185 ml/6 fl oz) water
1 medium onion, finely chopped
1 medium carrot, finely chopped
1 cup frozen peas
1 sprig fresh rosemary or 1 tsp dried
1 tsp chopped fresh thyme or ¼ tsp dried
¼ cup finely chopped parsley
1 tsp salt
freshly ground black pepper
about 1 Tbsp cornflour

Turn oven to 210°C (425°F). Make the pastry and chill for at least 15 minutes, then roll it out on a lightly floured board and cut into six 23 cm (9 in) circles.

Put the lamb and water in a pot and cook for about 10 minutes. Add the vegetables as they are prepared, the peas, then the herbs and seasoning. Cover and cook gently for another 40 minutes, or until the meat is tender and the vegetables cooked. Thicken with cornflour paste to hold the mixture together, then cool to room temperature.

Fill and shape one pasty at a time. Put about half a cup of cold filling on one half of a circle of pastry. Moisten the edges with water, then fold the pastry over to make a half circle. Press the edges together, removing as much air as possible. Moisten the edges, then fold over to make a double rim. Turn so the pasty sits with this rim uppermost, and flute the joined edges. Place in a sponge roll tin, again with the centre of the rim uppermost, and brush lightly with beaten egg to glaze.

Shape the remaining pasties the same way and bake for about 20 minutes, or until golden brown.

Cornish Pasties

Cheesy Pieburgers

This American recipe is easier to make than regular meat pies and is popular with all age groups. The filling is not pre-cooked, the pastry is very tasty, and the cooked pieburgers are freezable for school lunches, picnics and unexpected callers!

For 9 pieburgers:
1 recipe of Cheese Pastry (p. 150)
500 g (1 lb 2 oz) minced beef
1 packet (about 25 g/1 oz) mushroom sauce, or 1 packet (about 30 g/1 oz) french onion soup
¼ cup (60 ml/2 fl oz) tomato sauce
2 Tbsp plain flour
1 egg, lightly beaten

Turn the oven to 200°C (400°F). Make the cheese pastry, chill, then roll out thinly into 2 squares, each 30–35 cm (12–14 in) square.

Make the filling by combining all the ingredients (except half the egg) in a mixing bowl or food processor. Divide into 9 equal portions, and roll these into balls. Brush one square of pastry lightly with a little milk, mark it lightly into 9 equal squares (three rows of three) and arrange the balls of filling on these. Flatten each ball slightly.

Roll the other square of pastry round the rolling pin, so it is not stretched, then lay it on top of the balls. Using the rolling pin and your fingers, press the 2 layers of pastry together between and outside the mounds and cut air vents in the top of each.

Cut the pastry into 9 squares using a knife or serrated cutting wheel. Brush the 9 square pieburgers with the reserved beaten egg. If desired, reroll the pastry offcuts, cut them into strips and decorate the glazed tops of the pieburgers. Place on an oven tray covered with baking paper or a Teflon liner. Sprinkle with lightly toasted sesame seeds, if desired.

Bake for about 30 minutes, or until golden brown. Reduce the temperature after 15–20 minutes if they brown too quickly.

Serve hot, warm, reheated or cold. Refrigerate for up to 2 days or wrap individually and freeze for up to 3 months.

Variation: Make 16 smaller balls for smaller pieburgers.

Sausage Braid

The plaited pastry coating on this sausage meat really dresses it up! You can serve it hot, but I think it is better when it is cold.

For 4 servings:
400 g (14 oz) Margaret's Flaky Pastry (p. 150) or bought pastry
450–500 g (about 1 lb) sausage meat
1 onion, finely chopped
2 cups cooked, drained vegetables, chopped small*
1 tsp curry powder
2 tsp chicken stock powder or 1 tsp salt
pinch cayenne pepper
2 Tbsp finely chopped fresh herbs
1 egg

* Use a mixture of leftover cooked vegetables, or canned vegetables such as whole kernel corn.

Turn the oven to 220°C (425°F). Roll out the pastry to form a 45 cm (18 in) square. Put it on a sheet of baking paper which will later be put in a sponge-roll tin. Mark it lightly into thirds lengthways, using the back of a knife. Cut each outside third into 12 strips (so that the pastry looks rather like a stylised fern leaf).

In a large bowl, mix together the sausage meat, onion, vegetables, seasonings and herbs. Beat the egg, keep 2 tsp aside, then add the rest to the sausage mixture. Mix by hand until combined well.

Spread the filling down the centre third of the pastry. Starting at the far end, fold a strip from one side over the filling, at a slight angle, then one from the other side. Continue until all the filling is hidden by the strips which appear to be plaited.

Glaze the top with the reserved egg and bake at 220°C (425°F) for 15 minutes, until the pastry is golden brown, then at 180°C (350°F) for 10–15 minutes longer.

Serve with a selection of salad vegetables and new potatoes.

Minted Picnic Pie

Always popular and simply delicious!

For 8–12 servings:
400 g (14 oz) Margaret's Flaky Pastry (p. 150)
6 frankfurters or about 300 g (10½ oz) luncheon sausage
2–4 medium potatoes, cooked
2 cups cooked peas
¼ cup chopped mint
6 eggs
½ tsp salt
1 can (400 g/14 oz) whole tomatoes

Turn the oven to 220°C (425°F). Make the pastry. Cut in half and roll out both pieces very thinly to fit a 23 x 35 cm (9 x 14 in) sponge-roll tin or a roasting dish. Line the tin with one piece.

Slice the frankfurters or cube the luncheon sausage and arrange on the pastry in the tin. Spread the sliced or cubed potatoes on top, half the peas, then the chopped mint.

Cheesy Pieburgers

Break the eggs, one at a time, onto a saucer. Using a fork, beat each one enough to break the yolk, then tip over and around the mixture in the tin. Save about 1 Tbsp of beaten egg to glaze the top. Drop the remaining peas evenly over the egg, then sprinkle with salt.

Drain the tomatoes, saving the juice for another use, then slice thickly and drain again. Place evenly over the pie filling.

Lay the other half of the pastry over the filling. Trim the edges evenly, then dampen them with water and gently press down over the edge of the top crust. Brush the reserved egg over the surface and make about 12 holes in the top crust.

Bake at 220°C (425°F) for 15 minutes or until golden brown, then at 150°C (300°F) for about 15 minutes longer. (If you make the pie in a smaller tin, cook it for longer.) Serve warm or cold.

Variation: Replace frankfurters or luncheon sausage with ham pieces or 150 g cooked rindless bacon.

Little Meat Pies

These homemade pies are always popular!

For 12 pies:
6 onions
about 2 kg (4 lb 7 oz) chuck or blade steak
¾ cup plain flour
4–6 cups (1–1.5 litres/32–48 fl oz) water
2 tsp marjoram or oreganum
1 tsp thyme
about 2 tsp salt
about 800 g (1 lb 12 oz) flaky pastry, bought or homemade (p. 150)

Chop and brown onions in a large pan with as little oil as is needed to stop them sticking. For browner onions, stir 1 Tbsp of sugar into the partly browned onions.

Trim visible fat from the meat. Lightly flour, then brown the meat in batches, in large pieces, and cut these into smaller pieces after browning.

Simmer the browned meat and onions in the water with the herbs and salt for about an hour, until tender, then adjust seasonings. Cool the meat by standing the pot in cold water.

Roll the pastry out thinly until you can cut out 12 tops and bottoms for individual pie plates. Reroll scraps if necessary. Chill the pastry until needed.

Fill individual foil, 'tin' or non-stick pie plates with the large pieces of pastry, then add the cooled meat and gravy, filling two-thirds full. Dampen the underside of the pastry tops and set in place, pressing the edges together. Cut off overhanging pastry if necessary.

Bake in a preheated oven at 200°C (400°F) until the tops and bottoms are

Patricia's Pork Pie

golden brown and feel firm, about 20 minutes. Serve hot, or cool on racks, freezing those not required immediately.

Patricia's Pork Pie

Quick and easy! Serve hot, warm or cold.

For 4–6 servings:
double the recipe of Short Pastry (p. 150) or 400 g (14 oz) bought pastry
3 large slices wholegrain bread
2 large eggs
1 large onion, peeled and roughly chopped
about 6 leaves fresh sage or ½ tsp dried sage, crumbled
about ¼ cup chopped parsley
1 tsp salt
2 Tbsp sherry (optional)
400–500 g (about 1 lb) minced pork

Turn the oven to 200°C (400°F). Roll the pastry into two 30–35 cm (12–14 in) squares.

Break the bread into chunky pieces, crumble in a food processor, then remove.

Process the eggs until blended, then remove and put aside 1 Tbsp. Add the roughly chopped onion, sage, parsley, salt and sherry to the remaining egg and process until the onion is finely chopped. Add the crumbs and the minced pork, broken up into 4 or 5 chunks, then process in short bursts until all is evenly mixed.

Put one square of pastry on an oiled or lined baking tray and spread the filling on the centre of it, in a 25 cm (10 in) square.

Moisten the uncovered pastry with cold water, and place the other sheet on top, pressing it around the meat. Cut several air vents in the pastry. Trim the pastry edges then fold under the outside 1 cm (½ in) of pastry. Crimp or flute the edges.

Brush the pastry with the reserved egg mixed with 1 tsp water. If you like, cut the trimmings into shapes, arrange on top and brush with egg.

Bake at 200°C (400°F) for 15 minutes, then at 180°C (350°F) for 30 minutes.

See also
Filo Pastry Savouries, p. 28
Curried Fish Pie, p. 64
Old-Fashioned Fish Pie, p. 64
Stewart Island Seafood Pie, p. 64
Festive Chicken in Pastry, p. 87
Steak and Kidney Pudding, p. 125
Filo Lamb Samosas, p. 136
Tex-Mex Squares, p. 136
Cornbread-Crusted Chilli, p. 137
Cottage Pie, p. 138
Curried Sausage Pie, p. 141
Toad in the Hole, p. 142
Hearty Bean Pie, p. 166
Vegetarian Shepherd's Pie, p. 166
Beany Pie, p. 167
Pizza Pizzazz, pp. 186–189

Main Dish Salads

The idea of 'a meal in a salad bowl' is new to many of us! It is very practical, especially in warm weather, when a heavy meal has little appeal. Start by trying lunch salads, choosing ingredients that you know are popular. When you move from these to salads for the main meal, include a substantial ingredient such as pasta, rice, potatoes, couscous or bulgar. An interesting bread is a good accompaniment for many salads – in fact, you might consider completing the meal with crusty bread, your favourite cheese, and raw fruit.

Chicken and Crispy Noodle Salad

This tasty salad has a low-fat dressing, and makes a great lunch or dinner throughout the warmer months. Although it must be assembled at the last minute, the ingredients are prepared ahead.

For 2 servings:
2–3 cups coarsely chopped, crisp lettuce salad vegetables
2 boneless, skinless chicken breasts
1 tsp sesame oil
1 tsp Kikkoman soy sauce
about 1/4 cup (60 ml/2 fl oz) dressing (see below)
70–100 g (2 1/2–3 1/2 oz) Asian crispy noodles (bought)
1 Tbsp toasted sesame seeds or 2 Tbsp chopped roasted peanuts

Dressing
2 cloves garlic
1 cm (1/2 in) piece of fresh root ginger
1 small dried chilli pepper
1/4 cup (60 ml/2 fl oz) wine vinegar or rice vinegar
1/4 cup (60 ml/2 fl oz) Kikkoman soy sauce
2 Tbsp sugar
1 Tbsp sesame oil
1 Tbsp cornflour
1/2 cup (125 ml/4 fl oz) water

To make the dressing, roughly chop the garlic and ginger into a food processor or blender. Process with all the other ingredients except the water until very finely chopped, then add the water, process briefly and tip into a pot. Bring to the boil, stirring constantly, then pour into a lidded container and cool. Refrigerate for up to 2 days, shaking before use.

For the salad, cut the crisp lettuce into strips about 1 cm (1/2 in) wide and 6 cm (2 1/2 in) long. Place in a bowl with 2 or 3 other salad vegetables such as spring onion, fresh coriander, celery, cucumber, red pepper or sprouts, cut into pieces of

Chicken and Crispy Noodle Salad

similar size if necessary. Cover tightly and refrigerate until required.

Pound the chicken breasts between plastic until 1 cm (1/2 in) thick, coat with sesame oil and soy sauce, and grill or pan-grill for about 5–6 minutes, until the thickest part of the breast has turned milky white. (Cut to check this.)

Just before serving, slice the warm chicken breasts into diagonal strips 1 cm (1/2 in) thick, and toss in about 2 Tbsp dressing. Toss the salad mixture gently with another 2 Tbsp dressing.

Pile 2 layers each of salad and crispy noodles on each flat plate or salad bowl, and top with chicken strips. Sprinkle with the sesame seeds or peanuts and serve immediately.

Crunchy Chicken and Rice Noodle Salad

This salad is an interesting mixture of lettuce, crisp white noodles and smoked chicken in an Oriental dressing.

For 3 main servings or 6 starter-course servings:
400–500 g (about 1 lb) boneless smoked chicken
oil
100 g (3 1/2 oz) dry rice or bean vermicelli noodles
6–9 cups finely shredded lettuce
1/2 cup chopped spring onions
1/2 cup chopped fresh coriander
3 Tbsp sesame seeds, lightly toasted
1/4 cup pickled ginger, thinly sliced

Lemon-Honey Dressing
1 tsp finely grated lemon rind
1/4 cup (60 ml/2 fl oz) lemon juice
2 Tbsp each light soy sauce, salad oil and honey
1 Tbsp smooth Dijon mustard
1 Tbsp sesame oil
1 clove garlic, very finely chopped

Prepare all ingredients and assemble the salad just before serving.

Cut the chicken into small, thin strips, and chill in a plastic bag until required.

Heat 2 cm (3/4 in) oil in a deep pan or wok until smoking. Tear the noodles into 4–6 small handfuls. Add a handful to the hot oil, turn until puffed up, crisp and very lightly browned (about 30 seconds) then drain well on paper towels. Repeat with remaining noodles. Put aside in a sealed plastic bag if prepared ahead.

To make Lemon-Honey Dressing, shake all the ingredients together in a screw-top jar.

Just before serving, shred the lettuce finely and spread on a wide, shallow bowl or platter. Top with the smoked chicken, spring onion, coriander, sesame seeds, and ginger. Sprinkle the crisp fried noodles on top.

At the table drizzle dressing over the salad, toss gently to mix, and serve at once.

Easy Pasta Salad   V

Ready-made pasta sauce makes a really quick, flavourful dressing for pasta salad. The mixture may be refrigerated for two days if necessary.

For 4 servings:
250 g (9 oz) spirals or other pasta
about 1 cup (250 ml/8 fl oz) ready-made garlic pasta sauce
1/2 cup (125 ml/4 fl oz) oil (partly olive if possible)
1 Tbsp wine vinegar
1 tsp sugar
1/2 tsp salt
1 tsp ground cumin
1/2 tsp oreganum

Cook the pasta in boiling, lightly salted water with 1 Tbsp added oil until just tender. Drain thoroughly.

Mix together the next 7 ingredients in a food processor or shake together in a screw-top jar. Stir about half the dressing gently into the hot, drained pasta and leave to stand for at least 15 minutes, refrigerating it once it has cooked slightly.

Just before serving, chop the spring onions and stir into the salad. Add a little of the remaining dressing if you like.

Chicken Caesar Salad

This salad makes a great main course in hot weather. Prepare the individual components ahead, then quickly assemble them when you want a complete meal in a hurry.

For 2 servings:
croûtons, bought or homemade (see below)
2–4 Tbsp dressing (see below)
½ small iceberg lettuce or 1 small cos (Romaine) lettuce
200–300 g (7–10 oz) smoked chicken or freshly grilled chicken breast, sliced
freshly grated Parmesan cheese

Dressing

2–3 cloves garlic
1 small can anchovy fillets
2 Tbsp capers
1 Tbsp Dijon mustard
2 tsp sugar
1 cup (250 ml/8 fl oz) olive oil
2 Tbsp wine vinegar
2 Tbsp balsamic vinegar or extra wine vinegar
2 tsp minced chilli (optional)

To make croûtons, cut a bread roll (or the same length of french bread) into thin slices with a sharp knife. Mix together 2 Tbsp olive oil, 2 Tbsp grated Parmesan cheese and 1 crushed clove garlic, and brush the mixture on 1 side of each slice. Place, brushed side up, on a sprayed or Teflon-lined oven tray. Bake at 200°C (400°F) for 5–7 minutes, or until lightly browned and crisp. Use immediately or put aside in an airtight container for a few days, warming before use.

For the dressing, place all ingredients in a food processor. If you like the strong, savoury (but not fishy) taste of anchovies, use the oil as well, otherwise drain off and discard it. Do not add any salt since anchovies are very salty. Process until smooth, then transfer to a screw-top jar. Use immediately or store in the refrigerator for up to 2 weeks, warming before use, as olive oil sets when refrigerated.

For best results, prepare and refrigerate the crisp lettuce leaves several hours before the salad is to be eaten. Spread the washed leaves on a length of paper towel, then roll up like a sponge roll and refrigerate. (The leaves will stay cold, dry and crisp for hours.)

To assemble the salad, put the chilled salad greens in a bowl, drizzle over 2–3 Tbsp of dressing and mix gently (preferably with your fingers). Pile the dressed greens up in 2 shallow bowls or plates, with chunky pieces of chicken through them. Drizzle with extra dressing and top with the Parmesan cheese.

Peanutty Chicken (or Turkey) Salad

This is a good mixture to make when you have cooked chicken or turkey in the refrigerator, or when you have bought a rotisseried chicken on the way home.

The quantities below are suggestions only – alter them to suit.

For 4 servings:
2–3 cups shredded cooked chicken or turkey
2 spring onions
2 cups crisp, shredded vegetables, e.g. bean sprouts, celery, red pepper, firm crisp lettuce heart, water chestnuts, snowpeas
1 cup roasted peanuts
dressing as required

Dressing

¼ cup crunchy peanut butter
2 tsp tabasco sauce
1 tsp sesame oil
1 Tbsp dark soy sauce
1 Tbsp light soy sauce
½–1 tsp finely chopped garlic
½ tsp salt
2 Tbsp sugar
2 Tbsp balsamic vinegar or wine
¼–½ cup (60–125 ml/2–4 fl oz) water

Remove any bones from the poultry and cut it into thin strips.

Cut the spring onions lengthways into long, thin strips, then cut these crosswise into shorter lengths. Mix with the chicken.

Make a mixture of crisp vegetables, avoiding any that will make the mixture soggy.

Chop the roasted peanuts.

Keep the ingredients separate, in plastic bags or other containers, until serving time.

To make the dressing, combine all the ingredients except the water in a bowl or food processor, using a whisk or the metal chopping blade. When all are combined, add lukewarm water until the dressing is the consistency of cream. Put aside in a screw-top jar. Refrigerate unused dressing, warming it to room temperature before using, and thinning it with water if it thickens. Check the flavour before using, since it may need balancing after standing.

To serve the salad, gently mix together the prepared chicken or turkey, vegetables and peanuts, then moisten with as much of the dressing as you like. Serve in any of the following ways:

• packed into toasted, split pita breads;
• in split rolls or french bread;
• rolled up in mountain or naan bread;
• piled on shredded lettuce, alone or mixed with crispy noodles;
• tossed through room-temperature cooked pasta which has been moistened with the same dressing.

Chicken and Kumara Salad with Mango Dressing

Chicken salads coated with curry-flavoured mayonnaise have long been an American favourite, but I find creamy dressings based on sour cream are easier to make and even nicer.

For 2–3 servings:
150–200 g (5–7 oz) cooked chicken (see Chicken Waldorf Salad, opposite)
400 g (14 oz) golden-fleshed kumara
2–3 cups salad greens
mixed fresh salad herbs (optional)
¼ cup chopped roast peanuts or cashews

Dressing

¼ cup lite sour cream
1–1½ tsp curry powder or paste
2 Tbsp mango chutney, chopped
½ tsp salt
2–3 Tbsp chicken stock or water

To prepare dressing, stir together the first 4 ingredients until smooth. Thin with a little chicken stock or water until it is coating consistency, then put aside.

Scrub the kumara, cut off the ends, then wrap in cling film and microwave until the flesh 'gives' when pressed, probably 5–6 minutes. Leave to cool.

Wash the salad greens and herbs, break into suitable pieces, roll up in a paper towel (as you would roll a sponge roll), then refrigerate until needed.

To assemble, peel and slice the kumara. Toss it with the chicken, most of the nuts, the salad greens, herbs and the dressing.

Arrange on individual plates and sprinkle with the remaining nuts. Serve the extra dressing for diners to add as they wish.

Two-Minute-Noodle Salad   V

The essential ingredient in this salad is a packet of 2-minute noodles. It makes a good lunch dish and, with a few more additions, a good, easy, one-dish meal for a warm spring evening.

For 2–4 servings:
2 cups (500 ml/16 fl oz) water
1 packet 2-minute noodles (chicken or oriental flavour)
1½ Tbsp wine vinegar
3 Tbsp canola or other oil
½–1 tsp sesame oil
2–3 cups finely shredded cabbage
1 large carrot, shredded or cut into matchsticks
2–3 celery stalks, sliced thinly
2–3 spring onions, sliced
¼–½ cup chopped roasted peanuts

Optional

1–2 cups fresh bean sprouts
chopped fresh coriander
roast or smoked chicken, cut in strips

Chicken Waldorf Salad

Bring the water to the boil in a large pot. Break the block of noodles into small pieces and cook for 2 minutes. Drain off the water as soon as the noodles are cooked, leaving the noodles in the pot to cool to lukewarm.

Meanwhile, mix together the noodle seasoning, vinegar, canola and sesame oil. Shred the cabbage, using more or less as you like, then stir the cabbage and dressing through the lukewarm noodles.

Prepare the carrot and celery so you have long, thin strips. Stir them through the cabbage mixture with the spring onions and chopped peanuts. Taste and adjust seasonings if necessary, adding a little light soy sauce or fish sauce and a few more drops of sesame oil if you like.

Serve immediately or cover and refrigerate for up to 24 hours. Just before serving, toss through the bean sprouts and coriander. Fold in strips of room-temperature roast or smoked chicken if serving as a main meal.

Chicken Waldorf Salad

The contrasting textures of this chicken salad make it an interesting meal at times when summer fruits are not available.

For 2–3 servings:
150–200 g (5–7 oz) cooked chicken*
2–3 cups salad greens
mixed fresh salad herbs
1–1½ crisp red apples
2 Tbsp lemon juice
2 stalks celery
¼ cup shelled walnuts, roughly chopped

Dressing
1 Tbsp sugar
¾ tsp salt
1 tsp curry powder or paste
1½ tsp Dijon or mild mustard
2 Tbsp each lemon juice, lite sour cream and canola oil
2–3 Tbsp chicken stock or water

*Slice or dice flesh from breasts or legs of moist grilled, baked or roast chicken, rotisseried or smoked chicken. Using a sharp knife, slice it attractively, or cut in

1 cm (½ in) cubes. If not using immediately, cover tightly and refrigerate.

To prepare the dressing, whisk together the first 7 ingredients until smooth. Thin with a little chicken stock or water until it is coating consistency.

Wash the salad greens and herbs, roll up in a paper towel (as you would a sponge roll), then refrigerate until needed.

Assemble the salad a short time before serving. Cut the unpeeled apples into wedges or cubes, put them in a large bowl and sprinkle with lemon juice. Cut the celery into 5 mm (¼ in) thick slices or cubes, then add to the apples, along with the cooked chicken, walnuts and salad herbs. Add enough thinned dressing to coat, and toss together.

Make a bed of torn or chopped salad greens on individual plates or shallow bowls and pile the salad on top. Pass round the remaining dressing for diners to add as they like.

Salad Niçoise

Salmon and Pasta Salad

This tasty salad makes a can of salmon go a long way.

For 6 servings:

250 g (9 oz) small pasta shells or
  vegetable spirals
1 can (200 g/7 oz) salmon
1 cup pasta sauce (half a 500 g/1 lb 2 oz
  jar)*
¼ cup (60 ml/2 fl oz) olive or canola oil
½ cup sour cream
¼ cup (60 ml/2 fl oz) lemon juice
1 tsp sugar
½ tsp salt
2–3 Tbsp chopped fresh dill
4 spring onions, chopped

* Use your favourite 'ready-made' tomato-based pasta sauce.

Cook the pasta in plenty of boiling water then drain in a large sieve.

Place the salmon, with its liquid, in a large bowl and break it up, then add the drained pasta.

Shake the next 7 ingredients together in a screw-top jar, then stir gently through the warm pasta and salmon. Leave for 15 minutes or longer to soak up the dressing. Just before serving, stir in the spring onions. Serve with a cucumber salad.

Salad Niçoise

This salad makes a wonderful hot-weather main course. It looks best if you arrange the ingredients, one at a time, on individual dinner plates.

For 2 servings:

2 eggs
4–6 small new potatoes
100–150 g (3½–5 oz) green beans
mixed lettuce leaves, preferably small
2 medium or 8–10 baby tomatoes
10 cm (4 in) telegraph cucumber
1 can (185–200 g/6½–7 oz) tuna
2–4 spring onions, sliced diagonally
4–6 anchovy fillets, whole or chopped
8–12 black olives

Dressing

2 Tbsp lemon juice
6 Tbsp olive oil
1 tsp Dijon mustard
¼ tsp salt

At least 30 minutes before serving time, hard-boil the eggs and cook the potatoes and beans. Cool. Prepare the remaining ingredients while these cook.

Shortly before serving, make a bed of lettuce leaves on 2 dinner plates. Arrange on top the sliced potatoes, eggs (cut into 4 or 6 wedges), whole or sliced beans (depending on size), and whole or quartered tomatoes. Cut the cucumber in half lengthways, scoop out the seeds with a teaspoon, then cut in slices. Arrange with the other vegetables. Drain and flake the tuna, and place in the centre of the plates. Top with spring onions, anchovies and olives.

Just before serving, shake together the dressing ingredients and drizzle over the salads. Serve with french or garlic bread.

Fisherman's Salad with Kiwifruit Salsa

Use salt- or freshwater fish for this salad.

For 4 servings:
*1 cleaned, whole, 1 kg (2 lb 3 oz) fish,
  skin on
1 tsp each celery, garlic and onion salt
1 tsp hickory smoke salt
1 tsp lemon pepper
1 tsp ground cumin
1 tsp oreganum
2 lemons
fresh herb sprigs, if available
about 1 Tbsp canola oil*

Turn the oven to 180°C (350°F).

Cut several deep slashes on each side of the cleaned fish, and place it on a double layer of foil large enough to make a parcel. Sprinkle the dry seasonings in and over the fish. Squeeze the juice from 1 lemon in and over the fish. Slice the other lemon and place it in the cavity, with fresh herbs if available. Drizzle oil over the fish. Seal the fish in the foil so you can turn the parcel. Place in a large, shallow baking dish.

Bake a 1 kg (2 lb 3 oz) fish (5 cm/1¼ in thick, side to side) for about 20 minutes, until the thickest flesh is milky white and will flake. Cool for 10 minutes. Pour off, strain and save all juice. Discard the head, tail, fins and skin, then lift the flesh from the bones in chunks. Put in a dish with the juice (warm gently if it sets). Taste and add extra salt if needed.

Serve at room temperature with Kiwifruit Salsa (p. 346) tossed through the fish or alongside, and mayonnaise (p. 344).

Ten-Minute Salmon and Couscous Salad

Try this quick recipe for an easy dinner at the end of a long, hot summer day. Use whatever sized can of salmon you have.

For 2–3 servings:
*1 can (100–200 g/3½–7 oz) salmon
1½ cups (375 ml/12 fl oz) liquid (see
  method)
½ tsp minced chilli (optional)
¾ cup couscous
2 spring onions, chopped
2 cups chopped crisp lettuce leaves
about 1 cup chopped cucumber
1–2 stalks celery, chopped
fresh herbs, e.g. coriander, basil or dill
juice of 1 lemon
2–3 Tbsp olive oil
salt and pepper to taste
about 1 cup coarsely chopped tomatoes*

Drain the liquid from the salmon into a measuring jug and make up to 1½ cups with chicken stock or other stock. Add the chilli if using it, then bring to the boil in a pot or in the microwave.

Sprinkle in the couscous, remove from the heat, cover, and leave to stand for 6 minutes while you prepare everything else.

Chop all the vegetables except the tomatoes into a shallow salad bowl, varying the vegetables to suit your taste. Add whatever herbs you like. Cover and refrigerate if not using immediately.

Just before serving, toss the salmon through the room-temperature couscous with half the lemon juice and oil. Taste and season if necessary, then fork the mixture gently through the vegetables. Toss gently with the remaining lemon juice and oil, top with the tomatoes and serve straight away, piled in shallow bowls.

Variations: Top with cooked prawns or chopped marinated mussels, surimi or chopped hard-boiled eggs.

Seared Scallop Salad

Scallops are at their best when cooked briefly in a very hot pan. Served with this dressing, they make a memorable salad.

For 4 servings:
*about 6 cups mixed salad greens
1 avocado
about 1 Tbsp lime or lemon juice
about 10 cm (4 in) cucumber
½ cup chopped fresh coriander
about 500 g (1 lb 2 oz) scallops
1 tsp sesame oil
1 tsp soy sauce
oil for cooking
freshly ground black pepper
about 20 cherry tomatoes*

Dressing
*¼–½ tsp minced chilli
1 clove garlic, finely chopped
2 tsp finely grated ginger (optional)
1 Tbsp sugar
1 Tbsp wine vinegar or rice vinegar
¼ cup (60 ml/2 fl oz) water
2 Tbsp fish sauce
1 Tbsp sesame oil
1 Tbsp lemon or lime juice*

Shake the dressing ingredients together in a screw-top jar until well mixed. Refrigerate for up to a week.

Prepare the salad greens, putting them in a large plastic bag or covered bowl to chill. Just before you start to cook the scallops, slice the avocado and turn the slices in the lemon or lime juice, slice the cucumber into chunky pieces and chop the coriander.

Prepare the scallops, patting them dry, and toss in the sesame oil and soy sauce.

Heat a large, non-stick pan on a high heat until very hot. Add a film of oil then the scallops in batches. Toss for 2–3 minutes

so the surfaces brown lightly; do not overcook. Remove from the pan. Reheat the pan before cooking the next batch. When all the scallops are cooked, add pepper to taste, then spoon over a little dressing and leave to cool.

Just before serving, arrange the salad greens and other salad ingredients on individual plates. Arrange the scallops on top and sprinkle over the remaining dressing. Serve immediately, with warmed crusty bread rolls.

Variations: Cook salmon or other fresh fish in the same way, flaking it after the fish has cooled in the dressing. Freshly cooked mussels also make a good salad. Steam them open, remove them from their shells and leave to stand in the dressing.

Gado Gado Salad   V

This simple version of a popular peanut sauce is delicious on potatoes and other cooked vegetables.

*shredded lettuce
cold cooked potato, sliced
barely cooked cauliflorets
lightly cooked cabbage, chopped
cooked green beans, chopped, or raw
  bean sprouts
cucumber, chopped
hard-boiled eggs, quartered*

Peanut Sauce
*1 onion, finely chopped
1–2 cloves garlic, chopped
2 Tbsp oil
1 Tbsp brown sugar
2 tsp soy sauce
1 Tbsp lemon juice
about 1 cup water or vegetable liquid
½ cup peanut butter
tabasco or other chilli sauce
¼–½ cup (60–125 ml/2–4 fl oz) coconut
  cream (optional)
½–1 tsp salt (optional)*

To make the sauce, cook the onion and garlic in the oil in a covered pan for 3–4 minutes. Add the next 4 ingredients and simmer for 3–5 minutes. Stir in the peanut butter and chilli sauce to taste, and heat until blended. Stir in the coconut cream and salt if using. If desired, purée until smooth. If necessary thin to pouring consistency using water, more coconut cream or vegetable cooking liquid. Pour over the vegetables while warm.

To assemble the salad, line a individual plates with lettuce. Pile on plenty of potato, then add the rest of the vegetables in a random arrangement or in individual piles. Top with quartered eggs. Pour about ¼ cup of dressing over each serving of vegetables. Serve with crisp shrimp puffs.

Variation: Add sliced fried tofu for extra texture and protein if desired.

Mediterranean Meat Salad

A great way to serve meat on a hot day!

For 4–6 servings:
500 g (1 lb 2 oz) sliced roast (lean) beef fillet or lamb loin
1 red onion, thinly sliced

Dressing
¼ cup (60 ml/2 fl oz) canola oil
2–3 Tbsp wine vinegar
2 Tbsp chopped parsley
2 Tbsp chopped capers
1–2 tsp Dijon mustard
½ tsp oreganum
1 tsp salt
1 tsp Worcestershire sauce

Use meat that is cooked so it is rare or pink. Arrange the sliced meat and onion on a platter, in overlapping slices. Cover and refrigerate until needed.

Mix the dressing ingredients together in a small bowl or screw-top jar, using the smaller quantities of vinegar and mustard initially, adding extra after you have tasted the dressing, if necessary. Fifteen minutes before serving, drizzle the dressing over the sliced meat and onions, cover with cling film and refrigerate until you are ready to serve.

Note: The onion flavour will become milder on standing.

East-West Beef Salad with Coriander Dressing

The marked and delicious flavours in the dressing of this salad are intended for those who like strong Asian seasonings.

For 2 servings:
200–250 g (7–9 oz) rump steak, cut 2 cm (³⁄₄ in) thick
1 Tbsp fish or soy sauce
1 Tbsp canola oil
mixed salad leaves
cucumber chunks
cherry tomatoes
sliced cooked green beans
avocado slices
basil leaves

Dressing
1–2 cloves garlic, finely chopped
1 tsp finely chopped lemon grass
2 Tbsp sugar
1 Tbsp fish sauce
2 Tbsp fresh lime juice
2 Tbsp water
¼ tsp salt
⅛ tsp chilli powder or minced red chilli
2–3 Tbsp chopped fresh coriander
1 spring onion, chopped

Trim any fat from the steak, coat it with a little fish or soy sauce and oil and leave to marinate for at least 15 minutes, or up to 24 hours in the refrigerator. (The steak becomes more tender as it marinates.)

Prepare the salad ingredients, chilling them in a plastic bag or arranging them on 2 plates.

About 15 minutes before serving, preheat a heavy pan over high heat and pan-grill the steak in the dry pan for 1–2 minutes per side, until brown on the outside but pink in the middle. Place on a carving board and leave to cool.

To make the dressing, chop the garlic and thinly sliced lemon grass finely in a food processor or blender. Add the remaining ingredients and process until the coriander and spring onion leaves are finely chopped.

Just before serving, slice the warm or cool meat into thin strips and coat with some of the dressing. Arrange the slices on the individual salads and drizzle over extra dressing. Serve with crusty bread or with bowls of basmati or jasmine rice.

Note: Replace rump with sirloin, rib-eye or fillet steak if desired.

Thai Beef Salad

Although I have hopefully ordered beef salads in Thai restaurants many times, I have never been given a salad that compared with the first one I tasted in London many years ago. My only option, therefore, was to try to reproduce it myself. Here is my recipe. The dressing is delicious with the steak.

For 2 main or 4 starter-sized servings:
250–300 g (9–10 oz) rump steak, cut 2 cm (³⁄₄ in) thick
lettuce leaves of different types
chopped spring onions
cucumber slices
fresh coriander
fresh red chillies (optional)

Dressing
1–2 cloves garlic, crushed
about 3 cm (1¼ in) lemon grass stalk, thinly sliced
2 Tbsp sugar
1 Tbsp fish sauce
2 Tbsp fresh lime juice
2 Tbsp water
¼ tsp salt
very thinly sliced fresh chillies, or ⅛ tsp chilli powder
2 Tbsp chopped fresh mint
2 Tbsp chopped fresh coriander
1 spring onion, chopped

Trim the steak of all visible fat, and remove the membrane around the edges or snip it at intervals to prevent the steak curling. Rub the steak with a little soy sauce and oil, cover, and refrigerate until about 30 minutes before you want to serve it. Bring the steak to room temperature before cooking it.

Wash, prepare and chill the salad ingredients.

Pan-grill the steak in a heavy, preheated pan until nicely browned on both sides but still pink in the middle. Take care not to overcook it. Place it on a carving board and leave it to stand for 5–10 minutes while you make the dressing.

To make the dressing, put the garlic and thinly sliced lemon grass in a food processor or blender and chop very finely. Add the next 6 ingredients and process again. Add the mint, coriander and spring onion, and process until roughly chopped. (Taste and see if you like the balance of flavours, and add more salt if you like.)

Slice the meat thinly, then toss in some of the dressing.

Arrange the salad ingredients on individual plates, place the marinated meat on top and drizzle over the remaining dressing. Garnish with a coriander leaf, thinly sliced spring onions, sprigs of mint or a 'flower' made from a fresh red chilli.

Oriental Steak Salad

Pan-grilled skirt steak has a very good flavour and is cheaper than more commonly used steaks. It needs to be treated with care, however, or it may be tough.

The rules to remember if you want tender pan-grilled skirt steak are:

•marinate before cooking;
•cook to rare or medium only;
•slice thinly, across the grain.

A whole skirt steak will make two hot servings, and two delicious cold salad servings.

To pan-grill skirt steak:
Trim the thin edges from a whole skirt (or thin flank or flank-skirt steak). Lightly score diamond shapes on both surfaces.

Marinade
2 Tbsp dark soy sauce
2 Tbsp lemon juice
2 Tbsp corn or soya oil
2 cloves garlic, crushed

Place scored steak in a heavy, unpunctured plastic bag with the marinade. Squeeze the air from the bag and marinate for up to 1 hour at room temperature, or longer in the refrigerator.

Remove from the marinade and pan-grill in a heavy, preheated, very hot pan, allowing about 4 minutes per side. Cut the centre of the meat to check for doneness, cooking a little more if necessary. Leave to stand for 5 minutes or longer, then cut into very thin slices across the grain of the meat, with the knife at 45° to the board.

Oriental Steak Salad

Dressing
4 shallot bulbs, unpeeled
1–2 cloves garlic (optional)
¼ cup (60 ml/2 fl oz) corn or soy oil
¼ cup (60 ml/2 fl oz) lime or lemon juice
½ cup (125 ml/4 fl oz) light soy sauce
1 Tbsp sugar
pinch chilli powder

Combine all the dressing ingredients in a food processor. Mix, then strain, and bottle until required.

Assemble the salad just before serving. Arrange salad greens on individual plates and lightly coat with about a third of the dressing. Pour a third of the dressing over the thinly sliced warm or cold beef. Turn the slices gently to coat, then arrange over the salad greens. Drizzle over the remaining dressing, garnish with herbs or edible flowers such as nasturtiums or borage, and serve immediately.

Sausage and Potato Salad with Mustard Dressing

New potatoes and sliced precooked sausages taste great when mixed with this dressing! Make the salad with your favourite (precooked) speciality deli sausages, frankfurters, or even leftover barbecued sausages.

For 4 servings:
about 300 g (10 oz) new potatoes
200–300 g (7–10 oz) cooked sausages
4 gherkins (optional)
2–4 pickled onions (optional)
coarsely chopped crisp lettuce

Dressing
¼ cup grainy mustard
2 Tbsp brown sugar
2 Tbsp wine vinegar
1 large clove garlic, roughly chopped
1 Tbsp roughly chopped parsley
1 Tbsp roughly chopped chives or spring onions
1 Tbsp chopped fresh coriander (optional)
½ cup (125 ml/4 fl oz) olive or canola oil
¼ cup (60 ml/2 fl oz) warm water

Scrape the new potatoes and simmer in just enough lightly salted water to cover them. Cook until tender, testing with a sharp knife. Remove from the heat and leave to stand in the water for 5 minutes.

To make the dressing, measure the first 3 ingredients into a food processor or blender. If the grainy mustard you use is sweet, start with half the amount of brown sugar. Add the roughly chopped garlic, parsley, chives or spring onions, and coriander (this adds a lovely flavour but is not essential – add it if you can).

Add the oil slowly with the motor running, then add the water. Taste and add extra sugar if required. The finished dressing should be of a thickness somewhere between mayonnaise and french dressing. Use immediately or refrigerate in a covered container, bringing to room temperature before using.

Drain the potatoes, slice them, and while warm toss them gently in enough dressing to coat. Slice the sausages about 5 mm (¼ in) thick and toss in enough dressing

to coat. Leave to stand for a few minutes if possible, so the dressing flavours the sausages.

Gently mix the sausages and potatoes together and add the finely sliced or chopped gherkins and/or pickled onions if desired.

To serve, make a bed of torn or chopped lettuce on individual plates (or shallow bowls) and pile the sausage mixture on top.

Note: The dressing recipe makes more than you need for this salad, but ingredients are given in convenient quantities.

See also

Soused Trout, p. 62

'Two for One' Chicken Breasts, p. 77

Pork Stir-Fry Salad, p. 93

Oriental Pork Schnitzel, p. 95

Confetti Salad, p. 168

Tabbouleh, p. 170

Peanutty Rice Salad, p. 171

Brown Rice Salad, p. 173

Pasta Salad, p. 173

Tomato and Bread Salad, p. 175

Mexican Salad, p. 176

Pasta with Summer Sauce, p. 180

Caesar Salad, p. 205

Greek Salad, p. 207

Rice Salad, p. 209

Vegetarian Mains

There are many recipes throughout this book which are suitable for vegetarians or those who like to have non-meat meals several times a week. In this chapter I have gathered together a number of vegetarian recipes that I use often, sometimes for small family groups, at other times for gatherings of our friends. Check out the other recipes listed at the end of the chapter, and glance through the book for other recipes that are suitable for vegetarians (indicated by a 'V' symbol).

MEAL COMBINATIONS

When I am 'eating vegetarian' I sometimes make only one dish, but often prepare two or even three foods which I feel go together well to make a balanced meal. Each dish is of equal importance, rather than being accompaniments to one more important dish.

Curried Chickpeas

This dish is delicious served on its own or as part of an Indian-style meal.

For 6 servings:
4 cups chickpeas*
1 large onion, chopped
2 cloves garlic, chopped
1 Tbsp butter
1 tsp grated fresh ginger
1 tsp turmeric
1 tsp ground cumin
1/2 tsp cinnamon
1/4 tsp ground cloves
1/4–1/2 tsp chilli powder
1 can (425 g/15 oz) whole tomatoes
1 tsp salt
sugar (optional)

* If using dried chickpeas, soak 1 1/2 cups in water overnight then boil them in unsalted water for about 2 hours, or until tender. Otherwise use about 4 cups of drained canned chickpeas.

Cook the onion and garlic in the butter in a large pot until they are transparent but not browned, stir in the seasonings (using 1/4 tsp chilli for a milder flavour) and cook a few minutes longer. Add the tomatoes then the drained chickpeas and cook gently for about 15 minutes. If you prefer a thicker mixture break up slightly with a potato masher. Add salt and a little sugar to taste if you have started with dried chickpeas.

Serve in bowls with rice and curry accompaniments or a green salad.

Chickpea and Pumpkin Casserole

This is a delicious casserole, which has been popular with our family for years. I sometimes make it with dried chickpeas, but it is really easy if you use canned ones instead.

For 6 large servings:
750 g (1 lb 10 oz) peeled and deseeded pumpkin
1 large onion, chopped
1 tsp (1–2 cloves) minced garlic
50 g (2 oz) butter
1/2 tsp minced chilli
2 cups grated tasty cheese
1/2–1 tsp salt
black pepper
2 cans (each 310 g/11 oz) chickpeas, drained and rinsed (about 3 cups)

Turn the oven to 180°C (350°F). Cut the pumpkin into cubes and simmer in a little salted water until tender.

Cook the onion and garlic in the butter until transparent, then add the chilli and mash with the drained pumpkin, keeping the mixture slightly chunky.

Mix in the cheese. Taste, adding salt and pepper to taste. Gently stir in the drained chickpeas.

Spread the mixture in a large (23 cm/9 in square) non-stick sprayed or lightly oiled baking pan and heat through until bubbly at the edges and hot in the centre, 20–30 minutes.

Refried Beans

For 5–6 servings:
1 Tbsp oil
1 onion, chopped
1 clove garlic, finely chopped
1 bayleaf
1 tsp ground cumin
1/2 tsp oreganum
1/2 tsp chilli powder
1 can (400 g/14 oz) baked beans
1 Tbsp tomato paste (optional)

Heat the oil in a large frypan and cook the onion, garlic and bayleaf over moderate heat for 3–4 minutes.

Stir in the cumin, oreganum and chilli powder and cook a few seconds longer, then add the beans. Stir well and heat until the mixture comes to the boil. Taste, adding salt and sugar if necessary; add tomato paste for a more definite tomato flavour.

Remove the bayleaf and serve hot, warm or reheated in briefly warmed tortillas, with shredded lettuce and/or grated cheese and/or sliced avocado. Wrap in large, folded paper serviettes for a casual meal.

Don't hesitate to make small changes that will make a recipe suitable for vegetarians – it's often just a matter of replacing chicken stock with vegetable stock. I have done this with some recipes, but I'm sure there are others that are suitable too!

Canned vs Dried Beans

Canned beans save you time, but beans you cook yourself are cheaper.

A 440 g (15 oz) can of kidney beans provides 1 3/4 cups of drained beans, which weigh 350 g (12 oz).

One cup of dried kidney beans weighs about 200 g (7 oz) and gives you 2 1/2 cups (500 g/1 lb 2 oz) of cooked drained beans.

To prepare dry beans, pour 1 litre (4 cups/32 fl oz) of hot water over them and leave for between 1 and 24 hours. Drain, add 1 litre (4 cups/32 fl oz) of fresh water, boil briskly for 15 minutes, then simmer for about an hour, or until tender enough to crush with your tongue on the roof of your mouth. Do not add salt while cooking beans, but add garlic and herbs for extra flavour if you like.

After cooking, add salt and leave the beans to stand in their cooking liquid if you like.

Curried Chickpeas

Vegetarian Shepherd's Pie

This recipe is one most meat-eaters also enjoy. A shepherd's pie will 'pass muster' with no meat in it, but it certainly couldn't exist without its delicious potato top.

For 4–6 main servings:
6 medium-sized floury potatoes (about
 1 kg/2 lb 3 oz)
2 Tbsp butter
1 cup grated cheese
milk
2 large onions, chopped
2 Tbsp butter
1 red or green pepper, chopped
3 Tbsp plain flour
1 tsp vegetable stock powder
1 tsp each basil, oreganum, paprika and
 dark soy sauce
1½ cups (375 ml/12 fl oz) water, beer,
 wine, bean liquid, or a mixture
2 Tbsp tomato concentrate
1 can (440 g/15 oz) red kidney beans

Peel the potatoes and simmer until tender. Drain and mash with the first measure of butter, half the cheese and enough milk to make a good spreading consistency. After mashing, beat with a fork until light and fluffy.

Meanwhile, cook the onions in the second measure of butter in a large pot or frypan, until tender and medium brown. Add the chopped pepper and flour, and stir until the flour browns lightly. Add the remaining ingredients, except the beans, and bring to the boil, stirring constantly. Add the drained beans.

Vegetarian Shepherd's Pie

Spread the mixture into a lightly sprayed pan about 20 x 25 cm (8 x 10 in) and cover with the mashed potato. Sprinkle the remaining cheese over the surface. Refrigerate if not using immediately.

When required, cook uncovered at 180°C (350°F) for 20–30 minutes. Brown the top under a grill if necessary. Serve with a green vegetable such as brussel sprouts, beans or broccoli.

Short-Order Curried Beans

Plain canned baked beans are good, ready-to-eat, protein-rich food. Always keep some in your store cupboard so you don't get caught out when you have to produce a fast meal. Dress them up using this recipe – maximum reward for minimum energy!

For 2–3 servings:
2 onions
2 apples
2 Tbsp oil
1 tsp curry powder
2 tsp vegetable stock powder or ¾ tsp salt
½ cup (125 ml/4 fl oz) water
1 can (450 g/16 oz) baked beans
1–2 tsp cornflour
chopped fresh parsley, oreganum or basil
 (optional)

Peel the onions and apples and chop them into small cubes. Sauté in the oil in a small frypan until golden brown, then stir in the curry powder.

Meanwhile, microwave-bake potatoes, toast split rolls or bread, or reheat rice, pasta, etc.

Add stock powder (or salt) and water to the onion mixture and simmer for 5 minutes. Add beans and simmer until the mixture thickens, or thicken with a little cornflour and water paste.

Add herbs, taste, and adjust seasonings if necessary. Serve on the prepared base.

Note: Add any leftover cooked vegetables you have, either before or just after adding the water.

Hearty Bean Pie

The filling for this pie consists of cooked beans (or lentils) in a rich and delicious brown onion and mushroom sauce. Use canned beans when time is short, and add leftover cooked vegetables if you have them.

For 4–6 servings:
2 medium onions, finely chopped
2–3 cloves garlic, finely chopped
1 Tbsp oil
100 g (3½ oz) mushrooms, sliced
1 tsp sugar
½ tsp salt
½ tsp oreganum
¼ tsp thyme
black pepper to taste
1 Tbsp plain flour
1 cup (250 ml/8 fl oz) water
2 Tbsp sour cream (optional)
about 2 cups cooked beans or lentils
 (p. 344)
200–300 g (7–10½ oz) bought or
 homemade pastry (p. 150)

Turn the oven to 220°C (425°F). Sauté the onion and garlic in the oil in a large frypan. Add the mushrooms and sugar and cook until the onions are well browned. Stir in the salt, herbs, pepper and flour.

Pour in the water slowly, stirring constantly, until the sauce is the consistency of thick gravy. Remove from the heat and add sour cream if desired. Stir in the cooked, drained beans. Leave to stand and cool while preparing the pastry.

Roll out two-thirds of the pastry and line a 20–25 cm (8–10 in) pie dish. Spread the cooled filling evenly over the pastry. Dampen the exposed pastry with water.

Roll out the remaining pastry. Lay it gently over the top, pressing it onto the dampened edge. Trim, leaving a 1–2 cm (½–¾ in) overlap. Fold this under the sealed edge. Decorate with a fork or by fluting the edge with your fingers if you like. Bake for 20 minutes, or until golden brown.

Serve with mashed potatoes and cooked vegetables for a main meal, or alone or with bread for lunch.

Variation: Make several small pies or pastries rather than one big one.

Beany Pie

This is a great pie! Although it contains no meat it is substantial and filling, popular with meat-eaters and vegetarians alike.

For 6 servings:

short pastry using 2 cups plain flour
  (p. 150)
2 large onions, chopped
2 apples, sliced
1–2 Tbsp oil
1 tsp ground cumin
1 tsp oreganum
1/2 tsp chilli powder
1 can (440 g/15 oz) baked beans
1 cup grated tasty cheese

Turn the oven to 220°C (425°F). Make the pastry. Roll it thinly into two 30 cm (12 in) circles. Ease one circle into a 20 cm (8 in) round cake tin.

Cook the onion and apple in the oil until browned and tender. Remove from the heat and stir in the seasonings, beans and cheese. Turn into the uncooked crust.

Dampen the remaining pastry circle with water and place it over the filling, sealing the edges. Cut off extra pastry and use for decoration. Fold the edges double and pinch attractively. (Brush the surface with a little beaten egg for the best appearance.)

Bake at 220°C (425°F) for 20 minutes or until golden brown, then at 180°C (350°F) for 20 minutes longer. Serve warm, with a selection of salads.

Beanburgers

Dried beans can be prepared in many interesting ways to make inexpensive meals. These burgers only take a short time to make – their flavour depends on the seasonings added to the cooked beans.

For 4 servings:

about 2 cups cooked kidney beans
1 Tbsp butter or oil
1 large onion, chopped finely
1 tsp oreganum
1 tsp ground cumin
1 tsp curry powder
1 tsp salt
1 tsp sugar
1 egg
about 1/4 cup dried breadcrumbs

Drain the cooked beans thoroughly.

Heat the butter or oil in a frypan and cook the onion over medium heat for about 15 minutes, until evenly browned and tender. Stir in all the seasonings and remove from the heat.

Mash the drained beans with a fork and add to the onion. Mix in the egg with a fork, then add enough breadcrumbs to make the mixture just firm enough to form

Beany Pie

into 8 soft patties. Coat the patties with more crumbs, then cook in a film of oil in a large pan for about 10 minutes per side.

Serve with tomato relish, sauce, etc., in hamburger buns or with salads or cooked vegetables.

Mexican Beans

This mixture looks rather like mince. Serve it as you serve spaghetti sauce, wrap it in warmed flour tortillas, or pile it up and serve with corn chips.

For 4 servings:

2 Tbsp canola oil
1 onion
1 carrot
2 cloves garlic
1 tsp ground cumin
1/2 tsp oreganum
about 1/2 tsp chilli powder
about 1/2 cup (125 ml/4 fl oz) water
1 can (400 g/14 oz) red kidney beans
2 Tbsp tomato paste
1 Tbsp wine vinegar
about 1/2 tsp salt

Put the oil in a medium-sized pot, chop in the onion, carrot and garlic, add the cumin and oreganum and stir over moderate heat for 2–3 minutes, then stir in the chilli powder. Add the water and cook until the vegetables are tender, about 10 minutes.

Add the beans and their liquid, the tomato paste, vinegar and salt, and simmer for about 5 minutes. Chop the mixture coarsely in a food processor or mash with a potato masher. Serve as suggested above.

Curried Lentils

This dish has an interesting, spicy flavour and can be made in 30 minutes from store-cupboard ingredients.

For about 6 servings:

1 1/2 cups red lentils
1 or 2 bayleaves
2 cups (500 ml/16 fl oz) water
1/4 cup (60 ml/2 fl oz) olive or canola oil
  or 50 g (2 oz) butter
2 onions, chopped
2 cloves garlic, chopped
1 tsp turmeric
1 tsp ground cumin
1 tsp ground coriander
1 tsp ground ginger
3–4 cups chopped vegetables*
1 tsp salt
1 cup (250 ml/8 fl oz) hot water

* Use a selection of the following: potatoes, kumara, carrots, beans, cauliflower, cabbage, eggplant.

Simmer the lentils and bayleaves in the water for 15–20 minutes, until the lentils are tender and the water has disappeared.

Meanwhile, heat the oil or butter in a pan and add the next 6 ingredients. Stir over a low heat for 5 minutes, add the chopped vegetables, and stir for 2–3 minutes more. Add the salt and hot water, cover and cook for 5 minutes more, or until the vegetables are barely tender. Do not drain off cooking liquid. Combine the lentil and vegetable mixtures and stir over a very low heat for 5–10 minutes. Season to taste.

Serve on rice, with yoghurt spooned over if you like. Good with a cucumber and tomato salad.

Corn and Pea Patties

Although split green and yellow peas are often added to soups, they can also be used in the same way as red and brown lentils or dried beans. Here they add extra protein to an old favourite, corn fritters.

For 4 main-course servings:
1/2 cup split green or yellow peas
1 1/2 cups (375 ml/12 fl oz) water
1 clove garlic, crushed
1 tsp ground cumin
1 tsp oreganum
1 Tbsp oil
1 can (450 g/16 oz) whole kernel corn
2 tsp vegetable stock powder or 1 tsp salt
2 eggs
1 tsp paprika
1 tsp curry powder
1 cup self-raising flour
oil

Put the split peas, water, garlic, cumin, oreganum and oil (but no salt) in a medium-sized pot. With the lid ajar, cook gently for an hour, or until the peas are tender. After about 45 minutes, add the liquid from the corn.

When the peas are tender and most of the liquid is gone, cool to room temperature, add the stock powder or salt, the unbeaten eggs, corn, paprika and curry powder. Mix with a fork, then fold in the flour, mixing only until combined.

Heat about 5 mm (1/4 in) of oil in a frypan. Place several spoonfuls of mixture in the hot oil and cook, adjusting the heat so the bottom of each patty is golden brown after about 2 minutes. Turn carefully and cook the second side.

Keep the cooked patties hot on a paper towel in a warm oven until all are done.

Serve immediately, with cooked vegetables and/or salads, and salsa (p. 346), sauce or chutney if desired.

Confetti Salad

This combination of rice, lentils and vegetables makes a well-balanced meal.

Although the lentils lose their red colour, they finish up yellow and still look good.

For 6–8 servings:
1 large onion, chopped
2 cloves garlic, chopped
1/4 cup (60 ml/2 fl oz) soya or other oil
1 cup basmati or other long-grain rice
1/2 cup red lentils
3 Tbsp wine vinegar
2 tsp vegetable stock powder or 1 tsp salt
2 tsp sugar
2 tsp prepared mustard
3 cups (750 ml/24 fl oz) boiling water
french dressing (optional)

Optional additions
chopped parsley
sliced or chopped radishes
chopped spring onions
cooked green peas
grated or chopped carrots
chopped red or green pepper
chopped celery
cooked corn

To microwave:
Chop the onion into pieces about the size of rice grains. Put the onion, garlic and oil in a large covered microwave dish and microwave on High (100%) power for 2 minutes.

Stir in the rice, lentils, vinegar, stock powder or salt, sugar and mustard, then add the boiling water. Cover and cook on Medium (50%) power for 20 minutes, then stand for at least 10 minutes.

To cook conventionally:
Heat the oil in a large non-stick frypan with a lid and cook the onion and garlic until softened but not browned. Add the other ingredients, cover, and cook for 20–30 minutes, until the rice and lentils are tender, adding more water if the mixture looks dry before it is cooked. All liquid should be absorbed by the time the lentils are tender.

Add several of the optional ingredients to the cooked mixture and serve hot or cold, as is, or with french dressing tossed through just before serving.

Brown Rice and Lentil Loaf

This grain-based loaf is surprisingly solid, satisfying and well-flavoured. Leftovers also taste good cold.

For 4–6 servings:
1/2 cup brown rice
1/2 cup brown lentils
1 large onion, chopped
2 cloves garlic, chopped
2 Tbsp oil
1/2 cup sunflower seeds
1 tsp basil
1 tsp marjoram
1/2 tsp thyme
1 tsp sugar
1/2 tsp salt
1 Tbsp dark soy sauce
black pepper
1/4 cup wheatgerm
2 eggs
1 cup grated cheese
1/4 cup sunflower seeds
paprika

Cook the rice and lentils separately (p. 344), or use 1–1 1/2 cups each of pre-cooked rice or lentils.

Turn the oven to 180°C (350°F). Sauté the onion and garlic in the oil until lightly browned. Add the 1/2 cup sunflower seeds

and the herbs, and cook a few minutes more.

Mix the next 6 ingredients and half the cheese together in a large bowl. Stir in the cooked rice, lentils and onion, and mix until well combined. Transfer to a carefully oiled or lined loaf tin, and sprinkle with the remaining cheese, sunflower seeds and a little paprika.

Bake uncovered for about 45 minutes, until the centre feels firm when pressed. Leave to stand for 5–10 minutes before turning out. Serve with a selection of cooked vegetables, or a salad of your choice.

Cheesy Polenta   (Photo p. 196)

A pile of cheesy polenta topped with roasted, grilled or barbecued vegetables (pp. 202 and 203) makes a great summer meal. If you haven't used it before, polenta is a grainy yellow cornmeal that's rather like slightly grainy mashed potato – good 'comfort food'.

For 2–3 servings:
1 Tbsp olive oil or butter
1 tsp (1–2 cloves) minced garlic
1/4–1/2 tsp minced red chilli or chilli powder (optional)
1 cup quick-cooking or regular polenta
about 3 cups (750 ml/24 fl oz) vegetable stock or 3 tsp vegetable stock powder and 3 cups water
3 Tbsp grated Parmesan cheese
salt and pepper to taste

Heat the oil or butter, garlic and chilli in a medium-sized, non-stick frypan until it bubbles, then add the polenta and 2 cups (500 ml/16 fl oz) of the stock. Stir until smooth, then cover and simmer for about 5 minutes. Add more stock until it is like very sloppy mashed potato, then cover and cook for about 5 minutes for quick-cooking polenta or 10 minutes for regular. If necessary add extra stock or water to achieve mashed potato consistency.

Beat in the Parmesan cheese and enough salt and pepper to bring out its mild, pleasant flavour. (For extra flavour, stir in sun-dried tomato, basil pesto or tapenade.) Pile the polenta onto individual plates or bowls and top with roasted vegetables or other vegetable mixtures.

Creamy Herbed Polenta

Polenta is satisfyingly 'rib sticking' on a cold winter's night, especially when you team it with your favourite roasted winter vegetables and gravy! Although Cheesy Polenta is fine with this combination, here's another possibility, flavoured with herbs and cheese.

For 2–3 servings:
1 Tbsp butter
1 tsp (1–2 cloves) minced garlic
1 cup quick-cooking or plain polenta

*about 3 cups (750 ml/24 fl oz) vegetable
    stock or 3 tsp vegetable stock powder
    and 3 cups water*
1 Tbsp basil, rocket or coriander pesto
*¼ cup finely chopped parsley or other
    fresh herbs*
*about ¼ cup (60 ml/2 fl oz) sour or fresh
    cream*
salt and pepper to taste

Cook the polenta as for Cheesy Polenta
above. When it is cooked, beat in the
pesto, herbs and cream, and season to
taste. Pile into a bowl and serve with
roasted vegetables and Vegetarian Gravy
(p. 345), or with other hot cooked bean or
vegetable mixtures.

Pan-Browned Polenta Wedges

Cook polenta as for Grilled Polenta
Kebabs above. Pour it into a round pan,
and when set, cut into wedges. Brush the
wedges with oil or melted butter and
brown in a non-stick pan or on the solid
plate of a barbecue. Serve with fried eggs,
mushrooms, tomatoes, etc.

Grilled Polenta Kebabs

Cooked polenta can be left to cool and
set, then cut into cubes and browned in a
little oil. The polenta cubes can then be
threaded on skewers with vegetables, and
barbecued outdoors or heated on a small
electric table-top grill/barbecue.

For 4 servings:
2 cups (500 ml/16 fl oz) water
about 1 tsp salt
*1 tsp each chopped fresh thyme, basil and
    oreganum, or ½ tsp dried*
1 cup polenta
*1 cup grated cheddar cheese or ¼–½ cup
    grated Parmesan cheese*

Bring the water and salt to the boil. Add
the herbs then sprinkle the polenta into
the water while stirring thoroughly. Keep
stirring, over a low to moderate heat, for
about 5 minutes, until very thick. Remove
from the heat and stir in the cheese. (The
polenta may seem salty at first, but this
diminishes on standing.)

Pour into a buttered or oiled 20 cm (8 in)
square pan, and leave to cool for about
30 minutes. Turn out and cut into 2 cm
(³/4 in) cubes.

Brown the polenta cubes on all sides in a
little butter or oil in a non-stick pan.
Thread onto skewers, alternating with
vegetables such as mushrooms, cocktail
tomatoes and/or peppers. Barbecue when
required.

Persian Couscous

Colourful and tasty, with interesting
textures, Persian Couscous makes an
interesting side or even main dish.

For 2–4 servings:
1 cup couscous
2 tsp vegetable stock powder or 1 tsp salt
½ tsp sugar
grated rind of ½ an orange (optional)
2 cups (500 ml/16 fl oz) boiling water
¼–½ cup chopped almonds or pinenuts
¼–½ cup currants
2 Tbsp butter or olive oil
¼–½ cup dried apricots
2 spring onions, finely chopped
¼ cup chopped fresh coriander, if available

Stir the couscous, stock powder or salt,
sugar and grated orange rind together in a
bowl. Add the boiling water, cover and
leave to stand for 6 minutes.

Heat the nuts and currants in the butter or
oil in a small frypan over moderate heat,
until the nuts brown lightly and the currants
puff up. Chop and add the apricots.

Stir the hot nuts and fruit through the
couscous. Serve hot, warm or at room
temperature, adding spring onions and
coriander just before serving. Nice with a
green salad, or with broccoli and/or
mushrooms.

Persian Couscous

Convenient Couscous

Couscous is a busy cook's dream come true – it's invaluable for anyone who wants food on the table fast!

Although a relative newcomer to supermarket shelves (and often available loose, in bulk foods departments), it has become popular for its texture and flavour. Couscous is a good accompaniment when cooked plainly, but it can also be flavoured in many different ways. The quick-cooking couscous is, in fact, pin-head-sized pellets of pre-cooked pasta.

For 4 servings:
1 cup couscous
2 tsp butter or 1 tsp each pesto and olive oil
2 tsp vegetable stock powder in 2 cups (500 ml/16 fl oz) boiling water, or 2 cups stock
ground pepper (optional)
cooked flavourings (optional)
chopped parsley or other fresh herbs (optional)

Put the couscous in a bowl and add the butter, or the pesto and olive oil. Add the stock powder then stir in the boiling water, or add boiling stock. Cover and leave to stand for 5–6 minutes, while the liquid is absorbed.

Check seasonings and serve, or stir in pepper, any pre-cooked flavourings you like, and chopped herbs.

Note: When serving couscous alongside a 'saucy' dish, you can add 1½ instead of 2 cups of water, so it soaks up the sauce on the plate.

Kibbled Wheat and Kibbled Mixed Grains

Kibbled grains are chopped but not pre-cooked. They cook much more quickly than whole, unchopped grains, but take longer than bulgar.

1 cup kibbled wheat or mixed grains
1 Tbsp oil
2 cups (500 ml/16 fl oz) vegetable stock or 2 tsp stock powder in 2 cups water

Heat the kibbled wheat or grains in the oil over moderate heat for 4–5 minutes. Add the stock and cook gently, with the lid ajar, for 20–30 minutes. If the liquid is absorbed before the grains are as tender as you like, add more water and simmer for longer.

Serve as you would serve rice.

Wheat Pilaf

If you haven't used kibbled wheat before, experiment with it, using it in much the same way that you use rice to make savoury mixtures. It doesn't matter if you overcook kibbled wheat. It has a pleasantly nutty flavour, is higher in fibre than white rice, and costs less too, so it is worth a try!

This recipe will give you a starting point. You can add many other different vegetables to it. What you should not do is reduce the cooking time, unless you like a very chewy mixture.

For 4 servings:
2–3 Tbsp butter or oil
1 large onion, chopped
2 cloves garlic, chopped
¾ cup kibbled wheat
1 cup finely chopped celery
3 cups (750 ml/24 fl oz) water
2 tsp stock powder or 1 tsp salt
freshly ground pepper to taste
¼ cup chopped parsley
salt

Heat the butter or oil in a fairly large frypan or pot with a close-fitting lid. Add the onion and garlic and cook gently for 2–3 minutes without browning. Stir in the kibbled wheat. Keep stirring, with a wooden spoon or fish slice, until all the grains are hot and are coated with butter or oil. Add the celery and the water, cover, and cook for 20 minutes, or until most of the water is absorbed and the wheat is quite tender.

Stir in the stock powder or salt, and add a generous grinding of pepper. Add an extra ½ cup of water if you think the mixture looks dry, cover again, and cook for 5–10 minutes longer, until all the water has disappeared and the wheat is as tender as you like it. Stir in the chopped parsley, add salt to taste and serve.

Grainy Mix

Grains and lentils which have their outer coats attached take longer to cook than 'uncoated' varieties, but have definite nutritional advantages.

2 Tbsp oil
1 onion
2 stalks celery
1 carrot
1 clove garlic
1 tsp ground cumin
1 tsp oreganum
1 tsp salt
2 small chillies, very finely chopped
½ cup brown rice
¼ cup pearl barley
¼ cup brown lentils
3 cups (750 ml/24 fl oz) water
up to ½ cup chopped parsley

Heat the oil in a heavy, lidded pot or frypan. Chop finely, and add to the pot as they are prepared, the onion, celery, carrot and garlic. Stir in the cumin, oreganum, salt and chillies, then add the rice, pearl barley, lentils and water. Bring to the boil, cover tightly, and simmer until the grains and lentils are tender, about 45–60 minutes.

Remove from the heat, stir in the parsley and other herbs if you like. Leave to stand for 5–10 minutes. Serve alone or topped with yoghurt, salsa or Parmesan cheese.

Variation: Add quick-cooking vegetables to the mixture 10–15 minutes before the end of the cooking time – cauliflower, cabbage, spinach, corn, green beans or peas, peppers and mushrooms are all suitable.

Bulgar

Bulgar (or burghul) is a quickly prepared grain made from chopped wheat that has been pre-cooked and dried. It may be used in place of rice, by itself, or in mixtures. (It is not the same as kibbled wheat, which is chopped wheat that has not been pre-cooked.)

Basic Bulgar

1 cup of bulgar absorbs 1–1½ cups (250–375 ml/8–12 fl oz) of liquid. Either pour boiling vegetable stock over it and leave to stand for about 15 minutes, or bring the bulgar and stock to the boil, remove from the heat and leave to stand for 5–10 minutes, until the liquid is absorbed. Add herbs or other seasonings if desired. Serve in place of plain cooked rice, or leave to cool and add vegetables and dressing to make a salad.

Tabbouleh (Bulgar and Tomato Salad)

This salad makes a good lunch.

For 4–6 servings:
1 cup bulgar
2–3 cups (500–750 ml/16–24 fl oz) boiling water
2 spring onions, chopped
¼ cup (60 ml/2 fl oz) lemon juice
¼ cup (60 ml/2 fl oz) olive oil
½–1 cup chopped parsley
¼–1 cup chopped mint
2 cups cubed tomato (see below)
salt, pepper and sugar to taste

Pour the boiling water over the bulgar and leave for 30 minutes. Drain by pouring into a sieve lined with a clean cloth, then gather up and twist the ends of the cloth to force out excess water. Toss the drained bulgar in a bowl with the next 5 ingredients.

To prepare the tomatoes, halve them, shake out the seeds and juice, and chop. Add to the salad 30 minutes before serving.

Season the salad to taste and refrigerate until required. Serve at room temperature.

Variation: Replace bulgar with 1 cup couscous. Use 1½ cups boiling water and stand for 6 minutes before adding the other ingredients. Couscous does not require draining or squeezing.

Spiced Rice Scramble

Put together this delicious and unusual rice recipe for a main meal, and serve leftovers cold as a salad. The final assembly takes next to no time, but you must do a little preparation ahead.

For 4 servings:

4 cups cooked basmati rice (1½ cups raw)
1 cup Californian raisins
3 Tbsp balsamic or wine vinegar
3 Tbsp water
1 red and 1 yellow pepper (optional)

Sauce

2 Tbsp each tomato paste, water and sherry
1 Tbsp each sesame oil, oyster* or Hoisin sauce, and Thai sweet chilli sauce

Scrambled Eggs

4 eggs
3 Tbsp water or milk
¼ tsp salt
1 Tbsp butter or oil
1 Tbsp oil
¼–½ cup pinenuts
4 spring onions, finely chopped

* Oyster sauce is suitable for semi-vegetarians only.

Prepare the rice, raisins, peppers and sauce before you need them, up to several hours ahead.

Microwave the rice in a large covered bowl with 3½ cups boiling water and 1 tsp salt for about 20 minutes. Leave to stand for at least 10 minutes, until all the water is absorbed.

Boil the raisins in the vinegar and water in a small pot or frying pan for 5–10 minutes, until all the liquid has disappeared.

If using peppers, turn them under a grill for 5 minutes, or until their skins have charred on all sides. Cool in a plastic bag, peel off the skin and chop the flesh into small pieces.

Make the sauce by shaking all the ingredients together in a screw-top jar.

About 10 minutes before serving, assemble the dish.

Using a fork, beat the eggs with the water or milk and the salt. Heat a large non-stick frypan and scramble the eggs in 1 Tbsp butter or oil until they are set, then remove from the pan.

Add 1 Tbsp oil to the pan, lightly brown the pinenuts, then add the raisins and heat through. Tip in the rice and toss over fairly high heat until hot, then fold in the prepared peppers, eggs and spring onions and heat through. Add the sauce, and toss everything together. Serve alone or with tomatoes.

Spiced Rice Scramble

Spicy Red Rice

This makes a good main dish or snack. Simply top with cheese, pile on toast and grill, or top with a poached egg.

For 8 servings:

3 cups (750 ml/24 fl oz) boiling water
¾ tsp salt
1½ cups basmati rice
2 Tbsp oil
2 large cloves garlic, chopped
1 tsp freshly grated ginger
1 tsp ground cumin
1 tsp ground coriander
¼ tsp chilli powder
¼ tsp cinnamon
½ tsp turmeric
2 Tbsp tomato paste
1 can (440 g/15 oz) whole kernel corn
½ cup (125 ml/4 fl oz) liquid from corn
1 can (425 g/15 oz) chunky tomato and onion or tomatoes in juice

Add the salt to the boiling water and cook the rice in a covered dish in the microwave on Medium (50%) power for about 12 minutes, or until barely cooked. Leave to stand for 5–10 minutes.

While the rice cooks, heat the oil in a pan on the stove and cook the garlic, ginger and spices on medium heat for 2–3 minutes. Drain the corn, keeping ½ cup (125 ml/4 fl oz) of the liquid. Add the tomato paste and corn liquid to the pan and heat through, stirring until smooth. Add the tomatoes and drained corn, breaking up any large pieces of tomato.

Bring to the boil then stir through the hot cooked rice. Microwave on Medium (50%) power for 2–3 minutes.

Serve immediately or reheat when required.

Peanutty Rice Salad

This is one of my favourite salads. The sesame oil and peanuts give it an interesting nutty flavour and texture.

For 2–3 servings:

2 cups cooked rice
½ cup cooked peas
½ cup chopped roasted peanuts
about 4 radishes, sliced and chopped
2 spring onions, chopped
2 tsp sesame oil
2 Tbsp olive or other oil
1 Tbsp light soy sauce

Measure all the ingredients, in the order given, into a large plastic bag or serving bowl. Toss together lightly, taste, and add more sesame oil if you want a stronger flavour. Chill until needed.

Mushroom Risotto

Risottos require some attention while they cook, but this only takes about 20 minutes. The finished result should be creamy, but the rice grains should remain intact.

For 3 servings:
2–3 Tbsp oil
2 medium onions, chopped
2 cloves garlic, chopped
250 g (9 oz) mushrooms
1 cup arborio (or calrose) rice
½ cup (125 ml/4 fl oz) white wine
2–3 cups (500–750 ml/16–24 fl oz)
  mushroom, vegetable or chicken stock,
  or 3 tsp stock powder in 3 cups water
1 cup frozen peas
¼ cup (60 ml/2 fl oz) cream (optional)
¼–½ cup grated Parmesan cheese

Heat the oil in a large pot or frypan and cook the onion and garlic until soft. Add the mushrooms and cook until wilted, over a fairly high heat. Stir in the rice and continue to cook, stirring frequently until the rice has turned milky white.

Add the wine and stir until it has been absorbed by the rice. Pour in 1 cup of stock and stir frequently until it has been absorbed (about 5 minutes). Add another ½ cup of stock and leave to simmer, stirring fairly often and adding ½ cup (125 ml/4 fl oz) of stock whenever the rice seems dry. When the rice is cooked right through, after about 20 minutes, add the peas and the cream (if you run out of stock before the rice is cooked, add water). Cook over a low heat until the peas are tender, then remove from the heat and stir in the Parmesan cheese.

Serve immediately, with a tomato salad or Mixed Green Salad (p. 206).

Asparagus Risotto

Celebrate spring with this tasty risotto! Italian arborio rice is traditionally used to make risotto, but the cheaper calrose rice works pretty well too.

For 2–3 servings:
about 250 g (9 oz) asparagus
  (10 medium-sized stalks)
2 cups (500 ml/16 fl oz) vegetable stock
  or 2 tsp stock powder in 2 cups water
2 Tbsp butter
1 medium onion, finely chopped
1 tsp (1–2 cloves) minced garlic
1 cup arborio or calrose rice
¼ cup (60 ml/2 fl oz) dry white wine or
  extra stock
salt and pepper
½ cup grated tasty cheddar cheese
grated Parmesan cheese

Cut the asparagus stalks diagonally into 4 cm (1¾ in) pieces. Put them in a medium-sized pot with the vegetable stock, cover and boil for 3–4 minutes, until barely tender. Drain, reserving the cooking liquid. Put the asparagus aside.

In the same pot melt the butter, add the onion and garlic and cook for 3–4 minutes, until the onion is transparent but not brown. Stir in the rice and cook for about a minute, stirring frequently.

Add the wine to the reserved stock. Add ¼ cup stock to the rice, then add more, ¼ cup every few minutes, or as the rice soaks it up and seems dry. Stir at regular intervals (this makes the mixture creamy), covering between stirrings.

The rice should be tender after 20 minutes, with no uncooked core in the middle of the grains. If it is not, add ¼ cup water and cook longer. Stir in the asparagus and heat over very low heat for about 5 minutes.

At the end of this time, half an hour after you started cooking the onion, the rice grains should be soft and clumping together, with no liquid left. Add enough salt and pepper to bring out the asparagus flavour, then fold the grated tasty cheese through the risotto. Sprinkle with Parmesan cheese and serve immediately, alone or with a salad and warmed bread rolls.

Spicy Rice Pilaf

This is a very tasty alternative to plainly cooked rice.

For 4 servings:
2 Tbsp oil
1 medium onion, finely chopped
2 cloves garlic, finely chopped
¼–½ cup slivered or chopped almonds
1 cup long-grain rice
1 medium carrot, finely diced
¼ cup dried currants or sultanas
½ tsp each ground cumin, coriander, cinnamon and chilli powder
¼ tsp ground cloves
grated rind of 1 lemon or orange
3 cups (750 ml/24 fl oz) boiling vegetable stock, or 3 cups water plus 3 tsp stock powder

Cook the onion and garlic in the oil in a large frypan (or flameproof casserole) over a moderate heat for about 2 minutes. Add the almonds and cook until lightly browned.

Stir in the rice, carrot, currants and spices and cook a few minutes longer, stirring frequently. Add the grated rind and the stock. Bring the mixture to the boil, cover and simmer gently for about 15 minutes, until the rice is cooked and the liquid absorbed.

OR bake, covered with a close-fitting lid or foil, at 170°C (325°F) for 1 hour.

OR microwave in a covered dish on Medium-High (70%) power for about 15 minutes.

Green Rice with Tomatoes

This dish is good warm or reheated and served with salads, making an interesting family meal or addition to a summer buffet.

For 4–6 servings:
1½ cups long-grain rice
3 cups (750 ml/24 fl oz) boiling water
500 g (1 lb 2 oz) spinach
2 cups grated tasty cheese
1 tsp grated nutmeg
4 eggs, lightly beaten
1 cup (250 ml/8 fl oz) milk
2 cloves garlic, finely chopped
2 Tbsp chopped fresh herbs
1 can (425 g/15 oz) Mexican tomatoes or tomatoes in juice
1 cup grated tasty cheese

Turn the oven to 200°C (400°F). Cook the rice in the lightly salted, boiling water on the stove or for about 12 minutes on High (100%) power in the microwave. Allow to stand for 5 minutes if microwaved, then drain if necessary.

In another pot, cook the spinach until barely tender then drain well, squeezing out all the water. Chop finely and add to the cooked rice with the first measure of cheese, the nutmeg, eggs, milk, garlic and herbs. Bake uncovered in a roasting dish for about 15 minutes, or until it feels firm.

If using whole tomatoes chop them and mix with their juice. Spread the tomatoes and liquid evenly over the hot rice, sprinkle with the second measure of cheese, and bake for 10 minutes longer or until the cheese melts.

Serve hot, warm, or reheated, cut into squares, with a crisp leafy salad.

To cook brown rice

To cook short- or long-grain brown rice, allow 3 cups water and ½–1 tsp salt for each cup of rice. Simmer for 45 minutes to an hour in a pot with the lid ajar. If the pot seems dry before the rice is tender, add more water. If the rice is tender before all the water is absorbed, drain off excess water.

1 cup uncooked brown rice yields 2–3 cups of cooked rice. It may be refrigerated for up to 3 days, or kept in the freezer for up to a month.

Crusty Rice Cakes

These delicious little cakes are particularly good when made with brown rice, but they may be made with any cooked rice.

For 2–3 servings
1½ cups cooked brown rice
1 large egg
2 Tbsp grated Parmesan cheese
2 Tbsp pesto

Combine all the ingredients with a fork. Heat a little oil in a non-stick frypan, and drop in spoonfuls of the mixture. Cook over a moderate heat for about 10 minutes per side, until golden brown and crunchy.

Serve alone, with a salad, or in place of potatoes with meat and vegetables.

Brown Rice Salad

This salad has a lovely flavour. Served cold or warm it makes an excellent addition to a buffet and an interesting meal. Follow the instructions carefully for good results.

For 6 servings:

1 cup uncooked brown rice
1³/4 cups (435 ml/14 fl oz) water
1/4 cup (60 ml/2 fl oz) soy sauce
1/2 medium onion, finely chopped
3 spring onions, finely chopped
1 red pepper, chopped in tiny cubes
1/2 cup sultanas
1/2 cup roasted peanuts, coarsely chopped
1/2 cup each roasted sunflower, pumpkin and sesame seeds

Dressing

1/4 cup (60 ml/2 fl oz) olive or other oil
2 Tbsp lemon juice
1 tsp grated lemon rind
1 clove garlic, crushed
1 tsp grated fresh root ginger
1 tsp honey or sugar

Cook the rice in the unsalted water in a tightly covered pot for 45 minutes, until the rice is tender and the water is all absorbed.

Add the soy sauce and onion to the hot cooked rice, mix well, then leave for at least 2 hours (overnight if possible).

Shake the dressing ingredients together in a screw-top jar. Add the remaining ingredients to the salad and toss the dressing through just before serving it.

Pasta Salad

A creamy tomato dressing gives this useful salad lots of flavour.

For 4–6 servings:

250 g tortellini, spirals or other pasta shapes
1 Tbsp olive or canola oil
1/2 (125 ml/4 fl oz) cup tomato purée
2 Tbsp sour cream
1/4–1/2 (60–125 ml/2–4 fl oz) cup olive oil
1 Tbsp wine vinegar
1 tsp sugar
1/2 tsp salt
1 tsp ground cumin
1/2 tsp oreganum, crumbled

Optional

1 or 2 firm tomatoes, diced
2 spring onions, thinly sliced (white and green parts)

2 Tbsp finely chopped parsley
1 stalk celery, thinly sliced
1/4–1/2 cup small cubes of unpeeled telegraph cucumber
1/2 cup drained whole kernel corn

Cook the pasta until just tender in plenty of boiling, lightly salted water with the Tbsp of oil, then drain thoroughly. Take care not to under- or overcook the pasta if you want a good salad.

Pasta Salad, Roasted Pepper Salad (p. 209)

Mix together the next 8 ingredients, using olive oil if possible. Stir this dressing gently into the hot, drained pasta and allow to stand for at least 15 minutes, refrigerating after it has cooled slightly (during this time the pasta will absorb a lot of the dressing). Just before serving, stir in any of the optional ingredients.

Variation: For a milder dressing, use 1/4 cup (60 ml/2 fl oz) tomato purée.

Red Onion Frittata

Over the years my plain, light omelets have turned into the more substantial, firm, slowly cooked egg-and-vegetable mixtures found in Spain and Italy.

For 2 servings:
2 cloves garlic
3–4 red onions
1–2 stalks red silverbeet (optional)
1 Tbsp oil or butter

3 eggs
2 Tbsp grated Parmesan cheese
½ tsp fresh thyme (optional)
pinch of salt
freshly ground black pepper
1 Tbsp butter

Red Onion Frittata

Chop the garlic finely and cut the onions into 5 mm (¼ in) slices. If using silverbeet stalks, slice them the same thickness and save the leaves for later use.

Heat the oil or butter in an 18–20 cm (7–8 in) pan, then cook the garlic, onions and silverbeet stalks over a moderate heat for a few minutes. Add about 1 Tbsp water, cover, and cook until the water has evaporated and the vegetables are tender. Remove the lid and make sure any liquid has evaporated.

Using a fork, beat together the eggs, cheese, thyme, salt and pepper, until the whites and yolks are blended, then stir in the vegetables.

Add the second measure of butter to the hot (clean) frypan; when it foams pour in the egg mixture. Lower the heat and cook until the eggs are set around the sides and on the bottom, and the bottom is golden brown. Sprinkle over a little extra Parmesan cheese if desired.

To cook the top, cover with a lid while the bottom cooks, or put the frittata under a grill.

Serve hot or warm, or wrap leftovers to eat cold in packed lunches.

Variation: Replace the silverbeet with other vegetables such as broccoli, asparagus, spinach, new potatoes, kumara, leeks, etc.

Tomato and Bread Salad

Made with firm, red, flavourful tomatoes, this is an outstanding salad that can be served alone for a light meal. Firm-textured french bread produces the best results, but you can use whatever you have. Serve with cheese and fruit for a complete meal.

For 4 large servings:
20 cm (8 in) length french bread
about ¼ cup (60 ml/2 fl oz) olive oil
2 tsp basil (or other) pesto (optional)
4 ripe red tomatoes
¼ red onion or 2 spring onions
about 20 fresh basil leaves, if available
sprinkling of salt, sugar and black pepper

Cut the french bread in quarters lengthways. Mix the olive oil with the pesto, then brush lightly over all surfaces of the bread (the leftover oil is added later).

Ten minutes before serving, toast the long pieces of oiled bread under a moderate grill, turning so that all the edges are golden but no surfaces burn.

Chop the tomatoes into 1 cm (½ in) cubes and put in a large salad bowl with the finely chopped or thinly sliced onion and the basil leaves, whole or broken up by hand.

Just before serving, cut the warm, browned bread crosswise into 15 mm (½ in) chunks.

Sprinkle the tomato mixture with a little salt, sugar and pepper, toss gently, and when the juices start to run add the bread and toss to mix. Drizzle over the unused oil and serve immediately.

Note: Alter the proportions of tomato and bread to suit your taste.

Quick Corn Square

This is one of my easiest, most useful recipes.

For 6–8 servings:
4 large eggs
1 can (440 g/15 oz) creamed corn
½ cup sour cream
2 cups grated tasty cheese
½ cup self-raising flour
½ tsp garlic salt
2 spring onions, finely chopped
2–3 medium tomatoes, sliced (optional)

Turn the oven to 180°C (350°F). Beat the eggs, corn and sour cream together with a fork. Stir in the grated cheese, sieved flour and garlic salt. Add the spring onions and mix gently. Pour into a shallow, lightly buttered 20 cm (8 in) square dish. Arrange tomato slices on top.

Bake, uncovered, for 30 minutes, or until set in the centre and lightly browned on top. Serve while hot or refrigerate and reheat when ready to use.

Variation: Add up to 1 cup of other well-drained cooked vegetables with the spring onions.

Pumpkin Bake

A great way to serve pumpkin as one of the main parts of a meal.

For 4–6 servings:
800 g pumpkin, cooked
2 eggs
½ cup (125 ml/4 fl oz) cream
½ cup (125 ml/4 fl oz) milk
½ tsp ground cardamom (or cinnamon)
½ tsp salt
freshly ground black pepper to taste
1 cup grated tasty cheese

Turn the oven to 200°C (400°F). Using a tablespoon, scoop pieces of cooked pumpkin into a lightly sprayed or buttered casserole dish that is large enough to hold it in one layer.

Beat the eggs, cream and milk together with a fork. Add the cardamom, salt and pepper. Pour evenly over the pumpkin and top generously with grated cheese.

Bake for 20–25 minutes, or until the custard is set, the mixture has puffed up and the top is brown. Serve as soon as possible, since it deflates on standing.

Serve with a crisp green salad or Brown Rice Salad (p. 173).

Quick 'Roasted' Winter Vegetables

Use whatever amounts of several vegetables you like. Thinly peel kumara, pumpkin, potatoes and parsnip, and cut into even slices 1 cm (½ in) thick. Cut unpeeled zucchini diagonally into 1 cm (½ in) slices. Trim the stems of large flat mushrooms level with the gills. Cut white or red onions into 1 cm (½ in) thick rings, or in quarters or sixths lengthways.

Brush the vegetables with olive oil. Cook for 10–15 minutes in a double-sided contact grill heated to medium, or roast at 200°C (400°F) in a cast-iron baking dish or heavy roasting pan for 20–30 minutes, turning halfway through. Test at regular intervals, removing those which cook first when they are tender and attractively browned. If you like, brush with a little pesto diluted with oil in the last few minutes of cooking, or with Tex-Mex Dressing (p. 345).

Serve on pasta, polenta, focaccia, couscous, rice, etc., or pack into split bread rolls.

Crunchy Curried Cauliflower

The seasonings used in this recipe are interesting, but not too hot. Change the hotness by using more or less chilli powder if you like.

For about 6 servings:
2 Tbsp each sesame and cumin seeds
2 cloves garlic, finely chopped
1½ tsp grated fresh ginger
2 Tbsp roasted peanuts, finely chopped
½ tsp turmeric
¼ tsp chilli powder
½ tsp ground cloves
1 tsp salt
2–3 Tbsp oil
2 medium onions, chopped
1 large cauliflower, cut into walnut-sized florets
juice of ½ lemon
about ¼ cup (60 ml/2 fl oz) water

Toast the sesame and cumin seeds in a frypan without any added oil, then remove from the pan and grind. Mix with the next 7 ingredients and put aside.

Heat the oil and cook the onions until transparent and lightly coloured. Stir the spice mixture through the onion and cook for 2 minutes. Then add the cauliflower florets, lemon juice and about ¼ cup water.

Cover and cook over moderate heat, stirring and tossing the cauliflower occasionally, until it is tender-crisp, from 5–10 minutes. Taste and add extra salt if necessary.

Serve with rice and tomato or cucumber salad.

Curried Kumara

Mexican Salad

This is a good salad to serve with a grain-based dish for a main meal, or with bread rolls for lunch.

For 3–4 servings:
2 large tomatoes
1 or 2 stalks celery
1 red and 1 green pepper
1 cup drained whole kernel corn
1 cup of small cucumber cubes
1 cup cooked, chopped green beans

Dressing
1/2 cup olive or other oil
1/4 cup wine vinegar
1–2 Tbsp sugar
finely grated rind of 1 lime or 1/2 lemon
2 Tbsp lime or lemon juice
2 cloves garlic, crushed
1/2 tsp ground cumin
about 1/4 tsp chilli powder
1/2 tsp salt

Dice all the vegetables into pieces about the same size as the corn. Put into an unpunctured plastic bag or a covered bowl with the dressing ingredients. Use the larger amount of sugar if you like a fairly sweet dressing. Mix the dressing gently but thoroughly through the vegetables, then leave to stand in the refrigerator for about 15 minutes before serving.

Curried Kumara (or Butternut)

Served with rice, crisp poppadoms, cucumber in yoghurt, homemade chutney and quartered tomatoes this is delicious!

For 3–4 setvings:
2 Tbsp oil
1 tsp mustard seeds
2 tsp ground cumin
1 tsp ground coriander
1/2 tsp curry powder
1/2 tsp chilli powder
2 onions, chopped
2 large cloves garlic, finely chopped
1 tsp grated root ginger
500 g (1 lb 2 oz) kumara or butternut
1 can (400 g/14 oz) coconut cream
about 1/2 tsp sugar
about 1/2 tsp salt
2 Tbsp lemon juice
chopped fresh herbs

Heat the oil in a large frypan or pot, add the next 5 ingredients and heat gently until they bubble and smell aromatic. Add the onion, garlic and ginger and cook gently, without browning, for about 5 minutes. Add the kumara or butternut cut into about 10 mm (1/2 in) thick slices.

Add the coconut cream, cover and cook gently until the vegetables are tender, about 30 minutes, turning gently several times. As soon as the vegetables are tender remove the lid. Raise the heat if the liquid is thin, or add water if it is very thick. Add sugar, salt, lemon juice and fresh herbs to taste.

Kumara Patties

For 2–4 servings:
300 g (10 1/2 oz) kumara
oil
1 egg
2 Tbsp chopped coriander leaves
1 tsp green curry paste or curry powder
1/2 tsp salt
2 Tbsp plain flour

Scrub the kumara, trim off the thin ends, and lightly oil them. Bake at 200°C (400°F), or microwave on High (100%) power, until the flesh gives when pressed, as a baked potato does when cooked. Chop into fairly small pieces. This quantity should fill a 2-cup measure when tightly packed.

Using a fork, beat together the egg,

chopped coriander, green curry paste and salt. Add the kumara, mashing it into the mixture with the fork, then beat in the flour. Form into 8 flat cakes or patties.

Heat a little oil in a non-stick pan and cook the patties over moderate heat until golden brown on both sides, and heated through to the middle.

Serve with plainly barbecued meat, grilled chicken, or spicy meat mixtures.

Microwaved Curried Potatoes

This easy curry makes a good 'one dish' meal.

For 4 servings:
1 onion, chopped
8 small new or waxy potatoes (800–900 g/
* 1 lb 12 oz–2 lb)*
1 can (400 g/14 oz) coconut cream
2 tsp curry powder
1/2–1 tsp salt

1/2 tsp sugar
1–2 cups frozen peas
about 300 g (10½ oz) cauliflorets
* (optional)*
1–2 cups chopped cabbage (optional)

Put the chopped onion and the unpeeled, halved or quartered potatoes into a microwave dish with the coconut cream and seasonings, using the smaller amount of salt. Cover and microwave on High (100%) power for 12 minutes, or until the potatoes are barely tender.

Add the frozen peas and microwave for about 4 minutes, or add the peas, cauliflower and cabbage, stir to coat the vegetables, and microwave for 6–8 minutes, stirring at least once during the cooking time. Check that the cauliflower and cabbage are cooked to the tender-crisp stage and taste the sauce, adjusting the seasonings if necessary.

Serve immediately or leave to stand, reheating when required.

Making Homemade Vegetable Stock

To make quick homemade stock, grate coarsely or chop finely in a food processor 1 large carrot, 1 large onion and 2 or 3 stalks of celery. Add 1 tsp of minced garlic and 1/2 tsp of minced chilli. Simmer mixture in a large pot with 6 cups (1.5 litres/48 fl oz) of water for 20 minutes, adding some dried herbs and pepper as the vegetables cook. Strain, squeeze as much liquid as possible from the solids, then add 1 tsp each of salt and sugar. Use or freeze.

Frozen Homemade Stock

Keep homemade vegetable stock in lidded plastic tubs and cartons (or plastic milk or cream bottles) in the the freezer. Don't fill containers right to the top since stock expands during freezing. One-cup quantities are particularly useful since they thaw fast in the microwave or in your soup pot.

Faster Pasta

Pasta is a wonderful standby. Keep a few different shapes on hand so you can put together a good variety of easy pasta meals. Some of the following recipes use meat mixtures with the pasta, others pair pasta and tomatoes, and there are a number where pasta is teamed with cheese and other dairy products to make very satisfying meals. Remember that a good variety of pasta dishes will keep your family happy, so don't limit yourself to only a few.

Pasta with Salami and Broccoli

For best flavour and texture, combine the sauce, cooked pasta and broccoli just a few minutes before eating them. If you like, prepare the sauce ahead but do not cook the pasta or broccoli until the last minute.

For 2–3 servings:
150–200 g (5–7 oz) fettuccine or large
  spirals
about 200 g (7 oz) fresh broccoli
3 Tbsp butter
2 cloves garlic, finely chopped
1/2 cup (125 ml/4 fl oz) chicken stock or
  1/2 tsp chicken stock powder in 1/2 cup
  water
1/2 cup (125 ml/4 fl oz) cream or sour
  cream
1 tsp Dijon mustard
1/8 tsp cayenne pepper
50 g salami
3–4 spring onions, finely chopped
1/4 cup grated Parmesan cheese

Cook the pasta in plenty of lightly salted boiling water. Vary the amount, depending on appetites!

Cut the florets from the broccoli stalks and cook for 2–3 minutes in a covered pan in 1 Tbsp water and 1 Tbsp of the butter.

Melt the rest of the butter in a frypan or pot. Add the garlic and cook on moderate heat for 1–2 minutes, without browning. Add the stock, cream or sour cream, mustard and cayenne, and bring to the boil, stirring all the time. Remove from the heat and put aside.

Cut the salami into matchsticks and stir into the sauce with the spring onion and Parmesan.

Drain the pasta when cooked. Just before serving, gently toss together the hot pasta, broccoli (including cooking liquid) and sauce. Serve straight away, alone or with a salad.

Pasta with Salami and Broccoli

Orzo Dinner

Orzo is a macaroni product that is shaped like rice. It can be cooked like macaroni, or browned first then cooked in stock with vegetables to make a quickly cooked, tasty, one-pan dinner.

For 4–6 servings:
2 Tbsp butter
1–2 onions, sliced
1 1/2 cups orzo (rice-shaped pasta)
3 cups (750 ml/24 fl oz) boiling water
4 tsp chicken stock powder
2–3 cups finely diced vegetables*
1–2 cups diced cooked chicken
2 Tbsp chopped parsley

* Use carrots, peas, beans, celery, zucchini, red or green peppers. If using frozen vegetables, add them after the orzo has cooked for 7 or 8 minutes.

Melt the butter in a large frypan, then add the onion and orzo. Cook over medium heat until the orzo is straw-coloured. Lower the heat, add the hot water and stock powder, cover and simmer 3–5 minutes, then stir in the vegetables. Cover and simmer for 10 minutes, until the vegetables and orzo are tender and all the liquid absorbed. Add more boiling water if the mixture dries out before it is tender. Stir occasionally to prevent sticking.

Stir in the chicken and leave until it has heated through, then sprinkle with parsley and serve.

Egg and Tomato Orzo   V

This makes a very quick lunch or dinner. It looks colourful, too.

For 4–6 servings:
2 Tbsp butter
1 cup orzo (rice-shaped pasta)
2 1/2 cups (600 ml/20 fl oz) boiling water
3 tsp chicken or vegetable stock powder
2–4 eggs
2–3 medium tomatoes
2 Tbsp chopped parsley

Melt the butter in a frypan and add the orzo. Cook, stirring frequently, until the orzo is straw-coloured. Reduce the heat and add the hot water and stock powder. Cover and simmer gently for 10–15 minutes, until the orzo is tender and nearly all the water is absorbed; add more water if necessary.

Meanwhile hard-boil the eggs. Dip the tomatoes in boiling water for 15–20 seconds, cool them under the cold tap, then peel off their skins. Chop them, or cut each into 6–8 wedges.

When the orzo is tender add the tomato and replace the lid. Shell and quarter the eggs, add them to the mixture, and leave for a few moments to allow them to heat through.

Turn the mixture onto a heated plate, sprinkle generously with parsley and serve immediately.

Creamy Parmesan Pasta   V

This simple and delicious pasta sauce can easily be dressed up to form the basis of an elegant and substantial meal.

For 2–3 servings:
250–300 g (9–10 1/2 oz) fresh or dried
  pasta (any shape)
2 Tbsp butter
1/4 cup (60 ml/2 fl oz) cream
1/4 cup grated Parmesan cheese
freshly ground black pepper
extra Parmesan cheese to serve

Cook the pasta in plenty of lightly salted boiling water. Drain, then toss through the butter. Pour on the cream, then mix in the Parmesan cheese. Add black pepper to taste. Allow to stand for a minute or so, stir again, then serve with extra Parmesan.

Variation: To dress up, simply toss in one or two of the following: pesto, chopped fresh herbs, slivers of smoked fish, lightly cooked asparagus, zucchini, sugar peas or broccoli florets, thin strips of sun-dried tomato, halved cherry tomatoes, crumbled blue cheese.

Pasta with Summer Sauce

This mixture is a cross between a salad and a pasta sauce. You make the uncooked sauce, then pour the hot, drained pasta over it, stir, and leave it to stand. Serve it hot, warm or at room temperature, or reheat it later.

For 6–8 servings:
250 g (9 oz) large pasta spirals
2 spring onions, chopped
1 large clove garlic, chopped
4–6 sprigs fresh basil
about a cup of loose parsley sprigs
3–4 anchovy fillets, chopped
1 Tbsp drained, chopped capers
1 Tbsp caper liquid
¼ cup (60 ml/2 fl oz) olive or other oil
1 tsp sugar
¼–½ tsp chilli powder
½ tsp salt
about 6 ripe red tomatoes
6 black olives, chopped

Cook the pasta in plenty of boiling, lightly salted water for about 10 minutes, until just tender. Chop the next 6 ingredients by hand or in a food processor. Add the liquids and seasonings, and tip into a serving bowl.

Halve the tomatoes and discard the seeds by squeezing and shaking them. Chop finely, using a sharp knife or food processor, and add to the other ingredients with the chopped olives.

Drain the cooked pasta and tip it into the dressing. The pasta will soak up most of the dressing as it stands, over the next 15 minutes. Serve with crusty bread rolls.

Note: If the tomatoes do not have a lot of flavour, add 1 Tbsp tomato paste.

Pasta with Ham and Asparagus

Asparagus, tossed with pasta in a creamy sauce, always makes me feel that summer is just around the corner.

For the best flavour and texture, combine the sauce, pasta and asparagus just before they are to be eaten.

For 2–3 servings:
150–200 g (5–7 oz) fettuccine or large spirals
250 g (9 oz) fresh asparagus (about 20 stalks)
3 Tbsp butter
2 cloves garlic, finely chopped
½ cup (125 ml/4 fl oz) chicken stock, or ½ tsp chicken stock powder in ½ cup water
½ cup (125 ml/4 fl oz) cream or sour cream
1 tsp Dijon-style mustard
⅛ tsp cayenne pepper
100 g (3½ oz) ham
3–4 spring onions
¼ cup grated Parmesan cheese

Cook the pasta in plenty of lightly salted boiling water. Vary the amount, depending on appetites!

Trim the heads from the asparagus and cook them for 2–3 minutes in 1 Tbsp water with 1 Tbsp of the butter, in a covered pan. Cut the remaining stalks into 5 mm (¼ in) slices, peeling the bases of the stalks if they seem tough.

Melt the rest of the butter in another pan, add the garlic and asparagus stalks, and cook on moderate heat for 2–3 minutes.

Add the stock, cream or sour cream, mustard and cayenne, and bring to the boil, stirring all the time. Remove from the heat and put aside.

Cut the ham into matchsticks, chop the spring onions very finely, and stir them, with the Parmesan, into the sauce.

Drain the cooked pasta. Just before serving, gently toss together the hot pasta, buttered asparagus tips (with the cooking liquid) and hot asparagus sauce. Serve straight away, alone or with a salad.

Pasta with Bacon Sauce

This makes a complete, well-balanced meal that is enjoyed by people of all ages. To dress it up, serve it with heated bread rolls and a salad.

If possible, choose pasta with an irregular shape – more sauce sticks to shapes with many nooks and crannies!

For 4–6 servings:
250 g (9 oz) pasta crests
100–150 g (3 1/2–5 oz) bacon, chopped
1 large onion, chopped
1 Tbsp plain flour
1 can (400 g/14 oz) tomatoes
½ cup cream cheese
chopped parsley (optional)

Cook the pasta in a large pot of lightly salted boiling water until it is just tender. Once the pasta is cooking, make the sauce. The two should be ready at about the same time.

Gently cook the bacon and onion for 5 minutes in a large frypan over a moderate heat. (If you are not using a non-stick pan, you may need to add 1 Tbsp butter or oil.) Cook, stirring at intervals, until the bacon is crisp and the onion lightly browned. Stir in the flour, then the tomatoes, breaking them up as they cook. Heat until the mixture is boiling. Let the thickened sauce simmer for about 3 minutes, stirring occasionally.

Cut the cream cheese into cubes and add to the pan, squashing it into the tomato mixture and stirring well. Drain the pasta as soon as it is cooked, then stir it through the sauce. Sprinkle with chopped parsley and serve straight away.

Salmon and Seashells

Make this for a quick family meal.

For 4–6 servings:
2–2½ cups (250 g/9 oz) small seashell pasta
6–8 cups (1.5–2 litres/48–64 fl oz) water
1 tsp salt
1 Tbsp oil

Sauce
2 Tbsp olive oil or butter
1 large onion, finely chopped
2 large stalks celery, finely chopped
1 clove garlic, finely chopped
1 Tbsp plain flour
1 can (400 g/14 oz) tomatoes in juice
½ cup light cream cheese
1 can (about 200 g/7 oz) salmon
salt
freshly ground black pepper

Bring the water, salt and oil to the boil in a large pot. Stir in the pasta, boil uncovered until tender but not soft and floppy, then drain.

While the pasta cooks, make the sauce. Heat the oil in a large frypan, add the onion, celery and garlic, cover and cook gently for about 5 minutes, until tender but not browned. Stir in the flour then add the tomatoes and bring to the boil, stirring constantly.

As soon as the mixture thickens add the cream cheese in several spoonfuls. Stir over low heat until it is distributed evenly through the mixture.

Drain the salmon liquid into the mixture then break the salmon into small chunks and add it too.

Gently fold the drained pasta into the sauce and season with salt and black pepper to taste. Warm through and serve immediately, or transfer to a casserole or microwave dish and reheat when needed.

Variation: Replace the salmon with tuna, adding a cup of cooked frozen peas if you like.

Easy Ham and Mushroom Pasta

To fill a hungry family after an energetic day outside, make this quick and easy ham and mushroom pasta dish. It is a useful dish, based on staples from your store cupboard, freezer and refrigerator.

For 4 servings:
250 g (9 oz) macaroni or other small pasta shapes
1 packet (about 30 g/1 oz) mushroom soup
1½ cups (375 ml/12 fl oz) water
2 Tbsp sherry (optional)
¼–½ cup sour cream
1–2 cups frozen peas
about 1 cup finely chopped ham

Roast Pumpkin Ravioli

Cook the pasta in plenty of lightly salted boiling water until barely tender, then drain.

While the pasta cooks, heat the soup, water and sherry in a large frypan for 5 minutes, until thick and smooth. Stir in the sour cream. Simmer for 2–3 minutes, then add the peas, cook 2–3 minutes longer, then stir in the ham. Stir the drained pasta through the sauce and serve immediately in bowls.

Tortellini in Herbed Sauce   V

Make this with any pasta of convoluted shape, which will hold a lot of the delicious sauce. Tortellini look like little turbans. They hold a lot of sauce in their folds, and are particularly satisfying to eat.

For 2 large or 3 medium servings:
250 g (9 oz) tortellini or other pasta
butter or oil for pasta
2 cloves garlic
1 Tbsp butter
1 cup grated cheese
1 Tbsp plain flour
1/4 cup (60 ml/2 fl oz) white wine
1/2 cup (125 ml/4 fl oz) double cream or
* sour cream*
1–2 Tbsp finely chopped fresh thyme or
* sage*
salt to taste
hot pepper sauce (optional)

About 15 minutes before you want to eat, add the pasta to lightly salted boiling water and cook until tender, then drain and toss with a little melted butter or oil.

While the pasta cooks, chop the garlic and heat it in 1 Tbsp of butter in a fairly large microwave dish for about 30 seconds. Toss the cheese in the flour and add the wine, cream, and cheese to the garlic. Microwave on High (100%) power until the sauce bubbles vigorously around the edges. Stir well. If the sauce does not become smooth in a few seconds, cook it a little longer and stir again. Stir the herbs and salt into the smooth sauce.

Just before serving fold the sauce and pasta together, reheat if either has cooled down, taste and add extra salt and a little hot pepper sauce if desired. Serve straight away.

Note: You can use any fresh herbs – I use a mixture of parsley, chives, thyme, marjoram, sage and spring onions. Use just parsley and spring onions if these are all you have.

Variation: Stir small cubes of tomato through the sauced pasta.

Roast Pumpkin Ravioli   V

Wonton wrappers make quick ravioli. Serve a few in a bowl as a starter course, or a pile in a bigger bowl for a main course for two, with crusty bread and side salads.

For 12 wontons:
24 wonton wrappers
1 medium onion
400 g (14 oz) peeled and deseeded
* pumpkin*
1 Tbsp olive oil
2 tsp wine vinegar or balsamic vinegar
2 tsp sugar
100 g (3 1/2 oz) feta cheese
fresh herbs (optional)
2 cups (500 ml/16 fl oz) vegetable stock

Thaw the wonton wrappers if necessary. Turn the oven to 200°C (400°F).

Peel the onion and cut it in half from top to bottom, then into 8 wedges. Cut the pumpkin into 2 cm (3/4 in) cubes. Coat the onion and pumpkin with the olive oil and roast for about 30 minutes, until both are tender and lightly browned. Stir the vinegar and sugar through the vegetables after they have roasted for 20 minutes.

Mash the vegetables with the feta cheese. Taste and season if necessary, adding fresh herbs if you like, and moistening with a little stock, milk or cream if necessary.

Place spoonfuls of the filling in the centre of 12 wonton wrappers. Add a sprig of fresh herbs if desired. Brush around the filling with water, then top each 'filled' wonton with a plain wonton wrapper, pressing the tops and bottoms together carefully, without leaving any air bubbles. Leave the prepared ravioli square, or cut into rounds with a suitable cutter.

Simmer in the vegetable stock for 5–6 minutes, until the ravioli are cooked. Serve immediately, in a little stock, with basil pesto.

Variation: Cut the onion and pumpkin into slices 1 cm (1/2 in) thick, brush with oil and cook for about 10 minutes on medium heat in a double-sided contact grill.

Bacon, Egg and Pasta

I made this recipe regularly when my children were small. They always loved it! The egg and milk form a sort of custard which coats the pasta. Overcooking, however, turns the coating to scrambled eggs, so take care!

For 4 servings:
200 g (7 oz) spaghetti or macaroni
3–4 rashers bacon
4 eggs
¼ cup (60 ml/2 fl oz) milk
¼ tsp salt
pepper
chopped parsley, spring onions or other fresh herbs
paprika

Bacon, Egg and Pasta

Cook the pasta in plenty of boiling, salted water until just tender.

Chop the bacon finely and cook without draining in a medium-to-large frypan until crisp.

Using a fork, beat the eggs with the milk, adding salt and pepper to taste.

Drain the pasta and add it to the bacon in the pan, turning it until it is coated with bacon drippings. Pour the egg and milk mixture over the bacon and pasta and cook over a medium heat, turning the mixture with a fish slice as the egg heats through. As soon as the egg is no longer liquid, but is coating the pasta, serve garnished with spring onions or herbs and paprika.

Mushroom Stroganoff V

Mushrooms in a rich sauce make a quick meal with an interesting texture. Choose medium-sized, partly open mushrooms for maximum flavour and colour.

For 4–5 servings:
about 400 g (14 oz) fresh or dried spaghetti or other (green if you like) pasta
1 Tbsp butter, oil or pesto
750 g (1 lb 10 oz) mushrooms
1–2 Tbsp butter or olive oil
2 cloves garlic, chopped
1 Tbsp plain flour
1 cup (250 ml/8 fl oz) chicken or vegetable stock
1 Tbsp tomato paste
2 Tbsp sherry
¼–½ cup sour cream
1 bunch spring onions, chopped

Cook the pasta in plenty of boiling, lightly salted water until just tender. Drain and toss in a little butter, oil or pesto.

While it cooks, quarter the mushrooms and cook them in butter or oil with the garlic over high heat, until lightly browned. Stir in the flour and cook for about 3 minutes. Add the stock, tomato paste and sherry and simmer for 5 minutes. Stir in sour cream to taste, with half the spring onions.

Serve the sauce over the pasta and sprinkle with the remaining spring onions. Good with a crisp green salad.

After-School Spirals

This is an easy recipe that my children regularly made for themselves as an after-school snack. It's also a good quick lunch for pre-schoolers. You may also like to make larger quantities and serve it alongside plainly grilled or barbecued lean meat. As a change from spirals, use any other interestingly shaped pasta.

For 1 large or 2 small servings:
about 100 g (3½ oz) pasta spirals
½ tsp chicken stock powder
1 tsp cornflour
½ tsp sugar
¼ cup (60 ml/2 fl oz) water
1 tsp butter
¼ cup chopped parsley
basil or other fresh herbs (if available)
1 cup finely cubed tomato

Cook the pasta in about 4 cups of lightly salted boiling water for about 10 minutes, or until just tender.

Meanwhile, in a smaller pot, stir together the stock powder, cornflour and sugar, then add the water and butter and bring to the boil. Remove from the heat and stir in the parsley with a few leaves of finely chopped basil or other herbs.

Drain the cooked pasta, add the tomato to the sauce and bring back to the boil, then stir the two mixtures together. Leave to stand for 2–3 minutes before serving.

Macaroni and Vegetables V

You can eat this with meat for dinner, or serve it by itself for lunch or tea.

For 2 or 3 servings:
2 Tbsp butter
1 onion, chopped
1 stalk celery, chopped
1 cup (110 g/4 oz) macaroni
2 cups (500 ml/16 fl oz) hot water
1 or 2 tomatoes, chopped
3 tsp chicken or vegetable stock powder
1/4 cup (60 ml/2 fl oz) water
1/2 cup parsley

Melt the butter in a medium-sized frypan and add the onion and celery. After 2 minutes stir in the macaroni. Stir over moderate heat for 1 minute then add the hot water. Cover and simmer gently for about 10 minutes.

When the macaroni is almost tender and the water has nearly all disappeared, mix the last 4 ingredients together and add them to the pan. Stir gently, cover again and cook on low heat for 3–5 minutes.

> When using stock powder, make sure you use level measuring teaspoons or the recipe will be too salty.

Home-Fried Spaghetti

This quick, savoury egg-and-spaghetti dish is a cross between an omelet, a fritter and a pancake. It tastes good and is filling enough for the main part of a quick dinner. I like it with a sauce made of thickened stewed or canned tomatoes. It can also be served with a green salad in warm weather.

If you know you have to produce a meal in a very short time, you can do part of the preparation ahead. Cook the spaghetti and mix the eggs with the other ingredients earlier in the day, then combine the spaghetti and egg mixture just before you start cooking it. Although the bacon and onion are added to the egg mixture raw, their final flavour and texture is good, and it is not necessary to pre-cook them.

For 4 servings:
200 g (7 oz) spaghetti
4 eggs
1 1/2 tsp salt
1/2 tsp pepper
2 Tbsp onion pulp
1–2 rashers bacon, chopped finely
1/4 cup grated tasty cheddar cheese
2 Tbsp butter

Place the spaghetti, broken roughly into 5 cm (2 in) lengths, into a pot of rapidly boiling, lightly salted water. Cook until tender. Beat together the eggs, salt and pepper. Cut an onion in half crosswise and scrape the cut surface with a teaspoon to make the onion pulp. (Cut off a slice and scrape again to get more pulp.) Add the onion pulp, bacon and cheese to the egg. When the spaghetti is cooked, drain it and rinse in cold water. Add the spaghetti to the egg mixture just before you are going to cook it.

Coat a large frypan with non-stick spray. Heat the pan well, add the butter, and as it is bubbling pour in the egg and spaghetti mixture. Cover and cook over moderate heat, without stirring, for 4–5 minutes or until the bottom is golden brown and the top is no longer runny, then slide the half-cooked mixture out of the pan onto a plate and flip it over, back into the pan. Cook, uncovered, until the second surface has browned, then slide from the pan. Cut into wedges and serve with stewed, lightly thickened tomatoes, or with tomato salsa.

Savoury Lentil Sauce for Pasta V

This sauce, served over pasta, makes a satisfying vegetarian meal.

For 4 servings:
1 cup (190 g/16 1/2 oz) brown lentils
1 bayleaf
3 cups (750 ml/24 fl oz) water
2 large onions, chopped
2 or 3 cloves garlic, chopped
1 red pepper, chopped (optional)
2 Tbsp oil
1 can (440 g/15 oz) cream of pumpkin soup
1 can (400 g/14 oz) tomatoes in juice
cornflour (if necessary)
grated cheddar or Parmesan cheese

Simmer the lentils and the bayleaf in the water in a covered pot until the lentils are tender, about 45 minutes.

In another pot cook the onion, garlic and red pepper in the oil for 5 minutes. Add the (undiluted) pumpkin soup and the chopped or crushed tomatoes, and simmer for about 10 minutes. Put aside until the lentils are tender, then add them, with as much of their cooking liquid as you need to make a good sauce consistency (discard the bayleaf). If necessary, thicken with a little cornflour paste.

For a substantial vegetarian meal, spoon the sauce over boiled, drained spaghetti or other pasta. Top with grated cheddar or Parmesan cheese if desired and serve with a salad.

Clam Sauce for Spaghetti

Spoon this sauce over cooked, drained spaghetti which has been lightly buttered or tossed with a little pesto. A leafy green side salad is good with this.

For 3–4 servings:
1 Tbsp oil
1 red pepper, chopped (optional)
2 cloves garlic, chopped
1 onion, chopped
2 cans (each 400 g/14 oz) whole tomatoes in juice
1 Tbsp chopped fresh basil or pesto
2 tsp tomato paste
1 Tbsp soft butter
1 Tbsp flour
1 can (285 g/10 oz) baby clams
about 1 tsp sugar
about 1/2 tsp salt
about 200 g (7 oz) spaghetti

Heat the oil in a medium-sized pot and cook the red pepper, garlic and onion gently for about 10 minutes, without browning them. Add the tomatoes (and their liquid), the basil or pesto and the tomato paste, and simmer for about 30 minutes. Mix the butter and flour together until well blended, then stir or whisk into the tomato sauce. (It should thicken the sauce slightly without forming lumps, and it rounds out the flavour nicely.)

Drain the clams, reserving the liquid. Add the clams to the sauce, simmer a few minutes longer then taste and season carefully with all or some of the reserved clam liquid, salt and sugar, to balance the flavours.

Put aside, then reheat when needed. Serve over spaghetti.

Easy Spaghetti 'n' Meat Sauce

For 4–6 servings:
500 g (1 lb 2 oz) minced beef
1 onion, chopped
1 clove garlic, finely chopped
1/4 cup (60 ml/2 fl oz) tomato concentrate
1/2 tsp marjoram or oreganum
1 tsp salt
1 Tbsp sugar
1/2–1 cup chopped mushrooms (optional)
2 cups (500 ml/16 fl oz) water
400–500 g (14–18 oz) spaghetti

Heat a large frypan, add the minced beef, onion and garlic, and brown, stirring often, for about 5 minutes. (Add a little oil only if the mixture sticks.) Add all the other ingredients except the spaghetti, cover the pan tightly, and simmer for about 30 minutes, adding extra water if the mixture looks dry.

Cook the spaghetti in plenty of lightly salted boiling water in a large pot. Drain the cooked pasta, spoon over the sauce, and serve immediately.

Quick Bolognese Sauce

What we know and love as Bolognese sauce may bear little resemblance to the original Italian version, but it is still good, quick and versatile. The relatively short cooking time gives a nice fresh flavour.

For 4–6 servings:
2 Tbsp olive oil
1 medium onion, diced
2 cloves garlic, finely chopped
1 red or green pepper (optional)
2 medium carrots
2 stalks celery
400 g (14 oz) minced beef
1 Tbsp chopped fresh basil, if available
1/2 tsp oreganum
2 cans (each 400 g/14 oz) whole
  tomatoes in juice
2–3 Tbsp tomato paste
1/2–1 tsp salt
black pepper to taste
400–500 g (14–18 oz) long pasta
  (spaghetti, fettuccine, etc.)

Heat the oil in a large pan, then add the onion and garlic, and cook until the onion has softened.

Chop the pepper, carrots and celery into small (5 mm/1/4 in) cubes (or chop finely in a food processor), add to the onion mixture and cook for 4–5 minutes.

Add the minced beef and cook over high heat until lightly browned, stirring frequently to break up any lumps. Stir in the herbs then the tomatoes (and their juice) and the tomato paste. Crush or mash the tomatoes with the back of a spoon, then season to taste with salt and pepper.

Bring the mixture to the boil, stirring occasionally. Reduce the heat and leave uncovered to simmer gently while you cook the pasta in plenty of boiling water.

When the pasta is cooked, drain it quickly, then toss it with a little extra olive oil. Add the sauce and toss until evenly mixed.

Serve immediately, either from a large serving dish or on individual plates. Garnish with chopped fresh basil and plenty of freshly grated Parmesan cheese.

Summer Spaghetti V

This is a mild, light sauce that children love. Serve it on your favourite pasta.

For 2–3 servings:
200 g (7 oz) spaghetti or other pasta
2 tsp cornflour
1 tsp sugar
1 tsp chicken stock powder or 1/2 tsp salt
1 can (400 g/14 oz) tomatoes, chopped
1 Tbsp butter
2 Tbsp finely chopped parsley or mixed
  fresh herbs
1 Tbsp grated Parmesan cheese (optional)

Cook the pasta in plenty of lightly salted boiling water until tender.

In a medium-sized pot, stir the cornflour, sugar and stock powder together thoroughly. Mix until smooth with a little of the tomato, then add the rest. Heat, stirring until the sauce thickens and boils, then add half the butter.

Drain the cooked pasta, and toss through the rest of the butter, the herbs, and the Parmesan. Put the pasta into individual serving bowls, and top with the sauce.

Super-Special Macaroni Cheese V

Make a macaroni cheese dish that is really special! The sauce that coats the macaroni is very carefully seasoned, and tastes extra cheesy.

For 4–6 servings:
300 g (10 1/2 oz) macaroni or other pasta
2 Tbsp butter
2 Tbsp oil
1 tsp curry powder
1/4 cup plain flour
3 cups (750 ml/24 fl oz) milk
1 Tbsp Dijon or other mild mustard
1 tsp salt
1/4 tsp freshly ground pepper
1 tsp Worcestershire sauce
1/2 tsp tabasco sauce
1/2 tsp grated nutmeg
2 cups grated tasty cheese

Topping
1–2 Tbsp butter
1 cup fresh breadcrumbs
1/2 cup grated tasty cheese

Turn the oven to 180°C (350°F). Cook the pasta in a large pot of boiling, lightly salted water until tender. Rinse with cold water and leave to drain in a sieve.

Heat the butter and oil in a pot, add the curry powder then the flour and heat until it bubbles. Add the milk, 1 cup at a time, bringing the sauce to the boil and stirring constantly between additions. Stir the remaining ingredients in thoroughly without reheating. Carefully stir the macaroni and sauce together, and turn into a well-buttered or sprayed 12-cup (3 litre/96 fl oz) capacity ovenproof dish.

For the topping, melt the butter and remove from the heat. Stir in the breadcrumbs and grated cheese, and sprinkle over the surface of the macaroni cheese. Bake for 30 minutes, or until the sauce bubbles and the top browns.

Economical Lasagne M

Most lasagne recipes call for pre-cooking the pasta, a slowly simmered meat and tomato sauce, and a cheesy sauce topping. This, however, is one of my easier versions. All pre-cooking is eliminated, but the end result still has a good flavour and texture. What's more,

you can use only a small amount of meat to feed four or five people if you need to.

For 4–5 servings:
250–400 g (9–14 oz) minced beef
1 can (300 g/10 1/2 oz) tomato purée
1 can (440 g/15 oz) tomato soup
2 cloves garlic, chopped
1 tsp beef stock powder or 1/2 tsp salt
1 tsp each basil and oreganum
1 cup (250 ml/8 fl oz) boiling water
125 g (4 1/2 oz) uncooked lasagne noodles
1 1/2 cups (150 g/6 oz) grated cheese

Mix together the minced beef, tomato purée, soup, garlic, stock powder or salt, herbs and boiling water and stir well.

Butter or spray a fairly shallow microwave or ovenproof dish of at least 8-cup (2 litre/ 64 fl oz) capacity. Layer a third of the meat mixture, then half the noodles, then a third of the cheese. Repeat with the same proportions of meat, noodles and cheese, and top with the remaining meat. Do not leave the mixture to stand before cooking.

Microwave, covered loosely, on High (100%) power for 30 minutes, then sprinkle with the remaining cheese and microwave 1 minute longer to melt it.

OR cover and bake at 180°C (350°F) for 45 minutes, adding the cheese and cooking uncovered for the last 5 minutes.

Leave to stand for at least 15 minutes before serving.

Variations: Add 200–400 g (7–14 oz) sliced, sautéed mushrooms to the minced beef and tomato mixture.

Replace the minced beef with 2–3 cups thoroughly cooked, drained, brown lentils.

If you are baking the lasagne in the oven, after 40 minutes add the remaining cheese, then pour over it a mixture made by beating 2 eggs with 1 cup of milk. This sets to make a cheese custard when the lasagne is baked, uncovered, for about 15 minutes (instead of the 5 minutes suggested to melt the cheese).

Vegetable Lasagne V

Mixtures of savoury foods layered between lasagne noodles have become so popular in recent years that they are now considered part of our basic cuisine.

For 6 servings:

First Layer
1 onion, finely chopped
1 clove garlic, finely chopped
1 Tbsp olive oil
about 300 g (10 1/2 oz) mushrooms, sliced
1 tsp finely chopped fresh thyme
1 cup (250 ml/8 fl oz) vegetable stock
1 Tbsp cornflour
1/4 cup (60 ml/2 fl oz) water
salt and pepper to taste

Layered Macaroni Bake

Second Layer

*300 g (10¹/₂ oz) spinach or broccoli,
  chopped small*
1 cup (250 g/9 oz) cottage cheese
2 eggs
1 cup grated tasty cheese
salt and pepper

*250 g (9 oz) fresh lasagne sheets (spinach
  or plain)*
*1 can (425 g/15 oz) Italian seasoned
  tomatoes*
¹/₂ cup grated tasty cheese

Turn the oven to 180°C (350°F). To
prepare the first layer, cook the onion and
garlic in the oil until soft but not
browned. Add the mushrooms and thyme
and cook for 5 minutes more. Add the
stock, then thicken with the cornflour
mixed with the water. Season to taste.

To prepare the second layer, cook the
spinach or broccoli until barely tender.
Drain. Mix together the cottage cheese,
eggs, grated cheese, and salt and pepper
to taste. Stir in the drained broccoli or
spinach.

To assemble, butter or spray a casserole
dish about 20 x 30 cm (8 x 12 in). Cover
with a layer of lasagne sheets. Spread over
the mushroom mixture then top with a

second layer of lasagne. Spoon over the
cottage cheese mixture, and cover with
more lasagne. Pour the tomato mixture
evenly over the top, covering it completely.
Sprinkle with the grated cheese.

Cover and bake for about 40–45 minutes,
then uncover and bake for about
15 minutes longer, until the top is lightly
browned.

Layered Macaroni Bake   V

This basic, easy recipe is very popular
with children, and is a good way to use
up leftovers.

For 4 servings:

300 g (10¹/₂ oz) large macaroni shapes
1 Tbsp butter
1 Tbsp plain flour
*1 can (400 g/14 oz) tomatoes, chopped
cooked mushrooms, corn or other
  vegetables and/or chopped cooked
  chicken (optional)*
1 cup grated cheese
2 eggs
1 cup (250 ml/8 fl oz) milk

Turn the oven to 180°C (350°F). Cook the
macaroni in plenty of lightly salted
boiling water until tender. Drain, then stir
in first the butter, then the flour and

chopped tomatoes. Stir in additional
vegetables and/or chicken, and spread in
a large ovenproof dish. Sprinkle evenly
with the grated cheese. Beat the eggs and
milk to blend, and pour over the pasta.

Bake, uncovered, for 30–40 minutes or
until the cheesy topping is firm in the
centre. Stand for 5–10 minutes before
serving.

See also
Fish and Macaroni Casserole, p. 64
Spicy Pork on Noodles, p. 92
Fruited Couscous p. 105
Lamb Shanks with Macaroni, p. 113
Anne's Stroganoff, p. 131
'Buttons and Bows' Frypan Dinner,
p. 131
Macaroni Mix-Up, p. 131
Dinner for One, Please James, p. 132
Mushroom Lasagne, p. 138
'Home Alone' Special, p. 144
Easy Pasta Salad, p. 157
Salmon and Pasta Salad, p. 160
Pasta Salad, p. 173

Pizza Pizzazz

Many families are delighted to eat pizzas several times a week. You can save a great deal of money if you make your own pizzas, sometimes with a traditional yeasty base or, when time is short, mixing up some easier options. Once you start to think about toppings, the sky's the limit! You can even put different toppings on different sections of your pizzas, so you please everybody!

PIZZA PARTS

Pizza Bases
For the bready base of a pizza you can use uncooked scone dough, uncooked yeast dough, or some variety of cooked bread, split or not as you choose.

For a pizza that is the main part of a meal for 4 people, make a scone or bread dough using 2 cups of flour. You can add grated cheese, basil and marjoram to the base mixture if you like. It looks nice and you use less topping if you make 4 individual pizzas rather than one large one. Roll and pat them out directly on an oven tray that has been sprayed or buttered or lined with baking paper or Teflon liner, and make the outer edges a little thicker than the rest to enclose the topping.

If you roll out pizza dough on grainy cornmeal you may be able to slip the ready-to-cook pizza onto a pizza stone which has been preheated in a hot oven. This browns the base nicely.

Tomato Topping
Tomato topping is usually put next to the dough. Flavour this layer with fresh or dried basil and marjoram or oreganum.

Choose one of the following toppings:
- Fresh, firm sliced tomatoes;
- Drained canned or bottled tomatoes;
- Tomato purée;
- Slightly diluted tomato concentrate (paste);
- Packet soup boiled with 1 cup of water, then cooled;
- Ready-seasoned tomato pizza toppings;
- Canned spaghetti in tomato sauce (popular with children).

Extra Toppings
It's best to use foods that have a short cooking time or are already cooked, or those that can be eaten raw. Use a few tasty toppings rather than too many all mixed up!

Choose a few of the following toppings:
- Tomato paste, sun-dried tomato paste, dried tomato pesto, sliced tomatoes, drained canned tomatoes, commercially made tomato-based pizza toppings;

Roasted Vegetable Pizza

- Red, yellow and green peppers;
- Roasted pepper strips or wedges, eggplant, mushrooms, zucchini, etc;
- Onion slices, caramelised onions, chopped spring onions, roasted garlic;
- Sliced or sautéed mushrooms, sliced or whole olives, fresh and dried herbs, artichoke hearts;
- Anchovy fillets, salmon and shrimps;
- Salami, ham, bacon, cooked turkey and chicken;
- Cooked sausage varieties, frankfurters;
- Your favourite pesto;
- Cooked mince mixtures;
- Chilli bean mixtures;
- Chopped or sliced avocados;
- Creamed corn, corn kernels, small whole corn cobs;
- Olive oil.

Roasted Vegetable Topping
Toss a selection of suitable vegetables in a plastic bag containing a little olive or canola oil and roast them, uncovered, in a shallow baking pan for about 15 minutes while the oven is heating for the pizza.

Cheese Topping
Use plenty of any cheese you have or like, either sliced or grated. Cheese over the toppings mentioned above stops them from drying out. Experiment with different cheese varieties to see what you like best – try mozzarella, cheddar, blue cheese, camembert or brie, Parmesan or feta.

Baking
Bake uncooked-base pizzas at 200–225°C (400–425°F) until the base has cooked through and the bottom of the crust is golden brown. Thin-based pizzas cook faster than those with thick bases. The topping ingredients should be hot and bubbly by the time the base is cooked. Check that the dough and the topping in the centre is cooked before you take the pizzas from the oven.

Pizza toppings put on cooked bases may be baked or grilled, just long enough to heat the topping and melt the cheese, for a shorter time than those on uncooked bases.

Ceramic pizza 'stones' are used to produce crisper, browner bases on pizzas. They are useful but not essential.

Non-Traditional Toppings
These days some toppings are added to pizzas after they are baked. These include freshly cooked vegetables such as broccoli, salad greens and other salad vegetables.

Serving
Serve pizzas alone, with salad or after soup, as soon as possible after removing them from the heat. It is often easier to cut pizzas into pieces with kitchen scissors than to cut them with a knife. If reheating cooked pizza, add extra cheese and garnishes to stop the topping looking dry or meagre!

Quick Yeasty Pizza   V
This is my fastest yeasty pizza base recipe. I usually make six individual pizzas with it, although it can be used for one large pizza.

For 6–8 individual pizzas or one 25–35 cm (10–14 in) pizza base:
1¼ (310 ml/10 fl oz) cups warm water
2 Tbsp sugar
1 Tbsp active dried yeast
2 Tbsp oil
1 cup self-raising flour
2 cups plain flour
1 tsp salt

Turn the oven to 220°C (425°F). Measure the water and sugar into a mixing bowl or food processor. Stir or process to dissolve (double-check that the water is lukewarm), and add the yeast. Mix or process again briefly, and leave to stand for at least 5 minutes until the yeast starts to bubble.

Combine the oil, flours and salt in a large mixing bowl. Stir in the bubbling yeast mixture and mix well. If necessary add a little extra flour to make a dough that is firm enough to turn out and knead on a floured board. Knead until smooth and satiny, then cut into 6–8 pieces for individual pizzas or one large round. If making individual pizzas, roll each portion of dough out to form a 15–18 cm (6–7 in) circle and place on well-oiled oven trays. Leave to stand for a few minutes while you prepare the toppings you want, then bake for 10–15 minutes, until the dough is golden brown around the edges and lightly browned underneath.

Yeast-Based Pizza V

One of the joys of owning a breadmaker is how really easy it is to make good yeasty pizza bases! Simply measure in the ingredients, set to the dough cycle and go away. The hardest part becomes selecting your toppings!

**Makes 1 very large pizza,
2 medium pizzas, or 8 individual pizzas:**
2 tsp active dried yeast
*1 cup (250 ml/8 fl oz) plus 2 Tbsp warm
  water*
2 tsp sugar
1 tsp salt
2 Tbsp olive oil
3 cups high-grade flour

If using a breadmaker:
Carefully measure all the ingredients into a 750 g (1 lb 10 oz) capacity breadmaker, in the order specified by the manufacturer.

Set to DOUGH cycle and START. When the cycle is complete, take the dough out of the machine and shape and bake it as below.

(If you are short of time, turn the machine off 1 hour after it has started, remove the kneaded dough, and shape it as below. This results in only a small loss of quality.)

If handmaking dough:
Measure the first 5 ingredients into a large bowl with 1 cup of the measured flour and mix thoroughly. Cover and leave for 15 minutes, or longer, in a warm place. Stir in the remaining flour, adding extra if necessary, to make a dough just firm enough to knead.

Knead with the dough hook of an electric mixer or by hand on a lightly floured surface for 10 minutes, adding extra flour if necessary, until the dough forms a soft ball and springs back when pressed lightly.

Turn dough in 2–3 tsp of oil in the cleaned, dry bowl, cover with cling film and leave in a warm, draught-free place for about 30 minutes. Knead the risen dough lightly, then shape.

To shape and bake pizzas:
Heat the oven to 225°C (425°F). Roll dough into thin circles, according to the number and size of pizzas you require. Place in or on sprayed pizza pans, Teflon liners, baking paper or well-oiled oven trays.

Add your favourite toppings (p. 187) and bake until the underside is brown. For crisp, very thin pizza, bake before (and after) adding topping.

Quick Scone-Based Pizza V

A quick pizza like this makes a good weekend meal. All sorts of leftovers can be put on top of the tomato paste layer before the cheese is added!

For 2 servings:
1 cup plain flour
2 tsp baking powder
1 Tbsp oil
½ cup (125 ml/4 fl oz) milk
1 Tbsp tomato paste
½ tsp oreganum
½ cup grated cheese

Turn the oven to 220°C (425°F). Sift the dry ingredients into a bowl, add the oil and milk and mix to form a dough softer than pastry dough. Roll out to form a base about 30 cm (12 in) across. (Roll directly on a buttered baking sheet if you like.)

Spread with the tomato paste, sprinkle over the oreganum, add any other bits and pieces you have, then top with the grated cheese.

Fold the edges over to form a rim if you think it necessary, then bake for 10 minutes, or until the base is golden brown (lift it up with a fish slice to check).

Stromboli

This is wonderfully tasty and portable! Made from layers of pizza dough and your favourite fillings, stromboli is rolled up just like a strudel.

Make yeast-based pizza dough (above) in a bread machine or by hand. After the dough has risen for the last time, cut it in two. Working on a well-floured bench, roll the dough very thinly into a rectangle 40 x 50 cm (16 x 20 in), making sure it does not stick. Turn the oven to 200°C (400°F).

Use either of the following fillings:
¼ cup each diced ham, diced salami, grated tasty cheese and Parmesan cheese, OR 2–3 Tbsp basil pesto, ¼ cup each sun-dried tomato paste, diced salami, diced ham and 1 cup grated tasty cheese.

Spread the filling ingredients over the dough, then roll up as you would a sponge roll. Lift the filled roll carefully onto an oven tray lined with baking paper or a Teflon liner, so the join is underneath. Pierce at intervals from top to bottom to reduce the likelihood of the roll splitting as it cooks.

Bake for about 12 minutes, or until golden brown. Serve warm or cold, cut in diagonal slices.

Variation: Don't roll the dough out so thinly. Add the filling and roll up as described, then cut the filled roll into short lengths before baking. Place cut-side up on Teflon sheets or baking paper and bake at 210°C (425°F) until browned underneath.

Calzone V

Calzone is a pizza that is folded in half and sealed before it is baked.

Make yeast-based pizza dough in a bread machine or by hand, following the recipe above. After the dough has risen for the last time, cut it into 8 even pieces. Roll each piece into a circle 20 cm (8 in) across, adding enough flour to stop it sticking to the rolling pin and work surface.

Cover half of each circle with pizza toppings, leaving a small uncovered rim. Moisten the rim with water then fold the uncovered half over the top and seal the edges. Lift onto an oven tray, cut several air vents, then leave to rise for about 10 minutes.

Heat the oven to 220°C (425°F) and bake for about 10 minutes. Serve warm.

Note: Don't forget the air vents. They are very important – without them the calzone puffs up like a balloon!

Potato Pan Pizza

Potato lightens the base of this pizza, and adds bulk to the topping.

For 3–4 servings:
Base
1 cup self-raising flour
1 cooked potato
50 g (2 oz) butter, at room temperature
¼ tsp oreganum

Topping
*2 cups (total) cubed raw tomato, chopped
  red or green pepper, chopped
  mushrooms*
1–2 rashers bacon
¼ tsp basil
¼ tsp marjoram
1 cup cubed cooked potato
1½ cups grated or cubed cheese

Turn the oven to 200°C (400°F). Mix all the base ingredients together, using a food processor or your fingertips. Press the resulting dough into a well-sprayed 20 cm (8 in) loose-bottomed cake tin.

Measure all the topping ingredients into a bowl and stir to mix. Press the topping quite firmly onto the uncooked base and top with extra cheese if desired. Bake for 25 minutes.

When cooked, lift the pizza, on its base, away from the sides of the pan. Serve warm or cold.

If you often serve homemade pizzas for the main family meal of the day, make sure you include plenty of vegetables, plain or roasted, in the toppings you use, OR serve a mixed green salad with your pizza.

Hawaiian Pizza

Mushroom and Avocado Melt

V

Melts make quick, spectacular and substantial meals. Always make them just before they are to be eaten. Experiment with different toppings on the toasted bread base, beneath the melted cheese.

For 4 servings:
6 large flat mushrooms
Parmesan Dressing (below)
1 flat (focaccia-type) round bread, about
  25 cm (10 in) across
2 avocados
1–2 roast red peppers (p. 346)
grated or sliced cheese

Lightly brush the stem side of the mushrooms with Parmesan Dressing, then grill until the cheese bubbles, 2–3 minutes. Turn and brush the mushroom tops, then grill again.

Cut the bread through its middle, as you would a hamburger bun. Brush the cut surfaces with more of the dressing and grill until golden brown and crisp.

Slice the cooked mushrooms and pile on the toasted bread with slices of avocado and strips of red pepper. Top with grated or sliced cheese, using quantities to suit yourself. Grill until the cheese melts, then cut into wedges.

Variations: Try artichoke hearts, smoked chicken, smoked salmon, anchovies, tuna, olives, grilled eggplant, tomatoes, pesto, tapenade and different cheeses on melts.

Parmesan Dressing

1/4 cup (60 ml/2 fl oz) olive oil
1 Tbsp wine vinegar
2 tsp grainy mustard
1 clove garlic, finely chopped
1/4 tsp salt
1/2 tsp sugar
1/4 cup grated Parmesan cheese

Put all ingredients in the food processor and process until well mixed and thickened, OR shake all ingredients together in a screw-top jar.

Use immediately or refrigerate, warming to room temperature when required.

Brush over mushrooms and bread before grilling, or use as a dressing on salad greens.

Hawaiian Pizza

After you have made this a couple of times, you'll be able to make it really quickly and easily.

For 2 people:
1/2 cup (125 ml/4 fl oz) milk
1 Tbsp olive or other oil
1 cup self-raising flour
1 Tbsp tomato paste
1 Tbsp water
1/4 tsp crumbled oreganum

Toppings
1/2 cup chopped ham or 1/4 cup chopped salami
1/2 cup chopped canned pineapple

1 cup grated cheese
1/4 cup chopped tomato

Put the oven rack just below the middle and turn the oven to 220°C (425°F).

Put the milk and oil in a medium-sized bowl and mix well with a fork. Add the flour and mix with the fork, then your hand, to form a ball.

So the pizza doesn't stick, rub butter in a 30 cm (12 in) circle on an oven tray. Roll the dough out on this until it is 30 cm (12 in) round. Fold in the edges all round.

Mix together the tomato paste, water and oreganum and spread evenly over the pizza base. Cover with ham or salami and pineapple, then sprinkle cheese and tomato on top.

Bake for 12 minutes, or until golden brown underneath. Cut in wedges with kitchen scissors and eat before it gets cold.

A pizza needs to cook at a temperature high enough to brown its edge and cook the toppings. It must be in the oven long enough to cook the crust through and brown its lower surface. The time and temperature will depend on your oven, the oven slide or pizza pan you use, and the position of the pizza in the oven. A preheated pizza stone, or a pizza pan with a perforated base, makes the pizza base cook and brown faster.

189

Potatoes to Please

Never underestimate the appeal of potatoes! If you keep a bag of potatoes on hand in a cool (but not too cold), dark place, you can use them as the base for many interesting, family-pleasing recipes at a very reasonable price. Experiment with some of the different recipes in this section, and see how popular the results are!

POTATO POWER

Potatoes not only taste good, they're good for you! They contain many nutrients per calorie, and are high in complex carbohydrates.

A plainly cooked 100 g (3½ oz) potato contains almost no fat and less than 100 calories. When you cook potatoes in oil or butter, however, or add butter or cream before serving them, remember that you are adding calories!

Potatoes vary in size, shape, colour, flavour and texture, depending not only on the variety, but also the place where they were grown. Even if you always buy the same variety, those you buy today are unlikely to be exactly the same as those you bought a month ago, grown in another place, under different conditions.

Nevertheless, different varieties do have different characteristics. Choose potatoes that are known for their waxiness or flouriness – waxy potatoes slice best, and floury ones mash best.

Potatoes to Die For!　　V

This recipe is delicious, if rather sinful, since it contains rather a lot of sour cream. Serve it as an occasional treat.

For 4 main servings:
1.5 kg (3 lb 5 oz) waxy or all-purpose
　potatoes
3 large cloves garlic
¼ cup plain flour
½ tsp salt
2 cups sour cream
½ cup (125 ml/4 fl oz) milk
200 g (7 oz) gruyère cheese, grated

Turn the oven to 180°C (350°F). Scrub the potatoes, cut them into 5 mm (¼ in) slices, dropping them into a large container of cold water as you do so. Drain and transfer to a microwave dish or oven bag, cover the dish or tie the bag loosely, and microwave until the potatoes are tender, 12–15 minutes on High (100%) power.

Potatoes to Die For!

Make the sauce while the potatoes cook. Using a food processor if you have one, finely chop the garlic, then add the flour, salt, sour cream and milk. Process until smooth.

Butter or spray a large, shallow, oval or rectangular baking dish, about 23 x 30 cm (9 x 12 in). Overlap half the potatoes in the dish, drizzle almost half the sauce mixture over them, then sprinkle over almost half the cheese. Repeat with the remaining potatoes and sauce, then sprinkle the rest of the cheese evenly over the top.

Bake uncovered for about 30 minutes, until the potatoes have heated through and the topping is golden brown. Leave to stand in a warm place for 5–10 minutes before serving. Serve with a mixed green salad or a spinach salad.

Variation: Top with 200–300 g (7–10 oz) hot-smoked salmon, broken into flakes, after removing the potatoes from the oven.

Mediterranean Potatoes

It takes only a little effort to turn everyday potatoes into something that will delight everybody who eats them.

For 2 main servings:
about 800 g (1 lb 12 oz) waxy or all-
　purpose potatoes
2–3 Tbsp olive or other oil
1 or 2 large cloves garlic, very finely
　chopped
chilli powder or cayenne pepper
several sprigs of fresh thyme, rosemary or
　sage
salt or 2 tsp capers
2 tsp chopped anchovies
2 tsp caper vinegar
about ¼ cup chopped parsley
black olives (optional)

Scrub the potatoes with a soft brush to remove all dirt, then cut lengthways into large, chunky wedges or chip shapes. Rinse in cold water, then pat dry with a paper towel or clean teatowel.

Heat the oil in a large, heavy non-stick frypan. Add the potatoes, tossing them in the oil. Cover and cook, turning every 5 minutes, for about 20 minutes, until the potatoes are barely tender, and are lightly

browned on most sides. While turning the second time, add the garlic, sprinkle over the chilli powder or cayenne pepper, then mix well. Put several sprigs of herbs and the salt or capers on top of the potatoes.

As soon as the potatoes are tender, remove the herbs, add the anchovies and caper vinegar and cook for about 10 minutes longer, uncovered, turning occasionally.

Mix in the chopped parsley just before serving. Scatter the olives over the top.

Serve in bowls, alone, or topped with poached eggs, with spinach salad.

Friggione　　V

For this recipe to be at its best, do not hurry the cooking time. Although it loses its bright colour, it tastes better and better as the liquid disappears and the mixture browns.

For 4–6 servings:
about ¼ cup (60 ml/2 fl oz) olive oil
5 medium-sized waxy or all-purpose
　potatoes (750 g/1 lb 10 oz)
2 large red onions, sliced
2 red or green peppers, sliced
1 can (425 g/15 oz) Italian seasoned
　tomatoes or whole tomatoes in juice
1–1½ tsp salt
1 tsp sugar
freshly ground black pepper
chopped parsley (optional)

Heat the oil in a large frypan, preferably one with a non-stick surface. Scrub or peel the potatoes, cut them into 1 cm (½ in) cubes and pat dry with a paper towel. Add the potatoes, onions and peppers to the hot oil. Cover and cook over a moderate heat for 20 minutes, stirring several times, until the vegetables are tender and lightly browned.

Add the tomatoes and juice, breaking up the tomatoes if necessary. Cook uncovered over a medium heat for 15–30 minutes, until the mixture darkens and has reduced so there is only a small amount of liquid around the potatoes. Season to taste and sprinkle with chopped parsley before serving.

Serve alone, with a green salad, or as an accompaniment for grilled meat.

Corn and Potato Casserole V

Potato casseroles are a popular addition to any buffet meal. This recipe always looks good, and is easy to prepare and cook. It is baked uncovered for the whole of its cooking time, and should form an attractive golden-brown crust.

If possible, bake it in a dish of similar size to the one specified since the size of the dish affects the consistency of the mixture. If the dish is too deep the mixture turns out more liquid, and if too shallow it tends to dry out.

Serve the casserole as the main part of a vegetarian meal, or to accompany unsauced meat, with perhaps a salad.

1 kg (2 lb 3 oz) all-purpose potatoes
2 large onions, thinly sliced
2 cups grated cheese
1 medium or large can creamed corn
1 cup (250 ml/8 fl oz) chicken or
*   vegetable stock, or 1¹/₂ tsp chicken or*
*   vegetable stock powder in 1 cup water*

Turn the oven to 180°C (350°F). Scrub the potatoes, or peel them if you prefer, and slice thinly.

Butter or spray an ovenware dish 23 cm (9 in) in diameter, with sides about 5 cm (2 in) high. Arrange a third of the potatoes on the bottom of the dish. Cover with half the onion, half the corn (in little blobs if you find it hard to spread), and sprinkle with a quarter of the cheese. Repeat these layers, then top with the remaining potato slices, arranging them attractively in overlapping circles.

Pour the stock over the potatoes.

Sprinkle with the remaining cheese, and bake uncovered for 1¹/₄ hours, until the potatoes are tender and the top is lightly browned. Leave to stand for 15–30 minutes before serving.

Special Spanish Omelet

While the mild red onions from our garden last, from January until May, I use them with whatever peppers I have on hand to make big, substantial Spanish omelets. I serve these as whole meals, often with a salad alongside.

For 4–6 servings:
3 large all-purpose potatoes (about 750 g/
*   1 lb 10 oz)*
1 medium-sized red onion
3 Tbsp olive oil
1 red pepper
1 green or yellow pepper
3 large eggs
¹/₂ tsp salt

Scrub the potatoes and cut them into 1 cm (¹/₂ in) cubes. Chop the onion.

Heat the oil in a 20 cm (8 in) frypan (preferably non-stick). When hot, add the potatoes and onion. Cover and cook over moderate heat until the potatoes are just tender, about 10 minutes. (The potatoes need not brown, but it is nice if they and the onions colour lightly.) If you want to speed up the cooking, add about 1 Tbsp water to make steam.

Cut the peppers into 5 mm (¹/₄ in) cubes and add to the potatoes for the last 2–3 minutes of their cooking time.

Beat the eggs and salt with a fork until combined. Tip the hot potato mixture into the eggs and stir to mix thoroughly. Tip all this back into the pan and cook, uncovered, until most of the egg has cooked. Slide the omelet onto a plate, so the uncooked side is still uppermost, then flip the whole thing back into the pan to set and lightly brown the other side.

As it finishes cooking, push the edges down to compact them. Tip the omelet out onto a flat plate and cut it in wedges as you would a pie. Leftovers are good cold, in packed lunches.

Microwaved Herbed Potato Cake VM

For 4–5 servings:
about 25 g (1 oz) butter
4 medium all-purpose potatoes (600 g/
*   1 lb 5 oz)*
2 small onions, very finely sliced or
*   grated*
¹/₄ cup chopped fresh parsley
1 Tbsp chopped fresh thyme or marjoram
2 tsp green herb stock powder or 1 tsp
*   salt*
about 50 g (2 oz) thinly sliced or grated
*   cheese (¹/₂ cup)*
paprika

Melt the butter in a 6-cup microwave ring pan. Shred the scrubbed potatoes coarsely, putting them into a bowl of cold water as you do so, to prevent browning. Drain in a sieve, squeezing to remove excess water.

Mix the potatoes with the onion, herbs, stock powder or salt and melted butter. Press into the ring pan, cover and microwave on High (100%) power for 10 minutes, or until the potato is tender. Leave for 2 minutes then turn out onto a flat plate.

Place cheese slices or grated cheese around the top, sprinkle with paprika, and microwave for about 30 seconds, until the cheese melts.

Serve with meat or poultry and other vegetables.

Variation: Replace the onions with 3–4 chopped spring onions, using the leaves as well as the white part.

Mock Whitebait Fritters V

For best 'whitebait' appearance, shred potatoes into long, thin whitebait-like pieces.

For 4 servings:
1 tsp celery salt
1 tsp green herb stock powder or ¹/₂ tsp
*   salt*
1 Tbsp milk
2 eggs
2 waxy or all-purpose potatoes
1 onion
¹/₂ cup self-raising flour
oil

Put the celery salt, stock powder or salt and milk in a large bowl. Stir with a fork then break in the eggs and stir again until they are evenly mixed.

Scrub the potatoes and peel the onion, then shred or grate them. Quickly mix them with the egg before they go brown, then stir in the flour to make a fairly thick batter. Add extra flour to make a fritter consistency if necessary.

Fry dessertspoon lots of batter in hot oil about 5 mm (¹/₂ in) deep. Turn carefully (using tongs) when the first side is golden brown. The fritters should take about 5 minutes to cook. Keep cooked fritters hot on paper towels in a warm oven.

Serve with tomato sauce, with tomatoes, sausages or bacon, or a salad.

'Shortcut' Party Potatoes V

This recipe may be of help when you are preparing a meal for a crowd. The buttery herbed coating disguises the slightly different flavour and appearance of canned potatoes.

For 40 servings:
2–3 large cans (each 3 kg/6 lb 10 oz)
*   cooked potatoes**
6–8 Tbsp melted butter
about 1 cup chopped fresh herbs,
*   e.g. parsley, chives, thyme and*
*   oreganum, or parsley, chives and dill*

*Ask your grocer to get you large cans of small potatoes in brine. Each 3 kg (6 lb 10 oz) can should contain about 45 small potatoes. Allow 2–3 potatoes per person, depending on the age and appetites of your guests.

Put half a can of drained potatoes in a large, tough oven bag with ¹/₂ cup of the liquid from the can, and heat in the microwave on High (100%) power for 9–10 minutes.

Drain the potatoes but leave them in the bag. Turn in 1–2 Tbsp of melted butter per half can of potatoes, then sprinkle generously with about ¹/₄ cup of very finely chopped fresh herbs. (Chop dry herbs in the food processor for best results.) Mix gently to coat. Repeat this process with the remaining potatoes.

If you cannot microwave the potatoes just before you need them, as above, then keep them hot in their oven or roasting bags, in an insulated chilly bin type container, for up to an hour. Transfer to serving dishes just before the meal. (Roasting bags are light, compact, unbreakable and easily transportable. Close them loosely with rubber bands when microwaving.)

Serve as part of a buffet meal, as you would freshly cooked new potatoes. Use leftovers in potato salads, scalloped potato dishes, or sautéed.

Note: Leftover canned potatoes may be refrigerated in the bags for 3–4 days.

Cooked potatoes should never be left 'standing around' for long without refrigeration, especially in warm weather.

Special Scalloped Potatoes V

This recipe starts with cooked rather than raw potatoes, so the cooking time is reduced. A packet of soup is added for extra flavour.

For 6 servings:
1 kg (about 2 lb) cooked waxy or all-purpose potatoes
1 packet (about 30 g/1 oz) onion or vegetable soup mix
2 cups (500 ml/16 fl oz) milk
1/2 cup grated cheese

Turn the oven to 200°C (400°F). Cook the potatoes if necessary, boiling or microwaving them in a large covered container with 1/2 cup water. (This quantity of potatoes should cook in the microwave in about 10 minutes.)

Butter or spray a large, shallow ovenware dish about 23 cm (9 in) in diameter. Slice the potatoes and arrange them in layers in the dish. Sprinkle the soup mix over each layer, using it all. Pour the milk over the potatoes, dampening the soup mix, but do not worry if it does not cover the potatoes. If the underside of the top layer is above the milk, add up to 1/2 cup of water.

Sprinkle the grated cheese over the potatoes, then cover loosely with foil and bake for 15 minutes, then remove the foil and bake uncovered for 15–30 minutes, until the potatoes on top are golden brown.

Note: If you are in a hurry, brown the top under a grill after a total of 30 minutes in the oven.

If the sauce looks too thick before the potatoes are browned, add up to 1/2 cup boiling water. (Some potatoes absorb more liquid than others.)

Curried New Potatoes VM

This is an easy microwave recipe that I have made many times during cooking demonstrations in supermarkets. I am always surprised by the number of people who enjoy it so much they rush off to buy all the ingredients so they can cook it as soon as they get home.

For 4 servings:
1 onion, chopped
8 small waxy potatoes (800–900 g/ 1 lb 12 oz–2 lb), preferably Nadine
1 can (400 g/14 oz) coconut cream
2 tsp curry powder
1/2–1 tsp salt
1/2 tsp sugar
1–2 cups frozen peas
about 300 g (10 1/2 oz) cauliflorets (optional)
1–2 cups chopped cabbage (optional)

Put the chopped onion and the unpeeled,

halved or quartered potatoes into a microwave dish with the coconut cream and seasonings, adding the smaller amount of salt. Stir to mix, cover, and microwave on High (100%) power for 12 minutes, or until the potatoes are barely tender.

Add the peas and microwave for about 4 minutes, or add the peas, cauliflower and cabbage, stir to coat the vegetables, then microwave for 6–8 minutes, stirring at least once during this time. Check the cauliflower and cabbage are cooked to the tender-crisp stage and taste the sauce, adjusting the seasonings if necessary.

Serve immediately, alone or with a green salad, or leave to stand and reheat when required.

Variation: Quarter the recipe, reducing all the microwaving times to about a third of those suggested, and you have a good, quick meal for one.

Curried New Potatoes

Swiss Potato Cake

Swiss Potato Cake   V

I love Swiss Potato Cakes! I am sure my untraditional version would horrify a dedicated Swiss cook, but it works, is easy, and tastes very good.

For 1 serving:
2 medium all-purpose potatoes (about 300 g/10 oz), grated
about 2 Tbsp butter, melted
2 tsp oil
1/2 cup sautéed mushrooms
about 1/2 cup grated cheese
2 tsp finely chopped fresh herbs

Shred the scrubbed potatoes quite coarsely with a sharp cutter, e.g. the blade of a food processor which makes long shreds. Plunge them into cold water, leave to stand for at least 5 minutes, then drain in a colander and pat dry on a paper towel or teatowel. Melt the butter in a fairly large pot or microwave bowl, then toss the potato in it, lightly coating as many pieces as possible.

Heat the oil in a non-stick frypan. Coat the whole pan, then add the potato, pressing it down quite firmly. Put the lid

on lightly and cook the cake over moderate heat for about 15 minutes, until golden brown. Slide the potato cake onto the lid or a plate, then flip it back into the pan so the uncooked side is down.

Cook the second side for about 10 minutes, again with the lid on lightly. During the last 3 minutes, top with the sautéed mushrooms, put the grated cheese mixed with the herbs over the central part, and let the cheese melt slightly. Slide the potato cake onto a plate, with the cheese and mushroom topping uppermost.

Serve immediately as the main part of a meal, with a side salad and bread roll if you like.

Nelson Potatoes   V

Always cook considerably more of this than you think you will need!

For 4 servings:
2 medium onions, sliced
2 Tbsp butter or oil
3 medium apples, sliced
3 large waxy or all-purpose potatoes (600 g/1 lb 5 oz), sliced

1/2 cup (125 ml/4 fl oz) apple juice, wine, or stock powder and water
salt and freshly ground pepper
chopped fresh herbs, e.g. sage, thyme or oreganum

Cook the onion in a large, non-stick frypan in the butter or oil until transparent and browned on the edges. Raise the heat, add the apple and cook uncovered, stirring often, until it has browned slightly. Mix in the potato, then add the apple juice or other liquid. Cover the pan tightly and cook for about 20 minutes, until the potato is tender. Turn occasionally, adding extra liquid if the mixture becomes too dry.

Just before serving add freshly ground pepper, salt and herbs to taste.

Pizza Potatoes

Most children love the flavour of pizza. You can use the same combination of flavours in a baked potato, producing a stuffed potato which can be served as the main part of a meal.

For 1–2 servings:
1 large floury potato (about 200 g/7 oz)
1 cup grated cheese
2 spring onions, chopped
1 rasher bacon, chopped
1/4 cup chopped mushrooms or red or green peppers
1/4 tsp oreganum or marjoram
1 Tbsp tomato paste
liquid to thin

Choose the biggest potato in the bag! Scrub it and bake in the microwave on High (100%) power for 5–6 minutes, turning once, or in a regular oven at 200°C (400°F) for 1–1½ hours. (Allow 3–4 minutes' standing time when microwaving.) When cooked, the potato should 'give' when pressed.

While the potato cooks, mix together the cheese, spring onion, bacon, mushroom or peppers, and oreganum or marjoram. Add the tomato paste.

When the potato is cooked, cut it in half and scoop out the flesh with a spoon. Mash this with the other ingredients. Add yoghurt, milk or sour cream if the mixture is dry.

Pile the filling into the potato halves. Garnish with a little extra bacon, pepper, olives or anchovies if desired. Reheat in the microwave for 3–4 minutes, or in the oven for 15–20 minutes. Serve alone or with a salad.

Variation: Cook the chopped bacon and mushrooms or peppers in a frypan before mixing with the potato.

Bird's Nest Potatoes

Grate 1 large, floury or all-purpose potato per person onto an old teatowel. Squeeze the cloth to remove the liquid, then drop handfuls of potato into a very hot frypan containing a little oil. Flatten lightly, but do not pack down. Turn when golden, adding more oil if necessary.

Note: Work fast, since uncooked potatoes brown on standing.

Gold Nuggets

These taste as good as they look!

For 4 servings:
2 Tbsp oil
2 Tbsp butter
1–2 cloves garlic, finely chopped
4 medium all-purpose potatoes
salt
chopped parsley

Scrub or peel the potatoes and cut into 1 cm (1/2 in) cubes. Heat the oil and butter together in a large, non-stick frypan with a lid. Add the garlic and potato, turn the potato cubes to coat them, then cover the pan and cook over a moderate heat for 15 minutes, turning occasionally. Remove the lid and cook for 10–15 minutes longer, turning occasionally, until the potato cubes are golden brown and cooked through. Drain off any visible oil, sprinkle with salt and chopped parsley, mix well and serve.

Sautéed Potato Balls

Cut potato balls from raw, peeled all-purpose potatoes using a melon-ball cutter. Gently sauté in oil with 2 crushed garlic cloves for about 15 minutes, or until evenly browned and tender. Remove the garlic as soon as it browns.

Note: Boil the raw potato trimmings to make mashed potatoes for a later meal.

Banded New Potatoes

(Photo p. 99)

If you cook whole new potatoes without scraping them, their skins may burst. Scrub small, whole new potatoes with a soft brush, then peel a band of skin from the centre of the potato using a sharp vegetable brush or a small vegetable knife.

Simmer the new potatoes in a small amount of very lightly salted water in a covered pot until they feel cooked when pierced with a sharp knife. OR microwave them in an oven bag with all the air squeezed out, with 1 Tbsp water and 1/4 tsp butter per serving. Take care not to overcook the little potatoes, however you cook them.

Sautéed Potatoes

For 2 servings:

Slice 3–4 medium-sized, cold, cooked new potatoes (about 500 g/1 lb) into chunky pieces. Heat 3–4 Tbsp butter or oil in a non-stick frypan. When hot, add the potatoes and cook, uncovered, for 20–30 minutes, turning occasionally, until evenly crisp and golden. Sprinkle with chopped parsley before serving.

Variation: In a small pan, bring to the boil 2 Tbsp wine vinegar, 1 chopped clove garlic, 1 tsp finely grated lemon rind and 2 Tbsp olive oil. Pour over sautéed potatoes before serving.

Oven-Baked Chips (Photo p. 59)

It is much simpler to bake chips than fry them. As an added bonus, you also use much less oil.

Turn the oven to 230°C (450°F). Scrub all-purpose potatoes, then slice them as evenly as possible, making them a little thinner than normal chips. Drop the pieces into a bowl of cold water as you work. When all the potatoes are prepared and the oven is hot, drain then rinse the chips, and dry them as thoroughly as possible, using paper towels or teatowels.

Place the dried chips in a roasting pan or sponge-roll tin, lined with baking paper or a Teflon sheet. Drizzle over 1 Tbsp oil per potato. Mix the oil and potatoes thoroughly with your fingers, so that all the surfaces are oiled. Arrange in one layer. Bake for about 20 minutes, or until the potatoes are tender.

If the cooked chips are not brown enough, brown them under the grill, as evenly as possible. Serve straight away.

Barbecue Potato Packs

It always takes a while to get a barbecue fire to the right stage for cooking meat over hot embers. Before this stage is reached you can start cooking Barbecue Potato Packs because of their double foil coating. The packs take 30–45 minutes to cook, depending on the heat of the fire, and they are delicious!

For each pack tear off a piece of foil about 30 cm (12 in) long. Fold it in half so it is 15 cm (6 in) wide. Smear 1 tsp butter over the centre of the foil.

Scrub then slice 1 or 2 new potatoes. Overlap the slices on the top half of the foil, leaving the edges clear. Sprinkle with plain salt, or onion or celery salt, then add a pinch each of basil and marjoram (or other herbs).

Put a few small pieces of butter on top then fold the foil over the potatoes, squeeze to push out most of the air, then turn the edges several times to seal the packages.

Place on a rack over the barbecue fire. Turn every few minutes for the first 15 minutes, then turn occasionally. Open a pack after 30 minutes to see whether the potatoes are cooked. If not, reseal carefully.

Serve hot, warm or cool (but not chilled).

Variation: Add chopped bacon if desired.

Barbecued Potatoes

When you barbecue pre-cooked potatoes, all you have to do is brown and crisp the outside and heat them through.

Scrub large all-purpose potatoes, simmer until just tender or microwave them as follows: scrub and quarter lengthways 8 fairly large potatoes (about 1.5 kg/ 3 lb 5 oz). Put them in an oven bag with 25 g (1 oz) butter and 2 Tbsp water. Fasten the bag with a rubber band, leaving a finger-sized opening. Microwave on High (100%) power for 12–20 minutes, repositioning the potatoes in the bag twice, until the potatoes are barely tender. Leave them in the bag until you want to barbecue them, then put the quarters on a preheated, oiled grill rack or plate, and turn to brown all sides evenly, brushing with flavoured butter or oil only if they burn.

Barbecue time is likely to be 6–15 minutes, depending on conditions.

Barbecued New Potatoes

Microwave 750 g (1 lb 10 oz) small new potatoes with 1 Tbsp butter, 2 mint sprigs and 2 Tbsp water in an oven bag (see previous recipe) for about 8 minutes. Thread them onto skewers, alone or with other vegetables. Brush with melted butter or Garlic Herb Butter (p. 344) before cooking on an oiled grill rack until nicely browned.

Vegetable Accompaniments

Many of our mothers and grandmothers grew up thinking that a dinner plate should be filled with meat – vegetables, often overcooked, were served almost as a garnish on the side! We know better, getting the health message that our dinner plate should be two-thirds filled with vegetables, or with vegetables and some other complex carbohydrate. We now have such a variety of flavourful vegetables at our disposal, and so many interesting recipes to choose from, that we can often make vegetables the high point of our meal.

Buttered Asparagus

Select asparagus stalks of the same thickness so that they cook evenly.

Make the most of a small quantity of new season's asparagus by peeling the outer skin from the bottom 4–5 cm (1½–2 in) of the stalk; this way you can eat more of the stalk and the tender tips do not overcook while the bottoms finish cooking.

Lie the peeled stalks flat in a frypan, add just enough water to cover the bottom of the pan, cover and cook over a high heat until most of the water has evaporated and the stems are tender-crisp but still keep their bright colour, 2–4 minutes.

Drain off any remaining water, add ¼ tsp butter and 1 tsp lemon juice per serving, and freshly ground black pepper. Shake the pan to coat the asparagus, and serve immediately. (Asparagus turns olive green if left to stand in lemon juice, vinegar, etc.)

Valencia Asparagus

100–200 g (3½–7 oz) tender asparagus
1 Tbsp olive oil
salt
freshly ground pepper
a few drops balsamic vinegar or lemon
*   juice*

Wash the asparagus, snap off the tough ends, and cut into 3–4 cm (1½ in) lengths.

Heat the oil until very hot in a large, heavy pan. Add the asparagus, cover, and lower the heat. Cook, tossing the asparagus or shaking the pan frequently, for 2–3 minutes, until the asparagus is tender-crisp and has browned in a few places.

Sprinkle with salt, pepper and balsamic vinegar or lemon juice, and serve immediately.

Cheesy Polenta (p. 168) with Roasted
Summer Vegetables (p. 202)

Beans in Mustard Sauce

(Photo p. 198)

You can cook beans in this sauce, pour it over plain beans, or toss the cooked beans in the sauce just before you serve them. I like the last way best.

For 4 servings:
250 g (9 oz) fresh green beans
2–3 tsp butter
2 Tbsp chopped onion
1 tsp Dijon mustard
1 Tbsp wine vinegar
2 Tbsp water
1 Tbsp chopped fresh parsley or savory,
*   1 tsp chopped fresh tarragon, or ½ tsp*
*   fresh thyme*

Wash the beans and snip off the ends unless they are very young and tender. Cook over high heat in a little lightly salted water in a covered pan for a few minutes, until they are barely tender, and still bright green.

Heat the butter in a medium-sized frypan and cook the onion over medium heat until very lightly browned. Add the mustard, vinegar, water and herbs of your choice, cover and cook for 1–2 minutes.

Toss the cooked, drained beans in the sauce and serve immediately.

Note: If the beans are small and young, you will need to start the sauce before you cook the beans. If you want to cook the beans in the sauce, add a little extra water and a pinch of salt.

Beans with Almonds

For 2–3 servings:
250–300 g (9–10½ oz) runner or other
*   smaller green beans*
1 tsp butter
1 Tbsp finely sliced almonds

Trim and slice the beans if necessary. Cook over high heat in a little water in a covered, non-stick pan, so all the water has evaporated by the time the beans are cooked.

Meanwhile, in another pan heat the butter and toast the almonds. Toss the cooked beans and almonds together.

Savoury Beans and Tomatoes

An interesting sauce to give new life to yet more beans from the garden!

For 4 servings:
300 g (10½ oz) green beans
2 Tbsp olive or other oil
1 large clove garlic, chopped
1 onion, chopped
1 Tbsp sugar
2 Tbsp wine vinegar
1 Tbsp Dijon or other mild mustard
1 can (400 g/14 oz) tomatoes in juice
½ tsp salt
chopped fresh basil and/or sliced black
*   olives (optional)*

Trim the beans; if large, cut them diagonally into two or three. Cook in a small amount of water in a covered pan.

Heat the oil in another pan, add the garlic and onion, cover and cook until the onion is tender, then add the sugar, vinegar and mustard. Add the tomatoes and boil rapidly for 2–3 minutes, breaking the tomatoes into smaller pieces as the mixture boils down. Add salt to taste.

Add the drained beans to the sauce, or serve the sauce over the beans. Garnish with basil and/or olives if available.

Serve with crusty bread, new potatoes or on plainly cooked pasta, and grilled or barbecued meat.

How many servings of vegetables do you eat each day? If it is too many to count on one hand, then you are on the right track!

As well as the recipes in this chapter, look for vege-rich options in soups, salads, starters and lunches.

Sesame Broccoli   M

Sesame oil adds an interesting flavour to broccoli.

For 4 servings:
400–500 g (about 1 lb) broccoli
2 Tbsp water
1–2 Tbsp sesame oil
½ tsp salt
freshly ground black pepper

Cut off the broccoli florets, then peel the tough skin from the base of the stalks towards the tips. Cut the peeled stalks into short lengths.

Put all the ingredients in a microwave dish and cook on High (100%) power for about 3–4 minutes, tossing once during cooking, OR cook in a covered frypan over high heat for about 3 minutes, tossing to coat during cooking.

Serve immediately.

Variation: For Lemon Broccoli, omit the sesame oil and toss through 1–2 Tbsp lemon juice just before serving.

Brussels Sprouts in Mustard Dressing

Remove the loose outer leaves from brussels sprouts and cut a deep cross in the base of each so the centre cooks more quickly. Cook in a covered pot or microwave dish in a little lightly salted water, until barely tender. Do not overcook so the sprouts lose their lovely bright green colour.

Drain, saving the liquid for stock or gravy. Toss in a little butter (½ tsp for 4 servings) if desired, or serve with Mustard Dressing.

Mustard Dressing

2 Tbsp corn oil
2 Tbsp Dijon mustard
2 Tbsp hot water
2 Tbsp wine vinegar
1 Tbsp sugar
chopped parsley
1 tsp chopped fresh thyme
½ tsp salt
2 Tbsp olive oil (or extra corn or soya oil)

Shake all the dressing ingredients together in a screw-top jar, or mix in a food processor. (Dressing made in a food processor is thicker and does not separate as quickly.) Refrigerate for up to 4 days.

Savoury Cabbage

For 2 servings:
½ rasher lean bacon
1 clove garlic, chopped
few drops oil or ¼ tsp butter
200 g (7 oz) shredded cabbage
freshly ground black pepper
cornflour (optional)

Remove the rind and chop the bacon finely. Heat gently in a pot with the garlic and oil or butter until the bacon starts to sizzle, then add the cabbage with some water still clinging to the leaves. Add black pepper, cover, raise the heat, and toss occasionally until the liquid comes to the boil.

Cook until the cabbage is tender-crisp – it should still be bright green. The cooking time depends on the cabbage, but it may be as short as 3 minutes. Raise the heat and evaporate the liquid on the bottom of the pan, or thicken it with a little cornflour paste. Toss the cabbage in the thickened liquid and serve straight away.

Red Cabbage

This sweet-sour sauce gives cabbage new life! If you like to work ahead, it may be made the day before it is needed and reheated. It is best served with meat that has a strong flavour, and with plainly cooked or mashed potatoes.

For 4 servings:
1 Tbsp oil or butter
2 rashers bacon
1 large onion, sliced
1 apple, peeled and chopped
rind and juice of 1 orange (made up to
  ¾ cup (185 ml/6 fl oz) with water)
2 Tbsp sugar
½ cup (125 ml/4 fl oz) wine vinegar
1 tsp salt
4 cloves
1 bayleaf
6 peppercorns
½ red cabbage, sliced (about 500 g/
  1 lb 2 oz)
cornflour (optional)

Heat the oil or butter in a large pot. Remove the rind from the bacon, chop the bacon into small pieces and cook with the onion until both are lightly browned. Add the apple, cook about a minute longer, then add the finely grated orange rind, the juice and water, sugar, vinegar and seasonings.

Red Cabbage, Leeks in Cream Sauce (p. 200), Beans in Mustard Sauce (p. 197)

Shred the cabbage finely and add to the pot, cover, and heat until the cabbage has wilted. Cover tightly and cook for about an hour, stirring and turning occasionally, or transfer to a tightly covered casserole and bake at 180°C (350°F) for 1¹/₂ hours, turning once or twice.

Just before serving, taste and adjust seasonings if necessary. If you like, add a little cornflour paste. When the liquid is thickened lightly, it coats the cabbage and gives it a glossy appearance.

Puréed Potato and Celeriac

Celeriac is not commonly seen, but it is worth trying when you do come across it. I regard it as a winter treat. It is not a beautiful vegetable, being rather lumpy-looking, usually bigger than a tennis ball, with a number of stringy roots attached. When it is trimmed, peeled and cubed, then cooked and mashed with potatoes, it reminds me of Europe, where it is widely used in winter. It has a lovely celery flavour and a good texture.

Prepare equal quantities of potatoes and celeriac: peel them, cut into pieces of similar size, and boil together in lightly salted water. Mash with some butter, some of the cooking liquid, and a little nutmeg if you like. Whip well with a fork after mashing. Serve as you do mashed potatoes.

Cauliflower in Curried Tomato Sauce

This sauce turns cauliflower into something really special! It makes a good side dish, or may be served on rice as the main part of a meal.

For 4–6 servings:
500 g (1 lb 2 oz) prepared cauliflower
2 Tbsp butter
about 1 tsp curry powder
2 Tbsp plain flour
1 can (425 g/15 oz) chunky tomato and onion (or other savoury tomatoes)
¹/₂–1 cup grated tasty cheese

Break the cauliflower into 3 cm (1¹/₄ in) diameter florets and simmer until barely tender in lightly salted water. Drain, then arrange in one layer in a lightly buttered baking dish.

Make the sauce while the cauliflower cooks. Heat the butter and curry powder until bubbling, then stir in the flour. Add the tomato mixture and bring to the boil, stirring constantly. Thin with a little water if necessary, then pour evenly over the cauliflower. Sprinkle with as much cheese as you like, and put aside until needed.

Bake uncovered at 180°C (350°F), just until the cheese melts and the cauliflower heats through. Do not overcook.

'Fresh' Creamed Corn

This is a good way to use cheap corn, bought at roadside stalls. Refrigerate or freeze the mixture, but do not bottle it unless you use a pressure cooker to process the jars.

6 cups corn pulp
2 cups water
2 Tbsp sugar
1 Tbsp salt

Hold a cob of corn firmly and run down the tops of the kernels with a floating-blade potato peeler, without removing too much of each kernel. With a tablespoon held upside down, scrape down the cob, removing the contents of the kernels. Transfer the cut tips and scraped pulp into a measuring container (10 large, mature corn cobs produce about 6 cups of scraped pulp.)

Heat the corn pulp with the other ingredients, stirring constantly. As soon as it boils and thickens, remove from the heat. Refrigerate until required. Use in the same way as canned creamed corn.

Carrot Purée

If you start with carrots of a good colour, and you do not overcook them, you may be surprised by their bright, almost luminous colour. Use the suggested flavourings or add others to suit your taste. Processed carrots will be much smoother than mashed carrots.

For 6 servings:
400 g (14 oz) carrots
2 Tbsp butter
¹/₂ tsp chopped fresh thyme or a grating of nutmeg
¹/₂–1 tsp orange rind
about 2 Tbsp orange juice

Scrape the carrots and cut into rounds about 5 mm (¹/₄ in) thick. Cook in ¹/₄–¹/₂ cup of lightly salted water until tender – no longer than necessary if you want a fresh flavour and bright colour.

Drain, reserving the liquid, put into a food processor with the remaining ingredients and process until smooth, or mash with a potato masher. Taste, adjust seasonings, and add some of the reserved cooking liquid if the purée needs thinning, then fluff up with a fork.

Scalloped Carrots and Corn

This simple casserole is always popular when served as a vegetable at a buffet party. It can be prepared in advance then heated just before you serve it, needing no attention during this time. It doesn't spoil if it has to wait for late arrivals either, so it is a useful dish.

For 6 servings:
3 Tbsp olive oil
2 onions, chopped
3 Tbsp plain flour
¹/₂–1 tsp curry powder
1 tsp salt
1 tsp sugar
1 cup (250 ml/8 fl oz) liquid from corn, topped up with milk
about 1 cup canned whole kernel corn
about 1 cup diced cooked carrots
2 Tbsp butter
2 cups 5 mm (¹/₄ in) bread cubes

Put the oil in a pot, add the onion, stir, then cover and cook gently for 5 minutes, until tender but not browned. Add the flour, curry powder, salt and sugar. Drain the liquid from the corn and make it up to 1 cup with milk. Add half the liquid and bring to the boil, stirring constantly. Add the remaining liquid and bring to the boil again, stirring all the time. Fold in the corn and carrots. Turn into a sprayed, medium-sized ovenware dish.

Melt the butter, then remove it from the heat and toss the bread cubes in it. Spread the bread over the vegetables. Refrigerate until needed.

When required, bake uncovered at 190°C (375°F) for 30–45 minutes. Serve with grilled meat or poultry and a green salad.

Variation: Replace the carrots with cooked celery, peas, green beans or broccoli.

Orange-Glazed Carrots

For 2–3 servings:
3 medium (or more small) carrots
1 tsp cornflour
1 tsp sugar
1 tsp wine vinegar
2 Tbsp orange juice

Trim and slice carrots, and simmer in a small amount of unsalted water until tender. Drain, reserving the liquid.

In the order given, mix the remaining ingredients to a paste. Add ¹/₄ cup reserved liquid (and water if necessary). Pour over the carrots in the pan, and heat until the glaze evaporates, thickens and coats the carrots.

Carrot and Parsnip Purée

Slice about equal quantities of thinly peeled carrots and parsnips. Put the carrots into the pot before the parsnips.

Cook in a little water, tightly covered, until the vegetables are just tender. Drain, reserving the liquid. Mash or chop in a food processor, adding a little butter, plenty of pepper, and a little nutmeg and salt and sugar if necessary. If dry, add some of the reserved liquid.

Kumara Patties

For 2–4 servings:
300 g (10½ oz) kumara
oil
1 egg
2 spring onions, finely chopped
1 tsp ground cumin
1 tsp oreganum
½ tsp salt
2 Tbsp plain flour

Scrub the kumara, trim off the thin ends, and lightly oil them. Bake at 200°C (400°F), or microwave on High (100%) power, until the flesh gives when pressed, as a baked potato does when cooked. Chop into fairly small pieces. This quantity should fill a 2-cup measure when tightly packed.

Using a fork, beat together the egg, spring onions, cumin, oreganum and salt. Add the kumara, mashing it into the mixture with the fork, then beat in the flour. Form into 8 flat cakes or patties.

Heat a little oil in a non-stick pan and cook the patties over moderate heat until golden brown on both sides, and heated through to the middle.

Serve with coleslaw or a lettuce-based salad as a complete meal for two, or serve with pork for four.

Kumara and Corn Patties

Serve these as a vegetable dish with pork chops, sausages, roast poultry (or other meats) or serve as part of a vegetarian meal.

For 3–4 servings:
500 g (1 lb 2 oz) kumara
1 onion, roughly chopped
2 cloves garlic, chopped
1–2 corn cobs (optional)
2 spring onions, chopped
1–2 tsp green curry paste
about ½ tsp salt
2–3 Tbsp chopped fresh coriander
1 large or 2 small eggs
3 Tbsp self-raising flour

Peel the kumara thinly using a potato peeler, cut roughly into 2 cm (¾ in) slices, then put in a pot with just enough water to stop them burning while they cook. Add the onion and garlic, and a light sprinkling of salt, cover, and cook over moderate heat until the kumara is just tender when pierced with a sharp knife. Drain, then finely chop the vegetables in the pot with a sharp knife. You should have about 3 cups.

For easiest cooking, microwave the unpeeled corn cobs, allowing 3 minutes per cob. Remove the outer layers, then cut the kernels from the cobs and mix through the kumara with the spring onion, curry paste, salt and coriander. (For

children, use the smaller amount of curry paste.) Stir in the egg with a fork, then sprinkle the flour over the cool mixture and mix again.

Using a dessertspoon, form the mixture into 12 rough-surfaced patties. Barely cover the bottom of a pan with olive or other oil, heat, then add half the patties. Cook uncovered over moderate heat for about 5 minutes, until nicely browned, then turn and cook the other side. Keep warm while cooking the remaining patties.

Serve immediately or reheat under a grill or in the microwave.

Eggplant Kebabs

When eggplant is cubed, threaded on skewers, marinated, then grilled or barbecued, it assumes an importance which it never has when simply sliced.

When marinated in the following mixture, eggplant makes a good accompaniment for food from almost any part of the world!

For 4 servings:
200 g (7 oz) eggplant, cut into cubes
2 cloves garlic, finely chopped
¼ cup (60 ml/2 fl oz) olive oil
2 Tbsp sesame oil
2 Tbsp wine vinegar
1 Tbsp light soy sauce
1 tsp honey
1 tsp grated fresh ginger
½ tsp salt

Combine all the ingredients and marinate the eggplants for about 30 minutes. Thread cubes of eggplant onto wooden skewers that have been soaked for a few minutes in cold water.

Grill or barbecue until the cut flesh is evenly golden, about 10 minutes. Turn frequently and brush with extra marinade during cooking.

Leeks in Cream Sauce

For 4 servings: (Photo p. 198)
2–4 leeks
¼ cup (60 ml/2 fl oz) cream
1 Tbsp Dijon mustard
1 tsp fresh dill (optional)
½ tsp salt
pepper to taste
2 Tbsp chopped parsley

Wash the leeks thoroughly, making sure there is no dirt between the leaves. Cut into 1 cm (½ in) rings, using all the white parts and some of the green. Steam in a little water in a tightly covered pot until tender but still attractively coloured. Drain well.

Whip the cream with the mustard, dill, salt and pepper until thickened but not stiff. Just before serving, toss the warm leeks in the cream mixture, and garnish with chopped parsley.

Savoury Stuffed Mushrooms

This is a good, easy way to make stuffed mushrooms, and each is piled with a well-flavoured mixture.

For 4–6 servings:
12 brown mushroom caps
2 slices stale bread
50 g (2 oz) butter, at room temperature
4–6 anchovies
1 cup fresh parsley
2–3 large cloves garlic, peeled
black pepper to taste
juice of ½ lemon
about 2 Tbsp grated Parmesan cheese (optional)
chopped bacon or strips of red pepper (optional)

Turn the oven to 220°C (425°F). Wash the mushrooms only if they are gritty; do not peel. Cut across each mushroom, removing most of the stem and the frilly edge of the cap. Put the caps, stem up, in a shallow dish lined with baking paper or Teflon.

Put the stems and trimmings in a food processor with the crumbled bread. Add the butter, anchovies, parsley, garlic, pepper, lemon juice and optional Parmesan. Process until mixed, using the metal chopping blade, then divide the mixture between the mushrooms. Top with a few pieces of chopped bacon or strips of red pepper if you like, and bake for 10–12 minutes.

Serve warm or hot as appetisers or vegetables.

Sautéed Mushrooms

Sautéed mushrooms are delicious, but they can absorb a great deal of butter before they soften and cook. This way you can get very good results with a small amount of butter.

For each serving:
1 tsp butter
1 clove garlic, finely chopped
about 1 Tbsp dry white wine
chopped parsley and/or thyme
pepper
cornflour
salt

Heat the garlic in the butter, then add whole, halved, quartered or sliced mushrooms, and the wine. Cover and cook over high heat, adding more wine if the pan looks dry before the mushrooms soften and produce liquid. Add herbs to taste.

When the mushrooms are wilted, lightly thicken the liquid with cornflour paste, and coat the mushrooms. Raise the heat to evaporate excess liquid, and add a little salt to taste, if necessary.

Okra and Tomatoes

Okra is an interesting vegetable that looks very beautiful when sliced thinly across the pods. The cut pods contain a sticky substance which thickens the cooking liquid. Vary the proportions to suit yourself when making a mixture like this.

1 large onion, preferably red
butter or oil
6–10 okra pods
about 1 cup chopped fresh or canned
  tomatoes
¹/₂–1 tsp sugar
salt
hot pepper sauce

Chop the onion and cook until tender, but not browned, in as little butter or oil as possible. Cut the okra into 5 mm (¹/₄ in) slices and add to the onion. Cook for 2–3 minutes, then add tomatoes, sugar, a sprinkling of salt and a dash of hot pepper sauce. Cook a little longer, until the okra is tender but still bright green. Thin the sauce with a little water or tomato juice if it thickens too much. Adjust seasonings to taste.

Serve with plainly cooked steak, sausages, chicken or any grilled or barbecued meat, or spoon over pasta or rice.

Orange-Glazed Pumpkin Cubes

Pumpkin is one of our inexpensive, everyday vegetables – easy to take for granted. This is a pity, because its smooth texture, bright colour and sweet flavour are often popular with children. Try it lightly sprayed with oil and roasted in small cubes, or dress it up with a spicy orange glaze.

For 4 servings:
500–600 g (1 lb 2 oz–1 lb 5 oz) pumpkin
1–2 Tbsp butter
3 Tbsp marmalade
¹/₄ tsp thyme, ¹/₂ tsp ground coriander
  seed, or 1 tsp grated root ginger
chopped chives or spring onions

Remove the seeds from the pumpkin, scooping them out with a dessert spoon. Cut it into several pieces, remove the skin, then cut into 1 cm (¹/₂ in) cubes. Place these in a non-stick frypan with about ¹/₂ cup of water. Cover and cook over high heat until the pumpkin is barely tender. Test often since it may cook in 3–4 minutes. Remove the lid and let the last of the water evaporate, if it has not already done so.

Add the butter and marmalade. As soon as the butter melts, turn the pumpkin cubes in the mixture to coat evenly. Leave over low heat, stirring or shaking often.

Sprinkle with the thyme, coriander or ginger, and toss again. Serve as soon as possible, with grilled or barbecued meat.

Barbecued Vegetable Kebabs and vegetables cooked on a solid barbecue plate

Barbecued Vegetable Kebabs

Cut vegetables such as carrots, cauliflower, red and green peppers, parsnip, pumpkin, kumara and zucchini into chunky 2 cm (³/₄ in) cubes. Quarter larger onions or use whole small onions.

Pre-cook all vegetables by boiling them until barely tender in lightly salted water.

Thread on skewers in colourful combinations, adding quick-cooking mushrooms and lengths of spring onions if desired. Brush with melted butter, olive oil or seasoned oil and barbecue, turning so all sides brown evenly. Brush with a glaze in the last minute of cooking, if you like. Serve hot or warm.

Roast Yams

Little pink yams look like a child's drawing of clouds at sunset. They are related to oxalis and seem to grow and spread almost as easily. Plant a few of the yams that you buy as a vegetable, and see for yourself!

To roast yams, scrub them and put in a shallow baking dish. Drizzle or brush on a little oil, but don't roast them in a bath of oil. Roast uncovered at 180°C (350°F) for about 30 minutes, until tender.

Yams that are cut in half lengthways before cooking will cook more quickly, as you might expect, and the cut surface will brown attractively.

Cooked Vegetable Platters

Summer Squash

This is the American name for the zucchini family, whatever their colour, shape and size. They require very little cooking, especially early in the season.

Cut them into even pieces, cover and cook briefly with a little chopped garlic, water and butter, until barely tender. Aim to have all the cooking liquid evaporated when the vegetable is cooked.

Micro-Baked Tomato Halves   M

For 4 servings:
500 g (1 lb 2 oz) fairly large, red tomatoes
2 tsp butter
sugar
salt
basil, thyme, spring onions or parsley

Halve the tomatoes and place them close together, cut-side up, in a shallow baking dish. Dot the surface with butter; sprinkle with sugar, salt and herbs.

Microwave uncovered on High (100%) power for 2–4 minutes, until the tomatoes are just soft. The cooking time will vary with the temperature, and the ripeness and size of the tomatoes.

Sliced Microwaved Tomatoes   M

Arrange thickly sliced tomatoes on a buttered dish. Sprinkle with salt, sugar, pepper, chopped spring onions or other herbs. Microwave on High (100%) power until hot but not too soft, allowing about 30 seconds per tomato. Watch carefully to prevent overcooking.

Easy-Cook Tomatoes

This is an easy way to enjoy tomatoes when they are plentiful.

For each serving:
1 tsp butter
pinch each of salt and sugar
chopped parsley, spring onion or basil, if available
about 1 tsp cornflour in 1 Tbsp water (optional)

Quarter or halve tomatoes lengthways, cut out the tough stem-end core, and heat in a covered frypan with the butter, salt and sugar. Add parsley, spring onion or basil. If you like, thicken with cornflour paste.

Serve on pasta, rice or toast. For a more substantial meal, spoon the tomatoes over a poached egg or over sliced cooked sausages on pasta or rice.

Note: Out of the tomato season, heat, season and thicken canned tomatoes in the same way, using juice from the can instead of water.

Zucchini Ribbons (Photo p. 60)

A mixture of green and yellow zucchini is particularly attractive.

For 6 servings:

8 green and/or yellow zucchini
2 ripe tomatoes
1 clove garlic, finely chopped
3 Tbsp white wine vinegar
¼ cup (60 ml/2 fl oz) olive oil
2 Tbsp finely chopped fresh basil
½ tsp sugar
¼ tsp salt
pepper to taste

Chop the ends off the zucchini and cut them into thin ribbons using a potato peeler, or into matchsticks with a vegetable knife. Place in a large sieve, lower this into a pan of boiling water and cook for 30 seconds to 1 minute, until half cooked but not completely soft. Drain and cool.

Peel the tomatoes and remove the seeds, then chop the flesh into small cubes. Mix the remaining ingredients together in a screw-top jar and shake to mix.

Put the zucchini and tomato in a shallow salad bowl, and pour over the dressing. Toss gently to coat, and serve.

Waist-Watcher's Zucchini

Try this as a dieter's lunch or a vegetable.

For 4 side servings:

500 g (1 lb 2 oz) zucchini
¼–½ (60–125 ml/2–4 fl oz) cup water
2 cloves garlic, chopped
½ tsp each chicken and green herb stock powder, or ½ tsp salt
1 tsp cornflour
1 Tbsp cold water
¼ cup chopped parsley
black pepper to taste

Slice or shred the zucchini. Cook for 2–5 minutes, depending on the size of the pieces, with the water and garlic. Just before serving add the stock powders or salt and enough cornflour and water paste to thicken the juices. Sprinkle generously with the parsley and lots of black pepper.

Roasted Summer Vegetables (Photo p. 196)

Use amounts and types of vegetable to suit yourself. Quarter peppers of several colours, removing the seeds and pith, cut the stems of mushrooms level with their caps, cut eggplant into 1 cm (½ in) slices, zucchini into 1 cm (½ in) diagonal slices, and small red onions into quarters lengthways.

Brush vegetables on both sides with plain or seasoned olive oil. Cook in a double-sided contact grill preheated to medium for about 5 minutes, OR cook under a regular grill, turning half way through, for 10–15 minutes, OR roast uncovered at 200°C (400°F) for 20–30 minutes, removing mushrooms before other vegetables if necessary.

Brush with olive oil mixed with your favourite pesto, or with Tex-Mex Dressing (p. 345) before serving if desired.

Barbecued Summer Vegetables

Many summer vegetables taste very good when barbecued. They may have a slightly chewier texture than you are used to, but this can be an advantage rather than a failing. If you are intending to use your barbecue for other foods, consider cooking several vegetables on it as well. Adjust the heat and baste the vegetables frequently, so they don't burn before they cook.

Choose a colourful mixture of summer vegetables, such as red onions, eggplants, zucchini, red and yellow peppers, etc., and cut them into chunky pieces. Quarter onions so the pieces are held together by the root.

Brush with Seasoned Oil (below) and barbecue about 12 cm (5 in) from the heat, turning frequently so the vegetables cook before they burn. Allow vegetables to brown but not burn on the edges.

Seasoned Oil

½ cup (125 ml/4 fl oz) olive oil
2 cloves garlic, peeled
6 basil leaves, chopped
2 Tbsp fresh thyme
2 Tbsp fresh rosemary

Put all the ingredients in a food processor fitted with the metal chopping blade. Process until finely chopped. Leave to stand for at least 10 minutes then strain, discarding the flavourings.

Cooked Vegetable Platters

Vegetables are an important part of any dinner, and deserve as much care and attention as the main food being served.

Although you may make a point of keeping fresh fruit and vegetables in your refrigerator, or even growing them in your garden, you may find that they go uneaten unless you bring them out, cut them up, and present them on the table in an attractive way. Vegetables for two, on a small serving plate, can be presented as attractively as vegetables on a large platter, for a crowd.

Even the most ordinary vegetable can be given extra appeal with a little thought. If you have a large crop of one vegetable in your garden, or can buy a vegetable cheaply in bulk, you will have to use your imagination if you want your family to eat it several times a week until it is finished.

Take carrots as an example. If you grow them, pick and cook the thinnings for a special treat. If you have enough, freeze some, complete with some of the green stalks. Mature carrots do not freeze well, but baby carrots do. Young carrots need only a short cooking time, and are very tender and sweet. Cut mature carrots in rings sometimes, in strips at other times, and cook them whole when you can

allow the extra time. Experiment with your food processor and see the many different ways you can shred or chop carrots. Lying them flat in the feed tube and pressing down with the pusher fairly firmly, you can produce excellent julienne strips in a fairly short time. Carefully seasoned carrot purée or mashed carrot is interesting too. Make mixtures of carrots and other vegetables using small cubes sometimes and strips at others. Experiment with raw carrots, as dipping sticks or in shreds, and make salads with cooked carrots in dressing.

Most vegetables taste best when cooked until they are barely tender, in the smallest amount of water you need to stop them drying out. Whether they are cooked in a pan or in a microwave oven, you will find they need no salt during cooking if there is no water to throw out at the end of cooking time.

My own favourite way of serving vegetables which have been cooked like this is to add a tiny amount of butter, some freshly ground nutmeg or pepper, often a squeeze of lemon juice, and a few finely chopped herbs. If you vary the herbs, and occasionally add toasted sesame seeds or other finely chopped nuts, you can produce interesting vegetables with very little time and trouble.

Side Salads

A side salad should add interesting flavour, colour and texture to a meal. It is easy to get into a rut where salads are concerned, using the same few salad vegetables and dressing day after day! If you feel that your salad-making could do with a shake-up, this section should offer you a variety of new ideas.

In many cases the amount of dressing given in recipes on the following pages is more than you need for one salad, because I feel it is a waste of time making tiny quantities. Use just as much as you need to coat the vegetables and refrigerate the rest for later use.

Caesar Salad

Caesar salad is justifiably popular as a starter, side salad or main. Always make it it with a crisp, firm-leafed lettuce. Use cos (romaine) for first choice for crispness and bright leaf colour. If this is not available, use chunky pieces of iceberg lettuce in preference to soft-leaved green lettuce.

For 4–6 servings:
1 cos (romaine) lettuce
1/4–1/2 cup freshly grated Parmesan cheese
1/2–1 cup croûtons (p. 344)

Dressing
1 egg
1 clove garlic
juice of 1 lime or lemon
2 anchovy fillets
1 tsp Dijon or mild mustard
about 1/2 tsp salt
freshly ground black pepper
1/4–1/2 cup (60–125 ml/2–4 fl oz) olive oil

Wash the lettuce and roll up the damp leaves in a length of paper towels. Chill for several hours, or overnight, so the leaves are dry and cold when used.

Combine all the dressing ingredients except the oil in a food processor or blender. Blend until smooth then, with the motor running, add oil in a slow, steady stream until the dressing is as thick as pouring cream. Season to taste.

To assemble the salad, arrange whole or torn leaves in a large salad bowl. Just before serving, drizzle over the dressing, toss if desired, then sprinkle with the croûtons and Parmesan.

Variations: For a lighter dressing, leave out the egg. For Chicken Caesar Salad, serve larger portions, and add 50–100 g (2–31/2 oz) cooked chicken per serving.

Caesar Salad

Asparagus Salad

For 4 servings:
16–20 spears freshly cooked asparagus
1 Tbsp wine vinegar
1 Tbsp lemon juice
1/2 tsp salt
1 tsp Dijon or mild, smooth mustard
1/4 cup (60 ml/2 fl oz) olive or canola oil
2 Tbsp fresh or sour cream
1 Tbsp chopped parsley or chives
1 hard-boiled egg, chopped, or 1/2 red
 pepper, sliced

Drain the asparagus, but do not let it dry out. Measure the vinegar, lemon juice, salt, mustard and oil into a screw-top jar. Shake to mix, add the cream and herbs and shake again.

Arrange the asparagus on a platter or on individual plates, with the heads pointing in the same direction. Spoon over the dressing and garnish with chopped hard-boiled egg, or strips of red pepper.

'Taste of the Tropics' Salad

The dressing on this salad is wonderful. It seems particularly good on avocados and pawpaws (papayas), which have a melting texture. The peanuts and mild red onion make the texture more interesting.

For about 4 servings:
1 avocado
1/2 pawpaw or 1/2 small rock melon
1 small red onion, finely chopped
about 1/4 cup roasted peanuts, chopped
 coarsely

Dressing
2 Tbsp finely chopped fresh basil
2 tsp lime juice
2 tsp lemon juice
2 Tbsp fish sauce
1 Tbsp honey
1 Tbsp Thai chilli sauce

Deseed and peel the avocado and pawpaw or melon and cut them into small cubes or wedges. Add the onion and peanuts.

Combine all the dressing ingredients in a screw-top jar and shake well. Gently toss about half the dressing through the salad, taking care not to break up the avocado and pawpaw. Taste and add more dressing if necessary.

Halve avocados by cutting around them, then twisting the halves gently. To remove the stone, chop a sharp knife into the stone in the halved avocado and twist the knife.

Avocado with Mediterranean Dressing

Give avocados star status with this dressing! Serve as a starter course or side salad.

For 4 servings:
2 ripe avocados

Dressing
2 Tbsp olive oil
1/4 cup pinenuts
4 sun-dried tomatoes, chopped
2 tsp balsamic or wine vinegar
1 clove garlic, very finely chopped
1/4 tsp salt
freshly ground black pepper to taste

Warm a little of the olive oil in a frypan, add the pinenuts and heat until golden brown. Add the rest of the oil and the remaining dressing ingredients, then put aside until required.

Just before serving, halve the avocados and remove the stones. Spoon dressing into the cavities and serve promptly.

Wilted Cucumber Salad

For 4–6 servings:
1 telegraph cucumber
brine made with 1 tsp salt and 1 cup
 water
1 Tbsp toasted sesame seeds
1 tsp sugar
2 spring onions, chopped
1 small clove garlic (optional)
2 Tbsp wine vinegar
pinch of chilli powder

Halve the cucumber lengthways. Scoop out the seeds using a small teaspoon. Cut into thin slices and stand these in the brine for 10 minutes. Drain and pat the softened slices dry.

Crush the sesame seeds with the sugar in a pestle and mortar. Mix the cucumber with the spring onion, garlic, vinegar, chilli powder and sesame/sugar mixture.

Bean Salad

I keep changing the proportions of this useful, do-ahead salad, which I have made for years! It keeps for two or three days, is a good companion to plain tomatoes or avocados, and a tasty addition to filled rolls.

For 3–4 servings:
*1 can (310–400 g/11–14 oz) mixed beans
   or kidney beans
1/4 red onion, chopped
3 Tbsp olive or canola oil
2 Tbsp wine vinegar
1 Tbsp sugar
1/2 tsp ground cumin
1/2 tsp salt
about 1 cup chopped peppers (any colour)
1/4 cup chopped celery, optional*

Tip the beans into a sieve, saving about 2 Tbsp of liquid from the can if possible. Rinse under a tap.

Tip the beans into a container and add the next 6 ingredients. Add the reserved bean liquid or 1 Tbsp water, and mix gently until the sugar dissolves.

Cut the peppers and celery into 5 mm (1/4 in) cubes, stir into the bean mixture and leave for at least 15 minutes. Serve with a slotted spoon, so the remaining salad is covered with dressing. Refrigerate for up to 3 days, adding chopped parsley when serving, if you like.

'Brocauli' Salad

This salad of lightly cooked broccoli and cauliflower can be made at most times of the year. Eat it as soon as you coat the cooked vegetables with dressing, or make it up to 24 hours ahead.

For 4 servings:
*200–250 g (7–9 oz) prepared broccoli
250–300 g (9–10 1/2 oz) prepared
   cauliflower*

Dressing
*1/4 cup (60 ml/2 fl oz) olive or canola oil
3 Tbsp white wine vinegar
1 clove garlic, finely chopped
1/2 tsp oreganum, crumbled
1–2 tsp Dijon or mild, smooth mustard
salt and pepper to taste*

Cut the vegetables into bite-sized pieces, discarding any tough outer skin, then boil in a little lightly salted water until tender-crisp. Do not overcook. Cool to room temperature in very cold water, then drain and refrigerate in a plastic bag if not using immediately.

Put all the dressing ingredients except salt and pepper into a screw-top jar and shake well. Season to taste.

To keep the broccoli bright green, toss the vegetables in the dressing just before serving. For more flavour, but olive-coloured broccoli, mix the dressing and vegetables as soon as they are prepared and leave to stand.

Shredded Carrot Salad

This salad is very popular with children.

For 2 servings:
*200 g (7 oz) carrots
1 Tbsp oil
1 Tbsp orange juice
1 Tbsp very finely chopped parsley, spring
   onions, fresh basil, dill or other herbs
sugar and salt to taste*

Shred the carrots, making long matchsticks if you have the right sort of cutter. Toss with the oil, juice and herbs. Taste, add a sprinkling of sugar and salt, and taste again. When you have the balance right, refrigerate for 30 minutes, then toss again, drain off any liquid and serve.

Carrot Salad

Use this tasty carrot mixture as a salad, relish or sandwich filling.

For 4 servings:
*2 large carrots, shredded coarsely
1 spring onion, finely chopped
2–4 Tbsp finely chopped fresh mint or
   coriander
1 tsp finely grated root ginger
2 Tbsp lemon juice*

Toss all the ingredients together. Use immediately or refrigerate in a plastic bag for up to 2 days.

Memorable Coleslaws

Coleslaw is an amazingly useful and versatile salad which doesn't call for anything exotic or expensive! Its ingredients will keep in the refrigerator for days and are readily available throughout the year. It is one of the few leafy salads which may be made ahead, so it is suitable for pot-luck meals and picnics. Picky young eaters often like coleslaw because they know what it is. As well, coleslaw need never be boring because you can make so many variations.

For basic coleslaw, simply shred a quarter of a drum-head cabbage very finely, coarsely grate a scrubbed carrot or two, and toss the two together with your favourite coleslaw dressing – mine is Sesame Dressing (p. 345).

• Other suitable additions are thinly sliced celery, peppers, cauliflower and spring onions. Bean and pea sprouts give coleslaw a lovely, slightly nutty flavour.
• For sweetness add small cubes of unpeeled apple tossed in lemon juice, sultanas, currants or small, dark raisins.
• Grated cheese is a popular addition to basic cabbage, carrot and celery coleslaw.
• Add toasted seeds and nuts for a change.

Two-Minute Noodle Coleslaw

Partially break up the noodles from a packet of 2-minute noodles. Place on foil and heat under a moderate grill until the noodles turn golden brown (1–2 minutes). Break into smaller pieces and toss through coleslaw that has been tossed with Sesame Dressing (p. 345), just moments before it is to be eaten. Note: Don't do this too often since these noodles are usually fried in palm oil (a saturated plant oil) before you get them.

Easy Oriental Coleslaw

Using quantities to suit, shred cabbage and celery and grate carrot, by hand or in a food processor. Add bean sprouts if you have them, a few chopped roasted peanuts, and just enough Sesame Dressing (p. 345) to moisten everything. Serve immediately.

Marinated Florence Fennel

Florence fennel looks rather like celery with a swollen base and feathery leaves. It can be sliced like celery and used in salads, but it tastes particularly good when cooked, left to stand in an oil and vinegar dressing, then served warm or at room temperature.

Trim the feathery side leaves. Remove any tough or discoloured outer leaves, then cut the fennel in half from top to bottom. Cut each half in 2, 3, or 4 lengthways wedges, depending on its size. Lay the wedges in a covered pan with about a cup of water and a little salt. Simmer until the outer stalks are fairly tender, 5–20 minutes, depending on age, then drain off half the water. Add 1/4 cup (60 ml/2 fl oz) white wine vinegar and 1/4 cup (60 ml/2 fl oz) salad oil. Add 1/2 tsp sugar, then adjust other seasonings to taste. Sprinkle generously with chopped parsley, then cover and leave until required. Serve at room temperature.

Mixed Green Salad

No two of my green salads are the same as I use a wide variety of salad vegetables.

Choose from:
mixed young salad leaves (mesclun); iceberg lettuce, chopped; young spinach leaves; young nasturtium leaves; lamb's lettuce leaves; young celery leaves; watercress leaves; snow pea shoots; mild onion rings; cucumber, sliced thinly; green peppers; rocket leaves; mustard and cress; spring onions, sliced; avocado, sliced.

Prepare a selection of leaves. For best results, after removing damaged parts, stems etc., wash by immersing in a sink or container of cold water. Shake to remove most of the water then lie the leaves on a clean, dry teatowel or a long length of paper towels. Roll up like a sponge roll and refrigerate until needed (up to 12 hours).

Elizabeth's Favourite Salad

Just before serving, tip the dried, chilled leaves into a salad bowl, drizzle with Cumin Dressing (p. 208) or Rice Salad Dressing (p. 208). Toss to coat the leaves lightly and evenly.

Serve with any vegetarian, poultry or fish dish, for lunch or dinner.

Elizabeth's Favourite Salad

My granddaughter Elizabeth, given the ingredients and a sharp knive, makes this ever-popular salad willingly and efficiently, at the drop of a hat! It's good with almost any main course, or for lunch.

For 4 servings:
1 Tbsp lemon juice
1 tsp sugar
1/4 tsp salt
1 large avocado
2–3 firm, red tomatoes
10 cm (4 in) length telegraph cucumber
about 2 cups chopped crisp-leaf lettuce
1 or 2 spring onions
1 Tbsp olive oil
pepper to taste

Mix the lemon juice, sugar and salt in the bottom of a fairly large salad bowl. Remove the skin and stone from the avocado, cut it into 1 cm (1/2 in) cubes and turn gently in the lemon juice without breaking up.

Cut the tomatoes into slices 1 cm (1/2 in) thick, then into 1 cm (1/2 in) cubes. Discard excess juice and place on the avocado, without tossing. Cut the unpeeled cucumber in 1 cm (1/2 in) cubes and sprinkle over the tomato. Cut firm iceberg lettuce into 1–2 cm (1/2–3/4 in) squares, without separating the leaves, or cut romaine hearts into 1 cm (1/2 in) slices. Slice spring onions thinly and add to the bowl, without mixing.

Cover with cling film and refrigerate for up to an hour. When serving, sprinkle with the olive oil, freshly ground pepper, add a little extra salt if necessary, and toss gently to coat the ingredients without bruising or breaking them.

Quick Tomato Salad

For 2–4 servings:
3–4 ripe, red tomatoes
2–3 spring onions, chopped
about 2 Tbsp finely chopped mint
juice of 1 lemon
about 1 tsp sugar
1/4–1/2 tsp salt
few drops hot pepper sauce

Slice the tomatoes or cut them into chunks. Toss with the remaining ingredients. Cover and refrigerate for 15–30 minutes, then turn to coat the tomatoes with the dressing, and serve.

Greek Salad

This salad goes well with barbecued or grilled lamb kebabs, but is substantial enough for a main meal on a hot night, especially if you serve it with interesting, crusty bread rolls.

For 2 servings:
about 20 cm (8 in) telegraph cucumber
4 large tomatoes, sliced or cubed (or whole small tomatoes)
1 small red onion, sliced
oreganum
about 50 g (2 oz) feta cheese, sliced or cubed
about 10 black olives
olive oil
black pepper
lemon wedges (optional)

Cut the cucumber in half lengthways and scoop out the seedy area with a teaspoon. Cut into 1 cm (1/2 in) chunks and divide between 2 plates. Top with the tomato, and onion rings.

Sprinkle with oreganum, add the feta, and toss the olives over the top. Drizzle over olive oil, and add black pepper to taste. Squeeze lemon wedges over the salad if you like.

Note: Since olives and feta are salty, you will probably not need to add salt.

Spiced Tomato (and Cucumber) Salad

Really simple salads never go out of fashion. Serve this at picnics and barbecues, or with curries.

For 4–6 servings:
3–4 firm, red, flavourful tomatoes
1/4–1/2 telegraph cucumber (optional)
2 spring onions or 1/4 red onion
1 Tbsp sugar
1–2 tsp ground cumin
1/2 tsp salt
chopped fresh coriander (optional)

Cut the tomatoes and unpeeled cucumber into neat 1 cm (1/2 in) cubes. Slice the spring onions thinly or finely chop the red onion. Place the prepared vegetables in a serving dish.

A few minutes before serving, sprinkle with the sugar, cumin and salt, then mix gently. (Use the smaller amount of cumin if not using cucumber.) Sprinkle with fresh coriander, if available, and serve cold.

Kumara Salad

Kumara make very satisfying salads. Vary the additions to suit yourself. The dressing is good with or without the sour cream or yoghurt.

For about 6 servings:
3 orange-fleshed kumara (750 g/
 1 lb 10 oz)
1/4 cup sultanas
1 firm banana
1/4–1/2 cup shredded coconut (optional)
2 spring onions
roasted peanuts or cashews (optional)

Dressing
1/4 cup (60 ml/2 fl oz) olive or canola oil
1/4 cup (60 ml/2 fl oz) white wine vinegar
1 tsp Dijon or mild mustard
1–2 tsp grated root ginger
1/2 tsp salt
2 tsp sugar
1/4 cup (60 ml/2 fl oz) lite sour cream or
 plain low-fat yoghurt (optional)

To make the dressing, shake the first 6 ingredients in a screw-top jar. Add sour cream or yoghurt and shake again for a creamy dressing.

Scrub the kumara and microwave until tender. When cool enough to handle, peel and chop into bite-sized pieces.

Pour boiling water over the sultanas to plump them up then drain well and mix through the kumara. Add sliced banana, coconut, and spring onions.

Toss through half the dressing, adding more when serving if you wish. Sprinkle with chopped nuts.

Quick Vegetable Salad with Cumin Dressing

This is a salad that you can put together in a few minutes, with ingredients from your store cupboard. The dressing brings the vegetables to life!

For 6 servings:
1 can (425 g/15 oz) green beans
 or 2 cups chopped cooked green beans
1 can (440 g/15 oz) whole kernel corn
1 cup diced celery
1/2–1 red pepper, diced or 1 cup sliced
 cooked carrots

Dressing
1 Tbsp onion pulp
1/2 cup (125 ml/4 fl oz) salad oil
1/4 cup (60 ml/2 fl oz) cider vinegar
2 tsp ground cumin
1 tsp celery salt
1 tsp garlic salt
2 tsp oreganum
pinch chilli powder

Drain the beans and corn. Put in a serving dish with the celery and red pepper or carrots.

Make onion pulp by scraping the cut surface of an onion with a teaspoon. Place in a screw-top jar with the remaining dressing ingredients and shake well.

Just before serving, toss the vegetables with as much of the dressing as you like. Refrigerate the rest for up to a week.

Cumin Potato Salad

This interesting dressing adds zest to a potato salad.

Dressing
1/2 cup (125 ml/4 fl oz) olive or other oil
1/4 cup (60 ml/2 fl oz) wine vinegar
2 tsp ground cumin
1 Tbsp onion pulp
3/4 tsp salt
2 tsp crumbled oreganum
1 clove garlic, very finely chopped
black pepper to taste
hot pepper sauce to taste

Shake all the ingredients together in a screw-top jar (to get onion pulp, scrape the surface of a cut onion with a teaspoon).

Pour as much as you like over warm potato cubes or slices and cooked peas or chopped green beans. Sprinkle with finely chopped parsley, coriander, spring onions or chives.

American Potato Salad

This is a wonderful salad if made with good mayonnaise!

cooked waxy or new potatoes
wine vinegar
olive or other oil

For each 2 cups sliced or cubed potatoes:
1 spring onion, chopped
about 2 Tbsp chopped parsley
1/4 cup (60 ml/2 fl oz) mayonnaise
1 tsp wine vinegar
1 hard-boiled egg, chopped
 chives

For best flavour, moisten the cooked potatoes with equal amounts of wine vinegar and olive or other oil before they cool. Slice or cube the cooked potatoes into a bowl, and add the spring onion, 2 Tbsp parsley, the mayonnaise, 1 tsp wine vinegar and 1/2 the chopped egg. Mix gently, without breaking up the potato too much. Thin if necessary with a little water, lemon juice or milk. Serve at room temperature with the remaining egg, more parsley and chives.

Kiwifruit Salad

Try this as a curry accompaniment.

For 4 servings:
4 ripe kiwifruit
1 cup alfalfa, bean or pea sprouts
1 Tbsp lime or lemon juice
2 Tbsp olive or canola oil
1 clove garlic, finely chopped
1 tsp chopped red chilli
2 Tbsp chopped fresh coriander
1/4 tsp salt

A short time before serving peel the kiwifruit and slice it into a salad bowl. Sprinkle with the sprouts.

Mix the remaining ingredients together, taste, and add a little sugar if necessary. Just before serving, drizzle the dressing over the salad and toss lightly.

Variation: Replace the kiwifruit with apples, pears or fresh pineapple.

Spinach Salad

This popular salad may be served as a side salad, or in larger amounts as a full meal.

For 4–6 servings:
400–500 g (about 1 lb) small, good
 quality spinach leaves
4–6 rashers lean bacon
250 g (9 oz) button mushrooms
a few canned water chestnuts (optional)
avocado (optional)
1/2–1 cup small croûtons (p. 344)

Dressing
1/4 cup (60 ml/2 fl oz) canola or olive oil
about 1/4 tsp salt
1 tsp sugar
2–3 tsp Dijon or mild mustard
2 Tbsp wine vinegar

Wash the spinach carefully in a sink of cold water so you don't bruise it. Roll it in a clean teatowel or length of paper towels and refrigerate, making sure the leaves are dry before using them.

Remove rinds and grill the bacon until crisp. Chop or break into small pieces and set aside.

Mix the dressing ingredients together in a screw-top jar. Leave at room temperature until required.

Just before serving, wash, dry and slice the mushrooms, drain and slice the water chestnuts and slice the avocado. Put with the cold, dry spinach and the bacon in a large serving bowl or plastic bag, then pour over the dressing and toss gently until the spinach is coated. Arrange in individual bowls and sprinkle generously with croûtons. Serve promptly.

Rice Salad

Rice makes substantial salads which may be made some time before they are needed. On standing, their flavour becomes milder as much of the dressing is absorbed by the rice, so it pays to make plenty of dressing, and keep some aside to add to the salad just before it is served.

For 4–6 servings:

2–3 cups cooked brown or white rice
1 or 2 carrots, shredded
1 or 2 stalks celery, thinly sliced
about 6 radishes, sliced (optional)
2 or 3 spring onions, thinly sliced
¼ cup chopped parsley
chopped fresh herbs to taste

Dressing

½ cup (125 ml/4 fl oz) olive or canola oil
¼ cup (60 ml/2 fl oz) wine or cider vinegar
1 Tbsp Dijon or other mixed mustard
2 tsp sugar
1 tsp salt

Make this salad with leftover or freshly cooked rice; it should be cold or at room temperature.

Fold the carrot, celery and spring onion into the rice. Add the parsley and any other fresh herbs you like.

Shake the dressing ingredients together in a screw-top jar. Toss about half the dressing through the salad about 30 minutes before it is to be eaten, stopping when you like the way it tastes. For best flavour, add extra dressing just before serving. Serve as part of a buffet or picnic meal, with your favourite chicken dish.

Variations: Add chopped sultanas and chopped roasted peanuts with the carrot. Mix enough sesame oil into the dressing to give it a nutty flavour.

Add sweet chilli sauce for hotness and extra sweetness.

Roasted Pepper Salad

(Photo p. 173)

Peppers prepared this way have a wonderful flavour and interesting texture, quite unlike raw peppers.

4–6 plump, fleshy red, yellow or orange peppers
¼ cup (60 ml/2 fl oz) lemon juice
¼ cup (60 ml/2 fl oz) olive oil
freshly ground black pepper
salt to taste

Heat the whole peppers under a grill, over a barbecue rack, or on a gas burner, keeping them close to the heat and turning them as their skins blister and blacken. OR roast for about 30 minutes in a 220°C (425°F) oven.

When they have blackened in patches and blistered fairly evenly, put the peppers in a paper or plastic bag to stand for 5–10 minutes, then hold them, one at a time, under a cold tap and peel or cut off the skin. The flesh underneath should be brightly coloured and partly cooked.

Quarter the peeled peppers and trim away the seeds and pith. Cut into even shapes, put them in a shallow dish, and coat with the lemon juice and oil, using less or more depending on the amount of flesh you have. Refrigerate until you need them, up to 2 days.

Sprinkle with freshly ground pepper, add salt to taste, and serve at room temperature.

See also

Main Dish Salads, pp. 156–163
Tabbouleh, p. 170
Peanutty Rice Salad, p. 171
Spiced Rice Scramble, p. 171
Brown Rice Salad, p. 173
Pasta Salad, p. 173
Mexican Salad, p. 176
Pasta with Summer Sauce, p. 180

Quick Vegetable Salad with Cumin Dressing

Warm Weather Desserts

We all know that desserts are not an essential part of life! For many children, however, a dessert is the best part of dinner, and is something to be looked forward to several times a week. This chapter contains a number of simple, child-pleasing desserts, all of which have been thoroughly tested by my family! It also contains a number of desserts that are suitable when you have friends for dinner.

Tangelo and Banana Jelly

Jellies made from fruit juice, eaten the day they are made, are a treat well worth trying.

For 4–6 servings:
2 level measuring Tbsp gelatine
1 cup (250 ml/8 fl oz) cold water
1 Tbsp finely grated tangelo rind
1/4 cup (60 ml/2 fl oz) golden syrup
1/4 cup sugar
1 1/2–2 cups (375–500 ml/12–16 fl oz)
  tangelo juice
juice of 1 lemon
1/4 cup (60 ml/2 fl oz) sherry or extra juice
extra water if needed
1–2 bananas, very thinly sliced

Soften the gelatine in the cold water. While it is softening, add the tangelo rind, golden syrup and sugar.

After 5 minutes, heat the mixture enough to melt the gelatine and dissolve the sugar. Bring almost to boiling, but do not boil.

Strain to remove rind. Mix in the tangelo and lemon juice and the sherry, made up to 4 cups (1 litre/32 fl oz) with extra water or juice. Check that the mixture is only slightly warm, then add the banana and leave to cool. Spoon into individual dishes if desired.

> Always measure gelatine carefully, using level, standard measuring spoons, otherwise the texture of the pudding will be quite spoilt.

Tamarillo Delight

Tamarillos have a definite, quite strong flavour that some people do not like. In this recipe I think I have tamed this flavour without changing it.

For 4 servings:
4 tamarillos
1/2 cup (100 g/3 1/2 oz) brown sugar
1/4 cup (55 g/2 oz) white sugar
2 tsp gelatine
2 Tbsp cold water
1 cup (250 ml/8 fl oz) cream
1/2 tsp vanilla essence

*Tangelo and Banana Jelly and
Tamarillo Delight*

Pour boiling water over the tamarillos and leave to stand for 5 minutes. Replace the hot water with cold, and peel off the skins. Chop the fruit into a heavy pot, cover, and simmer gently until tender, about 10 minutes. Add the sugar and mash with a potato masher until the fruit is puréed and the sugar dissolved.

While the fruit is cooking, mix the gelatine with the cold water and leave it to stand and soften for 5 minutes. Once softened, tip it into the hot fruit and stir until it dissolves. Stand the pot in a large container of ice and water to cool it quickly.

Whip the cream with the vanilla. When the fruit starts to thicken, fold in the cream, leaving it a bit streaky if you like. Spoon into a bowl or individual dishes, and leave to finish setting in a cool place.

Variation: Spoon some of the jelly into bowls then fold the cream into the rest.

Lemon Jelly

Try this recipe if you have a lemon tree in the garden.

For 4 servings:
3/4 cup sugar
1 1/2 Tbsp gelatine
2 cups (500 ml/16 fl oz) cold water
3 lemons

Stir the sugar and gelatine together in a pot, add the water, stir again, and leave to stand while you peel the yellow skin from the lemons using a floating blade peeler. Do not peel off any of the white pith. Drop the peel into the gelatine mixture, then heat it until it comes to the boil and the gelatine dissolves. Remove from the heat.

Squeeze the lemons, which should yield 1/4–1/2 cup juice. Add to the pot with any pulp and seeds, stir well, then pour the jelly through a sieve into the dish in which it will set.

Serve with very cold, lightly whipped cream, plain or flavoured with thinly sliced preserved ginger, and some of the ginger syrup that surrounds it.

Variation: Replace about 1/2 cup sugar with golden syrup.

Whip 1/2–1 cup (125–250 ml/4–8 fl oz) cream. Stir into the jelly when it has set as thick as an unbeaten egg white.

Chocolate Velvet Pudding

I have made this pudding since my children were pre-schoolers. My grandchildren enjoy it just as much as their parents did!

For 8 servings:
1 can (400 g/14 oz) unsweetened
  condensed milk (evaporated milk),
  chilled*
2 Tbsp gelatine
1/2 cup (125 ml/4 fl oz) milk
6 level Tbsp cocoa
1 cup sugar
1/2 cup (125 ml/4 fl oz) water
1/2 tsp vanilla essence

*The condensed milk must be very cold if it is to beat up to a good volume. Refrigerate it 24 hours ahead; freeze it in a bowl until it is cold enough to form ice crystals; or if you are really short of time chill it quickly by covering it with cold water and lots of ice-blocks.

Stir the gelatine and milk together in a small bowl and leave to soften while you mix the cocoa and sugar in a pot. Add the water to the pot and bring to the boil, stirring all the time. Remove from the heat and stir in the softened gelatine and the vanilla. Stand the pot in cold water to cool the mixture until it is thick but not set. (If it sets, warm it until it liquefies again.)

Beat the chilled condensed milk in a large bowl until very thick and frothy. Slowly pour in the cold (but still liquid) gelatine mixture, beating all the time.

As soon as the two mixtures have been blended, pour into 2 large or about 8 individual bowls to set. Cover and refrigerate for up to 2 days. (The pudding will darken as it stands.)

Serve with canned peaches and lightly whipped cream, or top with whipped cream and chopped nuts.

Norwegian Trifle

This is a quickly made dessert of my childhood! As long as you have ice-blocks handy it can be made shortly before it is to be served. Ice-blocks in a little cold water provide a very quick way of cooling the gelatine mixture to the correct consistency.

4 level tsp gelatine
1/2 cup (125 ml/4 fl oz) cold water
2 eggs, separated
1/4 cup (60 ml/2 fl oz) liquid (sherry, rum,
* passionfruit pulp, fruit juice or syrup)*
1/2 cup sugar
2–4 Tbsp raspberry jam (optional)
1/2–1 cup whipped cream
crystallised cherries and/or toasted
* almonds (optional)*

Sprinkle the gelatine over the cold water in a small pot. When it has softened, after 2 or 3 minutes, heat it until the mixture is quite clear and free from grains. Stop heating before the mixture boils.

Add the egg yolks and the liquid to the warm gelatine and beat with a fork until well mixed. Stand the pot in a larger container of ice-blocks and water until it thickens to the consistency of unbeaten egg white.

Meanwhile, beat the egg whites until foamy, add the sugar and beat until meringue-like, forming peaks with turned tips. Fold carefully but thoroughly into the jelly, then turn into individual bowls or 1 large dish. Leave to set.

When set, spread raspberry jam over the top, then whipped cream, and decorate with toasted almonds and cherries if desired.

Dragon's Breath Pudding

Here's a traditional Danish dessert which my children named when I told them not to breathe out near candles on the table in case they caught alight! In fact the rum adds flavour, not alcohol, but the idea is fun!

For 4–6 servings:
4 level tsp gelatine
1/4 cup (60 ml/2 fl oz) cold water
1/4 cup (60 ml/2 fl oz) rum
3 eggs, separated
1/4 cup sugar
1 cup (250 ml/8 fl oz) cream

Sauce
200–250 g (7–9 oz) raspberries, fresh or
* thawed*
1/2 cup sugar
2 Tbsp cornflour or custard powder
1 cup (250 ml/8 fl oz) water
red food colouring

Sprinkle the gelatine over the cold water in a fairly small pot. Leave to stand for 2–3 minutes until it swells and softens,

then add the rum and stir over a very low heat until the gelatine dissolves. Remove from the heat and add the egg yolks. Stir to mix, then heat very gently until the mixture thickens (this happens before it boils). As soon as it thickens, remove from the heat and stand the pot in a bowl of ice-blocks in cold water. Remove when the mixture is thick but not set.

Beat the egg whites until foamy, then add the sugar and beat until the peaks turn over at the tops when the beater is lifted up. Fold the egg whites into the gelatine mixture. Beat the cream until thick (using same unwashed bowl and beater), then fold it gently but thoroughly into the mixture.

Spoon into an oiled mould or bowl that holds about 5 cups (1.25 litres/40 fl oz). A patterned ring mould looks best and sets fastest, but an ordinary bowl will do. Stand it in an ice-and-water mixture until it sets, then dip in warm water and invert onto a plate. Pour a little sauce over the pudding and pass the rest round separately.

To make the sauce, mix together the fruit, sugar, cornflour or custard powder and water. Bring to the boil, stirring constantly, then remove from the heat, add colouring if desired, and leave to cool.

Fruit Sorbet

If you have an icecream churn or a food processor, you can make interesting no-fat icecreams that have a lovely smooth texture but are made of little more than fruit. Use 1/4 cup sugar to 1 cup liquid, or 1/4 cup sugar to 1 1/4 cups thick fruit purée.

For about 4 servings:
1 tsp gelatine
1/4 cup (60 ml/2 fl oz) cold water
finely grated rind of 1 orange
1/4 cup sugar
about 1 cup puréed rock melon, apricots,
* peaches, etc.*
flesh of 1 orange
2 Tbsp lemon juice

Mix the gelatine with 1 Tbsp of the water. Leave to stand for about 5 minutes.

Heat the remaining water with the grated rind and sugar, boil for 1–2 minutes, then stir in the softened gelatine.

Purée the orange flesh with enough ripe rock melon (or other fruit) to yield about 1 1/2 cups purée altogether. Add the lemon juice, and stir together with the syrup.

Icecream machine method: freeze the mixture following the manufacturer's instructions. This mixture, put into a well-frozen canister fitted with an electric churning blade, will freeze to a softish 'snow-freeze' consistency in about

20 minutes. If the canister is then replaced in the freezer without the blade, the consistency will be suitable for scooping balls after about 20 minutes more.

Food processor method: freeze the mixture until solid in the coldest part of the freezer, break or chop the block into pieces and process until light-coloured, smooth and free from lumps. Work quickly so the soft mixture does not melt. To freeze so that it can be scooped, return to the freezer for about half an hour.

The sorbet will become too solid to scoop on prolonged freezing, but it can be returned to soft smoothness by more processing.

Variation: Spoon the mixture into plastic moulds, and refreeze them to make delicious fruity ice-blocks.

Note: The most efficient way to grate the orange is to peel off all the coloured skin thinly, with a floating blade peeler, then chop the peel with the sugar in a food processor.

One-Whip Orange Icecream

This recipe makes a delicious icecream with a slightly fruity flavour. It can be made in a few minutes, but the unsweetened condensed milk should be refrigerated for several hours beforehand.

For 6–8 servings:
1 orange
1 lemon
1 can (400 g/14 oz) unsweetened
* condensed milk, chilled*
1/4 cup sugar
1/2 can (200 g/7 oz) sweetened condensed
* milk*

Grate the orange and lemon rind, squeeze the juice from each, and mix them in a small basin.

In a large bowl beat the unsweetened condensed milk until it is thick. Add the sugar and beat again. If using an electric mixer, use the fastest speed.

Pour the sweetened condensed milk into the orange and lemon mixture and mix thoroughly. Add to the unsweetened condensed milk, beating just enough to combine the ingredients.

Pour into 2 icecream trays and freeze until firm. A second beating is not necessary.

Mocha Ripple Icecream

This recipe makes a rich, one-whip icecream which may be served straight from the freezer, since it never sets rock hard.

For about 1.5 litres (48 fl oz):
2 eggs, separated
1/2 cup sugar
1 Tbsp water
1 1/4 cups (310 ml/10 fl oz) cream, whipped
1 Tbsp instant coffee
1 Tbsp cocoa
1–2 Tbsp boiling water
1 tsp vanilla essence

Beat the egg whites until stiff, add half the sugar and beat again. In another bowl, beat the yolks with the water and remaining sugar until thick and creamy. Fold the whites, yolks and whipped cream together carefully but thoroughly. Spoon half the mixture into a freezing container.

Mix the instant coffee, cocoa and boiling water to a paste, then add the vanilla. Stir into the remaining mixture, then pour this over the unflavoured mixture. Stir to get a ripple effect. Freeze for several hours until firm.

Variation: Add 2 Tbsp rum or brandy with the vanilla.

Frozen Lemon Cream

The lemony flavour of this frozen dessert seems to take away from its richness.

For 6 servings:
1/2 cup wine or malt biscuit crumbs
2 Tbsp butter, melted
3 eggs, separated
1/2 cup sugar
juice of 1 lemon
rind of 1/2 lemon
2 Tbsp sugar
1 cup (250 ml/8 fl oz) cream

Line a 23 cm (9 in) round cake tin (preferably with a removable base) or a loaf tin with baking paper. Mix the biscuit crumbs with the melted butter and spread half the crumbs on the paper.

Mix the egg yolks, 1/2 cup sugar, lemon juice and rind together in a bowl and heat over boiling water, stirring frequently, until it thickens. Cool over an ice and water mixture.

Beat the egg whites until foamy. Add 2 Tbsp sugar and beat until the peaks turn over at the tips when the beater is removed.

Beat the cream until thick, then fold the 3 mixtures together carefully but thoroughly. Pour carefully onto the crumbs, then sprinkle the remaining crumbs over the top. Cover with another piece of baking paper or foil and freeze until set.

Turn out onto a flat plate for serving. Cut into wedges or slices.

Homemade Vanilla Icecream

Every now and then I make my own rich, creamy, dense, vanilla icecream. It doesn't take long to mix or freeze, if you have an efficient freezer.

Although you can keep this icecream for some time in the freezer, it does tend to go very hard. It is at its best eaten the same day it is made (or softened by food processing about 15 minutes before serving). The mixture is too rich and sweet to freeze well in an icecream maker.

1 Tbsp cornflour
pinch of salt
1/2 cup sugar
1 cup (250 ml/8 fl oz) milk
1 egg
1/2 tsp vanilla essence
about 1 cup (250 ml/8 fl oz) cold cream, lightly whipped

Before you start, half-fill a large bowl with cold water and ice-blocks, ready to cool the pot after the mixture thickens.

Stir together in a medium-sized pot (or in a bowl over boiling water) the cornflour, salt and sugar. Mix in the milk and egg, then stir with a wooden spoon or whisk over moderate heat until the custard thickens. (Do not let the egg curdle.)

Immediately stand the pot in the iced water, add the vanilla and stir frequently until it is very cold. (This is the quickest way to chill it.) Then put the pot in the freezer until it has ice crystals around the edge and bottom.

Fold in the cream. Freeze in a covered container, in the coldest part of the freezer, for several hours, or until firm enough to scoop out. If the icecream hardens on longer storage, stand it in the refrigerator for 15 minutes before serving.

Variations: For berry icecream, purée or mash about 1/2 cup frozen strawberries or raspberries. Sieve to remove raspberry seeds if you like. Swirl the purée through the partly frozen mixture, after the cream has been added.

Add chopped walnuts, pecans, roasted hazelnuts, etc.

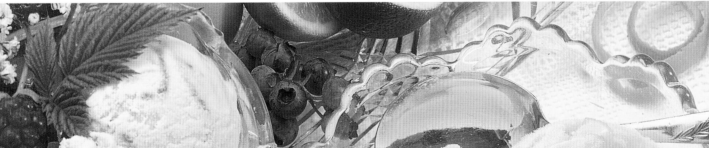

Homemade Vanilla Icecream with berries and Fruit Sorbet

Icecream Cake

It is not hard to make a decorative icecream cake based on bought icecream!

For about 12 servings:

½–1 cup sultanas (or other dried fruit), chopped
¼ cup (60 ml/2 fl oz) sherry or rum
1 Tbsp instant chocolate
1–2 tsp rum essence
1 tsp instant coffee
½ tsp almond essence
½ tsp vanilla essence
½ tsp cinnamon
¼ tsp ground nutmeg
¼ tsp ground cloves
1 or 2 egg whites
2 Tbsp castor sugar
300 ml (10 fl oz) cream
½ cup icing sugar
1 litre (32 fl oz) softened vanilla
  icecream*
toasted almonds (optional)
extra whipped cream for decoration

* Take the icecream from the freezer 20–30 minutes before mixing.

Chop the sultanas using a knife, mincer or food processor. Mix the sherry or rum with the dried fruit and the next 8 flavourings. Leave to stand for 30 minutes or longer so the liquid can soak into the fruit.

Beat the egg white until foamy, then add the castor sugar and beat until the peaks just turn over. Beat the cream until fairly thick, then add the icing sugar and beat again. (Do not whip until very stiff.)

Combine the softened icecream with the other mixtures and turn into a 23 cm (9 in) cake tin lined with baking paper. Freeze until firm.

Unmould and roll the sides with toasted almonds if desired. Place on a serving plate. Decorate with extra whipped cream, then freeze again.

Variations: Replace the first 10 ingredients with 1 cup Christmas mincemeat.

Scoop the mixture into individual dishes like ordinary icecream.

Nutty Lace Baskets

Make these brandy-snap-like baskets for special people, a special occasion and perhaps when you want to show off a little! Make them just a few hours before you serve them, or store them in airtight containers.

They require a little experimentation – this is not a recipe for beginners! Make sure you use standard measuring cups and spoons.

For about 12 baskets:

1 cup freshly shelled walnuts
½ cup sugar
¼ cup plain flour
125 g (4½ oz) butter
½ tsp almond essence
2 Tbsp milk

Turn the oven to 190°C (375°F). Put the walnuts, sugar and half the flour in the food processor and process with the metal chopping blade until the nuts are very finely chopped.

Melt the butter until liquid, then remove from the heat and stir in the essence, milk and the nut mixture. Cover an oven tray with baking paper or a Teflon liner and put a dessertspoon of the mixture in the middle. Spread it out evenly with the back of a spoon.

Place in the middle of the preheated oven and bake for about 5 minutes, until golden brown. If the mixture burns at the edges before it is golden in the middle, turn down the oven a little. If it runs too far, add some of the reserved flour.

Using a greased fish slice, lift the lacy disc from the tray as soon as you can pick it up without breaking it, and drape it over a small bowl or glass to shape.

Adjust the oven temperature and the

Nutty Lace Baskets, One-Whip Orange Icecream (p. 212)

mixture until you get everything right. Once you do, put 2 biscuits at a time on each oven tray, using 2 trays so you can bake one lot while you shape others.

Just before serving, fill with icecream etc. and garnish attractively.

Note: If you don't have a food processor, replace the walnuts with 100 g (3¹/₂ oz) ground almonds. You may need no flour at all with finely ground almonds.

Lacy Wafers

These are delicate little biscuits that are delicious served with icecream, or a cup of after-dinner coffee.

For about 50 7-cm (3-in) wafers:
125 g (4¹/₂ oz) butter
1 cup sugar
1 cup rolled oats
1 egg
1 tsp vanilla essence
¹/₂ tsp almond essence

Turn the oven to 170–180°C (325–350°F). Melt the butter in a microwave dish or shallow pot. When it is liquid but not hot add the sugar, rolled oats, egg and essences, and stir together until well mixed.

Cover a baking tray with baking paper or a Teflon liner. Put level teaspoons of the mixture on the tray, 10 cm (4 in) apart – use an ordinary household teaspoon but make sure it is not heaped. Bake for 5–8 minutes.

As they cook the biscuits first spread, then start to bubble, then brown. It does not matter if the outside rim is a little darker than the middle, but if the outside darkens while the middle is still very pale, reduce the heat a little.

Like brandy snaps, the biscuits are too soft to handle when they come out of the oven, and harden as they cool. Peel the Teflon or baking paper away from the biscuits as soon as they are cool enough to work with.

If you can work fast enough, and do not cook too many biscuits at once, press them into shallow patty pans to form baskets, or lie them over a rolling pin so they are curved. Biscuits that harden too soon may be reheated briefly to soften them.

When cold, store in an airtight container.

Sherried Fruit Sauce

This sauce turns plain icecream into something special.

2 Tbsp custard powder
2 Tbsp brown or white sugar
2 Tbsp sherry
1 cup (250 ml/8 fl oz) fruit syrup or juice*
1–2 Tbsp butter

* Make fruit syrup or juice up to 1 cup with water if necessary. Use the syrup drained from canned or bottled fruit.

Mix the custard powder, sugar and sherry together in a pot. Add the syrup or juice and stir over medium heat until the sauce thickens. Add the butter and stir well.

Serve warm over icecream, sprinkled with finely chopped nuts if you like.

Blueberry Topping

Crushed blueberries make a wonderful dark reddish-purple sauce.

For 4 servings:
1 pottle blueberries
¹/₂ cup (125 ml/4 fl oz) white wine or water
¹/₄ cup (60 ml/2 fl oz) orange juice
2 Tbsp sugar
1 tsp cornflour
pinch of cinnamon

Put half a cup of blueberries and all the other ingredients in a pot. Heat, stirring all the time, until the berries pop, about 3–4 minutes. Mash into a sauce with a fork or potato masher. Taste and add extra sugar if you like a sweeter sauce. Remove from the heat and immediately stir in the remaining blueberries.

Serve over icecream, wedges of cream sponge, or as a cheesecake topping.

Variation: To make an even more spectacular sauce, stir in 1 cup of raspberries while the sauce is still slightly warm.

Blackcurrant and Raspberry Sauce

Keep a supply of frozen raspberries and blackcurrants in your freezer so you can make this at any time of the year! You don't need to thaw the fruit before using it.

For about 6 servings:
2 cups blackcurrants (fresh or frozen)
1 cup sugar
2 Tbsp custard powder
1 cup (250 ml/8 fl oz) water
1 cup raspberries (fresh or frozen)
2–3 Tbsp rum or brandy (optional)

Put blackcurrants in a pot, add sugar and custard powder, stir well, then add the water and bring to the boil, stirring constantly. Remove from the heat and drop in the raspberries. Stir occasionally as they thaw. Cool the mixture; when it is at room temperature, stir in the rum or brandy.

Serve at room temperature over icecream, chill and serve with a little chilled cream or yoghurt, or spoon over slices of sponge roll, shortcake or pie.

Hot Spiced Peach Sauce

This warm sauce turns icecream into a cold-weather dessert!

25 g (1 oz) butter
¹/₄ cup brown sugar
1 tsp mixed spice
1 can (425 g/15 oz) sliced peaches
2 Tbsp sherry (optional)

Heat the butter and sugar in a large frypan until the sugar has melted and the mixture is bubbly. Add the spice, peaches (with juice) and sherry, stirring often until the syrup is thick.

Serve over icecream placed on a slice of sponge roll. Top with chopped nuts if desired.

Orange Caramel Sauce

Popular with all age groups!

For 4–6 servings:
2 Tbsp butter
1 cup brown sugar
¹/₂ cup (125 ml/4 fl oz) cream
1 orange, grated rind and juice

Melt the butter in a small pot. Add the sugar and cream and cook over medium heat, stirring until it comes to the boil. Add the grated rind, reduce the heat and cook gently for 3–4 minutes, or until all sugar lumps have disappeared and the sauce is a rich golden brown.

Remove from the heat and add the orange juice. While warm, pour into a small jug and serve with icecream.

Blackberry Sauce

If you like the flavour of blackberries but don't like a mouthful of seeds, make this sauce which has a beautiful colour and delicious blackberry flavour.

For about 4 servings:
2 cups blackberries
³/₄ cup (185 ml/6 fl oz) water
¹/₄ cup sugar
2 Tbsp custard powder
¹/₄ cup (60 ml/2 fl oz) water
1 Tbsp white, cider or wine vinegar, or 2 Tbsp lemon juice

Simmer the blackberries in ³/₄ cup water for 3–4 minutes, until the berries are soft. Mix the remaining ingredients to a smooth paste in a bowl. Stir in the hot blackberries, then transfer the mixture to the saucepan and stir over low heat until it thickens. Push through a sieve to get rid of the seeds. (If you use cultivated berries you will find sieving is unnecessary.)

Variation: For a special occasion, use ¹/₂ cup water instead of ³/₄ cup. Stir ¹/₄ cup sherry, port, brandy or liqueur into the sieved, warm sauce.

Best Berries

To see which fresh berry sauces give the best flavour and appearance I have done some experimenting. A cup of very ripe raspberries puréed with 1/4 cup (25 g/ 1 oz) of icing sugar, then sieved, did not taste as good as those puréed with 2 Tbsp castor sugar. If the purée was brought to the boil, then cooled, its flavour was much more intense and its colour very bright.

A cup of puréed raspberries, brought to the boil with 2 Tbsp castor sugar and 1 tsp cornflour, so that it thickened slightly, tasted best of all, and looked much nicer than either of the other sauces when it was cooled and spooned over icecream, carefully stirred through strawberries, or puddled under scoops of icecream. It also produced rave reviews when it was cooled and served over sliced ripe, raw peaches with very cold, lightly whipped cream mixed with apricot yoghurt. What's more, the cooked, lightly thickened sauce kept well in the refrigerator for several days.

Brandied Boysenberries

Keep a can of boysenberries on hand to make this easy, festive sauce.

For 4–6 servings:
1 can (455 g/16 oz) boysenberries
1/4–1/2 tsp cinnamon
pinch of ground cloves
2 Tbsp cornflour or custard powder
1/4 cup sugar
juice of 1 orange or 1/4 cup sherry
1–2 Tbsp brandy

Drain the boysenberries in a sieve, collecting the juice in a medium-sized pot. Add the cinnamon and cloves to the juice and boil them, uncovered, for 2–3 minutes.

Mix the cornflour or custard powder with the sugar and orange juice or sherry to form a smooth paste. Stir into the hot juice and simmer until smooth and thick. Put the sauce aside.

When ready to serve, warm the sauce, stirring frequently, until bubbling.

Stir in the drained berries carefully so they do not break up, then transfer to a serving dish. Warm the brandy, and pour it over the hot sauce.

Serve flaming sauce over scoops of icecream in individual dishes.

Note: For a more substantial dessert, put a slice of fresh or frozen sponge roll under the icecream.

Creamy Custard

This recipe is so easy that any custard-loving 10-year-old can make it without help.

For 4 servings:
3–4 level Tbsp custard powder
1/4 cup white or brown sugar
1 egg
2 cups (500 ml/16 fl oz) milk
1/2 tsp vanilla essence
1 Tbsp butter

Use standard measuring spoons for the custard powder; 3 Tbsp if you prefer a runnier custard, 4 Tbsp for a firmer mixture. Mix thoroughly with the sugar in a medium-sized pot. Break in the egg and mix well. Add the milk and vanilla.

Cook over moderate heat, stirring all the time. Add the butter as soon as the milk is warm enough to melt it. As soon as the custard thickens, take it off the heat. Serve warm or at room temperature.

Variation: Stir in a thinly sliced banana when the custard has cooled.

Chocolate Pear Custard

Pears and chocolate seem to be made to go together! This easy pudding is very popular with children.

For 4–6 servings:
2 Tbsp custard powder
3 Tbsp cocoa
3 Tbsp sugar
1 egg
1 1/2 cups (375 ml/12 fl oz) milk
1 can (425 g/15 oz) pears
1 Tbsp butter
1/2 tsp vanilla essence

Mix the custard powder, cocoa and sugar in a medium-sized pan. Beat in the egg, milk and juice from the pears. Bring to the boil, stirring constantly. When hot, add the butter and vanilla. Keep heating and stirring until the pudding is dark, thick and bubbling around the edges. Remove from the heat.

While the pudding cools, chop the pears into smaller pieces. Put into 4 to 6 individual dishes and pour over the pudding, or put the pudding into the dishes and put the pears on top.

Serve plain or top with a little runny cream, whipped cream or yoghurt and decorate with chopped nuts if you like.

Zabaglione

Zabaglione is an interesting, light and frothy special dessert for adults. Serve it over strawberries, or by itself, with crisp biscuits.

For 3–4 servings:
4 egg yolks
1/4 cup sugar
*1/4 cup (60 ml/2 fl oz) Marsala or 2 Tbsp
   sweetish sherry mixed with 2 Tbsp water*
1/4 cup (60 ml/2 fl oz) dry white wine

Combine the yolks and sugar in a stainless steel bowl, place it over a pot of

boiling water, and beat with a whisk until combined. Add the Marsala or sherry and water, and the white wine. Beat with the whisk for about 10 minutes, until the mixture heats up and gradually thickens. It will increase in volume while it cooks. (If you stop beating, the mixture will set on the sides of the bowl and form a type of scrambled eggs!)

When the mixture is thick enough to pile up, stop beating. If you want to serve it cold or warm, keep beating it until it cools down, over a container of cold water. Once cool, leave it untended.

Serve hot, warm or cold, by itself, in stemmed glasses, or spoon it over strawberries in stemmed dishes or small bowls.

Sabayon

I always enjoy measuring the sherry and sugar for this recipe. Choose the best half-shell – one without jagged edges.

For 3–4 servings:
4 egg yolks
5 half-shell measures sherry
2 half-shell measures sugar

Break the egg yolks into a heat-resistant glass or stainless steel bowl. Select an evenly broken shell, and use it to measure the sherry and sugar. Add these to the yolks. Beat until well combined, then heat over boiling water, beating constantly with an egg-beater or whisk for 10 minutes, or until the mixture is really thick and light.

Serve warm or cold, within an hour, in stemmed glasses or small dishes with crisp biscuits, or use as a sauce on cake.

Note: Try different wines for sabayons of different flavours. I like them all!

Praline Trifles

At a dinner party recently I served individual trifles which, to my surprise, really delighted my guests.

For 4 servings:

Praline
1/2 cup sugar
1/4 cup blanched almonds

Custard
1 Tbsp castor sugar
1 Tbsp cornflour or custard powder
3 large eggs
1/2 tsp vanilla essence
2 cups (500 ml/16 fl oz) milk

To assemble
about 120 g (4 oz) unfilled sponge
*2 Tbsp orange liqueur, sherry or fruit
   syrup*
1–2 cups raspberries
1 Tbsp castor sugar
whipped cream

Praline:

This is an important part of the pudding. It may be made some days before it is needed, if kept in a tightly closed screw-top jar.

To make praline, place the sugar and almonds in a shallow pan over low heat. Shake occasionally if you like, but do not stir. Leave over low heat until the sugar dissolves into a clear liquid, then cook at a slightly higher heat until the liquid has turned a rich brown colour. By this stage the almonds will have browned too.

Pour the mixture onto an oiled baking tray, a non-stick Teflon liner or buttered baking paper, with the almonds in a single layer. Cool. When cold and brittle, pulverise the nuts and toffee. Chop in a food processor, use a pestle and mortar, or put in a heavy plastic bag and bang with a rolling pin. However you do it, crush finely and evenly, then put in the airtight jar.

Custard:

Mix the sugar and cornflour or custard powder until smooth then add the eggs, vanilla and a little cold milk and beat to a smooth paste with a whisk or other stirrer. Make this mixture in a large microwave bowl, or in a pot with rounded corners. When quite smooth, add the remaining milk. Heat on High (100%) power in the microwave, stirring at regular intervals, or on moderate heat on the stove, stirring constantly. If you have kept the mixture well stirred, your custard should reach maximum thickness as soon as it bubbles around the edge. Give the thickened custard a final beat with a whisk and pour it through a sieve.

To assemble:

Cut the crusts from the sponge and break it into a bowl. Dampen with orange liqueur, sherry or fruit syrup then spoon into individual glasses, or one large bowl.

Putting a few berries aside for garnish, mix the raspberries and sugar together, breaking the berries only slightly. Arrange on the sponge. Pour or spoon over the cool custard.

At this stage you can refrigerate the trifles until close to serving time if you like. The praline is crunchy if it's put in and on the trifles a short time before they are eaten. If it is put in the trifle some hours before it is eaten it loses its crispness but still has a lovely flavour.

Whenever you choose, sprinkle praline quite thickly on top of the custard. Pipe on or spread with unsweetened, unflavoured, stiffly whipped cream. Refrigerate until serving time. A few minutes before serving, sprinkle a little praline on top of each trifle, and top with a few perfect raspberries.

Mexican Flans

Mexican Flans

These moulded caramel custards are a lower-fat variation of an old favourite. They are easy to make in bulk in deep muffin pans.

For 12 unmoulded custards:

1/2 cup sugar
4 large eggs
1/2 can (200 g/7 oz) sweetened condensed milk
2 1/2 cups (625 ml/20 fl oz) milk
1/2–1 tsp vanilla essence

Turn the oven to 150°C (300°F). Spray deep non-stick muffin pans with non-stick spray.

Put the sugar in a small, preferably non-stick frypan and heat gently, shaking the pan to move the sugar around. Do not stir. If the sugar starts to brown unevenly, lower the heat. (Dark brown caramel is bitter.) Pour the caramel into the prepared muffin pans, tilting to coat the bottoms evenly.

Beat together the eggs, condensed milk, milk and vanilla. Pour through a fine sieve into a jug, then pour into the muffin pans. Stand the tray in a roasting dish of hot water.

Bake uncovered for about 20 minutes, or until the centres feel firm and a sharp knife inserted in the middle of a custard comes out clean.

Cool to room temperature, then chill for at least 4 hours. Unmould carefully, pushing one side of the pudding down with your fingers until it flips over and sits caramel-side up on your cupped fingers. Slip onto individual dishes.

Serve with caramel liquid poured over each custard. Garnish with a fanned strawberry and a spoonful of lightly whipped cream if you like.

Old-Fashioned Rice Pudding

Mary Jane's Rice Pudding

Well-made rice pudding is delicious!

For 4–5 servings:

3 Tbsp short-grain rice
2¹/₂ cups (600 ml/20 fl oz) milk
1 Tbsp butter
2 Tbsp brown sugar
¹/₄ tsp salt
¹/₂ tsp vanilla essence

Mix the rice with the milk in a medium-sized pot. Add the butter and bring to the boil, then cover with the lid ajar, and simmer very gently until the rice is tender, about 30–40 minutes. Add the remaining ingredients and simmer a further 15–20 minutes. Taste and add extra sugar if necessary. Serve hot or cold.

Note: This pudding doesn't thicken up until the last 10 minutes of cooking; do not be tempted to add more rice. Thin the pudding a little before serving if necessary.

Old-Fashioned Rice Pudding

Show this golden-topped, creamy, old-fashioned rice pudding to pudding lovers like me and you may well be mobbed!

For 4 servings:

4 cups (1 litre/32 fl oz) milk
¹/₄ cup short-grain rice
about ¹/₄ cup white or brown sugar
1 vanilla pod or ¹/₂ tsp vanilla essence
1 strip orange peel (optional)
freshly grated nutmeg (optional)

Turn the oven to 150–180°C (300–350°F). Put the milk, rice and sugar into a baking dish that holds 4–6 cups (1–1¹/₂ litres/ 32–48 fl oz) and is about 20 cm (8 in) in diameter. Add the vanilla pod or essence and a strip of rind peeled from an orange with a potato peeler if you like a mild orange flavour. Grate a little nutmeg on top of the pudding before it goes into the oven if you like.

Bake uncovered, preferably without fan-bake, for about 1¹/₂ hours, stirring several times during cooking. A golden-brown skin will form on top as the pudding cooks. Stir this into the pudding every now and then, or remove it, depending on your taste. (Covering the pudding loosely with foil or baking paper will slow down skin formation.)

When the rice is very soft and the liquid is creamy, remove from the oven. Leave to stand for 15–30 minutes while it cools and thickens. Soon after taking it from the oven, remove and wash the vanilla pod for later use, and remove and discard the orange peel.

Serve warm, alone or with cooked or raw fruit and a dribble of cream, a scoop of plain vanilla icecream, or a spoonful of lightly whipped cream if desired.

Variation: Halve the amount of sugar and stir in about ¹/₄ cup sultanas or raisins, or ¹/₂ cup dates.

Junket M

Microwaved junket is easy – and children usually love it. My favourite junket has an odd (but good) combination of flavours.

For 4 servings:
*2¹/₂ cups (600 ml/20 fl oz) milk
2 Tbsp brown or white sugar
¹/₂ tsp vanilla essence
¹/₂ tsp almond essence
grated nutmeg
1 tsp rennet*

Measure everything except the rennet into a 1 litre (32 fl oz) Pyrex measuring jug (or similar). Microwave on High (100%) power until the mixture is at blood heat, about 2¹/₂ minutes.

Remove from the microwave, stir until the sugar has dissolved, and test the heat. If necessary, warm longer or cool to reach blood heat. Stir in the rennet then pour into individual dishes. Leave undisturbed at room temperature until the junket sets.

If you like, grate more nutmeg onto the surface of the junket before or after it sets. Refrigerate once set. Decorate with whipped cream and sliced bananas, passionfruit pulp, etc., if desired.

Note: For 1 serving, measure ³/₄ cup (185 ml/6 fl oz) milk and about a third of the flavourings into a dessert plate. Microwave on High (100%) power for 45–60 seconds, until the milk is blood heat, then stir in ¹/₂ tsp rennet.

If junkets don't set, it is usually because the milk has cooled down too much before the rennet can 'set' it. Microwave on High (100%) power for a few seconds, until the mixture warms and sets. (Do not overheat.)

For an easy test for blood heat, shut your eyes and put your little finger into the warm milk. If you can't feel when your finger goes into it, the milk is the right temperature.

Sago Cream

This delicious mixture is very popular with children and open-minded adults.

For 4–6 servings:
*¹/₂ cup sago (no more!)
3 cups (750 ml/24 fl oz) milk
¹/₄ tsp salt
¹/₄ cup brown sugar
2 eggs, separated
1 Tbsp white sugar
¹/₂ tsp vanilla essence*

Bring the milk and sago to the boil in a medium-sized pot, then simmer for 7–10 minutes, stirring occasionally. Add the salt and brown sugar, and bring to the boil again.

Mix a little hot sago with the egg yolks then pour them into the pot. Mix well and bring to the boil again, stirring all the time. Remove from the heat when boiling.

Beat the egg whites until foamy then add the sugar and beat until they form peaks that turn over at the top when the beater is lifted from them.

Fold into the hot sago with the vanilla, then tip the sago cream into serving dishes.

In summer put fresh strawberries or raspberries, slightly crushed and mixed with sugar, into the dishes just before serving, or make layers of fruit, sago cream and whipped cream for a treat.

Old-Fashioned Lemon Sago

An inexpensive dessert if you have a lemon tree in the garden.

For 4–6 servings:
*¹/₂ cup sago
3 cups (750 ml/24 fl oz) water
finely grated rind of 1 lemon
pinch of salt
¹/₂ cup (125 ml/4 fl oz) golden syrup
¹/₄ cup (60 ml/2 fl oz) lemon juice
1 Tbsp butter (optional)*

Put the sago and water in a medium-sized pot and bring to the boil, stirring all the time. Add the lemon rind and salt and cook gently, stirring occasionally, until the sago is clear, about 15 minutes. Stir in the golden syrup and lemon juice and remove from the heat. Add the butter and leave to cool. (The mixture will thicken on standing.)

Serve at room temperature with a little runny cream or yoghurt.

Tamarillo Sago

Tamarillo sago is popular with many children who find 'straight' tamarillo too strong.

For 4–6 servings:
*¹/₂ cup sago
2 cups (500 ml/16 fl oz) water
1–1¹/₂ cups chopped or sliced tamarillos
¹/₄–¹/₂ cup (60–125 ml/2–4 fl oz) orange,
  lemon or grapefruit juice
¹/₂ cup sugar*

Mix the sago and water in a medium-sized, heavy-bottomed pot and bring to the boil, stirring constantly. Simmer over very low heat for 5–10 minutes, until the sago is clear, stirring occasionally.

While the sago boils, prepare the tamarillos. Pour boiling water over the fruit, leave for 1–2 minutes, then pour cold water over them and skin them, OR halve them and scoop out the flesh with a sharp-edged teaspoon. Slice, chop or food process the flesh.

Add the citrus juice (or water). (The juice intensifies the red colour of the fruit.) Stir into the sago and simmer for 5 minutes, then add the sugar and remove from the heat.

Serve warm, preferably in stemmed glass dishes, with a little whipped or runny cream, fruity yoghurt or icecream.

Mini Pavlovas

Use this easy method to make these popular confections!

For 6 mini (or 1 large) pavlovas:
*1 cup castor sugar
2 tsp cornflour
¹/₄ tsp salt
1 tsp wine vinegar
¹/₂ tsp vanilla essence
¹/₂ cup (3–4) egg whites*

Turn the oven to 100°C (225°F). Using standard level cups and spoons for everything, measure the castor sugar, cornflour and salt into a clean, dry bowl. (Any trace of fat stops eggs beating up.) Stir together.

Add the vinegar and vanilla, then measure and add the egg whites, taking care to get absolutely no yolk in the mixture. Beat with an electric mixer at high speed for about 15 minutes, until a thick, non-gritty meringue forms. When you lift out the mixer blades, the peaks should stand up stiffly, or just bend over at the tips.

Shape the mixture into 6 mini pavs, almost as high as they are wide, on baking paper sheets, leaving space between them. Bake for 45 minutes, then turn off the oven and leave 15 minutes longer. Remove from the oven after this time.

Leave unwrapped, in a cool place, for up to 2 days. To serve, top with whipped cream and decorate with strawberries, kiwifruit, passionfruit or other fruit. Drizzle chocolate topping over strawberries, if desired.

Variations: If you prefer one large pavlova, bake for 1 hour and leave in the oven 15 minutes longer.

Use double quantities for a larger pav. Pile on baking paper or bake in a paper-lined round 20 or 23 cm (8 or 9 in) tin. Bake for 1¹/₄ hours then leave in the oven for 15 minutes.

Note: Because ovens vary, you may need to adjust cooking times. Pavlovas with space below the crust and compacted middles have been cooked too long. If the centres are not completely set, cook a little longer next time. Fan-bake for the first 10 minutes if you have this option. If fan-baking for the whole time, lower the temperature by about 10°C (50°F).

Strawberry Pavlova Roll

Don't despair if you can't make a pavlova! This pavlova roll is not only much quicker to cook, but it also looks interesting and impressive!

If necessary you can eat it half an hour after it goes into the oven, although it is really best to allow an hour, in case it takes longer to cool than you think.

For about 6 servings:
4 large egg whites
⅛ tsp salt
½ cup castor sugar
½ tsp vanilla essence
about 1 cup (250 ml/8 fl oz) cream
fresh strawberries

Turn the oven to 180°C (350°F) (or 170°C/325°F if using fan-bake).

Beat the egg whites, salt, sugar and vanilla together at high speed with an electric mixer until the mixture is stiff and the peaks of meringue stand upright, only a small tip turning over when the beater is lifted from them.

Line a sponge roll tin (about 23 x 33 cm/ 9 x 13 in) with a non-stick Teflon liner or baking paper, and spread the mixture over it evenly.

Bake for 10–15 minutes, until the surface is a light golden brown, the centre feels firm, and the mixture has puffed up. Take care not to overcook, as this shrinks the roll.

Wipe a sheet of baking paper over very lightly with soft butter, then sprinkle it with castor sugar. Remove the roll from the oven, turn it upside down onto the baking paper, and leave to cool. (The mixture will compact a little.)

When cold, spread with half the stiffly whipped, cold cream. Cover the surface of the cream with sliced strawberries, then roll up, using the paper to help you. It is usual to start rolling from a short side, forming a short, fat roll, but you can make a long thin roll if you prefer.

Place the roll, join down, on a long plate or board. Pipe the remaining cream decoratively along the top of the roll, then place a line of strawberries on it.

Cover loosely and refrigerate until serving, preferably the day it is made. Cut into slices with a serrated or sharp knife.

Note: This mixture should not be overcooked. Since ovens vary, be prepared to experiment, using a shorter cooking time if the cooked mixture shrinks excessively.

Economical Meringues

Although this seems a very odd mixture, I have never known it to fail. If completely dry, the meringues keep for weeks in an airtight container.

For 50–60 small meringues:
1 large egg white
¾ cup sugar
1 tsp vinegar
1 tsp vanilla essence
2 Tbsp boiling water

Turn the oven to 130–140°C (250–275°F). Stand a small bowl in a larger bowl of very hot water. Measure all the ingredients into the small bowl and beat with an electric beater until the mixture is smooth, stiff and piled high.

Run a piece of baking paper under the cold tap and place it wet-side down on a large oven tray. Using a forcer bag and star nozzle, a plastic bag with the corner cut out, or 2 teaspoons, shape the mixture into 50–60 small meringues. Bake for 1 hour or until dry right through.

Orange Mini Cheesecakes

Top these delicious little cheesecakes with strawberries, raspberries or passionfruit, depending on the season and availability.

Strawberry Pavlova Roll

For 10–12 servings:

75 g (2½ oz) plain, sweet biscuits
1½ Tbsp butter, at room temperature
1 Tbsp sugar
peeled rind of 1 orange
¾ cup sugar
500 g (1 lb 2 oz) cream cheese
3 large eggs
2 Tbsp orange liqueur or orange juice

Turn the oven to 150°C (300°F). Crumb the biscuits in a food processor. Add the butter and 1 Tbsp sugar and process until mixed. Press into 12 well-sprayed muffin pans.

In the unwashed processor, process the orange peel and ¾ cup sugar until the peel is finely chopped. Add the cream cheese in spoonfuls, the eggs and the orange liqueur or juice and process until smooth. Pour onto the crumbs in the muffin pans so each hole is almost full.

Bake for 15–20 minutes, or until the centres feel set. (Do not overcook.) Leave to stand for 5 minutes (they will shrink during this time) then go round each one carefully with a sharp knife. Place an oven tray covered with plastic, baking paper or a Teflon liner on top of the muffin tray and invert it carefully, then bang the lot against the flat surface on which you want to unmould the cheesecakes.

Serve at room temperature, topped with fruit, sprinkled with icing sugar and accompanied by whipped cream.

Dee's Ultimate Cheesecake

This is the best that I have ever made – or tasted!

For 8–12 servings:

1 packet (250 g/9 oz) digestive biscuits
100 g (3½ oz) butter
750 g (1 lb 10 oz) cream cheese
1 cup sugar
2 large eggs
1 tsp vanilla essence

Turn the oven to 160°C (325°F). Crumb the biscuits in a food processor or put them into a plastic bag and crush with a rolling pin.

Melt the butter and add the biscuit crumbs. Mix well and press onto the bottom and sides of a 20 or 23 cm (8 or 9 in) springform or loose-bottomed cake tin.

Beat the cream cheese and sugar until soft and fluffy. Add the eggs one at a time, then the vanilla. Pour the mixture into the prepared biscuit base.

Bake for 40–50 minutes, until the centre is firm, taking care not to brown the top too much. Leave in the oven to cool, then refrigerate until ready to serve.

Dee's Ultimate Cheesecake

To serve, pile fresh berries on top and sprinkle them with icing sugar. Spoon lightly whipped cream onto wedges.

Variation: Use fewer biscuits and less butter and coat only the base with them.

Bake for 1 hour, or until dry right through. When cold, store in airtight containers.

Summer Pudding

This is a delicious but practical pudding using up dry bread (fresh bread makes a pasty pudding). It can be made with a wide range of summer fruit. The fruit and juice are poured into a bread-lined bowl and left to stand until the juice seeps through the bread and the fruit thickens slightly. The pudding is usually turned out like a sandcastle, then cut into wedges and served with something creamy.

For 8–10 servings:

1 pottle (about 250 g/9 oz) each of
* raspberries, redcurrants and strawberries*
¾ cup sugar
8–10 slices day-old bread, crusts removed

You need about 3–4 cups of prepared fruit for a pudding which is to go in a bowl that holds 6 cups. Pick over the fruit carefully, and remove any stalks, leaves and imperfect bits.

Put the raspberries in a large pot with the sugar, bring to the boil and cook for about 1 minute. Stir in the redcurrants and the sliced strawberries. Mix gently to combine.

Line a 6-cup pudding bowl or Pyrex bowl first with a film of oil, then with the slices of stale bread, cut so they taper to fit the bowl. The bottom and sides of the bowl must be completely lined, so that the fruit is enclosed completely. Overlap the slices if you like but do not use too much bread.

Fill the bread-lined bowl with the fruit, but reserve some of the juice. Cover the fruit with a layer of bread, and trim away any of the bread lining the bowl which comes above the fruit. Place a saucer or plate smaller than the top of the bowl on the top piece of bread, and weigh it down with a can or something heavy. Refrigerate overnight.

To serve, carefully turn the pudding out onto a fairly large, flat serving plate. Brush the reserved syrup over any patches that are still light-coloured. Garnish with fresh berries, coating them with a dusting of icing sugar for a snowy effect. Serve with runny or lightly whipped cream.

Chocolate Mousse

This chocolate mousse is exceedingly rich and quite delicious.

For 8–12 servings:

500 g (1 lb 2 oz) good quality dark
* chocolate (not cooking chocolate)*
½ cup (125 ml/4 fl oz) hot water
2 tsp instant coffee
juice and zest of 2 oranges
3 eggs, separated

Heat the chocolate, water, coffee, orange juice and zest in the microwave on Defrost (30%) power until the chocolate has melted, 6–7 minutes. You should have a nice thick sauce. If you don't have a microwave oven, warm in a double boiler.

Remove from the heat, add the egg yolks and mix well.

Beat the egg whites until stiff and fold carefully into the mixture. Pour into 8–12 small glasses and refrigerate for at least 2 hours, or pour into a lined loaf tin, refrigerate for 1–2 days, then unmould and cut into slices.

Serve with chocolate curls (made by cutting a thin sliver of chocolate from the side of a warmed chocolate block), candied violets, mandarin segments and Apricot Balls (p. 347).

Kirsten's Chocolate Roll

As a child, my daughter Kirsten asked for this cake for every birthday party. It is quick but delicious.

For 6–8 servings:

3 large eggs, at room temperature
½ cup sugar
½ cup flour
2 Tbsp cocoa
1 tsp baking powder
1 Tbsp boiling water

Turn the oven to 230°C (450°F). Beat the eggs and sugar together until the mixture is very thick and creamy.

Sift the flour, cocoa and baking powder onto the egg mixture, then fold in carefully but thoroughly. Add boiling water and mix again. Spread the mixture evenly on a sponge roll tin (about 23 x 33 cm/9 x 13 in) lined with baking paper.

Bake for 8–10 minutes, or until the centre of the sponge springs back when pressed lightly with a finger. (Take care not to overcook.)

Working quickly, loosen the sponge from the sides of the tin, and turn it out onto a clean, old teatowel that has been wet, then wrung out as dry as possible. Lift the paper off the bottom of the sponge, and roll the sponge and cloth together, lightly but firmly. Roll either way, for a short,

thick roll, or a long, thin one. Stand the roll, still in the cloth, on a rack until cold then unroll carefully, spread with raspberry jam and whipped fresh cream or mock cream, and roll up again – without the cloth!

Sprinkle with icing sugar just before serving.

Chocolate Soufflé Roll

This light-textured spongy roll is rich and dark. It's not difficult to roll up if you make sure it doesn't overcook.

6 eggs, separated
½ cup sugar
½ cup cocoa

Turn the oven to 160°C (325°F). Line the bottom and sides of a sponge roll tin (about 23 x 33 cm/9 x 13 in) with baking paper or foil. Beat the egg yolks until creamy, add ¼ cup sugar and beat till it dissolves. Sift the cocoa and add gradually, mixing it in thoroughly.

In a separate bowl beat the whites to a stiff foam (until the peaks turn over), add the remaining sugar and beat until the peaks stand up. Fold the beaten whites carefully but thoroughly through the yolk mixture.

Spread the mixture in the prepared pan and bake until the centre feels firm and a toothpick poked into the centre comes out clean. Turn out onto a clean, dry teatowel sprinkled with icing sugar (or plain cocoa if you like a slightly bitter coating). Roll up immediately, incorporating the teatowel in the roll. Unroll when cold and carefully remove the towel. Spread the sponge with vanilla-flavoured whipped cream and re-roll.

Little Pots of Chocolate

This rich dessert is served in small quantities in stemmed glasses.

For 4–6 servings:

4 eggs, separated
1 Tbsp sugar
1 tsp vanilla essence
100 g (3½ oz) cooking chocolate

Beat the egg whites, add the sugar and beat until the peaks stand stiff and upright. Beat the yolks in another bowl with the vanilla.

Stand yet another bowl over a pot of hot, but not boiling water, break the chocolate into it and stir the chocolate. When it has melted, add the egg yolk and vanilla. Don't cook this, but mix before the bowl is removed from the hot water to prevent the chocolate setting again.

Now combine the whites and chocolate mixture, folding them together thoroughly. Divide the mixture between 4–6 glasses.

Chill overnight, or for at least 4 hours in the refrigerator. Top with brandy- or rum-flavoured sweetened whipped cream or plain whipped cream. Garnish with grated chocolate or chocolate curls made by cutting a thin sliver of chocolate from the side of a warmed chocolate block. Chill until serving.

Chocolate Fondue   M

People of all ages seem to enjoy sitting around a communal pot of Chocolate Fondue dipping into it. You may be surprised how quickly the fruit disappears! Be realistic – provide protection for clothes and furniture, or serve your fondue outside!

200–250 g (7–9 oz) dark, milk or cooking
* chocolate, or chocolate chips*
½ cup (125 ml/4 fl oz) cream
grated rind of 1 orange or 1–2 Tbsp
* brandy, rum or liqueur*

Break the chocolate into squares or small pieces and place in a flat-bottomed microwave dish. Pour over the cream then very finely grate all the coloured rind from the orange into the mixture.

Microwave on High (100%) power for 2 minutes, leave to stand for 1 minute, then stir until the chocolate and cream are evenly mixed. If there are any remaining lumps, microwave again in 20-second bursts, until the lumps disappear when stirred. If adding spirits, stir into the cooked mixture.

Pour the warm mixture into the serving dish, or put aside for later reheating and serving.

Pile generous amounts of bite-sized pieces of fruit on a flat plate around the hot chocolate dip. (The fruit may be prepared ahead and refrigerated in plastic bags until required.)

Suitable fruits include: apples, apricots, bananas, cherries, grapes, kiwifruit, melons, nashi, oranges, pawpaw, peaches, pears, pineapple and strawberries.

Variation: Leave out the orange flavouring and make with only chocolate and cream.

Quick Black Forest Cherry Cake

One of my favourite desserts is a chocolate sponge of three layers, sandwiched together with whipped cream and a cherry filling. If you are not too fussy about authenticity, you can call your concoction Black Forest Cherry Cake. Authentic or not, it tastes delicious.

For 8 servings:

Kirsten's Chocolate Roll (left)
1 can or jar cherries in syrup
cornflour or custard powder

2 Tbsp kirsch or brandy
300 ml (10 fl oz) cream
¼ cup icing sugar

Bake the chocolate roll, leave it to cool in the tin, then remove the paper from the bottom. Cut the cake into 3 even pieces crosswise.

Drain the cherries and remove the stones – if necessary, using your fingers. Boil the syrup until it is reduced to half its original volume, then thicken to sauce consistency with cornflour or custard powder mixed to a paste with water. When cool, stir in the cherries and add a small amount of kirsch or brandy if desired.

Spread the almost cold cherry mixture on 2 layers of sponge. Whip the cream until very stiff, adding icing sugar and kirsch or brandy when it is partly beaten.

Divide into quarters.

Put one cherry-topped layer on the serving plate and spread a quarter of the cream on it, then top with the other cherry-topped layer. Top this with another quarter of the cream, then add the last cake layer. Sprinkle with extra kirsch or brandy if desired, and coat the sides of the layer cake with the third quarter of the cream. Put the remaining cream on top of

the cake or spread about half of it on top and put the rest in a piping bag. If you like, sprinkle the top and sides of the cake with chocolate curls (cut from a warmed bar of dark chocolate with a floating blade peeler. The warmer the chocolate, the bigger the curls will be.) Pipe rosettes of cream on the cake, and top these with glacé cherries.

Refrigerate the cake for at least an hour, or up to 36 hours as long as the cream is fresh. This is a rich cake, so do not cut very thick slices.

Chocolate Mousse, Apricot Balls (p. 347)

Date and Walnut Cake

Date and Walnut Cake

You can't actually see the fruit and nuts in this delicious cake because they are so finely chopped. Serve it for dessert or for a special occasion, with coffee. You need a food processor and beater to make it.

For a 23 cm (9 in) round or ring cake:

1 cup chopped dates
1 cup walnut pieces
½ cup sugar
2 Tbsp flour
1 tsp baking powder
2 large eggs, separated
1 tsp vanilla essence

Turn the oven to 180°C (350°F), or to 170°C (325°F) if using a fan oven. Line the bottom of a round cake tin with baking paper and spray the sides with non-stick spray.

Put the dates and nuts in a food processor, add half the sugar, all the flour and baking powder, then chop until the dates and nuts are as fine as rolled oats.

In another bowl beat the egg whites with half (2 Tbsp) the remaining sugar until their peaks turn over when the beater is lifted. Beat the egg yolks with the rest of the sugar and the vanilla until thick and creamy.

Combine the 3 mixtures, folding them together lightly. Turn the mixture into the prepared tin. Bake for about 30 minutes, until the centre springs back when pressed. Leave for 10 minutes then turn onto a rack to cool.

Serve topped with whipped cream, quark or ricotta, decorated with a selection of chopped dried fruit and nuts, such as dates, dried apricots, walnuts and pecans.

Notes: Use good quality dried fruit and nuts, especially walnuts.

This cake may be made ahead and frozen. It is best decorated within 3 hours of serving.

Do not expect a high cake – it is meant to be fairly flat!

Almond Torte

This rich cake makes an unusual dessert that needs no last-minute attention.

For 9 servings:

100 g (3½ oz) unblanched almonds
1 cup plain or nut-flavoured biscuit
   crumbs
1 cup sugar
3 eggs, separated
2 tsp water

Turn the oven to 160°C (325°F). Chop the almonds as finely as possible, using a knife or blender. Check that you finish up with half a cup of chopped nuts. Crush biscuits very finely in a food processor, or put them in a plastic bag and crush with a rolling pin. Mix the nuts and biscuit crumbs together with ½ cup sugar.

Beat the whites until frothy. Add ¼ cup sugar and beat until the peaks stand upright. Beat the yolks and the water until thick and cream-coloured. Add the last ¼ cup of sugar and beat again.

Carefully but thoroughly fold together the egg white, yolk and nut mixtures. Turn into a 23 cm (9 in) square tin lined with greased paper. Bake for 30–40 minutes, until the centre feels firm. Turn out and cool.

Cut into 9 squares and top each with flavoured whipped cream and fresh fruit or firm canned apricot halves.

Note: The un-iced cake freezes well and thaws quickly.

Apricot and Almond Cake

This is a wonderful cake. You may find yourself inventing a special occasion so you have an excuse to make it!

For a 20 cm (8 in) ring cake:

140–150 g (5 oz) slivered almonds
2 tsp baking powder
20 (75 g/2½ oz) lightly salted crackers,
   e.g. Snax
½ cup dried apricots
3 egg whites
1 cup sugar
1 tsp vanilla
whipped cream or fromage frais to
   decorate

Turn the oven to 180°C (350°F). Butter the sides of a ring tin well or spray with non-stick spray. Line the bottom with a ring of baking paper or a non-stick Teflon liner.

Toast the almonds until evenly golden under a grill without letting them darken. Put aside about 1 Tbsp for garnish.

Put the rest of the nuts, the baking powder and the biscuits in a plastic bag and bang with a rolling pin until they are broken into small pieces, but not as fine as breadcrumbs. Wash the dried apricots and chop them into small pieces while wet, using a sharp knife or kitchen scissors. Mix with the crumbs, breaking up any clumps.

In a large, grease-free bowl, beat the egg whites until the peaks turn over when the beater is lifted out. Add the sugar and beat until the peaks stand up straight when the beater is removed. Fold the crumb mixture and the vanilla into the meringue.

Spoon the cake mixture into the prepared tin and bake for 30 minutes, then run a knife around the tin and tip the cake carefully onto a rack. As soon as it is cold, turn it right-side up onto a flat serving plate.

Decorate with whipped cream or fromage frais, piling it on top, then sprinkle with the reserved nuts and extra chopped apricots if desired.

Notes: Do not use a food processor to crumb the biscuits. If they are crushed too small the cake will be dry and too firm.

You can bake this cake in a 20 cm (8 in) tin without a central hole, but you may find the centre drops a little. Cook until the centre springs back and feels as firm as the part nearer the edge. You do not notice the depression in the middle if you fill it with cream.

Fromage frais is best chilled, stirred with a fork until smooth, and piled on the cake (or on individual servings) just before serving.

Kiwi Layer Cake

This 'dinner-party' cake is best eaten the day after it is made. If this is not possible, make it two days ahead!

For 8–12 servings:
1 unfilled sponge sandwich
1 Tbsp instant coffee
3/4 cup sugar
1/4 cup (60 ml/2 fl oz) water
1/2 Tbsp rum or brandy
1–1 1/2 (250–375 ml/8–12 fl oz) cups
  cream
6–8 kiwifruit
1/2 cup slivered almonds
1/2 cup canned mandarins (optional)

Split both sponge layers so you have 4 thin round layers. Put one of these aside for other use and place 3 side by side on a clean working surface.

Heat the coffee, sugar and water, stirring until the sugar dissolves, then boil without stirring until a drop between your thumb and forefinger forms a thread when you move them 1 cm (1/2 in) apart. Cool until you can put your hand on the bottom of the container, then stir in the rum or brandy.

Drizzle each of the 3 sponge layers with a third of the coffee syrup, covering the surface evenly.

Whip the cream stiffly, put a quarter on each of 2 layers, then cover with two-thirds of kiwifruit, thickly sliced. Stack these 2 layers on a flat serving plate, and cover with the remaining layer. Spread the remaining cream over the top and sides.

Toast the almonds under a grill until golden brown, and when they are cool press them into the cream on the sides of the cake, tilting it slightly and rotating it. Cover lightly, and refrigerate for at least

12 hours before serving. The texture changes during this time.

Just before serving, decorate the top with a ring of overlapping kiwifruit slices. Pile drained mandarin segments in the centre of the cake if desired.

Note: Refrigerate leftovers. The kiwifruit between the layers will look good a day later, but the fruit on the top may need to be replaced.

Orange Gâteau

This orange-flavoured layer cake makes a good dessert.

For about 8 servings:
1 sponge sandwich, unfilled
2 oranges, rind and juice
water or wine
1 cup sugar
1/4 tsp citric acid
1 tsp water
300 ml (10 fl oz) cream
1/4 cup icing sugar
2–3 Tbsp orange liqueur
brandy or rum
chopped nuts or coconut (optional)

Split the sponge sandwich into 4 layers. Grate the rind from the oranges and then squeeze them, making the liquid up to 1/2 cup with water or wine if necessary. Boil the rind, juice and sugar until the syrup thickens. Remove from the heat and add the citric acid dissolved in 1 tsp water. Drizzle the hot syrup over the 4 pieces of sponge.

Beat the cream until 'floppy', then add the icing sugar and liqueur and beat until stiff. Divide the cream into 4 equal parts and spread over each cooled 'syrupy' cake surface. Sprinkle the top and sides with chopped nuts or coconut if desired, and refrigerate for at least 12 hours.

Drained canned mandarins make a good decoration for this cake. They should be added just before serving.

Sponge (or Sponge Roll) with Summer Fruits

If you can whisk up a quick sponge you can use it as a base for all types of summer berry desserts.

If time is short you can always 'dress-up' a bought sponge, but it doesn't take much time or effort to make your own. This one is very light and eggy. If you want a sponge with a more solid texture and a greater volume, add an extra tablespoon of cornflour.

For 6–8 servings:
3 large eggs, at room temperature
1/2 cup sugar
1/4 cup cornflour
1/4 cup self-raising flour
1 tsp vanilla essence

Turn the oven to 190°C (375°F). Line the bottom of a 20 cm (8 in) square or round tin with baking paper and spray the sides or butter and flour them (or prepare two 18 cm (7 in) sponge sandwich tins).

Beat the eggs until light-coloured and thick, then add the sugar and beat again until very thick. Sift the cornflour and flour together 2 or 3 times, then sprinkle over the egg mixture. Add the vanilla. Fold in the dry ingredients and vanilla until no pockets of flour remain.

Pour the mixture into the prepared tin and bake for 10 to 20 minutes, until the centre springs back when pressed lightly with a finger. Leave to cool in the tin for about 5 minutes, standing the sponge, in the tin, upside down on a cake rack if desired, then loosen the edges and remove carefully.

Fill when cool, or wrap carefully and freeze until required. Top with whipped cream and one or more varieties of fresh berries, dusted with icing sugar.

Variation: For a sponge roll, spread the mixture in a 23 x 33 cm (about 23 x 33 cm/9 x 13 in) sponge roll tin which has had a piece of baking paper spread across the bottom and 2 sides. Bake at 190°C (375°F) for 12 to 15 minutes, or until the centre springs back. Quickly turn out of the oven onto a clean teatowel, remove the paper and trim the edges if necessary, then roll up in either direction, rolling the teatowel with the sponge.

Leave to cool, then unroll, fill with whipped cream, berries, etc., reroll, dust with icing sugar and cover lightly until serving.

See also

Cold Weather Puds, pp. 226–235

Sweet Pastries, pp. 236–245

Rum and Raisin Muffins, p. 264

Apricot Surprise Muffins, p. 266

Rhubarb and Fresh Ginger Muffins, p. 266

Strawberry Cream Cheese Muffins, p. 266

Chocolate Surprise Muffins, p. 267

Double Chocolate and Banana Muffins, p. 267

Upside-Down Nectarine Muffins, p. 267

Lemonade and Cream Muffins, p. 268

Caramel Malt Bar, p. 290

Warm Blueberry Cake, p. 297

Mississippi Mud Cake, p. 300

Yoghurt Cake, p. 302

Chocolate Orange Liqueur Cake, p. 304

Treats and Sweets, pp. 310–317

Cold Weather Puds

If you feel you need something to cheer up your family on cold and wintry days, the puddings in this chapter should do the trick! Many of them may be refrigerated or frozen and warmed up later, so I seldom make a smaller quantity, even if I am cooking for only two people. I prefer just to put aside the extra, since it is always useful later, and smaller amounts usually take just as long to prepare as the full recipe.

Peach Crisp with Sauce

This is a cross between a shortcake and a crumble. It is very quick and easy to assemble and mix.

For about 6 servings:
1 can (820 g/1 lb 13 oz) sliced peaches, drained
1 egg
1 Tbsp oil
1 tsp vanilla essence
1¼ cups self-raising flour
½ cup sugar

Peach Sauce
syrup from canned peaches
orange juice or white wine
2 Tbsp cornflour
2 Tbsp sherry
2 rounded dessertspoons golden syrup

Turn the oven to 180°C (350°F). Spray or butter an ovenware dish, about 23 cm (9 in) in diameter, and place the drained peaches in it.

Beat the egg, oil and vanilla in a medium-sized bowl until blended, then tip in the flour and sugar and toss with a fork until evenly dampened. Sprinkle this mixture over the peaches, without smoothing the surface at all, and bake for about 30 minutes, until the top is evenly crisp and lightly browned.

For the sauce, make the syrup up to 1½ cups with orange juice or white wine. In a pot mix the cornflour and sherry to a thin paste, then add the golden syrup and the juice mixture. Stir over moderate heat until clear and thick. Taste, adjust flavourings if desired, then cover and put aside until required.

Serve warm sauce over individual servings of Peach Crisp. Save any extra sauce to pour over icecream on another occasion.

Variation: Replace peaches with 2 cups (500 ml/16 fl oz) of any other drained, cooked fruit.

Citrus Sponge Pudding

This pudding is flavoured with coconut, orange and lemon. It forms a crust on top and a sauce underneath as it bakes.

For 4–6 servings:
75 g (2½ oz) butter, melted
1 cup sugar
4 large eggs
1 cup (250 ml/8 fl oz) milk
½ cup plain flour
¾ cup desiccated coconut
grated rind of 1 lemon
grated rind of 1 orange
½ cup (125 ml/4 fl oz) lemon juice
½ cup (125 ml/4 fl oz) orange juice

Turn the oven to 180°C (350°F). Butter a round baking dish 23 cm (9 in) across, or 6 individual dishes.

Beat the butter, sugar and eggs until thick. Add the milk, flour and coconut and beat until mixed. Add the grated rinds and juice, mix again.

Pour the mixture into the prepared dish (or dishes). Stand in a roasting pan with hot tap water halfway up the dish(es).

Bake for 20 minutes for small dishes, 40 minutes for a large dish, or until lightly browned and set to a depth of 1 cm (½ in). Remove from the roasting pan.

Serve warm, dusted with icing sugar.

Note: Undercooked puddings have too little crust and too much sauce; overcooked puddings are the reverse!

Baked Lemon Sponge Pudding

Make this when you want a really popular warm pudding. A lemon sauce forms under the sponge topping as it cooks. If overcooked, the sauce sets, but it still tastes good.

For 4 servings:
50 g (2 oz) butter
¼ cup plain flour
2 eggs, separated
¾ cup sugar
grated rind of 2 lemons
¼ cup (60 ml/2 fl oz) lemon juice
¾ cup (185 ml/6 fl oz) milk

Turn the oven to 180 or 190°C (350/375°F) (see below). Melt the butter in a medium-sized pot, add the flour and stir. Put the egg whites into an ovenproof dish that you can bake the pudding in (1 litre/32 fl oz capacity) and the yolks into the butter mixture.

Beat the whites until they form soft peaks. Add ¼ cup sugar and beat again until the tips of the peaks turn over when the beater is lifted from them.

Add the remaining ½ cup sugar to the butter mixture with the lemon rind and juice. Beat with the (unwashed) beater, then add the milk and beat again. Pour the lemon mixture over the beaten whites, and mix gently to combine.

Stand the baking dish in a larger bowl of hot water. Bake at 190°C (375°F) for about 40 minutes, or at 180°C (350°F) for about 60 minutes, until the centre is firm and golden brown.

Spiced Fruit Crumble

For best results the fruit you start with should be raw rather than cooked.

For 4 servings:
3 or more cups raw fruit
¾ cup rolled oats
½–¾ cup sugar
½ cup plain flour
1 tsp cinnamon
75 g (2½ oz) very cold butter

Turn the oven to 190°C (375°F). Lightly butter a 20–23 cm (8–9 in) ovenproof dish.

Prepare the fruit by grating unpeeled apples, finely chopping rhubarb, slicing peeled peaches, feijoas, etc. Place the fruit in the prepared dish.

Mix all the dry ingredients together, using extra sugar if the fruit is sour. Grate in the cold butter and rub together well, OR mix the cold, cubed butter into the other ingredients in a food processor. Sprinkle the crumbly mixture over the fruit.

Bake for 45 minutes, until the topping is firm and light brown. Serve warm, with icecream if you like.

Citrus Sponge Pudding

227

Chocolate Fruit Sponge

Peach Danish

I serve this cake warm from the oven for weekend coffee breaks, and for dessert with icecream or lightly whipped cream whenever I think anyone in the house needs a little TLC.

*1 or 2 cans (each 425 g/15 oz) sliced
  peaches**
75 g (2½ oz) butter
1 egg
½ cup (125 ml/4 fl oz) milk
¼ cup (60 ml/2 fl oz) juice from peaches
¼ tsp almond essence
½ cup sugar
1½ cups self-raising flour
½ cup icing sugar
2–3 tsp lemon or peach juice
¼ cup toasted flaked almonds

* You can make an adequate cake using one can of peaches, but two are nicer!

Turn the oven to 190°C (375°F). Drain the peaches in a sieve, keeping the liquid. Microwave or warm the butter on the stove, in a medium-sized bowl or pot, until it melts, then add the egg, milk,
¼ cup of the peach juice, and the almond essence; beat with a fork to combine.

Chop the peaches in the sieve roughly, then add about half to the liquids with the sugar and flour. Fold everything together until the flour is dampened, taking care not to overmix or break up the fruit. Stop mixing before the mixture is smooth.

Spray or line a 23 cm (9 in) square cake tin (or a roasting pan that is a little bigger), spread the mix over the bottom evenly, then arrange the remaining peaches over the top.

Bake for 15–30 minutes, depending on the size of the pan and whether the oven has a fan, until the centre of the cake springs back when pressed. Put the hot cake on a rack or leave in the pan if you can serve wedges straight from it.

Beat the icing sugar with enough liquid to make a thick cream. Drizzle this over the warm cake, then sprinkle with the toasted flaked almonds.

Chocolate Fruit Sponge

This pudding is lighter in texture than many sponge puddings. I usually consider a three-egg pudding extravagant, but this makes so many servings, has such a short list of other ingredients, and requires so little handling that it redeems itself!

For 8–10 servings:
4–6 cups hot cooked fruit
3 eggs
½ cup sugar
½ tsp vanilla or almond essence
½ cup cornflour
2 Tbsp plain flour*
2 Tbsp cocoa*
1½ tsp baking powder

* Use level measuring spoons, especially

for the flour and cocoa. Together (4 Tbsp) these should measure ¼ cup. Rounded household tablespoons will upset the recipe completely.

Turn the oven to 180°C (350°F). Cook the fruit until tender, adding very little sugar since the topping is quite sweet. Purée or mash the fruit, or leave it chunky. Do not have a lot of liquid, but do not drain it completely. Keep the fruit hot until the topping is ready.

Beat the eggs, sugar and essence in a large bowl in a sink of warm water (or in an electric beater) until thick and light-coloured. Sieve the dry ingredients together then fold into the eggs.

Put the hot fruit in a large dish or small roasting pan, about 20 x 30 cm (8 x 12 in), or 2 or 3 smaller dishes. Pour the topping evenly over the fruit; it should cover it completely, being 5–10 mm (¼–½ in) thick. Bake the pudding in one dish for about 30 minutes; smaller dishes will cook more quickly. When cooked the centre should spring back when pressed with a finger. The middle of a large pudding may not rise as much as the sides, but the sponge mixture usually falls a little after cooking anyway, and this does not matter.

Sprinkle the top with icing sugar and serve warm, preferably with a little cream or icecream.

Berry Buckle

If you have blackberries growing nearby, pick one or two cupfuls and make this pudding. If not, try it with blueberries.

For 6–9 servings:
50 g (2 oz) butter
1/2 cup brown sugar
1 egg
1 cup plain flour
1 1/2 tsp baking powder
1/2 tsp cinnamon
1/4 cup (60 ml/2 fl oz) milk
1–3 cups berries or cubed fruit
juice of 1/2 lemon (optional)

Topping
1/2 cup plain flour
1/4 cup brown sugar
1/2 tsp cinnamon
50 g (2 oz) cold butter
grated lemon rind (optional)

Turn the oven to 180°C (350°F). Heat the butter until liquid in a medium-sized pot, then remove from the heat. With a fork beat in the sugar and egg until creamy. Stir in the sifted flour and baking powder, cinnamon and milk until blended. Do not overmix. Spread into a buttered and floured (or sprayed) sponge roll tin or a 23 cm (9 in) square tin.

Sprinkle the berries over the uncooked batter, and squeeze lemon juice over the fruit if desired.

To make the topping, mix the flour, sugar and cinnamon into a bowl. Cut in the butter until the mixture resembles breadcrumbs. Add grated lemon rind if you like. Sprinkle the topping evenly over the fruit.

Bake for 45–60 minutes, until firm in the middle. Serve warm, cold or reheated, plain or with whipped cream.

Rhubarb Cobbler

As it is cooked in two steps, a cobbler takes a little longer to make than some simple puddings, but it is much faster and easier to make than a pie, and one large pudding may stretch over two or more meals.

For about 8 servings:
4 cups (about 500 g/1 lb 2 oz) sliced rhubarb
3/4 cup sugar
2 Tbsp cornflour
1/2 cup (125 ml/4 fl oz) orange juice or 1/4 cup (60 ml/2 fl oz) water and 1/4 cup orange juice
1 Tbsp butter

Topping
25 g (1 oz) butter
1 cup self-raising flour
1 tsp mixed spice
1 egg
1/2 cup (125 ml/4 fl oz) milk

Turn the oven to 200°C (400°F). Cut the rhubarb into 1 cm (1/2 in) slices. Place in a round or oval oven or microwave dish about 23 cm (9 in) across, or in a pot. Mix the sugar and cornflour together and sprinkle over the rhubarb, then add the orange juice. Stir to mix, add the butter, then heat in a microwave or on the stovetop until the mixture thickens and becomes clear. Transfer to a baking dish if necessary.

To make the topping, cut or rub the butter into the flour and spice in a bowl or food processor. Beat the egg and milk together with a fork and add to the dry ingredients. Mix just enough to dampen the dry ingredients.

Drop the batter in dessertspoonfuls onto the hot, thickened fruit. (It will spread to cover the whole surface as it cooks.)

Bake for 20 minutes, or until the centre feels as firm as the edges, then leave to stand until cooler. Serve warm with a small scoop of icecream.

Variation: Replace the rhubarb with other fruit, using less sugar and cornflour.

Apricot Custard Squares

This pudding always works! It can be prepared and cooked just before it is to be eaten, or it can be made up to a day ahead, and served cold or reheated. It is not suitable for freezing.

For 6–8 servings:
2 cups plain flour
100 g (3 1/2 oz) butter
1 can (850 g/1 lb 14 oz) apricot halves or pieces
1/2 cup sugar
1 tsp cinnamon
3 eggs
1 cup (250 ml/8 fl oz) syrup from apricots
1 1/4 cups (310 ml/10 fl oz) unsweetened condensed milk

Turn the oven to 180°C (350°F). Sift the flour into a large bowl and rub in the butter until crumbly, or chop the butter through the flour in a food processor.

Press this dry mixture into a 23 cm (9 in) square tin. (Use a tin with a loose bottom, or line the bottom and 2 sides with foil, so the cooked square can be lifted out easily.) Drain the apricots well and arrange the fruit evenly over the base. Cut the fruit into pieces if necessary. Mix the sugar and cinnamon and sprinkle evenly over the fruit. Bake uncovered for 20 minutes.

Beat the eggs, apricot syrup and condensed milk until blended but not foamy. (Replace the condensed milk with fresh or sour cream if you prefer.) Pour over the hot apricots and bake for 30 minutes longer, or until the custard has

set in the middle. Serve hot, warm or cold, with whipped cream.

Variations: Use 1–1 1/2 cups (250–375 ml/ 8–12 fl oz) of the milk or cream and alter the amount of syrup so the total liquid remains the same.

Replace apricots with peaches or pineapple.

Chocolate Upside-Down Cake M

This quick, easy pudding looks as if you have spent hours slaving over a hot stove!

For 6–8 servings:

Topping
1 can (425 g/15 oz) peaches or pears
1 Tbsp butter
1 tsp custard powder
1 Tbsp juice from canned fruit
2 Tbsp golden syrup
chopped walnuts or cherries (optional)

Cake
50 g (2 oz) butter
1/2 cup brown sugar
1 large egg
1 cup plain flour
2 Tbsp cocoa
1/2 tsp baking soda
juice from canned fruit, to mix

Drain the fruit in a sieve, saving all the juice.

Melt the butter for the topping in a lightly sprayed microwave ring pan. Stir in the custard powder, juice and golden syrup. Microwave on High (100%) power for about 45 minutes, or until the mixture boils and thickens slightly. Sprinkle walnuts or cherries in the ring pan, then arrange the drained fruit attractively around the dish.

To make the cake, soften the butter and beat it with the sugar and egg using a rotary beater, fork or food processor. Sift over the dry ingredients, add about 2 Tbsp of reserved juice, and mix together. As you mix, add extra liquid, using as much as you need to make a batter soft enough to drop from a spoon.

Drop this in spoonfuls evenly over the fruit. Don't worry if there are unfilled areas, as the cake mixture spreads as it cooks. Cover the dish with a lid, or for faster, more even rising, with vented plastic film.

Place in the microwave on a rack, or on an upturned plate, and cook on Medium-High (70%) power for 10–12 minutes, or until the mixture close to the central cone is cooked. If in doubt, cook a little longer.

Leave to stand for 2–3 minutes, then turn out onto a flat plate and lift away the ring pan. Serve warm, plain or with icecream.

Dutch Apple Cake with Lemon Sauce

Don't overcook this, because it tends to dry out, and don't forget the sauce that goes with it!

For 6 servings:
1½ cups plain flour
2 tsp baking powder
¼ tsp salt
2 Tbsp sugar
50 g (2 oz) butter
1 egg
½ cup (125 ml/4 fl oz) milk
2 large apples
½ tsp cinnamon
2 Tbsp sugar

Turn the oven to 200°C (400°F). Butter a 20 cm (8 in) square, or 23 cm (9 in) round, ovenware dish or plate.

Sift the flour, baking powder and salt together, add the sugar, and cut in the butter until the mixture resembles coarse breadcrumbs.

Beat the egg and half the milk with a fork.

Make a well in the centre of the dry mixture, add the egg and milk and enough of the remaining milk to make a dough that is softer than scone dough, but firmer than a buttercake mixture. Using a spatula or spoon, spread this mixture into the prepared dish.

Peel and core the apples, cut them into quarters then cut each quarter into three. Poke these pieces, rounded surface uppermost, into the dough as close together as possible. Cover the whole surface of the dough with apple.

Mix the cinnamon and sugar and sprinkle thickly over the surface of the apples and pudding. Bake for 25–30 minutes, or until the dough is firm in the centre. Meanwhile make a lemon sauce.

Lemon Sauce
rind of 1 lemon
1 Tbsp golden syrup
1 cup (250 ml/8 fl oz) water
2 Tbsp vanilla custard powder
1 Tbsp sugar
juice of 1 lemon
1 tsp butter

Heat together the grated lemon rind, golden syrup and nearly all the water.

Mix the custard powder and sugar with the remaining water, and add gradually to the boiling syrup. Stir well. When thick and transparent, add the lemon juice and butter, stir well, and remove from the heat.

Serve the apple cake hot with the hot or warm lemon sauce.

Apple Sponge

Fruit sponge is a good-natured pudding. You can make it with a little or a lot of fruit, and this can be freshly stewed, bottled or canned.

Just remember that the fruit should be drained so there is not too much syrup or juice around it, and it must be close to boiling when the topping is spooned onto it, otherwise the centre will be raw when the rest of the pudding is cooked.

For 4 servings:
500 g (1 lb 2 oz) apples, etc.
1–2 Tbsp water
about ¼ cup sugar

Sponge Topping
50 g (2 oz) butter
1 Tbsp golden syrup
½ cup sugar
1 egg, lightly beaten
1½ cups self-raising flour
1 tsp cinnamon
2 tsp mixed spice
½ cup (125 ml/4 fl oz) milk

Turn the oven to 180°C (350°F). Peel, core and slice the fruit, and put it in a covered pan with the water and sugar. Simmer gently until the fruit is tender but not necessarily mushy.

If using canned or bottled apples, check there is not too much liquid. Use 1–2 cups prepared fruit, and heat until boiling.

To make the topping, heat the butter and golden syrup in a medium-sized pot or microwave dish until the butter has just melted. Add the sugar and egg and beat with a rotary beater until the mixture looks light and creamy.

Sieve the flour, cinnamon and mixed spice onto this mixture, add the milk, then fold everything together.

Spray or butter an ovenware dish that is about 18 x 25 cm (7 x 10 in) and about 5 cm (2 in) deep. Spread the very hot fruit evenly in the dish (heat a glass or pottery dish before you do this, in case it cracks). Spoon the sponge mixture evenly over the fruit. It may not cover it all at this stage, but it will spread during cooking.

Bake for 40–45 minutes, until it is golden brown, the centre springs back when touched, and a skewer in the centre comes out clean.

Serve warm or fairly hot rather than straight from the oven. Dust with icing sugar before serving, and add a scoop of icecream or a little lightly whipped cream on special occasions.

Apple Betty

This may be an old-fashioned pudding but it is still popular and practical and a good way of using up stale bread.

For 4–6 servings:
2 cups soft breadcrumbs
6 cooking apples
¾ cup sugar
½ tsp cinnamon
½ tsp salt
2 Tbsp butter
1 lemon, grated rind and juice
¼ cup (60 ml/2 fl oz) water

Turn the oven to 190°C (375°F). Make soft breadcrumbs by crumbling stale bread, preferably in a food processor. Peel, core and slice the apples and place half in a casserole. Mix together the breadcrumbs, sugar, cinnamon and salt. Sprinkle half the crumbs over the apples, then dot with half the butter. Repeat with the remaining apples, crumbs and butter. Mix together the lemon rind, juice and water and sprinkle over the mixture. Bake uncovered for 45 minutes.

Apple Pancake

This is a quick and unusual dessert which you can make, start to finish, in only 20 minutes. Cook it in a frypan with a metal handle, or in a shallow flame-resistant dish which will go from stove top to oven without breaking.

For 3–4 servings:
2 Tbsp sugar
1 tsp cinnamon
2 Tbsp butter
2 medium apples
2 eggs, separated
2 Tbsp milk
3 Tbsp plain flour
½ tsp baking powder
¼ tsp salt
3 Tbsp sugar

Turn the oven to 200°C (400°F). Mix the sugar and cinnamon together. Melt the butter in a 23–25 cm (9–10 in) metal-handled, heavy-bottomed frypan. Sprinkle the cinnamon sugar evenly over the melted butter.

Peel and quarter the apples. Cut each quarter into 3 or 4 slices, then arrange all the slices neatly on the cinnamon sugar, working towards the centre. Leave to cook over low heat for 5 minutes while mixing the batter.

Add the milk to the egg yolks; stir to mix. Sift together the flour, baking powder and salt, and stir into the liquid mixture. Beat the egg whites until foamy, add the sugar and beat until the tips of the peaks turn over when the beater is lifted from them. Fold the whites into the yolk mixture, carefully but thoroughly. Spread the batter evenly over the hot apples in the pan.

Bake in the oven for 10 minutes, until puffy and golden brown. Loosen the edges and turn the pancake upside-down onto a flat serving plate. Serve immediately with cream or icecream.

Fruity Honey-Baked Apples

Fruity Honey-Baked Apples

Dress up baked apples with this recipe!

4 granny smith apples
8 dried apricot halves
2 Tbsp chopped pecans
2 Tbsp shredded coconut
2 Tbsp honey
¼ cup (60 ml/2 fl oz) orange juice
4 tsp butter

Turn the oven to 180°C (350°F). Remove the apple cores and cut a line around the 'equator' of each apple.

Chop the apricots into small pieces, and mix with the coconut, half the honey and half the orange juice.

Stand the apples in a shallow baking dish with the remaining orange juice.

Divide the filling in four. Press it into the core cavities. Top each apple with 1 tsp butter and drizzle over the remaining honey.

Bake for about an hour, basting occasionally with the surrounding liquid. Cover lightly with foil if the filling browns before the apples are tender.

Serve warm, with yoghurt, cream or icecream.

Variation: Cook without butter if desired, if the apples are to be served cold.

Fruity Dessert Cake

Fruity Dessert Cake

Make this delicious cake with one or more seasonal fruits and the nuts of your choice!

For 6–8 servings:
*¼ cup chopped walnuts, toasted almonds
  or toasted hazelnuts
1 Tbsp white or brown sugar
150 g (5 oz) butter
1 cup sugar
2 large eggs
1 tsp vanilla essence
1½ cups self-raising flour
1 tsp baking powder
1–2 cups cubed or sliced ripe, raw fruit*
½ cup berries (optional)*

*Suitable fruit includes peaches, nectarines, plums, apples, pears, kiwifruit, strawberries, raspberries, blueberries, blackberries. Drained canned fruit may also be used.

Choose whatever nuts complement the fruit you are using. Toast them lightly under a grill or in the oven as it heats to 180°C (350°F), then chop finely, mix with the 1 Tbsp sugar and put aside.

Melt the butter in a microwave bowl or pot until just liquid. Add the second measure of sugar, the eggs and vanilla and beat until blended. Sieve the flour and baking powder onto the mixture, then add half the nut and sugar mixture. Spread evenly in a buttered or sprayed 23–25 cm (9–10 in) round (preferably loose-bottomed) cake tin.

Prepare the fruit, slicing it or cutting it into 2 cm (³/4 in) chunks. Arrange the pieces, skin-side up, in the batter. Sprinkle with berries then with the remaining nut topping.

Bake at 180°C (350°F) for about 45 minutes, until the cake mixture has risen round the fruit and browned lightly, and the centre springs back when pressed.

Serve warm, cut into wedges, sprinkled with icing sugar if you like, with a little lightly whipped cream.

Linzer Torte

I don't like giving modified recipes their original names, but it is hard to describe this dessert in any other way. Since it is best made two days before it is eaten, it is a good dessert for a busy hostess-cum-cook-cum-housemaid-cum-mother!

For 6–8 servings:
*1 cup plain flour
½ tsp baking powder
50 g (2 oz) butter
½ cup almonds
¼ cup sugar
1 tsp instant coffee
½ tsp cinnamon
¼ tsp ground cloves
rind from ½ lemon
1 egg, beaten with a fork
¼ cup raspberry or blackcurrant jam*

Turn the oven to 180°C (350°F). Sift the flour and baking powder together. Cut in the butter until the mixture resembles coarse breadcrumbs. Chop the almonds very finely by hand, or chop them to a powder with the sugar in a food processor. Add the sugar, almonds, coffee, spices, lemon rind and three-quarters of the beaten egg to the flour. Stir with a fork, then knead lightly. Stand the dough in a cool place for 5 minutes.

Roll out three-quarters of the dough to fit a 23 cm (9 in) tin (with a removable base if possible). Make a slight rim around the edge. Spread the jam evenly over the dough. Roll out the remaining dough and cut it into strips. Arrange these across the jam to form a diamond pattern. Neaten the edges.

Brush the lattice with the reserved egg and bake for 30 minutes, or until it is firm in the centre. Cool, then store in an airtight tin. Leave for 1 or 2 days before serving if possible.

Spicy Apple Shortcake

Apple shortcake is always popular. The dough for this recipe is handled in a fast and easy way, so the shortcake does not take long to assemble. The spice in the apple filling makes it seem much richer than it is.

For 9 large servings:
*¼ cup dried apricots, chopped
½ cup (125 ml/4 fl oz) water
1 tsp cinnamon
1 tsp mixed spice
½ tsp ground ginger
½ tsp ground cloves
½ cup brown sugar
½ cup (125 ml/4 fl oz) orange (or other)
  juice
4 large apples
1 Tbsp cornflour*

Crust

125 g (4½ oz) butter
½ cup and 2 Tbsp sugar
1 egg
1 cup self-raising flour
1¼ cups flour

Turn the oven to 190°C (375°F). Boil the chopped apricots with the water in a large frypan. When the apricots are plump and the water has evaporated, remove from the heat and add the spices, sugar and orange juice. Bring the mixture to the boil then add the apples, which have been peeled, cored and cut into 5 mm (¼ in) cubes or chunks. Stir, then cover and simmer for 5 minutes.

Remove the lid and cook several minutes more, until most of the liquid has evaporated. Mix the cornflour to a paste with a little water, stir into the apples, then remove from the heat and cool by standing the pan in cold water.

To make the crust, combine the butter, sugar and egg, and beat until evenly mixed. Stir in the flours, then divide the mixture in half.

Press half the crumbly dough into a baking paper-lined sponge roll pan (20 x 30 cm/ 8 x 12 in). Spread with the cool filling, then crumble the remaining dough over this. (If the dough forms a solid ball, chill it, then grate it onto the filling.)

Bake for 35–40 minutes, or until the top is an even golden colour and the shortcake feels firm in the middle. Serve warm, sprinkled with icing sugar.

This shortcake freezes well – freeze cooked, individual servings.

Queen Pudding

A baked custard seems much more exciting when it has meringue on top! This satisfying pudding is easy to make for a special family meal.

For 4–6 servings:
¼ cup sugar
2 cups (500 ml/16 fl oz) milk
2 slices stale, toast-thickness bread
½ tsp vanilla essence
2 eggs, separated
¼ cup raspberry jam
pinch of salt
¼ cup sugar

Turn the oven to 180°C (350°F). Heat the first measure of sugar with the milk in a small pot until bubbles form at the side of the pan. Remove from the heat.

Break the bread into pieces and put in a baking dish that will hold about 4 cups of mixture, pour over some of the hot milk, and when soft break it up with a fork. Add the remaining hot milk and the vanilla.

Add the egg yolks to the mixture and mix in evenly. Stand the baking dish in a roasting dish half-filled with warm water, and bake uncovered for 20–30 minutes, or until a knife inserted in the middle of the custard comes out clean.

Spread the surface of the custard with raspberry jam (stir it first if it is firm). Beat the egg whites and salt until the peaks turn over when the beater is lifted from them, then add the sugar and beat until the mixture stiffens again and forms stiff peaks with turned tips when the beater is lifted from them. Put the meringue in smallish spoonfuls all over the custard, spread carefully with a knife without mixing the jam through it, and bake for 15 minutes longer, or until the higher parts are lightly browned. Serve warm or cool, rewarming if necessary.

Bread and Butter Pudding

The bread and butter puddings I make for special occasions are a far cry from the plain ones I remember as a child!

For about 4 servings:
3 toast-thickness slices white or light
  brown bread
about 6 dessert dates
2 eggs
2 Tbsp soft brown sugar
1 cup (250 ml/8 fl oz) milk
½ cup (125 ml/4 fl oz) cream
2 Tbsp rum (optional)

½ tsp vanilla essence
pinch of salt
about 2 Tbsp apricot jam

Turn the oven to 180°C (350°F). Butter or spray a fairly shallow dish of 4-cup (1 litre/32 fl oz) capacity.

Break, cut up or crumble the bread and put it in the prepared dish. (Crumbled bread mixes faster and better with the other ingredients.) Chop dessert dates into thin rounds and add half to the bread.

Combine all the remaining ingredients except the jam in a food processor or mixing bowl, mix well, and pour over the bread. Leave to stand for about 10 minutes so the bread can soak up the liquid. (If time is short, heat the milk before mixing it with the other ingredients.)

Sprinkle the remaining dates over the uncooked pudding, and stand it in a roasting pan. Pour boiling water around it to the depth of the pudding, and bake for 30 minutes, or until the custard is set everywhere except in the centre. This part will finish cooking as it stands.

Just before the pudding is due to come out of the oven, heat the jam in the microwave until it bubbles vigorously, and brush it over the surface to glaze it.

Serve warm, plain, with thin cream or a sauce made of puréed sweetened raw or cooked fruit. This pudding is best eaten half an hour after it is taken from the oven.

Bread and Butter Pudding

Sticky Date Pudding

When the weather is cold and wintry and you want to cheer up your family, make a sticky date pudding!

For 4 servings:
1 cup dates
1 tsp mixed spice
1/2 cup (125 ml/4 fl oz) water
25 g (1 oz) butter
1 rounded household Tbsp golden syrup
25 g (1 oz) butter
grated nutmeg to taste
1/2 cup (125 ml/4 fl oz) boiling water
1 cup self-raising flour
3/8 cup (100 ml/3 fl oz) milk

Bring the first 4 ingredients to the boil in a small pot. Stir until the dates break up, then remove from the heat and stand the pot in cold water to cool.

Put the golden syrup in a small microwave ring pan that holds about 6 cups, and will fit in a large pot or frypan. Cut the second measure of butter into about 6 cubes and dot these over the syrup, then add nutmeg to taste. Pour the boiling water on top, then stir to mix.

Next mix the flour with enough milk to make a fairly stiff dough, and roll this out on a floured board to about 20 x 28 cm (8 x 11 in). Spread the cool date mixture over the dough, leaving a 2 cm (3/4 in) strip on one long side uncovered. Dampen this strip with water and roll up, starting at the other side so the damp strip seals the roll. Cut the roll into 8 pieces with a sharp, serrated knife. Put the pieces, cut side down, in the syrup mixture in the ring pan, placing the larger, fatter pieces evenly around the ring, with the smaller pieces between them.

Place the ring pan in a heavy pot or pan, with boiling water to halfway up the sides of the ring pan. Cover the pot or pan tightly. Simmer for 20 minutes, or until firm when pressed in the centre.

Leave to stand for 5 minutes to thicken the sauce, then unmould and serve. On longer standing the syrup will be soaked up by the dough.

Serve warm, with a little lightly whipped cream, vanilla icecream or a mixture of cream and low-fat apricot yoghurt.

Variation: Bake the pudding instead of steaming it. Make the golden syrup mixture as above, in a shallow, round ovenproof dish about 20 cm (8 in) across, then pour on 1 cup of boiling water. Arrange the slices of date-filled dough in this, then bake uncovered at 180°C (350°F) for about 40 minutes, until the dough is lightly browned and cooked, basting occasionally. Serve the baked pudding without unmoulding it.

Marion's Oaty Pudding   M

This rich steamed pudding contains no flour, butter or oil. It has a lovely flavour, a really good dark colour, and a wonderful aroma.

For 4–6 servings:
1 cup (250 ml/8 fl oz) milk
1 cup (fine) rolled oats
425 g (15 oz) mixed fruit
1 egg
2 household dessertspoons golden syrup
1 tsp baking soda
1 tsp cinnamon
1 tsp mixed spice
1/2 tsp ground cloves
1/2 tsp lemon essence

Pour the milk over the rolled oats in a mixing bowl and leave for 5 minutes.

Put the dried fruit into a sieve, run hot water over it, then leave it to drain.

Add the egg and golden syrup to the rolled oats mixture. Beat with a fork to mix well, then stir in the clean, drained fruit. Sprinkle over the soda and spices. Add the lemon essence, and stir just enough to mix. If the mixture is so wet that some thin liquid separates out, add another 2 Tbsp rolled oats and leave to stand a few minutes longer.

To cook conventionally: butter or spray a 4-cup bowl well, and line the bottom with a circle of baking paper. Pour in the mixture, and stand the uncovered bowl on a saucer in a saucepan half full of boiling water. Cover tightly and simmer for 2 1/2–3 hours, adding more boiling water if necessary.

Leave to stand for 5 minutes, run a knife around the bowl, and turn out the pudding.

To microwave: line the bottom of a small microwave ring pan with a non-stick Teflon ring pan liner or a circle of baking paper. Pour in the mixture and cover with cling film. Make a few holes in this, and cook on Medium (50%) power for 12–15 minutes, until the mixture close to the central ring springs back when pressed. Leave to stand for 5 minutes before turning out onto a plate.

Serve with any steamed or Christmas pudding sauce, such as Creamy Custard Sauce (opposite).

Marmalade Pudding

Marmalade Pudding is good – and easy, quick, and cheap into the bargain.

For 4 servings:
1/4 cup marmalade
2 Tbsp brown sugar
2 Tbsp water
2 Tbsp butter
2 cups self-raising flour
1 cup (250 ml/8 fl oz) milk
1 cup (250 ml/8 fl oz) boiling water

Warm the first 4 ingredients together until blended, then put aside.

In a bowl, mix milk into the flour just until it is dampened. Do not overmix or beat until smooth.

Put the marmalade mixture in an 18 cm (7 in) casserole dish and stand it on a plate in a large pot of water. Drop the flour mixture in 4 'blobs' on top of the sauce. Do not cover the container the pudding is in.

Pour boiling water over and around the pudding, cover the pot tightly and simmer for 30–45 minutes, until a knife pushed into the centre shows no raw mixture. (Don't keep looking at the pudding as it cooks.)

Unmould onto a plate big enough to hold the marmalade sauce.

Variation: Make individual puddings, in 4 ramekins about 10 cm (4 in) across, or in old cups. Cook these, uncovered in a covered pot, for 12–15 minutes.

Fresh Plum Pudding   M

If you don't like heavy, rich puddings in summer, try a 'fresh plum' pudding some time during the festive season. This pudding should be cooked the day it is eaten or made the day before and reheated.

For about 6 servings:
75 g (2 1/2 oz) butter
2–3 tsp finely grated orange or tangelo rind
1/2 cup brown sugar
1 egg
1 cup plain flour
1 tsp baking soda
1 tsp mixed spice or cinnamon
1/2 tsp ground cloves
3/4 cup cold stewed plums, sieved
1/2 cup sultanas

Melt the butter in a medium-sized pot, remove from the heat, and add the rind, brown sugar and egg. Beat with a fork until mixed. Add the sifted dry ingredients but do not mix until the sieved plums and sultanas have been added. Fold all the ingredients together thoroughly but without overmixing.

Put into a buttered bowl, cover with foil and steam for about 2 hours, OR microwave in a ring pan covered with cling film for about 4 minutes, or until set close to the centre cone.

Serve hot or warm, with whipped cream flavoured with rum or brandy, Mary Alice's Rum Butter, Brandy Butter or Creamy Custard Sauce (all on next page).

> The fastest way to cook a steamed pudding conventionally is in an uncovered ring pan in a tightly covered pot or frying pan (microwaving is fast but is not suitable for some puddings).

Christmas Pudding

This is my favourite Christmas pudding!

For 10–12 servings:
100 g (3¹/₂ oz) butter
2 eggs
1 cup packed brown sugar
grated rind of 1 large lemon
grated rind of 1 orange or tangelo
3 cups mixed fruit
1 large apple, finely chopped or grated
2 cups flour
1 tsp cinnamon
¹/₂ tsp ground cloves
1 tsp baking soda
1 cup (250 ml/8 fl oz) liquid (see below)

Heat the butter until it is liquid, then add the eggs and brown sugar and mix thoroughly. Grate all the coloured rind from the citrus fruit and add to the butter mixture with the mixed fruit and chopped or grated unpeeled apple, then mix well. Sift in the flour, cinnamon, cloves and baking soda, but don't mix until you add the liquid.

Mix up 1 cup of liquid, using the juice of the orange or tangelo, and another orange or tangelo if available, but not the juice of the lemon. Make up to 1 cup (60–125 ml/2–4 fl oz) with ¹/₄–¹/₂ cup of sherry, or a mixture of sherry and rum, whisky or brandy. Add to the fruit mixture and mix until there are no pockets of flour.

Pour into 1 large or 2 smaller buttered bowls that will fit inside large pots. The mixture should no more than three-quarter fill the bowl(s). Cover the bowls with foil.

Lower each pudding bowl onto a saucer in a large pot containing enough boiling water to come halfway up the bowl. Cover the pot tightly, bring back to the boil, then simmer gently for 4 hours, adding extra boiling water to the pot if the level falls.

If making ahead, refrigerate until required then boil as before for 2–3 hours before serving.

Flaming a Pudding

To 'flame' a Christmas pudding, heat 1–2 Tbsp of brandy, whisky or rum to bath temperature. Pour it over the hot pudding and set alight. The brandy will not burn unless it is heated first. (The flame may not be visible unless the room is in darkness).

Mary Alice's Rum Butter

Delicious on Christmas pudding, mincemeat pies and even muffins. Make extra, as a gift for good friends!

100 g (3¹/₂ oz) softened butter
1 cup brown sugar
1 tsp freshly grated nutmeg
2 Tbsp rum

Beat or process all the ingredients until light and creamy. Cover and refrigerate for up to a month. Serve at room temperature.

Christmas Pudding

Brandy Butter (Hard Sauce)

Very rich and extra good!

125 g (4¹/₂ oz) softened butter
2 cups icing sugar
1 Tbsp brandy

Beat or process all the ingredients until light and creamy. Refrigerate until the butter hardens. Pile into a serving dish and serve at room temperature.

Variation: For a slightly grainy texture, use 1 cup castor sugar instead of icing sugar.

Creamy Custard Sauce

A less rich alternative to serve with steamed puddings!

¹/₄ cup custard powder
¹/₄ cup brown sugar
1 large egg
3 cups (750 ml/24 fl oz) milk
1 tsp vanilla essence
2 Tbsp butter
1 Tbsp brandy or 2 Tbsp rum (optional)

Stir the custard powder and sugar together in a pot. Add the egg and mix again. Stir in the milk and vanilla. Cook over medium heat, stirring constantly. When the milk is hot, add the butter. As soon as the custard thickens and bubbles, remove from the heat and add the brandy or rum. Serve warm.

Sweet Pastries

The inviting aromas of fruit, spices and pastry are irresistible to most people, perhaps because they awake childhood memories of coming home to mother at the stove, at the end of the day – mmm! If you like pies, I'm sure you will enjoy many of these recipes. I can't guarantee they are low in calories, but if you are strong-minded you may be able to cut very thin slices, and serve them without a small scoop of icecream or a dribble of fresh cream, or save them for high days and holidays!

Most of these recipes use homemade pastry, although you can use bought pastry instead. When used for lower crusts, however, bought pastry is not usually as crisp as homemade, because it generally contains more fat – homemade short pastry usually has about half as much fat as bought pastry. When buying pastry, read the packets carefully, selecting varieties with less fat if possible.

Rolled thinly, 350 g (12 oz) of bought pastry will make two crusts for a 23 cm (9 in) pie, or two single-crust pies the same size.

I fold the rims of pies back to form a double layer, and make sure the shells are large enough that if they shrink during cooking the filling won't run underneath. (Flaky and puff pastries shrink more than short pastry.)

Short Pastry

This is a good all-purpose pie pastry, which can be made by hand or in the food processor. It contains less fat than flaky pastry, and so is better for pie bottoms. Double-crusted pies made with short pastry look best when glazed.

1 cup plain flour
60 g (2¼ oz) cold, hard butter
3–4 Tbsp cold water
OR
1½ cups plain flour
100 g (3½ oz) cold, hard butter
4–6 Tbsp cold water

Traditional method:
Measure the flour into a mixing bowl. Cut, rub or coarsely grate in the butter using your fingertips, 2 knives or a grater, until the butter is cut in small pieces. Add the water a few drops at a time, tossing the mixture with a fork until it will form a ball when pressed with your fingers.

Food processor method:
Use the metal cutting blade. Put the flour and cold butter, cut into about 9 cubes, in the food processor but do not process.

Apple Cream Pie

Acidify the water with 1–2 tsp lemon juice for extra tenderness if you like. Using the pulse button, add water in a thin stream while chopping the butter through the flour. Test at intervals, stopping as soon as the particles are moist enough to press together to form a ball. (The mixture still looks crumbly at this stage. If a ball of dough forms in the processor, the mixture is too wet.)

Chill the ball of pastry for at least 5 minutes before rolling it out as required.

Note: Overmixing or too much water makes tough pastry.

Quick Flaky Pastry

This is an easy recipe which is flakier and richer than short pastry.

For 1 thinly rolled double crust 20 cm (8 in) pie:
1¼ cups plain flour
1 tsp baking powder
125 g (4½ oz) cold butter
about ½ cup (125 ml/4 fl oz) milk
1 tsp wine vinegar

Mix the flour and baking powder. Grate the butter or cut it into about 25 small cubes, and rub or cut it into the flour, by hand or with a food processor. (Pieces of butter should be visible when the pastry is rolled out.)

Mix the liquids, and add slowly to the flour mixture until it forms a fairly stiff dough. Chill for at least 5 minutes.

Double-Crust Apple Pie

A pie like this will make everyone's eyes light up!

For 6 servings:
Short Pastry (above), using 1½ cups flour
600–700 g (1 lb 5 oz–1 lb 9 oz) tart apples
½ cup sugar
¼ tsp ground cloves or 1 tsp cinnamon
2 Tbsp cornflour

Turn the oven to 220°C (425°F). Make the pastry. Use half to line a 23 cm (9 in) pie dish.

Slice the peeled apples into a mixing bowl. Sprinkle with the sugar, cloves or cinnamon, and cornflour (use half the cornflour if the pie is to be eaten cold). Toss to mix well, and turn into the uncooked pie shell. Cover with the remaining pastry, and glaze with milk or lightly beaten egg if desired. Cut several steam vents in the top crust.

Bake for 20 minutes or until brown, then bake at 180°C (350°F) for 20 minutes more.

Variations: For feijoa pie, thinly peel 500–600 g (1 lb 2 oz–1 lb 5 oz) feijoas. Chop or slice them, and mix with 2 Tbsp custard powder and ½ cup sugar.

Apple Cream Pie

This is one of my family's favourite pies.

For 6 servings:
Short Pastry (above), using 1½ cups flour
2 eggs
½ cup sugar
¼ cup (60 ml/2 fl oz) cream or sour cream
500 g (1 lb 2 oz) tart apples, unpeeled and coarsely grated

Turn the oven to 200°C (400°F). Make the pastry and roll it out thinly into 2 circles. Use one to line a 20–23 cm (8–9 in) flan tin. Run the rolling pin over the crust to cut off excess pastry.

Mix the eggs, sugar and cream or sour cream. Add the apple and mix well. Spread the apple mixture in the uncooked pie crust.

Cut the remaining pastry into strips and arrange them lattice-style over the filling (p. 347). Press the edges firmly to attach them to the bottom crust, and remove excess.

Bake for about 30 minutes, until the pastry is brown and the pie is set in the middle. Serve warm or reheated, dusted with icing sugar.

Variation: Use 400 g (14 oz) thinly sliced rhubarb, or peaches, plums, pears or apricots instead of apples.

Apple Crumble Pie

Cross an apple crumble with an apple pie and you have a winner!

Pastry
1 cup plain flour
60 g (2 oz) cold butter
about 1/4 cup (60 ml/2 fl oz) cold water

Filling
1/2 cup rolled oats
1/4 cup plain flour
1/4 cup brown sugar
1 tsp mixed spice
50 g (2 oz) cold butter
3–4 apples

Turn the oven to 220°C (425°F). To make the pastry, rub or cut the butter into the flour until it looks like breadcrumbs. Add the water a few drops at a time, tossing the mixture with a fork. Stop as soon as the particles are damp enough to press together to form a stiff dough. Refrigerate for at least 5 minutes, then roll out thinly and line a 23 cm (9 in) pie plate or flan tin.

To make the filling, mix the dry ingredients in a bowl or food processor. Rub or cut in the butter as above. Sprinkle a little mixture into the uncooked pie crust. Grate (or chop in the food processor) the unpeeled apples, spread them in the pie crust then top with the remaining crumble mixture.

Bake until the pastry browns, about 15 minutes, then turn the oven down to 180°C (350°F) and bake 10–15 minutes longer.

Blackberry and Apple Pie

When you find a patch of ripe, wild blackberries, add them to apples to make an extra-special dessert.

For a 20–23 cm (8–9 in) pie:
Short Pastry (p. 237), using 1 1/2 cups flour
1–2 cups blackberries
1–2 medium apples
1/2 cup (110 g/4 oz) sugar
2 Tbsp plain flour

Turn the oven to 220°C (425°F). Make the pastry and roll it into 2 circles to fit a 20 or 23 cm (8 or 9 in) pie plate. Put one in the pie plate.

Pick over the berries and mix them with the finely sliced or coarsely grated apple, the sugar and the flour. Tip into the uncooked pastry crust. Dampen the edges of the pastry, lay the second circle on top, and turn the edges under to make a good seal. Crimp the edges attractively. Cut several steam vents in the top. Glaze as desired.

Bake for 15 minutes, or until the edge is brown, then reduce the heat to 180°C (350°F) and bake 20 minutes more. Serve warm or cold.

Blueberry Pie

It's a pity to hide the colour of blueberries! A lattice top lets you see what's inside your pie!

For a 20 cm (8 in) pie:
3/4 cup plain flour
1/2 tsp baking powder
75 g (2 1/2 oz) cold butter, cubed
1/4 cup (60 ml/2 fl oz) milk
1/4 tsp vinegar
3 rounded Tbsp red jam
3 cups blueberries, fresh or frozen
3 Tbsp plain flour
1 tsp cinnamon
1/4 cup sugar

Turn the oven to 210°C (425°F). Put the first 3 ingredients in the food processor and cut the butter in coarsely, using the pulse button. Mix the milk and vinegar together and add slowly until the mixture will form a dough. Do not overmix. Cut the ball of dough in two. Roll each half out thinly on a floured surface, to form a 25 cm (10 in) circle.

Line a 20 cm (8 in) sponge sandwich tin with 1 circle, and cut the other into 10 strips.

Heat the jam until liquid, stir in the remaining ingredients, and pile into the uncooked crust. Dampen the pastry edges with water. Arrange the pastry strips in a lattice pattern over the filling (p. 347), cut off the pastry 2 cm (3/4 in) beyond the rim of the dish, then turn in the edges, enclosing the ends of the strips. Decorate the outer edge if you like, then bake until the pastry is golden brown, 25–40 minutes. Serve warm.

Variation: Use a metal, removable-base flan tin, removing all the pastry that lies beyond the edge of the tin by pressing it down on the edge.

Feijoa Crumble Pie

Aromatic feijoas make an interesting pie. Replace the coconut with extra rolled oats if you prefer.

For 4–6 servings:
Short Pastry (p. 237), using 1 cup flour
400–500 g (about 1 lb) feijoas

Topping
1/4 cup plain flour
1/4 cup coconut
1/4 cup rolled oats
1/4 cup brown sugar
50 g (2 oz) cold butter

Turn the oven to 200°C (400°F). Prepare the pastry and press it together to make a firm dough. Chill for 10 minutes then roll out to fit a 23 cm (9 in) flan tin.

Next prepare the topping, mixing the dry ingredients together, then cutting in the butter (using a food processor if available) until the mixture is crumbly.

Peel the feijoas thinly and slice them about 5 mm (1/4 in) thick. Work quickly to prevent browning. Place half the fruit in the uncooked pastry shell. Sprinkle with 1/4 cup of the topping. Cover with the remaining fruit, then the rest of the topping, spread evenly over fruit.

Bake for 20 minutes or until the pastry browns lightly, then reduce the heat to 180°C (350°F) and bake 15–20 minutes longer. Serve warm with icecream or whipped cream.

Sour Cream Raisin Pie

This is a lovely spicy pie with a firm texture. This quantity makes a fairly shallow 23 cm (9 in) pie, or a deeper 18–20 cm (7–8 in) pie.

For 4–6 servings:
Short Pastry (p. 237), using 1 cup flour
1/4 cup brown sugar
1 Tbsp flour
1/2 tsp cinnamon
pinch of cloves
1 large egg
1/2 cup sour cream
1/2 cup sultanas
1/2 cup chopped walnuts

Turn the oven to 220°C (425°F). Make the pastry, then roll it out thinly to fit your pie plate. Dampen the edges with cold water and fold them under to make a double edge.

Mix the sugar, flour and spices together in a food processor or bowl. Add the egg and sour cream and mix until smooth. Pour boiling water over the sultanas in a sieve, cool to bath temperature, then stir into the filling mixture with the nuts. Pour into the unbaked crust.

Bake for 10 minutes, then reduce the heat to 180°C (350°F) and bake for 15 minutes, until the filling has set. Serve warm, cold or reheated.

Spiced Fruit Pie

For 6–8 servings:
Short Pastry (p. 237), using 1 cup flour
3 eggs, separated
3/4 cup sugar
25 g (1 oz) butter, melted
1 Tbsp wine vinegar
1/2 tsp cinnamon
1/2 tsp mixed spice
3/4 cup sultanas
2 Tbsp sugar

Turn the oven to 220°C (425°F). Prepare the pastry then roll it out thinly to line a 23–25 cm (9–10 in) pie plate. Fold under the edge then flute it if desired.

Combine the egg yolks, sugar, butter, vinegar and spices. Chop the sultanas with a hot, wet knife and fold into the mixture. Beat the egg whites until the peaks turn over, add the sugar and beat again until the peaks stand up. Fold this meringue through the yolk mixture and pour into the unbaked crust.

Bake for 10 minutes, then reduce the heat to 180°C (350°F) and bake 20–30 minutes longer, or until the centre is set. Serve warm or cold.

Coconut Fruit Pie

This versatile pie can be made and cooked very quickly. If it isn't all eaten warm for dessert, cut it into small pieces and serve for in-betweens, or pack it in school lunches.

For 4–6 servings:
Short Pastry (p. 237), using 1 cup flour
2–3 Tbsp raspberry, strawberry or plum jam
1/2 cup sultanas or currants
50 g (2 oz) butter
1 cup sugar
2 eggs
1/2 tsp vanilla essence
2 cups coconut

Turn the oven to 220°C (425°F). Make the pastry, refrigerate it for 5 minutes then roll it out thinly to line a 23 cm (9 in) square pan or a sponge roll tin 23 x 35 cm (9 x 14 in). Spread the pastry with jam, then sprinkle it with rinsed and dried sultanas or currants.

Melt the butter in a pot, remove it from the heat and add the sugar, eggs and vanilla. Mix thoroughly, add the coconut and mix again. Spread evenly over the jam.

Bake for 10 minutes, then reduce the heat to 180°C (350°F) and bake 10–15 minutes longer, until the coconut topping is golden brown.

Variation: Use apricot or other jam, and crushed pineapple, almonds or cashew nuts instead of dried fruit.

Pumpkin Pie

This pie is dark in colour, spicy and rich.

For about 8 servings:
Short Pastry (p. 237), using 1 cup flour
1 cup cooked pumpkin
1 1/4 cups (310 ml/10 fl oz) cream
1 cup loosely packed brown sugar
1 large egg
1 tsp cinnamon
1 tsp vanilla essence
1/4 tsp ground cloves
1/4 tsp ground ginger

Turn the oven to 220°C (425°F). Make the pastry, chill it for about 5 minutes then roll it out thinly to fit a 23 cm (9 in) pie plate or flan tin.

For speed and extra smoothness, measure all the remaining ingredients into a food processor and process until smooth and

Swiss-Style Rhubarb Tart

well blended. OR measure everything into a bowl, stir well with a whisk, fork or wooden spoon, then push the mixture through a sieve into the uncooked pie crust.

Bake for 15–20 minutes, until the edge of the crust browns, then reduce the heat to 180°C (350°F) and bake 15 minutes longer, or until the centre of the filling has set.

Variation: For a larger pie with a lighter colour, milder flavour and softer texture, replace the cream with a 400 g (14 oz) can (or 1 1/2 cups) of unsweetened condensed milk (evaporated milk) and use 2 large eggs instead of 1. All the other ingredients are the same. The initial cooking time and temperature is unchanged but this pie needs about 15 minutes longer at the lower temperature to set the custard in the centre.

> For best results, keep pastry cool while working with it. Roll it evenly on a board floured just enough to prevent sticking.
>
> Leave rolled pastry for up to 10 minutes before shaping, if possible. Take care not to stretch pastry out of shape when transferring it to baking pans.

Swiss-Style Rhubarb Tart

The cream in this tart 'softens' the acidity of the rhubarb, with delicious results!

For 6–8 servings:
1/2 recipe Quick Flaky Pastry (p. 237)
2–3 cups finely sliced rhubarb
2 eggs
1/2 cup sugar
1/4 cup (60 ml/2 fl oz) cream or sour cream

Turn the oven to 220°C (425°F). Make the pastry, chill it for at least 5 minutes, then roll it out thinly on a floured board. Line a well-sprayed 23 cm (9 in) pie plate with the pastry, trim the edge 15 mm (3/4 in) beyond the edge of the pie plate and brush with water. Fold the edge of the pastry inwards, and press firmly. Decorate the edge of the pie if you like.

Cut the rhubarb into 5 mm (1/4 in) slices and place in the uncooked shell.

Mix the eggs, sugar and cream or sour cream until smooth in a food processor or bowl. Pour over the fruit and bake for 15–20 minutes, until golden brown, then reduce the heat to 180°C (350°F) until it is set in the middle and the fruit is tender. Serve hot or warm, sprinkled with icing sugar.

Citrus Tart

Use oranges, mandarins, tangelos or limes to make this tart. If none of these are available, use two extra lemons.

For 8 servings:

Quick Flaky Pastry (p. 237), using
  1¼ cups flour
rind and juice of 1 large or 2 small citrus
  fruit
½ cup sugar
3 eggs
juice of 2 lemons
½ cup (125 ml/4 fl oz) sour cream

Turn the oven to 220°C (425°F). Make the pastry, then wrap it in cling film and refrigerate it for about 20 minutes, if you have time. Roll it out on a lightly floured board into a circle big enough to fit a 23 cm (9 in) shallow flan tin with a removable base. Ease the pastry into the tin and remove the surplus by running the rolling pin over the top. Prick the base in several places with a fork. Bake for about 5 minutes while you prepare the filling.

Remove all the coloured rind from the fruit with a potato peeler and chop it very finely, processing it with the sugar in the food processor if you have one. Add the remaining ingredients and mix evenly.

Pour the filling into the partially baked pastry shell and return it to the oven,

turning the heat down to 180°C (350°F). Cook for another 8–10 minutes, or until the filling has set and the pastry is golden brown. Leave to cool slightly before removing the outer ring of the tin.

When required, warm through, dust lightly with sifted icing sugar and serve with lightly whipped cream or icecream.

> To bake blind, line (paper-lined) uncooked pastry crust with dried beans kept especially for this purpose. Remove the beans and paper when the pastry is firm. Return the crust to the oven until lightly browned.

Lemon Meringue Pie

Lemon meringue pie obviously doesn't go out of fashion, judging by the popularity of this recipe. It has several short cuts to make it easier.

For a 20 cm (8 in) pie:

Short Pastry (p. 237), made with 1 cup flour

Filling

1 cup (200 g/7 oz) sugar
rind and juice of 2 large or 3 small lemons
½ cup (60 g/2 oz) cornflour or custard
  powder
1½ cups (375 ml/12 fl oz) water
2 Tbsp butter
3 egg yolks

Topping

3 egg whites
pinch of salt
¼ cup castor sugar

Turn the oven to 230°C (450°F). Make the pastry, chill it for 5 minutes, then roll it out and shape it over the outside of an upturned 20 cm (8 in) pie plate. Trim, dampen and fold back the edges, and prick all over so it will not puff up as it cooks. Bake, still upturned, for about 10 minutes, or until lightly browned. Cool until you can lift the cooked shell off the tin, then stand it right side up in a bigger pie plate or a flat plate.

To make the filling, put the sugar in the unwashed processor bowl. Remove the lemon rind with a potato peeler and chop it very finely with the sugar, then mix in the cornflour or custard powder. Tip into a microwave dish, mix with the water and microwave on High (100%) power until clear and evenly thick, stirring every 2 minutes. Do not hurry this step.

Stir in the butter and egg yolks, mix well and heat again until it bubbles and thickens even more. Do not overcook. Stir in the lemon juice (squeezed with the food processor attachment) but do not cook again. Pour into the cooked shell.

Beat the egg whites and salt with an electric or rotary beater until the peaks

Citrus Tart

turn over, then add the sugar and beat again until the peaks are stiffer, turning over only a small amount at the top. Pile onto the filling in the pie shell. Swirl attractively, making sure the meringue is touching the shell at the edges, then bake at 190°C (375°F) for 5–10 minutes, until the tips of meringue are lightly browned. Do not overcook.

Serve warm, or at room temperature.

Almond Rum Fudge Tart

This rich tart is ideal for a special occasion dessert. It does require a little time and effort, but your friends and family should really enjoy it! When cut, a dark, delicious, soft centre is revealed.

For 8–10 servings:

Base
1 packet (250 g/9 oz) digestive biscuits
100 g (3¹/₂ oz) butter

Filling
3 large eggs
1 cup sugar
3 Tbsp cocoa
1 cup ground almonds
¹/₂ cup (125 ml/4 fl oz) cream
2 Tbsp dark rum

Turn the oven to 180°C (350°F). Crumb the biscuits, using a food processor if available, or put them in a plastic bag and crush with a rolling pin.

Melt the butter, add the biscuit crumbs, and mix well. Using the back of a spoon, press the mixture onto the bottom and about 4 cm (1³/₄ in) up the sides of a 23 cm (9 in) springform or loose-bottomed cake tin. Refrigerate while you make the filling.

Use a food processor or electric beater to beat the eggs and sugar together until thick and fluffy. Add the cocoa, ground almonds, cream and rum, and mix briefly to combine.

Pour the filling into the prepared base and bake for 25–30 minutes, until the top and edges of the cake feel firm, but the centre is still soft. The cake will firm up as it cools, but should be very soft in the centre. Leave to stand overnight, or at least for several hours. When it has cooled, neaten the edges of the crust if necessary by trimming them carefully with a sharp knife, and carefully remove from the tin.

Serve at room temperature with lightly whipped cream, sprinkled with toasted slivered almonds if you like. Slice with a hot, wet knife.

Variation: Replace the rum with orange juice or very strong coffee.

Crumb Crusts

Crumb crusts are particularly useful if you are making a pie with an uncooked filling, because the crumb crust doesn't need cooking either. Crumb crusts can be cooked, in which case about 2–3 Tbsp sugar is usually added. Cooked crumb crusts are a little crisper than uncooked ones.

For extra flavour, add ¹/₂–1 tsp spice (e.g. cinnamon, mixed spice, ginger) to crumb crusts.

Frozen crumb crusts are very hard to cut (or bite) if they contain too much butter.

125 g (4¹/₂ oz) wine biscuits (1 cup fine crumbs)
50 g (2 oz) butter, at room temperature
2–3 Tbsp sugar (optional)

Break the biscuits into pieces, put them in the food processor fitted with the metal chopping blade, and process until all the biscuits are crumbs. Add the butter (which should be soft enough to spread), cut into 3 or 4 cubes, and add sugar only if the crust is to be baked, so it is crisper and firmer. Process until the butter is well mixed with the crumbs.

Tip the mixture into a 20–23 cm (8–9 in) pie plate or flan tin and press firmly onto the bottom and sides, or the bottom only, if you prefer. If baking, bake at 180°C (350°F) for 10 minutes.

Easy (Uncooked) Cheesecake

This easy cheesecake is especially good when topped with strawberries. It can be eaten a few minutes after it is made, but it can also be refrigerated and left for 24 hours.

For 8 servings:
crumb crust (above)
250 g (9 oz) cream cheese*
¹/₂ cup icing sugar
¹/₂ cup (125 ml/4 fl oz) cream
¹/₂ tsp vanilla or almond essence

Optional Glaze
¹/₄ cup redcurrant jelly or firm apricot jam
1–2 tsp water or white wine

* For a firm filling, do not use a soft or spreadable cream cheese.

Make the crumb crust, press it into a 20–23 cm (8–9 in) pie plate or loose-bottomed cake tin, and refrigerate.

Spoon the cream cheese into a food processor in 4 or 5 pieces. Add the icing sugar, cream and essence, and process in bursts until smooth, with no lumps of cream cheese remaining. Spoon into the crumb crust and top with fruit, e.g. strawberries, pressing them into the filling if desired.

Glaze the fruit if you like. To make the glaze, heat the redcurrant jelly or apricot jam with the water or wine. When the jelly has softened and the mixture is smooth, spoon or brush it over the berries, then leave it to set.

Variation: Replace 1 or 2 Tbsp cream with sherry, brandy, rum or kirsch. Leave out the essence.

Baklava

This Greek dessert is made of layers of filo pastry layered with sweetened spiced nuts, and soaked in a honey syrup after it is cooked. It is an interesting and different dessert for a group of eight or more.

For 16–20 pieces:
1 cup walnut pieces
1 cup almonds
1 cup pinenuts, or extra walnuts and almonds
¹/₄ cup sugar
2 tsp cinnamon
¹/₄ tsp ground cloves
12 sheets filo pastry
50 g (2 oz) melted butter for brushing

Syrup
1 cup sugar
1 cup (250 ml/8 fl oz) water
¹/₂ cup honey
thinly peeled rind and juice of 1 lemon
1 tsp cinnamon
¹/₈ tsp ground cloves

Turn the oven to 150°C (300°F). Roughly chop first the walnuts, then the almonds, and mix them with the pinenuts, sugar, cinnamon and cloves.

Spray the base and sides of a 32 x 25 cm (13 x 10 in) baking dish with non-stick spray.

Working quickly, brush butter onto 2 sheets of filo pastry and stack them with a third (unbuttered) sheet on top. Make 3 more 3-sheet filo 'sandwiches'. Place one in the baking dish. Sprinkle evenly with a third of the nut mixture, then top with 2 more layers of filo and nuts, finishing with a filo layer. If the sheets are a little bigger than the dish, fold the edges over towards the centre or trim them off.

Cut the baklava lengthwise (through all the layers) into 4 or 5 strips, then into diamond shapes, using a sharp, serrated knife. Sprinkle or spray lightly with water to prevent the edges of the top layer curling. Bake for 1 hour, until crisp and golden brown. Lower the heat if the filo browns too much.

While it cooks, prepare the syrup. Put all the ingredients in a pot and boil gently for 15 minutes. Strain and cool.

Pour or spoon the cooled syrup over the hot cooked baklava. Leave several hours before serving. Eat within 2–3 days.

Apple and Hazelnut Filo Pie

Filo Apple Strudel

Made with filo pastry, this dessert is much lighter and crisper than a traditional strudel.

For 6 servings:
1/4 cup blanched almonds
1 slice (toast thickness) bread
3 apples
1/2 cup sultanas
1/4 cup sugar
1 tsp cinnamon
1/2 cup sour cream
1 egg yolk, lightly beaten
9 sheets filo pastry
oil or butter for brushing

Turn the oven to 180°C (350°F). Chop the almonds roughly in a food processor. Add the bread and process until crumbed. Quarter the unpeeled apples, remove the cores, cut the apples into rough slices and add to the bowl. Process in bursts until the apples are chopped to the size of peas. Add the next 5 ingredients and mix until just combined.

Take 3 sheets of filo pastry and, working quickly on a dry bench, lie them side by side, with the long sides slightly overlapping. Brush each sheet lightly with oil or butter. (Use no more than 1 tsp per sheet, as the whole surface need not be covered.) Cover with 3 more sheets, oil or butter in the same way, then top with the remaining 3 sheets. You will end up with a large rectangle, 3 layers thick.

Place the prepared filling along one of the short edges of the large rectangle, spreading it out into a strip 20–23 cm (8–9 in) wide, then roll it up loosely like a partly filled sponge roll, starting at the filled end. Cover the ends of the roll with foil so the filling will not fall out during cooking.

Place on an oven tray and bake for 15–20 minutes, until golden brown. Serve soon after cooking, hot or warm, with whipped cream.

Note: If you have a small processor, you may have to process the filling in 2 batches. (It may also be mixed after chopping the nuts and apples by hand.)

Filo Pear Triangles

These delicious little triangles are flavoured with pears, ginger and nuts.

For 4 servings:
1/2 slice toast bread
1/4 cup roasted cashews
6 pieces crystallised ginger, roughly chopped
3 winter nelis pears
2 Tbsp sugar
1/4 cup sour cream
1 egg yolk, lightly beaten
6 sheets filo pastry
oil or melted butter for brushing

Apple and Hazelnut Filo Pie

500 g (1 lb 2 oz) apples, peeled, cored and sliced
1 Tbsp butter
1/4 cup (60 ml/2 fl oz) orange juice
1/2 cup (125 ml/4 fl oz) white wine
8 dried apricots, finely chopped
1/4 cup sugar
1 Tbsp plain flour
1/4 cup toasted hazelnuts, chopped
8 sheets filo pastry
about 2 Tbsp melted butter
4 Tbsp apricot jam
sieved icing sugar for dusting

Turn the oven to 190°C (375°F). Heat the first 5 ingredients in a large pan. Mix in the sugar and flour, and cook gently until the apples are just soft, in a lightly thickened sauce. Stir in half the nuts.

Trim the filo pastry into squares. Brush one square lightly with melted butter. Lay the next square on top at a slightly different angle and brush lightly with melted butter. Repeat with the remaining sheets, making an 8-layer pile.

Place the layered filo in an oiled 23 cm (9 in) pie plate. Spoon in the prepared filling, sprinkle with the remaining nuts and fold the filo corners back over the filling, wrinkling and folding them attractively. (Some filling should remain visible in the centre of the pie.)

Bake for 20–30 minutes, until the base of the pie is golden. Brush exposed filling with warmed jam, then dust the filo with icing sugar.

Variations: Replace the hazelnuts with walnuts, or leave out the nuts completely. Leave out the dried apricots too, if you like.

Turn the oven to 180°C (350°F). Put the bread, cashews and ginger into a food processor and process until roughly chopped. Chop the unpeeled pears roughly, and add with the sugar, sour cream and egg yolk. Process briefly until the pieces of pear are pea-sized. Take 3 sheets of filo pastry and, working quickly on a dry bench, brush 1 sheet lightly with oil or butter. (Use no more than 1 tsp per sheet. The whole surface need not be covered.) Cover with another sheet, oil or butter it the same way, then top with the third sheet. Cut the sandwiched sheets into 4 even strips crosswise. Put an eighth of the filling at the end of one strip. Fold the end over to form a triangle, then continue folding to encase the filling completely, always forming triangles (diagram p. 148).

Repeat with the remaining pastry and filling. Brush the folded parcels with a little more oil or butter.

Place on an oven tray and bake for 15–20 minutes, until golden brown. Serve hot or warm, with whipped cream.

Almond and Peach Tarts

This recipe uses ground almonds instead of flour to make really delicious individual flans that are always popular for parties. Served warm, these tarts make a wonderful dessert too, so give your family a treat.

For 6 servings:
Short Pastry (p. 237) using 1 cup flour

Filling
1can (820 g/1 lb 13 oz) peach halves
1 cup blanched whole almonds
¾ cup sugar
150 g (5 oz) butter, softened
2 large eggs
1 Tbsp brandy, pear liqueur or sherry

Turn the oven to 150°C (300°F). Make the pastry as instructed, chill for few minutes in the refrigerator then divide into 6 even portions. Roll out each portion and line 6 individual 10 cm (4 in) flan tins or pie plates.

Drain the peaches and pat them dry with paper towels. Place one half or several slices in each pastry-lined tin.

Put the almonds and sugar in the food processor and process until finely ground. Add the butter, eggs and liquor and process until well combined. Spoon over and around the peaches.

Bake for 30 minutes, or until golden brown and set in the middle. Brush with apricot glaze or sieved, heated apricot jam. Serve warm or cold, with whipped cream.

Variation: Replace the peaches with pears.

Passionfruit Cream Pie

This rich passionfruit cream pie is one of the nicest and most popular desserts I make. It is the perfect dessert for a dinner party since it can be made and refrigerated 8–24 hours before it is needed.

Freeze several half-cup measures of passionfruit pulp when they are in season so you can make it at any time.

For 8 servings:
½ cup (125 ml/4 fl oz) fresh passionfruit pulp
¾ cup sugar
¾ cup (185 ml/6 fl oz) water
1 lemon jelly
250 g (9 oz) cream cheese
crumb crust (p. 241)
1 cup (250 ml/8 fl oz) cream

Heat the passionfruit pulp, sugar and water in a medium-sized pot until boiling. Add the jelly crystals, remove the pot from the heat and stir until the crystals dissolve. If necessary warm the pot gently to dissolve all the crystals. Leave to cool to room temperature.

Soften the cream cheese slightly by beating it with a fork or wooden spoon. Pour about ¼ of the jelly mixture through a sieve into the cream cheese, and beat until smooth. Sieve in the remaining jelly mixture, pressing all the pulp from around the seeds through the sieve, but discarding the seeds themselves. Beat until smooth, then chill until quite cold and partly set.

While mixture sets, make the crumb crust and press it into a 23 cm (9 in) flan tin.

Whip the cream until thick, and fold it into the partly set jelly. Pour into the prepared crust, and leave to set in the refrigerator. Cover with cling film as soon as the filling is firm enough.

Decorate just before serving with stiffly whipped cream. If you like, serve extra passionfruit pulp separately so diners can help themselves.

Variation: Serve the filling in 6 individual dishes instead of pouring it into a pie shell.

Impossible Custard Pie

This is an interesting and easy recipe which forms a heavier crust-like layer on the bottom of the baking dish, and a lighter custardy mixture on top.

For about 6 servings:
2 large eggs
¼ cup sugar
¼ cup self-raising flour
1 cup (250 ml/8 fl oz) milk
1½ Tbsp melted butter
1 tsp almond or vanilla essence
2 Tbsp coconut (optional)
nutmeg or cinnamon sugar (p. 11)

Turn the oven to 180°C (350°F). Put the first 7 ingredients in a food processor fitted with the metal chopping blade and process for a few seconds, or mix with a whisk in a bowl. Pour the mixture into a buttered or sprayed 20 cm (8 in) pie plate.

Sprinkle with grated nutmeg or cinnamon sugar and bake for 30–35 minutes, or until the centre of the pie is no longer liquid. Serve warm, preferably with a little lightly whipped cream.

Variations: For a 23 cm (9 in) pie plate, use 1½ times the mixture.

Leave out the coconut. Soak ½ cup sultanas or Californian raisins in 1 Tbsp rum overnight (in a plastic bag). Drop these into the pie plate after adding the processed mixture.

Note: If the pie should rise alarmingly during cooking, simply stab the bump with a sharp knife. It should flatten immediately!

Improbable Pumpkin Pie M

I always find it exciting to mix together all these ingredients, pour them into a pie plate, and find that the mixture, when cooked, has separated into a firmer bottom part, which closely resembles a crust, and an upper part with a regular baked pie filling consistency.

This mixture makes quite a large pie, but it can be reheated for serving a second time.

For a 23–25 cm (9–10 in) pie:
1½–2 cups cooked pumpkin (650–700 g/ 1 lb 7 oz–1 lb 9 oz raw)
1½ cups (375 ml/12 fl oz) evaporated milk, or ½ cup milk and 1 cup sour cream
2 large eggs
¾ cup brown sugar
½ cup self-raising flour
2 tsp cinnamon
1 tsp mixed spice
2 tsp vanilla essence

Turn the oven to 180°C (350°F). Cook the pumpkin until tender, press the pulp into a measuring cup then food process it or press it through a sieve. Add the evaporated milk (or milk and sour cream), eggs, brown sugar, flour and flavourings, and process or beat with a rotary beater until everything is combined. (Do not mix more than necessary.)

Spray or butter a 23–25 cm (9–10 in) pie plate and pour in the mixture.

Bake for 45–60 minutes, until a knife in the centre comes out clean; or microwave on 70% power for 20–22 minutes, to the same stage.

Leave at least 15 minutes before serving.

Christmas Mincemeats

I've never yet tasted bought Christmas mincemeat that could hold a candle to the three mixtures I make myself.

Traditional Mincemeat

I have made this easy recipe ever since I bought my first food processor. It can be eaten raw as well as cooked.

rind of 1 lemon
rind of 1 orange
1/2 cup sugar
1/2 cup brown sugar
3 small sturmer apples
juice of 1 lemon
2 cups sultanas
2 cups mixed fruit
1 tsp cinnamon
1 tsp mixed spice
1 tsp grated nutmeg
1 tsp salt
1/2 tsp ground cloves
1/4 cup (60 ml/2 fl oz) brandy, whisky or rum

Remove all the coloured rind from the lemon and orange with a potato peeler, then chop it with the sugar in the food processor until very fine. Add the brown sugar, chunks of unpeeled apple, lemon juice, half the sultanas and half the mixed fruit. Process until the apple is finely chopped. Add the remaining fruit and flavourings, and process briefly.

Spoon into sterilised jars and top with a little more spirits. Top with boiled plastic or metal screwtops, and refrigerate for up to a year, or freeze in plastic containers.

Cooked Mincemeat

This is a thickened mixture. I like it because it does not soak into the pastry. Pies, tarts or filo triangles remain crisp a lot longer.

75–100 g (2 1/2–3 1/2 oz) butter
1 cup brown sugar
1 tsp mixed spice
1/2 tsp cinnamon
1/4 tsp ground cloves
2 eggs, beaten slightly
2 cups currants
1/4–1/2 cup mixed peel
rind and juice of 1/2 orange
2 apples, finely chopped, or 1 cup
  drained canned apples
2 Tbsp sherry
2–3 Tbsp brandy or other spirits

Melt the butter in a microwave or in a metal bowl over a pot of boiling water. Stir in the next 8 ingredients. Chop, coarsely grate or process the unskinned apples. Stir in with the sherry.

Microwave on High (100%) power for about 8 minutes or simmer over boiling water for 20–30 minutes, stirring regularly. The mixture thickens when cooked. Cool, add the brandy, store in the refrigerator and use within 2 months. Use as a filling or spread.

Light Fruit Mincemeat

For a change, try this light-coloured, fresh-flavoured fruity mixture instead of traditional darker fruit mincemeats. This delicious mixture has a gold colour and a tangy fruit flavour.

1 1/2 cups fruit medley*
about 1/4 cup pinenuts or chopped
  almonds
1/2–1 cup (125–250 ml/4–8 fl oz) orange
  juice
1/2–1 cup (125–250 ml/4–8 fl oz) white
  wine
6 cloves or 1/8 tsp ground cloves
1 cinnamon stick or 1/2 tsp ground
  cinnamon
1/4–1/2 cup sugar
1/4–1/2 cup (60–125 ml/2–4 fl oz) sherry
  (or brandy or rum)

* Available from bulk food departments, or make your own by tossing together chopped dried apples, dried apricots and sultanas.

Put the fruit medley in a medium-sized pot. Make up 1 1/2 cups liquid, using orange juice and wine in any proportions you like, then add this and the spices to the fruit. Bring to the boil and simmer for 5 minutes.

Remove from the heat, stir in the amount of sugar you want, and leave to cool. Add the sherry, spirits, or a mixture of the two, and spoon the mixture into a jar.

Refrigerate for up to 3 months, stirring in extra juice, wine, sherry or spirits if the fruit looks too thick or dry.

Use as icecream topping, crêpe filling, and an interesting filling for sweet filo triangles or mincemeat tarts.

Christmas Mince Pies

If you have time, turn some of your Christmas mincemeat into mince pies before you get too busy with other festive tasks, and hide them in the freezer. When time is short, make filo triangles instead.

Traditional Mince Pies

This mixture is easy to work with, although it takes some time to shape. It makes pies that freeze and reheat well.

Pastry
100 g (3 1/2 oz) butter
1/2 cup sugar
1 egg
1 cup plain flour
1 cup self-raising flour

Turn the oven to 170–180°C (325–350°F). Soften but do not melt the butter; beat in the sugar and egg until well combined. Stir in the unsifted flours and mix well to form a dough. If too dry, add a little milk. If too soft to work with, refrigerate rather than adding more flour.

Roll the pastry out on a lightly floured board. Using a glass, round lid, or fluted cutter, cut out circles for the bottom of the pies (the size will depend on the muffin pans in which the pies will be baked.) Cut circles for the tops with a smaller cutter, or small biscuit cutters that form hearts, stars, diamonds, etc.

Ease the dough into (medium or mini) muffin pans, then spoon in the mincemeat mixture of your choice (see above) and top with the smaller shapes or circles of pastry, pressing the edges lightly.

Bake for 10–15 minutes, removing them from the oven as soon as the edges start to brown. Cool in the tins for 2–3 minutes then carefully transfer onto cooling racks. Serve warm, dusted with icing sugar.

Filo Mincemeat Triangles

Each Christmas I make one large batch of traditional mince pies, followed by many of these quick triangles. For best results, use thickened fillings unless the triangles are to be eaten soon after they are cooked.

Turn the oven to 180°C (350°F). Take 3 sheets of fresh filo pastry, lightly brush them with melted butter, then stack them. Cut crosswise into 3–5 strips. At one end of each strip put a spoonful of mincemeat. Fold the filo over the filling, forming a triangle. Keep folding to form triangular pastries, enclosing the filling completely. Brush with more melted butter. (See folding instructions on p. 148.)

Bake for about 10 minutes, or until golden brown. Serve warm rather than hot, dusted with icing sugar.

Carol's Butter Tarts

This recipe was given to me by a Canadian friend. The melt-in-your-mouth tarts are best made with equal parts of butter and lard, since lard makes the pastry very tender and flaky. If you find lard difficult to find, however, you can replace it with extra butter without worrying too much.

For about 24 tarts:

Pastry
75 g (2 1/2 oz) cold butter
75 g (2 1/2 oz) lard or extra butter
2 cups plain flour
1/2 tsp salt
1 egg yolk
2 tsp wine or cider vinegar
1/4–1/2 cup (60–125 ml/2–4 fl oz) water

Filling
50 g (2 oz) butter
1 cup sugar
1 egg
1 egg white
1 tsp vanilla essence
1/4 cup (60 ml/2 fl oz) milk
1 cup currants

Put the cold, cubed butter, the lard, flour, salt and egg yolk in a food processor. Mix the vinegar and water together, then drop it down the food processor tube in a thin stream, while processing in bursts. Don't mix more than you need to. Stop adding liquid as soon as you can press the mixture together to form a fairly stiff dough. Discard the unused liquid.

Wrap the pastry in cling film and leave it in the refrigerator for at least 15 minutes, while you heat the oven to 180°C (350°F) and prepare the filling.

Melt the butter, and mix it with the sugar, egg, egg white, vanilla and milk in a food processor or with a rotary beater until well combined but not frothy. Stir in the currants.

Roll the pastry out thinly on a lightly floured board and cut it into circles about 8 cm (3 in) in diameter, using a biscuit cutter or a lightly floured glass. Spray a tray of shallow patty pans with non-stick spray, carefully lift the pastry circles with a knife or spatula and ease them into the tray. Prick each pastry case several times with a fork.

Half to three-quarter fill the uncooked pastry shells with the filling, then bake for about 20 minutes. The tarts will puff up during cooking and may look as if the filling will spill over the sides, but the filling should subside without problems.

Let the tarts cool slightly in the tins then transfer them to a wire rack to cool completely.

Berry Tartlets

Filo pastry makes quick, crisp, light containers for glazed berries. You can make these any size you like.

Use the filling recipes that follow as a guide, and experiment with other fruit.

Turn the oven to 180°C (350°). Place a sheet of filo on a dry surface, brush lightly with melted butter or oil, then cover with another sheet. (The whole surface does not need to be coated.) Cut into squares that will fit your baking pans (i.e. medium or large muffin pans, or round individual pie dishes), allowing for frilly edges.

Take 2 of the sandwiched squares, place one over the other so the corners form an 8-pointed star, then press them lightly into buttered or sprayed pans. Repeat until all the pans are filled. (Use 3 squares instead of 2 if you prefer.)

Bake for 5–15 minutes, until the pastry is evenly coloured and golden brown. (Lower the heat if the corners brown too fast.)

Fill the freshly baked (or recrisped) cases with warm, thickened berry mixture 5–30 minutes before serving. Dust the fruit and pastry with sifted icing sugar. (The icing sugar on the berries disappears.)

Traditional Mince Pies, Filo Mincemeat Triangles

Blueberry Filling
1 punnet (about 350 g/12 oz) blueberries
½ cup (125 ml/4 fl oz) red or white wine
½ tsp cinnamon
¼ cup sugar
2 tsp cornflour
2 Tbsp red fruit jam or jelly

Boil ½ cup of the blueberries with the wine and cinnamon until the berries are soft. Mash well, or press through a sieve.

Mix the sugar and cornflour thoroughly then stir into the cooked berry mixture. Add jam or jelly, and boil until the mixture is thick and smooth, stirring often. Lift off the stove, stir the remaining berries through the hot sauce and spoon the warm filling into cooked filo shells.

Raspberry Filling
1 punnet (about 350 g/12 oz) raspberries
½ cup (125 ml/4 fl oz) red or white wine
¼ cup sugar
2 tsp cornflour
2 Tbsp red jam or redcurrant jelly

Boil ½ cup of raspberries with the wine, mash or sieve the mixture, stir in the thoroughly mixed sugar and cornflour, add the jam or jelly and proceed as for Blueberry Filling.

Strawberry Filling
1 punnet (about 350 g/12 oz) small
  strawberries
¼ cup (60 ml/2 fl oz) orange juice
¼ cup (60 ml/2 fl oz) water
¼ cup sugar
2 tsp cornflour
1 tsp finely grated orange rind
2 Tbsp apricot jam or redcurrant jelly

Hull and halve the strawberries. Boil ½ cup of them with the orange juice and water until soft, then mash or sieve. Mix the sugar and cornflour well, stir into the liquid, add the orange rind and jam or jelly, then proceed as for Blueberry Filling.

Filo pastries are best eaten within a few hours of the time they are made.

Yeast Breads and Buns

Cooking with yeast is very satisfying! Whether you stir together dough which requires no kneading, use a bread machine to prepare and cook dough, or mix, knead and shape the bread by hand, you are likely to fill the house with wonderful aromas and produce bread that gets eaten very promptly! Try some of the following recipes – they have delighted the people in my house and given me a lot of pleasure too.

White Bread

This is a basic white bread that I have made for many years. It improved noticeably when I started to use high-grade or bread flour and a yeast mixture which incorporated bread improvers.

For 1 kg (2 lb 3 oz) cooked bread:
6 tsp Surebake or Muripan yeast
1 Tbsp sugar
2 cups (500 ml/16 fl oz) lukewarm water
3 cups high-grade flour
2 Tbsp oil, melted butter or lecithin
  granules
2 tsp salt
2–3 cups extra (high-grade) flour

Put the first 3 ingredients in a large bowl in the order given, and mix well. When the yeast has dissolved, stir in the first measure of flour. Cover the bowl with cling film, a plate or an oven tray, then put it in a warm place for about 30 minutes until it rises to about twice its size.

Stir the risen mixture to deflate it, then stir in the oil, melted butter or lecithin, salt and as much flour as you need to make a dough that is firm enough to form into a ball. Turn it out on the floured bench to knead. Make sure you get all the bits of dough and flour from the bowl. Knead the dough for 5–10 minutes, adding just enough extra flour to stop it sticking to the bench and your hands. After a while the dough stops sticking, starts to spring back when you poke it, and feels satiny.

Make the dough into 2 loaves (to bake in medium-sized loaf tins). Use any buttered baking tins (or empty fruit cans) but make sure they are no more than half full at this stage. Stand the tins in a warm place for about 30 minutes, or until risen to twice the original size. Brush with milk, beaten egg or melted butter if you want them to brown nicely. Top with grated cheese, poppy seeds or toasted sesame seeds if you like.

Bake at 200°C (400°F) for about 30 minutes, until lightly browned. The loaves are ready when they sound hollow after being removed from their tins and tapped. Cool on racks and eat within 2 days.

No-Knead Brown Bread

No-Knead Brown Bread

You can make a firm-textured bread with brown (wholemeal) flour without kneading it at all. This is a well-flavoured, nutritious loaf, especially useful for anyone who is eating little or no meat.

For a 900 g (2 lb) loaf:
1½ tsp active dried yeast or 2½ tsp
  Surebake or Muripan yeast
2 cups (500 ml/16 fl oz) lukewarm water
1 Tbsp golden syrup
1 Tbsp oil or butter
4 cups wholemeal flour
1½ tsp salt

Use the larger amount of yeast if you want the dough to rise faster.

Put the yeast, water and golden syrup in a bowl big enough to add the flour to later. Stir to mix in the syrup, then cover and leave to stand in a sink of warm water, or in the sun for about 20 minutes, or until you can see little bubbles bursting on top.

Add the oil or butter (heated just enough to melt it), flour and salt. Stir together thoroughly, then beat with a wooden spoon (this helps the bread to rise).

Butter or oil a loaf tin that will hold 8 cups, or 2 large fruit cans. Put a piece of baking paper on the bottom of the tin to prevent bread sticking, then spoon the mixture evenly into the tin. Level the top with the back of a wet spoon.

Cover the tin with cling film and stand it in a sink of warm water (cover the sink with an oven tray), in the sun or in a turned-off oven. Leave to rise until twice its original size (probably about an hour).

Preheat the oven to 200°C (400°F). Sprinkle the loaf with sesame seeds if you like, put it in the middle of the oven, and bake for about 45 minutes. Turn the oven down if the top of the loaf gets too brown.

The top of this loaf stays fairly flat, so don't let this worry you. Pierce the middle of the loaf with a skewer – if the loaf is cooked, the skewer should come out without any uncooked dough or crumbs on it. Tip the loaf out of the tin and tap its bottom. It should sound hollow when it is cooked. If you think it needs a little longer, put it back in the oven for about 5 minutes, out of its tin.

Cool on a wire rack. When cold, put it in a plastic bag in the refrigerator. It will keep for about 4 days. It is easier to slice thinly after it has stood for a few hours.

High-grade or bakers' flour makes much better bread than plain, all-purpose flour. It also makes good scones and fruit cakes.

Yeast mixtures containing improvers such as Surebake and Muripan produce better breads than active dried yeast. If substituting, I use 1½ tsp Surebake or Muripan instead of 1 tsp active dried yeast.

To knead, push the heel of one hand into the dough firmly, pushing it away from you, then collect the dough and bring it towards you, with a circular movement of your other hand. Once you get under way the dough should move in a circle on the bench.

For best results when using a bread machine, lift the lid and check the dough consistency 5 minutes or so after the kneading starts. If necessary, add a little extra flour or water to make a soft-looking ball of dough that moves around the container as it is kneaded by the turning blade.

An oven that has been turned on for 3 minutes, then turned off, is usually about the right heat for rising bread. If necessary, take the partly risen dough from the almost cold oven, reheat it for another 2 or 3 minutes, then put the dough in to rise again. NEVER leave rising dough in an oven while it is on.

Mixed Grain Bread

This recipe makes a light-textured loaf, flecked with kibbled grains.

Makes 1 large loaf (8-cup pan):
1/2 cup mixed kibbled grains
1 1/4 cups (310 ml/10 fl oz) cold water
3 tsp Surebake or Muripan yeast
2 Tbsp olive oil
2 Tbsp sugar
1 1/2 tsp salt
1 Tbsp lecithin granules
1 cup wholemeal flour
2 1/2 cups high-grade flour

Cover the kibble mix with 2–3 cups water. Bring to the boil, then simmer for 1–2 minutes. Drain well in a sieve.

To make by hand:
Mix the prepared kibbled grains with the cold water in a large bowl. Add all the other ingredients except the high-grade flour. Mix thoroughly, cover and leave for 15 minutes in a warm place.

Stir in the high-grade flour, and add a little extra water or flour if necessary, to make the dough firm enough to knead. Knead with the dough hook of an electric mixture or by hand on a lightly floured surface for 10 minutes, adding extra flour if necessary, until the dough forms a soft ball that springs back when pressed gently. Turn the dough in 2–3 tsp oil in the cleaned, dry bowl, cover with cling film and leave in a warm, draught-free place for 30 minutes.

Knead the dough lightly in the bowl for a minute, then shape. Pat the dough into a square a little longer than the baking pan. Roll it into a cylinder, then put it into the buttered or sprayed pan, pressing it into the corners and levelling the top. Leave to rise in a warm, draught-free place for about an hour, or until double its original size.

Heat the oven to 200°C (400°F). Brush the loaf with beaten egg or egg glaze and sprinkle with poppy seeds or sesame seeds if desired. Bake for about 30 minutes, until the unmoulded loaf has a browned bottom and sides, and sounds hollow when tapped.

To make with a bread machine:
Carefully measure all the ingredients, including the prepared kibble mix and the cold water, into a 750 g (1 lb 10 oz) capacity bread machine, in the order specified by the manufacturer. Set to WHITE bread cycle, MEDIUM crust and START. After 5 minutes check that the dough has formed an even, roundish ball; if too sticky, add 1–2 Tbsp extra flour, if too dry, add 1–2 Tbsp extra water.

> Yeast needs to be mixed with water no hotter than a baby's bath water. If the water is too hot the yeast will be killed and the bread will not rise.

Bread to Shape and Bake

Using this basic recipe, then shaping it in different ways, you can make a selection of interesting breads such as quick rolls, pizza, pita bread, calzone, focaccia and breadsticks.

For about 900 g (2 lb) bread:
3 tsp Surebake or Muripan yeast
2 tsp sugar
1 1/2 cups (375 ml/12 fl oz) lukewarm water
2 Tbsp olive or canola oil
4 cups high-grade flour
3 Tbsp non-fat milk powder
1 1/2 tsp salt

To make by hand:
Mix the yeast, sugar and lukewarm water together, add the oil, cover and leave to stand in a warm place for 10 minutes or longer, until the yeast starts frothing.

Warm the flour in a microwave oven for about 45 seconds on High (100%) power or in an oven that has been turned to 150°C (300°F) for 5 minutes then turned off. Stir the milk powder, salt and enough warm flour into the bubbly yeast to make a dough firm enough to knead. Knead until smooth and satiny, about 5 minutes.

Turn the dough in a dribble of oil in a microwaveable bowl. Cover the bowl and leave to rise. The fastest way is to give it 1 minute, 30% power, bursts in the microwave every 5–10 minutes, or when the bowl of dough feels cold. The microwave is a good place to leave it to stand between bursts, too.

Otherwise use a pre-warmed oven (see box, p. 247) or stand the covered bowl in a sink of lukewarm water that has been covered with an oven tray. When the dough is twice its original size, knead it again thoroughly, and shape it as you like. If it rises before you are ready for it, give it a short knead, cover it again, and leave it to stand at room temperature. Keep doing this as it rises again, until you are ready to work with it more.

To make with a bread machine:
Carefully measure all the ingredients into a 750 g (1 lb 10 oz) capacity bread machine, in the order specified by the manufacturer. (If you have a machine of smaller capacity, reduce the ingredients proportionately.) Set to the WHITE bread cycle, MEDIUM crust and START (or use the DOUGH cycle and shape and bake by hand.) Check dough after 5 minutes (see box).

Quick Rolls

Shape the dough into about 20–24 rolls, dribble about 1 Tbsp olive oil onto a shallow dish and turn the rolls in this. Place on an oven tray and sprinkle with grated parmesan or other cheese, toasted sesame seeds or poppy seeds, etc. Cover lightly with cling film and leave in a warm place until they rise to almost twice their size. Bake at 220°C (425°F) for 10–15 minutes, until the tops and bottoms are browned.

Pizza V

Press or roll the dough out to form a large circle, 10–12 small circles or to fill two sponge roll pans. Use grainy cornmeal to stop shaped pizzas sticking to the oven tray. Top with your favourite pizza toppings (p. 187) and bake at 220–230°C (425–450°F) until the cheese melts and the base is browned slightly, 5–15 minutes, depending on size and thickness.

Pita Bread V

Cut the dough into 10–12 equal parts, roll each out 15–18 cm (6–7 in) across on a well-floured or cornmealed work surface, then leave to stand for about 10 minutes. Heat the oven to its highest temperature, with an oven tray, cast iron pan or griddle heated in the middle of it. Slide the first rolled circle onto a piece of cardboard, then slide it quickly onto the heated oven tray. In 1–2 minutes the bread should rise into a ball, then deflate. Lift out with tongs after no longer than 3 minutes, and put another bread in to cook. Pile the cooked pita breads in a plastic bag so they do not dry out.

Calzone

Roll the dough into 6–8 circles. Cover one half of each with pizza toppings (p. 187), leaving a small uncovered rim. Moisten this with water, then fold the uncovered half over the covered half. Lift onto the oven tray. Cut several air vents, leave to rise for about 10 minutes, then bake at 220°C (425°F) for about 10 minutes. Serve hot.

Focaccia V

Press the dough into olive-oiled sponge roll pans, making finger-hole depressions. Top with chopped olives, sauteed onion rings, sage or rosemary, sun-dried tomatoes, etc., then drizzle over 2–3 Tbsp olive oil. Leave to rise in a warm place for about 15 minutes. Sprinkle with grated Parmesan cheese if desired, then bake at 220°C (425°F) until golden brown, about 10–15 minutes. Serve warm, in rectangles.

Bread Sticks

Roll the dough into about 24–30 long, thin sticks, each about 20 cm (8 in) long. Place on an oiled oven tray, brush with lightly beaten egg white, then sprinkle liberally with Parmesan cheese.

Focaccia, Pan Bread, Knotted Rolls (rosettes)

Leave to stand for 10–20 minutes, then bake at 180°C (350°F) for about 20 minutes, until dried through and lightly browned. Store in airtight containers. Make fewer, thicker bread sticks, and cook at a higher temperature for a shorter time, if you want them to be soft in the middle.

Knotted Rolls

Cut the dough into about 18 pieces and roll each into a 25–26 cm (10 in) long 'pencil'. Knot each strip loosely, folding under the ends to make rosettes if you like. Put the shaped rolls on a lightly oiled oven tray. Cover lightly with cling film and leave in a warm place to rise to almost twice their size. Brush very gently with beaten egg or egg glaze then sprinkle with poppy seeds, toasted sesame seeds or finely grated cheese. Bake at 220°C (425°F) for 10–15 minutes, until golden brown.

Pan Bread

Melt 2 Tbsp butter in an electric frypan, then turn the pan off; it should be warm, not hot, to rise the bread.

Roll the dough into 25–36 even-sized balls, then turn in the melted butter in the frypan. Arrange the rolls so they all fit, and flatten each one slightly. Put the lid on and leave the rolls to rise for about 15 minutes.

When the dough has risen to almost double its original size, turn the pan on to 150°C (300°F). Keep the lid on and the steam vent closed. After about 5 minutes the rolls should have risen more, be fairly firm and dry (and white) on the top, and golden brown on the bottom. Turn over, one at a time, or in one piece. Cook for 3–5 minutes longer with the steam vent open, so the tops of the rolls are still warm, but some steam can escape.

Variation: Use 2 small, round heavy-based frypans instead of a large electric frypan. Heat gently so the bread does not burn before it is cooked.

'Shortcut' Bread

This 'shortcut' bread recipe makes three brown, crusty twists that are very light and white inside.

For 3 twisted loaves, each 400 g (14 oz):
2 cups (500 ml/16 fl oz) lukewarm water
1 Tbsp sugar
5 tsp Surebake or Muripan yeast
2 Tbsp olive oil
3 cups self-raising flour
1 tsp salt
about 3 cups high-grade flour

Put the warm water in a bowl, sprinkle over the sugar, then the yeast and olive oil. Stir, then leave to start working. Measure the self-raising flour and salt into a large bowl.

As soon as the yeast mixture starts to froth, stir it into the self-raising flour and beat vigorously with a wooden spoon. Cover the bowl with cling film and stand in a warm place. When it has risen until it has doubled its bulk, beat in enough of the high-grade flour to make a dough just firm enough to knead. Knead on a floured board until the dough springs back when pressed with a finger. Cut the dough in three.

Divide each piece in half, and roll out to make long sausages. Twist pairs of sausages together. (You get better-shaped loaves by starting to twist in the middle of each length, working towards the ends.) Place on greased baking trays and leave to rise until almost double in size. (Do not over-rise the dough.) Brush the risen loaves with beaten egg or egg glaze and sprinkle with poppy seeds, sesame seeds or coarse salt if desired. Bake at 220°C (425°F) for 15 minutes, or until well browned. Cool on racks. Serve warm or reheated.

Homemade bread is best eaten the day it is made, served warm and fresh.

Bagels

Bagels

Make your own wonderfully chewy bagels for about a tenth of the price of bought ones, in a surprisingly short time! Spoil yourself with the traditional toppings of cream cheese and smoked salmon. Bliss!

For 8 plump bagels:

3 tsp Surebake or Muripan yeast
1¼ cups (310 ml/10 fl oz) lukewarm water
1 Tbsp honey
1 Tbsp sugar
1½ tsp salt
½ cup wholemeal flour
2 Tbsp gluten flour (for chewier texture)
1½ cups high-grade flour

To make with a bread machine:

Carefully measure all the ingredients into a 750 g (1 lb 10 oz) capacity bread machine, in the order specified by the manufacturer.

Set to the DOUGH cycle and START (see box on p. 247). After 40 minutes stop the machine and remove the dough, even though the cycle is not complete. Shape and bake by hand as below.

To make by hand:

Measure the first 6 ingredients into a large bowl and mix thoroughly. Cover and leave for 15 minutes or longer in a warm place.

Stir in the gluten (which makes the bagels chewier) and high-grade flour, adding extra flour or water if necessary, until the dough is just firm enough to knead.

Knead with the dough hook of an electric mixer or by hand on a lightly floured surface for 10 minutes, until you have a soft dough that is smooth and satiny, and springs back when pressed gently.

Turn the dough in 2–3 tsp oil in the cleaned, dry bowl, cover with cling film and leave in a warm, draught-free place for 30 minutes.

Knead the dough lightly for a minute, then cut into 8 equal pieces. Roll each into a 'snake' about 26 cm (10 in) long, then dampen the ends with water and press together firmly, forming even rings. Place the rings on a sheet (or individual pieces) of oiled baking paper in a warm place and leave for 20–30 minutes, or until nicely risen.

Put about 10 cm (4 in) water in a large pot and bring to the boil.

Meanwhile turn the oven to 220°C (425°F).

Carefully lower 2 or 3 bagels at a time into the boiling water, lift away the paper, and cook for 45–60 seconds per side. Drain on paper towels, then put on a large baking tray lined with baking paper or a non-stick Teflon liner, leaving space for rising.

Brush as far down the sides as you can with beaten egg or egg glaze and sprinkle with poppy or toasted sesame seeds.

Bake for 10–12 minutes, until browned top and bottom. Cool on a rack and serve warm or toasted within 24 hours, or freeze in an airtight container as soon as they are cold.

Panini   V

Over the last few years, little, flat, oval breads called panini have become available. At first, they were available only in lunch bars, where they were displayed split and filled, ready for heating between hot, ridged plates after they were ordered. Now the unfilled, unsplit breads are in some bakeries and supermarkets.

If you can't find ready-made panini to fill and grill for a quick and delicious snack, make your own 'little breads' and refrigerate or freeze them until you want to fill and grill them.

For 8 panini:

2 Tbsp olive oil
1 cup (250 ml/8 fl oz) lukewarm water
2 tsp Surebake or Muripan yeast
2 tsp sugar
1 tsp salt
3 cups high-grade flour

To mix in a bread machine:

Put all the ingredients in a bread machine in the order listed and set it to the DOUGH cycle. Turn on and check the dough after 5 minutes. One hour after the machine starts kneading the dough, turn it off completely and take out the risen dough.

To mix by hand:

Mix all the ingredients (except the last half cup of flour) in a bowl. Add enough extra flour to make a ball that is just firm enough to knead. Knead by hand for 5–10 minutes, adding extra flour if the dough is too soft to work with. When the dough is smooth, elastic, and springs back when pressed with a finger, put it back in the bowl, cover with cling film and leave it to rise in a warm place for 1 hour.

To shape the dough:
Knead it lightly, then cut into 8 even pieces. Roll each (floured) piece into an oval shape, 18 x 8 cm (7 x 3 in). Arrange these on baking-paper-lined oven trays, then leave in a warm place to rise until double their original thickness, about 45 minutes.

Heat the oven to 180°C (350°F) and bake for about 12 minutes, until firm but not browned. Turn over after 10 minutes, for even cooking. Cool the cooked panini on a rack, brushing them evenly with olive oil while warm. Use immediately, or wrap, then refrigerate or freeze.

To fill panini:
Halve them (like hamburger buns). Spread with pesto. Fill with sliced cheddar, raclette or other cheese, and sliced tomato. If desired, add roasted or grill vegetables such as asparagus, peppers, onion, aubergine, mushrooms or zucchini. If available, add fresh basil and sliced ham, chicken or salami. (OR choose other fillings, but always include cheese.)

To cook the filled panini:
Place in a preheated double-sided grill, on medium or high heat, until the cheese melts and the bread browns. OR cook in a hinged, double-sided wire holder, on a barbecue or under a grill. OR heat on a preheated heavy frypan, pressing down on the panini as it cooks with a fish slice or something similar. (For best results, the filled panini should be under some pressure as they cook.)

English Muffins

These are made from a soft yeast dough and coated with cornmeal to stop them sticking to any surface they touch.

For 8 English muffins:
3/4 cup (185 ml/6 fl oz) hot water
1/2 cup (125 ml/4 fl oz) milk
1 Tbsp active dried yeast
2 tsp sugar
2 cups high-grade flour
1 tsp salt
2 Tbsp melted butter or oil
about 1/4 cup cornmeal (optional)

In a large bowl, mix the hot water and milk together to make a liquid slightly warmer than body temperature. Stir in the yeast and sugar until the yeast dissolves and leave to stand in a warm place for 5–10 minutes, until the surface bubbles. Measure the flour and salt into a microwaveable bowl and heat it on High (100%) power in 10-second bursts, until it feels warm (2 cups flour takes 20–30 seconds). Add the butter or oil to the yeast mixture, then beat in the warmed flour, mixing thoroughly. Leave to stand in a warm place until the mixture doubles in size (about 30 minutes).

Stir the mixture back to its original size and add enough extra flour so you can turn the mixture onto a board without it sticking. Keep the dough very soft, adding as little flour as possible. Cut into 8 pieces and roll into balls with well-floured hands. Roll the balls in cornmeal (to stop them sticking), then place each one on a 10 cm (4 in) square of sprayed or oiled baking paper or cling film and leave to rise in a warm place for 15–20 minutes, until light and puffy.

Carefully place the muffins, paper side up and top side down, into an electric frypan or griddle preheated to 150°C (300°F) then lift off the plastic or paper. Cook for about 2 minutes, then carefully turn. Cook the second side for 5–7 minutes, turn again and cook a further 5 minutes. (This produces muffins with even-sized cooked surfaces.) Cool on a rack.

Before serving, brown each side under the grill, then split and eat while hot with your favourite sweet or savoury topping. Alternatively, split the muffins, then brown them in the toaster.

> You can use a microwave to rise dough, warming the dough on Defrost (30%) power for 1 minute every 5–10 minutes. Feel the temperature of the dough before and after microwaving, taking care not to overheat.

Panini

Easter Wreath

This wreath is something really special! It may seem rather complicated the first time you try it, but it will be received so enthusiastically that you will want to make it again. Simplify the shaping if you like.

Dough

3 tsp active dried yeast
1¼ cups (310 ml/10 fl oz) lukewarm milk
1 Tbsp sugar
1½ tsp salt
50 g (2 oz) butter, softened
3 cups plain flour

Filling

50 g (2 oz) butter
2 Tbsp sugar
¼ cup plain flour
¾ tsp almond essence
½ cup each toasted almonds and dried apricots, chopped
¼ cup each red and green glacé cherries, chopped

To make in a bread machine:
Carefully measure all the ingredients into a 750 g (1 lb 10 oz) capacity bread machine, in the order specified by the manufacturer.

Set to the DOUGH cycle and START. When the cycle is complete, remove the dough and fill, shape and bake as below.

To make by hand:
Measure the first 5 ingredients into a large bowl with 1½ cups of the flour. Mix thoroughly then cover and leave for 15 minutes or longer in a warm place.

Add the remaining flour and stir to make a soft dough, adding a little extra flour if necessary to make a dough just firm enough to knead. Knead with the dough hook of an electric mixer, or by hand on a lightly floured surface for 10 minutes, adding extra flour if necessary, until the dough forms a soft ball that springs back when pressed gently.

Turn the dough in 2 tsp oil in the cleaned, dry bowl, cover with cling film and leave in a warm draught-free place for 30–40 minutes.

Prepare the filling by beating together the softened butter, sugar, flour and essence, then fold in the fruit and nuts.

Knead the dough lightly for a minute, then roll it out into a rectangle 25 x 75 cm (10 x 30 in), on a well-floured surface.

Dot the filling evenly over the dough then roll it up tightly, starting from a long edge. Cut the roll in half lengthwise using a sharp knife, then twist the 2 strands loosely together so the cut surfaces are outermost. Form into a ring, pinching the ends together, on a floured oven tray. Leave to rise in a warm, draught-free place for 40–60 minutes or until double its original size.

Heat the oven to 200°C (400°F). Brush the ring lightly with beaten egg and bake for 20 minutes, or until lightly browned. If you like, while warm, drizzle with icing made by mixing 1 cup sifted icing sugar with 2 Tbsp lemon juice until smooth.

Easter Wreath

Crumpets

Crumpets are like pikelets that are risen with yeast instead of baking powder. They have tunnels which run from bottom to top and a special different texture because they are made from a very runny dough. They are very popular and disappear very fast, topped with butter, syrup or honey.

For about 10 crumpets:
1½ cups (375 ml/12 fl oz) hot water
1 cup (250 ml/8 fl oz) milk
1 Tbsp active dried yeast
1 tsp sugar
2 cups high-grade flour
1 tsp salt

In a large bowl mix the hot water and milk together to make a liquid slightly warmer than body temperature. Stir in the yeast and sugar until the yeast dissolves. Leave to stand in a warm place until the surface bubbles, usually 5–10 minutes. Measure the flour and salt into a microwaveable bowl and heat on High (100%) power in 10-second bursts until it feels warm (2 cups flour takes 20–30 seconds).

With a wooden spoon, beat the warmed flour and salt into the yeast mixture, mixing thoroughly for several minutes. Cover with cling film and leave to stand in a warm place for about 30 minutes, until the mixture is bubbly and has doubled in size. (Use the microwave, warming the dough on Defrost (30%) power for 1 minute every 5–10 minutes. Feel the temperature of the dough before and after microwaving, taking care not to overheat.) Do not stir the risen mixture.

Heat a well-buttered or sprayed frypan to 150°C (300°F) or a griddle to a temperature lower than you would use for cooking pikelets. Spray or butter some 10 cm (4 in) metal rings. (I use clean tuna cans with both ends cut out.) Place the rings in the frypan and spoon in enough dough to fill the ring 1 cm (½ in) deep.

Cook the crumpets for about 5 minutes. As they cook, bubbles rise up and burst, leaving tunnels. If the bubbles do not burst, you can pop them with a buttered skewer towards the end of the cooking time. After 3–4 minutes, the edges should be cooked and you will probably be able to remove the baking ring. Turn the crumpets when the top is set, and cook for 1–2 minutes to dry the surface. Place on a rack to cool.

Before serving, brown both sides under a grill or in a toaster. Eat while hot, topped with butter and golden or maple syrup, honey or jam.

Note: For ease, speed and minimum mess, you can mix and rise half this mixture in a food processor bowl. (Do not microwave the metal blade though.)

Cream Buns

Cream buns are always popular with young children, but they are not cheap when you buy them regularly. It is worth making your own occasionally. Even if they are not perfect, nobody minds.

Extras can be frozen as soon as they have cooled, then thawed and filled, but they are really nicer eaten the day they are made.

For 18 buns:
½ cup (125 ml/4 fl oz) lukewarm water
1 tsp sugar
4 tsp Surebake yeast
50 g (2 oz) butter
1½ cups (375 ml/12 fl oz) milk
¼ cup (55 g/2 oz) sugar
½ tsp salt
1 egg
4–5 cups high-grade flour
½ cup sultanas or currants (optional)

Filling
¼–½ cup raspberry jam
1–2 cups sweetened whipped cream

Stir the first 3 ingredients together and leave to start working while the other ingredients are prepared.

Melt the butter in a large metal bowl then add the milk. Keep warming the bowl until the milk is body temperature. Add the sugar, salt and egg.

Measure the flour and warm it in the oven for a few minutes in cold weather.

Combine the egg and yeast mixtures and 3 cups of the flour. Beat well with a wooden spoon, cover the bowl with cling film or foil, and leave to stand in a warm place until twice its original bulk. Add the dried fruit and enough of the remaining flour to make a dough just firm enough to knead.

Knead by hand or in a mixer with a dough hook for about 10 minutes until the dough feels smooth, and springs back when poked with a finger.

Cut the dough into 18 pieces, then form each into a ball. Put these in two 23 cm (9 in) square, buttered cake tins. Cover with cling film so they don't dry out. Leave to rise in a warm place until they are twice their original bulk. (Do not over-rise or under-rise the dough at this stage.) Uncover and bake at 200°C (400°F) until lightly browned on the top and bottom, about 10–15 minutes. Cool on a wire rack.

When cool or cold, slice diagonally and fill with raspberry jam and whipped cream. Dust with icing sugar if desired. Eat the day they are made.

> Glazes and toppings can make your home-made breads look irresistible. Bread machine instruction books often tell you how to make machine-made breads look extra-special.

Bread Glazes and Toppings

What you put on the surface of the bread you make affects its appearance a lot.

Floury-Topped Breads

A floury top gives a 'cottagy', home-baked look to a loaf or rolls. Sprinkle the flour onto the risen loaf using a shaker with small holes or a sieve. If you lightly wet the surface first, the flour sticks better, and the crust tends to be firmer. If you score the crust of the risen loaf with a very sharp blade after flouring it, before baking it, the cuts will be an attractive, contrasting colour.

Egg Glaze for Breads

If you brush the surface of the risen loaf with beaten egg or egg glaze just before it is baked, it will brown better and have an attractive shine. The crust will be thin and fairly tender.

Shake together in a tightly closed jar, or beat with a fork in a bowl 1 egg, 1 Tbsp water, ½ tsp sugar. This will keep in the refrigerator for 2–3 days.

An egg glaze also sticks a topping onto a loaf. Brush the uncooked bread with the glaze then sprinkle with poppy seeds, sesame seeds, sunflower or pumpkin seeds, coarse cornmeal, etc.

Note: Take care. Toppings such as kibbled grains harden during cooking. Do not break your teeth!

Milk-Glazed Breads

For a slightly glazed appearance and a thin crust, brush the bread with milk instead of egg glaze. Milk containing some fat works better than very low-fat milk.

Water and Steam

For a crusty loaf, put a roasting pan containing water 1 cm (½ in) deep on the bottom shelf of the oven 5 minutes before you put the bread in. For extra crustiness, spray the crust with water several times during cooking. Remove the pan of water 5 minutes before you take the bread from the oven. Spraying by itself, without the pan of water in the oven, is not very effective.

A longer cooking time produces a crustier loaf, but you must be careful not to overcook the bread.

Golden Syrup Glaze

To give a shiny brown glaze to sweet buns and bread, make a syrup by bringing to the boil 1 Tbsp each of golden syrup, honey and water. Brush on buns and breads (which have not been egg-glazed) as soon as they come from the oven. This glaze softens the crust, too.

For a darker glaze replace the honey with extra syrup. For a lighter glaze, use all honey and no syrup.

Baking Powder Breads

Loaves risen with baking powder are usually quick and easy to mix, and bake reliably with little attention. They keep for several days – if they get the chance – will freeze well, and are popular sliced and buttered, in school lunches or at home at any time of day. They are usually less rich than cakes, and they often have the bonus of containing fresh or dried fruit, vegetables and bran, in a form that nearly everybody enjoys. I hope you enjoy baking and eating them as much as my family does.

Date and Walnut Loaf

For best flavour, leave this for 24 hours before cutting. It keeps for up to a week.

75 g (2½ oz) butter
1 cup chopped, pitted dates
¾ cup brown sugar
finely grated rind of 1 orange
1 cup (250 ml/8 fl oz) boiling water
1 egg
2 cups plain flour or 2 cups wholemeal flour
3 tsp baking powder
½ tsp salt
½ cup chopped walnuts

Turn the oven to 180°C (350°F). Cut the butter into cubes and put it in a bowl (or pot) with the dates, brown sugar and grated rind. Pour over the boiling water and leave to stand for about 10 minutes, stirring occasionally until the butter melts. Cool to room temperature before adding the other ingredients.

Meanwhile, line the long sides and bottom of a 7-cup (1¾ litres/56 fl oz) capacity tin with a strip of baking paper. Butter or spray the ends of the tin.

Beat the egg until frothy. Stir the remaining ingredients together until well combined. Tip the egg and the mixed dry ingredients on top of the cooled date mixture, then fold the three mixtures together, stirring only until everything is dampened, but not smooth. (If overmixed, the loaf will rise to a peak and be tough.)

Turn into the prepared tin and bake for about 40 minutes, or until a skewer pushed into the centre of the loaf comes out clean.

Coconut Loaf

This loaf is easy to make. Although it contains no butter or oil it is a moist loaf with a lovely flavour. Enjoy it the day it is made as a cake, or served warm as a dessert, with fruit and whipped cream. After this, butter it and eat it within 4 or 5 days.

Coconut Loaf, Date and Walnut Loaf with Orange Cream Cheese (p. 346)

2 eggs
1 tsp vanilla essence
¼ tsp almond essence
¼ tsp salt
1½ cups (375 ml/12 fl oz) milk
1½ cups coconut
1½ cups sugar
2 cups self-raising flour

Turn the oven to 180°C (350°F). Prepare a loaf tin as for the Date and Walnut Loaf, above.

Beat the first 5 ingredients together until combined.

Measure the coconut, sugar and flour into another container and mix well. Stir gently into the egg mixture until combined, but not smooth. Do not overmix. Pour into the prepared tin.

(If you have a food processor, process all the ingredients except the flour until mixed well. Add the flour and mix very briefly, in bursts, just enough to dampen the flour. Turn into the tin as above.)

Put the loaf in the oven and turn the heat down to 160°C (325°F), so the top doesn't brown too fast. Bake for 40–60 minutes, until the centre feels firm and a skewer pushed down to the base comes out clean.

Cool in the tin for about 5 minutes, then turn onto a rack.

Sultana Tea Bread

Although it is recommended, my family never manage to leave this loaf for 24 hours before cutting it. By this time it has always been eaten!

1 cup sultanas
1 tsp mixed spice
1 tsp cinnamon
25 g (1 oz) butter
1 cup (250 ml/8 fl oz) hot tea
1 cup (packed) brown sugar
2–2¼ cups self-raising flour

Turn the oven to 180°C (350°F). Put the sultanas, mixed spice, cinnamon and butter into a medium-sized bowl. Pour over hot, recently made tea and leave to stand until cold. When the mixture is cool, add the brown sugar and flour. (If you use 2 cups of flour the loaf will be cake-like and moister, whereas 2¼ cups will give you a larger, bread-like loaf.) Mix only enough to dampen the sugar and flour. Do not overmix or the loaf will be tough.

Line a 20 cm (8 in) cake tin, or a 23 x 12 cm (9 x 5 in) loaf tin, with baking paper and pour the slightly lumpy-looking mixture evenly into it. Bake for 35–45 minutes in the cake tin, or 1 hour in the loaf tin, until a skewer pushed into the middle comes out clean.

Store in a covered container when cold. It is said to be best if left for 24 hours before cutting! Serve sliced, buttered or spread with cream cheese.

Fruity Bran Loaf

This is a quick, easy loaf to mix. Always put the Allbran and milk into the bowl first, so it can soak while you get everything else ready.

1 cup Allbran
1 cup (250 ml/8 fl oz) milk
1 cup chopped dates, sultanas or mixed fruit
1 cup brown sugar
1 cup self-raising flour

Turn the oven to 190°C (375°F). Put the Allbran and milk in a mixing bowl and leave for at least half an hour (or longer) before you add the flour.

Meanwhile, chop the dates or break up any lumps of sultanas or mixed fruit. Put the fruit in a sieve and run very hot water over it to clean and soften it, then put it in with the bran and milk. Stir in the brown sugar.

At least half an hour after the bran and milk were mixed, stir in the flour (without overmixing). Spoon the mixture into a loaf tin lined with baking paper across the bottom and the long sides.

Bake for 45 minutes, until the loaf feels firm and a skewer pushed into the middle comes out clean.

Sharon's Banana Bread

This is my favourite, and probably easiest, banana bread.

125 g (4½ oz) butter, softened
1½ cups sugar
3 eggs
*500–600 g (1 lb 2 oz–1 lb 5oz) ripe bananas**
2½ cups self-raising flour

* This is the unpeeled (as bought) weight. Very ripe bananas which have clearish, soft flesh give the best flavour and texture.

Turn the oven to 180°C (350°F). Soften, but do not melt the butter. Put it in a food processor or bowl, add the sugar and mix until light-coloured and creamy.

Mix in the eggs one at a time, adding a spoonful of the flour between each egg so the mixture does not curdle.

Peel the bananas and mash them with a fork, then mix half the bananas into the mixture with half the remaining flour. Repeat with the rest of the bananas and flour.

Line the bottom and long sides of one very large (8-cup capacity) or two smallish (3–4 cup capacity) loaf tins with a folded piece of baking or greaseproof paper, then lightly butter or spray the ends of the tins. Spoon in the mixture. Do not fill any tin more than two-thirds full.

Bake for about 45 minutes for 2 loaves, and slightly longer for 1 large loaf, until a skewer pushed into the middle of the loaf comes out clean. Leave to stand for 5 minutes before removing from the tin.

Eat unbuttered slices on the day of making, and butter them after this.

Sticky Lemon Loaf

The crunchy sweet-sour topping on this loaf makes it interesting and different.

100 g (3½ oz) butter, softened
¾ cup sugar
finely grated rind and juice of 2 lemons
2 eggs
1½ cups plain flour
1 tsp baking powder
½ tsp salt
½ cup (125 ml/4 fl oz) milk
¼ cup sugar

Turn the oven to 180°C (350°F). Cream the butter and the first measure of sugar. Add the lemon rind, then the eggs one at a time, beating well after each addition.

Sharon's Banana Bread

Sift together the flour, baking powder and salt, then add alternately with the milk to the creamed mixture.

Line the bottom and long sides of a loaf tin (about 23 x 13 cm/9 x 5 in) with a sheet of greaseproof or baking paper. Turn the mixture into the tin and bake for 1 hour, or until the loaf shrinks from the sides of the tin and a skewer pushed into the middle of the loaf comes out clean.

While the loaf cooks, mix the lemon juice with the second measure of sugar (do not heat them) and sprinkle, spoon or brush this over the top of the hot loaf as soon as it comes out of the oven. Remove from the tin and brush any extra lemon on the sides and bottom. Leave to cool on a wire rack.

Slice when cold, and serve buttered or plain.

Note: You can make this load in a food processor; chop the thinly peeled lemon rind into the sugar before adding the butter, then proceed as above.

Gingerbread

This is a soft-textured, light-coloured gingerbread. It is best eaten within a few days.

100 g (3¹/₂ oz) butter
¹/₂ cup (packed) brown sugar
¹/₂ cup (125 ml/4 fl oz) boiling water
¹/₂ cup (125 ml/4 fl oz) golden syrup
2 large eggs
2 cups plain flour
1 tsp baking powder
¹/₂ tsp baking soda
2 tsp ground ginger
1 tsp cinnamon

Turn the oven to 200°C (400°F). Line the bottom and 2 sides of a 23 cm (9 in) square tin with baking paper.

Cut the butter into small squares and put it in a large bowl with the brown sugar. Pour over the boiling water, then add the syrup (measured with a hot, wet measuring cup). Add the eggs and beat with a rotary egg beater until the last pieces of butter have dispersed and the egg is mixed thoroughly. Sift in the dry ingredients and give a brief 'burst' with the beater to combine the liquid and dry ingredients.

Pour the fairly thin mixture into the prepared tin. Put in the oven and turn the heat down to 180°C (350°F). Bake for about 25 minutes, until the centre springs back when pressed and a skewer comes out clean. Cool for 5 minutes then invert onto a cooling rack.

Serve buttered, or reheat and serve as a hot pudding with a topping of whipped cream and chopped nuts, or puréed apples or stewed fruit.

Fresh Gingerbread

This wonderful, spicy gingerbread is best eaten warm, topped with lightly whipped cream.

125 g (4¹/₂ oz) butter
1 tsp grated lemon rind
¹/₂ cup (125 ml/4 fl oz) boiling water
¹/₂ cup (firmly packed) brown sugar
¹/₂ cup (125 ml/4 fl oz) golden syrup
1 large egg
1 Tbsp finely grated root ginger
1³/₄ cups plain flour
1 tsp baking soda
1 tsp grated nutmeg
¹/₄ tsp ground cloves
¹/₂ tsp cinnamon

Turn the oven to 180°C (350°F). Prepare a ring pan or loaf tin that holds at least 7 cups (1³/₄ litres/56 fl oz), lining the bottom with baking paper or a non-stick liner and lightly buttering the sides.

Cut the butter into 16 cubes, put in a pot, add the lemon rind and pour over the water. Heat until the butter melts, then remove from the heat. (Do not let the mixture boil.) Cool to bath temperature.

Whisk in the brown sugar, golden syrup, unbeaten egg and root ginger, and cool to lukewarm in cold water.

Add the sifted dry ingredients and beat with a whisk or beater until the mixture is relatively free of lumps, without beating more than you need to. Pour into the prepared tin and bake for 40 minutes, until a skewer inserted deeply comes out clean. Cool in the tin for about 5 minutes, then transfer to a serving plate.

Dust lightly with icing sugar and serve warm, plain or with fresh fruit and lightly whipped cream.

Food Processor Carrot Loaf

Quickly and easily made, this loaf always disappears fast!

200 g (7 oz) carrots, cubed
¹/₄ cup (60 ml/2 fl oz) canola or other oil
³/₄ cup brown sugar
1 tsp vanilla essence
¹/₄ tsp salt
¹/₄ cup (60 ml/2 fl oz) apple or orange juice
¹/₂ cup coconut
³/₄ cup wholemeal self-raising flour, or wholemeal flour plus 1¹/₂ tsp baking powder
1 tsp baking soda
1 tsp cinnamon

Turn the oven to 180°C (350°F). Put the cubed carrots in a food processor and chop very finely. Add the oil, sugar, vanilla, salt and juice and process to combine. Add the coconut, flour, soda and cinnamon and process briefly.

Line a loaf tin with baking paper. Pour the mixture into the tin and bake for 30 minutes, until a skewer comes out clean and the centre springs back when pressed.

Serve plain or spread with butter, cream cheese or Apricot Conserve (p. 325).

Flour Tortillas

If you can't easily buy flour tortillas, or if you want a cheaper alternative, considering making your own. They're not difficult and they taste very good.

For 8–12 tortillas:
2 cups plain flour
1 tsp baking powder
1 tsp salt
¹/₄ cup (60 ml/2 fl oz) canola oil
1 cup (250 ml/8 fl oz) bath-temperature water

Combine the flour, baking powder and salt in a bowl. Add the oil and mix lightly until the dough is crumbly, as for pastry. Stir in the water and mix lightly until the dough forms a ball.

OR put the first 4 ingredients in a food processor. Add the water while mixing (pulse mode) until the mixture forms a soft, easily worked ball. Knead the dough on a lightly floured surface until it is smooth and elastic (about 5 minutes). Put the dough in a plastic bag and let it rest in a warm place for at least 30 minutes, or up to 2 hours.

Divide the dough into 8–12 portions. Roll each portion with your hands to form a ball then, on a lightly floured surface, roll each ball out to form a very thin circle about 20 cm (8 in) or more in diameter. Layer the tortillas between pieces of plastic wrap or baking paper.

Heat a heavy frypan or griddle, or a flat barbecue plate, until it is smoking. Brush the surface lightly with oil. Place a tortilla on the hot surface and cook for about 30 seconds, pressing down with a spatula as it puffs up. Turn and cook the other side until it is speckled with brown but still soft enough to fold.

Remove from the heat and, before each tortilla cools, slip it into a plastic bag, making a pile. Fold the top of the bag over to keep the tortillas moist, and to ensure they stay soft enough to wrap around fillings.

Cook the remaining tortillas in the same way. (Bagged tortillas may be kept refrigerated for up to 3 days.)

See also:
Scones, p. 259

Scones, Pikelets and Pancakes

These quick breads are wonderful standbys. It is well worth perfecting the art of making them, so you can whip up a batch without a second thought. Scones hot from the oven and pikelets and pancakes warm from the pan will fill your family and provide a welcome for unexpected guests, and may well make your reputation as a good baker. How nice to think that simple, plain baking can be so popular!

Scones

If you can make a batch of scones quickly and easily, it doesn't matter if you run out of bread. Remember that practice makes perfect!

For about 9 scones:
2 cups self-raising flour
1/4 tsp salt
2 tsp sugar (optional)
25 g (1 oz) butter
1/2 cup (125 ml/4 fl oz) milk
1/4–1/2 cup (60–125 ml/2–4 fl oz) water

Turn the oven to 220°C (425°F). Sift the flour, salt and sugar into a mixing bowl. Heat the butter until it melts, and tip with the milk and the smaller amount of water into the flour.

Mix with a knife or spatula until blended but not overmixed, adding extra water to make a soft dough. Turn onto a floured bench and roll out lightly, about 22 cm (9 in) square. Cut into 9 rough squares, place them about 1 cm (1/2 in) apart on an oven tray, and bake in the middle of the oven for about 10 minutes, until the tops and bottoms of the scones are lightly browned.

Serve hot or warm, with your favourite spreads.

Note: Last time I priced them, homemade scones cost half the price of everyday bread, weight for weight!

Pan-Cooked Scones

These cook in a covered frypan, saving your time and fuel.

For about 6 wedges:
Make scone dough as above, and roll out on a lightly floured board into a 20–23 cm (8–9 in) circle, to fit a heavy frypan. Cut into 6 wedges, and put these close together in the lightly buttered, preheated frypan.

Cover and cook over low heat until the bottoms are browned, then carefully slide out of the pan onto a flat lid or plate, flip back, raw side down, and cook uncovered. Break or cut into wedges, and serve warm.

Scones

Note: Make sure the centre is cooked before taking the scones from the pan, as the cooking time varies with the thickness and heat of the pan etc. If they are not cooked right through, split each one, put a little butter in the pan, and cook a little longer, split side down.

Scone Pinwheels

Warm scone pinwheels taste so good! Make them with sweet or savoury fillings.

Turn the oven to 220°C (425°F). Make scone dough as above and roll out thinly on a well-floured surface, so it is about 30 x 20 cm (12 x 8 in).

Spread with a little melted butter and cinnamon sugar (p. 11), with grated cheese and chutney or tomato sauce, or with savoury leftovers, leaving about 2 cm (3/4 in) uncovered on the long side that is away from you. Dampen this strip with water.

Roll up so the dampened edge is rolled last. Cut into 1–2 cm (1/2–3/4 in) slices with a sharp knife, lay each piece flat on an oven tray lined with baking paper, and bake until lightly browned top and bottom, turning down the heat a little if the filling darkens too much.

Scone Twists

If you feel your scones leave a little bit to be desired, don't make plain scones, where every imperfection shows, but try an interesting variation.

scone dough (see above)

Filling
1/4 cup brown sugar
1 tsp cinnamon
1 Tbsp cold butter
1/4 cup coconut

Turn the oven to 200°C (400°F). Make scone dough as above and roll out into a long, thin rectangle, about 40 x 20 cm (16 x 8 in).

Put the filling ingredients in a food processor, and process just enough to combine them. (If you don't have a food processor, melt the butter then mix it with the other ingredients.)

Spread the filling on the half of the dough farthest away from you, leaving 1 cm (1/2 in) on the far edge uncovered. Dampen this strip, then fold the uncovered half over the covered dough. Press together firmly, then cut into 1 cm (1/2 in) strips crosswise. Twist each strip twice, and transfer to an oven tray lined with baking paper. Press each end down firmly.

Bake for 10–15 minutes, until lightly browned. Serve warm, buttered or plain.

Barbecued Savoury Scones V

For about 8 scones:
2 cups self-raising flour
2 Tbsp grated Parmesan cheese
1/4 cup chopped fresh herbs
2 tsp sugar
1/4 cup (60 ml/2 fl oz) cream
about 1/2 cup (125 ml/4 fl oz) milk

Measure the flour, cheese, herbs and sugar into a mixing bowl. Add the cream then enough milk to form a soft dough that is just firm enough to form a ball. Coat with a little more flour and pat out to form a 20–23 cm (8–9 in) circle (to fit a frypan that has a lid). Thoroughly butter the bottom and lower sides of the frypan, put the circle of dough in it, pat it out further if necessary so that it covers the whole base, then mark it into eighths with a floured knife. Put the lid on the pan and take it outside to stand until needed; up to an hour.

Place the covered pan on the barbecue and cook over fairly high heat until the pan heats up. It should take about 6 minutes for the scones to become light brown on the bottom and cook through to the centre. Turn the gas higher or lower to achieve this if necessary.

Turn the segments of scone with a spatula or fish slice, and cook the second side for 4–5 minutes, or until similarly browned. Leave the lid ajar while the second side cooks. Serve soon after cooking.

Lemonade and Cream Scones

Lemonade and Cream Scones

This untraditional scone recipe is so easy and reliable I make it often. Try for yourself!

For 8 large square scones:
2 cups self-raising flour
¼ cup sugar
½ tsp salt
½ cup (125 ml/4 fl oz) cream
½ cup (125 ml/4 fl oz) plus 2 Tbsp lemonade

Turn the oven to 230°C (450°F), or 220°C (425°F) for a fan oven. Put the dry ingredients into a large bowl and toss to mix. Add the cream and lemonade, and mix to make a soft dough. Flour the dough lightly and turn it onto a floured board.

Knead lightly half a dozen times then pat or roll the dough out until it is about 2 cm (³/₄ in) thick, and twice as long as it is wide. Cut it in half lengthways, and in four crosswise, using a floured knife.

Arrange the scones on a baking tray (close together if you like soft sides, or further apart for crusty sides). For a good colour, brush the tops with a little milk or melted butter. Bake for 10–12 minutes, until the tops and bottoms are lightly browned.

Serve warm (or reheated), split, with butter and jam, or jam and whipped cream. Fresh strawberries or raspberries make an excellent addition.

Note: These scones stay fresh and soft for 48 hours – if they get the chance!

When making scones, fork the flour until light before measuring it, then spoon it into the measuring cup lightly.

Pikelets

Pikelets are great for a quick snack or when you have unexpected company. Spread them with butter and jam, top them with hundreds and thousands for small children, or 'dress them up' with whipped cream, jam and fresh berries.

For 12–20 pikelets:
1 household Tbsp golden syrup
25 g (1 oz) butter
1 Tbsp sugar
½ cup (125 ml/4 fl oz) milk*
1 large egg
1 cup self-raising flour

* For very tender pikelets replace the milk with ³/₄ cup (185 ml/6 fl oz) buttermilk.

Heat a frypan (use the second highest setting if it is electric).

Dip a household tablespoon in hot water, then measure the syrup into a bowl. Add the butter, warm to soften both, then mix in the sugar, milk and egg.

Sprinkle the flour over the top, then mix briefly with a whisk or beater, just until smooth.

Rub the surface of the hot frypan with a little butter on a paper towel. Drop 1 or 2 Tbsp of mixture into the pan, pouring it off the tip of the spoon to make nice round pikelets. (If the first pikelets are too thick and do not spread, add a little extra milk to the mixture.)

As soon as you see bubbles begin to burst on the surface, turn the pikelets over. (Turn the heat up if the pikelets are not brown enough, or turn it down if they are too brown when the first bubbles burst.) When the centres of the second side spring back

when touched, the pikelets are ready. Cook in batches until all the batter is used.

Cool the pikelets in a clean, folded teatowel; transfer to a plastic bag when cold. Serve warm, as described above.

Variations: Leave out the golden syrup and use 3 Tbsp sugar.

Replace the butter with 2 Tbsp canola oil and add a pinch of salt.

Peg Eason's Chocolate Pikelets

These pikelets are deliciously different!

For about 20 pikelets:
1 Tbsp butter, melted
1 large egg
½ tsp vanilla essence
½ cup sugar
½ cup (125 ml/4 fl oz) milk
1 cup plain flour
1–2 Tbsp cocoa
½ tsp baking soda
1 tsp cream of tartar
pinch of salt

Put the melted butter in a bowl big enough to mix all the ingredients in. Add the egg, vanilla, sugar and milk, and beat with a whisk or egg beater until well mixed.

Put a sieve over the bowl and measure the dry ingredients into it (use the extra cocoa for a darker colour and strong chocolate flavour). Sift into the bowl on top of the liquid mixture, then whisk or beat in very briefly, stopping mixing as soon as everything is combined. (Overmixing toughens pikelets.)

Heat a lightly buttered, heavy frypan then drop in dessertspoonfuls of mixture. Turn the pikelets as soon as the first bubbles burst on the top.

Thin the mixture with a little extra milk if necessary, but keep it and the pikelets fairly thick if they are to be split later.

Cool the pikelets in a clean, folded teatowel. When cold, transfer to a plastic bag. To serve, split with a very sharp knife, leaving a small hinge; fill with raspberry jam and whipped cream flavoured with icing sugar and vanilla (especially if they are to be transported). Or top with jam and whipped cream.

Pancake Rolls

Rolled pancakes are useful for school lunches, adding variety, and fitting easily into lunchboxes. They can also be made in just a few minutes.

These pancakes have the consistency and thickness of pikelets. I use just less than half a cup of batter to make each one and I drop currants or sultanas onto the middle of the pancake as soon as I have put it in the pan. If you do this promptly the dried fruit sinks into the batter and doesn't affect the surface of the second side.

For 6 pancakes:
50 g (2 oz) butter
2 eggs
1/4 cup sugar
1 cup (250 ml/8 fl oz) milk
1 1/2 cups self-raising flour
sultanas or currants

Melt the butter until liquid, then remove from the heat. Break the eggs into the same pot or bowl and add the sugar. Beat with a whisk or fork until smooth then add the milk, then the flour. Whisk again, just until the flour is mixed in – overbeating toughens the pancakes.

Heat a frypan until a drop of water dances around it (about 190°C/375°F). Oil or spray the surface of the pan (before the first pancake only) then pour in half a cup of batter. Tilt the pan slightly so the mixture forms an even circle and drop a handful of currants or sultanas in the centre. Flip the pancake over with a fish slice as soon as bubbles start to break on its surface. Cook the second side until it is golden and the centre of the pancake is cooked (test with a knife if you are not sure). Remove from the pan, place on a paper towel or teatowel and roll both up together, forming a reasonably tight cylinder. Cool on a rack. Unwrap and fill when cold.

Suitable fillings include grated cheese and jam, cottage cheese or cream cheese with jam, lemon juice-dipped slices or strips of banana with jam, cottage cheese, etc.

Crêpes

These thin, delicate, tender pancakes are made in a small pan. As long as they are kept from drying out, they may be made ahead and refrigerated or frozen till required. This recipe makes 8 crêpes using 2 Tbsp (1/8 cup) of batter for each one, allowing for a few experimental failures.

2 eggs
3/4 cup (185 ml/6 fl oz) milk
1/2 cup plain flour
1/2 tsp salt

Combine the ingredients in the order given, in a food processor or blender. If mixing in a bowl, add the egg then the milk to the dry ingredients and beat until smooth.

Heat a small, sprayed or buttered pan, then pour in a measured quantity (e.g. 2 Tbsp) of the batter. Immediately tilt the pan so the batter covers the bottom in a thin film. If it does not spread thinly, add more milk to thin the batter down before making the next crêpe. Don't worry if the crêpes are not even circles.

When the batter no longer looks wet in the centre, ease the edges of the crêpe from the pan. (The underside should be golden-brown by this time. Raise or lower the heat before making the next crêpe if necessary.) Lift carefully with your fingers or a fine-bladed food turner. Dry the second side, without necessarily browning it. Remove from the pan.

Stack the crêpes until required, placing them on a plate in a plastic bag to prevent them drying out.

To freeze crêpes:
Freeze crêpes in a stack, putting a piece of plastic film between each one so they can be removed easily. Slide the stack of crêpes into a plastic bag with a piece of cardboard underneath to keep them flat. Remove the air from the bag and seal with a rubber band. They thaw quickly when required.

Filling crêpes:
Place one crêpe at a time on a board. Either spread several spoonfuls of filling evenly over the whole surface, or place it in a line down the centre. Roll or fold the filled crêpe, and place it on a lightly buttered, shallow, microwavable or ovenproof dish. Cover with plastic film (or foil), and microwave (or bake) until warmed through. The time needed will depend on the number, and whether they are tightly packed, etc. Serve hot or warm.

Top sweet crêpes with a sprinkling of lightly toasted slivered almonds or a dusting of icing sugar, and whipped cream, if desired.

Variation: Place a spoonful of jam in the middle of each crêpe, and fold the sides over it to make a square package. Place each package, smooth side up, in a lightly buttered pan. Brown lightly, then turn and brown the top. Serve warm, with sour cream or crème fraîche.

Peg Eason's Chocolate Pikelets

Savoury Crêpe Filling Suggestions

- Roll asparagus spears in crêpes spread with cream cheese or cheese sauce. Top with more cheese sauce and/or grated cheddar cheese. Heat.
- Sauté apple wedges in butter with sliced onions and chopped bacon. Roll, top with grated cheese and grill to brown, or fold in quarters and serve with maple syrup.
- Fill with sautéed mushrooms in thickened cheese or white wine sauce, with or without herbs. Sprinkle with Parmesan cheese and brown under the grill.
- Fill with chilli con carne or other mince mixtures in thickened sauce. Top with grated cheese and brown under the grill.
- Fill with smoked fish in white wine or cheese sauce. Use a mixture of seafood if desired. Top with extra thinned sauce or grated cheese and brown under the grill.
- Fill with sautéed chicken livers in lightly thickened sauce.
- Mix lightly cooked vegetables such as broccoli, corn, sweet peppers or mushrooms with grated cheese. Cover with cheese sauce and grill or bake.
- Mix chopped smoked salmon with cream cheese or scrambled egg. Roll up and serve promptly.
- Coat cooked chicken with mayonnaise. Add almonds or sautéed mushrooms and roll. Sprinkle with Parmesan or grated cheese and reheat under the grill.

See also:

Blueberry Buttermilk Pancakes, p. 13

Fruity Pancakes, p. 13

Giant Baked Pancake, p. 13

Crêpes, p. 33

Apple Pancake, p. 230

Make a Muffin

You can gain a reputation as a great baker by making only muffins! Besides being enormously popular, muffins are so easy to mix and bake that you are likely to become an expert in no time. There are so many interesting flavours to choose from that you should never get bored – in fact, your only problem is likely to be deciding what type of muffin to make next!

TIPS FOR MARVELLOUS MUFFINS

Muffins are very quick and easy – but to make your reputation as a MARVELLOUS muffin maker, you need to know the finer points!

- When making muffins, do as you should for all baking and always spoon the flour you are using into the cup measure lightly. Do not bang the cup, or pack the flour down with a spoon or you will be adding more flour than you should.

- Combine the dry ingredients in a bowl that is big enough to mix all the ingredients in later. Mix them well, so they are light and airy.

- Mix the liquids in another container. Melt butter in the microwave or on the stove, add the other liquids and egg, and mix with a fork, beater or whisk, so that you end up with a mixture that is at room temperature.

- Extra ingredients may be mixed with the liquids, they are sometimes stirred through the dry mixture, or they may be added separately, depending on the recipe.

- The way you combine the dry and wet mixtures is vital. Add all the liquid and extra ingredients at once. Fold them together with as little mixing as possible, until no pockets of flour are left. Stop while the mixture looks rough and lumpy. NEVER give it a quick beat or stir for good measure!

- Muffins can stick like crazy! Use pans with a non-stick finish, clean them well, but without scratching them, and always use a light, even coating of non-stick spray as an extra precaution.

- Spoon muffins into prepared pans, helping the mixture off with another spoon. Put as few spoonfuls in each pan as possible and let the mixture mound naturally – do not smooth or interfere with the surface. Add toppings if you like.

Crunchy Lemon Muffins, Chocolate Banana Muffins

- Bake at a high temperature until the centres spring back when pressed. If this is hard to judge, push a skewer into the centre. When it comes out clean, the muffins are ready. If you have the temperature right, the outsides should be attractively browned by this stage.

- The cooking times given are only a guide. My muffins are cooked in an oven with a fan. Without a fan, use higher temperatures or allow more time.

- After cooking, let muffins stand in pans for 3–4 minutes. They loosen themselves in this time! Press down gently round the edges with several fingers of one hand, and twist slightly. As soon as the muffins turn freely, lift them out.

- Muffins are best served warm. They stay warm for some time, without going soggy, in a napkin-lined basket. Reheat when necessary in a microwave oven, or in a paper bag at about 150°C (300°F) in a conventional oven. (Do not overheat.)

- Muffin tins vary in size. Most of my recipes make 12 medium-sized muffins (normal muffin pans), 24–30 mini-muffins, or 6 'monster' Texan muffins.

Crunchy Lemon Muffins

A great favourite! The lemon and sugar topping gives a tangy flavour and an interesting sugary crunch.

For 12 medium muffins:
2 cups plain flour 8 oz
3/4 cup sugar 6
75 g (2½ oz) butter
1 cup (250 ml/8 fl oz) milk
1 egg
grated rind of 1 large or 2 small lemons
¼ cup (60 ml/2 fl oz) lemon juice
¼ cup sugar

Turn the oven to 200°C (400°F). Toss the flour and the first measure of sugar together.

Melt the butter, add the milk, egg and rind, and beat well with a fork.

Add the liquids to the dry ingredients and fold together until the dry ingredients have been lightly dampened but not thoroughly mixed.

Divide the mixture evenly between well-sprayed muffin pans and bake for 10 minutes.

Stir together the lemon juice and second measure of sugar without dissolving the sugar, and brush over the hot muffins as soon as they come out of the oven. Leave the muffins to stand in the pans for just a few minutes after this, in case the syrup hardens as it cools and sticks the muffins to the pans.

Serve for afternoon tea, or as a dessert with lightly whipped cream and fresh berries or other fruit.

Chocolate Banana Muffins

This recipe is well worth trying. The banana flavour is strongest when you use overripe bananas.

For 12 medium or 24 mini-muffins:
2 cups self-raising flour
½ cup castor sugar
½ cup chocolate chips
½ tsp salt
100 g (3½ oz) butter
1 cup (250 ml/8 fl oz) milk
1 egg
1 tsp vanilla essence
1 cup (2 or 3) mashed bananas

Turn the oven to 220°C (425°F). Stir the flour, castor sugar, chocolate chips and salt together with a fork.

Melt the butter, remove from the heat, add the milk, egg and vanilla and beat well with a fork.

Mash and measure the bananas. Stir them into the liquid mixture and mix well. Add to the dry mixture and fold everything together carefully until all the flour is dampened; stop before the mixture is smooth.

Spoon into sprayed muffin pans and bake for 12–15 minutes, until they spring back when pressed in the centre.

Serve at any time of the day; fresh or frozen mini-muffins are very popular for school lunchboxes.

For muffin mixing and baking details see p. 263.

Blueberry Bran Muffins

For 12–15 medium or about 30 mini-muffins:

1 cup baking (wheat) bran
¼ cup wheatgerm or extra bran
½ cup (125 ml/4 fl oz) canola oil
¾ cup plain or fruity yoghurt
1 large egg
1 tsp cinnamon
¾ tsp salt
1 cup sugar
1–1½ cups frozen blueberries
1½ cups plain flour
1 tsp baking soda

Turn the oven to 200°C (400°F). Measure the first 8 ingredients into a bowl, mix well with a fork, then leave to stand.

Separate clumps of frozen blueberries then stir into the mixture. Shake in the flour and soda through a sieve, then fold through the mixture. If it looks dry, add ¼ cup (60 ml/2 fl oz) extra yoghurt or milk.

Spoon into well-sprayed muffin pans and bake for 10–15 minutes, until the centres spring back when pressed.

Variation: Make a lemon glaze, mixing together 2 Tbsp each lemon juice and sugar. Brush over the hot muffins.

Banana Bran Muffins

I often make these during my cooking shows, to prove that muffins which contain no butter or oil, but a lot of bran, can be moist and taste absolutely delicious. See for yourself!

For 18 medium or 36 mini-muffins:

2 cups baking (wheat) bran
½ cup sultanas
½ cup chopped walnuts
½ cup plain flour
1 tsp baking powder
1 tsp baking soda
1 tsp cinnamon
½ cup (125 ml/4 fl oz) golden syrup
1 cup (250 ml/8 fl oz) milk
1 large egg or 2 egg whites*
2 large bananas, mashed

* Use 2 large egg whites for diets that exclude egg yolks.

Turn the oven to 200°C (400°F). Put the bran into a large bowl, add the sultanas and nuts. Shake the flour, baking powder, soda and cinnamon onto the bran through a sieve and stir to mix evenly.

Warm the tin of golden syrup in a bowl of hot water until it is runny. Put the required golden syrup into another bowl, using a hot, wet measuring cup. Add the milk and egg, and beat with a fork until well mixed. Mash the bananas with a fork and stir into the liquid.

Tip the liquid mixture into the dry ingredients and fold together just until the bran is evenly dampened. Do not overmix. Put into well-sprayed muffin pans using 2 spoons.

Bake for about 7 minutes for mini-muffins and 10 minutes for larger muffins, or until they spring back when pressed in the middle. Watch them carefully, as muffins containing a lot of golden syrup burn easily. Leave in the pans for 2–3 minutes then twist and remove them.

Eat warm, freezing leftovers. Spread large muffins with low-fat cottage cheese and jelly. Serve mini-muffins plain.

Spiced Apple Muffins

Make these muffins only after you know what consistency a muffin mixture should be. Raw apple gives muffins a lovely fresh apple flavour, but when you use it, you never know exactly how much milk will be needed.

For 12 medium or 24 mini-muffins:

1 cup self-raising flour
1 cup (fine) rolled oats
¾ cup brown sugar
2 tsp mixed spice
2 tsp cinnamon
½ tsp ground cloves
½ tsp baking soda
½ tsp salt
75 g (2½ oz) butter
1 egg
¾–1 cup (185–250 ml/6–8 fl oz) milk
1 cup chopped or grated raw apple

Turn the oven to 200°C (400°F). Mix the first 8 (dry) ingredients together with your fingers to ensure the rolled oats and brown sugar are mixed through evenly.

Melt the butter then add the egg and ¾ cup (185 ml/6 fl oz) of the milk, and beat with a fork until mixed. Grate or chop the apple in a food processor, press it into the cup, removing air bubbles, then stir it into the liquids. (Work quickly so it doesn't brown.)

Add the liquid mixture to the dry ingredients and mix lightly to dampen them, adding as much of the extra ¼ cup (60 ml/2 fl oz) of milk as you need to reach muffin consistency.

Spoon into sprayed muffin pans and bake for 12–15 minutes, or until the muffins spring back when pressed.

Good for morning tea or brunch, in packed lunches, and as after-school snacks.

Rum and Raisin Muffins

I make these muffins for a cold-weather treat. If I am going to serve them with coffee, I top them with a glaze flavoured with rum essence. For dessert, I reheat them in the microwave and serve them with delicious Rum Butter – try it!

For 12 medium or 24 mini-muffins:

1 cup small dark raisins
2 Tbsp rum
2 cups plain flour
1½ tsp baking soda
2 tsp cinnamon
2 tsp mixed spice
¼ tsp ground cloves
¾ cup sugar
½ cup chopped walnuts
75 g (2½ oz) butter
1 egg
1 cup yoghurt (any flavour)
¾ cup (185 ml/6 fl oz) milk

Turn the oven to 210°C (425°F). Put the raisins and rum into a small plastic bag, knead gently and leave to stand in a warm place while you mix the other ingredients.

Sieve the flour, soda and spices into a large bowl. Add the sugar and chopped walnuts and stir to mix thoroughly.

Melt the butter, add the egg, yoghurt and milk, then the raisins and any remaining liquid, and mix well.

Add the liquid mixture to the dry ingredients, but don't overmix. Spoon into well-sprayed muffin pans and bake for 10–12 minutes, or until the centres spring back.

Serve for holiday brunches, with coffee in midwinter, or for dessert on any occasion. Top with Cinnamon Sugar (p. 11) before cooking OR mix ¼ cup icing sugar with ½ tsp rum essence and about 1 tsp milk – enough to make a thin icing – and drizzle over warm muffins on a rack OR serve warm, halved, with Rum Butter (p. 346).

Date and Yoghurt Muffins

A favourite with date lovers.

For 12 large muffins:

1 cup chopped dates
½ cup chopped walnuts
2 cups baking (wheat) bran
1½ cups plain flour
1½ tsp baking powder
1½ tsp baking soda
½ cup (125 ml/4 fl oz) oil
1 cup brown sugar
2 large eggs
1½ cups yoghurt (any flavour)

Turn the oven to 200°C (400°F). Mix the first 6 ingredients together in a large bowl.

In another bowl, beat together the oil, sugar, eggs and yoghurt with a fork. Pour the liquid into the dry ingredients, then fold the 2 mixtures together until just combined. Spoon into well-sprayed, deep muffin pans.

Top with Cinnamon Sugar (p. 11) if desired then bake for 10 minutes, or until the muffins spring back when pressed lightly in the middle.

Apricot and Walnut Muffins

Dried fruits and nuts always make good additions to muffins! New Zealand dried apricots are best in this recipe – they give an extra-strong apricot flavour to the mixture, since they break up after being heated in the water or juice.

For 12 medium or 24 mini-muffins:

2 cups plain flour
1 tsp baking soda
1 cup brown sugar
1 tsp cinnamon
½ cup chopped dried apricots
¼ cup (60 ml/2 fl oz) water or orange juice
100 g (3½ oz) butter
2 large eggs
1 cup yoghurt
rind and juice of 1 large orange
½ cup chopped walnuts

Turn the oven to 190°C (375°F). Mix the first 4 (dry) ingredients together in a large bowl, making sure the brown sugar is mixed through evenly.

Microwave the apricots with the water or juice until all the liquid is absorbed – about 1 minute on High (100%) power. Add the butter, warming again if necessary, then mix in the eggs, yoghurt and grated rind.

Make the juice from the orange up to half a cup with water if necessary, and add to the mixture with the chopped walnuts.

Fold the liquid and dry mixtures together, taking care not to overmix. Add a little extra liquid to make nice soft muffins if necessary.

Spoon into well-sprayed muffin pans and bake for about 12–15 minutes, or until the muffins spring back when pressed lightly.

Serve for a weekend brunch or with coffee; also good in packed lunches, as after-school snacks, and on picnics.

Best Orange Muffins

When you break these muffins open, their wonderful golden colour surprises you; if you have a food processor and an orange in the house, try them!

For 12 medium muffins:

1 orange (about 200 g/7 oz)
1 cup sugar
1 large egg
½ cup (125 ml/4 fl oz) milk or orange juice
100 g (3½ oz) butter, melted
1½ cups plain flour
1 tsp baking powder
1 tsp baking soda
½ cup sultanas or chopped dates
½ cup chopped walnuts (optional)

Turn the oven to 200°C (400°F). Cut the unpeeled orange into quarters then each quarter into 4 pieces crosswise. Put into a food processor with the sugar and process with the metal chopping blade until very finely chopped. Add the egg, milk or juice and melted butter, and process until combined.

Sift the dry ingredients into a large bowl, tip in the orange mixture, sprinkle over the sultanas or dates, and add the nuts. Fold together, taking care not to overmix; stop as soon as the dry ingredients are dampened, but before the mixture is smooth.

Spoon into buttered or sprayed muffin pans and bake for 12–15 minutes, until the tops are golden brown and the centres spring back when pressed.

Serve warm, plain, buttered or topped with cream cheese or cottage cheese.

Best Orange Muffins

Glazed Passionfruit Muffins

For muffin mixing and baking details see p. 263.

Rhubarb and Fresh Ginger Muffins

The tartness of rhubarb, the spiciness of fresh ginger and a hint of orange make these muffins surprisingly different.

For 12 medium muffins:
2 cups plain flour
1 cup sugar
2 tsp baking powder
1/2 tsp baking soda
grated rind and juice of 1/2 orange, made up to 1 cup (250 ml/8 fl oz) with milk
1 large egg
1 Tbsp grated root ginger (fresh or frozen)
1 cup finely sliced raw rhubarb
50 g (2 oz) butter, melted
1/4 cup (60 ml/2 fl oz) canola oil

Turn the oven to 220°C (425°F). Mix the first 4 ingredients together thoroughly with a fork.

Grate the rind from half an orange and squeeze the juice into a 1-cup measure. Add milk to make up to 1 cup. Tip into a bowl, add the rind, egg and ginger, and beat with a fork until well combined. Carefully stir in the rhubarb, sliced no more than 4 mm (1/4 in) thick with a very sharp knife. Add the melted butter and oil.

Tip the liquids into the dry ingredients and gently fold together, until the flour is just moistened. Do not overmix.

Spoon into well-sprayed or lightly buttered muffin pans and bake for 12–15 minutes, or until the muffins spring back when pressed.

Serve warm for breakfast, for morning or afternoon tea, or with lightly whipped cream for dessert.

Variation: Stir together 1/4 cup sugar and the juice of 1 lemon. Brush over the hot muffins straight from the oven.

Apricot Surprise Muffins

These muffins are a favourite of mine. When you bite into them, you find a delicious filling of dried apricots and almonds. Make them for special occasions or for your best friends – but be sure to keep some for yourself!

For 12 medium muffins:
1 3/4 cups self-raising flour
3/4 cup sugar
1/4 tsp baking soda
1/2 tsp salt
1/2 cup sour cream
1/2 cup (125 ml/4 fl oz) milk
1 egg
1/2 tsp almond essence

Filling
40 g (1 1/2 oz) dried apricots
1/2 cup (125 ml/4 fl oz) water
2 Tbsp ground almonds
2 Tbsp sugar
2 Tbsp wine biscuit crumbs

Turn the oven to 200°C (400°F). Mix the first 4 ingredients together thoroughly.

Beat together the sour cream, milk, egg and almond essence. Tip into the dry mixture and fold together without overmixing.

To make the filling, chop the apricots into small pieces and boil with the water for 3–4 minutes, until the water has disappeared. Cool, then mix with the almonds, sugar and biscuit crumbs.

Half-fill sprayed muffin pans with the muffin mixture. Make a small depression in each muffin with a damp teaspoon. Divide the filling into 12 and place a portion carefully in each depression. Spoon the remaining muffin mixture over the filling, covering it completely.

Bake for 12–15 minutes, until the muffins spring back when pressed. Dust with icing sugar and serve warm with coffee, or with whipped cream as a dessert.

Glazed Passionfruit Muffins

These muffins are a special treat for lucky people who grow their own black passionfruit, or have a friend who grows enough to share! (If you freeze unsweetened pulp you can make these muffins out of season, too.)

For 12 medium muffins:
50 g (2 oz) butter
1/2 cup sour cream
1/4–1/2 cup (60–125 ml/2–4 fl oz) fresh passionfruit pulp
up to 1/4 cup (60 ml/2 fl oz) orange juice
2 large eggs
3/4 cup sugar
2 cups self-raising flour
1/4 cup icing sugar to glaze

Turn the oven to 210°C (425°F). Melt the butter in a large bowl, then stir in the sour cream.

Scoop out fresh passionfruit pulp with a teaspoon, putting aside 2 Tbsp for the glaze. You need at least 1/4 cup in the muffins to get a good flavour. Add orange juice to make the pulp up to 1/2 cup. Add to the butter mixture.

Break the eggs into the mixture, add the sugar, then beat with a fork until well blended.

Sprinkle or sieve the flour onto the mixture then fold it in, taking care not to overmix. Spoon into buttered or sprayed muffin pans and bake for 10–15 minutes, until the tops spring back when pressed.

Meanwhile, mix the reserved passionfruit with the icing sugar to pouring consistency (or use bought syrup). Brush over the muffins as soon as you take them from the oven.

Serve preferably on the day they are made, cold or slightly warm, unbuttered.

Strawberry Cream Cheese Muffins

The lovely strawberry flavour of these muffins reminds me of a summer day! This is a good way to use frozen strawberries, or to make a few ripe, fresh berries go a long way.

For 12 medium or 24 mini-muffins:
2 cups self-raising flour
3/4 cup sugar
1/4 tsp salt
1/2 cup cream cheese
1 cup (250 ml/8 fl oz) milk
1 egg
1 tsp finely grated orange rind
1 cup frozen or fresh strawberries, chopped

Turn the oven to 200°C (400°F). Whisk the flour, sugar and salt together in a large bowl.

Beat the cream cheese until smooth, warming it if necessary. Add the milk, egg and orange rind and combine with a whisk or beater.

Chop the fresh or frozen berries into more or less 5 mm (1/4 in) cubes. Combine the 3 mixtures, stirring as little as possible.

Spoon into sprayed muffin pans and bake for about 12 minutes for fresh berry muffins, about 15 minutes for frozen berry muffins, until the centres spring back when pressed.

Dust with icing sugar, or halve and serve with Orange Cream Cheese (p. 346) and more berries, or halve and serve with icecream. Serve for afternoon tea or dessert.

Chocolate Surprise Muffins

You can make these muffins with or without the surprise! I like them best with raspberry jam but they are very good without it too.

For 12 medium muffins:
1 3/4 cups plain flour
4 tsp baking powder
1/4 cup cocoa
1/2 cup sugar
1/2 cup chocolate chips
75 g (2 1/2 oz) butter
2 large eggs
3/4 cup (185 ml/6 fl oz) milk
3/4–1 cup raspberry jam
extra chocolate chips

Turn the oven to 200°C (400°F). Sift the flour, baking powder and cocoa into a bowl, add the sugar and chocolate chips and toss with a fork to mix.

Heat the butter gently until it is just liquid. Remove from the heat, add the eggs and milk, and beat with a fork until well combined and smooth.

Pour the liquids into the dry ingredients and fold together, mixing as little as possible.

Half-fill sprayed muffin pans by spooning about a tablespoon of the mixture into the tins, helping the mixture off with another spoon rather than letting it drop off by itself. Using a damp teaspoon, make a small hollow in each muffin and fill it with a teaspoon of jam. Divide the remaining muffin mixture between the muffins, ensuring the jam is completely covered.

Sprinkle with extra chocolate chips and bake for about 10 minutes, or until the centres spring back when pressed.

Serve warm, dusted with icing sugar if you like. Good with coffee, or served with fresh berries and whipped cream or icecream.

Upside-Down Nectarine Muffins

I experimented with these muffins in the middle of winter, using Californian nectarines. They looked so beautiful and smelt so appetising as they cooled on the rack that they really brightened the day!

For 12 medium muffins:
50 g (2 oz/12 tsp) butter
1/2 cup brown sugar
3 fresh nectarines
2 cups self-raising flour
3/4 cup sugar
1 tsp mixed spice
3/4 tsp salt
2 large eggs
3/4 cup plain or orange yoghurt
1/4 cup (60 ml/2 fl oz) canola oil
1 tsp vanilla essence

Turn the oven to 200°C (400°F). Spray or lightly butter 12 medium-sized muffin pans.

Melt the butter, put a teaspoon in each pan, then add 2 tsp brown sugar, spreading it evenly over the bottom.

Quarter the nectarines and cut each quarter into 3 slices. Arrange 3 slices on top of the butter-sugar mixture in each pan.

Stir the dry ingredients together well.

Lightly beat together the eggs, yoghurt, oil and vanilla.

Gently fold the liquid mixture into the dry ingredients, until the flour is just moistened. Spoon into the nectarine-lined pans and bake for 12–15 minutes. (The muffins may be flat-topped – this is not a problem!)

Leave to stand for 2 minutes after removing from the oven, then press down gently on each muffin and rotate it about half a turn, and lift the muffins onto a rack. The topping usually lifts off with the muffin if you get it at the right stage. Reposition any fruit that stays in the pans.

Serve warm or reheated, within a few hours of cooking. Good at any time of day, from breakfast to dessert!

Double Chocolate and Banana Muffins

These are rich, dark and moist – delicious!

For 12 medium or 24 mini-muffins:
2 cups self-raising flour
2 Tbsp cocoa
3/4 cup sugar
1/2 cup chocolate chips
1/2 tsp salt
1/4 tsp baking soda
1 cup (2–3) mashed bananas
1/2 cup (125 ml/4 fl oz) canola oil
3/4 cup (185 ml/6 fl oz) milk
1 large egg
1 tsp vanilla essence

Turn the oven to 210°C (425°F). In a large bowl, mix the first 6 ingredients together with a fork.

Mash the bananas, and mix well with the remaining ingredients.

Fold the liquid mixture through the dry ingredients until the flour is dampened; stop before the mixture is smooth. Do not overmix.

Spoon into sprayed muffin pans and bake for 10–15 minutes, until the centres spring back when pressed.

Upside-Down Nectarine Muffins

Easy Jaffa Muffins

These muffins, which have an interesting orange tinge, are popular after school and at parties. They are simple enough for kids to make. A 12-year-old in our family replaced the orange fizz with lemonade to make 'Elizabeth's Dalmatian Muffins'!

For 12 medium or 24 mini-muffins:
2 cups self-raising flour
½–¾ cup sugar
½ tsp salt
½ cup chocolate chips
¼ cup (60 ml/2 fl oz) oil, preferably canola
1 cup (250 ml/8 fl oz) orange 'fizz', e.g. Fanta
1 large egg

Turn the oven to 200°C (400°F). Mix the flour, sugar, salt and chocolate chips together with a fork. (Use the larger amount of sugar if you have a sweet tooth.)

Whisk together the oil, fizzy drink and egg with a fork.

Pour the liquid into the dry ingredients then fold gently together until the flour is just moistened. Do not overmix.

Spoon into well-sprayed muffin pans and bake for 10–15 minutes, or until firm when pressed in the centre.

Serve the day they are made. Freeze extra muffins in plastic bags and put them, frozen, in school lunches.

ABC Muffins

A for apple, B for banana, C for chocolate! These freeze well for lunchbox use.

For 12 medium or 24 mini-muffins:
1 cup (2–3) mashed ripe bananas
½ cup brown sugar
¼ tsp salt
¼ cup (60 ml/2 fl oz) canola oil
1 large egg
½ cup (125 ml/4 fl oz) milk
½ cup chocolate chips
1 apple, unpeeled, grated or finely chopped
2 cups self-raising flour

Turn the oven to 200°C (400°F). In a large bowl, mix together the mashed banana, sugar, salt, oil, egg and milk until well mixed. Stir in the chocolate chips and the unpeeled apple, coarsely grated or chopped in a food processor.

Sieve the flour onto the mixture and fold together until just dampened. Do not overmix. Spoon into sprayed muffin pans and bake for 10–12 minutes, or until golden brown.

Variation: Mix together 2 Tbsp each lemon juice and sugar, and brush over the hot muffins.

Lemonade and Cream Muffins

These light-textured, very easy (and very good) muffins are a summertime treat! Their texture is almost as light as that of a sponge cake. Serve them warm, split, with jam and/or fresh strawberries and whipped cream, with a cup of tea or coffee, or any time as a summer dessert.

For 12 medium muffins:
2 cups self-raising flour
½ cup sugar
¼ tsp salt
½ cup (125 ml/4 fl oz) lemonade
½ cup (125 ml/4 fl oz) cream
1 large egg

Turn the oven to 200°C (400°F). Toss the flour, sugar and salt together with a fork.

Mix the lemonade, cream and egg with a fork until combined.

Pour the liquid into the dry ingredients, then fold gently together until the flour is just moistened. Do not overmix.

Spoon into sprayed or buttered muffin pans and bake for 10–15 minutes, until the muffins are a light golden colour and firm when pressed in the centre.

Serve freshly made; they are especially good with whipped cream and fresh berries.

Easy Cheesy Muffins

These are very popular for lunch, and warm mini-muffins make excellent party snacks.

For 12 medium or 24 mini-muffins:
2 cups self-raising flour
2 cups grated tasty cheese
1 large egg
1 cup (250 ml/8 fl oz) lager or beer (flat or bubbly)
about 2 Tbsp chutney (optional)

Turn the oven to 220°C (425°F). Mix the flour and cheese together in a large bowl.

Using a fork, beat the egg enough to thoroughly mix the white and yolk. Add the lager or beer and stir briefly, then pour the mixture onto the flour and cheese.

Fold together until the flour is dampened; do not overmix. If you like the idea, fold in some chutney so that it stays in streaks.

Spoon into buttered or sprayed muffin pans and bake for 10–15 minutes, until the muffins are nicely browned and the centres spring back when pressed.

Serve warm or cold the day they are made, or reheated the next day.

For muffin mixing and baking details see p. 263.

Cheese and Pepper Muffins

These savoury muffins are just the right size to pop in your mouth easily at a buffet meal.

For 20–25 mini-muffins:
2 cups grated tasty cheese
1½ cups self-raising flour
½ tsp salt
1 Tbsp sugar
pinch of cayenne pepper
1–2 Tbsp chopped fresh coriander (optional)
1 red pepper, roasted and chopped (p. 209)
1 egg
1 cup (250 ml/8 fl oz) milk

Turn the oven to 200°C (400°F). Put the cheese, flour, salt, sugar and cayenne in a large bowl. Add the coriander and roasted pepper, and mix lightly with your fingertips.

Beat the egg and milk together, then pour onto the dry ingredients. Fold together, taking care not to overmix.

Spoon into well-sprayed muffin pans, sprinkle with paprika if desired, and bake for about 12 minutes, or until the muffins are golden brown and spring back when pressed lightly in the centre.

Sweet Spicy Pumpkin Muffins

These muffins make marvellous after-school snacks.

For 12 medium or 24 mini-muffins:
2 cups self-raising flour
1½ cups brown sugar
½ tsp baking soda
1 tsp cinnamon
½ tsp grated nutmeg
½ tsp ground ginger
¼ tsp ground cloves
100 g (3½ oz) butter
2 large eggs
*1 cup cooked, mashed pumpkin**

* Cook cubed pumpkin until tender then mash with a fork. Don't use buttered, peppered purée or pumpkin that is overcooked, dark and soggy.

Turn the oven to 200°C (400°F). Toss the first 7 (dry) ingredients together with a fork until thoroughly combined.

Warm the butter until melted, add the eggs and beat well. Stir in the mashed pumpkin. Add to the dry mixture and fold together gently. Do not overmix.

Spoon into sprayed muffin pans and bake for 15–18 minutes, until they are golden brown and spring back when pressed in the centre.

Serve warm for lunch, after school, or for dessert with Rum Butter (p. 346) or split, with whipped cream and fresh fruit.

Kumara, Bacon and Onion Muffins

Sizzled Sausage and Sage Muffins

Stretch a small amount of plain sausage meat to feed a crowd or use your favourite 'gourmet' sausages (skinned) in an interesting, different way. Change the herb to suit your sausage, trying, for example, chopped frankfurters and fresh fennel!

For 12 medium muffins:

1¹/₂ cups self-raising flour
1 cup grated tasty cheese
¹/₄ cup chopped parsley
¹/₂ tsp salt
1 tsp sugar
pinch of cayenne pepper
2 Tbsp oil
1 onion, chopped finely
250–350 g (9–12 oz) sausage meat
2 Tbsp finely chopped fresh sage or 1 tsp
   dried sage, crumbled
1 egg
1 cup (250 ml/8 fl oz) milk

Turn the oven to 210°C (425°F). Toss together the first 6 ingredients with a fork.

Heat the oil in a medium-sized frypan. Add the chopped onion and the sausage meat, breaking it into small pieces as it cooks until browned. Blot off any fat with a paper towel, then stir in the sage and cool.

Beat the egg and milk together. Pour over the dry ingredients, with the cooled sausage mixture. Stir just enough to combine.

Spoon into sprayed muffin pans and bake for 12–15 minutes, until the muffins spring back when pressed.

Serve as fingerfood, as the main part of lunch, or as a light evening meal.

Variation: Sprinkle each muffin with a little extra grated cheese and paprika or chilli powder.

Kumara, Bacon and Onion Muffins

These have a mild but definite flavour and texture, and are a very popular addition to luncheon soup and salad buffets, especially when overseas visitors are present.

For 12 medium or 24 mini-muffins:

2 rashers (100 g/3¹/₂ oz) lean bacon,
   chopped
1 small onion, diced
2 Tbsp canola or olive oil
2 cups self-raising flour
1 cup grated tasty cheese
1 tsp mild curry powder
¹/₂ tsp salt
1 cup (250 ml/8 fl oz) milk

1 large egg
1 cup cooked, roughly mashed kumara*

* Use golden kumara if possible, as they give the muffins a definite gold colour. Scrub about 300 g (10¹/₂ oz) kumara, cut off any hairy protrusions, then microwave for 4–5 minutes, until the thickest flesh gives when gently squeezed. When cool, peel off the skin and mash roughly.

Turn the oven to 200°C (400°F). Cook the bacon and onion in the oil until the bacon begins to brown.

Meanwhile, toss the flour, cheese, curry powder and salt together well with a fork.

Mix the milk and egg together with a fork until blended, then stir in the roughly mashed kumara and mix again, leaving some chunky pieces.

Tip the cooked bacon and onion, then the kumara mixture, into the flour. Gently fold together until the flour is moistened. Do not overmix.

Spoon into lightly buttered or sprayed muffin pans and bake for 12–15 minutes, or until golden brown on top and firm when pressed in the centre.

These are good hot, warm or cold. Buttering is not necessary.

For muffin mixing and baking details see p. 263.

Bacon Brunch Muffins

Get the weekend off to a good start by serving a basket of bacon-flavoured muffins and a bowl of fresh fruit salad (with yoghurt) for brunch or breakfast.

For 12 medium or 24 mini-muffins:
2–3 Tbsp oil
4 rashers (200 g/7 oz) lean bacon, chopped
2 cups plain flour
4 level tsp baking powder
3/4 tsp salt
1 1/2 cups grated tasty cheese
pinch cayenne or chilli powder (optional)
1 large egg
1 cup (250 ml/8 fl oz) milk

Turn the oven to 220°C (425°F). Cook the bacon in the oil until it is lightly browned.

Mix the flour, baking powder, salt, cheese and cayenne or chilli together in a large bowl. (Use absolutely level teaspoons of baking powder or the muffins will taste of soda.)

Mix the milk and egg together with a fork. Add the bacon and any pan drippings, and the milk and egg, to the dry ingredients. Fold together until the flour is wet; do not overmix.

Spoon into buttered or sprayed muffin pans and bake for 10–12 minutes, or until the muffins spring back when pressed.

Serve warm or cold. Mini-muffins certainly don't need buttering.

Note: Less bacon means less flavour! Don't scrimp – use an extra rasher (and less salt) if you have it!

Avocado and Bacon Muffins

Just about everyone likes the combination of avocado, cheese, bacon and spring onions. Serve these muffins as a complete lunch.

For 12 medium muffins:
2 cups plain flour
4 tsp baking powder
3/4 tsp salt
1 Tbsp sugar
pinch of cayenne pepper
1 cup grated tasty cheese
4 spring onions, chopped
3 rashers bacon, finely chopped
75 g (2 1/2 oz) butter
1 egg
1 cup (250 ml/8 fl oz) milk
1 avocado
about 1 Tbsp lemon juice

Turn the oven to 200°C (400°F). Mix the first 6 ingredients together in a large bowl, then stir in the spring onions.

Grill or fry the bacon until crisp. Keep the bacon drippings.

Melt the butter, add the egg, milk and bacon drippings, and beat to combine. Halve the avocado, scoop out the flesh with a spoon, then cut it into 7 mm (3 in) cubes. Sprinkle with lemon juice to prevent browning. Add to the liquid mixture.

Add the bacon to the liquid mixture then fold both mixtures together, stirring only to dampen the flour. Do not overmix.

Spoon into sprayed muffin pans and bake for about 10 minutes, or until the muffins spring back when pressed lightly in the centre.

Always serve these warm or reheated.

Herbed Mini-Muffins

Serve these very special little green-flecked muffins hot from the oven. Use your favourite herbs, or whichever teams best with your fillings or toppings, e.g. dill with salmon, basil with sliced tomato.

For about 12–18 mini-muffins:
1 cup plain flour
2 tsp baking powder
1 cup grated tasty cheese
1/4 cup chopped parsley
1 Tbsp chopped fresh herbs
1 spring onion, chopped
1/2 tsp salt
1 tsp sugar
1/8 tsp cayenne pepper
1 large egg
1/2 cup (125 ml/4 fl oz) + 2 Tbsp milk

Turn the oven to 200°C (400°F). Toss the first 9 ingredients together well.

Beat the egg and milk together with a fork or whisk. Tip into the dry ingredients and fold together, stirring just enough to dampen the flour. Do not overmix.

Spoon into sprayed muffin pans and bake for 10–12 minutes, until the centres spring back when pressed.

Serve hot whole or split from top to bottom, with savoury spreads, smoked salmon, shaved meats, sliced tomato, etc.

Herbed Pumpkin Muffins

Mashed pumpkin gives these muffins a wonderful colour. Herbs intensify both the pumpkin and the cheese flavours.

For 12 medium or 18 mini-muffins:
2 cups self-raising flour
1/2 tsp salt
1 Tbsp sugar
2 cups grated cheese
1 1/2 tsp ground cumin
1 tsp oreganum
1/4–1/2 tsp cayenne pepper
1 large egg
1 cup (250 ml/8 fl oz) milk
1 cup (250 g/9 oz) mashed cooked pumpkin
1–2 Tbsp pumpkin kernels

Turn the oven to 220°C (425°F). Toss the first 7 ingredients together well, crumbling the oreganum a little as you add it, and adding cayenne to suit your taste.

Beat together the egg, milk and mashed pumpkin until well mixed. Pour the liquids into the dry mixture and fold together without overmixing.

Spoon into sprayed muffin pans and sprinkle over a few pumpkin kernels. Bake for 12–14 minutes, until the muffins are golden brown and the centres spring back when pressed.

Serve warm as finger food for a party, or with soup for lunch.

Avocado and Bacon Muffins

Cornmeal Muffins (Photo p. 100)

If you like making 'different' muffins, look for metal moulds shaped like corncobs. Otherwise try this recipe using regular muffin pans.

I make these muffins using very fine cornmeal that does not have a gritty texture, but does have quite a distinctive flavour, and a soft beige-gold colour.

For 12 large muffins:
50 g (2 oz) butter
1 egg
1 cup (250 ml/8 fl oz) milk
1/2 tsp salt
2 Tbsp sugar
1 cup grated tasty cheese
1 cup plain flour
1/2 cup fine cornmeal
1 Tbsp baking powder

Turn the oven to 210°C (425°F). Melt the butter in a large bowl. Add the egg, milk, salt and sugar and beat with a fork until the egg is completely mixed. Sprinkle over the cheese.

Measure the flour carefully, stirring it then spooning it lightly into the cup, without shaking or packing it down. Sift the flour, cornmeal and baking powder onto the liquid ingredients.

Fold the 2 mixtures together, stopping as soon as the flour is dampened. The mixture should look lumpy. Do NOT beat until smooth.

Spoon into well-sprayed or oiled muffin pans, filling each one half full. If using gem or cornstick irons, oil them well and preheat them for 5 minutes in the oven. Drop the mixture into the very hot irons from the side of the spoon, filling each about half full.

Bake for 12–15 minutes, or until the centres spring back when pressed. Leave to cool for 3–5 minutes before carefully loosening from the pans.

Note: If you like, turn cornsticks over in their moulds as soon as they are firm enough to lift. This puts a corn-cob pattern on both sides.

Fresh Asparagus Muffins

These muffins have a definite asparagus flavour. The asparagus stays bright green as long as you don't overcook it.

For 12 medium or 24 mini-muffins:
1 1/2 cups self-raising flour
1–1 1/2 cups grated tasty cheese
1/2–1 tsp salt
1 large egg
1 cup (250 ml/8 fl oz) milk/asparagus cooking liquid
about 1 cup finely chopped, cooked asparagus*

* Cook 200–250 g (7–9 oz) asparagus in

Fresh Asparagus Muffins

1/4 cup (60 ml/2 fl oz) water (without salt) until tender-crisp (2–4 minutes in a pot or microwave-proof bag). Cool it quickly so it does not overcook and lose its colour. Pour the cooking liquid into a cup, then slice the asparagus into 4 mm (1/4 in) lengths with a sharp knife. This should produce about a cup of 'pressed down' asparagus.

Turn the oven to 210°C (425°F). Toss the flour, cheese and salt together with a fork. (Use the smaller amount of salt with the larger amount of cheese.)

Make the asparagus liquid up to 1 cup with milk, and beat it with the egg.

Combine the dry ingredients, liquid and drained, cooled asparagus, folding everything together just enough to dampen the flour. Do NOT stir until smooth.

Spoon into well-sprayed muffin pans. Sprinkle with a little grated cheese and some paprika if desired, or top with a few pumpkin kernels.

Bake for 10–14 minutes, according to size, until the tops and sides are browned and the centres spring back when pressed.

Serve warm or reheated, preferably in a basket lined with a paper or cloth napkin.

Spicy Corn and Cheese Muffins

These muffins have an interesting flavour and texture, and may be seasoned to suit your taste. They are as good with a bowl of warming soup in autumn and winter as they are for a summer picnic, or with a spring luncheon salad.

For 8–12 medium or 20–24 mini-muffins:
1 cup creamed corn
2 large eggs
1/2 cup (125 ml/4 fl oz) milk
2 cups plain flour
4 tsp baking powder
3/4 tsp salt
1 1/2 cups grated tasty cheese
1 tsp ground cumin (optional)
1/2 tsp oreganum (optional)
1/2 tsp chilli powder (optional)

Turn the oven to 220°C (425°F). Mix the corn, eggs and milk together with a fork. (The amount of corn does not need to be exact. If you are using up corn left in a can add a little more or less milk to achieve the right consistency.)

Mix the remaining ingredients together, using more or less of the optional flavourings according to your taste. (If you like, put the dry ingredients and chunks of weighed cheese into a food processor and chop finely, instead of grating it.)

Tip the dry ingredients (with the cheese) into the corn mixture and fold together until evenly dampened but not smooth. Add a little extra milk if the mixture is not as soft as uncooked muffins usually are.

Spoon into buttered or sprayed muffin pans and top each with a piece of cheese or some grated cheese and a sprinkling of paprika. Bake for 9–12 minutes, until the centres spring back when pressed and the sides and tops are golden brown.

Best served straight from the oven, but also good cool and cold.

Variation: Add the chopped leaves and stems of 2 spring onions if not using the spices.

Bake a Biscuit

Many of us remember what fun it was to climb up on a chair and help our mother or grandmother make biscuits on baking day. How satisfying it was to stir and shape them carefully, and to pop the odd uncooked bits of mixture into our mouths, wondering why biscuits needed cooking when they tasted so good raw. Some of my biscuits are made from recipes my mother gave me, while others are new ideas from friends and books from other countries. Some are meant for filling empty corners in lunchboxes, others are to offer friends who pop in, or to give as gifts. See which of my favourites YOU like best!

Cheese Crisps

Serve these buttered or plain, with tea, coffee or cocktails.

1½ cups plain flour
1½ tsp baking powder
½ tsp salt
½ tsp mustard
½ tsp paprika
shake of pepper
150 g (5 oz) cold butter
1½ cups grated tasty cheese
cold water

Turn the oven to 190°C (375°F). Measure the flour, baking powder and seasonings into a large bowl or a food processor. Cut, grate or chop in the butter and cheese, using 2 knives or the chopping blade, so the mixture stays as cold as possible. When it resembles rolled oats, add water a little at a time until the particles will stick together to make a firm dough. Do not overmix.

Flour the dough lightly and roll out thinly and evenly on a lightly floured board. Cut into squares, rectangles or fingers, and bake for 10–15 minutes, or until golden.

Lift onto a rack with a spatula or fish slice and leave to cool.

Homemade Crackers

These seem much nicer than bought crackers, and are a quarter of the price!

2 cups plain flour
1½ tsp baking powder
½ tsp salt
25 g (1 oz) very cold butter
1 Tbsp golden syrup or malt
about ½ cup 125 ml/4 fl oz water

Turn the oven to 190°C (375°F). Sift the flour, baking powder and salt into a bowl. Grate or rub in the cold butter.

Christmas Tree Biscuits (p. 278)

Mix the golden syrup or malt with the water. Add, a few drops at a time, to the flour mixture, tossing with a fork at the same time until the mixture is damp enough to form a rollable dough.

Roll out thinly on the floured bench, then cut into rounds or shapes using pastry cutters, or into squares or oblongs with a sharp knife. Prick each biscuit in a few places, and bake for 10–15 minutes, or until a pale golden colour.

When cold, store in an airtight container. Serve crackers plain, buttered, or with interesting toppings, depending on the occasion.

Variations: Use an extra Tbsp butter for flakier crackers.

Add a few Tbsp Parmesan cheese, poppy seeds or toasted sesame seeds if you want flavoured crackers.

Scroggin Biscuits

Extra-good when made with the nutritious optional ingredients, these biscuits are good for play lunch or after-school snacks.

For about 60 biscuits, depending on size:
200 g (7 oz) butter
1 cup soft brown sugar
1 cup white sugar
1 large egg
¼ cup (60 ml/2 fl oz) milk
½ tsp baking soda
1 tsp vanilla essence
1 cup flour
3 cups rolled oats (not wholegrain oats)
½ cup sultanas (optional)
½ cup chopped walnuts (optional)
½ cup sunflower seeds (optional)

Turn the oven to 180°C (350°F), or 170°C (325°F) for fan-bake. Melt the butter in a large pot or microwave bowl, removing from the heat when liquid. Stir in the sugars and egg, then the milk, soda and vanilla stirred together.

Sprinkle over the flour, rolled oats and optional additions and mix well with a stirrer, spoon or fork until well combined.

Drop teaspoonfuls of the mixture onto an oven tray sprayed with non-stick spray or covered with baking paper, leaving room for spreading. Bake for 10–12 minutes, or until the biscuits are golden brown and feel firm. Shape another trayful of biscuits while the first one cooks.

Lift onto a wire rack while warm. When cold, store in airtight containers.

Peanut Brownies

Peanut brownies never lose their popularity.

For 30–50 biscuits:
125 g (4½ oz) butter
1 cup sugar
1 large egg
1 cup plain flour
2 tsp baking powder
2 Tbsp cocoa
1½ cups lightly roasted peanuts

Turn the oven to 190°C (375°F). Melt the butter in a medium-sized pot over low heat until liquid but not hot. Remove from the heat, add the sugar and egg, and stir to combine. Add the sifted dry ingredients and the peanuts and stir until well combined.

Roll into balls about the size of a walnut or, using 2 teaspoons, put spoonfuls of the mixture on a lightly sprayed or Teflon-lined oven tray, leaving room for the biscuits to spread. Bake for 10–12 minutes. Do not let the biscuits darken around the edges.

Leave to stand for about 5 minutes then lift onto a wire rack. When cold, store in an airtight container.

Roast Peanuts

To lightly roast peanuts to use in baking or as a snack, bake raw peanuts at 150°C (300°F) for 15 minutes. Cool before using in biscuits. Rub off skins from roast nuts if required.

Peanut Plus Cookies

Whatever age you are, I think you'll enjoy a glass of milk and one of these peanutty cookies, full of good things! Make them giant-sized for fun, or regular size to last longer.

For 24 10-cm (4-in) biscuits or up to 60 smaller ones:
50 g (2 oz) butter
1/4 cup (60 ml/2 fl oz) golden syrup
3/4 cup peanut butter (crunchy or smooth)
1 large egg
1 tsp vanilla essence
1/2 cup white sugar
1/2 cup brown sugar
1/2 cup each sultanas, roasted salted peanuts and chocolate chips
1/2 cup sunflower seeds (optional)
1 3/4 cups plain flour
1 tsp baking soda

Turn the oven to 180°C (350°F), or 170°C (325°F) for fan-bake. In a large pot or microwave bowl melt the butter and the golden syrup (measured with a hot, wet measuring cup) just until you can stir them together without any lumps of butter showing. Stop heating, then stir in the peanut butter until the mixture is smooth.

Add the egg, vanilla and sugars, beat with a fork or stirrer until evenly mixed, then add the sultanas, roughly chopped peanuts, chocolate chips and sunflower seeds.

Sieve the flour and soda into the mixture, and mix until evenly combined.

With wet hands, divide the mixture into balls. For giant biscuits make 24 balls. Place 6 at a time on a baking tray lined with baking paper, then flatten with wet fingers until the biscuits measure 9 cm (about 3 1/2 in) across. The biscuits will spread about 1 cm (1/2 in) during cooking.

For smaller biscuits, make 36–60 balls, then flatten them until they are about 7 mm (1/4 in) thick.

Bake one tray at a time for 7–10 minutes, until evenly golden brown. Remove from the oven before they brown around the edge. (Use a slightly shorter time for chewy biscuits.)

Cool on a rack and store in sealed plastic bags or other airtight containers.

Note: To cook giant biscuits more evenly, reduce the heat by 10°C (25°F) and cook 2–3 minutes longer, if you prefer.

Colleen's Biscuits

Melting butter then mixing the ingredients in a pot is really fast and easy! These biscuits are good for school lunches and general family snacking.

For about 100 biscuits:
250 g (9 oz) butter
3/4 cup (185 ml/6 fl oz) golden syrup
1 tsp baking soda
1/4 cup (60 ml/2 fl oz) warm water
1 1/2 cups sugar
2 cups plain flour
2 cups desiccated coconut
2 cups rolled oats

Turn the oven to 180°C (350°F). Melt the butter in a large pot. Add the golden syrup, removing the pot from the heat once it is melted and liquid. Add the baking soda to the warm water. Add the sugar, flour, coconut and oats to the pot, then the water and soda. Stir thoroughly.

Place teaspoonfuls on trays, leaving room for spreading. Flatten the biscuits with your hand after you have filled each tray. Bake for about 12 minutes.

Easy-Mix Oaty Cookies

These biscuits are always popular. Keep them airtight, so they stay nice and crisp.

For about 60 biscuits:
100 g (3 1/2 oz) butter, melted
2 household Tbsp golden syrup
1 cup sugar
2 cups rolled oats
1 cup plain flour
1 tsp baking soda
2 Tbsp water

Turn the oven to 170°C (325°F). Melt the butter in a medium-sized pot. Take off the heat and add the golden syrup, stirring until it dissolves. Stir in the sugar, rolled oats and flour, then the baking soda dissolved in the water. Mix well, then put teaspoonfuls on sprayed oven trays, leaving room for the biscuits to spread.

Bake one tray at a time for about 8–15 minutes, or until the biscuits are evenly golden brown. Transfer them to a rack to cool and become firm.

Chocolate Chip Biscuits

Great for lunchboxes or with a glass of milk after school.

For 20–30 biscuits:
75 g (2 1/2 oz) butter
1/2 cup white sugar
1/2 cup brown sugar
1 large egg
1 cup plain flour
1/2 tsp baking soda
1/2 cup chocolate chips or 100 g (3 1/2 oz) dark chocolate, chopped

Turn the oven to 180°C (350°F). Melt the butter until just liquid. Remove from the heat, add the sugars and egg, and beat with a fork.

Sift the flour and baking soda and add with the chocolate to the butter mixture. Stir until well combined.

Place teaspoonfuls on oven trays that have been lightly buttered, sprayed or lined with baking paper or a non-stick Teflon liner. Leave room for the biscuits to spread.

Bake for 8–10 minutes, or until golden brown. Transfer to a cooling rack.

When cold, store in an airtight container.

Variation: For 'Orange Chippies', add the finely grated rind of 1 orange.

Hokey Pokey Biscuits

Another biscuit mixture that can be stirred together very quickly in a pot.

For 36–48 biscuits:
100 g (3 1/2 oz) butter
1 Tbsp milk
1 household Tbsp golden syrup
1/2 cup sugar
1/4 tsp salt
2 cups plain flour
1 tsp baking soda
1/2 cup currants or sultanas

Turn the oven to 180°C (350°F). Melt the butter in a medium-sized pot until liquid. Remove from the heat and add the milk, syrup, sugar and salt. Sift in the flour and baking soda, and add the currants or sultanas. Mix until all ingredients are combined.

Roll teaspoonfuls of mixture into balls, flatten slightly and place on cold, unbuttered oven trays, leaving room for spreading. Flatten with a fork dipped in water.

Bake one tray at a time, for 15–20 minutes, until the biscuits are an even, rich golden brown. Cool on a wire rack and store in an airtight container.

Note: Measure carefully. If your biscuits don't spread, you have used too much flour. If they spread too far, you have not used enough.

Foam Biscuits

These plain biscuits are somehow different from any other biscuit I make – there's something about their texture and flavour that makes them special. Everyone who passes the jar where they are stored helps themselves, until every biscuit disappears!

1/4 cup (60 ml/2 fl oz) milk
3/4 cup sugar
1/2 tsp baking soda
125 g (4 1/2 oz) butter
1/2 tsp vanilla essence
2 cups plain flour
1 tsp cream of tartar

Turn the oven to 180°C (350°F). Measure the milk, sugar and baking soda into a medium-sized pot or microwave dish and bring to the boil. Remove from the heat, add the butter cut into several pieces, stir until it is melted then set aside to cool, standing the pot in cold water if necessary. Stir in the vanilla.

Sift the flour and cream of tartar into the cooled liquid. Mix well.

Roll out the dough thinly on a lightly floured board, then cut it into interesting shapes with biscuit cutters. OR form it into an even cylinder about 3 cm (1¹/₂ in) across, wrap it in plastic and chill it until very firm in the refrigerator or freezer, then cut it into thin, even slices ready for baking.

Bake on a lightly sprayed, oiled or lined oven tray for 5–7 minutes, or until the biscuits are crisp and show signs of browning very slightly around the edges.

When cool, store in airtight containers.

Malt Biscuits

I love the flavour of malt, but I have found it can be quite a tricky ingredient to cook with if it's heated too much when it is being softened.

The thickness of these malty biscuits depends on the amount of sugar and flour used. Biscuits made with ¹/₄ cup sugar and 1¹/₂ cups flour do not spread far, and retain their fork marks. Those made with ¹/₂ cup sugar and a tablespoon less flour flatten and are very crisp. I like the second variety best, although some people would consider them failures. Please yourself!

For about 36 biscuits:
125 g (4¹/₂ oz) butter
¹/₂ cup malt
¹/₄ or ¹/₂ cup sugar
1 level tsp baking soda
about 1¹/₂ cups plain flour

Turn the oven to 170°C (325°F). Heat the butter in a pot or microwave dish until it is liquid. In cold weather stand the tin of malt in hot water and use a hot, wet cup to measure it. Off the heat, stir the malt into the butter.

Add the sugar, using the smaller amount if you want thicker biscuits with fork marks showing. Use the larger amount if you want flat, thin biscuits. Stir the baking soda into the warm mixture, then stir in nearly all the flour, reserving about 2 Tbsp.

Cook a few trial biscuits. Roll teaspoonfuls of the fairly soft mixture into small balls and put them onto oven trays lined with baking paper or non-stick Teflon liners. Press down with a fork dipped in hot water. Bake these for about 8 minutes, until evenly golden brown. If you think they are too flat, add the rest of the flour. Shape and cook the rest.

Cool on a rack. When quite cold and crisp, store in an airtight container.

Note: The uncooked mixture tastes absolutely delicious. Especially if you have children helping you bake, do not leave the dough unattended, or you may finish up with a very small number of cooked biscuits!

Speculaas

Speculaas are Dutch spiced biscuits. Refrigerating the mixture for an hour, or overnight, makes it easier to handle, so that even little hands can help with cutting out the biscuits. To make it easier for helpers, remember to roll out the dough on a lightly floured board, dip the cutters into extra flour before using them, and lift the shapes carefully with a fish slice, without distorting them, when putting them onto trays.

3 cups plain flour
2 tsp baking powder
1 tsp salt
2 tsp cinnamon
¹/₂ tsp each ground cloves, coriander, nutmeg and cardamom
225 g (8 oz) butter
1¹/₄ cups brown sugar
¹/₄ cup (60 ml/2 fl oz) milk

Turn the oven to 180°C (350°F). Sift the flour, baking powder, salt and spices into a large bowl. Rub the softened, but not melted, butter through the dry ingredients, then add the sugar and milk. Mix with your hands until it forms a ball, then transfer to a plastic bag and refrigerate or freeze until firm.

Roll out on a well-floured surface, and cut into shapes with floured cutters. Using a fish slice, carefully place on an oven tray lined with baking paper, without distorting the shapes. Bake for 15 minutes, or until lightly browned. Cool on a rack, then store in an airtight container.

The full flavour of these crisp little cakes does not develop until a few hours after baking. They are not decorated in any way.

Variation: If you prefer, shape the dough into a cylinder or long rectangle. Chill, then slice thinly. Prick each slice in a few places and bake as for cut-out biscuits.

Foam Biscuits and Malt Biscuits

Kirsten's Biscotti

Kirsten's Biscotti

Although this mixture starts as a loaf, the slices are baked again. A few slices in a small cellophane bag, tied with pretty curling ribbon, make a good small gift.

For about 40 biscotti:

3 eggs
1/2 tsp salt
1/2 cup sugar
1/4 tsp almond essence
1/2 tsp vanilla essence
finely grated rind of 1 orange
1 cup plain flour
1 1/2 cups raw almonds, preferably with
  skin on
1 1/2 cups red glacé cherries

Turn the oven to 180°C (350°F). Beat the eggs, salt, sugar and essences until light and fluffy, then add the rind.

Mix the flour, almonds and cherries together, then fold into the egg mixture.

Turn the mixture into a loaf tin about 9 x 23 x 8 cm (4 x 9 x 3 1/4 in), lined with a non-stick Teflon liner or baking paper, making sure the top is evenly flattened. Bake for 45–50 minutes, or until the loaf is lightly browned and the centre springs back when pressed.

When cool, remove from the tin, wrap and refrigerate for at least 24 hours, then cut into about 40 thin slices with a sharp, serrated knife.

Bake the slices on a lined oven tray at 125–150°C (250–300°F) for about 30 minutes, until they colour slightly. Cool on racks then store in airtight containers.

Variations: Leave out the cherries altogether.

Shape the original mixture into a long, thin roll rather than baking it in a tin.

Chocolate Crunchies

This is a simplified, quick version of afghans. Sometimes I ice the biscuits, but they are also good without icing.

For about 50 biscuits:

125 g (4 1/2 oz) butter
1 cup sugar
3 Tbsp cocoa
1 tsp vanilla essence
1 large egg
1 cup self-raising flour
1 1/2 cups malted wheatflakes or cornflakes

Optional Icing

2 tsp cocoa
2 Tbsp water
about 1 cup icing sugar
50 walnut pieces or halves

Turn the oven to 170°C (325°F). In a pot big enough to hold the whole mixture, melt the butter until it is barely liquid, then remove from the heat. Add the sugar, cocoa, vanilla and egg, and mix well with a fork. Put the flour and wheatflakes on top of the mixture and stir until evenly mixed.

Using 2 teaspoons, put small, compact heaps of the mixture on oven trays that have been lightly buttered or covered with baking paper. Leave room between them. The biscuits spread a certain amount as they cook, but if you want them to be large and flatter, flatten the unbaked biscuits gently, using several fingers.

Bake for 8–12 minutes, until they look evenly cooked but have not darkened round the edges. Transfer to a cooling rack while warm.

To make the icing, bring the cocoa and water to the boil in a small frypan, stirring all the time. Take off the heat. While still quite hot, stir in enough icing sugar to make a thin icing. Spread on the biscuits while both the icing and the biscuits are warm. Top with walnuts before the icing sets.

Store iced or un-iced biscuits in an airtight container to keep them crisp.

Coconut Haystacks

These delicious biscuits are something out of the ordinary. They contain no flour, and are quick and easy enough for a child to make.

For 30 haystacks:

50 g (2 oz) butter
1/2 cup sugar
1/2 tsp almond essence (optional)
1 egg
2 cups desiccated coconut

Turn the oven to 180°C (350°F). Melt the butter in a pot. Add the remaining ingredients and mix until well combined.

Use 2 teaspoons to shape the biscuits – take a spoonful of the mixture, and push it onto a sprayed oven tray with the other spoon. The biscuit will stay almost the same size and shape after baking.

Bake for 12–15 minutes, until the bottom edges are golden brown and the rough pieces on the top colour slightly. Watch closely towards the end of the cooking time.

Cool on a wire rack and store in an airtight container.

Margaret Payne's Coffee Creams

My mother's little biscuits, sandwiched together with delicious coffee cream, were always irresistible to the hundreds of her friends and guests who enjoyed them.

125 g (4½ oz) butter
½ cup sugar
1 egg, beaten with a fork
1 Tbsp instant coffee
1 Tbsp hot water
about 2 cups plain flour
2 tsp baking powder

Filling
2 tsp instant coffee
2 tsp hot water
3 Tbsp butter
about 1 cup icing sugar
1 tsp vanilla essence

Heat the oven to 180°C (350°F). Beat together the soft (not melted) butter, sugar and egg in a bowl or food processor. Dissolve the instant coffee in the hot water and add with the sifted flour and baking powder. Mix to form a dough, adding a little extra flour if the mixture is too soft to work with.

Roll into a long, 4 cm (1¾ in) diameter cylinder, wrap in cling film or greaseproof paper, and chill in the refrigerator or freezer until firm enough to cut without flattening; cut into about 60 slices, 5 mm (¼ in) thick. Bake on a lightly buttered tray until very lightly browned, about 10 minutes. Cool on a rack.

To make the filling, dissolve the instant coffee in the water in the unwashed container, add the remaining ingredients and mix until icing consistency; add extra icing sugar or water if necessary. Put the filling on half the cooked biscuits, as evenly as possible. When all the filling has been distributed, top with the other biscuits. Leave on a rack until firm.

Variations: Add ¼ cup finely chopped walnuts to the dough.

Reserve 2 tsp beaten egg and rub a little on top of half the uncooked biscuits, then top with extra finely chopped walnuts.

Custard Kisses

I can think of nothing nicer than being given a batch of small custard kisses as a gift – in a pretty box or jar, or packed in a cardboard tube wrapped as a Christmas cracker.

For 25 kisses:
175 g (6¼ oz) butter
¾ cup icing sugar
1 tsp vanilla essence
1½ cups plain flour
½ cup custard powder
1 tsp baking powder

Icing
2 Tbsp butter
½ cup icing sugar
1 Tbsp custard powder
few drops vanilla essence

Turn the oven to 170–180°C (325–350°F). Soften, but do not melt, the butter. Cream with the icing sugar and vanilla then stir in the sifted flour, custard powder and baking powder. Mix well, then form into about 50 small balls. Flatten these in your hand, put them on a lightly sprayed oven tray then make a pattern with a dampened fork, the dimpled surface of a meat hammer, or the bottom of a patterned glass.

OR form the mixture into a cylinder and refrigerate it until it will cut without flattening. Cut into slices, put on a tray and decorate as above.

Bake for 12–15 minutes, depending on the thickness of the biscuits. When done they should feel firm but should not have browned. Cool on a rack.

Stick cold biscuits together with icing made by mixing together the softened (but not melted) butter and other icing ingredients.

Store biscuits in airtight tins once the icing has set. Freeze if desired.

Custard Kisses

Shirley's Shortbread

This shortbread is a favourite with my family. The castor sugar is essential for good texture, so don't replace it with plain sugar or icing sugar.

225 g (7½ oz) butter
½ cup castor sugar
2 cups sifted plain flour
1 cup cornflour, stirred

Turn the oven to 200°C (400°F), or 180°C (350°F) for fan-bake. Using a beater or wooden spoon, cream the softened (but not melted) butter, add the sugar and beat until light and fluffy. Stir in the sifted flour and cornflour. Chill the dough if necessary to make it easier to handle.

Roll out about 1 cm (½ in) thick on a floured board, and cut into rectangles or festive shapes using biscuit cutters. Reroll scraps until all the dough is used. Prick the shapes with a fork.

Bake on an oven tray lined with baking paper for about 15 minutes, watching carefully towards the end of the cooking time. Take the shortbread from the oven before it starts to brown.

Belgian Biscuits

These spicy biscuits are very popular filled or unfilled.

For 90–100 biscuits:
1 cup brown sugar, packed
200 g (7 oz) butter
1 large egg
1 tsp cinnamon
2 tsp mixed spice
2 cups plain flour
2 tsp cream of tartar
1 tsp baking soda

Turn the oven to 180°C (350°F). To make in a mixer or by hand: cream the butter and sugar until light coloured. Add the egg and spices, and mix to combine. Sift in the flour, cream of tartar and baking soda. Fold into the creamed mixture.

To make using a food processor: put the egg, sugar and softened butter in the processor. Mix, then add all the dry ingredients except the flour. Process again, add half the flour, and process until just mixed. If the food processor is strong enough, add the remaining flour and process in short bursts until mixed, or remove the blade and stir it in with a spatula.

Turn the dough out onto a floured board and gently form it into 3 sausage-shaped rolls, each about 5 cm (2 in) in diameter. Chill in the freezer or refrigerator until firm enough to cut into thin slices. Each roll should yield 25–30 thin biscuits.

Place the biscuits on a lightly buttered or sprayed oven tray, leaving enough space for them to spread a little. Bake for about 10 minutes. Remove from the oven as soon as the edges begin to darken. Cool on a rack and bake the next batch.

Store the biscuits in an airtight container as soon as they are cold, or sandwich together with raspberry or blackcurrant jam. If desired, top with icing made from 2 cups icing sugar, 25 g (1 oz) butter and enough lemon juice or water to make a fairly soft icing. Sprinkle a few coloured sugar crystals (mix a few drops of cochineal through 2 Tbsp sugar) or red jelly crystals on the icing.

Lebkuchen

Try making these rock-hard Christmas tree biscuits with your children. The uncooked dough tastes wonderful, so do not expect the impossible!

50 g (2 oz) butter
1 cup honey
3/4 cup brown sugar
1 Tbsp lemon juice
1 Tbsp finely grated lemon rind
2 tsp cinnamon
1 tsp ground cloves
1 tsp nutmeg

1 tsp allspice
1/2 tsp baking soda
3–4 cups plain flour

Turn the oven to 170°C (325°F). Measure all the ingredients except the baking soda and flour into a medium-sized pot. Stir over low heat until blended and the sugar is no longer grainy. Do not boil. Remove from the heat and cool to room temperature.

Stir in the baking soda sifted with 1 cup of the flour. Stir well then add more flour, about half a cup at a time, until the dough is firm enough to roll out. The more flour you add, the harder and longer-lasting the biscuits will be.

Roll out the dough on a floured board, to about 5 mm (1/4 in) thick, and cut into shapes using biscuit cutters, etc. Before cooking, make a hole with a gently twisted straw so you can thread red ribbon or wool through later.

Bake for about 10–20 minutes, or longer, until the edges brown lightly. (Longer-baked biscuits are harder.)

Cool on a rack. Leave plain or decorate with water icing, or make an icing of piping consistency, adding water and a little butter to icing sugar, and pipe on designs.

Christmas Tree Biscuits

(Photo p. 272)

Shape and decorate these biscuits so they can be hung on a Christmas tree, or pack them in pretty glass containers for gifts.

150 g (5 oz) butter
1/4 tsp almond essence
1 tsp ground cardamom (optional)
1/2 cup castor sugar
1 egg, separated
2 Tbsp milk
about 2 cups flour

Turn the oven to 150°C (300°F). Cream the softened (but not melted) butter, essence, cardamom and sugar together until light coloured and fluffy. Add the egg yolk and milk and beat again, then add enough flour to make a dough that is firm enough to roll out and cut in shapes.

Cut into festive shapes with suitable cutters. If you don't have any special cutters, cut out large circles with a glass, then cut smaller circles from the centres of these using the tops of small bottles.

For biscuits to hang up, cut a small circular hole with a straw before baking. For almond wreath biscuits, beat the egg white until bubbly, brush it onto the uncooked circles of dough, and arrange flaked almonds in a pattern. Decorate other biscuits after baking.

Bake for about 15 minutes, or until very lightly browned. Cool on a rack. Make white icing by beating the remaining egg white with sifted icing sugar until the mixture is of good spreading consistency. Spread with a small knife. Neaten up the edges by running a finger along them. Decorate iced biscuits with slices of cherries, silver cachoux, etc. before the icing hardens.

Attach biscuits to the tree with silver or gold thread, or with tartan ribbons and fine wire, etc.

To keep them crisp, store in airtight containers.

Note: Biscuits that have been hung on trees for several days or longer are not suitable for eating later.

Painted Biscuits

These are great fun for children to make at Christmas for grandparents and other friends! They are cut into shapes then painted before baking. They look rather like animal biscuits, but are not as sweet.

100 g (3 1/2 oz) butter
1/2 cup castor sugar
1 egg, separated
1/2 tsp vanilla essence
1 1/2 cups plain flour
1/2 tsp baking powder

Turn the oven to 170°C (325°F), or 160°C (just under 325°F) for fan-bake. Beat the butter and castor sugar together until well mixed. Add the egg white then the essence and stir well. Sift in the flour and baking powder and stir until mixed.

Put the dough in a cold place for 5 minutes, then roll out thinly on a floured board and cut into circles with a glass or into shapes using fancy cutters. (Dip cutters in flour so they do not stick.)

Using a lightly floured fish slice or spatula, put the biscuits on an oven tray covered with a non-stick Teflon liner or baking paper. Handle carefully so you don't distort the shapes.

Stir the egg yolk with a fork and divide it into 3; colour each part with food colouring then paint the biscuits, using watercolour painting brushes. Turn round biscuits into happy/funny faces and paint on details to suit other shapes. (Add silver cachoux for eyes, etc. if you like.)

Bake for 5–10 minutes, until the edges are very lightly browned. The time will depend on the temperature and the thickness of the dough. Do not let the colours darken.

Cool on a rack. When cold, pack on pretty paper plates covered with plastic wrap so they are airtight.

'Heart of Glass' Biscuits

'Heart of Glass' Biscuits

'Stained glass' heart biscuits are fun to make occasionally when you want a special effect. You can shape the dough in two ways, rolling it into a long rope, then forming bits of the rope into heart shapes, or rolling it out thinly and cutting the shapes with larger and smaller heart-shaped biscuit cutters. The first way is rather fun and requires no cutters, the second produces neater biscuits.

225 g (8 oz) butter
1¼ cups sugar
½ tsp baking soda
¼ cup (60 ml/2 fl oz) water
3–4 cups plain flour
clear red boiled sweets ('Lifesavers')

Turn the oven to 180°C (350°F), or 170°C (325°F) for fan-bake. Soften (but do not melt) the butter. Add the sugar and cream thoroughly in a beater or food processor.

Mix the baking soda with the water, beat into the creamed mixture, then add the flour – if you intend to roll the mixture into a rope and shape it by hand, add 3 cups (375 g/13 oz) flour.

Chill the dough if it is too soft to work with, then roll small amounts into a rope about 7 mm (¼ in) in diameter. Shape lengths of this into hearts.

If you are going to roll out the mixture and cut shapes from it with cutters, add 4 cups (500 g/18 oz) flour. Roll the dough

out thinly then cut heart outlines, first using a larger heart cutter, then using a smaller heart cutter to remove the centre portion, leaving a space to fill with candy.

Place the heart-shaped outlines on a non-stick Teflon liner or on foil and bake for about 4 minutes. Remove from the oven and sprinkle finely crushed red Lifesavers or other red toffee-like sweets into the centre of each heart. Bake again for 2–3 minutes, until the toffee melts and bubbles, and the biscuit mixture is lightly coloured. Remove from the oven and let the 'glass' centre cool and harden before lifting the biscuits from the tray.

Store immediately in airtight containers or the toffee will become soft and sticky.

Gingerbread Houses

Make gingerbread houses (or gingerbread people) to delight children at Christmas.

For 4 small houses:
50 g (2 oz) butter, cubed
100 g (3 1/2 oz) brown sugar
1/4 cup (60 ml/2 fl oz) golden syrup
1/4 cup (60 ml/2 fl oz) plus 1 Tbsp treacle
2 large eggs, separated
2 1/2 cups plain flour
1 Tbsp ground ginger
1/2 tsp baking soda

Turn the oven to 180°C (350°F). Cut 3 shapes from cardboard. (Each will be used twice to cut gingerbread shapes for one cottage.) Cut an 8 x 10 cm (3 1/4 x 4 in) rectangle for each side of the roof, and a 6 x 8 cm (2 1/2 x 3 1/4 in) rectangle for each side wall. To make the gabled walls, draw a 10 x 6 cm (4 x 2 1/2 in) rectangle, then make a mark 4 cm (1 3/4 in) from one end on each long side, and another mark in the middle of the short side nearest the other 2 marks. Join this mark to the other 2, then cut out.

Heat the first 4 ingredients together and mix until smooth. Stir in the egg yolks then the sieved dry ingredients. Knead to form a smooth dough, adding a little water or flour if necessary.

Cut into 4 even pieces and wrap until ready to use. Roll one piece out about 3 mm (1/4 in) thick on a floured board, so it is just large enough to cut 2 each of the 3 cardboard shapes, rerolling dough scraps if necessary. Bake on an oven tray lined with a non-stick Teflon liner or baking paper for about 7 minutes or until lightly and evenly browned. Cool on a wire rack. Repeat for the other houses.

For the icing, whisk one of the unused egg whites until foamy. Beat in about 1/2 cup sifted icing sugar at a time, until the icing will hold its shape when piped from an icing bag, or a tough plastic bag with a small hole in one corner. Decorate the walls and roof with shingles, doors, windows, etc. Stick the walls together (on a piece of cardboard) with icing, then place the roof on top. Leave in a warm place to set.

If you like, fill houses with small surprises before fastening the roof to the walls.

Nutty Lemon Wafers

These are crisp, lemony and delicious. If you grow Lisbon lemons, use one of these in preference to a Meyer lemon, as the lemon-lime flavour of the rind tastes particularly good. If you prefer, leave out the nuts.

For about 120 biscuits:
finely grated rind of 1 large lemon
1 cup sugar
125 g (4 1/2 oz) butter, softened
1 egg
1 3/4 cups plain flour
1/4 cup cornflour
1 tsp baking powder
*1/2–1 cup pinenuts, or chopped walnuts or
    almonds (optional)*

Turn the oven to 170°C (325°F). Cut all the coloured rind from the lemon, using a potato peeler. Process the rind and sugar until very fine in a food processor. Add the butter and egg, and process until light and fluffy.

Sift the dry ingredients into the butter mixture and process until mixed. Add the nuts and mix briefly using the pulse button.

Form the (quite soft) dough into two 20 cm (8 in) rolls on plastic or baking paper. (The shape need not be perfectly regular.) Roll the plastic or baking paper around the rolls to keep them in more or less cylindrical shape

Chill in the freezer for about 30 minutes, or until firm enough to cut easily. Cut each roll into about 60 very thin (3 mm/1/8 in) slices, using a sharp (or

Gingerbread Houses

serrated) thin-bladed knife. Before they soften, put the slices onto oven trays lined with a non-stick Teflon liner, or baking paper, leaving space for spreading. Bake for about 12 minutes, until the biscuits are very lightly browned. Transfer to a rack before the biscuits cool and harden.

If you like, refrigerate some of the dough for a day or two, or keep it in the freezer. You should be able to cut the frozen dough into thin slices if you have a good sharp serrated knife, but if you can't, let it thaw in the refrigerator for 30 minutes before slicing it.

Little Lava Rocks

These delicious, rich little 'rocks' have a special texture and a spectacular mottled appearance. Don't worry about making too many – I hate to tell you how fast these disappear in our house!

For 80 little rocks:
250 g (9 oz) dark chocolate
100 g (3½ oz) butter
½ cup castor sugar
1 tsp vanilla essence
3 large eggs
1¼ cups plain flour
¼ cup self-raising flour
¼ cup cocoa
about 1 cup icing sugar

Turn the oven to 170°C (325°F). Break the chocolate into even squares. Heat gently with the cubed butter over low heat in a fairly large pot, stirring often, until you have a smooth mixture. Do not heat more than necessary.

Remove from the heat and beat in the sugar and vanilla, then the eggs, one at a time, with a wooden spoon or spatula. Sieve the flours and cocoa into the chocolate mixture and mix until well combined. Chill in the freezer or refrigerator until firm enough to roll into balls.

Sift the icing sugar into a large, round, dry, flat-bottomed bowl. (Unsifted icing sugar will not coat the biscuits well.)

Divide the mixture into 4, and form each portion into 20 little balls with your hands. Drop 4 or 5 balls at a time into the icing sugar and rotate the bowl until the balls are thickly coated. Without brushing off any icing sugar, place the balls on oven trays covered with baking paper or non-stick Teflon liners. Leave at least 5 cm (2 in) between them.

Bake for about 10 minutes, until the centres feel soft and springy when you touch them. The rocks will spread slightly and have a cracked surface if you used enough icing sugar. Handle and store carefully to prevent the icing sugar smudging.

Almond and Cherry Biscuits

Often when I travel around the country cooking at fund-raising functions, I am given interesting recipes. These biscuits were brought to my motel by a kind woman who thought I might like something to nibble when I made a cup of tea! She was absolutely right, and the biscuits disappeared fast! The recipe arrived in the mail a few days later.

For about 36 biscuits:
175 g (6 oz) butter
½ cup sugar
¾ cup icing sugar
¼–½ cup chopped glacé cherries (red, green or a mixture)
¼ cup flaked almonds
¼ tsp almond essence
½ tsp vanilla essence
1 cup plain flour
½ cup self-raising flour
½ cup cornflour
2 Tbsp cold water

Turn the oven to 170°C (325°F). Cream together the butter, sugar and icing sugar until light in colour. Add the cherries, almonds and essences. Sift the flours together and stir into the mixture, taking care not to break up the cherries too much. Add water if the mixture is dry.

Cover an oven tray with a non-stick Teflon liner or baking paper. Roll the mixture into walnut-sized balls, put on the tray and flatten slightly with a wet fork or your fingers. Bake for about 15 minutes, until the edges start to colour.

Leave to cool slightly, then lift onto a wire rack. When cool, store in an airtight container.

Almond Rosettes

To make a present for someone special, fill a decorative glass jar with a tightly fitting lid with these pretty biscuits. If you don't have a forcing bag, shape them by pushing them through a heavy plastic bag with the corner cut out.

For 24–36 biscuits:
2 egg whites
¼ cup plus 1 Tbsp castor sugar
125 g (4½ oz) ground almonds
¼–½ tsp almond essence*
¼ tsp salt
8–16 glacé cherries

* Vary the amount of almond essence, depending on its strength. The biscuits should taste definitely, but not strongly, of almonds.

Turn the oven to 180°C (350°F), or 170°C (325°F) for fan-bake. Put the first 5 ingredients into a food processor. Mix until well blended and fairly smooth. If the mixture looks too soft to keep its shape, add more ground almonds.

Spray an oven tray thickly with non-stick spray, or use a non-stick Teflon liner, since these biscuits stick easily. Pipe or otherwise shape them into rosettes, making 24–36 biscuits. They don't rise during cooking, so you can put them quite close together.

Cut the cherries into halves or quarters, and press one or more pieces into the uncooked dough. Bake for about 20 minutes, until the biscuits are golden brown all over. If they appear to be browning too soon, turn the oven down to 170°C (325°F), or 160°C (just under 325°F) for fan-bake.

Cool on a rack, then store in airtight jars, where they will stay crisp for about a month.

Note: To make them without a food processor, beat the egg whites until bubbly but not stiff, add the remaining ingredients, and beat well with a wooden spoon until the mixture becomes quite stiff.

Coconut Macaroons

It was surprising how often Coconut Macaroons cropped up in various books I read as a child! I was an adult before I found a recipe and made them myself.

For 30–40 biscuits:
3 egg whites, at room temperature
¼ tsp salt
1 cup castor sugar
½ tsp vanilla or almond essence
2 Tbsp flour
1½ cups coconut
40 blanched almonds

Turn the oven to 150°C (300°F). Beat the egg whites with the salt until they form peaks which turn over, then add half the sugar and beat until the peaks stand upright when the beater is removed from the mixture. Stir in the essence.

Mix together the remaining sugar, the flour and coconut, then fold into the egg whites.

Shape the mixture (helping it off the end of a dessertspoon with another spoon) to form 30–40 biscuits. Try to keep them evenly round, and allow space for spreading. For easiest removal after cooking, use a non-stick Teflon liner rather than baking paper on the oven tray. Top each biscuit with a blanched almond.

Bake for 20–25 minutes. The biscuits should feel quite firm on the outside, but be chewy inside. The larger the biscuits, the longer they will take to cook.

Transfer to a cooling rack, then store in airtight jars when cold.

Small Cakes

Sometimes, when I decide to bake something, I feel that muffins, biscuits and large cakes are not exactly what I want, and I decide to make one of the recipes in this chapter. Fast work is called for, however, since I know that unless I work fast and get some of my handiwork into the freezer promptly, my small cakes will disappear like magic as people pass through the kitchen, sampling as they go! I think it is the texture as much as the flavour of these little cakes that makes them so 'moreish'!

Sponge Drops

For years I did not realise how easy sponge drops were to make. You may need to experiment with a few batches to find exactly the kind and amount of flour that works best, but you should soon be able to turn out sponge drops with very little time and trouble.

For 10–12 sponge drops:
1/2 cup self-raising flour
2 large eggs
1/4 cup castor sugar
extra castor sugar
about 1/2 cup (125 ml/4 fl oz) cream,
* whipped*
strawberry or raspberry jam

Turn the oven to 180°C (350°F). Spoon the flour into the measuring cup and level it off carefully.

Break the eggs into a fairly large bowl, stand it in a larger bowl or sink of warm water and beat with an electric or rotary beater until frothy. Beat in the sugar about 1 Tbsp at a time, until the mixture is very thick and lemon-coloured. To judge the thickness, make a figure 8 on the mixture with the beater. The part you shaped first should not have disappeared by the time the last part is shaped.

Sieve the flour twice. Sieve half on top of the mixture in the bowl, then fold it in with a knife or stirrer. Repeat, mixing in the flour evenly, but do not beat or stir vigorously or you will lose some of the air beaten into the eggs.

Line oven trays with baking paper or non-stick Teflon liners, then drop spoonfuls of mixture onto the tray, allowing space for spreading. Drop the mixture from the tip of the spoon, rotating it as the mixture comes off it, to get even shapes. (Drops will spread and flatten as they cook.)

Lightly sprinkle more castor sugar on top of each drop to give a slight crust, then bake for about 7 minutes, or until they are golden and the centres spring back when lightly pressed.

Sponge Drops

Remove from the oven, leave on the oven tray for about 10 minutes, then transfer to a cooling rack. About an hour before serving, sandwich pairs of sponge drops together with a little jam and plain or vanilla-flavoured whipped cream. (The cream softens the drops.) Unfilled sponge drops that have dried and cooled on a rack keep well, softening when filled.

First Aid: If your sponge drops flatten and spread too much as they cook, layer three together, with halved strawberries and whipped cream. Dust the tops with icing sugar, give them another name, and serve them for dessert!

Note: Experiment if necessary, using an extra Tbsp of flour, or replacing some flour with cornflour, until you produce good sponge drops.

Ginger Kisses

I make ginger kisses a little smaller than the commercial variety – that way I feel better if I cannot resist eating several.

I use modern technology to help me make these old-fashioned favourites easily. Of course you can still make ginger kisses without these aids, but they do help. Careful measuring is important, however. You need standard cup and spoon measures.

For 36 halves, each 5 cm (2 in) across:
125 g (4 1/2 oz) butter, softened
3/8 cup (80 g/2 1/2 oz) sugar
1 large egg
1 tsp ground ginger
1 tsp cinnamon
1 rounded household dessertspoon
* golden syrup*
75 g (2 1/2 oz) or 1/2 cup + 1 Tbsp plain
* flour*
75 g (2 1/2 oz) or 1/2 cup + 1 Tbsp cornflour
1/2 tsp baking powder
1/2 tsp baking soda

Turn the oven to 220°C (425°F). Soften but do not melt the butter. Put it in a food processor with the next 5 ingredients. (Measure the syrup with a spoon that has

been heated in hot water. It should be gently rounded but not heaped.) Process until smooth and light-coloured.

Weigh or measure the dry ingredients carefully, directly into the food processor; process enough to produce a smooth mixture.

Spoon the mixture into a piping bag with a plain nozzle, or shape small, even blobs with a spoon onto baking paper or non-stick Teflon liners. The piped mounds should be about the size of a half-walnut shell. They rise a lot, and you need to leave space between them. They will fill 2 oven trays.

Place the kisses in the preheated oven and turn it down to 210°C (420°F) as soon as the door is shut. Cook for about 5 minutes, reducing the heat during this time if the bottoms brown before the centres spring back when pressed. Watch carefully, as they burn easily.

Sandwich together with mock cream, or with whipped cream, if they are to be eaten soon after filling.

Mock Cream
50 g (2 oz) butter, at room temperature
1/2 tsp vanilla essence
1/2 cup sieved icing sugar
about 2 Tbsp water

Put the butter, vanilla and icing sugar in a food processor. Add 1 Tbsp of hot water, and process until smooth. Gradually add about 1 Tbsp cold water. You should finish up with a light-coloured, fluffy cream. Add more water if it is absorbed, if you like. Store filled ginger kisses in a cool place, so the filling hardens.

Note: If your kisses run all over the tray, you have used too much butter or not enough flour. If they do not spread enough, you have used too little butter or too much flour. Correct these mistakes next time. The failures are quite edible and are excellent stacked with berries and whipped cream for dessert.

Chocolate Lamingtons

Lamingtons are very easy to make and even young children love to help with them. Freeze what you do not plan to eat in the next day or so.

For 24 or 25 lamingtons:

500 g (1 lb 2 oz) bought, unfilled sponge
  (preferably a rectangular block)
1/4 cup cocoa
1/2 cup (125 ml/4 fl oz) water
1/4 cup raspberry jam
3/4 cup (185 ml/6 fl oz) hot water
2 cups icing sugar
about 1 1/2 cups fine coconut

Cut the sponge into 24–25 cubes. I like to cut off the brown top before I do this so the sponge soaks up the syrup better, but this is not essential.

Put the cocoa and the first measure of water into a small pot or microwave jug. Stir thoroughly to make sure there are no lumps, then boil until the colour darkens and the mixture thickens. Add the jam, stir again and bring back to the boil. Add the hot water then stir in the icing sugar, making a fairly thin mixture that will coat the sponge evenly. It will not be completely smooth and can be strained, but I don't think this is really necessary.

Dip the sponge cubes one by one into the chocolate syrup, turning to coat them evenly. Flick to remove excess icing, then turn in the coconut. I find the best way to do this is to put about 1/4 cup coconut into a plastic bag or a lidded plastic bowl. Shake, making sure you enclose some air in the plastic bag. (If you put too much coconut in the container at a time it tends to discolour.)

Leave the lamingtons to dry on a cake rack then store in airtight containers. Keep in the refrigerator up to 2 days or freeze.

To serve, split and fill with a teaspoonful of raspberry jam and whipped cream.

Cassie's Rock Cakes

My husband's mother made these rock cakes regularly and my daughter makes them too. When she was five, our grand-daughter Elizabeth was not impressed with their name, but enjoyed them all the same.

For 30–40 rock cakes:

125 g (4 1/2 oz) butter
1/2 cup sugar
1/2 tsp vanilla essence
1 egg
3/4 cup self-raising flour
1 cup plain flour
1 cup currants, sultanas, or mixed fruit

Turn the oven to 180°C (350°F). Soften but do not melt the butter. Add the sugar and vanilla, beat or process to combine, then add the egg and 1 Tbsp of the flour,

and beat or process until light-coloured. Add the remaining flour and mix just enough to combine. Add the dried fruit and stir or process very briefly.

Using 2 spoons, form into mounds on a non-stick Teflon-lined or lightly buttered oven tray, leaving a little space for rising. Bake for 10–15 minutes, until golden at the edges and firm in the middle. Cool on a rack, then store in an airtight container.

Note: For best results, stir the flour with a fork before spooning it into the cup measures.

Neenish Tarts   (Photo p. 288)

Neenish tarts are not made in a matter of moments. Even so, I occasionally make a batch because I have never bought a Neenish Tart that comes up to my expectations!

Tart Shells

100 g (3 1/2 oz) butter
3/4 cup icing sugar
1 cup plain flour
1/2 cup cornflour
milk, if necessary

Filling

1 tsp gelatine
1 Tbsp water
50 g (2 oz) butter
1/2 cup icing sugar
2 Tbsp warm water
1/4–1/2 tsp rum essence

Icings

1/2 recipe Everyday Chocolate Icing (p. 347)
1/2 cup icing sugar
1 Tbsp butter, at room temperature
about 2 tsp hot water

Turn the oven to 170°C (325°F). To make the shells, cream the butter and icing sugar until light. Stir in the flour and cornflour. If the mixture is too crumbly, add milk. Form into a cylinder about 6 cm (2 1/2 in) in diameter and chill for 15 minutes to firm up.

Slice the chilled dough into 3 mm (1/4 in) thick rounds, and press evenly into shallow, well-sprayed patty tins. Prick with a fork. Bake for 10 minutes, or until they darken slightly. Cool briefly in the tins, rotate carefully to ensure they have not stuck, then lift onto a rack to cool.

To make the filling, sprinkle the gelatine onto the cold water, leave to soften for 2–3 minutes, then heat briefly to dissolve. Cool.

Mix the softened butter and the icing sugar together in a food processor. Blend in the warm water and essence, then add the cooled gelatine. Process to combine. Chill until cold but not set hard.

Fill the cooked tart shells with the chilled filling and level off with the back of a knife blade.

You need to make two icings for Neenish Tarts. Make half the recipe of Everyday Chocolate Icing, then mix together the icing sugar, butter and hot water to make white icing.

Cover half the filled shell with the chocolate icing then refrigerate. Use a straight knife blade to ensure the edge between the two icings is straight, then cover the rest with the white icing. Leave to set before storing in the refrigerator.

Nana's Cheesecake Tarts

My mother (Nana to my children) always had a tin of these little tarts, which were enjoyed by four generations of our family. I was quite overwhelmed when my daughter brought me a batch of them, several years after my mother's death.

If you don't want to make the pastry, use very thinly rolled bought flaky pastry instead.

For 18–24 tarts:

Pastry

1 cup plain flour
75 g (2 1/2 oz) cold butter, cubed
3–4 Tbsp water

Filling

125 g (4 1/2 oz) butter, cubed
1/2 cup sugar
2 large eggs
1 cup plain flour
1 tsp baking powder
1 tsp vanilla essence
1/4 cup raspberry jam

Turn the oven to 190°C (375°F), or 180°C (350°F) for fan-bake. If using homemade pastry, make it first. Measure the flour and cold, cubed butter into a food processor. Process briefly while adding just enough water, a few drops at a time, to make the particles stick together. Remove from the food processor, form into a ball, and chill while you make the cake mixture.

Whisk or process the softened (but not melted) butter and sugar together until creamy. Add one egg and half the flour, mix until just combined, then add the remaining egg, flour, baking powder and vanilla, and mix briefly.

Roll out the pastry very thinly, and cut circles to fit 18–24 small patty pans. Place about half a teaspoon of jam on each pastry circle, then add a spoonful of the cake mixture. If you like, reroll pastry scraps, cut into strips 5 mm (1/4 in) wide and about 3 cm (1 1/4 in) long and place one or two strips on the uncooked cake.

Bake for about 15 minutes, until lightly browned, and until the centre of each little cake springs back when pressed. Remove from the tins, cool on a cake rack, then store in an airtight container. Eat within 2 days.

Mini Carrot Cakes for Easter

If you get the urge to bake over Easter, try this recipe. It is not as spicy as Hot Cross Buns but it has an interesting flavour. You can cook the mixture as mini-cakes, as one big cake in a roasting pan, or in muffin pans. All are good, and are made even better by the cream cheese icing! The big cake is only about 1.5 cm (½ in) high, and should be cut into generous squares.

For 8 mini-cakes, 1 large cake or 18 large muffins:

½ cup chopped walnuts
½ cup sultanas
2 large carrots, grated
1¼ cups plain flour
1 tsp salt
1 tsp baking soda
2 tsp cinnamon
1 tsp ground allspice
3 eggs
¾ cup brown sugar, tightly packed
½ cup sugar
¾ cup canola or other oil

Cream Cheese Icing

½ cup cream cheese
25 g (1 oz) butter
1 tsp vanilla essence
3 cups icing sugar

Turn the oven to 180°C (350°F). Mix the chopped walnuts with the sultanas and stir in the grated carrot.

Sift together the flour, salt, baking soda and spices.

In a large bowl, thoroughly beat together the eggs, sugars and oil. Stir the mixed carrots, nuts and sultanas into the egg mixture until thoroughly combined, then fold in the dry ingredients, mixing no more than necessary.

Carefully prepare your baking pans, as this mixture sticks: line the bottoms of 8 small tins 10 cm (4 in) across (e.g. smoked fish cans), OR line the bottom and 2 sides of a small roasting pan (about 25 x 30 cm/ 10 x 12 in) and butter or spray the other sides, OR butter or spray muffin pans.

Spoon the mixture into the prepared pans, half-filling the muffin pans, and bake in the oven. The mini-cakes will take about 20 minutes, the large cake 20–30 minutes, and the muffin-sized cakes about 12–15 minutes. The cakes are cooked when the centres spring back and/or a skewer comes out clean.

Cinnamon Oysters

Cinnamon oysters are not difficult to make, as long as you measure carefully.

For 12–18 cinnamon oysters:

2 large eggs, separated
pinch of salt
½ cup minus 2 Tbsp castor sugar
1 Tbsp golden syrup
½ cup plain flour
1 tsp cinnamon
¼ tsp ground ginger
½ tsp baking soda

Turn the oven to 180°C (350°F). Beat the egg whites with the salt until foamy. Add the sugar and continue beating until the whites are stiff and the mixture forms peaks with tips that fold over when the beater is lifted from them.

Measure the golden syrup using a household spoon. Dip it in hot water, then measure a slightly rounded spoonful. Add the syrup to the whites and beat until well combined. Beat in the egg yolks.

Sift together the carefully measured dry ingredients and fold into the egg mixture with a knife or flexible stirrer.

Lightly butter or spray shallow patty tins, and spoon in rounded household tablespoons or dessertspoons of the mixture.

Bake for 8–10 minutes, or until the centres spring back when lightly pressed. (They will dry out, toughen and shrink if overcooked.) Cool slightly in the patty tins then gently turn them to loosen, or run a knife around them. Cool on a wire rack.

Cut through, leaving a hinge, using a sharp serrated knife. They may seem tough and leathery at this stage, but they soften once they are filled. Fill with plain or vanilla-flavoured, lightly sweetened whipped cream, and leave to stand for about an hour to soften. Freeze at this stage if you like. Before serving, dust with sieved icing sugar.

To freeze, place uncovered on a flat plate or tray in the freezer, until hard, then pack into a container and cover tightly.

Cinnamon Oysters

Butterfly Cakes

These little cakes are based on an old, traditional pound-cake recipe, where the same weights of eggs, butter, sugar and flour are used. My cakes are always popular, even though I mix them untraditionally in the food processor instead of creaming them painstakingly by hand.

For 12 cakes in large paper cups:
2 large eggs (150 g/5 oz)
150 g (5 oz) butter
³/₄ cup castor sugar 4¹/₂ ozs.
1¹/₂ cups plain flour 60zs
finely grated rind of 1 orange
pinch of salt
1¹/₂ tsp baking powder

To decorate
whipped cream
raspberry or strawberry jam

fresh strawberries or raspberries
icing sugar

Turn the oven to 170°C (325°F). Weigh the eggs, then weigh the same amounts of butter, sugar and flour.

Mix the warmed, but not melted, butter and half the sugar together in the food processor. Add the finely grated rind, then the egg yolks, and process again.

In a fairly large bowl, beat the egg whites with a pinch of salt until light and frothy. Add the remaining sugar and beat until the mixture stands in peaks and just the tips turn over when the beater is lifted from them.

Fold into this meringue first the mixture from the food processor, then the flour sifted with the baking powder. Do not overmix.

Butterfly Cakes

Spoon the mixture into 12 large paper cases, standing them in patty tins or muffin tins. Bake for 15–20 minutes, until they are lightly browned and spring back when gently pressed in the centre.

When cool, cut the top off each cake carefully so the underside of the part removed is cone-shaped. Fill the depression that is left with raspberry or strawberry jam and vanilla- or orange-flavoured whipped cream. Carefully cut each top in half and arrange the 2 pieces, cut edges down, in the cream, rather like butterfly wings. Decorate the cream between the wings with a small piece of strawberry or a small raspberry, and sprinkle with icing sugar through a fine sieve.

Cup Cakes

Any little cakes that are not filled may be stored in an airtight container in a cool place for several days. These may be eaten as they are, iced with orange butter icing, or dusted with icing sugar.

Butter Cake (Pound Cake)

The mixture may be baked in a baking paper-lined loaf tin as a butter cake. Bake it at 170°C (325°F) for about an hour, until the edges start to shrink from the tin, the centre springs back when lightly pressed, and a skewer in the centre comes out clean. This cake keeps well, if it gets the chance, for up to a fortnight.

Cream Puffs

Cream puffs and chocolate éclairs are usually regarded as a special-occasion treat, but are much easier to make than you might think.

The mixture is soft and wet, and the puffs rise dramatically in the oven due to the steam formed inside them during baking. The eggs then set the outside crust, forming a crisp, firm shell with a large cavity in the middle.

¹/₂ cup (125 ml/4 fl oz) water
60g (2 oz) butter
¹/₂ cup flour
2 large eggs

Put the water into a medium-sized saucepan with the butter, in eight or nine small cubes. Measure the flour carefully without packing it into the measuring cup. If you are not an experienced choux pastry maker, break the eggs into a measuring jug and beat them with a fork so you can pour them from the jug in a controlled way.

Get all these things ready, and make sure the oven is preheated to 200°C (400°C) before you start beating and mixing.

Bring the water and butter to the boil. Heat it until the water bubbles vigorously and the butter melts completely. Tip in all the flour and stir briskly with a wooden stirrer until the mixture forms a ball which leaves the sides of the pot, then take the pot off the heat.

If you have a food processor, drop the hot mixture into it in four or five 'blobs'. Put the top on the machine and pour half the egg through the feed tube onto the mixture. Process (with metal chopping blade) for about 10 seconds then pour in half the remaining egg and process again. You should add as much egg as possible without making the dough too liquid. You will probably use all of 2 large eggs – you may need a third egg if the eggs are not very big. Lift out the blade and remove mixture from it, and the sides of the bowl, with a scraper.

If you are beating the egg into the hot mixture in the pot by hand, let it cool for about 2 minutes, add 1 egg and beat vigorously, then add the remaining egg as above. Put about 12 spoonfuls of mixture on a sprayed or oiled oven slide, leaving plenty of room for rising.

Bake at 200°C (400°C) for about 40 minutes, lowering heat if puffs brown too soon. You must allow the shell time to set properly, otherwise it will soften and collapse on cooling.

To serve, split and fill with sweetened whipped cream, and dust the tops with icing sugar or ice with chocolate glaze (see Chocolate Eclairs).

Chocolate Eclairs

For Chocolate Eclairs, make the cream puff mixture following the preceding recipe. Form mixture into 12–15 sausage shapes using a forcer bag or heavy plastic bag with the corner cut out. Bake as for cream puffs.

Ice with chocolate glaze before splitting and filling with plain or sweetened whipped cream.

Chocolate Glaze: Heat 2 level Tbsp of cocoa with ¼ cup (60ml/2 fl oz) of water in a small frypan or milk saucepan. As soon as this thickens and starts to look dry, remove from the heat and stir in ½ tsp of vanilla essence. Sift 1 cup of icing sugar. When the pan has cooled so that you can touch the bottom of it with your hand, add half the icing sugar. Like magic, the dryish chocolate mixture turns into a thin, dark brown, shiny mixture.

Add enough icing sugar to make the icing a manageable consistency. Tilt the pot or pan and dip the top of an Eclair or Puff in it. The icing should run down the sides a little bit when turned right way up again. If it runs too far, add more icing sugar. If it doesn't run at all, add a little water, but do not heat the pan in an effort to thin the icing.

Chocolate Brownies

Brownies are deliciously rich, with a unique texture, and have been an American favourite for a long time.

125 g (4½ oz) butter
¼ cup cocoa
1 cup sugar
2 large eggs
¼ tsp salt
1 tsp vanilla essence
1 cup plain flour
1 tsp baking powder
½ cup chopped nuts (e.g. peanuts, walnuts)

Turn the oven to 180°C (350°F). Melt the butter in a medium-sized pot. Remove from the heat when liquid, add the cocoa, sugar, eggs, salt and vanilla, and mix thoroughly. Sift in the flour and baking powder, and add the chopped nuts. Stir until all the ingredients are combined.

Pour the mixture into a 20–23 cm (8–9 in) square tin lined with baking paper. Bake for about 30 minutes, until firm in the centre. (Don't worry if the brownie mixture is higher at the edges than the middle. Whatever its height, it will taste fine!)

When cold, cut into rectangles. Serve with tea or coffee, or at the side of a plate of stewed fruit or icecream for dessert.

Jaffa Nut Brownies

Make these as a treat for yourself, or to give away! Their special, rich texture makes them very popular. What's more, they are really easy to make.

For 18 pieces:
100 g (3½ oz) butter
75 g (2½ oz) dark cooking chocolate
2 large eggs
¾ cup sugar
1 tsp vanilla essence
rind of 1 orange
½ cup chopped walnuts
½ cup plain flour

Turn the oven to 180°C (350°F). Cube the butter and break the chocolate into pieces. Put both in a microwave bowl and heat for 2 minutes on Medium (50%) power, or warm in a medium-sized pot over low heat, until the butter has melted and the chocolate softened. Remove from the heat and stir until smooth and combined.

Add the eggs, sugar, vanilla, rind and chopped nuts, and stir until well mixed. Sift the flour and fold together, but do not overmix.

Line the bottom of a 20 cm (8 in) square cake tin with baking paper and spray the sides with non-stick spray. Spread the mixture into the tin and bake for about 15 minutes, or until the centre feels firm when pressed. (Don't worry if the sides rise more than the centre.)

Cool, then cut into 6 pieces lengthways and 3 crosswise. Store in an airtight container. Dust lightly with sieved icing sugar just before serving.

Chocolate Bubble Cakes

Even young children enjoy making rice bubble cakes. For ease of handling later, fill paper cases (in patty pans) with the mixture, or put a rich caramel filling between two layers of the mixture to make a square for the sweet-toothed!

Chocolate Mixture
1 cup Kremelta (or Copha), melted
¼ cup cocoa
1 cup icing sugar
4 cups rice bubbles or similar cereal
½ cup chopped dried apricots, sultanas,
* walnuts or coconut (optional)*

Caramel Filling
50 g (2 oz) butter
2 rounded household Tbsp golden syrup
200 g (7 oz) sweetened condensed milk
* (half a can)*
1 tsp vanilla essence

To make the chocolate mixture, melt the Kremelta (or Copha) in a medium-sized pot over low heat. When liquid remove from the heat, sift in the cocoa and icing sugar, stir to mix, then add the rice bubbles.

For Bubble Cakes:
Stir in 2 of the optional additions for extra flavour and texture.

Line 20–30 mini or medium-sized muffin pans (depending on the size of cakes you wish to make) with paper patty tin liners and spoon the mixture into the cases. Leave to set in a cool place.

For Chocolate Bubble Caramel Square:
To make the caramel filling, put the butter, golden syrup and condensed milk, in that order, in a medium-sized pot. Bring to the boil over low heat, stirring constantly, and cook for about 5 minutes or until a little of the mixture dropped in cold water forms a soft ball. Remove from the heat and add the vanilla. Leave to cool slightly.

Line a 20 or 23 cm (8 or 9 in) square cake tin with cling film. Pour half the chocolate mixture into it, spread evenly, then chill until set. When firm, spread over the cooled caramel filling then top with the remaining chocolate mixture. (Reheat it over a low heat if the chocolate starts to set before you get to this stage.)

Chill until the chocolate has set. Cut into squares or rectangles with a serrated knife.

See also
Bake a Biscuit, pp. 272–281
Super Slices, pp. 288–295

Super Slices

One of the reasons slices are so popular is that they are easier and quicker to shape than anything that has to be baked and iced individually. They can also be cut into pieces of any size, depending on appetite and situation. Although there are exceptions, slices are often topped with delicious mixtures that are quite irresistible! They make great lunchbox treats, often take the place of desserts when served with coffee – in fact, they are popular with tea, coffee or cold drinks right through the day, as many cafés will testify! I hope you will try a number of these slices, since it would be a pity to stop at the first one you make, however good it may be!

Chocolate Caramel Bars

This slice is always popular. I think I make the whole batch for the same price as two or three pieces bought from a café or lunch bar!

Crust
100 g (3¹/₂ oz) butter
¹/₄ cup castor sugar
1 cup plain flour

Filling
100 g (3¹/₂ oz) butter
200 g (7 oz) sweetened condensed milk
(half a can)
¹/₂ cup (125 ml/4 fl oz) golden syrup
¹/₄ cup chopped walnuts

Easy Chocolate Icing
¹/₂ cup icing sugar
1 Tbsp cocoa
1 Tbsp butter, at room temperature
2 tsp boiling water

Turn the oven to 170°C (325°F). Cream the softened butter and the castor sugar, then stir in the flour. Press into a sponge roll tin lined with baking paper or a non-stick Teflon liner. The size of the tin is not critical – a smaller tin makes a deeper bar.

Bake until the centre feels as firm as the edges, usually 6–8 minutes. Do not overcook or it will be hard to cut.

To make the filling, put the butter, condensed milk and golden syrup into a pot. Bring to the boil over medium heat, stirring all the time, then cook for 10 minutes over a fairly low heat, stirring often, until the mixture is a deep golden colour and a drop forms a soft ball in cold water.

Chocolate Caramel Bars, Neenish Tarts (p. 284)

Remove from the heat, stir in the chopped walnuts and pour over the cooked base straight away, smoothing it out if necessary. Leave to cool.

Measure the icing sugar, cocoa and butter into a bowl, add the boiling water, and beat until smooth with a knife or stirrer with a flexible blade. Spread the icing over the cold, or nearly cold, caramel layer with a knife.

Leave at least 2 hours then cut into rectangles of desired size. Store at room temperature for up to 4 days.

Kirsten's Custard Squares

For as long as I can remember I have had a great weakness for custard squares. Few bought custard squares taste as good as I hope they will be, so I was delighted when my daughter, as a teenager, made me a custard square birthday cake!

For 16 squares:
about 200 g (7 oz) flaky pastry (p. 237)
¹/₂ cup (65 g/2 oz) vanilla custard powder
¹/₄ cup (50 g/2 oz) brown sugar
2¹/₄ cups (560 ml/18 fl oz) milk
2 eggs
¹/₂ tsp vanilla essence

Vanilla Icing
1 cup (110 g/4 oz) icing sugar
2 tsp soft butter
¹/₄ tsp vanilla essence
water to mix

Turn the oven to 200°C (400°F). For best results, use a 20–23 cm (8–9 in) square tin with a removable base. You can make a pretty good square without a tin, but you may have to trim more from the edges to get neat squares.

Roll the pastry out thinly to make two squares about 2 cm (1 in) bigger than your tin. If you are not using a tin, roll them out about 25 cm (10 in) square.

Prick the pastry evenly all over with a fork and bake for 7–8 minutes, or until golden brown on both sides. If using a tin, trim the cooked pastry to fit. Put one square in the tin.

To make the filling, mix the custard powder and brown sugar in a heavy-bottomed pot. Add the milk and stir constantly over low heat until the mixture thickens. Stand the pot of custard in a frypan containing enough water to come about 2 cm (1 in) up the sides of the pot. Keep the mixture simmering, stirring often, for about 5 minutes, until the custard loses its uncooked flavour. Beat the eggs with the vanilla until well combined but not foamy, stir into the custard, and keep stirring until it thickens again.

If using a tin, pour the filling into the pastry-lined tin straight away. If not using a tin, let it cool for 2 or 3 minutes, then spoon it onto one piece of pastry, trying to spread it evenly without it running over the edges. Cover the hot custard with the second pastry layer immediately.

Ice the top layer of pastry when the custard filling is cool. Mix the icing sugar, butter and vanilla in a bowl, then stir in small amounts of warm water until you get the right consistency.

Leave for at least 30 minutes, then cut into 16 squares with a sharp knife. Refrigerate any squares not eaten the day they are made, and eat within 2 days.

Variation: Mix the icing with passionfruit pulp or lemon juice instead of water.

> Because oven temperatures vary, always check 5–10 minutes before the suggested cooking time, to prevent over-cooking.

Kirsten's Orange Slice

As a child, Kirsten liked this in her school lunch – so much so that she made it quite often. It is one of our favourite uncooked slices.

Base
100 g (3¹/₂ oz) butter
³/₄ cup (half a can) sweetened condensed milk
1 cup coconut
grated rind of 1 orange or tangelo
1 packet (200 g/7 oz) wine biscuits, crushed

Icing
1 cup icing sugar
2 Tbsp soft butter
orange or tangelo juice to mix

Melt the butter in a medium-sized pot, stir in the condensed milk until well mixed, then remove from the heat. Stir in the coconut, orange rind and biscuit crumbs. (The crumbs should be fairly even but not powdered. Put the biscuits in a plastic bag and crush them with a rolling pin – crumbs made in a food processor are often too fine.)

Butter a sponge roll tin or line it with baking paper. Press the mixture lightly into the tin so it is about 15 mm (¹/₂ in) thick. It doesn't matter if the whole tin is not filled.

To make the icing, measure the icing sugar and soft (but not liquid) butter into a bowl and add juice a few drops at a time until it is a spreading consistency. Spread thinly over the slice then run a fork over it in wavy lines, so the biscuit mixture shows through.

Refrigerate, then cut into rectangles of desired size. Store in a tin with greaseproof paper between the layers.

Caramel Malt Bars

This bar is especially easy when mixed in a food processor. If you are making it without a food processor, use the conventional creaming method, adding the eggs after the butter and sugar are well mixed.

2 eggs
1 cup firmly packed brown sugar
150 g (5 oz) butter
¹/₂ tsp vanilla essence
1 rounded household Tbsp golden syrup
¹/₄ cup malted milk powder or drinking chocolate powder
1¹/₂ cups plain flour
1 tsp baking powder
¹/₂ cup sultanas

Turn the oven to 180°C (350°F). Process the eggs and the sugar using the metal chopping blade. Add the butter, warmed until it is just liquid, vanilla and golden syrup, and process until thoroughly mixed. Add the milk or chocolate powder, flour, baking powder and sultanas and process just long enough to mix evenly.

Line with greaseproof paper or thoroughly spray a 23 cm (9 in) square pan with sides at least 2 cm (³/₄ in) high. Pour in the mixture and bake for about 30 minutes, or until the centre feels firm when lightly pressed.

Leave for 4 minutes before removing from the tin. When cold, cut into fingers and store in airtight tins. Although this bar keeps quite well, it is best eaten within a few days.

Variations: Cut into squares and serve warm for dessert, with hot apple purée, warm custard sauce or icecream.

Ice with lemon or vanilla icing.

Ginger Crunch

Ginger crunch is popular with nearly everyone I know, especially if I make a generous amount of icing!

For about 30 pieces:

Base
125 g (4¹/₂ oz) butter
¹/₄ cup sugar
1 tsp baking powder
1 cup plain flour
1 tsp ground ginger

Ginger Icing
2 Tbsp butter
2 tsp ground ginger
2 rounded household Tbsp golden syrup
1 Tbsp water
2 cups icing sugar

Heat the oven to 180°C (350°F), or 170°C (325°F) for fan-bake. If using a food processor, cut cold butter into 9 cubes, then process in brief bursts with the other base ingredients, until the mixture is like coarse breadcrumbs.

If mixing by hand, warm the butter until soft, mix it with the sugar, then stir in the sieved dry ingredients.

Spray or line a 23 cm (9 in) square tin or a 20 x 30 cm (8 x 12 in) sponge roll tin with baking paper. Spread the crumbly mixture evenly into the tin and press it down firmly and evenly. Bake for about 10 minutes, or until lightly browned. It will still feel soft while it is hot.

Make the icing while the base cooks, since the base should be iced while hot.

Heat the butter, ginger, golden syrup and water, without boiling, until melted. Remove from the heat, sift in the icing sugar and beat until smooth.

As soon as the base is cooked, remove it from the oven. Pour the warm icing onto the hot base and spread so it covers the base evenly.

Leave to cool and set, marking it into pieces while still warm. Do not remove from the tin until it has cooled completely.

Note: If you like a really thick icing, use one and half times the icing recipe!

Chocolate Lunchbox Squares

These are irresistible as long as the base is not overcooked. Time the baking carefully, since I know of no other way to tell when the base is ready.

For 20–30 pieces:
150 g (5 oz) butter
¹/₄ cup (60 ml/2 fl oz) golden syrup
1 cup sugar
1¹/₂ cups plain flour
1 Tbsp cocoa
2 cups malted wheatflakes or cornflakes
¹/₂ cup sultanas

Turn the oven to 160°C (325°F). Melt the butter and golden syrup together, add the sugar and stir until well mixed. Sift the flour and cocoa and add with the wheatflakes and sultanas to the butter mixture. Fold together until combined.

Press the mixture into a 23 cm (9 in) square cake tin that has been lightly buttered, sprayed or lined with baking paper or a Teflon liner. Bake for 20 minutes.

Allow to cool slightly before icing with Everyday Chocolate Icing (p. 347) or Sour Cream Chocolate Icing (p. 347). Cut into squares when cold. Store in an airtight container.

Microwaved Chewy Fudge Squares M

¹/₂ Short Pastry recipe (p. 237)
1 can (400 g/14 oz) sweetened condensed milk
1 cup chocolate chips
few drops rum essence or ¹/₂ tsp vanilla essence
¹/₄ cup slivered almonds

Roll out the pastry so it is bigger than the baking dish (about 17 cm/7 in square or 15 x 20 cm/6 x 8 in). Place flat on baking paper and prick well. Microwave on High (100%) power for 3–4 minutes, or until just firm. Cut to fit a microwave-proof baking pan, leaving the paper intact on two sides so it can be lifted easily into the pan.

Put the condensed milk in a bowl and heat on High (100%) power for 1¹/₂ minutes. Stir in the chocolate chips until they melt, then add essence.

Pour onto the baked crust and microwave for 2 minutes. Sprinkle with almonds and bake 1 minute longer, or until barely firm in the centre. Cool, then lift out the square still on its paper, and cut into squares of desired size. These harden on cooling.

Butterscotch Fingers

This bar tastes good anytime and may be hidden in the freezer for weeks.

For about 20 slices, depending on size:

125 g (4¹/₂ oz) butter
¹/₂ cup sugar
1 large egg
1 tsp vanilla essence
1 cup self-raising flour
1 cup plain flour

Filling

100 g (3¹/₂ oz) butter
2 rounded household Tbsp golden syrup
1 can (400 g/14 oz) sweetened condensed milk

Turn the oven to 180°C (350°F). Line a 23 cm (9 in) square baking tin or a small sponge roll tin with 2 strips of baking paper, so the paper goes well up all sides.

Cut the butter into 9 pieces and warm on the stove or in the microwave until it starts to melt. Take off the heat and beat in the sugar, egg and vanilla with a fork or stirrer.

Stir in the flours until the mixture is crumbly, then squeeze it into a ball with your hands. Break three-quarters of the dough into bits, place these evenly in the prepared baking tin and pat them fairly flat, putting a piece of plastic between the mixture and your fingers if you like. Put the rest of the dough in the refrigerator or freezer.

To make the filling, melt the butter, measure the syrup with a hot, wet spoon, and stir in. Add the condensed milk, mix well, then pour over the unbaked mixture in the tin.

Coarsely grate the remaining (cold) dough on top of the filling, using a grater with large holes. Bake for 30–45 minutes, until the crust is golden and the filling has browned. (It may take a little longer in an oven without a fan.)

Leave for 2 hours, then remove from the baking tin and cut into pieces using a sharp knife dipped in hot water. Store in a covered container, refrigerating for up to a week or so, or freezing for longer.

Chocolate Fudge Squares

This delicious (unbaked) fudge square is simple enough to be made by quite inexperienced young cooks – if shown how to do it once or twice, they should then easily make it themselves.

For 12–24 slices, depending on size:

1 packet (250 g/9 oz) malt, wine or digestive biscuits, crushed
¹/₂ cup brown sugar
¹/₄ cup cocoa
3 Tbsp milk
75 g (2¹/₂ oz) butter
about 1 cup chopped walnuts or chopped sultanas, or a mixture
1 tsp vanilla essence

To crush the biscuits, put them in a large plastic bag, fasten loosely with a rubber band, then bang and roll with a rolling pin until quite evenly crushed. (You can crumble broken biscuits in a food processor, but don't make evenly fine crumbs.)

Mix the sugar and cocoa in a medium-sized pot, then add the milk and butter. Bring to the boil, stirring all the time.

Remove from the heat, add the crushed biscuits, chopped nuts and/or sultanas and the essence, and stir together.

Line a 20 x 30 cm (8 x 12 in) sponge roll tin with baking paper. Press the mixture into the tin (you do not have to cover the whole tin) until it is the depth you like. Flatten the surface with the back of a spoon.

Ice with Everyday Chocolate Icing (p. 347) or Sour Cream Chocolate Icing (p. 347). Cut into pieces when firm. Store in the refrigerator in hot weather.

Variations: Add peppermint essence to both the base and the icing.

Use finely grated tangelo or orange rind in the base and/or the icing for a jaffa flavour.

Add rum essence to the base and icing instead of, or as well as, the vanilla.

Chocolate Fudge Squares, Butterscotch Fingers

Ginger Date Slice

Especially popular with ginger lovers.

2 eggs
1 cup brown sugar
100 g (3½ oz) butter, melted
1 tsp vanilla essence
1½ cups plain flour
½ cup rolled oats
1 tsp baking powder
pinch of salt
1 cup chopped dates
1 cup chopped walnuts
½ cup chopped crystallised ginger

Icing

1 Tbsp butter
1½ tsp ground ginger
1 rounded Tbsp golden syrup
1 cup icing sugar
1–2 tsp water

Turn the oven to 180°C (350°F). Beat the eggs, sugar, melted butter and vanilla in a bowl or food processor until well mixed.

Measure the dry ingredients, dates, walnuts and ginger into a large bowl, and toss with a fork to mix. Pour in the egg mixture, and mix well without breaking up the fruit and nuts too much.

Spread into a 23 cm (9 in) square cake tin lined with baking paper. Bake for about 30 minutes, until the centre looks and feels like the edge.

To make the icing, heat the butter, ginger and golden syrup until melted (do not boil). Add the sifted icing sugar and beat well with a fork or wooden spoon until smooth, adding enough water to form a spreadable consistency.

Ice while still warm. When the icing is set, cut into fingers with a sharp knife.

Spicy Lemon Slice

An irresistible combination of textures and flavours.

125 g (4½ oz) butter, softened
½ cup sugar
1 egg
2 cups plain flour
2 tsp baking powder
1 tsp mixed spice
1 tsp cinnamon

Ginger Date Slice, Spicy Lemon Slice

Filling

2 Tbsp sugar
¼ cup apricot jam
¼ cup coconut
¼ cup currants
25 g (1 oz) butter
1 egg, beaten
rind and juice of 1 lemon

Lemon Icing

1 Tbsp butter, softened
finely grated rind of ½ lemon
1 cup icing sugar
3–4 tsp lemon juice

Turn the oven to 180°C (350°F). Cream the slightly warmed butter and sugar, add the egg and mix again, then add the dry ingredients. (These do not need to be sifted if you are mixing in a food processor.) Divide the mixture in two and press one half into a 20 cm (8 in) square baking tin lined with baking paper (preferably one with a loose bottom).

Roll the other half out the same size on a piece of plastic.

To make the filling, heat the sugar, jam, coconut, currants and butter until the mixture boils. Cool, then beat in the egg, finely grated lemon rind and juice with a fork. Spread over the mixture in the tin, cover with the second layer, lift away the plastic and press gently into the corners. Bake for 25–30 minutes, until evenly cooked.

To make the icing, soften the butter in a mixing jug or bowl, add the finely grated lemon rind and sifted icing sugar. Add lemon juice 1 tsp at a time, mixing well each time, until the icing is a smooth, spreadable consistency.

Spread on the nearly cooled slice, running a fork over it to form a wave pattern. When the icing has set, cut into about 24 fingers with a sharp knife.

Sticky Lemon Slice

This square has a delicious lemon custard topping. It is so popular I thought I should include it so that owners of food processors and lemon trees could try it! Unless you have the processor, forget it – just turn the page quickly!

For 16–20 pieces:

Base

2 cups plain flour
½ cup icing sugar
150 g (5 oz) cold butter

Topping

1½ cups sugar
thinly peeled rind of 1 lemon
3 large (or 4 medium) eggs
¼ cup (60 ml/2 fl oz) lemon juice
¼ cup self-raising flour

Turn the oven to 160°C (325°F). Press a large piece of baking paper into a 23 cm (9 in) square pan or a smallish sponge roll tin, folding the paper so it covers the bottom and all sides of the pan. Fold rather than cut the paper at the corners so the filling cannot run underneath it.

Measure the flour, icing sugar and cubed butter into a food processor fitted with a metal chopping blade. Process until the butter is chopped finely through the dry ingredients. Tip the mixture into the prepared tin and press down firmly and evenly with the back of a large spoon or a fish slice. Bake for 15–20 minutes, or until firm and straw-coloured. While the base cooks, prepare the topping.

Put the sugar in the (unwashed) food processor with half the rind (peeled from the lemon with a potato peeler). Process until the rind is very finely chopped through the sugar, then add the eggs, lemon juice and flour. Process until smooth.

Pour onto the partly cooked base, then bake for about 30 minutes longer, or until top is lightly browned and the centre does not wobble when the tin is jiggled.

When quite cold, cut into squares or fingers, pressing a heavy, lightly oiled knife straight down through the topping and base. Store, lightly covered, for 3 or 4 days. Sift icing sugar over the squares just before serving if you like.

Sticky Lemon Slice

Microwaved Date Bars M

Maybe this microwaved bar is not quite the same as a bar baked traditionally, but I find that it is never left to get stale!

Filling
2 cups dates, chopped
1/2 cup (125 ml/4 fl oz) water
1/4 cup sugar
1/4 cup (60 ml/2 fl oz) lemon juice

Base
100 g (3 1/2 oz) butter
1/2 cup brown sugar
1 cup rolled oats
1 cup plain flour

Place all the filling ingredients in a medium-sized bowl. Microwave on High (100%) power for 4–5 minutes, until fairly thick when stirred.

Combine the base ingredients in a food processor or pastry blender to make a crumbly mixture. Keep one cupful aside and press the rest into lightly buttered 20 cm (8 in) square microwaveable baking dish. Microwave on Medium (50%) power for 5 minutes.

Spread the date filling on the base, sprinkle with reserved mixture, and microwave, uncovered, on High (100%) power for 5 minutes. Cool and cut into small squares or rectangles.

Peanut Bars

This bar is good with or without the peanuts. If you buy roasted peanuts you are best to rinse them briefly under hot water, then dry them between paper towels to remove the salt. If you buy raw peanuts, spread them in a sponge roll tin or roasting pan and cook for 20–30 minutes at 180°C (350°F), until they brown slightly.

1 1/2 cups rolled oats
2 Tbsp butter or oil
1 cup coconut
1/4 cup wheatgerm
1/4–1/2 cup chopped roasted peanuts
1/2 cup honey
1/4 cup peanut butter

Put the rolled oats and butter in a frypan over low heat and stir until the rolled oats brown slightly and start to smell 'toasty'. Transfer to a bowl.

Brown the coconut in the pan over low heat for a toasted coconut flavour, or mix untoasted coconut with the cooked oats. Stir in the wheatgerm. Chop the peanuts finely and stir into the other ingredients.

Heat the honey and peanut butter gently in the frypan, stirring constantly, squashing the lumps of peanut butter and mixing it with the honey as it cooks. When drops of mixture harden in cold water to make a chewy ball, remove from the heat and stir in the dry ingredients.

Press into a buttered tin, leave to harden, then cut into bars with a serrated knife. Store in an airtight jar or tin.

Note: If you have difficulty cutting the bars when they are cold, mark the mixture into bars while it is hot, or simply roll the warm mixture into cylinders before it sets. If your bars are too chewy, cook the honey more next time. If they are too hard to chew easily, cook the honey for a shorter time.

Sesame Muesli Bars

Although these bars don't come into the 'budget' category, they are far cheaper than similar commercially made products.

1/2 cup toasted sesame seeds
1 cup coconut
1 cup rolled oats
2 Tbsp butter
1/4 cup wheatgerm
1/2 cup honey

Toast the sesame seeds in a dry frypan over low heat, then transfer to a large bowl. Tip the coconut into the pan and stir over low heat until golden. Do not overcook the coconut – some will remain white, while some colours. Add to the sesame seeds.

Put the rolled oats and butter in the pan and stir until the oats are coated with butter and start to have a cooked smell. Tip into the bowl, add the wheatgerm and mix well.

Measure the honey into the pan and heat gently, stirring frequently until a drop in cold water hardens to form a fairly hard ball (firmer than a soft ball, but not hard enough to crack when bitten). Remove from the heat and stir in the mixture from the bowl. Mix thoroughly, then press the mixture into a buttered tin.

When cold, saw into bars with a serrated knife. Store in airtight jars or wrap individual pieces in cling film.

Sticky Lemon Slice (p. 292), Cherry Slice

Cherry Slice

This is a recipe I worked out after trying a delicious but expensive bought slice in London. (It was so good that my sister and I ate our purchase before we left the store, giving the check-out clerk the empty wrapping!) My version is quick (if you have a food processor) and a fraction of the price!

For about 16 pieces:

Base

1 cup plain flour
¼ cup sugar
100 g (3½ oz) very cold butter

Filling

¼–½ cup raspberry jam
½ cup chopped crystallised cherries

Topping

1½ cups medium or fine desiccated
* coconut*
1 cup sugar
½ cup plain flour
½ cup flaked almonds
50 g (2 oz) cold butter
2 large eggs
¼ tsp almond essence

Turn the oven to 180°C (350°F). Spray a 23 cm (9 in) square tin with non-stick spray.

First make the base. Put the flour and sugar in the food processor (with the metal chopping blade). Add the cold butter, cut into about 9 small cubes. Process until the butter is cut into very small crumbs, then press the mixture into the prepared tin with the back of a fish slice or similar. To make the base without a food processor, melt the butter and stir it into the other ingredients.

Bake the base for 15 minutes. While it bakes, prepare the filling and topping.

Chop the cherries fairly finely and put aside.

Combine the first 4 topping ingredients in the (unwashed) food processor. Add the butter, cut into 9 cubes, then process with the metal chopping blade until the butter is cut through the mixture. Add the eggs and essence and blend until well mixed. If you don't have a food processor, melt the butter then stir in everything else.

Take the partly cooked base from the oven. Spread it with the jam then sprinkle over

the cherries. Cover this with teaspoonfuls of topping mixture, dropping it on with 2 spoons. Spread the topping lightly so the jam and cherries are almost covered, trying to avoid mixing the 2 layers.

Bake for another 20–30 minutes, until the topping browns lightly and is firm when touched. Leave to cool on a rack for 15 minutes then cut carefully into squares or fingers. Pack pieces between layers of plastic in an airtight container. Refrigerate for up to a week or freeze for longer.

Apricot Slice

This slice has a lovely caramel and apricot flavour.

150 g (5 oz) dried apricots, chopped finely
finely grated rind of 1 orange and ¼ cup
* (60 ml/2 fl oz) juice*
75 g (2½ oz) butter, melted
200 g (7 oz) sweetened condensed milk
* (half a can)*
½ cup brown sugar
1 packet (250 g/9 oz) wine or malt
* biscuits, finely crushed*
½ cup desiccated coconut
extra coconut

Cook the apricots with the orange rind and juice in a large pot until there is no liquid left. Add the butter and stir over low heat until it melts. Add the condensed milk and brown sugar, then heat gently, stirring often, until the sugar is no longer grainy and the condensed milk is golden brown.

Remove from the heat and stir in the crushed biscuits and the coconut. (Crush the biscuits in the food processor, or put them in a large plastic bag, seal with a rubber band, and bang them with a rolling pin. Sieve the crushed biscuits, and crush any large remaining pieces.)

Stir the mixture together then press into a 20 cm (8 in) square tin lined with baking paper. Sprinkle over some extra coconut, refrigerate for at least 2 hours then cut into small rectangles. Turn these in more coconut. Store in the refrigerator for up to a week.

Walnut Cheesecake Slice

Serve as a dessert the day it is made, or cut into smaller pieces for later use.

Base
1 cup plain flour
1/4 cup brown sugar
75 g (2 1/2 oz) cold butter

Topping
250 g (9 oz) cream cheese
1/4 cup brown sugar
1 large egg
1/2 tsp vanilla essence
1/2–3/4 cup chopped walnuts

Turn the oven to 180°C (350°F). Process or rub together the flour, brown sugar and cubed butter until crumbly. Press into a 23 cm (9 in) square tin lined with baking paper. Bake for 10 minutes.

Soften the cream cheese and stir in the brown sugar, egg and vanilla. Mix or process until smooth. Pour over the hot, partly cooked base, sprinkle with finely chopped nuts and bake for 20–30 minutes, or until the cream cheese mixture has set in the centre.

Cut into pieces when cool. Store in the refrigerator for up to 3 days.

Orange Snacking Cake   M

Although this may be cooked in a loaf tin, I like it best as a flatter, thin cake, cut in pieces and served straight from its baking pan.

grated rind and juice of 1 orange
water
1 egg
1/4 cup sour cream
50 g (2 oz) very soft butter
1/2 cup brown sugar
1 cup plus 2 Tbsp cake or plain flour
1/2 tsp baking soda

Orange Icing
2 tsp butter
reserved orange rind and juice
1 cup icing sugar

Reserve 1/2 tsp of the orange rind and 1 Tbsp of the juice for the icing. Make the rest of the juice up to 1/2 cup with water. Combine with the rind and the remaining ingredients. Mix only until blended (about 10 seconds in a food processor).

Turn into a 20 cm (8 in) square microwave pan. Cover with a lid, greaseproof paper or cling film, and elevate on an inverted plate. Microwave on Medium-High (70%) power for 7 minutes, or until just firm in the centre. Uncover, leave to stand for about 5 minutes, then ice.

To make the icing, heat the butter, reserved rind and juice for 10 seconds in the microwave. Add the icing sugar and beat until smooth. Spread over the warm or cooled cake.

Minted Fruit Square

I imagine this square should keep for at least a week, but I have never managed to have it in any sort of container for longer than two or three days!

about 200 g (7 oz) flaky pastry (bought or
*   half the recipe on p. 237)*
1 cup currants
1 cup mixed fruit
1/2 cup brown sugar
1 cup fresh mint leaves
25 g (1 oz) soft butter
1/2 tsp mixed spice

Turn the oven to 190°C (375°F). Roll the pastry out thinly to form one 20 cm (8 in) square and another 23 cm (9 in) square. Prick all over with a fork, and leave to stand while you mix the filling.

Chop the fruit, sugar and mint together, using a large knife on a large wooden board, or a food processor. If using the food processor, take care not to process the mixture so much that it loses all its texture and becomes a dark paste.

Add the butter and spice, and mix through evenly.

Put the bigger pastry square in a baking paper-lined 20 cm (8 in) square tin so that it comes up the sides, all round, then spread over the filling. Cover with the smaller sheet of pastry, pinching or forking the edges together.

Bake for 25–35 minutes, until the pastry is evenly brown. Press the pastry down if it has risen unevenly, leave it to cool completely, then cut into small squares with a sharp, serrated knife.

Fruit and Nut Bars (or Balls)

With a food processor you can make fruit and nut bars (or balls) with a lovely fresh flavour. They are not as expensive as you might think. Although it is difficult to specify bar sizes and numbers, this mixture makes about 36 balls the size of small walnuts.

As the coconut absorbs liquid the mixture becomes firmer, but it does not become as firm as buttery truffles do, so do not use wet fruit which will soften the mixture excessively.

1/2 cup dried apricots, roughly chopped
1/4 cup (60 ml/2 fl oz) orange or lemon
*   juice*
1/2 cup roasted (lightly salted) peanuts
1/2 cup sultanas
1/2 cup currants, dates or chopped figs
1/4 cup toasted sesame seeds
1/2 cup coconut
extra coconut for coating

Boil the apricots in the juice for 5 minutes, or until the juice has disappeared. Put freshly roasted peanuts in the food processor with the metal chopping blade and chop roughly using the pulse, on-off technique. Add the sultanas, currants or other fruit, sesame seeds and the hot, softened apricots. Process to the desired consistency.

Add coconut and process until mixed. If the mixture is too wet to shape into bars or balls with wet hands, add extra coconut.

Shape as desired, and roll in extra coconut. Refrigerate for 24 hours, uncovered or lightly covered, in one layer. After this time, store balls in a covered container, or wrap bars individually.

Variations: Replace the sesame seeds with peanuts.

Boil the apricots with finely grated orange rind as well as juice.

Note: Different fruit combinations may alter the consistency – use more or less coconut to compensate.

> When baking in a microwave, always check before the suggested cooking time, since individual ovens vary.

See also

Brownies, p. 287

Jaffa Nut Brownies, p. 287

Aunt Lucy's Mistake, p. 301

Christmas Panforte, p. 306

Fudge Squares, p. 315

Orange Fudge Squares, p. 315

Peanut Butter Squares, p. 315

Create a Cake

A cake is often used as a symbol of something special! We bake a cake to welcome a baby, we put candles on decorated cakes as we count our birthdays, we make them at Christmas and Easter, originally to celebrate the fact that warmer weather was on the way, I guess. Last but not least, a wedding wouldn't be the same without a cake for the bride and groom to cut together. On a smaller scale, we may make a cake for dessert when we ask friends to dinner or for coffee, and we may celebrate family achievements with a cake. You may also do as I do, and sometimes bake a cake just because you feel like it, and because you know it will please the people who eat it!

Warm Blueberry Cake

You can enjoy blueberries all through the year if you keep a package of them in your freezer, replacing them as they are used. Serve this delicious cake warm, with lightly whipped cream, with coffee or for dessert.

For a 23 cm (9 in) square cake (6–9 servings):
75 g (2½ oz) butter
1 large egg
¾ cup (185 ml/6 fl oz) orange juice
¾ cup sugar
1½ cups self-raising flour
½ cup walnuts
¼ cup sugar
3 tsp cinnamon
1–2 cups fresh or thawed blueberries

Turn the oven to 180°C (350°F). Spray or line a 23 cm (9 in) square tin.

Melt the butter in a bowl big enough to mix the cake in. Put aside 1 Tbsp of melted butter to add to the nut mixture. Add the egg and orange juice to the butter in the bowl and mix with a fork until combined. Sprinkle the sugar and flour over the egg mixture and fold together until the flour is dampened, but not smooth.

Mix together the reserved butter, finely chopped walnuts, sugar and cinnamon. Sprinkle two-thirds over the cake mixture, then spoon the mixture into the prepared tin so the nut mixture is marbled through it. Sprinkle the blueberries evenly over the top, press them down lightly, then sprinkle with the remaining nut mixture. Bake for 45 minutes, or until evenly browned and fairly firm. Serve warm, reheating if necessary.

Variation: Replace the blueberries with 1–2 cups other fresh or thawed berries, e.g. raspberries or chopped strawberries.

Apricot Party Cake (p. 301)

Peachy Coffee-Time Cake

This cake makes morning coffee very special. Ring the changes by replacing the peaches with seasonal raw fruit or berries.

For a 23 cm (9 in) square cake:
¼ cup sugar
1 Tbsp cinnamon
¼ cup chopped almonds, walnuts or pecans
1 can (425 g/15 oz) peaches
100 g (3½ oz) butter
2 eggs
½ cup sour cream
1 tsp vanilla essence
½ tsp almond essence
1 cup sugar
2 cups self-raising flour

Turn the oven to 180°C (350°F). Spray or line a 23 cm (9 in) square tin.

Mix the first 3 ingredients together for the topping and put aside. Drain the peaches, reserving the juice.

Melt the butter in a large pot or microwave dish. Add the eggs, sour cream, vanilla and almond essence, sugar and 2 Tbsp of the peach juice (or orange juice). Beat thoroughly with a fork or egg beater, then fold in the sifted flour.

Spoon about half the mixture into the prepared tin. Sprinkle over half the sugar topping. Spoon on the remaining mixture, then arrange the drained peaches on top. Sprinkle with the remaining topping and bake for 30 minutes, or until a skewer in the centre comes out clean.

For an optional glaze, mix ½ cup icing sugar with about 1 Tbsp lemon juice, to pouring consistency, and drizzle it over the partly cooled cake.

Variation: Replace the peaches with 1–2 cups sliced raw strawberries, blueberries, feijoas, etc. and add an extra ¼ cup sugar to the topping.

Chocolate Apple Cake

This cake is just as popular served with coffee as it is packed in lunchboxes.

For a 23 cm (9 in) cake:

Crunchy Topping
¼ cup brown sugar
2 Tbsp plain flour
1 tsp cinnamon
25 g (1 oz) cold butter
2 Tbsp chopped walnuts

Alternative Topping
¼ cup slivered almonds

Cake
2–3 apples
125 g (4½ oz) butter, melted
1 large egg
1 cup sugar
1½ cups plain flour
2 Tbsp cocoa
1 tsp cinnamon
1 tsp baking soda

Turn the oven to 190°C (375°F). Spray a 23 cm (9 in) square or round tin, or line it with baking paper.

Prepare the topping in a food processor, using the metal chopping blade to chop everything briefly, or rub the ingredients together by hand. Put aside.

Chop the unpeeled apples in the (unwashed) food processor (or grate them into a bowl). Add the remaining ingredients in the order given, sieving the last 4 ingredients onto the others if mixing by hand. Mix briefly to combine. (Always check baking soda for lumps by pressing it with a spoon against the palm of your hand before adding it with the other ingredients.)

Turn the mixture into the prepared tin. Sprinkle with prepared topping or slivered almonds. Bake for about 30 minutes, until the centre springs back when pressed. Cool for a few minutes then turn out of pan. Serve with whipped cream or icecream.

Lindsay's Apple and Walnut Cake

Here is my version of a friend's very popular cake. Enjoy it for dessert or with coffee.

For a 23 cm (9 in) ring or 20 cm (8 in) round cake:
125 g (4¹/₂ oz) butter
1 cup sugar
1 large egg
2 tsp mixed spice
1 tsp cinnamon
2 medium apples
1¹/₄ cups plain flour
¹/₂ tsp baking soda
¹/₂ cup each chopped walnuts and sultanas

Turn the oven to 190°C (375°F), or 180°C (350°F) for fan-bake. Melt the butter in the microwave or on the stove. Take off the heat and stir in the sugar, egg and spices until evenly mixed.

Chop the unpeeled apples into pieces about the size of sultanas, or slice chunky pieces from 1 apple into the food processor and chop in bursts with the metal chopping blade, then repeat with the second apple. Stir into the butter mixture.

Shake in the flour and soda through a sieve, add the chopped walnuts and sultanas, and fold everything together.

Thoroughly coat a 23 cm (9 in) ring tin or a 20 cm (8 in) round tin with non-stick spray then spoon the cake mixture into it evenly.

Bake the ring cake for 30 minutes, and the round cake for 35–45 minutes, or until the centre springs back when pressed and a skewer in the centre comes out clean.

Serve warm, dusted with icing sugar, plain or with lightly whipped cream.

Variation: For a firmer, more substantial cake, to be eaten the day it is made, use 1¹/₂ cups flour.

Rhubarb Cake

I think rhubarb is at its best in this cake, which has a definite, but not overpowering, and pleasantly tart flavour. This is one of my favourite fruity coffee cakes!

For a 23 cm (9 in) square cake:
150 g (5 oz) butter
³/₄ cup sugar
3 eggs
1¹/₂ cups plain flour
2 tsp baking powder
¹/₄ cup (60 ml/2 fl oz) milk

Topping
500 g (1 lb 2 oz) rhubarb
¹/₂ cup sugar
1 Tbsp flour
1 tsp cinnamon
icing sugar

Turn the oven to 190°C (375°F). In a food processor or bowl, cream the warm but not melted butter with the sugar, then add the eggs one at a time. Stir in the dry ingredients alternately with the milk, until they are combined.

Line a 23 cm (9 in) square tin with two strips of paper 23 cm (9 in) wide, so all the sides and the bottom are covered. Spoon in the mixture in 16 spoonfuls, without spreading them smoothly.

Remove the tough strings from the rhubarb and cut it into 1 cm (¹/₂ in) lengths. Toss it in the sugar, flour and cinnamon, then sprinkle over the surface of the dough so that much of the rhubarb is between the batter rather than on top of it. Sprinkle the remaining sugar mixture over the batter.

Bake for 40–45 minutes, until the centre is golden brown, and springs back when touched.

Cool in the tin for 15 minutes, then lift away from the sides of the tin, and remove the paper at the sides of the cake. Sprinkle evenly with icing sugar, using a fine sieve.

Serve warm or reheated, cut into squares or rectangles.

Grape Cake

This unusual grape cake is a modification of a German recipe. Try it with whatever grapes are available, but remember that varieties with few or no seeds will give best results. It can be eaten warm or cold.

Lindsay's Apple and Walnut Cake

For a 23 cm (9 in) square or round cake:
2 eggs
3/4 cup sugar
1 tsp vanilla essence
finely grated rind and juice of 1 lemon
1 1/2 cups self-raising flour
3–4 cups (500 g/1 lb 2 oz) grapes

Preheat the oven to 200°C (400°F). Line the bottom of a 23 cm (9 in) square or round tin with baking paper and butter the sides.

Beat the eggs, sugar and vanilla together until very thick (preferably with an electric beater). Add the lemon rind, juice and the sifted flour, folding each in thoroughly. When evenly mixed, gently stir in the grapes.

Spread the mixture in the prepared tin. Turn the oven down to 180°C (350°F) and bake for about 40 minutes, until the centre springs back when pressed lightly.

Leave to stand for 2–3 minutes then turn the cake out onto a rack and remove the paper. Turn right side up on a serving plate when required, and dust the top generously with icing sugar. Cut into slices with a sharp, preferably serrated knife.

Lemon Yoghurt Cake

Because this cake contains oil and yoghurt rather than butter, it is very easy to mix. It also has a really lovely texture and flavour.

For a 23 cm (9 in) ring cake:
rind of 2 lemons
1 cup (250 ml/8 fl oz) canola oil
2 eggs
1 3/4 cups sugar
1/2 tsp salt
1 cup plain or flavoured yoghurt
3 Tbsp lemon juice
2 cups self-raising flour

Turn the oven to 180°C (350°F). Butter and flour a 23 cm (9 in) ring pan of at least 7-cup capacity.

Grate all the coloured peel from the lemons into a mixing bowl. Add the oil, eggs and sugar, and beat with a rotary beater until thick and well blended. Add the salt, yoghurt and lemon juice and beat again briefly.

Pour into the prepared pan and bake for 30 minutes, or until the sides start to shrink, the centre springs back when pressed and a skewer comes out clean. Leave to cool for 10 minutes then turn carefully onto a rack.

Serve plain, sprinkled with a little icing sugar or topped with whipped cream.

Variation: For a lower-fat cake, replace 1/4 cup of the oil with yoghurt.

Pineapple Carrot Cake

The flavour of this cake is truly delicious. You can identify different ingredients in every mouthful.

For a 23 cm (9 in) square cake:
2 cups self-raising flour
1/2 tsp baking soda
1 cup sugar
3/4 cup coconut
1/2 cup chopped walnuts
1 tsp salt
2 tsp cinnamon
2 cups grated carrot
3 eggs
1 cup (250 ml/8 fl oz) oil
1 tsp vanilla essence
1 can (225 g/8 oz) crushed pineapple

Turn the oven to 160°C (325°F). Line a 23 cm (9 in) square baking pan with baking paper or a non-stick Teflon liner.

Sieve the flour and baking soda into a large bowl, and add the sugar, coconut, walnuts, salt, cinnamon and grated carrot. Mix well with a fork.

In another bowl, or food processor, beat the eggs, oil and vanilla. Stir in the pineapple (and its liquid). Combine the 2 mixtures, stirring until combined. (This mixture is firmer than many carrot cakes.)

Pour into the prepared tin and bake for 45–50 minutes, or until the centre springs back when pressed.

Serve with yoghurt or lightly whipped cream, with coffee or for dessert, or top with a lemon (p. 292), orange (p. 295) or cream cheese icing (p. 285).

Pear Ginger Cake

This pear ginger cake is easily made and has an interesting texture because of its oil content. Although I usually press quarters of ripe, raw pears into the mixture before I cook it, sometimes I make it plain and serve it with raw or cooked pears.

For a 20–23 cm (8–9 in) round cake:
1/2 cup (125 ml/4 fl oz) canola oil
1/2 cup brown sugar
1 egg
1 tsp vanilla essence
1 cup plain flour
1/2 tsp baking soda
1 tsp ginger
1 tsp mixed spice
1 tsp salt
3 ripe pears, quartered
2 Tbsp sugar

Turn the oven to 180°C (350°F). Butter or spray a 20–23 cm (8–9 in) round baking pan.

Beat the oil, brown sugar, egg and vanilla until thick and creamy using a beater or food processor. Sift in the dry ingredients

and fold together without overmixing. Spread the fairly stiff batter in the prepared tin.

Peel and quarter the pears into lightly salted water to stop them discolouring. Drain them, then press them into the dough, core side down, stem end towards the centre, fairly close to the edge of the dish. Sprinkle evenly with sugar and bake for about 30 minutes, until the centre springs back when pressed.

Serve warm, with whipped cream flavoured with the syrup from preserved ginger and slivers of preserved ginger, or with a sauce made by bringing to the boil a mixture of 1/2 cup brown sugar, 1 tsp ginger, 50 g (2 oz) butter and 2 Tbsp cream. This sauce thickens to thick cream consistency as it cools. Serve it at room temperature.

Variations: Replace the raw pears with well-drained cooked pears.

Cook the cake without the pears. Serve it warm with ripe or cooked pears, cream, sauce, etc. on the same plate.

Kirsten's Chocolate Cake

My daughter uses this recipe often, making excellent layer cakes, and birthday cakes of all shapes and sizes.

125 g (4 1/2 oz) butter
2 rounded household Tbsp golden syrup
2 large eggs
2 cups plain flour 8 ozs.
2 Tbsp cocoa
2 tsp baking powder
2 tsp baking soda
1 cup sugar 7oz
1 1/2 cups (375 ml/12 fl oz) milk

Turn the oven to 180°C (350°F). Warm the butter and golden syrup until just melted. Stir to combine.

Put the remaining ingredients, in the order given, in a food processor. Mix in brief bursts, then add the golden syrup and butter mixture, and process for two 30-second bursts.

Bake in two 20 cm (8 in) round tins (with high sides) if you want a cream-filled sandwich cake or a four-layer cake. For a rectangular, unfilled cake, bake in a pan about 22 x 27 cm (8 1/2 x 11 in) with rounded corners. Line tins with baking paper or non-stick Teflon liners.

Bake for 25 minutes, or until the centre springs back when pressed, and a skewer in the centre comes out clean. Ice with Everyday Chocolate Icing (p. 347).

This cake is best the day it is made, although it will last for 3 days.

Note: Some people have great success with this recipe, while others do not produce such good results. I don't know why!

Chocolate Banana Cake

This cake is moist, soft and well-flavoured, with a light texture. It is lovely eaten slightly warm.

For two 23 x 10 cm (9 x 4 in) loaves, or one 23 cm (9 in) ring cake:
200 g (7 oz) butter
1½ cups sugar 10½ozs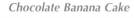
1 tsp vanilla essence
2 large eggs
1 cup (about 2) ripe mashed bananas
½ cup (125 ml/4 fl oz) buttermilk, or
  ½ cup milk with 1 tsp wine vinegar
2 cups plain flour 8oz
3 Tbsp cocoa
1 tsp baking powder
¾ tsp baking soda

Chocolate Banana Cake

Turn the oven to 180°C (350°F). Mix the soft (but not melted) butter, sugar and vanilla until fluffy. Add the eggs one at a time, beating well each time.

Mash and measure the banana and mix it with the buttermilk. If using a food processor, pour this mixture on top of the butter mixture, with the dry ingredients on top. Process in brief bursts to mix. If mixing in a bowl, fold the 3 mixtures together.

Bake in two 23 x 10 cm (9 x 4 in) loaf tins, each lined with a strip of baking paper going across the long sides and the bottom. The mixture is rather big for a 23 cm (9 in) ring pan, but it works well and makes an attractive cake if you build up the sides and centre with baking paper stuck in place with a little butter. Line the bottom of the ring pan with paper.

Bake the loaves or the ring cake for 30–40 minutes, or until a skewer in the middle comes out clean and the centre springs back when pressed.

Dust the top with icing sugar before serving, or ice with Everyday Chocolate Icing (p. 347) or Sour Cream Chocolate Icing (p. 347) when cold.

Store, uncovered, in a cool cupboard.

Jane's Banana Cake

For best flavour, this cake should be made with overripe bananas.

For a 20 cm (8 in) ring cake:
1½ cups self-raising flour 6oz.
1 tsp baking soda
3 ripe bananas
125 g (4½ oz) butter, at room temperature
¾ cup sugar 6
2 large eggs
2 Tbsp milk
1 tsp vanilla essence

Turn the oven to 180°C (350°F). Line a 20 cm (8 in) ring pan with baking paper or a non-stick Teflon liner.

Sieve the flour and baking soda into a large bowl.

Mash the bananas roughly with a fork, put in a food processor with the remaining ingredients and process until smooth. Add to the flour and mix until just combined.

Pour into the prepared pan and bake for 35–40 minutes, or until a skewer comes out clean.

Serve dusted with icing sugar, or topped with Cream Cheese Icing (p. 285), lemon (p. 292) or chocolate icing (p. 347).

Mississippi Mud Cake

What a wonderful name for a dense, dark chocolate cake!

For a 23 cm (9 in) ring cake, about 8 servings:
1 Tbsp instant coffee
½ cup (125 ml/4 fl oz) water
100 g (3½ oz) dark cooking chocolate or chocolate chips
100 g (3½ oz) butter
1 cup sugar
2 Tbsp sherry, whisky or brandy
2 large eggs
1 tsp vanilla essence
1¼ cups flour
½ tsp baking soda

Turn the oven to 150°C (300°F). Warm the instant coffee, water, broken up chocolate, butter and sugar until the chocolate has melted and the sugar dissolved, stirring at intervals if microwaving, and all the time in a pot. Cool to room temperature, then stir in the liquid.

Beat the eggs with the vanilla in a food processor or bowl.

Sieve the flour and baking soda together, then combine the 3 mixtures. Process or whisk just enough to get a smooth mixture that is thinner than most cake mixtures.

Line the bottom of a ring tin (at least 6-cup capacity) with baking paper or a non-stick Teflon liner, and butter or spray the sides carefully. Pour the cake mixture into the tin and bake for about an hour, or until the sides of the cake shrink away from the tin, and a skewer in the thickest part comes out clean.

Cool in the tin for about 10 minutes, then run a knife around the sides and invert onto a serving plate.

Serve dusted with icing sugar, with icecream or lightly whipped, chilled cream, and a dribble of coffee-flavoured liqueur if you like.

Three-Minute Chocolate Sponge

A popular 'all in together' cake!

For a 20 cm (8 in) cake or a 23 cm (9 in) ring cake:
75 g (2¹/₂ oz) butter
3 large eggs
³/₄ cup sugar
2 Tbsp milk
1 cup plain flour, minus 2 Tbsp
2 tsp baking powder
2 Tbsp cocoa

Turn the oven to 175°C (350°F). Line a 20 cm (8 in) square or round cake tin, or a ring tin, with baking paper or a non-stick Teflon liner. Butter or spray uncovered sides.

Melt the butter until just liquid in a bowl that will hold the whole mixture. Add the eggs, sugar and milk. Sift in the carefully measured flour, baking powder and cocoa.

Using an electric beater or a good hand beater, beat until the mixture is well mixed, looks creamy and is slightly paler in colour, about 30–60 seconds.

Turn into the prepared tin and bake for about 20 minutes, or until the centre springs back when pressed.

Dust with icing sugar or ice when cold, using one of the icings on page 347.

Variation: For Jaffa Cake, add the finely grated rind of 1 orange and replace 1 Tbsp of milk with 1 Tbsp orange juice.

Cornflour Sponge

Castor sugar gives this sponge a fine texture. Beware of overcooking it – the time required will vary with tin size and different ovens. Remove the sponge from the oven as soon as the centre springs back, even if it has only cooked for 10 minutes. If you leave it in the tin for a few minutes it will dry out less, and won't be crusty.

For a 20–23 cm (8–9 in) cake:
3 large eggs, separated
¹/₂ cup castor sugar
¹/₄ cup cornflour, stirred
¹/₄ cup plain flour
1 tsp baking powder

Turn the oven to 190°C (375°F). Butter and flour a 20–23 cm (8–9 in) square tin, shaking off excess flour.

Beat the egg whites until they form soft peaks. Add the sugar and beat until the peaks are stiff. Add the yolks and beat just enough to blend them with the whites.

Sift the cornflour, flour and baking powder 2 or 3 times for extra lightness. Add to the egg mixture in 2 or 3 parts, folding in carefully but thoroughly after each addition. Turn into the prepared tin and bake for 12–20 minutes, or just until the centre springs back when pressed with the finger.

Leave to cool in the tin for 2–3 minutes then invert on a cake rack.

Split the smaller sponge and fill with jam and whipped cream. Top the larger sponge with whipped cream and fresh berries.

Aunt Lucy's Mistake

Aunt Lucy was the much-loved aunt of a friend. Once, in an absent-minded moment, she muddled up a recipe while baking, to make a cake that was better than the original.

For a 20–23 cm (8–9 in) cake:
1 cup sugar
3 large eggs
200 g (7 oz) butter
¹/₄ cup cocoa
¹/₄ cup (60 ml/2 fl oz) boiling water
1¹/₂ cups (200 g/7 oz) plain flour
2 tsp baking powder
1 cup desiccated coconut
¹/₂ cup (125 ml/4 fl oz) milk

Turn the oven to 180°C (350°F). Put the sugar and eggs in a food processor and process until thick and creamy. Gradually add the softened, but not melted, butter and mix well.

Measure the cocoa into a cup or small bowl, add the boiling water and stir until mixed. Put in the food processor and without mixing add the flour and baking

powder. Process briefly – do not overmix. Add the coconut and milk and process again until just combined.

If you use an electric mixer, cream the butter, sugar and eggs, beat in the cocoa mixture, fold in the sifted flour and baking powder, then stir in the coconut and milk at the end.

Line a 20–23 cm (8–9 in) cake tin with baking paper or a non-stick Teflon liner. Pour the mixture into the tin and bake for about 30 minutes, depending on the tin size. The cake is cooked when it starts to shrink at the edges and springs back in the middle.

Ice with Everyday Chocolate Icing (p. 347).

Apricot Party Cake

(Photo p. 296)
Extra-easy and absolutely delicious!

For 1 large (or 2 smaller) ring cakes:
250 g (9 oz) butter
1¹/₂ cups sugar
1 can (445 g/15¹/₂ oz) or 2 cups unsweetened apricot pulp
finely grated rind of ¹/₂ lemon
2 tsp vanilla essence
2 tsp ground cardamom
2 Tbsp lemon juice
3 large eggs
2 cups plain flour
1 cup (140 g/5 oz) ground almonds
2 tsp baking powder
1 tsp baking soda
¹/₂ cup dried apricots, finely chopped

Turn the oven to 180°C (350°F). Melt the cubed butter gently in a large pot. Remove from the heat, add the sugar and apricot pulp, then the next 5 ingredients in the order given. Beat with a fork or whisk until well combined.

Shake the flour, ground almonds, baking powder and soda into the mixture through a large sieve, then tip in any remaining ground almonds. Sprinkle the apricots on top, then fold everything together, mixing to an even consistency that is a little thinner than normal.

Use a large, fluted pan (10-cup capacity), 2 smaller pans or 1 smaller pan and a muffin tray. Spray thoroughly with non-stick spray, then cover evenly with sieved flour. Shake off excess flour.

Fill the pans two-thirds full, then bake until the centres feel firm and a skewer pushed to the bottom comes out clean; about 45 minutes for the large pan, less for smaller pans.

Cool for 5 minutes, then carefully invert onto a cake rack. Dust with icing sugar before serving.

Variation: Leave out the cardamom.

Yoghurt Cake

Anne's Almond Cake

This is one of the nicest cakes I make. It is a moist, fairly rich, buttery cake, with a good texture and a slight but not strong almond flavour. It keeps well and is served in fairly small slices.

The surface of the cake should stay fairly level – if it peaks, it is a sign that you have used too much flour. If the top sinks a little, you have not used quite enough flour.

For a 20 cm (8 in) square cake:
225 g (8 oz) butter
1 cup castor sugar
4 large eggs
1 tsp almond essence
1¹/₃ cups plain flour
1 tsp baking powder
1 cup ground almonds

Turn the oven to 170°C (325°F). Line a 20 cm (8 in) square tin with greaseproof paper.

Cream the butter and castor sugar until light in colour. Add the eggs one at a time, beating well each time. Stir in the almond essence.

Sift the flour and baking powder together and mix with the ground almonds. Fold into the creamed mixture. Spoon the mixture (which should look fairly wet) into the tin and bake for 1 hour, or until the sides of the cake start to shrink from the tin and the centre springs back when pressed.

Cool the cake in the tin. When cold, ice with butter icing flavoured with a little almond essence. Decorate with toasted slivered almonds if desired.

Variation: If a flat-topped cake worries you, make three-quarters of the mixture and cook it in a 23 cm (9 in) ring pan. A ring cake is always useful if you are

dealing with a damp mixture that tends to sink in the middle.

Yoghurt Cake

Here is the recipe for a light, plain cake that is delicious served with berries. It makes two loaves, one to serve straight away, and one to freeze.

For 2 loaves:
75 g (2¹/₂ oz) butter
1 cup sugar
2 eggs
1 tsp vanilla essence
1¹/₂ cups plain flour
1 tsp baking soda
¹/₄ tsp salt
300 g (10 oz) plain or flavoured yoghurt

Turn the oven to 180°C (350°F). Line 2 loaf tins with a strip of baking paper along the long sides and bottom.

Melt the butter until it is liquid but not hot. Put the sugar, eggs and vanilla in the food processor, add the melted butter and process to mix thoroughly.

Add the flour, baking soda and salt, then the yoghurt, and process very briefly until combined. The mixture will be airy and puffy. Do not beat it or you will lose some of its lightness. Handle it as little, and as gently, as possible.

If you don't have a food processor, use a beater to combine the first 4 ingredients, then fold in the sifted dry ingredients and the yoghurt, taking care not to overmix.

Turn the mixture into the loaf tins and bake for 30 minutes, or until the centre springs back when pressed lightly and a skewer comes out clean.

Dust the top with icing sugar. Serve slices topped with fresh berries and extra yoghurt of the same flavour, or whipped cream.

Orange Cake

Make this cake by the conventional creaming method or in a food processor. Serve it with coffee or tea at any time of the day, or enjoy it warm for dessert, in slices topped with drained mandarin segments and lightly whipped cream flavoured with orange liqueur.

For a 23 cm (9 in) ring cake:
1 large or 2 small oranges
1 cup sugar
125 g (4¹/₂ oz) butter
3 large eggs
1 cup self-raising flour
³/₄ cup plain flour
water
1 Tbsp lemon juice

Turn the oven to 180°C (350°F). Thinly peel the orange with a floating blade peeler. Put the peel in the food processor with the sugar and process with the metal chopping blade until very finely chopped. Add the softened, but not melted, butter and the eggs and process until thoroughly mixed. Add the flours, then the juice from the orange(s) made up to ¹/₂ cup with water, and the lemon juice. Process briefly, just enough to mix, then spoon into a well-buttered or sprayed 23 cm (9 in) ring pan.

Bake just below the middle of the oven (with or without the fan) for 35–50 minutes, until a skewer comes out clean. Leave to stand for 5–10 minutes, then remove from the pan and cool on a rack. To serve, dust generously with icing sugar.

Coconut Cherry Meringue Cake

This is a really popular cake! Everyone who tries it comes back for another piece.

For a 23 cm (9 in) ring cake, about 8 servings:
100 g (3¹/₂ oz) butter
¹/₂ cup sugar
2 egg yolks
¹/₄ tsp almond essence
¹/₂ tsp vanilla essence
1 cup plain flour
1 tsp baking powder
2 Tbsp coconut
¹/₄ cup glacé cherries
¹/₄ cup (60 ml/2 fl oz) milk

Meringue Topping
2 egg whites
5 Tbsp sugar
¹/₄ tsp almond essence
1 tsp cornflour
1 cup coconut
¹/₄–¹/₂ cup glacé cherries

Turn the oven to 160°C (325°F). Line a 23 cm (9 in) ring tin with baking paper or a non-stick Teflon liner.

Warm the butter until it is soft, but not liquid. Beat it with the sugar until light-coloured, in a bowl or food processor. Add the egg yolks, almond and vanilla essences, and beat again.

Toss together the flour, baking powder, coconut and cherries, then tip them with the milk onto the creamed mixture. Fold in or process briefly until mixed.

Drop the mixture into the tin in blobs, then spread it as evenly as possible.

Beat the egg whites for the topping until foamy. Add the sugar and beat until the peaks stand up, without turning over, when the beater is removed. Add the essence, cornflour and coconut, and beat or fold in.

Spread over the uncooked cake and decorate with cherries, cut in pieces or left whole. Bake for 45–55 minutes, until the top is a light golden brown, and the sides start to shrink from the tin.

Leave to stand for 10 minutes, then remove carefully from the tin. (Cover the top with more baking paper and put soft teatowels over this. Turn out carefully upside-down onto a plate then turn right side up onto a serving plate. Remove the teatowels and baking paper.)

When cold, store on a flat plate in a lightly covered container, at room temperature, up to a few days. Refrigerate, tightly covered, for longer.

To cut the cake neatly, use a sharp serrated knife. If the meringue sticks or breaks, dip the knife in hot water.

Holiday Surprise Cake

This cake is really easy to mix and, if you add the filling and topping, full of surprises!

For a 23 cm (9 in) ring cake:
250 g sour cream
2 large eggs
1 cup sugar
1 tsp vanilla essence
1³/4 cups self-raising flour
1/4 tsp baking soda
1/2 tsp salt

Optional Topping
25 g (1 oz) cold butter
1/4 cup each sugar and chopped nuts
2 Tbsp flour
1 tsp cinnamon

Optional Filling
1/2 cup dried apricots
1/2 cup (125 ml/4 fl oz) water
1/4 cup each ground almonds, sugar and wine biscuit crumbs

Turn the oven to 180°C (350°F), or 170°C (325°F) for fan-bake. Line the bottom of a 23 cm (9 in) ring tin (of 7-cup capacity) with baking paper, and butter or spray the sides.

Put the sour cream, eggs, sugar and essence in a bowl or food processor.

Whisk or process until smooth, then sift in the flour, baking soda and salt; stir (or process briefly) to mix thoroughly but not more than necessary. Pour into the prepared pan.

To make the topping, cut or rub the butter into the remaining ingredients until it is crumbly.

For the filling, chop the apricots finely then boil them with the water for 3–4 minutes, until the water has disappeared. Cool, then mix with the ground almonds, sugar and biscuit crumbs.

Drop teaspoonfuls of the filling on the surface of the uncooked cake, leaving the edges clear. (The filling sinks to the middle of the cake during cooking.) Sprinkle the topping evenly over the surface.

Bake for 40–45 minutes, until the thickest part of the cake springs back when pressed, and the edges start to shrink from the sides of the pan. Leave to stand in the tin for 10 minutes, then run a knife around the sides and invert carefully. Invert it again onto a plate and dust with icing sugar or ice with chocolate icing (p. 347).

Serve warm with coffee, or with lightly whipped cream for dessert.

Variation: Replace the apricot filling with Christmas mincemeat or raspberry or apricot jam.

Henry's 'Eating Cake'

My father would describe cakes like this as 'eating cakes'! He meant they were not to be saved for special occasions, but enjoyed regularly with cups of tea or coffee.

For a 20 cm (8 in) square or 23 cm (9 in) round cake:
1 orange or 2 tangelos
125 g (4¹/2 oz) butter
1 cup sugar
2 eggs
1 tsp baking soda
¹/2 cup (125 ml/4 fl oz) water
1 tsp vanilla essence
2 cups plain flour
1 cup sultanas

Turn the oven to 150°C (300°F). Spray or line a 20 cm (8 in) square or 23 cm (9 in) round cake tin.

Cut the fruit into 8 chunky pieces, remove the seeds and central pith, then chop finely with the metal chopping blade of a food processor. Tip the pulp into another container.

Without washing the bowl or blade, add the softened, but not melted, butter, the sugar and eggs. Process for about 20 seconds. Add the baking soda dissolved in the water, the vanilla, flour and sultanas. Using the pulse blade in brief bursts, mix in the orange pulp until everything is combined.

Turn into the prepared tin and bake for 1–1¹/4 hours, or until the cake springs back when pressed lightly in the centre and a skewer comes out clean.

Holiday Surprise Cake

Rich Chocolate Rum Cake

This is a recipe I brought home from New York after a promotional tour. It is delicious!

For about 12 servings:

75 g (2¹/₂ oz) good quality dark chocolate
1 cup sugar
¹/₄ cup (60 ml/2 fl oz) boiling water
150 g (5 oz) soft butter
3 egg yolks
¹/₂ cup sour cream
1 Tbsp dark rum
1 cup plain flour
1 tsp baking powder

Glaze

75 g (2¹/₂ oz) dark chocolate
25 g (1 oz) butter
¹/₄ cup icing sugar
2 Tbsp dark rum

Turn the oven to 180°C (350°F). Line the bottom of a 23–25 cm (9–10 in) round flan or cake tin with baking paper, and spray or butter the sides.

Break the chocolate into squares and put it in the food processor with the sugar. Process until finely chopped.

Add the boiling water to melt the chocolate, then drop in the soft, but not melted, butter. Mix well then add the egg yolks, sour cream and rum. The mixture should be creamy and well mixed.

Add the flour and baking powder and process just enough to blend them in.

Spoon the mixture into the prepared tin and spread evenly. Bake for 30 minutes, or until the cake springs back when pressed in the middle. (It will rise, then fall, during cooking.) Leave to cool for 5 minutes, then turn out onto a rack.

Make the glaze as soon as you put the cake in the oven, so it will have cooled and hardened enough to spread by the time the cake has cooled.

Break the chocolate into squares and put it with the other glaze ingredients in a small frypan over low heat. As soon as the chocolate is soft enough, mix to a smooth cream, heating no more than necessary. Cover with cling film and leave to cool. Spread over the cold cake, and leave to set.

Chocolate Orange Liqueur Cake

Make this wonderful cake to celebrate a very special occasion! It owes its outstanding texture to a high proportion of dark chocolate and ground almonds. A 20 cm (8 in) cake will make 8–10 servings. Freeze the second cake, or halve the recipe if you like.

For one 23 cm (9 in) or two 20 cm (8 in) round cakes:

250 g (9 oz) dark chocolate
¹/₄ cup (60 ml/2 fl oz) orange liqueur
rind of 1 orange
1 cup castor sugar
250 g (9 oz) butter, softened
6 large eggs, separated
¹/₄ tsp citric acid
1 tsp water
1 cup ground almonds
³/₄ cup plain flour

Icing

125 g (4¹/₂ oz) dark chocolate, broken up
100 g (3¹/₂ oz) butter
1–2 Tbsp orange liqueur

Turn the oven to 180°C (350°F). Break the chocolate into even pieces. Melt it with the liqueur in a bowl over a pot of hot water, stirring until well combined. Put aside to cool.

Peel the orange with a potato peeler. Put the rind in a food processor with ³/₄ of the castor sugar and process until very finely chopped. Add the softened – but not melted – butter, process until light and fluffy, then beat in the egg yolks and the citric acid dissolved in the water. Add the cooled chocolate mixture, ground almonds and flour, and mix in lightly.

In another bowl, beat the egg whites until they form soft peaks. Add the remaining castor sugar and beat until the mixture forms peaks that turn over when you lift the beater. Do not overbeat. Carefully fold the chocolate mixture through the beaten egg whites.

Line the bottom and sides of one 23 cm (9 in) or two 20 cm (8 in) round baking tins with baking paper or non-stick Teflon liner(s). Pour the mixture into the tin(s). Bake for about 45 minutes for a 23 cm (9 in) cake, and about 30–40 minutes for the 20 cm (8 in) cakes, until the centre feels as firm as the edges, and a skewer pushed into the middle comes out clean. Leave for 10 minutes then turn out onto a wire rack.

Combine all the icing ingredients and heat in a bowl over hot water until

Chocolate Orange Liqueur Cake

melted. Mix well. Cool before spreading on the cake. Decorate as desired.

Variations: Replace the orange liqueur with rum or brandy.

Leave out the orange rind, citric acid and water if desired.

Easy Fruit and Nut Cake

A slice of this flavourful cake is an excellent high-energy, nutrient-rich snack. It is compact, easily portable and long-keeping (if it gets the chance). The recipe may be modified to make a richer cake for a special occasion.

For a 23 cm (9 in) cake:
4 cups mixed fruit*
1/2 cup (125 ml/4 fl oz) orange juice
150–200 g (5–7 oz) butter
1 cup (packed) brown sugar
about 1 cup walnuts, pecans or almonds, chopped
4 large eggs
1 cup self-raising flour
1 cup wholemeal or plain flour
cherries and almonds, optional

* Buy mixed fruit or use a mixture of sultanas, currants and small, dark raisins.

Turn the oven to 150°C (300°F). Simmer the dried fruit and orange juice in a large, covered pot for about 5 minutes or until all the juice is soaked up by the fruit, stirring at intervals. Take off the heat and stir in the butter (the larger amount makes a richer cake) cut into 1 cm (1/2 in) cubes, and the sugar. Stir until the butter melts and the sugar is no longer grainy, then stand the pot in cold water to cool the mixture, stirring occasionally. Stir in the nuts.

When the mixture has cooled to room temperature, add the eggs, beating them in with a fork. When thoroughly mixed, sprinkle the flours over the mixture and fold them in without overmixing.

Pour the mixture into a 23 cm (9 in) square tin or 2 fairly large loaf tins lined with one or more strips of baking paper to cover the bottom and sides. Level the top, pressing on cherries and almonds for decoration if desired.

Bake the cake for 60–75 minutes, and loaves for about 45 minutes. When the cake is ready the centre should feel firm and spring back when pressed, and a skewer pushed into the middle (right to the bottom) will come out clean. A 20 cm (8 in) square cake takes longer.

Sprinkle over a few tablespoons of rum, whisky or brandy if desired. Cool in the tin. For best flavour, leave 2 days before cutting.

Variation: For a richer Christmas cake, use 1 kg (2 lb 3 oz) dried fruit, 3/4 cup orange juice and 250 g (9 oz) butter.

Simnel Cake

I was taught that Simnel Cake is a traditional English cake, originally made by young women 'in service' to take home to their mothers on Mothering Sunday.

I love the layer of homemade almond icing baked in the middle of Simnel Cake. In this recipe an excellent result is obtained with a layer of semolina flavoured with almond essence.

For a 20 cm (8 in) cake:

Filling
50 g (2 oz) butter
1/2 cup semolina
1/2 cup sugar
1/4 cup (60 ml/2 fl oz) water
2 tsp almond essence

Cake
125 g (4 1/2 oz) butter
1/2 cup sugar
2 eggs
1 tsp vanilla essence
1/4 cup rolled oats
1/2 cup plain flour
1/2 cup self-raising flour
1 tsp mixed spice
1 tsp cinnamon
3 cups mixed dried fruit
1/4 cup (60 ml/2 fl oz) sherry

Turn the oven to 150°C (300°F). Make the filling first. Melt the butter in a (non-stick) frypan, then stir in the semolina and cook over a moderate heat for about 2 minutes, without browning. Add the sugar and water and cook uncovered, stirring frequently, until it leaves a wide band on the bottom of the pan when the spoon is pulled across it (about 4–5 minutes). Stir in the essence, then stand the pan in cold water to cool.

Make the cake by the conventional creaming method, or use a short-cut method if you have a food processor. Cut the butter into cubes and microwave it until soft but not melted. Put in the food processor (fitted with a plastic mixing blade) with the sugar, eggs, vanilla, rolled oats and half the plain flour. Process only after adding all these. Add the remaining flour and the spices, process again until evenly blended, then add the dried fruit and mix briefly, using the pulse action. If the mixture is very thick, add 1–2 Tbsp sherry to make it easier to spread.

Line the bottom and sides of a 20 cm (8 in) round or square tin with baking paper or a non-stick Teflon liner, and spread over half the cake mixture. Spread the almond mixture over this. If it is fairly firm, flatten pieces with wet hands. If it is too wet to handle, put it on in little blobs, and try to spread these evenly. Top with the remaining cake mix, and bake for 1 3/4–2 hours, until the centre springs back and a skewer comes out clean.

Drizzle the sherry over the cake while it is still very hot, putting more round the sides than the middle. Cool on a rack, then remove the lining paper.

If desired, decorate traditionally with pale green icing and Easter eggs.

Almond Ring

Although this almond ring is not strictly a cake, I think of it as closer to being a cake than a pastry. A real treat for anyone who likes almonds, it is something festive to serve with coffee after dinner, or with drinks. It looks pretty and makes an attractive gift, especially if you stand it on a flat glass plate and wrap it in clear film.

200 g (7 oz) flaky or puff pastry (p. 237)
1 1/2 cups ground almonds
3/4 cup sugar
1/2 tsp grated lemon rind
1/2 tsp almond essence
1 large egg
12 red crystallised cherries
1 cup apricot jam
angelica or green cherries

Turn the oven to 220°C (425°F). Roll the pastry out into a long, thin rectangle 60 cm (24 in) by 12 cm (5 in).

Measure the next 4 ingredients into a bowl. Beat the egg to combine the white and yolk, then add half to the almond mixture. Mix well. Add more egg until the mixture is moist enough to roll. Reserve about a teaspoonful of egg to glaze the pastry. If the mixture still looks dry, beat a second egg and add a little of this.

Either roll the almond mixture into a long, thin roll (the length of the pastry) or put it on the pastry in small blobs and shape it into a roll with damp hands. Halve all the cherries. Press 16 of the halves into the almond mixture, and pinch the mixture over them. Moisten the far side of the pastry with water.

Fold the undampened side of the pastry over the almond mixture. Fold the pastry-coated almond mixture over the dampened pastry, then bring the ends round in a circle, so the visible long join of the pastry is on the inside of the circle. Pinch the joined edges together firmly.

Transfer onto a lightly buttered or sprayed oven tray. Brush with lightly beaten egg. Do not prick the pastry.

Bake for 10–15 minutes, or until the pastry is golden brown. Remove from the oven and immediately brush with apricot jam. Decorate with the remaining cherry halves and angelica, and replace in the oven for about 2 minutes.

Note: If you do not like traditional Christmas cake, consider making almond rings instead, freezing them until just before you need them.

Christmas Panforte

This is a chewy, very firm, dark and compact flat cake, of Italian origin. Wedges from a round cake, or rectangular pieces cut from a square cake, carefully gift-wrapped, make a dozen or so special and unusual gifts for good friends. (When sold in speciality food stores, panforte is usually cut in small slices and prewrapped.)

For about 12–15 servings:
75 g (2¹/₂ oz) butter
¹/₂ cup chocolate chips
1 cup blanched almonds
1 cup hazelnuts
1 cup pecans
1 cup fruit cake mix
¹/₄ cup castor sugar
¹/₂ cup honey
¹/₂ cup plain flour
¹/₄ cup cocoa
2 tsp cinnamon

Turn the oven to 160°C (325°F), or 150°C (300°F) for fan-bake. Melt the butter and chocolate chips together in a fairly large bowl in the microwave oven on Medium (50%) power for about 2 minutes, or in a bowl over a pot of hot water. Put the nuts in a shallow baking dish in one layer, and roast lightly in the oven as it preheats. Check every 5 minutes – the almonds should be light beige when all the nuts are ready, after about 10 minutes. Tip the hot nuts into the melted butter and chocolate, add the fruit cake mix and stir together.

Warm the sugar and honey together over low to moderate heat, stirring until the sugar has dissolved. As soon as the mixture bubbles all over the surface, pour it into the nut mixture and stir again. Sift the flour, cocoa and cinnamon onto the mixture and stir until blended.

Line the bottom and sides of a round tin about 24 cm (9¹/₂ in) across, or a 23 cm (9 in) square tin, with a non-stick Teflon liner or baking paper. Pour the warm mixture into the tin and pat it out evenly, with a piece of plastic between the cake and your hand, if necessary.

Bake (on fan-bake if possible) for 30–45 minutes, or until the centre looks and feels as cooked as the part 5 cm (2 in) from the edge. Longer cooking gives a firmer, more toffee-like cake. Straight after cooking, the mixture feels much softer than a cake normally does, but it becomes firmer on cooling. It should be left for at least 24 hours in a cool place before it is cut, with a very sharp or serrated knife.

Dust with icing sugar before serving, or leave plain. Store wrapped pieces in the refrigerator or freezer if you are making it some weeks before it is needed.

Variations: Replace the cocoa with extra flour for a milder chocolate flavour.

Replace half the cinnamon with another spice.

Note: The mixture contains no baking powder, soda or eggs.

Tips for Better Fruit Cakes

There's more to a successful Christmas cake than just a recipe! A perfectly reliable recipe can fail if you misinterpret or modify the instructions.

Washing Fruit

It is important that dried fruit be plump, moist and never gritty. I now wash and 'plump up' premixed fruit as well as currants, raisins, sultanas, etc. Put the measured fruit in a colander or large sieve, pour boiling water over it, drain well, then dry it in the sun on a teatowel, in a low oven in a roasting pan, or in a microwave oven on paper towels. Unless especially soaked ahead according to your recipe, fruit should be dry, cooled and 'plumped' before it is added to other ingredients. Wash it the day before you plan to make your cake.

Which Flour?

Do not use cake flour or self-raising flour alone for fruit cakes. Use flour that is recommended for scone-making or bread-making as it holds up the fruit better.

Baking Powder

Baking powder and baking soda are not essential in a rich fruit cake. Both make the cake rise slightly. Baking soda tends to make a darker cake.

Curdling

Cake mixtures often curdle as the eggs are added. You can prevent this by adding 1–2 Tbsp of the measured flour between each egg.

Tin Sizes

A cake cooked in a tin smaller than that specified will be deeper and will probably take longer to cook.

Papering Tins

If you use a recipe that has been used by your great-grandmother, remember that your stove differs from hers! In today's well-regulated ovens you can make an excellent cake in a tin lined with a non-stick Teflon liner or one layer of baking paper.

Cooking Times

The cooking time given in a recipe can never be exact because different ovens have different characteristics. Use the given time as a guide only – look at and test your cake during the last hour of cooking. When ready, the cake will have shrunk slightly from the edge of the tin and be firm in the middle. A skewer pushed into the middle should come out clean, with no uncooked mixture on it. Never leave a rich cake to turn itself off in an automatic oven. A cake that sinks in the middle on cooling is probably not cooked right through.

Splits and Peaks

A cake which splits or peaks needs a larger tin, a lower temperature or ¹/₄–¹/₂ cup less flour.

Alcohol

Some recipes call for sherry or spirits to be added to the raw mixture. Others call for spirits to be sprinkled over the cake when it is taken from the oven. This won't hurt the cake as long as it is cooked! Put more round the edges than in the middle.

First Aid for Dry Cakes

Brush all surfaces liberally with sherry, brandy and/or spirits. Place the cake in a plastic bag and refrigerate it for at least a day. Repeat applications until the cake is as moist as you like it!

Maturing and Storage

Make your cake several weeks before you need it so it has time to mature.

Cakes should not be stored in completely airtight containers unless they are to be refrigerated or frozen. (Rich cakes freeze well for up to 6 months.)

Cakes stored at room temperature may go mouldy when stored in airtight plastic bags, foil or airtight plastic boxes. Use greaseproof paper, clean teatowels and storage containers which allow some air circulation.

Decorating Rich Cakes

To make a rich cake look as attractive as possible for a special occasion, decide how you want to decorate it before you put it in the oven.

- Place nuts and/or crystallised cherries on the surface of the cake before you bake it. Place them at random, or arrange them in a pattern. Use plump and perfect nuts. Brush with lightly beaten egg 15 minutes before the end of baking time for a glossy finish.
- You can stick halved or sliced nuts and pieces of crystallised fruit on the surface of an undecorated, nearly cooked cake which is to be eaten within 10 days, if you brush its surface with golden syrup or a thick sugar syrup half an hour before the cake is cooked. Quickly place the fruit and nuts in place, and brush the whole surface with thinned syrup

2 or 3 times during the next half-hour.

- Cakes decorated like this should have an attractive shiny surface, which will look good with a paper frill or a wide ribbon around the cake. Place a sprig of holly or a Christmas ornament in the centre. Marzipan fruit (see below) piled on top also looks pretty.
- Cakes that are to be iced should be brought to room temperature first. The first coating is usually a layer of almond icing. The cake is brushed with jam so the icing will stick to it, then the icing is rolled out and laid on the cake. This ensures that the top layer of icing is not discoloured by the cake, and makes the top layer more smooth.
- The top coat may be made of bought or homemade 'plastic' icing. This is rolled out and placed on top of the almond icing, which should be moistened with a little water or sugar syrup. The idea is to finish up with a smooth surface, so cut off any overhanging pieces rather than folding them over.
- Royal icing may be used as a top coat instead of plastic icing. Decorations are usually made of almond icing or royal icing.

Homemade Almond Icing

Almond icing may be used as a layer under the top coat of icing, and for decorations such a marzipan fruits. It is easy to make. This recipe is enough for a medium-sized cake. Double the quantity if you want enough for a very thick layer, for icing down the sides, or for marzipan fruit.

100 g (3½ oz) ground almonds
1 cup icing sugar
½ cup castor sugar
1 egg yolk
2 Tbsp lemon juice, strained
¼ tsp almond essence (optional)

Combine the ground almonds and sugars in a food processor or mixing bowl. Mix the egg yolk with half the lemon juice and add to the almond mixture with a little almond essence if desired. Add the remaining lemon juice a little at a time, until you have a paste that is easy to roll.

Warm a little apricot jam, sieve it and brush it over the cake, then roll out the almond paste on a dry board sprinkled with icing sugar. Place over the cake smoothly, using a rolling pin.

Plastic Icing

Plastic icing is not really difficult to make, as long as you have some experience of working with icing.

1 Tbsp gelatine
3 Tbsp cold water
3 Tbsp liquid glucose
2 tsp glycerine
1 kg (2 lb 3 oz) icing sugar

Decorating Rich Cakes

Mix the gelatine and cold water together, stand for 3–4 minutes, then warm in a microwave or over low heat just until the gelatine has dissolved. Add the liquid glucose and glyerine (warm liquid glucose until pourable if the weather is cold).

Sift the icing sugar into a large bowl, pour the warm liquid glucose mixture into the centre, then mix it with a dough hook or a wooden spoon. As soon as it is reasonably firm mix it with your hands until you have a smooth, workable dough (you may need to add a little hot water).

Roll out on a board dusted with icing sugar and place over moistened almond icing. Prick any air bubbles with a needle and put a smooth surface on the icing by polishing it with a square of smooth, shiny card. As you rub the card round and round, you will find that a lovely smooth, shiny surface forms.

Royal Icing

The top coat of icing on a fruit cake is sometimes made of royal icing, rather than plastic icing. Royal icing is very white, sets hard and is easy to pipe into rosettes, lines, dots, etc. for decorations.

1 egg white
1 tsp lemon juice, strained
2 cups sifted icing sugar
½ tsp glycerine (optional)

Mix the egg white and lemon juice in a food processor or bowl, just until frothy. Add the icing sugar a few Tbsp at a time, mixing well each time. Stop when the icing is the consistency you want. Mix in the glycerine.

Use the icing immediately, or store it in an airtight bag for up to 2 or 3 days. For piping, thin it down with a little water if necessary.

Notes: If you want to pipe royal icing into elaborate shapes such as leaves and roses, use icing sugar that does not contain cornflour.

Glycerine is supposed to keep royal icing softer than it would be otherwise, but it is not essential.

Extra-Special Mini Christmas Cakes

Small Christmas cakes, packed with candied fruit and nuts, and topped with brazil nuts and cherries, make very special Christmas gifts. This recipe makes four small cakes, or six tiny cakes. (Work out sizes by volumes, if you like. The total recipe makes about 8 cups of mixture.) Line little cake containers with baking paper, and spray or butter this for good measure, since the mixture has a tendency to stick.

For 4 small or 6 tiny cakes:
2–3 cups whole brazil nuts
1 cup whole almonds
1 cup whole cashew nuts
1 cup red glacé cherries
1 cup green glacé cherries
2–3 cups glacé mixed fruit
2 cups dried fruit
1½ cups plain flour
1 cup brown sugar
2 tsp cinnamon
1 tsp baking powder
1 tsp salt
4 large eggs
1 tsp vanilla essence

Put aside about 12 brazil nuts for decoration; put the rest of the nuts in a large bowl. Put aside about 12 glacé cherries, and add the rest to the nuts. Choose a variety of glacé fruits, e.g. pineapple, pears, papaya, crystallised ginger, mixed peel. (Do not replace glacé fruits with dried fruits.) Chop the fruit into 1 cm (½ in) cubes, measure it, then mix with the nuts, etc. For the dried fruit, use sultanas, currants, sticky raisins, dried apricots and prunes. Stir into the rest of the fruit and nuts.

Measure the flour, sugar, cinnamon, baking powder and salt into the bowl with the fruits and nuts. Stir well to coat everything evenly.

Beat the eggs and vanilla with a fork until the whites and yolks are combined, then add to the other ingredients, mixing thoroughly with your (very clean) hands. Press the mixture into prepared cake tins, then mix the reserved cherries and nuts in the small amount of batter left in the bowl, and arrange them carefully on top of the cakes.

Preheat the oven to 150°C (300°F), but turn it down to 130°C (250°F) when the cakes are put in the oven. Bake for 1–1¼ hours, until the mixture around the fruit and nuts in the centre of each cake feels quite firm when pressed.

Leave to cool for 5 minutes then remove from the lined containers. If you think it will be hard to remove the baking paper later, do it straight away.

When the cakes are cold, brush all the surfaces with whisky, brandy or rum. When this is dry, oil the palm of your hand and lightly rub the tops of the cakes to polish them.

Extra-Special Mini Christmas Cakes

They will keep in a cool cupboard for several months, wrapped loosely in greaseproof paper. (To 'refresh' them, brush with sherry or spirits, leave for 24 hours in a plastic bag, then rub lightly with oil, as above.)

Boiled Pineapple Cake

If you want to make a Christmas cake that can be eaten soon after it is made, that has a lovely flavour, but isn't too rich, large or expensive, try this cake. Follow the recipe carefully since mistakes can cause a soggy, gluey result.

For a 20 cm (8 in) cake:
100 g (3½ oz) butter
1 cup sugar
1 can (450 g/16 oz) crushed pineapple
300 g (10½ oz) sultanas
200 g (7 oz) mixed fruit
1 tsp cinnamon
1 tsp mixed spice
½ tsp baking soda
grated rind and juice of 1 tangelo or ½ an orange
2 large eggs
1 cup self-raising flour
1 cup plain flour

Put the butter, sugar, pineapple and juice, dried fruit, spices, soda, grated tangelo or orange rind and juice in a 23 cm (9 in) pot. Boil, uncovered, stirring often, for 15 minutes. The mixture must boil fast enough to evaporate some of the juice, but not fast enough to burn the fruit. (If you are worried about this, measure the mixture as soon as it comes to the boil, then again at the end. It should lose half a cup of liquid.)

Stand the pot in a sink of cold water and leave it until it is absolutely cold. (If you are impatient, your cake will be gluey!)

Beat the eggs until light coloured and thick, then stir into the cold fruit. Next stir in the flours without overmixing. If the mixture looks wetter than a normal light sultana cake, add up to ¼ cup more plain flour. Turn into a 20 cm (8 in) tin lined with baking paper.

Bake at 160°C (325°F) for 30 minutes, then at 150°C (300°F) for 1–1½ hours, until a skewer in the middle comes out clean and the centre is springy when pressed. Remove the cake from the tin as soon as it is cool enough to handle, and leave it to finish cooling on a rack.

Easy-Mix Fruit Cake

Here is a spiceless, essenceless cake which is a modest size and is very little trouble to put together. Its outstanding flavour comes from the soaked, dried fruit. I have made a number of cakes from the same basic recipe. All were popular and were eaten with great enthusiasm.

My favourite was flavoured with rum and sherry.

Read 'Tips for Better Fruit Cakes', p. 306, before you start.

For a 20 cm (8 in) square cake:
1 kg (2 lb 3 oz) small, dark raisins
½ cup liquid (125 ml/4 fl oz) (see below)
200 g (7 oz) butter
2 cups plain flour
1 cup sugar
1 tsp baking soda
½ tsp salt
¼ cup (60 ml/2 fl oz) golden syrup
½ cup (125 ml/4 fl oz) milk
2 large eggs

Put the raisins in an unpunctured plastic bag with ½ cup (125 ml/4 fl oz) cold tea, fruit juice, sherry, rum or brandy, or a mixture of 2 or more of these, and leave to stand in a warm place for 24–48 hours, until the fruit has soaked up all the liquid. (A mixture of rum and sherry gives the cake an outstanding flavour.)

When ready to make the cake, turn the oven to 150°C (300°F). Cut or rub the cold butter into the flour, sugar, baking soda and salt, using a food processor, a pastry blender or your fingers.

Measure the golden syrup in a hot, wet measuring cup, then warm the syrup and milk just enough to combine them. Beat in the eggs, then mix with the prepared fruit and the dry mixture. Turn into a lined 20 cm (8 in) square tin.

If you do not intend to ice your cake, decorate the top with a pattern of blanched almonds, cherries, etc.

Bake for 2¼–2½ hours, until a skewer inserted in the centre, pushed down to the bottom, comes out clean.

If you have decorated the top of the cake with nuts, 'polish' them by rubbing a little oil on the palm of your hand and rubbing your hand over the surface of the cake until the nuts shine.

Cover with bought or homemade almond icing and plastic or royal icing if you like (p. 307).

Peter's Special Cake

This is a lovely, dark, moist, fruity cake containing no essences. I like to add small amounts of several spices, but you can leave out those you don't have. Before you start, read 'Tips for Better Fruit Cakes', p. 306.

For a 23 cm (9 in) square or round cake:
500 g (1 lb 2 oz) sultanas
500 g (1 lb 2 oz) raisins
500 g (1 lb 2 oz) currants
½ cup (125 ml/4 fl oz) sherry
rind of 1 lemon
rind of 1 orange
1½ cups brown sugar
250 g (9 oz) butter, softened
1 Tbsp treacle
5 large eggs
2 cups flour
½ tsp each ground allspice, cardamom, cinnamon, cloves, coriander and nutmeg

One to two days before the cake is made, put the dried fruits in a plastic bag with the sherry. Turn the bag every now and then, and leave it in a warm place until all the sherry has been absorbed.

Turn the oven to 150°C (300°F). Remove the coloured rind of the lemon and orange with a potato peeler and process it with the sugar until very finely chopped. Add the butter, process until soft and fluffy, then add the treacle and mix again. Add the eggs one at a time, with 1 Tbsp of the flour between each egg.

Mix the rest of the flour and the spices with the fruit in a very large bowl. Add the creamed mixture, and mix until soft enough to drop from your hand. If the mixture is too dry, add up to ¼ cup (60 ml/2 fl oz) extra sherry or spirits.

Put the mixture into a 23 cm (9 in) round or square tin lined with baking paper. Decorate the top with almond or cherries if you like.

Bake at 150°C (300°F) for 1 hour, then turn the oven to 140°C (275°F) and cook for about 3 hours, or until a skewer in the centre comes out clean. Start testing after 1½ hours.

If you like, drizzle ¼ cup (60 ml/2 fl oz) rum or brandy over the cake while it is very hot. Leave it for an hour before removing it from the tin.

Treats and Sweets

My sisters and I, like many other children, started cooking by making sweets. What an incentive, to finish up with more sweets than our pocket money could buy, after a wet Sunday afternoon having fun in the kitchen. Over the years we learnt a lot by trial and error, and eventually could turn out batch after batch of smooth, creamy fudge – quite an achievement! Whether you are just starting to cook sweets, or whether you are an expert, I think you will find recipes to suit you in this section. I hope you have as much fun as we did, and enjoy eating the results.

Rich Chocolates

At Easter I often get the urge to make some homemade sweets for my friends. I have a very good time making these truffles (which are more suitable for adults than children), but I must admit that rather a lot of them never leave the kitchen!

Don't leave making these until the last minute. I find it is best to leave the mixture to chill for two days in the refrigerator before shaping it into balls. Before this the truffle mixture is rather soft and difficult to shape.

It is easier to coat truffles with cocoa than dip them in chocolate, but cocoa-coated truffles soften at room temperature and must be refrigerated until a few minutes before they are eaten. If you coat them with chocolate and let the coating set completely, you can leave them at room temperature for hours. You have the added bonus, too, of biting through firm chocolate and finding inside it a filling which is considerably softer. To me, this texture is one of the best things about truffles.

For about 24 truffles or chocolate fillings:
200 g (7 oz) dark cooking chocolate
2 Tbsp rum
200 g (7 oz) butter
1–2 tsp finely grated orange rind (optional)
2 egg yolks

Break the chocolate into small pieces and put it in a round-based metal bowl over a pot containing hot water. The water should not touch the bowl.

Add the rum to the chocolate and heat the water until the chocolate melts, stirring during this time. Cut the butter into 12 pieces. (Don't use any type of easily spread butter or the truffles will not be firm enough.) Add the butter to the chocolate and keep stirring and heating the water in the pot. As soon as the butter has melted, lift the bowl off the pot, then add the orange rind and the egg yolks.

Rich Chocolates

Beat thoroughly until the egg is evenly mixed in. Don't worry if the mixture is a little rough, as it becomes smooth when cold. Leave in the metal bowl or transfer to a smaller container, cover and refrigerate for 2 days.

When the mixture is cold and fairly firm, it can be shaped into small balls. The easiest way to get evenly shaped balls is to use a melon ball cutter. With some care, a teaspoon may be used to produce egg shapes or ovals with flat bases. Warm the metal spoon or melon baller for best results. If you shape balls with your hands, start with a small piece of mixture cut out with a spoon. Cool your hands in cold water, then dry them.

To coat with cocoa, sift cocoa into a flat-bottomed bowl, drop in a few balls at a time, and roll them around. Refrigerate, then brush off excess cocoa, pack as desired, and refrigerate again.

To coat with chocolate, melt about 100 g (3½ oz) Chocolate Melts with 1 tsp oil in a small heatproof bowl over a small pot containing hot water. Don't let the water mix with the chocolate. Place a cold (uncoated) truffle on a fork, quickly dip it in the melted chocolate to coat it completely, then transfer to a piece of cling film on a metal sponge roll pan. Refrigerate until the coating is hard, then peel off the plastic. (If you find any uncoated areas, patch them with melted chocolate or redip them.)

I find it best to complete my truffles or chocolates 3 or 4 days before they are to be eaten. Their flavour develops nicely in this time.

Liqueur Balls   (Photo p. 313)
These are rich, smooth and delicious.

150 g (5 oz) dark cooking chocolate
2 Tbsp orange-flavoured liqueur
2 Tbsp butter
1 egg yolk
¼ cup cocoa

Break the chocolate into pieces and microwave with the liqueur for 3–4 minutes on 30% power, until the chocolate is soft and will mix easily with the liqueur.

Add the butter and egg yolk and mix well. (The warm chocolate will melt the butter.) Leave for 3–4 hours at cool room temperature then roll into walnut-sized balls. Roll each ball in cocoa. Store in the refrigerator or freezer.

Note: See the previous recipe for more detailed instructions.

Smooth Chocolate Fudge

1 cup sugar
¼ cup cocoa powder (optional)
100 g (3½ oz) butter
¼ cup (60 ml/2 fl oz) golden syrup
1 can (400 g/14 oz) sweetened condensed milk (not low-fat)
1 tsp vanilla essence
¼ cup chopped walnuts (optional)

Butter or spray a tin, ideally a loose-bottomed one. Put the sugar and cocoa in a dry bowl, stir well. Cut the butter into 9 cubes and put them on top of the sugar. Add the golden syrup, using a measure that has been dipped in hot water, then tip in the condensed milk.

Microwave on High (100%) power for about 10–12 minutes, stirring every 2 minutes. The fudge is ready when half a teaspoonful dropped in cold water forms a soft ball.

Leave for 2 minutes on the bench, then stir in the vanilla and nuts. Stir for several minutes, until the fudge gets thicker and less shiny. Working quickly before it gets too hard, pour it into the tin. Smooth the surface with a knife.

Leave to set in a cool place, then cut into squares with a sharp knife. Eat straight away, refrigerate for 2–3 days, or freeze for longer.

Melt-in-the-Mouth Chocolate Fudge

If you can master the finer points of making wonderful creamy fudge, your reputation as a good sweet-maker will be assured! Good fudge must be cooked just enough, beaten carefully, and turned out just before it starts to set.

For 64 squares:

3 cups sugar
¼ cup cocoa
¼ tsp cream of tartar
1 cup (250 ml/8 fl oz) milk
50 g (2 oz) butter
1 tsp vanilla essence

Stir the sugar, cocoa and cream of tartar together in a medium-sized pot until no lumps remain. Add the milk and the butter cut into 4 cubes, then cook over a low to moderate heat, stirring all the time, until the sugar melts. There should be no grains of sugar left on the sides of the pot. (If there are, remove them with a spatula or put the lid on for 1–2 minutes.)

Raise the heat until the mixture is bubbling vigorously all over the surface, but is not climbing too high up the sides of the pot! Start to test the fudge after 5 minutes, dropping a half-teaspoonful into a bowl of cold water at least 5 cm (2 in) deep. The fudge is ready when the mixture in the water can be pushed into a soft ball that keeps its shape when lifted out (probably after 8–10 minutes).

Cool the pot until you can hold your hand against the bottom, then beat the mixture constantly with a spatula until you can see the fudge starting to set around the edges. Quickly pour it into a buttered 20 cm (8 in) square container before it sets. Swirl the top, then leave it to finish setting. Cut into 8 squares each way.

Note: If you are new to fudge-making, make half-quantities, reducing the boiling time to about 5 minutes until you get the feel of the mixture. Hard fudge means it has cooked too long, but will still be enjoyed! Fudge that does not set may be warmed with a little sour or fresh cream to make fudge sauce for icecream.

Easy Fudge

This mixture, a cross between fudge and chocolate, is easier to make than other mixtures with a similar smooth, rich texture.

500 g (1 lb 2 oz) chocolate*
1 can (400 g/14 oz) sweetened condensed milk
½ tsp vanilla essence
walnut halves
glacé or maraschino cherries

*Use dark cooking chocolate, Energy chocolate, White, Milk or Dark Melts.

Break up the chocolate if using a block. Heat the condensed milk with the chocolate in a heavy pot over low heat, stirring frequently, until the chocolate has melted and the two are well blended. If you do not have a heavy, flat-bottomed pot, stand a lighter pot in a bigger pan of water and heat this, or combine the chocolate and milk in a bowl resting over the top of a pot half-filled with water.

Add the vanilla and turn into a tin about 20 cm (8 in) square, lined with baking paper or a non-stick liner. Leave overnight or until firm then cut into 36 squares. Top each with a perfect walnut half, a cherry, or any other suitable garnish.

Cover and store out of sight, in a refrigerator or cool place, for up to a week.

Gift-pack your chocolates a short time before you give them away. Place each square in one of the small paper cases available from specialist sweet or cake decorating shops, or put the chocolates straight onto a baking paper liner in a decorative box.

Ginger Fudge   (Photo p. 317)

This is the creamy fudge my sweet-toothed sisters and I used to make on wet Sunday afternoons when we were teenagers.

Fudge-making requires some practice and expertise. If you overcook the fudge, or overbeat it, you finish up with hard, dry, grainy fudge. A candy thermometer may help, but it will not be the answer to all your problems, and is not essential.

2 cups sugar
½ cup (125 ml/4 fl oz) milk
50 g (2 oz) butter
½–1 tsp ground ginger
1 Tbsp golden syrup
½ tsp vanilla essence
2 Tbsp chopped walnuts

Put the sugar, milk and butter into a medium-sized pot. Add the ground ginger and the golden syrup. Bring to the boil over medium heat, stirring occasionally. Do not stir after the mixture starts boiling.

Boil until ¼ teaspoon of the mixture dropped into cold water forms a soft ball that holds its shape, or until a candy thermometer reads 235°F. (They all seem to be calibrated in Fahrenheit.) The fudge is cooked at this stage. Remove from the heat and leave until the pot is cool enough to touch.

Add the vanilla and chopped nuts and beat with a wooden spoon until the fudge shows signs of thickening. Pour it quickly into a buttered sponge roll tin, swirling the top with a knife before it sets hard, if possible. Cut as soon as it is firm, in case you have overcooked it, in which case it will harden so it is difficult to cut neatly.

Chocolate for Dipping

Foods dipped in chocolate look so professional (if you have done a good job) that you will really impress your friends and family! There is nothing like 'hands on' experience to teach you. Start by dipping biscuits or dried apricots, then move on to strawberries, chocolates, etc. The following pointers should help you to get a good result.

- The coating must be the correct consistency. If it is too thick it is hard to work with and will be 'gluggy'. If it is too thin, it will coat the food too lightly, and run off.
- You can coat foods with dark, milk, or white chocolate. Often you need to thin the chocolate you have melted with a little Kremelta (Copha). This makes it flow better and coat the food more smoothly. If you add too much, however, you dilute the chocolate flavour, make the coating too thin, and slow down the setting. A dipped chocolate, for example, will finish up standing on a solidified, spread-out puddle of thin, fragile chocolate. Add a little at a time, dipping something each time to check the consistency.
- If you melt a little Kremelta (Copha) in the bowl before you add the chocolate, it will melt more easily.
- The temperature also affects the consistency of the dip. Melt the dipping mixture in a bowl over hot water. Take it off the heat when ready, but leave the bowl standing over hot water so it does not cool down and thicken while you are dipping.
- Although you can remelt solidified coating for later use, you should try to melt little more chocolate than you need. A bowl, ramekin or cup may be better than a bowl with a wide base. You want to be able to submerge the food you are dipping.
- When you are dipping a chocolate and want a completely smooth surface, stand the uncoated chocolate on a fork with the prongs bent almost at right angles to the handle, or use a purpose-made dipping tool.
- After dipping, hold the coated food above the chocolate dip so that it can drip, then slip it off its holder onto a piece of plastic. When the chocolate has set, peel away the plastic.
- Chocolate sets faster on chilled food, but the food must not be damp. Do not dip warm foods, since the coating will run off them.
- Try dipping biscuits, Brazil nuts, almonds, dried apricots, dehydrated kiwifruit slices, candied peel, dried tangelo slices, truffles, strawberries and chocolates.

Marzipan Chocolates

1 cup (100 g/3¹/₂ oz) ground almonds
1 cup icing sugar
¹/₂ cup castor sugar
1 egg yolk
2 Tbsp strained lemon juice
¹/₄ tsp almond essence (optional)
50–60 blanched almonds (optional)

Combine the ground almonds and sugars in a mixing bowl or food processor. Mix the egg yolk with half the lemon juice and add to the almond mixture with a little almond essence if desired. Add the remaining lemon juice a little at a time until you have a mixture that is easy to work with. Roll the paste into small balls and chill until firm.

Dip in chocolate as described in Chocolate for Dipping. Top each with a blanched almond if desired, and refrigerate until set. Decorate with chocolate squiggles if desired. Store in the refrigerator for up to a month.

Homemade Chocolates

This recipe is one I have worked out to suit beginners. For the most interesting results, use a variety of essences to flavour the cream fillings. When you make fruit-flavoured fillings, you need to add acid as well to bring out the flavour. You can use citric or tartaric acid, but the powder or crystals must be dissolved before adding.

Fillings

2 Tbsp (25 g/1 oz) butter
¹/₄ cup sweetened condensed milk
1¹/₂–2 cups icing sugar
food colouring
flavourings (see below)
citric or tartaric acid

Flavourings

Several of the following:
peppermint essence
butter-rum essence
orange essence
lemon essence
raspberry essence
strawberry essence
vanilla essence

Coating

100 g (3¹/₂ oz) easy-to-melt chocolate
1–2 tsp Kremelta (Copha) (optional)

Melt the butter in a medium-sized pot. Take off the heat as soon as it has melted. Add the condensed milk and stir until mixed. Add 1¹/₂ cups of the icing sugar and stir well to mix it thoroughly. Knead it with clean hands, adding more icing sugar if the mixture is too soft to handle.

Divide the mixture into 3 or 4 balls and make a dent in the top of each ball with your finger. Drop a few drops of food colouring and a few drops of essence into each dent. (Wash and dry your hands carefully when changing fillings, so you do

From the top: Liqueur Balls (p. 311), Melt-in-the-Mouth Chocolate Fudge, Homemade Chocolates, Chocolate-Dipped Apricots

not mix colours and flavours.) If you are using fruit flavours, dissolve ¹/₄ tsp citric or tartaric acid in ¹/₂ tsp water, and mix a few drops with the colours and flavours. Taste small samples, and add extra essence, etc. until the fillings taste the way you like them. Add extra icing sugar at this stage if the fillings have softened when the flavourings were added.

Form each coloured and flavoured ball into a cylinder, wrap each cylinder in cling film and put in the refrigerator (or freezer) to set. Cut into slices when cold.

To make the chocolate coating, see 'Chocolate for Dipping' above. Working quickly, drop a slice of the cold filling into the chocolate, then lift it out onto a piece of plastic until it sets hard.

White Chocolate Truffles

200–250 g (7–9 oz) sponge cake
¹/₂ cup red glacé cherries, roughly chopped
2 Tbsp Kirsch
100 g (3¹/₂ oz) white chocolate, melted

Crumb the cake in a food processor or by hand. Mix the cake crumbs, cherries and Kirsch together, add the melted chocolate and mix well. Roll into small balls.

Coat balls with coconut while still moist, then store in the refrigerator; chill them then roll them in icing sugar just before serving, or chill then dip in white chocolate.

Variation: Replace the Kirsch with sherry and add a little almond essence.

Rum and Raisin Truffles

For 30 truffles:

¹/₄ cup chopped raisins
2 tsp dark rum
150 g (5 oz) cooking chocolate
1 egg yolk, beaten
25 g (1 oz) soft butter
¹/₂ cup icing sugar

Coating

150 g (5 oz) dark chocolate

Soak the raisins in the rum for 10 minutes or longer.

Break the chocolate into pieces and melt it in a bowl over a pan of hot water. Remove the bowl from the pan, and mix in the egg yolk, butter, icing sugar, raisins and rum. Chill until almost set then shape into small balls. Chill until firm.

Dip as described in 'Chocolate for Dipping' (opposite).

Christmas Pudding Truffles

I like these truffles decorated so that they look like mini-Christmas puddings. If you prefer, serve them as plain truffles rolled in coconut. They taste very good both ways.

1 cup currants
2 tsp very finely grated orange or tangelo rind
¼ cup (60 ml/2 fl oz) rum, whisky, brandy or citrus juice
2½ cups (250 g/9 oz) crumbs from a chocolate or plain cake
⅝ cup (125 g/4½ oz) chocolate chips

Decoration
75 g (2½ oz) white chocolate
1 tsp oil
about 6 red cherries
about 6 green cherries

Pour boiling water over the currants in a sieve then put them in a bowl with the rind and the spirit of your choice, or juice from the orange or tangelo.

Leave to stand while you crumb the cake and melt the chocolate chips, heating them until liquid. This will take about 4–5 minutes on Medium (50%) power in a microwave, or a little longer in a large metal bowl over a pot of hot, but not boiling, water. When the chocolate has melted, stir in the crumbs, then the currant mixture.

Mix well, then roll into small walnut-sized balls, or balls that will fit nicely into small foil or fluted paper confectionery cups. (Roll in coconut if not decorating further.) Refrigerate until cold.

Warm pieces of white chocolate with the oil in a clean bowl, either in the microwave for 3 minutes on Medium (50%) power or over hot water as before. Stir until smooth.

Chop the cherries, making the red pieces chunky, and the green pieces pointed like leaves.

Spoon a little of the warm white chocolate on top of each little pudding, helping it to look as if it is flowing, if necessary. This takes a little practice, but is mainly a matter of having the truffles cold and the melted chocolate semi-liquid. Before the white chocolate sets, put about 3 little red berries in the middle of the icing, and a couple of green leaves around them.

Rich Mocha Truffles

These soft-textured truffles contain only coconut to firm them up. Make them small, and keep them in the refrigerator.

100 g (3½ oz) butter
2 cups icing sugar
¼ cup cocoa
½ cup chopped sultanas
¾ cup fine coconut
1 tsp instant coffee
1 Tbsp sherry or rum
extra coconut for rolling

Mix the softened butter with the sifted icing sugar and cocoa.

Chop the sultanas with a wet knife. Add to the butter mixture with the coconut and the coffee dissolved in the sherry or rum. For easier handling, chill the mixture until firmer.

Form into small balls with a teaspoon, and roll in more coconut. Refrigerate until firm, then put in a container. Keep in the refrigerator or freezer.

From the top: Fruity Nutty Balls (p. 316), Peanut Butter Squares, Tipplers' Treats, Orange Fudge Squares

Dried Milk Truffles

I make these (and all my other truffles) in the food processor, but you can of course mix everything in a large bowl. For recipes like this, the amount of liquid required to mix the truffles to a firm dough will vary with the temperature, the fruit used, etc. Always add the liquid after all the other ingredients have been combined.

100 g (3½ oz) butter, softened
2 cups full cream milk powder
½ cup cocoa
1 cup icing sugar
1–1½ cups sultanas, chopped
½–1 tsp almond or rum essence
1 tsp vanilla essence
3 Tbsp milk, sherry or brandy
coconut or cocoa for coating

Soften the butter, add the milk powder, cocoa and icing sugar, and mix in a food processor or bowl.

If you use the metal blade of your food processor, the fruit will be chopped as it is mixed in; if you are mixing by hand, chop the fruit with a sharp knife. Add the dried fruit, then whatever essences you like, and mix well.

Add the liquid a tablespoon at a time, mixing until the dry ingredients are dampened enough to form a firm dough. Roll into balls the size of small walnuts, and coat with coconut or cocoa.

Refrigerate uncovered on a tray until firm, then store in jars in the refrigerator.

Variation: Leave out the dried fruit, and shape each truffle around a well-drained maraschino cherry. If you have gone this far, you may decide to take one final step and dip each truffle in melted chocolate (see 'Chocolate for Dipping' above).

Tipplers' Treats

These little truffles have a definite flavour from the spirits that are used in them. They contain a smaller proportion of butter to biscuit crumbs than richer truffles.

50 g (2 oz) butter
1 rounded household Tbsp golden syrup
¼ cup (60 ml/2 fl oz) whisky, brandy, rum or sherry
¾ cup icing sugar
1 Tbsp cocoa
1 packet (200 g/7 oz) wine or malt biscuits, crumbled
cocoa or icing sugar to dust

Heat the butter until it is liquid, then add the golden syrup (measured with a hot, wet spoon) and the spirit of your choice. Stir in the sifted icing sugar and cocoa, then crumb the biscuits very finely, add them to the mixture and stir thoroughly to combine.

If the mixture seems dry, add a little extra melted butter. If it is too moist to handle, add more crumbs or coconut, or chill the mixture before rolling it. (The mixture varies from batch to batch, and judgement is called for.)

Roll into small balls and chill until firm. Coat with cocoa or icing sugar just before serving or arranging in a box.

Jaffa Truffles

Chocolate and orange rind give these little truffles a flavour that should please all jaffa lovers!

1 cup (dried) currants
2 tsp very finely grated orange rind
¼ cup (60 ml/2 fl oz) rum, brandy or orange juice
2½ cups chocolate cake crumbs
½ cup chocolate chips, melted
coconut, cocoa or icing sugar to dust

Plump up the currants by pouring boiling water over them in a sieve. Dry them on paper towels then put them in a bowl with the rind and the spirits or orange juice.

Crumb the cake in a food processor or by hand. Add the crumbs and the melted chocolate to the currant mixture. Mix well, then roll into small walnut-sized balls. Roll the balls in coconut, cocoa or icing sugar. Store in the refrigerator or freezer.

Wendy's Brandy Balls

This recipe makes a large number of little balls which are a useful standby, especially over the Christmas season. Their texture varies depending on the method used. If you have fine, even crumbs, the texture of the biscuits will be fine and firm, the mixture will be drier and it will form neat balls. If you have large crumbs, the mixture will be softer and the balls will tend to be irregular. Both are delicious!

1 packet (200 g/7 oz) wine biscuits
200 g (7 oz) butter
½ cup cocoa
¾ cup coconut
2 cups icing sugar
1 tsp instant coffee
3 Tbsp brandy
3 Tbsp sherry
½ cup sultanas, chopped
¼ cup finely chopped walnuts
coconut

Crush the biscuits by putting them in a plastic or paper bag and using a rolling pin, or break them up about a quarter at a time and whiz them in a food processor.

Cream, but don't melt, the butter. When light and fluffy, add the cocoa, coconut, icing sugar and instant coffee. Beat with a wooden spoon until well blended, then add the liquid, sultanas (use a wet knife to

chop them) and walnuts. Then add the biscuit crumbs.

Form the mixture into small balls, roll in your hands until round, then roll in coconut. If the mixture is too soft to work with, chill it until the butter hardens.

Stand the brandy balls on a tray with a little extra coconut, in the refrigerator, until they have set, then place them in an airtight tin or jar. Leave for 24 hours for the flavours to blend. Store in the refrigerator. Serve after dinner, with a cup of coffee.

Orange Fudge Squares

In warm weather hide these in the fridge and enjoy them chilled.

250 g (9 oz) wine biscuits, finely crushed
100 g (3½ oz) butter
200 g (7 oz) sweetened condensed milk (half a can)
finely grated rind of 1 orange
2 Tbsp orange juice or orange liqueur
about 36 walnut halves (optional)

Crush the biscuits in a food processor or in a plastic bag with a rolling pin.

Melt the butter, add the condensed milk and mix well in a bowl or food processor. Stir in the rind and orange juice or liqueur. Add the crumbs, then press the mixture into a 20 cm (8 in) square tin lined with baking paper.

If you like, press freshly shelled walnut halves into the top of the warm fudge, in 6 rows. Refrigerate until set, then cut into 36 squares. Store in the refrigerator or freezer.

Peanut Butter Squares

These make a good addition to a box of mixed confections.

100 g (3½ oz) butter, cubed
½ cup smooth or crunchy peanut butter
1 cup wine biscuit crumbs
1 cup icing sugar
¼ tsp each almond and vanilla essence
100 g (3½ oz) white chocolate
2 tsp butter

Microwave the butter and peanut butter on High (100%) power for 2 minutes then stir thoroughly. (This can also be done in a pot over low heat.) Add the biscuit crumbs, icing sugar and essences. Mix well and press into a shallow pan about 20 x 30 cm (8 x 12 in) lined with baking paper. (Don't use the whole tin if you want thicker, smaller squares.) Chill.

Using gentle heat, melt the white chocolate and the second measure of butter until they mix together smoothly. Spread over the chilled mixture. Cut into small squares before the topping sets.

Peanut Honey Balls

This mixture is particularly nice to work with and is very popular with children who like peanutty sweets.

1/4 cup honey
1/2 cup smooth peanut butter
about 3/4 cup dried milk powder (non-fat or full-cream)
about 1/4 cup finely chopped roasted peanuts

Mix these balls in a food processor if you have one. If not, mix in a bowl.

Warm the honey until it is quite runny. Add the peanut butter and mix until smooth, then stir in milk powder until you have a mixture that is easy to work with.

Knead well with your hands to get it really smooth. Roll into balls, then flatten the balls slightly, pressing one or both sides in the finely chopped peanuts. The mixture will harden somewhat on standing but will never become very hard.

Variation: Coat the shaped, flattened balls with melted chocolate; see 'Chocolate for Dipping' (p. 312).

Fruity Nutty Balls (Photo p. 314)

These have a lovely fresh flavour which bought fruit confections seldom achieve.

1 cup sultanas
1 cup walnuts
1 cup chopped dates
1 cup cornflakes or malted wheatflakes
orange juice, sherry or brandy
1/2 cup desiccated coconut
1 tsp cinnamon

Pour boiling water over the sultanas in a sieve, drain well, then chop roughly in a food processor. Add the walnuts and roughly chopped, pitted dates and process again to chop into smaller pieces, but do not purée. Add the cornflakes or other breakfast cereal, process again and moisten with the liquid of your choice, until the mixture is soft enough to form into balls.

Roll into small balls with wet hands and drop into a bowl or plastic bag containing the coconut and cinnamon. Shake to coat. Refrigerate or freeze.

Plain Toffee and Peanut Toffee

Both of these toffees are good to eat yourself or give to someone special. Always keep toffee in airtight jars to stop it getting sticky.

1 cup sugar
1/4 cup (60 ml/2 fl oz) water
1 Tbsp wine vinegar
2 Tbsp (25 g/1 oz) butter
1 cup roasted peanuts (for peanut toffee)

Put the sugar, water and vinegar in a small pot over low heat. Stir just until the sugar dissolves, then add the butter and raise the heat. Heat so bubbles cover the surface but the toffee does not boil over or brown. (Do not stir at all after the sugar has dissolved.)

Every few minutes put a few drops of toffee into a dish of cold water. When a cold drop will break when you bite it, the toffee is cooked enough. Raise the heat a little until the toffee turns light brown, like a caramel.

For plain toffee, drop little rounds onto a buttered oven tray.

For peanut toffee, warm the peanuts in the microwave on High (100%) power for 45 seconds. Tip the warm peanuts into the pot of toffee and stir with a dessertspoon. Drop teaspoonfuls into buttered mini-muffin pans or pour onto buttered trays and mark in squares when partly set. Break when cold and hard.

Store in an airtight jar as soon as the toffee is cold and hard.

Caramel Suckers

1/2 cup white sugar
red food colouring (optional)
raspberry or strawberry flavouring (optional)
ice-block sticks

Rub a metal tray or sponge roll tin with butter and have some ice-block sticks ready.

Sprinkle the sugar into a clean, dry frypan. Hold the pan over medium heat until the sugar melts. Watch that the temperature is not too hot, or the sugar will brown in some places before it melts in others. You can tilt the pan to move the sugar, but do not stir it at all.

When the sugar has melted, and is light golden brown, add 2–3 drops of red food colouring, and a few drops of flavouring if you like. Tilt the pan and drop teaspoons of toffee onto the greased tray. Put the sticks on the hot toffee, and drop on more toffee to cover the sticks.

Wrap the suckers in thin plastic so they do not go sticky.

Note: Fill the pan with hot water to clean it. Be very careful not to burn your fingers when you make toffee.

Peppermint Chews

These lollies are a variation of an old recipe. One of my friends has the recipe for them handwritten in an old cookbook, under the name Stick-jawettes! Try them if you like something chewy and different!

1 Tbsp butter
2 Tbsp sugar
1/4 cup golden syrup
3/4–1 cup skim milk powder
1 tsp peppermint essence

Heat the butter, sugar and syrup gently, stirring only until the sugar has dissolved. Boil the mixture until quarter-teaspoonfuls dropped into a bowl of cold water form a soft ball. (Keep the heat low so the mixture does not darken as it boils, or the sweets will taste burnt.)

Take the pot off the heat, add 3/4 cup of milk powder and the essence, and stir with a wooden spoon until it is thoroughly mixed and cool enough to touch. If the mixture seems very soft, add the rest of the milk powder.

Knead the mixture until it is smooth, then roll it into 2 or 3 long, thin sausages. Cut the sausages into little pieces with buttered kitchen scissors or a buttered knife or break off pieces with your fingers, roll them into balls, then squeeze the balls between your finger and thumb.

When cool, store in an airtight screw-top jar.

Christmas Candies

I use this recipe with great success to make jars of rum-flavoured toffees, twisted red and white raspberry-flavoured candy canes, and modelled toffee animals.

Because the toffee must be handled while warm and partly set, you should make several small batches rather than one large one.

1/2 cup sugar
2 Tbsp water
2 Tbsp honey
2 Tbsp butter
rum or raspberry essence
red food colouring (optional)

Put the sugar, water, honey and butter in a small pot and bring to the boil, stirring frequently. As soon as it boils, stop stirring and lower the heat. Heat gently, without stirring, until a little toffee dropped in cold water forms a hard ball that breaks cleanly (or snaps) when you bite it. If you heat it quickly the toffee will brown before it reaches this stage.

Take the toffee off the heat and let it cool a little. Add about 1/2 tsp rum or raspberry essence, or other essence. Swirl the toffee in the pot to mix the essence through it. Do NOT stir it. Tip it out onto a well-buttered, shallow plate. If you are making candy canes, tip half of it out and add red colouring to the half remaining in the pan, then tip the coloured toffee into a second buttered dish.

Ginger Fudge (p. 312), Peppermint Chews

As soon as the toffee has cooled enough to handle, pick it up with buttered hands. Pull it into a long string, put the ends together and pull again. Repeat at least 10 times. It becomes more evenly shaped as pulling progresses. Twist each string or strand.

To make toffees, cut the long strand into short lengths with buttered kitchen scissors to make small, pillow-shaped toffees. As soon as these are cold put them in an airtight jar.

To make candy canes, twist together 2 pulled strands, one red and the other light-coloured, to form a rope. Cut into suitable lengths and bend to candy cane shape. Wrap each in airtight cling film or seal in plastic bags.

To make toffee animals, work fast. Shape the strands after pulling them. Cut toes, mouths, ears, etc. with kitchen scissors. Poke holes or stick on small balls for eyes, spots, etc. Pieces of toffee pressed together while fairly hot stick better than pieces pressed together when cooler. These sometimes pop apart when the animal is cold.

When you start making animals, shape a coiled, ready-to-strike snake as your first effort – then progress to lizards, etc.

Cinnamon Popcorn

For 6 cups popcorn:

Put ¼ cup popping corn and 1 Tbsp canola oil in a large pot or pan, preferably with a glass lid. Cover and heat, shaking the closed pot every 30 seconds or so. After a few minutes the corn will start to pop. Turn the heat to low, and keep the lid on to stop hot corn popping out! Shake the pot at intervals. When all the popping has stopped, open the pot.

Mix ¼ cup icing sugar and ¾ tsp cinnamon. Shake over hot, buttered popcorn with ¼ cup each sultanas and roasted peanuts. Mix well.

Spiced Nuts

These nuts are particularly useful during the holiday season. Make enough for yourself, as well as for gifts.

2 Tbsp egg white
1 Tbsp honey
½ tsp salt
1 tsp ground ginger
1 tsp mixed spice
3 cups mixed raw nuts
1 Tbsp castor sugar

Turn the oven to 150°C (300°F). Beat the egg white slightly before measuring it. Warm the honey until liquid, then mix it with the egg white and the next 3 ingredients. Add the nuts, stirring to coat evenly.

Spread in a lightly buttered or sprayed roasting dish (or on a non-stick Teflon liner), sprinkle with the castor sugar, and bake for 15–20 minutes, until a halved nut looks beige. (The nuts will not be crisp until they have cooled.) Remove from the oven, cool slightly, and stir to separate, if necessary.

Pack in screw-topped jars with airtight tops when cool. Attach a label and decorate lids if desired.

See also

Kirsten's Biscotti, p. 276

Custard Kisses, p. 277

Christmas Tree Biscuits, p. 278

Lebkuchen, p. 278

'Heart of Glass' Biscuits, p. 279

Gingerbread Houses, p. 280

Almond Rosettes, p. 281

Super Slices, pp. 288–295

Refreshing Drinks

We all need plenty to drink, and although we know that water is a perfectly good thirst-quencher, we often like it 'jazzed up' a little. I have hazy memories of days when the man behind the counter of a little, dark store beside a sportsground mixed up his own fizzy drinks to sell to thirsty kids. I have always made cordials and other drinks 'from scratch', often using fruit from our garden to flavour them, partly because I like to know exactly what is in our drinks, and partly because I object to the price of commercially made, sweetened fizzy water. If you have similar feelings, you may like to try some of these recipes.

'Loaves and Fishes' Cordial

I make this drink with oranges, tangelos, mandarins and grapefruit. It takes only a few minutes, and all variations seem popular. Use your common sense regarding the size of the fruit. You will need several mandarins or 2 tangelos to replace 1 orange. From 1 orange you get 16 large glasses of orange drink, with a good orange flavour. You can see how the drink got its name!

For 3 cups cordial:
1½ cups (375 ml/12 fl oz) water
2 cups sugar
rind and juice of 1 orange
1½ tsp citric acid
½ tsp Epsom salts

Microwave the water and 1 cup of sugar on High (100%) power for 2 minutes, or bring it to the boil in a medium-sized pot on the stove, to dissolve the sugar.

Remove the coloured skin from the orange with a potato peeler. Chop this very finely in a food processor with the remaining sugar, the citric acid and the Epsom salts.

Tip the orange mixture into the syrup and heat for another 2 minutes, or until boiling. Add the orange juice, then strain into a second container to get rid of all the rind.

If you are going to drink the cordial in a few days, pour it into any suitable bottle. If you want to keep it for longer, bring it to the boil again and pour it into bottles that have been washed with hot water, then rinsed with boiling water. Top immediately with screw-tops that have been standing in boiling water. Dip bottle tops and lids in melted wax if you think the tops may not be airtight.

Dilute the cordial with water or soda water when required, using 1 part cordial to 4 parts water, or a little more or less according to taste.

Lemon Cordial

Variation: If you don't have a food processor, boil all the sugar with the water, then add the very finely grated rind with the acid and Epsom salts. Because a lot of the flavour comes from the rind, you will need to grate every bit of coloured rind, or use 2 oranges.

Berry Cordials

This recipe is one I use for wild blackberry cordial, but you can use other berries, fresh or frozen, to make similar cordials.

8 cups blackberries
1 cup (250 ml/8 fl oz) water
sugar
citric acid

Crush the berries using a food processor or potato masher. Heat them with the water for 30 minutes in a bowl over boiling water, stirring occasionally. Strain through muslin or other cloth into a sieve or colander. Do not squeeze the bag. Leave overnight.

The next day measure the juice and add 1 cup sugar and 1 level measuring tsp citric acid to every 2 cups juice. Stir until dissolved, without heating if possible. Pour into small, clean glass soft-drink bottles with screw tops, leaving 3 cm (1¼ in) headspace. (Use bottles of the same height.) Put cleaned screw tops on loosely.

Stand the bottles on a rack in a deep pot, with water up to the level of the cordial. Heat to 85°C (190°F). At this temperature little bubbles form on the sides of the pot, then burst on the surface of the water. (The surface of the water should not be heaving with large bubbles.) Keep at this temperature for 20 minutes. Lift out the bottles and screw the tops on tightly. When cool, dip the bottle tops and necks of the bottles in melted wax to make quite sure no air can get in. Store in a cool, dark place.

Once the cordial has been opened drink it within 2–3 days, or store it in the refrigerator for up to 6–8 weeks. Try the syrup, undiluted, drizzled over icecream, plain or with bananas.

Note: For blackcurrant cordial use 1 cup (250 ml/8 fl oz) water to 500 g (1 lb 2 oz) fruit.

Lemon Cordial

This cordial is good with iced water, soda water, iced tea, gin, whisky and rum. If you are making it only for adult use, you may like to add an extra teaspoon of each of the acids.

4 cups (1 litre/32 fl oz) water
5 cups sugar
rind and juice of 4 lemons
5 tsp citric acid
3 tsp tartaric acid
3 tsp Epsom salts

If you have a food processor, peel the yellow skin from 2 or 3 lemons with a potato peeler and chop them with a cup of the sugar using the metal chopping blade. Otherwise grate them, removing most of the coloured skin but no white.

Bring the water, sugar and grated rind to the boil, then remove from the heat and add the juice and the carefully measured acids and Epsom salts (use level measuring spoons). Stir until dissolved, then strain into clean glass soft-drink bottles. Screw on the tops tightly.

Store in the refrigerator. For long storage, bottle immediately, cover tightly, then dip the tops in melted candle wax when cool.

'Cold Cure'

This is a wonderful nightcap. Whether it cures your cold or not, it is sure to make you feel better.

1 Tbsp brown sugar
thinly peeled rind and juice of ½ a lemon
½ cup (125 ml/4 fl oz) water
1–2 cloves (optional)
1–2 Tbsp whisky (optional)

Measure all the ingredients into a mug. Microwave on High (100%) power for 30–45 seconds, until hot but not boiling.

V9 Juice

Go one better than the canners who make juice from eight vegetables! The redder the vegetables, the better the colour.

1 kg (2 lb 3 oz) ripe, red tomatoes,
  quartered
1–2 cups grated carrot
1/2–1 cup finely sliced celery
1 small beetroot, grated
1/2 red pepper
1/2 red onion
1/2 cup grated zucchini
1 cup thinly sliced greens (silverbeet,
  lettuce, etc.)
large sprig parsley
1 1/2 tsp salt
1/2 slice white or wholemeal bread

Combine all the ingredients in a large, covered microwave dish or pot. Cook on High (100%) power or simmer until the vegetables are soft, up to 15–20 minutes. Purée in a blender or food processor, then sieve. Refrigerate for up to 3 days or freeze for later use. Pour over ice to serve.

Elderflower Cordial

Collect elderflowers in late spring and enjoy this cordial over the next month or so. Add ice and a slice of lemon, and you have a lovely drink for a summer day.

12–20 heads of elderflowers
1 1/2 cups (375 ml/12 fl oz) cold water
1 1/2 cups sugar
1 1/2 tsp citric acid

Pick the elderflowers from wild land, preferably not too close to busy roads. Put the flowers in water as you would any other bunch of flowers. Make the cordial as soon as possible.

Using the tines of a fork, push most of the flowers off the stalks. Get rid of as many green stalks as possible, but do not fuss if a few remain.

Pour the cold water over the flowers and leave them to stand for at least 8 hours, or up to 24 hours. (They will brown if warm or hot water is used.)

Strain through a fine sieve or a piece of coarsely woven cotton into a jug or bowl. Add the sugar then the citric acid (use level standard measures) and stir or whisk at intervals until the sugar dissolves. Strain again if necessary, into bottles cleaned in detergent and water then rinsed in very hot water. Close with screw tops.

Store in the refrigerator for up to a month, diluting it to the strength you like using about 5 parts water or soda water to 1 part cordial.

Variation: After you have tried the recipe once, make it again with more or less sugar and citric acid, according to your taste.

Boston Cream

I remember a shop that made and served this drink to children! It is an old-fashioned homemade instant fizzy drink which you should not expect to be the same as commercially bottled fizz! The drink bubbles for just a few seconds after the baking soda is added so it should be drunk very quickly – don't serve it in large glasses.

1 cup sugar
2 cups (500 ml/16 fl oz) water
1 Tbsp tartaric acid
1 tsp lemon essence
1 lightly beaten egg white (optional)
plain or whipped cream (optional)
baking soda

Heat the sugar and water until the sugar dissolves. Remove from the heat and add the carefully measured tartaric acid and lemon essence.

If you like, beat an egg white until foamy but not stiff, mix it into the cool drink mixture, and bottle it. (The egg is supposed to trap the bubbles later, but the drink bubbles quite well without it.)

To serve, shake the cordial bottle then pour about 1 Tbsp into a small glass. Add about 1 tsp cream or a squirt of aerosol cream if you like, top up the glass with cold water, then add a pinch (about 1/16 tsp) of baking soda. Drink while bubbly!

Note: Experiment until you get the proportions of cordial to liquid just right. Try it with and without the cream and see which you like best. It is too sour without the baking soda, which neutralises some of the acid, forming bubbles of carbon dioxide.

Soya Milk

It is not difficult to make an inexpensive and nutritious 'milk' from soya beans. One cup of dried beans yields 6 cups of liquid, which may be used for drinking 'straight', making flavoured cold drinks, hot chocolate drinks, in baking, and even for milk puddings.

The flavour is not the same as cows' milk, but it is a great help to those who cannot or do not want to drink cows' milk.

(Soya milk needs added calcium and vitamin B12 to give it a nutritive value similar to that of cows' milk. See the note at the end of the recipe.)

Follow the instructions exactly; the milk will have a strong flavour if boiling water is not used during the grinding.

For about 6 cups:
1 cup dried soya beans
4 cups (1 litre/32 fl oz) lukewarm water
7 cups (1.75 litres/56 fl oz) boiling water

Flavourings
2–3 Tbsp honey, malt or brown sugar
1 tsp vanilla
about 1/2 tsp salt

Pour the lukewarm water over the soya beans and leave to stand for 2–4 hours, until the beans have softened right through. Change the water, and rub the beans to halve them, if you are in a hurry. Leave the beans to soak for longer if you like.

Drain the beans and pour over 1 cup (250 ml/8 fl oz) boiling water. Rinse a food processor with hot water, then discard the soaking and rinsing waters. Put half the hot, drained beans in the food processor. Process to chop finely, then add 2 cups boiling water and process until very finely chopped. Pour into a large sieve lined with a clean cloth, over a large bowl. Repeat with the remaining beans.

Tip the beans from the cloth back into the processor, process again to chop more finely, then add the remaining 2 cups (500 ml/16 fl oz) boiling water and process about a minute longer. Pour into the cloth-lined sieve. Squeeze and twist the bag to get out as much liquid as possible, then heat all the strained liquid in a microwave until it boils, or in a covered bowl over boiling water for 30 minutes.

Add extra boiling water to make up to 6 cups if necessary, then stir in the flavourings, varying quantities to taste. Cover and refrigerate for up to 4 days.

Fortified Soya Milk
To fortify soya milk so it is about the same composition as cows' milk, add to the warm liquid with the flavourings:

2 Tbsp oil
1 Tbsp (about 2 g) powdered calcium
  carbonate
1 tablet (25 µg) vitamin B12, crushed

Buy the powdered calcium carbonate and vitamin B12 from a chemist. Shake the bottle of soya milk before using it.

Note: In 2000, homemade soya milk, without flavourings or additions, cost about 30 cents per litre.

Chocolate Syrup

Keep this syrup in the refrigerator to use as the base for different drinks.

1/2 cup cocoa
1/2 cup sugar
3/4 cup (185 ml/6 fl oz) water
1 tsp vanilla essence

Measure the cocoa and sugar into a medium-sized pot and mix well, making sure there are no lumps. Add the water and vanilla, stir well and bring to the boil. Boil for 2 minutes then remove from the heat.

Cool to room temperature, store in a bottle or jar and refrigerate for up to a week.

Iced Mocha

A cooling, milk-based drink for a hot day!

For 1 serving:
1 tsp instant coffee
1 Tbsp hot water
1 Tbsp Chocolate Syrup (above)
1 cup (250 ml/8 fl oz) milk, chilled
4–6 ice-blocks

Stir the instant coffee and hot water together in a medium-sized jug. Add the chocolate syrup and chilled milk and stir or whisk until combined. Pour over ice-blocks into a tall glass and serve with a straw.

Chocolate Egg Nog

A meal in a glass – just the thing for an adult who needs some TLC.

For 2 servings:
3 Tbsp Chocolate Syrup (above)
1½ cups (375 ml/12 fl oz) milk
1 egg, separated
few grains of salt
1 Tbsp sugar
1–2 Tbsp rum (optional)

Beat together the chocolate syrup, milk and egg yolk. Heat until the mixture bubbles around the edges and thickens slightly. Do not boil.

Beat the egg whites with a few grains of salt until foamy. Add the sugar and beat until the peaks turn over.

Strain the hot chocolate mixture into the beaten egg white and whisk again until the whole mixture is evenly coloured. Stir in the rum.

Chocolate Spider

You may find that adults enjoy this as well as children.

1 scoop chocolate icecream
Coca Cola, chilled

Measure the icecream into a tall glass. Pour over chilled Coca Cola and whisk with a fork until the mixture is fluffy. Serve with a long straw.

Variation: For a Jaffa Spider, pour chilled orange-flavoured fizzy drink over chocolate icecream.

Kirsten's Mulled Wine

Mulled wine makes a good party drink in cold weather, as long as you take care not to boil the wine.

For 30 150 ml (5 oz) glasses:
1 cup (250 ml/8 fl oz) water
2½ cups sugar
2 Tbsp whole cloves

6 cinnamon sticks, broken
2–3 crushed nutmegs
rind of 3 lemons
rind of 2 oranges
4 cups (1 litre/32 fl oz) orange or other juice
1 cask (3 litres/96 fl oz) red wine

Bring the first 5 ingredients to the boil. Peel the rind from the lemons and oranges and add to the syrup. Cover and simmer gently for 15 minutes, then strain. Mix the syrup and juice together, ready to reheat when needed. Use 1 part of this to 2–3 parts wine.

If you are making mulled wine for a large number of people, combine all the wine with all the juice mixture and heat it all at once, to hot drink temperature, but not to boiling. If you are serving it to three or four people, mix enough to fill a 4–8 cup jug (1–2 litres/32–64 fl oz). It is very convenient if you can warm the jug in the microwave. For one or two people, mix and heat the mulled wine by the glass.

Remember to provide paper serviettes to make it easy for your guests to hold the hot glasses.

FROZEN TREATS

Homemade frozen 'ice-lollies' are always popular in hot weather. Use plastic moulds and wooden ice-block sticks to make them, then remove them from the moulds and store, wrapped in plastic in the freezer, until required.

Orange Juicicles

Mix concentrated orange juice with about three-quarters as much water as is needed to reconstitute it to juice consistency. I use 1 Tbsp bottled concentrated orange juice with 3–4 Tbsp water. For every ½ cup of liquid, allow ¼ tsp gelatine softened in 2 tsp cold water, then warmed until it dissolves. Stir into the juice, pour into moulds, and freeze quickly. If you use regular strength juice, sweetened it a little, then add gelatine in the same proportions as above.

Jelly Quixicles

I make these in two flavour combinations, combining pineapple jelly and banana Quik, or strawberry Quik with raspberry or strawberry jelly. I add milk powder for extra smoothness and protein.

2 Tbsp jelly crystals
½ cup (125 ml/4 fl oz) boiling water
½ cup (125 ml/4 fl oz) milk
1 tsp banana or strawberry Quik
2 Tbsp dried milk powder (optional)

Measure the jelly crystals into a small bowl. Add the boiling water and stir until dissolved, then add the milk, and stir or whisk in the Quik and milk powder. Pour into 5 or 6 moulds and freeze quickly.

Fruity Ice-Blocks

Dilute fruit cordials to make a stronger drink than usual, for best texture adding gelatine in the same proportions as for Orange Juicicles above. For milky fruit ice-blocks, use part water, then part milk, judging the quantities by taste. Add gelatine as in Orange Juicicles.

Milkshake Ice-Blocks

Most kids love these, and they are easy, cheap and nutritious. They are based on a concentrated milk mixture.

½ tsp gelatine
1 Tbsp cold water
4 tsp sugar
½–1 tsp vanilla essence
½ cup (125 ml/4 fl oz) milk
¼ cup full-cream milk powder

Put the gelatine in a small glass bowl, add the water and leave to stand for 2–3 minutes to soften the gelatine. Microwave or warm over hot water until the gelatine melts, then stir in the sugar and ½ tsp vanilla. Add the milk, then whisk in the milk powder until the mixture is smooth. Taste. If it does not taste like a milk shake, add more vanilla.

Pour into 4 moulds or more ice-cube holders and freeze, inserting sticks when half-frozen if desired.

Banana Pops

Purée banana in a food processor, measure and add about half the volume of yoghurt, and sweeten to taste with icing sugar, or apricot or raspberry jam if you like. Add vanilla essence if you have not added jam. Spoon or pour into moulds and freeze.

See also

Golden Whirl, p. 14

Malted Banana Float, p. 14

Orange and Banana Cream, p. 14

Orange Julia, p. 14

Sal's Special, p. 14

Strawberry Dream Cream, p. 14

Tofu Temptation, p. 14

Banana Egg Nog, p. 15

Banana Smoothie, p. 15

Golden Morning, p. 15

Kiwi Smoothie, p. 15

Orange Milk Shake, p. 15

Prunaroonie, p. 15

Raspberry Smoothie, p. 15

Tofu Shake, p. 15

Jams and Jellies

These days few of us grow much fruit, and are not concerned about using seasonal excesses the way our grandmothers were. Our supermarkets stock a wide range of everyday jams at reasonable prices. As a result, the 'bulk' jam and jelly-making that was part of our grandmothers' lives is not part of ours. This does not mean, however, that some of us, at least, do not make jams and jellies in small quantities. We often use interesting and unusual fruits that commercial manufacturers do not use. We use a high proportion of fruit and make jams with intense flavours. We put them in beautiful jars, with homemade labels, enjoy them on our own tables and give them to our friends, with pride, as special gifts. Best of all, perhaps, we get a great deal of pleasure from the fruits of our labours!

Lime Marmalade

This marmalade has a most distinctive, definite flavour.

Since relatively small amounts of fruit are used, I slice it with a very sharp knife instead of mincing or blending it. In the past I have been disappointed with lime marmalade prepared in a food processor or blender.

The recipe takes less than an hour from start to finish. It doesn't matter what size cup you use, as long as you use the same measure for everything.

1½ cups thinly sliced limes
½ cup thinly sliced lemons
6 cups (1.5 litres/48 fl oz) water
4 cups sugar

Halve the limes lengthways, then slice them as thinly as possible with a very sharp stainless steel knife. Pack the slices into the cup measure so there are no large air gaps, but don't squeeze them in.

Slice and measure the lemons similarly, discarding the seeds. Put the fruit in a large pot, add the water, and simmer uncovered until the peel is tender, about 30 minutes.

Add the sugar and boil briskly. Test as for Kumquat Marmalade. When cooked, leave to cool for 15 minutes, then stir to mix the peel evenly through the marmalade. Pour into sterilised bottles and top with sterilised screwtop lids immediately, or put in jars with plastic tops and refrigerate until eaten.

Kumquat Marmalade, Lime Marmalade

Kumquat Marmalade

Kumquats are small, round or oval citrus fruit, with a strong, distinctive flavour. They make really delicious, slightly bitter, rather tart marmalade, with a strong orange flavour.

1 kg (2 lb 3 oz) kumquats
8 cups (2 litres/64 fl oz) water
35 g (1¼ oz) powdered jam-setting mix
  (½ packet)
2 kg (4 lb 7 oz) sugar

Scrub the kumquats with a soft brush. Process them to a purée in 3 or 4 batches, without adding any water, then put the pulped fruit into a coarse sieve over a large bowl.

Measure out the water, use some of it to rinse out the food processor, and tip it through the sieve with most of the remaining water. Press as much pulp through the sieve as possible, then wrap the remaining pulp and chopped seeds in a handkerchief-sized piece of coarsely woven cloth, form it into a partly filled bag around the kumquat mixture, and tie firmly with string.

Put the strained pulp, all the water, and the filled cloth bag in a large pot or jam pan, and leave to stand for 1–2 hours, then heat to a rolling boil and boil for 30 minutes. Remove the bag, squeeze out as much liquid as possible, then add the jam-setting mix to the liquid and boil 5 minutes longer, stirring several times. Add the sugar, raise the heat, and stir until it boils. Boil uncovered for 15–30 minutes, until a tablespoon of the marmalade on a clean, dry saucer, left to stand for 2–3 minutes, forms a skin that wrinkles when you draw your finger over it.

Turn off the heat, remove any scum with a spoon, and pour the marmalade into hot jars. Top tightly with metal screwtop lids that have been soaked in boiling water for 5 minutes.

Note: For a less bitter marmalade, remove the seeds before puréeing the fruit. If you do this, don't bother to sieve the pulp, or boil it in the bag.

Seville Orange Marmalade

Seville oranges are bright orange and very sour – they make delicious sour marmalade that is also bright orange. If you buy them, make your marmalade straight away, since the oranges lose their special sourness and slight bitterness as they ripen, and don't make such good marmalade.

1 kg (2 lb 3 oz) Seville oranges
juice of 2 lemons
8 cups (2 litres/64 fl oz) water
2 kg (4 lb 7 oz) sugar

Quarter the fruit and cut away any blemishes and the central pithy and seedy part. Boil the pips, etc. in a pot with some of the measured water for about an hour then strain and discard the solids, and add the water to the soaking fruit.

Slice or process the quartered fruit, add the lemon juice and all the water, and leave it to stand overnight.

The next day boil the mixture quite vigorously in a large, uncovered pot or jam pan until it is soft. Add the sugar, stir until it dissolves, then proceed as for Kumquat Marmalade.

Note: Seville oranges may be quartered, pulped or sliced, then frozen until you want to make marmalade. Always use a little less sugar and water when making marmalade (or jam) from frozen fruit.

Blackberry Jelly

Sometimes wild blackberries have too many seeds to make good jam. Blackberry jelly requires a little more work, but it tastes and looks marvellous.

4 cups blackberries
1/2 cup (125 ml/4 fl oz) water
sugar

Crush the blackberries in a medium-sized pot and add the water. Bring to the boil and simmer for 10–15 minutes. Pour through a sieve into a clean bowl and leave to drain overnight, or push or bang the sieve to force the juice and some of the pulp through if you don't mind slightly cloudy jelly. Discard the seeds in the sieve.

Measure the juice. For each cup of juice add 3/4 cup sugar. Bring to the boil. Do not skim. Test as described in Tips for Jam and Jelly Making (above), and when cooked pour into hot, clean jars.

Note: This recipe makes less jelly than jam, as much of the fruit is discarded as seedy pulp.

Quick Blackcurrant Jelly

This quickly made jelly is not crystal clear because it is strained through a sieve rather than being dripped through a cloth for hours. All the same, it is a delicious spread.

500 g (1 lb 2 oz) fresh or frozen
*   blackcurrants*
2 cups (500 ml/16 fl oz) water
1 1/2 cups sugar

Simmer the blackcurrants and water in a large pot for 10 minutes, crushing the fruit at intervals. Push and bang it through a sieve, then discard the skins.

Make the juice up to 2 cups with more water if necessary. Add the sugar and bring to the boil, stirring until the sugar dissolves. Boil briskly, uncovered, and test as described in Tips for Jam and Jelly Making (above).

When cooked, pour into clean, dry jars, leave until the jelly is bath temperature, then cover with a metal screwtop, melted paraffin or candle wax, or cellophane.

Variations: For Spiced Blackcurrant Jelly, boil a broken cinnamon stick and 5 whole cloves with the blackcurrants.

For Blackcurrant and Rum Jelly, add 1–2 Tbsp dark rum just before pouring the jelly into jars.

Passionfruit Jelly

If you have a flourishing passionfruit vine, consider making some of this gourmet jelly as gifts for your friends. Use an intensely flavoured wine for best results.

1/2 cup passionfruit pulp
1/2 cup (125 ml/4 fl oz) white wine
30–35 g (1–1 1/4 oz) powdered pectin
*   (jam-setting mix)*
1 cup (250 ml/8 fl oz) water
2 cups sugar

Sieve the passionfruit pulp to remove the seeds, then measure it. Put the pulp, wine, pectin and water into a large pot, stir well to mix, then boil for 5 minutes. Add the sugar, bring the mixture back to the boil and boil briskly for 5–10 minutes, testing as described in Tips for Jam and Jelly Making (above left). Pour into clean, hot jars and seal.

Quince Jelly

Quince jelly is tart and interesting. Eat it on cheese, bread, scones or pikelets, or serve it with mutton, hogget or turkey as you would redcurrant jelly or cranberry jelly. It makes a good glaze for fruit tarts, too, and can be used instead of marmalade on the breakfast table.

Allow 4 cups (1 litre/32 fl oz) water for every kg (2 lb) of quinces. Quarter the quinces, put them in a large pot with the water, cover, and simmer. Try not to mash the softened fruit with the water or you will get less liquid from the mixture when you pour it into a jelly bag and leave it to drip. If you don't have a jelly bag, use an old pillow slip or a teatowel, or a Chux cloth in a colander. I find I get about 2 cups juice from 1 kg (2 lb) fruit after the mixture has dripped several hours or overnight.

Measure the juice into a large pot, add the same amount of sugar, and boil briskly, uncovered. Test for setting as described in Tips for Jam and Jelly Making (above left) and as soon as the jelly is cooked remove the pot from the heat and pour the jelly into clean, hot jars. Seal with wax then cellophane.

(Ruby red quince jelly looks beautiful but has usually been overcooked. The mixture usually gels when it is pinkish rather than deep red.)

Autumn Jellies

This jelly is made from a mixture of autumn fruits. Choose several from the following: apples, quinces, crab apples, pears, grapes, passionfruit, blackberries and rosehips. A few stalks of rhubarb may be added, along with the odd lemon. I try to include in each brew a fruit that makes good jam or jelly, because it sets well.

Chop the fruit into a big pot or jam pan, leaving in all skins and cores, removing only any bad bits, or any discoloured, insect-eaten areas of skin. Chop the fruit into pieces no bigger than grapes. Some fruit, like crab apples, is best chopped in the food processor, but others are best cut with a heavy knife or cleaver.

In general, add about 1 cup (250 ml/ 8 fl oz) water to every 500 g (1 lb 2 oz) fruit. Add no water for watery fruit such as grapes, and a bit more than a cup for hard, pectin-rich (good-jellying) fruit such as crab apples. When all the fruit is chopped into the container, the water usually comes three-quarters of the way up to its level.

For spiced or citrus-flavoured jelly, add cinnamon sticks, whole cloves, slices of root ginger and lemon or orange peel, without any white pith.

Boil the mixture for about half an hour, until the fruit is quite soft. Depending on the fruit used, the final mixture may be chunky with thin juice, or pulpy with only a little thick juice. Thin-juiced mixtures may be strained quickly through a fine sieve, but thick mixtures should be tipped into a cloth bag, or old pillow slip, so the liquid can drain from the pulp over a longer time. For clear jelly the pulp should not be pressed or the bag squeezed, but for home consumption this is not an important issue.

Next, measure the juice or stock, into a large, wide pot or pan. Work with no more than 4 cups at a time. Add 3/4 cup sugar for every 1 cup juice. Stir constantly while it comes to the boil, then adjust the heat so that it boils briskly in the centre, and a scum of little bubbles forms round the edge. Remove this as soon as it is firm enough.

As soon as the mixture comes to the boil, start testing it to see if it sets, as described in Tips for Jam and Jelly Making (above left). Sometimes the jelly needs 10 or more minutes' boiling before it sets. At other times it may be so concentrated that it wants to set before it boils and clears. If this happens, add 1/4–1/2 cup water, wine or commercially made juice to dilute it, and boil again.

Traditionally, jelly is bottled in glasses rather than jars, so it may be tipped out like sandcastles when it is served. Glasses or jars should be clean, and preheated in a low oven. Pour in the hot jelly, then seal with a lacquered metal screwtop, or leave until set, and seal with melted wax and a cellophane top.

Jelly is particularly good on muffins, melted to glaze fruit tarts, etc. or melted into sweet-sour sauces for meat.

Apricot Conserve

Bottled sunshine, to brighten any breakfast table, or enliven plain, warm scones.

1 kg (2 lb 3 oz) ripe, raw apricots
1 can (450–500 g/1 lb–1 lb 2 oz) crushed
* pineapple*
grated rind and juice of 1 orange
grated rind and juice of 1 lemon
2¹/₂ cups sugar
¹/₂ cup slivered almonds (optional)
2–4 Tbsp Grand Marnier or Cointreau
* (optional)*

Slice the apricots into a large, shallow pot or jam pan. Add the crushed pineapple (and juice), then the grated rind and the juice of the orange and lemon. Boil until the apricots are tender, stirring often.

Add the sugar and boil for about 10 minutes, stirring often, until the jam thickens. Test as described in Tips for Jam and Jelly Making (p. 324). When cooked, remove from the heat, and add the almonds and Grand Marnier. Pour the hot conserve into hot, sterilised jars and seal with boiled metal lids.

Kiwi Conserve

Kiwifruit and pineapple are combined in this conserve (or jam), which makes a good breakfast spread and an interesting topping for cheesecakes. When you make it, add a little green colouring so the finished jam is the same clear green as a fairly ripe, raw kiwifruit.

2 cups chopped kiwifruit flesh
1–3 tsp finely grated fresh root ginger
juice of 1 lemon
1 cup canned pineapple
* (and juice)*
2¹/₂ cups sugar
green food colouring

If you like jam without many seeds and are using kiwifruit that are not too expensive, remove both the central core and the area with the most seeds before you chop the flesh.

First, halve the fruit lengthways. To cut out the central core and remove some of the seeds, use a sharp, serrated knife and cut a 'V' lengthways from each half. Hold the halved fruit in one hand then, with a teaspoon or dessertspoon, scoop out the remaining flesh. Press this firmly into a 2-cup measure if you do not want to weigh it.

Kiwi Conserve

Peel the root ginger and grate it finely. (If you use frozen root ginger, use at least twice as much, since it grates as a powdery dust.)

Boil the kiwifruit, ginger and lemon juice for 3–4 minutes. Add the pineapple juice and the pineapple cut into small pieces. Boil for 5 minutes longer, then add the sugar. Boil briskly, stirring frequently, for about 10 minutes, testing as described in Tips for Jam and Jelly Making (p. 324). When cooked, pour into clean, hot jars and seal immediately with metal lids soaked for at least 5 minutes in boiling water.

Lemon Honey

Lemon honey is a smooth, easily spread, lemon-flavoured mixture with many uses. It is delicious spread on pikelets, used as a filling for tartlets, put between the halves of a plain sponge sandwich, and is particularly tasty spread on pavlovas (as well as cream) since its tartness counteracts the sweetness of the meringue.

Although lemon honey does not keep as well as jams or jellies, it can be kept, covered, in the refrigerator for several weeks.

50 g (2 oz) butter
1 cup sugar
2 tsp finely grated lemon rind
3 eggs, slightly beaten
¹/₂ cup (125 ml/4 fl oz) lemon juice

Melt the butter in the top of a double boiler, or a basin over a pot of boiling water, and add the sugar and lemon rind.

In another basin beat the eggs just enough to blend the yolks and whites, and strain with the lemon juice into the mixture over boiling water. Heat, stirring occasionally, for 15–20 minutes, or until the mixture has thickened. (Do not heat over direct heat once the eggs have been added.)

Pour into jars that have been cleaned and heated in a cool oven (100°C/225°F) for 30 minutes. Seal with metal screwtop lids that have been soaked in boiling water for 5–10 minutes.

Uncooked Strawberry Jam

Basic Jam Recipe

You can turn even 2 cups of fruit into jam which will add a wonderful freshness and flavour to bread, toast, scones and pikelets. If you want to make jam with a particular fruit, but don't have a recipe, try these general instructions.

Boil the prepared fruit or berries in a fairly large pot, uncovered, over quite a high heat until soft. You may need to add a few tablespoons of water, orange juice or lemon juice to stop the fruit sticking at first, until it makes it own juice. (Add lemon juice to fruit that is not sour, e.g. peaches, blackberries and strawberries, since this helps the jam set.)

Measure the amount of cooked fruit pulp. Add ³/4 cup sugar for each cup of pulp. Bring to the boil over a low heat, stirring frequently, until the sugar is dissolved, then boil briskly over a higher heat until the jam is cooked to the setting stage. Test at 3-minute intervals, and bottle in clean, hot jars when cooked, as described in Tips for Jam and Jelly Making (p. 324).

Plum Jam

Slightly underripe plums make good jam, so if you find a fruiting plum tree by the side of the road, pick enough to make a few jars. Children like plum jam much better if you remove the plum skins and stones, so it is worth taking a few minutes to do this as you make it.

about 500 g (1 lb 2 oz) plums
about ¹/2 cup (125 ml/4 fl oz) water
sugar

Boil the plums and water in a large pot, stirring regularly so the fruit does not stick on the bottom. When the plums are soft, push the pulp through a coarse sieve or colander to get rid of the skin and stones.

Measure the sieved pulp, add a cup of sugar for each cup of pulp, and boil the mixture, stirring often. Test then bottle as described in Tips for Jam and Jelly Making (p. 324).

Banana Passionfruit Jam

I produced one of the most delicious jams I have ever made when I was given a bag of wild banana passionfruit. I tried unnamed samples on a dozen tasters. Everyone liked the jam, describing the flavour as a mixture of apricot and orange. It is the colour of apricot jam but it sets better. If you know where there's a vine growing, and you live in a fairly warm climate, try a small batch. (Fruit grown in cooler climates does not have a strong flavour.)

500 g (1 lb 2 oz) ripe banana passionfruit
1¹/2 cups (375 ml/12 fl oz) water
about 2 cups sugar

Passionfruit Honey   M

I make passionfruit honey each year using fresh or frozen pulp. I have always enjoyed this, and find that it keeps well as long as it is stored in the refrigerator, both before and after the jar is opened.

Lemon rind gives the passionfruit honey a distinct lemony flavour – if you like this, add the finely grated rind of a lemon. Without it, the flavour is more passionfruity.

Because it is so easy, I cook my passionfruit honey in the microwave oven. This works beautifully, as long as you don't overcook it and get a grainy instead of a satin-smooth texture. If you prefer, cook it as for Lemon Honey (p. 325).

For 2 cups:
75 g (2¹/2 oz) butter
1 cup sugar
1 Tbsp cornflour
2 eggs
¹/2 cup passionfruit pulp
¹/4 cup (60 ml/4 fl oz) lemon juice

Melt the butter in the microwave, then stir in the sugar and cornflour until there are no lumps. Add the eggs and beat with a whisk, fork or wooden spoon until they are well mixed, but not frothy. Stir in the fresh or thawed passionfruit pulp and the lemon juice. Microwave on High (100%) power for 1 minute, then stir thoroughly.

Keep microwaving in 1-minute bursts, stirring thoroughly after each minute, until the passionfruit honey is evenly thick. It should take 4–6 minutes, and will thicken round the edges first. (It will thicken more as it cools.)

Spoon the hot passionfruit honey into small jars that have been boiled for 5 minutes, and top with lids that have been boiled. Store in the refrigerator before and after opening, for up to 3 months.

Use as a topping for pikelets, scones, bread or toast, or to fill small cooked tart shells. Top tarts with a little lightly whipped cream if you like.

Cut the washed fruit into 1 cm (¹/₂ in) slices – skin, seeds and all – and put in a large pot with the water. Bring to the boil and simmer uncovered for 15 minutes, or until the skins are tender. Press the mixture through a sieve, using a wooden spoon. Use your fingers to get as much pulp as possible away from the seeds. Discard the seeds.

Measure the pulp back into the pot, adding sugar cup for cup (I had 2 cups pulp). Bring to the boil and boil briskly for 5–10 minutes. When the mixture boils, start testing as described in Tips for Jam and Jelly Making (p. 324). Remove it from the heat and bottle it as soon as it is cooked. Seal the jars as soon as they are cool, with screwtop lids or melted paraffin wax. This quantity of fruit makes about 2 full jam jars.

While experimenting I found:

- Less water makes very firm, rubbery jam.
- 'Blending' the fruit instead of slicing it produces a different flavour – obviously it is best not to break the seeds, which are bigger and harder than black passionfruit seeds.
- The bubbles on the surface of the boiling jam looked and sounded different when the setting point was reached. This test for readiness isn't obvious with all jams, so you may like to watch for it here.

Blackberry Jam

Wild blackberry jam has a wonderful colour and flavour – worth a few scratches! Sometimes it doesn't set as well as it might. If this happens, use it as an icecream topping.

250 g (9 oz) blackberries
1¹/₄ cups sugar
2 Tbsp lemon juice

Combine all the ingredients in a medium-sized pot. Mash with a potato masher, and leave to stand for an hour. Bring to the boil and simmer briskly, stirring occasionally, until it sets. See Tips for Jam and Jelly Making (p. 324) for testing and bottling instructions.

Cape Gooseberry Jam

Cape gooseberries have an unusual and distinctive flavour. If you have a Cape gooseberry plant in the garden you can pick the berries as they ripen, and freeze them as they are, until you have saved enough to make jam. To make Cape gooseberries go further, and to produce a jelly-like jam, I make a pectin base from apples before I make the jam. This doubles the yield, without changing the flavour noticeably.

500 g (1 lb 2 oz) barely ripe apples
2 cups (500 ml/8 fl oz) water
500 g (1 lb 2 oz) hulled Cape gooseberries
2¹/₂–3 cups sugar

Chop the apples, without removing the skins or cores, and boil them briskly in the water for about 15 minutes, uncovered. Drain off the liquid though a sieve – there should be about 1¹/₂ cups. If there is not enough, add extra water to the apples and recook and strain them to get more liquid.

Put the apple liquid and the Cape gooseberries in a large pot and boil until the berries are tender enough to crush with a potato masher (10–15 minutes). Measure the volume of the mixture – there should be about 3 cups. Add 1³/₄ cups sugar for every 2 cups liquid and bring to the boil, stirring frequently. Boil briskly, uncovered, for 10 minutes.

Pour the jam into small jars and leave to cool. If it seems runny rather than jelly-like after 12 hours, boil it up again for another 5 minutes. Bottle in screw-topped jars that have been thoroughly cleaned and heated in an oven at 150°C (300°F) for 10 minutes. Top while hot with metal lids that have been soaked in boiling water for 5 minutes.

Uncooked Strawberry Jam

When you open a jar of uncooked strawberry jam in the middle of winter, you will be amazed by its bright, almost luminous colour, and its wonderful, raw strawberry flavour.

If you decide it is too runny to serve as jam, you can always give your family a treat and serve it as an icecream sauce, over pancakes, or as a plain, hot pudding. The flavour is intense, and little is needed.

In this jam, lemon juice is added to the strawberries for extra acid, powdered commercially made pectin is added to the acidified fruit, then sugar is stirred in. Because the jam is not heated, it takes some time for the pectin and sugar to dissolve. Don't be impatient!

3 cups hulled, sliced strawberries
¹/₄ cup (60 ml/2 fl oz) plus 2 Tbsp lemon juice
¹/₂ cup (60 g/2 oz) powdered pectin
4 cups castor sugar

Choose strawberries with good flavour and colour. They should be ripe, but not overripe. Prepare then measure them into a fairly large container (I use a straight-sided 2 litre/64 fl oz microwave casserole).

Mash with a potato masher, add the lemon juice, and mash a little more to mix.

Stir in the powdered pectin. This will not dissolve straight away. Stir, every now and then, for 30 minutes, or until it dissolves.

Add the sugar. (It may seem a large amount, but the jam will not set if you use less.) Cover, and leave to stand at room temperature until the sugar has dissolved, stirring several times each day. It may take 2 or 3 days until you feel no gritty sugar on the bottom of the container.

Spoon or pour the jam into clean, dry, small jars. If you plan to use the jam within 3 months, seal the jars with metal lids and keep them in the refrigerator. If you plan to keep it longer, seal the jars with a couple of layers of plastic cut from a plastic bag and store in the freezer. (The plastic allows the jam to expand as it freezes, whereas a metal top may cause the jar to break when it is frozen.)

Notes: This jam does not boil down, so you finish up with a greater yield for the amount of fruit. You use much the same amount of sugar to produce this volume of cooked jam.

> Glass becomes slippery in the freezer. Make sure that freezer jam jars cannot fall out and break.

Mixed Berry Freezer Jam

This jam is not made by the usual method, and is thinner than cooked jam, but it keeps all the wonderful colour and flavour of fresh berries. It will keep in the refrigerator for a week or so, or in the freezer for a year. It may be used as a spread, or spooned over icecream.

1 cup sliced fresh strawberries
1 cup tightly packed raspberries (fresh or frozen)
¹/₄ cup (60 ml/2 fl oz) lemon juice
35 g (1¹/₄ oz) powdered jam-setting mix (¹/₂ packet)
2¹/₂ cups castor sugar

Slice the strawberries and pack them firmly into the cup. Pack the raspberries tightly. Mix the prepared berries in a fairly large bowl and leave to thaw completely, if they have been frozen.

When thawed, mix in the lemon juice and jam-setting mix and stir until the powder dissolves. After this, stir in the sugar. Stir at intervals until the sugar dissolves, then pour into sterilised bottles and cover as desribed in Uncooked Strawberry Jam (above). The jam should thicken over the next few days. Store in the refrigerator if you will be using it soon, or freeze for long-term storage.

> **See also**
> Anne's Traffic Light Pepper Jellies, p. 340

Preserves for the Pantry

To me, preserving is more than filling bottles with fruit, and processing them for later use. There are certainly some recipes for bottled fruit here, because I think everyone needs to know what an easy process it can be. There are also recipes for some foods that have interested me and made me want to make my own versions – candied citrus fruit, fashionable quince paste, candied angelica and the like. I have included these because it is hard to find instructions for making them, and I thought that if I wanted to know how to make them, someone else was sure to, too.

Easy Preserved Fruit

If you can buy cheap fruit at the height of its season, or if you are given fruit from a friend's garden, it is worth preserving some of it. Don't worry if the fruit is blemished or spotted. As long as you don't leave it to sit around and deteriorate, small blemishes and bad bits can be cut out and thrown away, leaving you with a perfectly good product.

Collect some unmarked, unchipped jars which have metal screwtop lids. Wash them carefully and heat them in the oven at about 100°C (225°F) for about 10 minutes. (If you pour hot fruit into cold jars, the jars will crack.) Clean the lids and boil them in a pot for a few minutes to soften the inner flexible seals.

Peel, slice and cook the fruit just as you do when you stew it to eat straight away. If you are cutting up a lot of fruit, put it in a bowl of lightly salted, cold water until it is all ready (use 1 tsp salt to 4 cups (1 litre/32 fl oz) water). This stops it going brown.

Drain the fruit and boil it in a syrup made from about 1/2 cup (110 g/4 oz) sugar to 1 cup (250 ml/8 fl oz) water. Don't use more liquid than you need to cook the fruit in, so you finish up with tightly packed fruit in the jar. As soon as the fruit has boiled thoroughly and feels as if it is barely cooked, ladle it (with some syrup) into the hot jars until they are overflowing. Using a clean cloth or paper towel, wipe the rims clear of fruit, and immediately screw on the boiled lids tightly.

When the jar and fruit have cooled the centre of the lid should be sucked in slightly. Do not loosen or tighten the lid after you screw it on initially, or you will destroy the seal. Wash and dry the jar and lid, label it, and store it in a cool, dry place until you want to use it.

Easy Preserved Fruit

If the lid is hard to undo when you want to open it, run it under a hot tap.

Warning: If the lid bulges at any time, do not eat the fruit. Throw it out. If the fruit looks or smells funny in any way, do not eat it. The fruit can spoil if you have not cleaned the jars and lids properly, have not heated the fruit enough or have broken the seal on the jars.

It is not safe to preserve vegetables, meat or fish in this way. Preserve only fruit like this.

Patricia's Perfumed Peaches

This is a good way to give home-grown peaches an extra-special flavour. Use wine that has a fruity flavour.

1 cup water
1 cup white wine
12 cardamom pods
rind of 1 orange
1 cup sugar
about 1 kg (2 lb 3 oz) golden queen
  peaches

Put the water, wine, crushed cardamom pods and orange rind (peeled with a potato peeler) in a pot, cover and simmer for about 10 minutes. Add the sugar, bring to the boil, then remove the orange peel.

Peel and quarter the peaches, add them to the syrup and bring them to the boil. Bottle the fruit as above.

For best flavour, leave the peaches for at least a month before opening. Serve plain, or sprinkled with lightly toasted almonds, with yoghurt, lightly whipped cream, or icecream.

Brandied Fruit

Brandied Fruit makes a special dessert, alone or with cream or icecream. If the price of commercially prepared fruit frightens you, make your own!

You can brandy any fruit you bottle conventionally. I have made brandied peaches, apricots, pineapple, pitted cherries, boysenberries and loganberries.

Pack the raw fruit in small decorative jars that hold about 1–1 1/2 cups, with lacquered metal lids. When you want a gift, simply take a jar from your cupboard, polish it until it shines, and cover the top with a circle of fabric secured with a rubber band then a ribbon. Attach a little card giving a few particulars of the contents of the jar.

Pack the prepared fruit into thoroughly cleaned jars all of the same height. Add suitable whole spices if you like. Spoon 2–3 Tbsp brandy (or light rum) into each jar. Fill the jars to 1 cm (1/2 in) from the top with heavy syrup made by boiling 1 cup of sugar with 1 cup of water. Place lids loosely on the jars so air can escape as the contents heat.

Place the jars on a rack or crumpled foil in a large pot and add bath-temperature water up to their necks (boiling water might break the jars). Cover the pot. Bring to a gentle boil, then simmer for 20 minutes.

After this, working quickly, ladle out some of the water from around the jars, until you are able to lift the jars one at a time onto a wooden board or a pad of newspapers. Using cloths to protect your hands, quickly tighten the jar lids and leave them to cool away from draughts.

Check that the lids have sealed when the jars are cold. You may hear them 'pop' as the centres of the metal lids are sucked down as the jars cool. You know that the jars have sealed when the centres of the metal lids are slightly concave. Store in a cool, dry place until required.

> Fruit preserving is easy, and if you can get ripe fruit free or cheaply, and save empty jars with screw-top metal lids, it will cost you almost nothing!

Candied Mandarin Peel

It is easier and quicker to candy mandarin peel than it is to candy any other citrus peel. Use it as a sweet, or chop it up for baking. Chocolate-dipped peel makes a special treat.

Refrigerate or freeze mandarin peel in a plastic bag until you have enough to candy.

peel from 8–10 mandarins
water to cover
about ½ cup sugar
¼ tsp citric acid
1 tsp water
extra sugar for coating
about 100 g (3½ oz) easy-to-melt cooking
  chocolate (optional)

Cover the pieces of peel with water and simmer for about 30 minutes, until they are very tender. Pour off and measure the liquid, then return it to the pot with the same volume of sugar (i.e. ½ cup liquid needs ½ cup sugar). Boil gently, uncovered, until a small amount dropped into cold water forms a soft ball.

Remove from the heat and add the citric acid dissolved in the water. Work fast after you do this, because the liquid sets like marmalade when the acid is added.

Pick out the pieces of peel and turn each one in sugar, then leave the peel sitting on the sugar until it is cool and fairly firm. Before it has cooled completely cut the pieces into strips, and make sure the cut edges are sugar-coated.

If you are going to use the peel for cooking, store it in an airtight container in the freezer.

If you want to coat it with chocolate, melt the chocolate in a small bowl over hot water, stirring it until it is liquid. Easy-to-melt chocolate does not need anything added, but other chocolate may need a little Kremelta (Copha) to make it liquid enough to work with. Dip one side of each strip of peel into the chocolate, then put it on a piece of plastic. If you like, dip the ends instead of one side of the strips.

Refrigerate the chocolate-coated strips on the plastic until the chocolate solidifies, then lift them off. Store in a cool, dry place until required.

Note: If you boil the syrup too long, the peel will be hard. If you don't boil it enough, it will be soft and sticky.

Candied Angelica

Candied angelica is not readily available, but it may sometimes be bought in specialist food stores. The green stems look rather like crystallised celery stems and are sliced thinly for decorating desserts, etc.

Angelica (*Angelica archangelica*) is a large plant that grows and seeds itself easily. The stems and leaves are bigger than rhubarb, and in its second year, when it flowers, the white flower heads are 2–3 metres tall. The strongly scented, light green, round, hollow leaf stalks are covered with many reddish hairs, and may be 1 metre (3 feet) long. These stems may be candied. (There is another plant known as angelica, which has dark green, very shiny leaves. This has no flavour or aroma, and should not be cooked or candied.)

The leaf stems are best picked for candying before, or just after, the flower stem starts to develop, usually at the start of the plant's second year.

Cut the stems into convenient lengths and boil them in lightly salted water until they are tender (about 15 minutes). Drain them and scrape off the hairy outer layer. Put the cleaned stems in a stainless steel pot or frypan which will not be needed for the next 5 or 6 days. Cover the angelica with a syrup of 1 cup sugar to 1 cup water. Add a little green food colouring if you like. Simmer, uncovered, for 15 minutes, then cover and leave the angelica to stand in the syrup. Each day for the next 5 days, boil it again for 15 minutes.

The syrup should become more concentrated daily, finishing up like runny honey. Until the last day it should not be concentrated enough to form a soft ball in cold water. If necessary, thin it down with water. If it seems too thin, concentrate it gradually by adding extra sugar. The last day, boil until the syrup will form a very soft ball in cold water.

Lift out the angelica stems, drain them and roll them in castor sugar. Leave them to dry out on a rack in the sun (or a very low oven).

To keep the best texture and flavour, store the stems in the freezer. When stored in airtight jars they sometimes turn sticky, while stored in an open container they may dry out too much.

Note: Angelica seeds should be planted within a few weeks of ripening on the plant. They are very slow to germinate, taking over 6 months at times.

Sun-Dried Tomatoes

Cut red-fleshed Italian tomatoes into slices 1 cm (½ in) thick. Lay the slices on the racks of a dehydrator and, with the dehydrator set to moderate heat (i.e. halfway round the dial if it has adjustable temperatures), dry the tomatoes until they no longer contain any damp pulp. Turn the slices occasionally, moving those in the centre of the tray closer to the edge as the slices shrink. The slices I dry take about 12 hours, but the time may vary.

Your aim is to produce quite dry tomatoes, without browning them.

Store the sun-dried tomatoes in plastic bags in the freezer, bringing them out only a few hours before you plan to use them. (Tomatoes which have not dried completely may spoil and become unsafe to eat if left to stand in oil at room temperature.)

If you don't have a dehydrator, dry the tomato slices on a rack in a fan-assisted oven, on the lowest heat. Oven-dried tomatoes darken more quickly than dehydrated tomatoes. You can try turning off the oven heat at intervals, using only the fan if you like. The drying time should be much the same as in a dehydrator, but you must judge by texture rather than going by time.

Pear and Grape Butter

Fruit butters are a cross between jams and jellies. The cooked fruit is puréed before being heated with sugar. The result is thicker than jam, and it is used as jam is, especially spread on toast or bread.

about 500 g (1 lb 2 oz) ripe pears
about 500 g (1 lb 2 oz) fairly ripe grapes
grated rind and juice of 1 orange
juice of 1 lemon
½ tsp cinnamon
sugar

Chop the pears, without removing the cores or skin. Add the grapes, orange rind and juice, and lemon juice. Add the cinnamon, cover and cook in a microwave or on the stove until the pear is soft.

Tip the mixture into a food processor and purée it, then shake it through a coarse sieve; or push it through the sieve without puréeing it first. Bang the sieve to get as much pulp through as possible.

Measure the pulp into a large, non-stick frypan, then add 1 cup of sugar to every 2 cups pulp. Cook over moderate heat, stirring (wear a rubber glove, so you don't get burnt by hot spatters). As the mixture gets thicker it does not spit so much. Cook for about half an hour, or until the mixture is as thick as you want it. Test the thickness by pouring a little onto a cold, dry saucer and letting it cool.

For thinnish butter, spoon into hot, clean jars and seal as soon as cool with melted wax.

Ginger Root Syrup

Fresh ginger root is available from the greengrocer or supermarket at most times of the year. If you are not already familiar with this interesting root, buy a little and smell the cut surface. It has a wonderful aroma, and is much more aromatic and lemony than other forms of ginger.

When ginger roots look particularly young, tender, plump and fleshy, I buy enough to make this hot, spicy ginger syrup. I keep it in a small screwtop soft drink bottle in the refrigerator and use it in a number of different ways:

- Put 1 or 2 Tbsp ginger syrup in a glass with soda water and ice. You get a drink like ginger ale, with more 'pep'. For a sweeter drink with a milder flavour, replace the soda water with lemonade.
- For apple ginger, add ginger syrup, to taste, to half a glass of apple juice and half a glass of soda water. Top with a sprig of mint.
- Use the syrup, to taste, with whisky, soda and ice.
- Make a ginger 'spritzer' – half white wine, half soda water and 2 or 3 tsp ginger syrup.
- Add 2–3 tsp ginger syrup to milk for a ginger milkshake. Whiz the syrup, cold milk and a generous scoop of icecream.
- Pour ginger syrup over fresh fruit – e.g. sliced plums, nectarines, peaches, watermelon, banana or fruit salad.
- Add to stewed fruit such as pears or peaches.
- Flavour whipped cream with ginger syrup.
- Drizzle ginger syrup over vanilla, white chocolate or hokey pokey icecream for a quick dessert.

After reading such a list, don't you wonder how you have managed to live without ginger syrup?

100 g (3½ oz) root ginger
1 cup (250 ml/8 fl oz) water
juice and thinly peeled rind of 1 lemon
2 cloves
cinnamon stick (optional)
½ cup honey
1 cup sugar

Do not peel the ginger. Grate or chop it, then pulverise it in a food processor or blender. Add the water during this process, or at the end of it.

Leave the mixture to stand for half an hour, then boil it for 15 minutes. Strain through a fine sieve and discard the solids. Boil the liquid with all the remaining ingredients for 10 minutes.

Strain again into a small jar or bottle. Cover tightly and refrigerate until needed.

If you find this syrup is too hot for your taste, and too concentrated, dilute it with more honey, sugar and water.

Variations: Add grated or thinly peeled orange rind and/or vanilla flavouring or a vanilla pod during the second boiling.

If you think the colour is boring, modify it using food colouring or a few drops of gravy browning.

Quince Pâté

Quince Pâté

I think quince pâté is a very special confection. It is firmer than a jelly, being more like Turkish Delight in texture. It could also be called quince leather or cheese, but none of these names really describes it adequately.

Quarter or roughly chop 500 g–1 kg (1–2 lb) quinces. Don't peel or core them, but cut away any blemished bits. Put them in a heavy-bottomed pot with about ½ cup (125 ml/4 fl oz) of water and ½ cup (125 ml/4 fl oz) lemon juice – enough to make steam and stop the fruit burning, but not too much. Cover and simmer for half an hour then press the quince flesh and liquid through a sieve, discarding the skin, seeds, etc.

OR microwave quartered quinces in a covered container on High (100%) power in ¼ cup (60 ml/2 fl oz) water and ¼ cup (60 ml/2 fl oz) lemon juice for about 15 minutes, or until tender. Discard the cores and purée everything else in a food processor, then shake or bang through a sieve.

Measure the volume of the purée and put it in a frypan with a non-stick finish, with the same volume of sugar (i.e. use 2 cups sugar for 2 cups purée). Simmer uncovered for half an hour, stirring regularly with a wooden spoon (wear a rubber glove so the very hot spatters don't burn you).

Pour the hot mixture onto another non-stick surface or a pan lined with a roasting bag. Spread it so it is about 1 cm (½ in) thick and leave it to cool.

When it is cold you should be able to lift it up in a sheet, put it on a board sprinkled with castor sugar and cut it into cubes. Coat the cubes with sugar and leave them to stand, uncovered, in a warm, well-ventilated place to dry out further. If the sheet of quince paste still feels soft, coat it with sugar but don't cut it up – leave it to stand on a rack for 24 hours or longer until it is firm enough to cut. Store it, if you can, in a cool, dry place in a shallow container with the lid ajar.

OR pour the mixture into hot, boiled jelly jars or glasses and seal with paraffin wax when cold. Store as you do jam, or freeze. Turn out (like sandcastles) after thawing. Slice and serve with meat or with cheese on crackers.

See also
Jams and Jellies, pp. 322–327
Pickles, Relishes and Chutneys, pp. 332–341

Pickles, Relishes and Chutneys

Vinegar is wonderful stuff! I never cease to be amazed when I taste an everyday fruit or vegetable that has been transformed by treatment with vinegar, salt, sugar and a few spices. My interest in pickling was sparked by North American and Northern European pickles, which were totally different from the English-style pickles I had eaten previously. Recently there has been an awakened interest in a variety of chutneys – let's hope it continues!

PICKLING HINTS

- Bottle pickles and chutneys in clean, hot jars. Wash them carefully then heat them in the oven at about 100°C (225°F) for about 10 minutes.
- For long-term storage, seal jars with preserving jar seals or metal screwtop lids that have been soaked in boiling water for at least 5 minutes. This sterilises the lids and softens the rubber seals. Once cool, the lids should be slightly concave.
- For short-term storage, seal jars with plastic tops and keep in the refrigerator.

Late Summer Pickle

This is a pretty pickle! I make it whenever I see cheap red peppers. It is chopped, boiled and bottled in a matter of minutes. It disappears quickly so make plenty.

2 cups cooked whole-kernel corn
6–8 cups chopped cabbage
3 onions, chopped
3 red peppers, chopped
3 green peppers, chopped
1 cup sugar
1 Tbsp salt
1 Tbsp celery seeds
1 Tbsp mustard seeds
1 Tbsp mustard powder
2½ tsp turmeric
2 cups (500 ml/16 fl oz) white vinegar
¼ cup cornflour
½ cup (125 ml/4 fl oz) water

Prepare the vegetables and put them in a large pot. Use drained canned or fresh corn, and don't chop the cabbage too finely. Cut onions and peppers the same size as the corn.

Add all the remaining ingredients, mixing the cornflour and water before adding them. Simmer, stirring constantly, for 15 minutes, then pack into hot sterilised jars and seal with boiled metal screwtops.

Note: Celery and mustard seeds are available in large grocery stores. Do not leave them out.

Pumpkin Pickle, Maharajah's Chutney (p. 338)

Pumpkin Pickle

This unusual pickle recipe came from a Latvian friend. Served with hot (and later cold) roast turkey, it glowed like 'bottled sunshine' on a drab winter's day!

500 g (1 lb 2 oz) prepared pumpkin
juice and rind of 1 lemon
3 cups sugar
1 cup (250 ml/8 fl oz) white vinegar
1 cup (250 ml/8 fl oz) water
3 cm (1 in) fresh root ginger, sliced
4 whole cloves
1 cinnamon stick
½ tsp salt

Cut the trimmed, peeled pumpkin into 1 cm (½ in) cubes. Remove all the coloured peel from the lemon in several long strips, then squeeze the juice. Boil these and all the remaining ingredients uncovered in a large pot for 5 minutes, then add the pumpkin and simmer for 30–40 minutes, until it is transparent.

Almost fill small, clean, hot jars with the pieces of clear pumpkin. Top with syrup almost to the rim of the jar, then screw on boiled, lacquered metal lids.

Note: Make sure you have plenty of syrup, since the pumpkin soaks up more while in the jars.

Mixed Autumn Pickle

(Photo p. 339)

An especially good pickle for gardeners.

4 cups neatly chopped or diced mixed autumn vegetables (beans, cauliflower, zucchini, corn kernels, etc.)
2 Tbsp plain salt
2 onions, finely diced
2 red peppers, finely diced
1½ cups sugar
½ tsp celery seeds
1 tsp mustard seeds
1 cup (250 ml/8 fl oz) cider vinegar
1½ Tbsp cornflour

Dice the vegetables the size of corn kernels. Sprinkle with the salt, cover with water, and leave to stand for 30 minutes.

Meanwhile, prepare and measure into a large pot the onions, red peppers, sugar, seeds and vinegar. Drain and rinse the salted vegetables, discarding the liquid. Add the vegetables to the pot. Bring to the boil, stirring regularly. Boil for no longer than about a minute.

Mix the cornflour to a paste with a little more vinegar, stir into the vegetable mixture and bring back to the boil. The mixture should thicken slightly. (It will thicken more as it cools.)

Pour into hot, sterilised jars to within 1 cm (½ in) of the top, and seal with boiled metal lids.

Notes: Refrigerate after opening, to prevent the vegetables softening.

Pumpkin and carrots are not good in this.

Add ¼ tsp turmeric with the sugar to intensify the colour of the vegetables if you like. Add ½–1 tsp to colour the liquid around the vegetables.

Garlic-Flavoured 'Capers'

Nasturtium buds and immature green seeds may be pickled in garlic-flavoured vinegar, and used in the same way as capers. If you can, pick buds rather than seeds, since they have the best texture.

nasturtium buds or seeds
1 cup (250 ml/8 fl oz) wine or cider vinegar
2 large cloves garlic, chopped
1 Tbsp salt
1 bayleaf
1 tsp black peppercorns
2 whole cloves
1 small dried chilli, crumbled

Fill small, clean jars with small nasturtium buds, or soft green nasturtium seeds.

Simmer the remaining ingredients for 10 minutes, then strain the liquid onto the nasturtium buds or seeds to cover all.

Cover, but do not necessarily seal the jars, and leave to stand for at least a month before using both the 'capers' and liquid.

Stan's Pickled Gherkins

This is the easiest and best recipe I have used to make traditional sweet-sour gherkins. If possible, pickle the gherkins within 24 hours of picking them.

3 kg (6 lb 10 oz) small, freshly picked
  gherkins
1 cup salt
10 cups (2.5 litres/80 fl oz) boiling water
2 Tbsp pickling spice
9 cups (2.25 litres/72 fl oz) cider vinegar
3 cups (375 ml/12 fl oz) water
3 cups sugar

Wash the gherkins, removing any soil with a small, soft brush if necessary.

Bring the salt and first measure of water to the boil. Pour over the gherkins and leave to stand until cool, then pour off the brine, rinse the gherkins with cold water and drain.

Tie the pickling spices loosely in a piece of clean cloth and bang gently with a rolling pin or hammer to crack them. Heat the bag of spices with the vinegar, second measure of water and the sugar until boiling. Pour over the drained gherkins (or add the gherkins to the pot) and leave to stand overnight.

Heat the gherkins in the vinegar mixture until boiling, then turn off the heat. Pack the hot gherkins into clean, heated jars, and fill to within 5 mm (1/4 in) of the top with the hot pickling liquid, making sure the gherkins are covered.

Heat the uncovered jars one at a time in a microwave on Medium (50%) power until the liquid bubbles, then remove and seal with boiled metal lids.

Use within 1 year, refrigerating after opening.

Stan's Pickled Gherkins

Zucchini Pickle

This pickle goes well with hot dogs and hamburgers, it spreads easily for sandwiches, and is good with crackers and cheese. Try it with sausages, and see if you like it, as I do, with plainly cooked fish.

If possible, use some bright yellow zucchini or scallopini to make the pickle prettier.

For 7–8 cups:
1 kg (2 lb 3 oz) zucchini
750 g (1 lb 10 oz) onions
1/4 cup salt
2 red peppers
4 cups (1 litre/32 fl oz) water
2 cups sugar
1 Tbsp mustard seeds
2 tsp celery seeds
1 1/2 tsp turmeric
2 cups (500 ml/16 fl oz) white or cider
  vinegar
1 Tbsp cornflour

Cut the zucchini and onions roughly into 2 cm (3/4 in) cubes. Chop these a handful at a time to the size of wheat grains, using the metal chopping blade of a food processor. (Take care not to reduce them to a pulp.)

Put the chopped pieces in a large bowl and mix with the salt. Chop the peppers finely and mix them with the other vegetables. Leave for half an hour, then add the water, stir again, and pour through a large, coarse sieve or colander. Discard the salty liquid.

Put the drained vegetables, sugar, seeds, turmeric and vinegar in a large, heavy-bottomed pot or jam pan. Bring to the boil, then simmer for 30 minutes, stirring often. Mix the cornflour to a paste with 2–3 Tbsp cold water, stir into the pickle, and boil for 5 minutes longer.

Pour into clean, heated jars and seal with boiled metal lids, or for relatively short-term storage cover with plastic screw-on lids and refrigerate. Refrigerate all opened jars.

Old-Fashioned Cucumber Pickle

After I discussed cucumber pickles on a radio programme many listeners wrote with questions about their own pickling recipes and techniques, and five people sent me their favourite cucumber pickle recipe. Four out of the five were the same pickle, a very old recipe according to one of the senders. For a few days my house smelt like a pickle factory as I experimented with this recipe, making half quantities.

I finished up with two variations, both delicious. I added mustard seeds and celery salt because I like these flavourings, but the pickles made without them are very good too. Please yourself!

2 telegraph cucumbers
2 tart apples
2 medium onions
1 cup sugar
1½ cups (375 ml/12 fl oz) cider vinegar
1 Tbsp turmeric
1 Tbsp mustard seeds
2 tsp salt
1 tsp celery salt
¼ tsp cayenne pepper

Peel the cucumbers only if their skins are tough. Halve them lengthways, scoop out the seeds and slice thinly. Thinly slice the quartered, unpeeled apples and quartered onions about the same size as the cucumbers.

Bring the remaining ingredients to the boil in a large pot, and add the sliced apple, onion and cucumber. Bring the mixture back to the boil, then spoon it into small, clean, heated jars. Fill to overflowing. Do not pack the pickle so tightly that you finish up with leftover liquid. Seal with boiled metal screwtop lids. Keep in the refrigerator once opened.

Variation: Using a food processor, chop the unpeeled apples, then the onions, then the cucumbers fairly small, but not to a mush. Add them to the boiling liquid. Bring back to the boil then thicken with 1 Tbsp cornflour mixed with 2 Tbsp water. Bottle and seal as above, or pour into clean, hot jam jars. When cool, cover with melted paraffin or candle wax then with cellophane tops.

Crunchy Celery Pickle

The celery in this pickle stays very crisp and crunchy, so it is a good one to serve with soft-textured cheese on crackers or in sandwiches. It is good with cold meat, especially poultry.

4–5 cups finely sliced celery
4 medium onions, sliced
1 green pepper, sliced
1–2 red peppers, sliced
1½ cups sugar
1 cup (250 ml/8 fl oz) water
4 tsp salt
1½ Tbsp mustard seeds
1½ cups (375 ml/12 fl oz) cider vinegar
½–1 tsp turmeric
2 Tbsp cornflour
¼ cup (60 ml/2 fl oz) water

Slice the celery, onions and peppers finely, all about the same size, and mix them together. Cover with boiling water and leave to stand for 10 minutes.

Meanwhile measure the sugar, water, salt, mustard seeds, vinegar and turmeric into a large pot. Use the smaller amount of turmeric to intensify the colour of the vegetables, and the large amount for a bright yellow pickle. Bring to the boil and add the drained vegetables. Bring back to

the boil, stirring constantly, and boil for 5 minutes.

Mix the cornflour and water to a paste, and stir into the pickle. Boil for 2–3 minutes more, then pour the pickle into clean, heated jars. Seal immediately with boiled metal screwtops, or close with plastic screwtops and keep in the refrigerator.

Pickled Asparagus

Pickled asparagus looks most attractive, and turns a lunch of bread and cheese into something special. It makes an interesting gift too.

This product is NOT the same, in texture or flavour, as plain canned asparagus. Do not dilute the vinegar used in the pickle, or modify this recipe, or you may finish up with a product that is unsafe to eat.

plump, freshly picked asparagus
wine, cider or white vinegar (see method)
2 Tbsp sugar for each 1 cup (250 ml/
   8 fl oz) vinegar
1 Tbsp salt for each 1 cup (250 ml/8 fl oz)
   vinegar

To find how much pickling liquid you need, pack a jar with asparagus spears that have been trimmed to fit, then boiled for 1 minute. Now fill this jar with water, up to the top. Pour the water into a measuring container and note its volume before discarding it. You will need this volume of vinegar with proportionate amounts of sugar and salt to make the pickling liquid for each jar. Mix the vinegar with the sugar and salt, and heat to dissolve them.

Work with one jar at a time, keeping the jars hot until you need them. Cut the asparagus heads so the tips come 5–7 mm (about ¼ in) below the jar rims, then drop a few more than you will need to fill a jar into a pot of boiling water for 1 minute.

Pack the hot stalks tightly into the jar, drain off any water, then fill the jar of hot asparagus to within 5 mm (¼ in) of the top with the boiling vinegar mixture. If the asparagus and liquid cool a little, microwave the uncovered jar on Medium (50%) power until the liquid bubbles. The vinegar and asparagus MUST both be as hot as possible when used.

Screw on hot metal tops tightly to seal. If the jars are properly sealed, the lids should be concave when cold. Leave for a month before using, refrigerating after opening. If the jars are not sealed, store them in the refrigerator for 2 weeks, then use.

Vinegar is an essential ingredient in pickles, relishes and chutneys. Never reduce the proportion of vinegar, shorten the processing time, or simplify the sealing procedures, or they may spoil and be unsafe to eat.

Green Tomato Chow Chow

Unripe, end-of-season tomatoes make a good mustard pickle. Although it has no added thickening, the vegetables thicken it to a good consistency.

A couple of red peppers chopped with the green tomatoes and onions make this a pretty pickle, but if you can't get red peppers, don't worry. Although it won't look quite so nice, the flavour will still be good.

2 large onions
2 red peppers (if available)
about 6 cups chopped green tomatoes
¼ cup salt
1 Tbsp mustard seeds
2 tsp celery seeds
1 Tbsp pickling spice
2 cups (500 ml/16 fl oz) white or cider
   vinegar
1 cup sugar
2 tsp mustard powder
½ tsp ginger
1 tsp turmeric

Chop the onions and peppers into 5 mm (¼ in) cubes and put them in a 2 litre (64 fl oz) container. Chop the green tomatoes into pieces the same size, and add them to the container until it is full, with the vegetables tightly packed. Sprinkle over the salt and leave to stand for 1 hour, stirring occasionally.

As soon as the vegetables have been salted, crush the mustard and celery seeds and the pickling spice roughly with a pestle and mortar or a hammer. Put them in a bag made from cheesecloth, muslin or an old teatowel, and tie the bag with string, leaving it long enough to tie to the handle of a pot.

Put the vinegar, sugar, mustard powder, ginger and turmeric into a large pot. Bring to the boil then remove from the heat, leaving the bag of seasoning to stand in the mixture until the vegetables are ready. After an hour, tip the salted vegetables into a colander or large sieve and discard the brine. Rinse them with cold water and leave to drain for a few minutes, then add to the pot. Simmer over moderate heat, stirring frequently, for 30 minutes. Remove the bag of spices in the last few minutes.

Pour the pickle into sterilised jars and seal with boiled metal screwtop lids.

Variation: If you get the pickle-making urge but don't have any green tomatoes, replace them with marrow, cucumber, cauliflower and beans, etc., keeping the total quantity of vegetables the same.

See 'Pickling Hints', p. 333, for detailed bottling instructions.

Pickled Olives

You can pickle green (unripe) and burgundy (ripe) olives using this recipe. The pickled olives may be flavoured with whatever herbs you like, or the herbs may be left out altogether.

This is not a recipe you can complete in an afternoon – the whole process takes at least a month!

8 cups green to burgundy olives
1 (level) Tbsp caustic soda
4 cups (1 litre/32 fl oz) lukewarm water
4 Tbsp salt
1/4 cup (60 ml/2 fl oz) white vinegar
4 cups (1 litre/32 fl oz) cold water
3 Tbsp salt
1/4 cup (60 ml/2 fl oz) white vinegar
4 cups (1 litre/32 fl oz) cold water
garlic cloves
dried chillies (optional)
fresh herbs, e.g. oreganum, basil or thyme
olive oil

Handle the olives with care to avoid bruising them. Pick out any with bad bits on them.

Handling the caustic soda with great care, measure it into a stainless steel container and dissolve it in the first measure of water. Add the olives and leave to stand for 12–20 hours, depending on their size. Weight the olives down if necessary to ensure they are completely submerged.

Drain off and discard the caustic solution and rinse with clean, cold water, changing it every hour for several hours. After this, change the water twice a day for 4 days. The olives may be ready sooner than this – you can stop rinsing them as soon as litmus paper (bought from a chemist) pressed against the surface of one of the olives does not turn blue.

Drain the olives and cover with a brine made by combining the first measures of salt, vinegar and cold water. Cover and leave to stand in a cold place for at least a month, and up to 3 months.

Drain and discard the liquid. Place the olives in clean jars and cover with a new brine mixture using the second measures of salt, vinegar and water. To each jar add 1 or 2 crushed garlic cloves, 1 or 2 dried chillies (optional), and a few sprigs of any Mediterranean-type herb.

Seal the jars by covering the olives and brine with olive oil 1 cm (1/2 in) thick.

Store in a cool, dark place for up to a year.

See 'Pickling Hints', p. 333, for detailed bottling instructions.

Pickled Walnuts

Pickled walnuts are a real delicacy. Serve them with cheese, bread, cold meat, etc., use them in savoury mixtures, or give them away to special friends. The walnuts must be picked when they are a reasonable size, but before the woody shell forms inside the fleshy green cover. Do not pickle walnuts if a darning needle will not pass through them easily.

walnuts
For each 4 cups (1 litre/32 fl oz) water,
  1 Tbsp whole cloves
  1 Tbsp whole allspice
  1 small cinnamon stick
malt or cider vinegar
sugar

Prick each nut in several places, and put them in a plastic bucket. Cover with water, and change it every day for a week.

Place the soaked nuts in a large pot and cover them with fresh water, measuring the amount used. Add cloves, allspice and cinnamon sticks in proportion to the water. Boil until tender, 1–2 hours, then pour off and discard the liquid and spices.

Boil up enough sweetened vinegar to cover the nuts, using 1 cup sugar to each 1 cup of vinegar. Pour the hot liquid over the nuts, leave to stand for a week, then strain it off, bring it to the boil again, and pour it over the nuts again.

Cool and pack into clean jars. Screw plastic or other lids onto the jars and put away to mature. (The jars do not need heat sealing.) Store for at least 2 months before using.

Warning: Walnut juice discolours your hands, and everything else that comes in contact with it. Wear rubber gloves if this bothers you.

Pickled Orange Slices

Jars of golden orange slices look beautiful and make unusual gifts. They give an interesting flavour to roast or cold pork, poultry or lamb.

5 or 6 small oranges
2–4 cups (500 ml–1 litre/16–32 fl oz)
  water
2 cups sugar
1/4 cup (60 ml/2 fl oz) wine or cider
vinegar
2 cinnamon sticks
12 cloves

Choose oranges with unblemished skins. Clean them and put them in a pot just big enough to hold them, cover with water and simmer for 15 minutes.

When the oranges are cooked, save 2 cups of the cooking water and discard the rest. Put the fruit on a board to cool slightly. Add the sugar and vinegar to the saved water, add the cinnamon stick broken into several smaller pieces, and the cloves, and simmer for about 10 minutes.

While the syrup boils, cut the oranges into thick (7 mm/1/4 in) slices with a sharp (serrated) knife. Discard the end slices, bring the other slices to the boil in the spiced syrup, then spoon them into clean, hot bottles, positioning them attractively with a skewer or fork. Work quickly, with everything as hot as possible. Pour boiling syrup and some of the spices over the slices, removing air bubbles with the skewer. Fill to within 3 mm (1/8 in) of the tops of the jars, top immediately with boiled, very hot lids, and screw them on tightly.

Leave for a month before using.

Pickled Beetroot

You can bottle beetroot using the overflow method as long as you put them in a vinegary liquid. However, if you dilute the vinegar too much, or pack the beetroot so closely that there is little room for liquid between the slices, you will need to boil the filled jars in a water bath. Bottle beetroot while it is young and tender, when the slices will be tender and crisp.

600 g (1 lb 5 oz) prepared beetroot
1 cup (250 ml/8 fl oz) malt vinegar
1/2 cup (125 ml/4 fl oz) water
1/4–1/2 cup sugar
11/2 tsp salt
1–4 cloves (optional)
1 bayleaf (optional)
1–2 cloves garlic (optional)

Cut the leaves from the beets, leaving 1–2 cm (1/2–3/4 in) of stalk above the root. Do not cut off the long thin root below the beet. Weigh the beetroot after cutting off the leaves. Scrub the roots so they are fairly free of soil, but do not peel them. Put them in a large pot, cover with water, and simmer until a large beet feels tender when pierced with a sharp knife, and its skin comes off easily when it is held under the cold tap. The time may vary from 15 minutes to 1 hour, depending on the size and maturity of the beets.

Drain off the boiling water and replace it with cold water. When the beets are cool enough to handle, squeeze them and remove their skins by hand. Slice them evenly and put in a pot with the remaining ingredients. (Do not reduce the amount of vinegar.) This amount of liquid should fill a 1 litre (32 fl oz) preserving jar containing about 500 g (1 lb 2 oz) cooked, sliced beetroot.

Bring everything to the boil. Taste and add extra sugar if you like.

Ladle the boiling mixture into clean, hot

jars, filling them to overflowing. Top with boiled preserving seals and screw the bands on tightly, or top with boiled screwtop metal lids.

Notes: Do not pack cool beet into jars, then fill them with boiling liquid, unless you are planning to process the jars in a water bath after sealing them.

Beetroot spoils quickly after cooking, before the vinegar is added, so always do the whole process at once – sliced boiled beetroot, left overnight, may become slimy and spoil.

Uncooked Mint Chutney

This is a quick chutney which keeps well and is excellent served with cold meat or poultry. With cheese, it makes a good cracker topping or sandwich filling.

3 medium-sized firm, red tomatoes
1 Tbsp salt
3–4 red-skinned apples
4–5 large onions
1 cup raisins
¼ cup chopped fresh mint
1 cup (250 ml/8 fl oz) vinegar, scalded
  and cooled

Remove the skins from the tomatoes, cut them in 5 mm (¼ in) cubes, and sprinkle with salt. Put aside for an hour.

Wash the polished apples, cut them into quarters and remove the cores. Cut the peeled onions into large pieces. Chop the apples, raisins and onions in a mincer or food processor.

Discard the liquid from the tomatoes and add the drained tomatoes, chopped mint and vinegar to the minced ingredients. Pack into sterilised jars, remove any air bubbles, and seal with boiled metal screwtops.

Keep this chutney for at least 1 week before using. Store it in a cool place for up to 1 year.

Pickled Vegetables

It is not difficult to make attractive pickled vegetables. They can be eaten after a few weeks, by which time they should be quite highly flavoured, but still quite crisp. Serve before a meal, by themselves or with cheese, or use to add interest to cold meat.

3 cups prepared small carrots
2 cups prepared beans
2 cups prepared celery
3 cups prepared cauliflower
2–3 red or yellow peppers

Brine
½ cup salt
8 cups (2 litres/64 fl oz) cold water

Pickled Vegetables

Pickling Liquid
8 cups (2 litres/64 fl oz) white wine vinegar
1 Tbsp black mustard seeds
1 Tbsp yellow mustard seeds
1 Tbsp celery seeds
1 cup sugar
¼ tsp chilli powder

Choose vegetables that are fresh, crisp and barely mature. Cut peeled carrots lengthways. String beans if necessary. String celery, and halve it lengthways. Cut the carrots, beans and celery into suitable lengths. Cut the cauliflower into florets related in size to the other vegetables. Cut seeded peppers into attractive pieces.

Stir the salt and cold water together. Cover the vegetables (without mixing them) in the brine, in plastic bags or bowls, and stand for an hour, making more brine if necessary. Drain the vegetables, rinse them with fresh water, then drain again.

Bring all the ingredients for the pickling liquid to the boil, then divide it between the drained vegetables in smaller pots. Simmer the vegetables until each is two-thirds cooked, then drain the pickling liquid back into one large pot.

Working fast, using tongs or spoons, arrange the vegetables attractively to within 1 cm (½ in) of the top, in clean, hot jars (see Pickling Hints, p. 333. Jars with rubber rings must be boiled in water for 5 minutes.)

Bring the pickling liquid to the boil and pour over the vegetables, leaving 1 cm (½ in) headspace. Screw on boiled metal lids, or tighten glass lids with wire fasteners over the rubber ring on the jar. Invert jars with glass lids after sealing. Jars should not leak, or show a stream of bubbles, as they cool.

Leave for at least 2 weeks before opening.

All-Season Relish

This tasty relish can be made at any time of the year.

1–2 cups sliced green beans
1 cup chopped celery
1 cup chopped onion
1 red pepper, chopped
1 tsp celery seeds
1 tsp mustard seeds
1 tsp turmeric
1½ cups (375 ml/12 fl oz) wine or cider
* vinegar*
1 can (440 g/15½ oz) whole kernel corn
¾ cup sugar
1 Tbsp cornflour
2 tsp salt

Measure the first 8 ingredients into a pot, bring to the boil and boil for 5 minutes. Drain, then add the corn and sugar.

Bring back to the boil, stirring carefully, then add the cornflour and salt mixed to a thin paste with a little extra vinegar.

Simmer for 2 minutes, then bottle or store in the refrigerator for up to a month.

Fresh Kiwi Relish

2 cloves garlic
2 spring onions, roughly chopped
1 tsp green peppercorns in brine, drained
* and crushed*
2 Tbsp wine vinegar
1 Tbsp Thai yellow chilli sauce
1 tsp salt
¼ cup fresh coriander, chopped
4 kiwifruit, halved and quartered

Peel the garlic and put it in the food processor with the spring onion and green peppercorns. Process until finely chopped. Add the vinegar, chilli sauce and salt and process to mix, then add the coriander and the quartered kiwifruit. Process carefully, using the pulse button, until the kiwifruit and coriander are fairly finely and evenly chopped.

For best flavour, leave to stand for 1–2 hours before using. Refrigerate for up to 2 days if desired.

Mary White's Feijoa Relish

Here is my version of an old recipe, where the aromatic flavour of feijoas is not lost, but blends nicely with the mixed spice.

1¼ cups (310 ml/10 fl oz) cider or malt
* vinegar*
1 large onion
1 large apple
8 large feijoas
1½ cups sugar
1 Tbsp mixed spice
1½ tsp salt
¼ tsp cayenne pepper
¼ tsp celery seeds (optional)

Put the vinegar in a large pot. Chop the onion and apple finely, and peel and cube the feijoas, adding each to the pot as soon as it is prepared. Stir in all the remaining ingredients in the order given. Simmer over low heat for about an hour, stirring at intervals to make sure the bottom does not burn.

When fairly thick, ladle into sterilised jars. Top with boiled metal lids, or leave until cool then top with screw-on plastic lids and store in the refrigerator.

Tomato Relish

This relish improves sausages, burgers, filled rolls, sandwiches, and many other foods. Make it when tomatoes are really ripe, plentiful, full of flavour, and cheap.

1 kg (2 lb 3 oz) ripe tomatoes, skinned
3 large onions, finely chopped
2 cups sugar
1 cup (250 ml/8 fl oz) malt or cider vinegar
1 Tbsp salt
1 Tbsp mustard powder
1 Tbsp curry powder
1 Tbsp cornflour
¼ cup (60 ml/2 fl oz) extra vinegar

Put the tomatoes in a large bowl, cover with boiling water and leave for a minute. Pour off the water, run cold water over the tomatoes, and peel off the skins. Chop the peeled tomatoes into a large pot. Add the onion, then the sugar, vinegar and salt, bring to the boil, and cook gently for 15 minutes.

Measure the mustard, curry powder and cornflour carefully (using level measuring spoons) and stir them to a smooth paste with the extra vinegar. Stir into the tomatoes and boil for 5 minutes longer.

Pour the hot relish into clean, heated jars and top immediately with boiled screw-on metal lids, or keep in the refrigerator in a large jar with a plastic screwtop.

Pineapple Chutney

This chutney can be made quickly and easily at any time of the year. With cheese, it makes good sandwiches and topping for crackers.

2 large onions, finely chopped
2 cups crushed pineapple
2 cups sugar
2 cups (500 ml/16 fl oz) white or cider
* vinegar*
2 tsp curry powder
2 tsp turmeric
2 tsp salt
2 Tbsp flour

Put the onions in a large pot with the pineapple and simmer until the onion is tender. Add the sugar and nearly all the vinegar and bring to the boil.

Mix the remaining ingredients to a thin paste with the last of the vinegar and add

to the boiling mixture, stirring until it thickens. Taste, and add more curry powder and seasonings if desired. Simmer for 10–15 minutes, until thick.

Pour the hot chutney into clean, heated jars, and top immediately with boiled screw-on metal lids, or keep in the refrigerator in a large jar with a plastic screwtop.

Maharajah's Chutney

(Photo p. 332)

This mixture is delicious, unusual and very popular with my family and friends.

10 plump cloves garlic, chopped
500 g (1 lb 2 oz) onions, chopped
2 tsp grated fresh root ginger
1 Tbsp black mustard seeds
5 small dried chillies
3 Tbsp coriander seeds
2 Tbsp cumin seeds, crushed
1 Tbsp cinnamon
2 tsp turmeric
½ cup (125 ml/4 fl oz) oil
2 Tbsp salt
2 cups (500 ml/8 fl oz) malt vinegar
2 cups sugar
500 g (1 lb 2 oz) sultanas, roughly
* chopped*
grated rind and juice of 2 lemons

Prepare and mix the garlic, onions and ginger in a bowl.

Using a pestle and mortar, a coffee and spice grinder or a heavy-duty plastic bag and a hammer, break up the next 4 ingredients together. Heat them in a large, heavy-based pot until fragrant, then add the cinnamon and turmeric, and heat through. Add about 2 Tbsp oil, then the onion mixture, and cook for about 5 minutes.

Add the remaining ingredients, including the rest of the oil. Bring to the boil and simmer for about 1 hour, stirring frequently.

Pour the hot chutney into clean, heated jars, and top immediately with boiled screw-on metal lids, or keep in the refrigerator in a large jar with a plastic screwtop.

Blueberry Chutney

This chutney is delicious with lamb, beef, game and poultry, or simply with cheese and crackers.

3 cups fresh or frozen blueberries
1 large onion
1 apple
2 cloves garlic
1 cup sultanas
½ tsp each cinnamon, allspice, curry
* powder and ginger*
¼ tsp ground cloves
¼–½ tsp chilli powder
½ tsp salt

1 cup soft brown sugar
3/4 cup (185 ml/6 fl oz) wine or cider vinegar

Put the blueberries in a fairly large pot. Chop in a food processor or mince together the onion, unpeeled apple, garlic and sultanas. (The pieces should be evenly small, but not puréed.) Add to the blueberries with the flavourings, sugar and vinegar, and simmer gently for 1–2 hours, until the mixture thickens. Check the flavour during this time and add extra chilli if desired.

Pour the hot chutney into clean, heated jars, and top immediately with boiled screw-on metal lids, or keep in the refrigerator in a large jar with a plastic screwtop.

Green Tomato Chutney

Here is an old English recipe for a sweet brown relish which uses end-of-season tomatoes that look as if they may not ripen.

For 4 cups:
750 g (1 lb 10 oz) green (unripe) tomatoes
2 large onions
2 Tbsp salt
2 large pears
1 large apple
1 cup sultanas
1/2 cup chopped dates
1 1/2 cups brown sugar
1 tsp mixed spice
1/4–1/2 tsp cayenne pepper
1 Tbsp freshly grated root ginger
1 3/4 cups (435 ml/14 fl oz) malt vinegar
1 (level) Tbsp cornflour
1/4 cup extra vinegar

Cut the whole, unskinned tomatoes into small pieces. Cut the onions into pieces about the same size. Put in a bowl, sprinkle with the salt, barely cover with water and leave to stand for 1–2 hours.

Pour off and discard the salted water and put the tomatoes and onions in a large pot. Add the pears and apple, thinly peeled and cut into small cubes. Add the next 7 ingredients, using the larger amount of cayenne for a hotter relish. Boil for 45 minutes, stirring regularly.

Mix the cornflour to a paste with the second measure of vinegar, stir it into the chutney, and bring the mixture back to the boil. (It will thicken more as it stands in the jars.)

Pour the hot chutney into clean, heated jars and top immediately with boiled screw-on metal lids, or keep it in the refrigerator in a large jar with a plastic screwtop.

Leave to stand for at least 24 hours for the flavour to develop before using.

Date, Pineapple and Banana Chutney

This is not as concentrated and strongly flavoured as chutneys which cook for a longer time. It makes an interesting accompaniment to meat, and goes well with cheese in sandwiches.

For 6 cups:
1 large onion, chopped
1 can (450 g/16 oz) crushed pineapple
2 tsp coriander seeds, crushed
2–3 tsp grated root ginger
1 1/2 cups (375 ml/12 fl oz) cider vinegar
1 Tbsp pickling spice
6 bananas (1 kg/2 lb 3 oz)
1 1/2 tsp salt
1 cup brown sugar
250 g (9 oz) dates, sliced

Put the onion, pineapple (and juice), coriander seeds, ginger and vinegar in a large pot or jam pan. Add the pickling spices loosely wrapped in an open-textured cloth or a piece of Chux cloth. Bring to the boil then simmer for 5 minutes.

Add the sliced bananas, salt and brown sugar, bring to the boil again and boil for 5 minutes.

Add the sliced dates and boil the mixture for a further 5 minutes, checking regularly to make sure the mixture doesn't stick on the bottom. Remove the pickling spices.

If you have room to keep this chutney in the refrigerator, pour it into clean, heated jars with plastic screwtops. Otherwise, pour the hot chutney into clean, hot jars and top immediately with boiled screwtop metal lids. Do not open the jars and break the seal until you are going to use the chutney. Once opened, keep the jar in the refrigerator.

Green Tomato Chutney, Mixed Autumn Pickles (p. 333)

Anne's Traffic Light Pepper Jellies

Anne's Traffic Light Pepper Jellies

This jelly is tasty and colourful, very good on crackers with cream cheese when you want something instant and savoury to serve with drinks before dinner.

Serve it with roast lamb, other cold meat and cheese. Add it to the sauce for a casserole, or to gravy when you think that a gentle pepper flavour is called for. In decorated jars (with serving suggestions) it makes colourful Christmas gifts.

2 large red, green, yellow or orange
  peppers
4 small dried chillies
1 cup (250 ml/8 fl oz) wine vinegar
35 g (1¼ oz) powdered jam-setting mix
  (½ packet)
½ cup (125 ml/4 fl oz) water
2 cups sugar
food colouring (optional)

Select peppers of one colour only. Remove and discard the stems and seeds. Chop the flesh very finely, preferably in a food processor, then tip it into a medium-sized pot, add the chillies and rinse out the processor bowl with the vinegar. Boil gently for 3–4 minutes, then add the jam-setting mix stirred into the water, and boil briskly, uncovered, for 5 minutes.

Add the sugar and bring back to the boil, stirring frequently. (If the jelly is not a vivid colour, add a few drops of the appropriate food colouring, especially if using green peppers which turn olive green when cooked.)

Boil the mixture for 4–5 minutes or until a teaspoon of the jelly, left to stand on a dry saucer for a few minutes, forms a skin that wrinkles when you run your finger across it.

Lift out and discard the small chillies. Pour the jelly into hot, sterilised jars and seal with boiled metal lids.

Note: This is not strictly a jelly, since it has pieces of pepper through it, but these are barely visible, and the mixture is generally known as a jelly.

Peach Chutney

This peach chutney is delicious, easy and economical. Since it comes out a fairly dark colour you can make it with slightly speckled fruit that is too ripe for stewing or bottling.

For about 2½ cups:
1 kg (2 lb 3 oz) peaches, peeled and
  sliced
2 large onions, chopped
1 clove garlic, chopped
¼–½ cup raisins or sultanas (optional)
2 cups brown sugar
1 cup (250 ml/8 fl oz) malt vinegar
1 Tbsp salt
1–2 tsp ground ginger or 1 Tbsp grated
  fresh ginger
2 tsp dry mustard
¼ tsp cayenne pepper
1 tsp ground cloves

Put all the ingredients into a large pot, or add the peaches once the rest of the mixture has come to the boil. The latter method will stop the peaches darkening. Boil over a moderate heat until the mixture starts to thicken (about an hour).

Pour the hot relish into clean, heated jars, and top immediately with boiled screw-on metal lids, or keep it in the refrigerator in a large jar with a plastic screwtop.

Note: Use the larger quantity of ground ginger if you want a strong ginger flavour.

Red Onion Marmalade

A boiled-down mixture of chopped onion, lemon juice, vinegar and sugar is usually called onion marmalade, although it doesn't really jell at all but forms a thick paste like a jam or chutney. Whatever it is called, it tastes good!

250 g (9 oz) red onions
juice of 1 large lemon
1 Tbsp balsamic vinegar
¼ cup sugar
¼ tsp salt
2 pinches chilli powder

Skin the onions and chop them finely, preferably in a food processor. Put in a pot with all the other ingredients, and simmer over low heat for 15–30 minutes or until fairly thick and tender. The mixture will thicken more as it cools.

Spoon or pour into a clean, heated jar while hot, and close with a boiled screwtop metal lid or a plastic lid.

Keep in the refrigerator before and after the jar is opened, and use it within a month. Serve on crackers or as a relish with any rich or dark-fleshed roasted meat.

Variations: Replace the lemon juice and balsamic vinegar with ¼ cup red or white wine vinegar, or sherry vinegar, if you do not have balsamic vinegar.

Use other onions when red onions are not available.

Plum Sauce

If you grow, can pick, or are given some ripe or nearly ripe plums, turn some of the less-than-perfect fruit into plum sauce. This will liven up your barbecued sausages and brighten up cheese or cold meat sandwiches or snacks. It can even be thinned with a little orange juice to form a puddle on which you can overlap slices of smoked eel or peppered mackerel for a dinner party starter!

This is an easy recipe, producing a sauce that you can admire less than an hour after you start to make it. Use nearly ripe or ripe plums.

For 4 cups:

1 kg (2 lb 3 oz) plums
1 cup (250 ml/8 fl oz) cider, white or malt vinegar
1 large onion, finely chopped
6 cloves garlic, finely chopped
3 cm (1 in) root ginger, finely chopped
2–3 small dried chilli peppers
6 cloves
2 tsp coriander seed
2 tsp allspice (pimento) berries
1 tsp black peppercorns
1 cinnamon stick, about 8 cm (3 in)
1 tsp salt
1½ cups brown sugar

Put the plums and vinegar in a large pot and cook over low heat until you have prepared and added all the other ingredients.

Chop the onion, garlic and ginger finely. Add to the plums. Crush the chillies, cloves, coriander seed, allspice berries and peppercorns, using a hammer or a pestle and mortar. Add the cinnamon stick, broken into small pieces, and heat in a dry frypan or under the grill until the spices smell aromatic. DO NOT BURN them. Add to the plum mixture.

Put a lid ajar on the pot and simmer for 20–30 minutes, until the plums have turned to pulp and the onion is very tender. At this stage add the salt and sugar and bring the mixture back to the boil. Remove from the heat and, if you have time, leave it to stand for 15 minutes before pushing it through a coarse sieve. You should finish up with less than ¼ cup of stones and spices to throw out. If you throw out too much at this stage, your sauce will be thin and watery.

Pour the hot sauce into clean, heated glass bottles, and immediately screw on the hot metal tops tightly. If you use bottles with tops that do not seal, dip the tops of the cold bottles in melted wax to make an airtight seal.

Refrigerate after you have broken the seal. Most homemade fruit sauces will ferment if left to stand in a warm cupboard.

Hot Garlic Sauce

I use this black sauce to flavour gravies, stews and casseroles. I occasionally use a few drops directly on plainly cooked foods, too. Although it looks like Worcestershire sauce, it doesn't taste the same!

For about 5 cups:

4 cups (1 litre/32 fl oz) malt vinegar
1½ cups treacle
50 g (2 oz) garlic, chopped
25 g (1 oz) fresh root ginger
1 large onion, chopped
¾ cup brown sugar
½–1 Tbsp small dried whole chillies
1 Tbsp whole cloves
1 Tbsp salt

Combine all the ingredients in a stainless steel pot. Leave to stand overnight, then simmer for an hour and strain into small bottles.

This sauce does not need to be sealed but the bottles should be covered.

Like Worcestershire sauce, it is almost everlasting!

'Everlasting' Tomato Sauce

The lady who gave me this recipe said the sauce does not need to be refrigerated after it is opened. I took the bottle home, enjoyed its flavour with some cold meat the same night, then I left it in my pantry for a month, during warm weather. The sauce remained unchanged! Try it for yourself!

Don't cut down the spices or the cooking time, or you won't get the same results.

3 kg (6 lb 9 oz) ripe tomatoes
1 kg (2 lb 3 oz) unpeeled apples
1 kg (2 lb 3 oz) unpeeled onions
3 large garlic cloves
100 g (3½ oz) common salt
750 g (1 lb 10 oz) brown sugar
30 g (1 oz) whole allspice (pimento) berries
30 g (1 oz) whole cloves
7 cups (1.75 litres/56 fl oz) malt vinegar

Chop the tomatoes, apples and onions into chunks, and put them in a fairly large jam pan. Chop the garlic, and add with the salt and sugar.

Wrap the allspice and cloves in a piece of loosely woven cloth and fasten it with string, leaving space for the spices to swell. Put the bag in the pan, add the vinegar and simmer for at least 4 hours. Remove the spice bag and push the sauce through a mouli, or purée it in a food processor then push it through a coarse sieve.

Pour into sterilised bottles and top with boiled lids. When cold, dip the tops of the bottles in wax. Unopened, this sauce will keep for years.

Spiced Apricot Sauce

This sauce has a fresh flavour because it doesn't need hours of cooking. To get the texture I like best, I chop the fruit in the food processor before I cook it rather than processing or sieving the sauce after it is cooked.

For 4 cups:

3 cloves garlic
1 kg (2 lb 3 oz) fresh apricots
2 tsp cumin seed
1 tsp coriander seed
2 cups sugar
2 tsp salt
1 tsp mustard powder
1 tsp ground cloves
⅛ tsp cayenne pepper
2 cups (500 ml/16 fl oz) vinegar

Chop the garlic and apricots roughly, then chop until fine in the food processor (process in 2 batches for best results).

Lightly roast the cumin and coriander seeds in a dry frypan. Grind with a mortar and pestle or in a coffee grinder.

Put all the ingredients in a large pot and boil for 30 minutes, stirring frequently so the sauce does not catch on the bottom of the pan and spoil the flavour. Ladle into clean, hot bottles and seal with boiled metal screwtops.

Especially good with plainly barbecued or roast chicken and lamb.

FLAVOURED VINEGARS

Vinegars flavoured with summer herbs, fruit and flowers make attractive gifts. These are useful in winter months when fresh herbs and other flavourings are not readily available. Top and label the jars attractively, suggesting uses for the contents.

Mint Vinegar

Bruise sprigs of mint and pack them tightly into a coffee jar. Season with a little salt and sugar if desired, pour over enough cider vinegar to cover, then screw on the lid. Leave to stand for 3 or 4 days, shaking the jar occasionally. Pour the strained vinegar over 1 or 2 flowering sprigs of mint in a pretty bottle. Colour the vinegar pale green with food colouring if its colour is unattractive.

Use for dressings with lamb, or on fruit salads.

Lavender Vinegar

Fill a jar with the heads of flowering English lavender. Cover with white wine vinegar and leave in a warm place, away from direct sunlight, for 2 or 3 days. Pour off the vinegar, which will be a startling purple, put more lavender flowers into the jar with the old ones and cover with more vinegar. Leave in a warm place for about a week, then pour off the liquid and mix with the earlier lavender vinegar. Add a few fresh sprigs of lavender for decoration.

Lovely with tomato salads or as a facial splash!

Strawberry Vinegar

Pour wine vinegar over clean, ripe, but not mushy berries in a jar, covering them generously. Cover and stand in a dark place at room temperature. Pour off the liquid after about 2–4 weeks, leaving any sediment behind. The colour fades with time, but the flavour remains.

Sprinkle over sugared strawberries or use in dressings for green salads and avocados.

Reference Recipes

The recipes in these pages have all been referred to earlier in the book, sometimes in several different chapters. Sometimes they are part of a finished dish, and at other times they are served with it. I find it easier to locate such recipes when they are grouped together at the end of a book. I feel sure that you will find this collection as useful as I do!

Homemade Chicken Stock

Homemade chicken stock, frozen in 2-cup containers, is a wonderful ingredient to have on hand. It gives body and flavour to soups and sauces for very little cost. There are several different ways to make it.

Stock from Raw Chicken

Freeze raw chicken trimmings and giblets (except livers which make bitter stock) in a bag in the freezer, adding to the bag until it is full. Alone, or with fresh chicken back bought specially, they make good stock, as long as other flavourings are added.

For 8 cups:
about 1 kg (2 lb) raw chicken bones,
  chicken backs, skin, giblets, feet, etc.
1 tsp finely chopped garlic
1 onion, chopped
2–3 bay leaves, optional
about 12 peppercorns
4 whole cloves
12 cups (3 litres/96 fl oz) water
1 tsp dried oreganum, crumbled
1 tsp fresh or dried thyme
1/4 cup chopped parsley
salt and pepper

Simmer whatever chicken bits you have, with everything except the salt and pepper in a very large pot, for 3 hours.

Strain through a sieve and discard the solids. Skim off and discard the fat from the surface.

Season to taste and refrigerate for up to 2–3 days or freeze for up to 6 months.

Stock from Chicken Bones

The skeleton and other remains of roast, barbecued, grilled or baked chicken may be used to make useful, small amounts of good stock. Start cooking the stock while you do the dishes, while you still have the bones, drippings and vegetable trimmings from dinner close at hand.

For 2–4 cups:
cooked carcass, chicken bones, giblets,
  skin, fat, etc.
1–2 cloves garlic
1 carrot
1 onion
1 stalk celery (optional)
1 Tbsp light soy sauce
1/2 tsp salt
6 peppercorns or 1 dried chilli
water to cover

Put all the chicken remains in a fairly large pot, with any of the cooking juices scraped from the original cooking pan, and any suitable vegetable trimmings (chop vegetables fairly finely for maximum flavour). Add the remaining ingredients, cover and simmer for about 2 hours.

Strain off stock and refrigerate for short storage or freeze in covered containers for up to 6 months.

Chicken Giblet Stock

Giblets (available from many supermarkets) make quite a strongly flavoured stock with minimum cost, mess and effort.

For 8 cups:
500 g (1 lb) chicken giblets
1–2 cloves garlic
1–2 slices fresh ginger, optional
1 Tbsp light soy sauce
1 Tbsp sherry, optional
freshly ground black pepper
8 cups (2 litres/64 fl oz) water

Put everything in a large pot and simmer for about 3 hours. Strain, keeping the giblets for other uses if you like.

Refrigerate stock for up to 3 days, or freeze for up to 6 months.

Stock from a Boiling Fowl

When you boil an old hen, you get stock with an intense chicken flavour, for a very low price.

Look for frozen birds with labels such as Pot Roasters, Table Hens, or Roasting Fowls (at a fraction of the price of younger birds) at specialist Asian food stores, some supermarkets and butchers, and some egg producers.

Put the thawed hen on to simmer for 4–5 hours in 8 cups (2 litres/64 fl oz) water with 1 tsp each of finely chopped (or bottled) garlic and ginger, and 2 Tbsp each of soy sauce and sherry. Spoon the fat from the top of the stock before refrigerating or freezing it in suitable quantities.

Brown Beef Stock

Although you can make stock from any beef bones, bones which contain marrow are generally regarded as best.

For about 10 cups:
1–2 kg (2–4 lb) beef bones, cut into small
  sections
2–3 onions
2 carrots
2 stalks celery, optional
2 cloves garlic
1–2 bayleaves
10 peppercorns
1 tsp salt
1/2 tsp dried thyme
1/2 tsp dried oreganum
several parsley stalks (optional)
about 12 cups (3 litres/96 fl oz) water

For a good brown colour and the best flavour, heat the bones and the roughly chopped vegetables under a grill or in a very hot oven until the edges char. Turn bones and vegetables so they brown on both sides.

Transfer bones and vegetables to a very large pot, add the flavourings and water, cover and simmer for 4–5 hours

Sieve the stock and leave to stand in a cool place until the fat rises to the surface and solidifies. Remove fat and refrigerate for up to 2–3 days or freeze for up to 6 months.

Variation: If you do not have the time to brown bones, cook all the above ingredients in a large pot without browning them first. The colour will not be as brown, nor the flavour quite the same but both will still be quite acceptable.

Roasted Peppers (p. 346)

Croûtons

Croûtons add interesting texture to many soups and salads. Spoon or sprinkle them onto individual servings, at the last minute.

2 Tbsp olive or other oil or butter
1 clove garlic
2 thick slices white bread

In a frypan, over a low heat, warm the oil or butter with the sliced garlic. Remove garlic before it browns.

Cut the bread into small cubes, toss in the hot pan, then cook on medium heat, turning frequently, until croûtons are golden brown, for 5–15 minutes.

If preferred, brown under a grill, while watching carefully. Or bake at 150°C for 10–15 minutes or until golden brown. Store in airtight containers if not using immediately.

Melba Toast

Cut stale bread rolls or french bread into very thin (2–3 mm) slices, using a sharp serrated knife. Bake at 150°–180°C in one layer on an oven tray until the bread browns very lightly. Cooking time will vary with the type of bread, its thickness and its staleness. Start to check after 3–4 minutes.

When cold, store in airtight jars or plastic bags for up to a month, although they are best in the few days after they are made. Refresh for 10 minutes at 150°C before serving if you like.

Garlic Herb Butter

This is a very useful mixture to keep on hand.

3–4 peeled garlic cloves
1 cup parsley sprigs
½ tsp thyme, dill, sage, or basil
200 g (7 oz) soft but not melted butter
a little lemon rind
1–2 Tbsp lemon juice
black pepper
hot pepper sauce to taste

Chop together very finely in a food processor the garlic, parsley and herbs. Add the butter, lemon rind and juice and season with pepper and pepper sauce. Process to mix, then refrigerate in a covered dish until needed (will keep up to two weeks). Melt small quantities to brush over fish, skinned chicken breasts, or vegetable kebabs before barbecuing.

Garlic Bread

This bread makes a soup meal much more substantial and interesting, especially for family members who are not 'wild about soup'! Make it ahead and cook or reheat when needed.

1 loaf french bread (or other long bread rolls)
50g (2 oz) butter
2 cloves garlic
2–4 Tbsp finely chopped parsley or other fresh herbs

Cut french bread into diagonal slices 1 cm thick, without cutting through the bottom crust, so the loaf (roll) holds together.

Soften but do not melt the butter, then mix in the finely chopped garlic and herbs. Spread the flavoured butter on one side of each cut slice, wrap the loaf in foil, leaving the top exposed, and bake at 200°C for about 10 minutes, or at a lower temperature for longer, until the top crust is crisp and the loaf has heated right through.

Variation: If preferred, cut bread rolls in half lengthways. Spread both cut surfaces with the flavoured butter and heat at 200°C, butter side up, uncovered, until edges brown, or brown under a grill.

Cooking Brown Lentils

Lentils which are undercooked will put you off recipes which are excellent if made with properly cooked lentils. Nearly cooked lentils are not good enough.

Cover lentils with about four times their volume of cold water. Bring to boil, add a tablespoon of oil to prevent excess frothing, and simmer with the lid ajar to prevent boiling over. You can flavour the lentils with garlic, onion, and herbs during cooking if you like, but you must not add salt, sugar, lemon juice or tomato products until the lentils are completely tender, since these toughen the lentils. They are cooked when they are tender enough to squash with your tongue against the roof of your mouth.

Approximate cooking time for brown lentils is 40–60 minutes. Use these times as a guide only, since times vary with the age and quality of the lentils. Add about ½ tsp salt to 1 cup of lentils, after cooking. Refrigerate up to 3–4 days. (Liquid drained from cooked lentils makes good stock for soups and sauces.)

Brown Rice

Brown rice is much more nutritious than white rice, and has a lovely nutty flavour. It is the ideal food for people who eat little or no meat. While it is easier to cook than white rice, because the grains do not stick together, it does take longer. But if you serve it undercooked, you will probably put your family off it forever.

Simmer 1 cup of short or long-grain brown rice in 3 cups of water with ½–1 tsp salt in a tightly covered pot for about 45 minutes. If it looks dry before it is tender, add more water. (Drain any excess water into soup in cold weather.)

Or put the same amount of rice, salt and water into a covered ovenproof dish and bake it while you cook something else. It will take about 45–60 minutes, depending on the heat of the oven, and whether you start with hot or cold water. It does not matter if you leave brown rice 10 minutes longer than you meant to, as long as there is some water left in its pot or casserole. If you like soft rice, use 4 cups of water instead of 3 cups, and cook it for an hour instead of 45 minutes. Very soft, overcooked brown rice may be eaten just as you eat porridge – it tastes very good like this. Brown rice does not need to have oil or butter added during cooking, since it is unlikely to stick together unless it is really overcooked.

Pilaf

This makes a tasty alternative to rice, on occasion.

2 Tbsp oil or butter
1 medium onion, chopped
1 cup ribbon noodles, broken into 1–2 cm (½–1 in) pieces
½ cup burghul (bulghar)
2 cups (500 ml/16 fl oz) chicken stock
1 cinnamon stick

Heat the oil or butter in a large frypan and cook the onion until golden brown.

Add the broken noodles and bulgar, cook until lightly browned. Add the chicken stock (use 2 tsp instant stock in 2 cups water if necessary) and the cinnamon stick and cook over a medium heat for about 10 minutes, or until the liquid is absorbed and the noodles and bulgar are tender. Add a little extra water if the liquid disappears before this.

Mayonnaise

Quick and easy to make in the food processor, this sauce is delicious and versatile. It puts most bought mayonnaise to shame!

1 egg
½ tsp salt
½ tsp sugar
1 tsp Dijon mustard
1 Tbsp wine vinegar
about 1 cup (250 ml/8 fl oz) olive or other oil

Measure the first 5 ingredients into a food processor or blender. Turn on and add the oil in a thin stream until the mayonnaise is as thick and creamy as you like it. Keep in a covered container in the refrigerator for up to 3 weeks.

Horseradish Cream

Add small quantities of dried horseradish powder (wasabi), very finely grated horseradish root (frozen or fresh), or commercially prepared grated horseradish to crème fraîche or cream cheese until you have the strength of flavour you like. Add salt to taste.

Alternatively, purée horseradish root in a food processor with white vinegar, a little salt and sugar, then add to crème fraîche or cream cheese. This mixture will keep in the refrigerator for several months.

Sesame Dressing

This strongly flavoured dressing is addictive! It turns the simplest coleslaw vegetables into something exciting, but also dresses tomato, sprout, mesclun, cooked vegetable and pasta salads successfully. It keeps well and may be refrigerated for weeks.

For 3/4 cup dressing:
1/4 cup (60 ml/2 fl oz) canola oil
2 Tbsp sesame oil
2 Tbsp wine vinegar
1 Tbsp lemon or lime juice
2 Tbsp sugar
1 Tbsp Thai sweet chilli sauce
1 Tbsp Dijon or mild mustard
1 tsp salt
1 tsp balsamic vinegar if available

Measure all ingredients into a screwtop jar and shake together. Use about 2 tsp dressing to 1 cup of compact salad, or 1 tsp per cup of salad leaves.

For a milder dressing use only 1 Tbsp sesame oil.

Tex-Mex Dressing

Use this assertive dressing to liven up gently flavoured foods – spoon it into avocado halves and stir it into drained canned beans to make spicy bean salads.

For 3/4 cup dressing:
1/2 cup (125 ml/4 fl oz) olive oil
1 tsp ground cumin
1 tsp salt
1 tsp sugar
1/2 tsp dried oreganum
1/2 tsp paprika
1/4–1/2 tsp chilli paste
1–2 cloves garlic, very finely chopped
2 tsp prepared smooth mustard
1 Tbsp tomato paste
1 Tbsp wine vinegar
2 Tbsp boiling water

Measure the first 7 ingredients into a screwtop jar and shake well to mix.

Mix the very finely chopped garlic, mustard, tomato paste and wine vinegar in a cup or small bowl. Stir in the boiling water to make a smooth paste, then transfer to the jar holding the other ingredients and stir well, then shake thoroughly until smooth and thick.

Leave to stand for at least 30 minutes before using. Refrigerate for up to a week.

Hollandaise Sauce

2 egg yolks
1 Tbsp lemon juice
100 g (3 1/2 oz) butter

Place egg yolks and lemon juice in a food processor bowl fitted with a metal chopping blade.

Cut the butter into cubes and melt it in the microwave oven in a microwaveable jug covered with a lid or plate to avoid splattering. Heat on High (100% power) for 2–3 minutes or until it's very hot, popping and bubbling vigorously.

Before the butter has time to cool at all, turn on the food processor and pour the very hot butter in a steady stream onto the egg yolks. The hot butter should cook and thicken the egg yolks. Once thickened, the sauce is remarkably good-natured and stable as long as you don't heat it above bath temperature. Transfer it to a small bowl and cover it.

Reheat by standing the bowl of sauce in a larger container of bath-temperature water for about 15 minutes, stirring it occasionally. It will curdle if the water around it is too hot.

Notes: In cold weather, heat the bowl and blades of the processor in very hot water before putting the egg and lemon juice in it. Pour out the water but do not dry the bowl or blades.

Add a teaspoon of finely grated orange rind to the egg yolk. Serve with salmon, young carrots and asparagus.

Gravy

Gravy is very nice with meat loaf and roast meats. Take meal from pan and drain off all fat, leaving 1–2 Tbsp of the pan drippings. If necessary, add a tablespoon of oil or butter to the baking pan, brown 2–3 Tbsp flour in it over moderate heat, then add about a cup of the lightly salted vegetable cooking liquid. Stir until the gravy thickens and boils. Add extra water, stock or vegetable liquid to thin to desired consistency. Simmer for a couple of minutes. Pour through a sieve to get rid of any lumps, adjust seasonings, and serve with the meat.

Vegetarian Gravy

To many of us, gravy is 'comfort food'. Serve this gravy in a jug, and let your family and friends pour it over their main course, mashed potoatoes, or whatever they like. You will probably be surprised by their pleasure!

2 medium-sized onions
2–3 cloves garlic
2 Tbsp oil or butter
1 tsp sugar
2 Tbsp flour
2 cups (500 ml/16 fl oz) water
2 Tbsp dark soy sauce
black pepper to taste
1/4–1/2 tsp salt

Finely chop or mince the onions and garlic. Heat the oil or butter in a large frypan or pot, add the onions and garlic, and cook, stirring occasionally until they brown. Stir in the sugar and flour and cook for about a minute longer.

Add half the water, stirring to remove any lumps, bring to the boil and allow to thicken before adding the remaining water and soy sauce. Bring to the boil again, season with black pepper and salt to taste, then serve!

Mustard Sauce

Serve this sauce with carrots, cauliflower, and lightly cooked, 'teenage' zucchini, as well as with boiled cured meat. Made with butter beaten in at the end it has a stronger flavour than it does when cream is added at this stage.

For 2 servings:
2 tsp butter
1 Tbsp finely chopped onion or shallot
1/2 tsp Dijon mustard
1/2 tsp grainy mustard
1/4 cup (60 ml/2 fl oz) white wine
1/4 cup (60 ml/2 fl oz) water
2–3 tsp extra butter or 2 Tbsp cream

Melt the butter in a small, preferably non-stick pan with a lid.

Add the very finely chopped onion or shallot, cover pan, and cook gently for 5 minutes or until the onion is tender.

Stir in both mustards, then add the wine and water and boil briskly, stirring often, until reduced to half its volume. Beat in teaspoon lots of the second measure of butter with a whisk, stopping when the sauce is smooth and thick enough to coat food; or add the cream and boil down further, until sauce is of coating consistency.

Parsley Sauce

1 Tbsp butter
2 Tbsp flour
1/2 cup (125 ml/4 fl oz) milk
1/2 cup (125 ml/4 fl oz) cooking liquid or chicken or vegetable stock or extra milk
about 1 Tbsp dry sherry or white wine (optional)
2–3 Tbsp chopped parsley

Melt the butter in a small pan. Stir in the flour, then add the milk and the stock if used. Bring to the boil, stirring constantly. Add sherry or white wine if desired, then stir in chopped parsley. Season to taste.

Let the sauce simmer gently for a few minutes, then add extra milk or cooking liquid to bring it to a fairly thin coating consistency. Adjust seasonings to taste.

Quick Satay Sauce

Brush small amounts of this sauce over chicken pieces before cooking.

1/2 cup chopped roasted peanuts
4 pieces crystallised ginger
1 Tbsp brown sugar
1/2 tsp ground coriander
2 cloves garlic, chopped
juice of 1 lemon
2 Tbsp light soy sauce
3–4 drops tabasco sauce
1 Tbsp oil
1 cup (250 ml/8 fl oz) coconut milk

Using a food processor or blender, chop the first 5 ingredients together until very fine, then add the next 4 ingredients and process again. Gradually add the coconut milk until the sauce is the consistency of thin gravy. Heat until it boils and thickens.

Kiwifruit Salsa

2 cups chopped kiwifruit
3 spring onions, sliced
1/2 cup basil leaves, chopped
1/4–1/2 tsp finely chopped red or green chilli
1 tsp ground cumin
1/4 cup (60 ml/2 fl oz) lemon juice
salt and pepper to taste

Gently stir all ingredients together so the kiwifruit keeps its shape. Refrigerate for up to 24 hours in a covered container, or fold through cold flaked fish as desired.

Variation: Replace the kiwifruit with any other fresh, raw fruit.

Easy Tomato Salsa

You can make this fresh-tasting salsa all year round. It's best the day it's made, but can be refrigerated for up to 3 days.

1/4 red onion or 2 spring onions
1 large clove garlic
1–2 Tbsp pickled Jalapeno peppers
1 Tbsp liquid from jar of Jalapeno peppers
1/2–1 tsp ground cumin
1/2 tsp oreganum
1 can (400 g/14 oz) whole tomatoes in juice or 4 large fresh red tomatoes, roughly chopped
1/2–1 tsp salt
1/2–1 tsp sugar
2–3 Tbsp chopped coriander leaves

Chop the first 6 ingredients together in a food processor or by hand. Add tomatoes and process until mixed but still chunky. Add salt and sugar to taste (fresh tomatoes need more than canned tomatoes) and add coriander leaves if you have them. Leave for about half an hour before using.

Use as a dip with corn chips, mix with mashed avocado to make an easy Guacamole, or spoon over poached eggs (my favourite!) and Mexican mixtures.

Mango Salsa

1 can (400 g/14 oz) mango slices in light syrup or 1 cup finely chopped fresh mango
1 spring onion
1 Tbsp lemon (or lime) juice
1/2 tsp minced red chilli or chilli powder
1/2 tsp salt
1–2 Tbsp chopped coriander leaf

Drain the mango slices and cut the flesh in to 5 mm cubes. Thinly slice the spring onion then mix with the cubed mango, lemon or lime juice, chilli, salt and chopped coriander in a small bowl.

Simple Salsa

Make this when time is really short, tasting it as you go, so you season to suit your own palate.

Prepare a bowl of chopped, blanched, seeded tomatoes, spring onion leaves and chopped coriander leaves or fresh basil. Toss together lightly, and season with salt, sugar and a dash of balsamic or wine vinegar.

Pesto

A spoonful of pesto dropped into tomato soups and some other vegetable soups at serving time adds an 'explosion' of flavour and makes the soup much more exciting. It also livens up many 'basic' sandwiches. Make it during basil's short growing season and keep for later use.

2 cups lightly packed basil leaves
1/2 cup parsley sprigs
2 cloves garlic
2–4 Tbsp Parmesan cheese
2 Tbsp pinenuts, almonds or walnuts
1/4–1/2 cup (60–125 ml/2–4 fl oz) olive oil
about 1/2 tsp salt

Wash the basil to minimise later browning, then drain on a cloth or paper towel. Removing tough stems, put the basil, parsley and peeled garlic cloves in a food processor bowl or blender with the Parmesan cheese and nuts. Process, adding up to 1/4 cup oil, until finely chopped. Keep adding oil until you have a dark green paste just liquid enough to pour. Add salt to taste.

Store in the refrigerator in a lidded container for up to 2 months or freeze for longer storage.

Hint: Pesto may darken at the top of the jar. Put a layer of oil at the top of each jar, to slow discolouration.

Sun-Dried Tomato Paste

Use sun-dried tomatoes to make a paste to spread on toasted or fresh French bread.

sun-dried tomatoes (equivalent of 3 tomatoes)
2 Tbsp wine vinegar – sherry or balsamic
1/4 small red onion, chopped
3–4 Tbsp olive oil, or oil from tomatoes
1/2–1 roasted, peeled red pepper
salt and pepper (optional)
sugar
fresh or dried chilli

Chop the (drained) sun-dried tomatoes in a food processor or blender with the best quality vinegar you have, then add the other ingredients.

If you've stored your sun-dried tomatoes in oil, use some of this to make the paste, otherwise use olive oil.

Leave to stand in the food processor/ blender for about 15 minutes then add more vinegar or oil to make a thin paste and process again. Taste and season as you like, using some or all of the suggested flavourings.

Roasted Peppers (Photo p. 342)

To cook whole or halved peppers, place under the grill and grill until blackened and swollen, turning several times to roast evenly. Or cook in a roasting dish at 220°C for 30–40 minutes until the skin and edges blacken and the flesh softens.

Remove the peppers from the oven and allow to stand in an oven bag for about 5 minutes. Remove from the bag and peel off the skin, while holding under cold water.

Basic Couscous

Couscous is very easily prepared. For 6 servings, heat 3 cups (750 ml/24 fl oz) chicken stock (or 2 tsp instant stock powder and 1 tsp sugar in 3 cups water) until boiling. Stir in 1 1/2 cups of couscous, turn off the heat and leave to stand in a warm place for 5 minutes or until all the water is absorbed. Fluff the couscous with a fork and serve as you would rice.

Orange Cream Cheese

This spread is much more interesting than plain butter or margerine!

Beat together until smooth 1/2 cup cream cheese (or quark) with 1 tsp finely grated orange, mandarin or tangelo rind and 1 Tbsp icing sugar. Serve on hot toast, toasted muffins, bread rolls, carrot or zucchini loaf, etc.

Rum Butter

This mixture is as good on a warm fruity muffin as it is on a steamed pudding. Try it – it is addictive!

Beat or process together 100 g (3 1/2 oz) softened butter, 1 cup brown sugar, 1 tsp freshly grated nutmeg, and 2 Tbsp rum, until light and creamy. Serve at room temperature.

Lattice-Topped Pies

A lattice top is easy when you know how!

Roll the pastry in 2 circles, each a little bigger than the pie plate or flan tin. Line plate or tin with one circle of pastry and trim edges. Arrange cold filling on pastry so surface is flat or slightly rounded.

Cut the second circle into even, parallel strips, about 1 cm wide. Drape alternate strips over the pie crosswise. Put the shorter strips nearer the edge of the pie (Fig. 1). Place the longest remaining strip (A) at a right angle to the others, in the middle of the pie. Take care not to stretch any strips. Fold every second strip back over strip A, then place strip B beside A (Fig. 2).

Replace the folded strips to their original position. Strip B is now under these strips. Now fold back the alternate strips which lie underneath strip B and place strip C in position (Fig. 3).

Continue in this way, folding back alternate strips until the edge of the pie is reached. Then remove strip A (Fig. 4). Now work in the other direction. Fold back the strips which lie under strip B and lie strip A in its final position (Fig. 5). Continue until the edge of the pie is reached, and the whole surface is latticed. Press edges against lower crust and cut away end pieces.

Centre of flan is now completed. Edge of pie looks neater if remaining strips are used to form a circle, covering the edges. For best results brush pastry with beaten egg before baking.

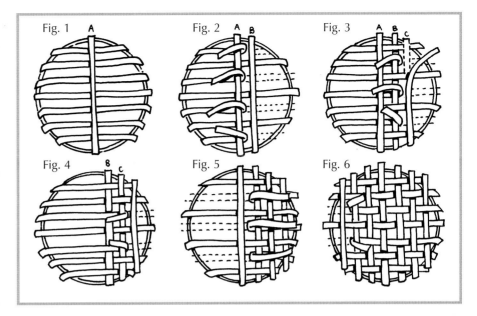

Apricot Balls   (Photo p. 223)

Easy, colourful, delicious and popular!

rind from 1/2–1 orange
1/2 cup castor sugar
250 g (8 oz) dried apricots, chopped
juice of 1/2 orange
1 3/4 cups desiccated coconut

Finely chop the orange rind with the sugar in a food processor, then add the apricots and process until all is finely chopped. Make the orange juice up to 1/4 cup with either lemon juice, sherry or brandy then add to sugar mixture and process briefly again.

Add 1 cup of coconut, process, then add extra coconut until mixture sticks together nicely. With wet hands form into small balls, and coat with the remaining coconut.

Refrigerate uncovered until firm. (Freeze if desired.)

Orange Icing

25 g (1 oz) butter
1 cup icing sugar
about 1 Tbsp orange juice

Put the butter in a clean bowl. (It should be soft enough to mix easily, but not melted.) Add the icing sugar and enough juice to mix with a stirrer, or table knife so it will spread smoothly over the base. To pattern the icing, make wiggles on top with a fork.

Everyday Chocolate Icing

1 Tbsp cocoa
1 1/2 Tbsp boiling water
2 tsp butter
1/4 tsp vanilla
1 cup icing sugar

Put the cocoa in a small bowl. Pour on boiling water and mix to a paste. Add room-temperature butter, vanilla and sifted icing sugar, then beat until smooth and thick. Add a little extra water or icing sugar to adjust thickness if necessary.

Spread on cake or slice, etc., using a knife or spatula.

Sour Cream Chocolate Icing

50 g dark, milk or white chocolate,
chocolate melts or 1/4 cup chocolate chips
2 Tbsp sour cream

This mixture never hardens completely.

Break up chocolate, if necessary, and heat with sour cream over boiling water or in a microwave until the chocolate has melted. Stir until well combined.

Cool to spreadable consistency if necessary. Spread on cakes or slices.

Variation: For a biscuit icing which sets hard, use half the amount of sour cream.

Chocolate Glaze

This makes a firm, dark, shiny glaze.

2 Tbsp cocoa
1/4 cup (60 ml/2 fl oz) water
1/2 tsp vanilla
1 cup icing sugar

Heat the cocoa and water together in a small pot. As soon as the mixture thickens and begins to look dry, remove from the heat and stir in vanilla.

Cool pot until you can touch the bottom with your hand. Stir in half the sifted icing sugar. Like magic the dryish chocolate mixture will turn into a thin, dark brown shiny mixture. Add enough of the remaining icing sugar to make the glaze the thickness you want.

Dip the tops of chocolate éclairs into the mixture.

Melting Chocolate

Take care when melting chocolate. A small amount of water can prevent chocolate from melting to a smooth glossy mixture. Do not cover chocolate when melting it, or water may drip in from the lid. Always stir with a dry spoon.

While melting chocolate, do not heat it more than necessary.

Melt chocolate, in small, even pieces, in a glass, stainless steel or china bowl over or in a pot or pan of water.

I usually melt block chocolate on my stove, but sometimes microwave chocolate chips on Medium power, stirring them every 30 seconds. (Microwaved chocolate keeps its shape, until stirred.)

If there are melting instructions on the chocolate you use, follow them!

Leftover melted chocolate which has hardened may be remelted later.

Different brands and types of chocolate, and different room temperatures and humidity will affect melting times, so watch carefully, rather than using specific times. A very small amount of Kremelta (copha) melted with chocolate thins it down. Use small amounts to start with (e.g. 1/4–1/2 tsp).

Index